READINGS IN AMERICAN DIALECTOLOGY

READINGS IN
AMERICAN
DIALECTOLOGY

edited by

Harold B. Allen
University of Minnesota

Gary N. Underwood
University of Arkansas

APPLETON·CENTURY·CROFTS

EDUCATIONAL DIVISION

New York MEREDITH CORPORATION

711-1

Library of Congress Card Number: 78-111877

PRINTED IN THE UNITED STATES OF AMERICA
390-02100-8

SPECIAL ACKNOWLEDGMENT TO

American Council of Learned Societies for permission to reprint: figure 1.1 in E. Bagby Atwood, "The Methods of American Dialectology" (reprinted on p. 17).

Centre International de Dialectologie Générale and respective authors for permission to reprint: Arthur M. Z. Norman, "A Southeast Texas Dialect Study," *Orbis* 5.61-79, 1956 (reprinted on pp. 135-151); Harold Orton, "An English Dialect Survey: Linguistic Atlas of England," *Orbis* 9.331-48, 1960 (reprinted on pp. 230-244); W. Nelson Francis, "Some Dialectal Verb Forms in England," *Orbis* 10.1-14, 1961 (reprinted on pp. 225-264); Carroll E. Reed, "Double Dialect Geography," *Orbis* 10.308-19, 1961 (reprinted on pp. 273-283); Trevor Hill, "Phonemic and Prosodic Analysis in Linguistic Geography," *Orbis* 12.499-454, 1963 (reprinted on pp. 343-349).

Cercle Linguistique de Copenhague and Walter Bloch for permission to reprint: Bernard Bloch, "Postvocalic /r/ in New England Speech," *Actes du quartième Congrès internationale de linguistes* (Copenhagen: Munksgaard, 1939), pp. 195-199 (reprinted on pp. 196-199).

Charles C Thomas and Professor Maurer and Dr. Vogel for permission to reprint: David W. Maurer & Victor H. Vogel, "The Argot of Narcotics Addicts," *Narcotics and Narcotic Addiction*, 3rd ed. (Springfield, Ill.: Charles C Thomas, 1967), pp. 318-346 (reprinted on pp. 500-523).

Columbia University Press and the respective authors for permission to reprint: Gordon R. Wood, "Dialect Contours in the Southern States," *American Speech* 38.243-256, 1963 (reprinted on pp. 122-134); Sumner A. Ives, "Pronunciation of *Can't* in the Eastern States," *American Speech* 28.149-157, 1953 (reprinted on pp. 169-177); Alva L. Davis & Raven I. McDavid, Jr., "*Shivaree:* An Example of Cultural Diffusion," *American Speech* 24.249-255, 1949 (reprinted on pp. 178-184); Walter S. Avis, "*Crocus Bag:* A Problem in Areal Linguistics," *American Speech* 30.5-16, 1955 (reprinted on pp. 185-195); George B. Pace, "Linguistic Geography and Words Ending in < i >," *American Speech* 35.175-187, 1960 (reprinted on pp. 216-227); W. Nelson Francis, "Some Dialect Isoglosses in England," *American Speech* 34.234-257, 1959 (reprinted on pp. 255-264); Robert P. Stockwell, "Structural Dialectology: A Proposal," *American Speech* 34.258-268, 1959 (reprinted on pp. 314-323); Beryl L. Bailey, "Toward a New Perspective in Negro English Dialectology," *American Speech* 40.171-177, 1965 (reprinted on pp. 421-426; figure 1.6 in E. Bagby Atwood, "The Methods of American Dialectology" (reprinted on p. 26).

English Language Institute, University of Michigan, for permission to reprint: Harold B. Allen, "The Primary Dialect Areas of the Upper Midwest," *Studies in Languages and Linguistics in Honor of Charles C. Fries* (Ann Arbor, Mich.: 1964) (reprinted on pp. 83-93).

Florida Foreign Language Reporter and William A. Stewart for permission to reprint: W. A. Stewart, "Sociolinguistic Factors in the History of the American Negro Dialects," *Florida FL Reporter* 5:2.1-4 (1967) (reprinted on pp. 444-453); W. A. Stewart, "Continuity and Change in American Negro Dialects," *Florida FL Reporter* 6:1.3-4, 14-16, 18 (1968) (reprinted on pp. 454-467).

Linguistic Circle of New York for permission to reprint: Gino Bottiglioni, "Linguistic Geography: Achievement, Methods, and Orientations," *Word* 10.375-387, 1954 (reprinted on pp. 287-299); Uriel Weinreich, "Is A Structural Dialectology Possible?" *Word* 10.388-400, 1954 (reprinted on pp. 300-313).

Linguistic Society of America and the respective authors for permission to reprint: Carroll E. Reed, "The Pronunciation of English in the Pacific Northwest," *Language* 37.559-564, 1961 (reprinted on pp. 115-121); Walter S. Avis, "The 'New England Short o': A Recessive Phoneme," *Language* 37.544-558, 1961 (reprinted on pp. 200-215).

Longmans, Green & Co. and Professor Kurath for permission to reprint: Hans Kurath, "British Sources of Selected Features of American Pronunciation: Problems and Methods," *In Honor of Daniel Jones*, Dennis B. Fry et al., Eds., (London: Longmans, Green, 1964), pp. 146-155 (reprinted on pp. 265-272).

Modern Language Association and Professor McDavid for permission to reprint: Raven I. McDavid, Jr., "Sense and Nonsense about American Dialects," *PMLA* 81.7-17, 1966 (reprinted on pp. 36-52).

Mouton and Co. and the respective authors for permission to reprint: Hans Kurath, "Interrelation between Regional and Social Dialects," *Proceedings of the Ninth International Congress of Linguistics* (The Hague: Mouton, 1964), pp. 135-143 (reprinted on pp. 365-373); Marvin D. Loflin, "On the Structure of the Verb in a Dialect of American Negro English," *Linguistics*, in press (reprinted on pp. 428-443).

National Council of Teachers of English and the respective authors for permission to reprint: Lee A. Pederson, "Some Structural Differences in the Speech of Chicago Negroes," *Social Dialects and Language Learning*, Roger W. Shuy, Ed. (Champaign, Ill.: NCTE, 1964), pp. 28-51 (reprinted on pp. 401-420); Raven I. McDavid, Jr., "A Checklist of Significant Features for Discriminating Social Dialects," *Dimensions of Dialect*, Eldonna Evertts, Ed., (Champaign, Ill.: NCTE, 1967), pp. 7-10 (reprinted on pp. 468-475); William Labov, "Stages in the Acquisition of Standard English," *Social Dialects and Language Learning*, Roger W. Shuy, Ed. (Champaign, Ill., NCTE, 1964), pp. 77-104 (reprinted on pp. 476-499).

Speech Association of America for permission to reprint: C. K. Thomas, "The Phonology of New England English," *Speech Monographs* 28.223-232, 1961 (reprinted on pp. 57-66).

University of Alabama Press and the respective authors for permission to reprint: Audrey R. Duckert, "The *Linguistic Atlas of New England* Revisited," *Publications of the American Dialect Society* 39.8-15, copyright © 1963 by the American Dialect Society (reprinted on pp. 67-73); Albert H. Marckwardt, "Principal and Subsidiary Dialect Areas in the North-Central States," *Publications of the American Dialect Society* 27.3-15, copyright © 1957 by the American Dialect Society (reprinted on pp. 74-82); Harold B. Allen, "Minor Dialect Areas of the Upper Midwest," *Publi-*

cations of the American Dialect Society 30.3-16, copyright © 1958 by the American Dialect Society (reprinted on pp. 94-104); David W. Reed, "Eastern Dialect Words in California," *Publications of the American Dialect Society* 21.3-15, copyright 1954 by the American Dialect Society (reprinted on pp. 105-114); Janet B. Sawyer, "Social Aspects of Bilingualism in San Antonio, Texas," *Publications of the American Dialect Society* 41.7-15, copyright © 1964 by the American Dialect Society (reprinted on pp. 375-381); Lee A. Pederson, "Terms of Abuse for Some Chicago Social Groups," *Publications of the American Dialect Society* 42.26-48, copyright © 1964 by the American Dialect Society (reprinted on pp. 382-400); and figure 1.5 in E. Bagby Atwood, "The Methods of American Dialectology" (reprinted on p. 25).

University of Michigan Press for permission to reprint: figures 1.2, 1.3, 1.4 in E. Bagby Atwood, "The Methods of American Dialectology" (reprinted on pp. 19, 21, 22 respectively).

University of North Carolina Press and Professor McDavid for permission to reprint: Raven I. McDavid, Jr., "Dialect Geography and Social Science Problems," *Social Forces* 25.168-72, 1946 (reprinted on pp. 357-364).

University of Texas Press and Mary B. Atwood for permission to reprint: E. Bagby Atwood, "Grease and Greasy: A Study of Geographical Variation," *Studies in English* 29.249-260, 1950 (reprinted on pp. 160-168).

The publisher and Mary B. Atwood for permission to reprint: E. Bagby Atwood, "The Methods of American Dialectology," *Zeitschrift für Mundartforschung* 30:1.1-29, 1963 (reprinted on pp. 5-36).

Preface

The immediate motivation for preparing this collection of 41 articles is like that which earlier led to a companion anthology, *Readings in Applied English Linguistics*. College and university libraries, although they may buy multiple copies of books for reference use, can rarely afford multiple copies of journals. Students thus find it difficult to obtain a journal article when they need it, to say nothing of reading several such articles in an assigned sequence. Furthermore, the field of American dialect study is actually not very well represented in libraries by the specialized journals. Even the two American publications, *American Speech* and *Publication of the American Dialect Society*, have limited distribution, and the international journal *Orbis* is found in only a few major universities. This anthology, then, makes more accessible a number of basic and representative articles; with one exception, complete chapters as well as excerpts from books easily available are deliberately excluded.

A more pervasive motivation is our desire to stimulate further a speaker's interest in his own language. For several generations the schools have thwarted and frustrated this interest by limiting language content to prescriptive rules taught as guides to "correct" usage. This content is now increasingly being replaced in schools and colleges by a body of content studied for its own sake and drawn from newer grammars, first structural and more recently transformational generative. Even so, the new content seems to be offered only rarely in a way consistent with our basic position that the study of the English language is more than a study of grammatical rules and internal structure. Indeed, grammar—albeit a different grammar—is still emphasized heavily.

The study of variations, as this collection stresses, is one very interesting and significant part of the larger body of language content. Until quite recently dialect study, first recognized as legitimate in the mid-nineteenth century, confined its concern to regional, or horizontal, dialects. Most of the articles in this collection quite properly deal with this kind of inquiry and in particular with the work and findings of the regional dialect research in the United States. Such research is generally known as dialect geography or linguistic geography.

vii

At first, the editors intended to include also several of the recent articles about Canadian English; but, in apportioning their list of desirable articles to the space available, they were compelled to put to one side all the Canadian materials in the belief that English in our sister country has already become the object of so much study that it soon will deserve its own anthology.

Within the past two decades dialect study has achieved a new dimension, the vertical. The recognition of vertical or social variations, of class dialects, has usually been restricted to the specification of departures from the canons of "correct" English. Deviations from a fairly formal literary standard were looked upon as more or less culpable errors, unworthy of scholarly attention except as evils to be shunned. But realization of the central role of language in the critical social ferment of our day has led to careful study of non-standard variants, now considered less as discrete items than as interrelated features of a different linguistic system. The relationship of this development in the new interdisciplinary field of socio-linguistics to the earlier study of regional varieties is obvious. Indeed, this development results from the application of the principles and methods of linguistic geography by researchers first trained in dialect field methods. For that reason, it seemed imperative to include in this book a second, though smaller, section, devoted to a few of the already significant contributions to the understanding of non-standard dialects and hence to the treatment of the problems of bidialectalism.

Whatever universals, innate or not, contemporary theoretical linguists may eventually settle upon as essential in human language—those underlying links that bind the facts of linguistics with those of psychology and philosophy—the correlations of overt language manifestations with place and social class will always prove, at the other end of the scale, equally interesting and far from trivial. This collection focuses upon these correlations and their significant interpretations.

The making of the collection would have been impossible, of course, without the generous willingness of our colleagues and their publishers to allow their articles to reappear here. We are grateful to them all. Specific acknowledgment accompanies each article. We are particularly grateful to Rudolph Troike, who has consented to first publication of his article here instead of in a journal.

HAROLD B. ALLEN

GARY N. UNDERWOOD

Contents

Single Feature Studies

The Comparative Approach

Dialect Theory

Part Two

SOCIAL DIALECTS

Part One

REGIONAL DIALECTS

An Overview

This anthology, devoted to the study of dialect in the United States, begins appropriately with articles by two of the three men who have done most to encourage that study and to stimulate graduate students to direct their research to that end. The third man, Hans Kurath, is represented later in the collection.

So excellent is the first article, the late E. Bagby Atwood's "The Methods of American Dialectology," that it remarkably serves as the underpinning of much that follows. No other scholar has produced so compendious and yet so concise a statement of the background, procedures, and current state of linguistic geography in this country.

Aside from specific dissertations and the merging of the two Pacific Coast atlases under the direction of David W. Reed at the University of California, Berkeley, probably the chief recent developments since Atwood wrote are these three. First, upon the retirement of Hans Kurath from his professorship at the University of Michigan and the unlikelihood that atlas research would continue there, the data files of the atlases of the Middle and South Atlantic states were transferred to the University of Chicago, where Raven I. McDavid, Jr., with the support of the university and of The University of Chicago Press, is editing them for publication. Second, in 1966 the National Endowment for the Humanities provided the first federal aid to a linguistic atlas project when it made a grant to the Linguistic Atlas of the Upper Midwest, a grant that received a one-year renewal for 1968–69. With this aid the first volumes of the projected four-volume work are due for completion in the summer of 1971. Third, hope has arisen for the long-needed establishment of the linguistic atlas of the Gulf States and Inner South. In April, 1968, Lee Pederson of Emory University received support from the Southeastern

Regional Educational Laboratory for a meeting of dialectologists to outline plans for that project. Subsequently, the Laboratory indicated its
willingness to seek funds to underwrite the field investigation, but its
application to the federal government was not approved. Further explora-
tion of funding possibilities was undertaken at a dialectology conference
at the University of Tennessee in April, 1970.

From a different and somewhat less impersonal viewpoint McDavid,
in the second article, clarifies certain misconceptions about dialect work
and provides orientation for the reader unsure of its status in the world
of scholarship. At the same time, he anticipates the focus of the second
part of this collection by offering the necessary transition from attention
upon regional varieties to that upon social dialects.

The Methods of American Dialectology

E. BAGBY ATWOOD

1.1 LEXICOGRAPHY

THE EARLIEST OBSERVATIONS of what would nowadays be called "dialect" covered a variety of linguistic categories but tended to concentrate on lexical and grammatical peculiarities. They were, moreover, largely prescriptive, at least by implication, and observers usually regarded the collected material as something to be avoided. Probably the first collection that could be called in any sense systematic was that of the Rev. John Witherspoon, who published a series of papers on usage in the *Pennsylvania Journal and Weekly Advertiser* during the year 1781[1]. He is credited with having coined the term *Americanism* to designate "ways of speaking peculiar to this country"[2]. Some of his examples, however, were neither American in origin nor "peculiar" to the United States; for example, *fellow countrymen* for *countrymen* and *notify* with its modern meaning of "inform". Witherspoon also collected a number of "vulgarisms", which were undoubtedly genuine and which are common even today: *knowed* for *knew*, *this here* for *this*, *drownded* for *drowned*, *attacted* for *attacked*, and others[3].

The most famous of American lexicographers, Noah Webster, need not be treated in detail, since a vast body of material has been published concerning him. However, as far as I know, the effect of the regional American dialects, particularly those of New England, on his recording of words and meanings remains to be determined. Certainly his first dictionary, that of 1806[4], was

---

Reprinted by permission of Mrs. E. Bagby Atwood and the editor from *Zeitschrift für Mundartforschung*, 30.1.1–29 (1963). The late Professor Atwood was a member of the department of English of the University of Texas and the author of *A Survey of Verb Forms of the Eastern United States* and *The Regional Vocabulary of Texas*.

[1] See M. M. Mathews, *The Beginnings of American English* (Chicago, 1931), p. 14.

[2] *Ibid.*, p. 16; H. L. Mencken, *The American Language*, 4th ed. (New York, 1938), pp. 4–7; G. P. Krapp, *The English Language in America*, 2 vols. (New York, 1925), I, 46–47; 72.

[3] Mathews, *Beginnings*, pp. 20–23.

[4] Noah Webster, *Compendious Dictionary of the English Language* (Hartford and New Haven, Conn., 1806).

attacked for seeming to sanction "Americanisms and vulgarisms", and Webster felt need to defend himself for having included such terms as *docket, decedent, dutiable,* and even *lot* (of land)—as well as such "cant words" as *caucus*[5]. In his *American Dictionary* of 1828[6] he recorded a considerable number of Americanisms, or at least new terms observable in America, including such controversial verb usages as *to notice, to advocate,* and *to progress,* all of which had been condemned by Benjamin Franklin[7]. We can only wish that Webster had recorded more "cant" terms.

The numerous glossaries of Americanisms that appeared during the course of the nineteenth century are to a great extent the work of amateurs whose observation tended to be somewhat random and impressionistic. Among the compilers of such lists were David Humphries (1815)[8], John Pickering (1816)[9], Robley Dunglison (1829–30)[10], John R. Bartlett (1848)[11], and John S. Farmer (1889)[12]. None of these was primarily concerned with folk speech, yet occasionally items of considerable dialectal interest are entered and commented on; for example *be* (for *am, are*—Be you ready?), *clapboard* (siding), *poke* (bag), *run* (small stream), and *tote* (carry)[13]. All of these appear as early as Pickering, and most are recorded in Webster's first dictionary.

By far the greatest of the early collectors of American usages was Richard H. Thornton, an Englishman who migrated to the New World in the 1870s[14]. Toward the end of the century he began to accumulate a carefully documented body of material, in which the source and the date of every usage were on record. His *American Glossary* was published in 1912 and later years[15]; although it is not primarily a dialect dictionary[16] it still serves as a model of lexicographic procedure.

The idea that popular (in the sense of uneducated) speech is worthy of serious scholarly study arrived perhaps somewhat later in America than in Western Europe. The first public manifestation of interest on the part of scholars was the organization of the American Dialect Society (ADS), which

[5] Mathews, *Beginnings*, pp. 49–50; Krapp, *English Language*, I, 360.

[6] *An American Dictionary of the English Language*, 2 vols. (New York, 1828).

[7] Mathews, *Beginnings*, pp. 52–54; Mencken, *American Language*, p. 7.

[8] Humphries attached a glossary to one of his plays, *The Yankey in England*. See Mathews, *Beginnings*, pp. 56–63.

[9] *A Vocabulary, or Collection of Words and Phrases Which have been Supposed to be peculiar to the United States of America* . . . (Boston, 1816).

[10] In a series of articles appearing in the *Virginia Literary Museum* beginning in December, 1829. Reprinted in Mathews, *Beginnings*, pp. 99–112.

[11] *A Dictionary of Americanisms* (New York, 1848). Subsequently re-edited a number of times.

[12] *Americanisms Old and New* (London, 1889).

[13] All of these have been shown by the Linguistic Atlas materials to have clear geographical limits. See the discussion of linguistic geography, below.

[14] For further biographical information see *Dialect Notes (DN)*, VI, Part XVIII (1939), 715–718 [American Dialect Society, University, Alabama].

[15] R. H. Thornton, *An American Glossary*, 2 vols. (London, 1912). The third volume was published piecemeal in *DN*, VI (1928–39).

[16] Of course, it contains many words of regional currency; for example, *bayou, chaparral, snake doctor, you-uns*.

took place at Harvard University in 1889. Evidently the idea was first suggested by Charles H. Grandgent, and the organization meeting was attended by twenty-eight persons, including Edward S. Sheldon, Francis J. Child, J. B. Greenough, George L. Kittredge, and others of their stature—men who were, or were to be, among the leading philological scholars of their time[17]. The avowed object of the Society was "the investigation of the spoken English of the United States and Canada, and incidentally of other non-aboriginal dialects spoken in the same countries"[18]. By January of 1890 there were 158 members[19], and the official organ of the Society, *Dialect Notes*, began publication in that year.

As Louise Pound has pointed out, the early dialect scholars must have been strongly influenced by German thought and method. The first four presidents of the ADS had all studied in Germany, and George Hempl, the eighth, took his doctorate at Jena[20]. The Wenker methodology, however, seems not to have been adopted as a basis for dialect collection, except to a limited extent and in a modified form. Hempl prepared a standard questionnaire of something over 90 items which he published in 1894[21], requesting the collaboration of his colleagues in its circulation. Hempl's questions were awkward and unwieldy[22], and it is difficult to see how most of them could have produced useful results. I believe that the only publication based on this material was Hempl's article on the pronunciation of *grease* (verb) and *greasy*, which appeared in 1896[23].

From an early date, the ADS took the position that the great majority of members could make their most valuable contribution in the field of vocabulary. In various circulars, instructions were given as to the kinds of usages to be collected and the methods to be followed[24]. It was the hope, obviously a rather naive one, that there might be assembled "*a complete record of American speech-forms in our day*, say in 1900", and that in the following years there might be published "an authoritative dictionary of American usage, which would supersede all other work in that line"[25]. Indeed, the idea of a dialect dictionary has always been prominent among the membership of the ADS; many have hoped that we might have a work comparable to Joseph Wright's monumental *English Dialect Dictionary*[26].

[17] *DN*, I, Part I (1890), 1–2. See also Louise Pound, "The American Dialect Society: A Historical Sketch," *Publication of the American Dialect Society (PADS)*, No. 17 (1952), 4–5. [American Dialect Society, University, Alabama.]
[18] "Constitution," *DN*, I, Part I (1890), 3.
[19] *DN*, I, Part I (1890), 30–32.   [20] Pound, "The ADS," pp. 7–9.
[21] George Hempl, "American Speech-Maps," *DN*, I, Part VII (1894), 315–318.
[22] For example, "Is '*a bunch of cattle*' familiar to you?" "What does the word 'to *squint*' first suggest to you? Mention other meanings in the order of their familiarity." "Which of the following words usually have *a* as in 'cat', or nearly that?" *Ibid.*, pp. 316–317.
[23] George Hempl, "*Grease* and *Greasy*," *DN*, I, Part IX (1896), 438–444. [See p. 154 in this book.]
[24] Pound, "The ADS," pp. 4–5; see also "The 1895 Circular," *DN*, I, Part VIII (1895), 360–367.   [25] *Ibid.*, p. 360.
[26] Joseph Wright, *English Dialect Dictionary*, 6 vols. (London, 1898–1905). The English Dialect Society, founded in 1873, regarded its work as complete when Wright's material was ready for publication; accordingly the Society disbanded toward the end of 1896.

Unfortunately the contributions to *Dialect Notes* were extremely uneven, both in completeness and in reliability. Even after some 40 years of collection, only a few names stood out for thoroughness of work—names such as L. W. Payne[27], H. Tallichet[28], Louise Pound[29], and Vance Randolph[30]. Most reports were pitifully meager, and the total mass fell far short of original expectations.

During the period when Louise Pound was president of the ADS (1938–41) she arranged, "as a private person, not as president of the society"[31], for the publication of the available dialect materials by the Crowell Company. On her recommendation, Harold Wentworth was chosen as editor. Within a relatively short time his *American Dialect Dictionary* had been prepared and published[32], although without the official sanction of the ADS. In answer to criticisms of her arrangements, Miss Pound replied that "a standstill of more than half a century seemed long enough. When an opportunity offered, why not seize it?"[33]

Wentworth's *Dictionary* must be regarded as an abridged one, whether so planned or not. It is very doubtful that all available material was included; and, in any case, the project was unfortunate in its timing. At least three important collections were being made during this period, of which publication was under way or would shortly begin. These were the materials of the *Dictionary of American English*[34], the *Linguistic Atlas of New England*[35], and the Mencken Supplements to *The American Language*[36]. Moreover, the G. & C. Merriam Company must have had in its files a great deal of valuable dialectal material which would ultimately see publication.

In recent studies of the vocabulary of the Southwest and other areas I have had occasion to refer to Wentworth many times. Although I frequently find valuable material, I am often annoyed by the absence of terms that are of considerable dialectal significance. I cite 40 such instances (out of a considerably larger number): *acequia* (irrigation ditch), *angledog* (earthworm), *banquette* (sidewalk), *belly band* (saddle girth), (*blue*) *norther* (sharp north wind), *burro* (donkey), *buttonwood* (sycamore tree), *Cajun* (Acadian), *chaparral* (bushy country), *charivari* (serenade), *clearseed peach* (freestone peach), *coon* (Negro), *cope!* (horse call), *corral* (horse pen), *devil's darning needle* (dragonfly), *dogie*

[27] L. W. Payne, "A Word-List from East Alabama," *DN*, III, Part IV (1908), 279–328, and III, Part V (1909), 343–391.

[28] H. Tallichet, "A Contribution towards a Vocabulary of Spanish and Mexican Words Used in Texas," *DN*, I, Part IV (1892), 185–195. Augmented in later issues.

[29] I believe the first of a considerable series of Miss Pound's dialect publications was "Dialect Speech in Nebraska," *DN*, III, Part I (1905), 55–67.

[30] Vance Randolph's publications on the Ozark area (Arkansas) are well known to folklorists as well as to dialectologists. Among many others, see "A Word-List from the Ozarks," *DN*, V, Part IX (1926), 397–405.

[31] Pound, "The ADS," p. 25.

[32] Harold Wentworth, *American Dialect Dictionary* (New York, 1944).

[33] Pound, "The ADS," p. 26.

[34] William A. Craigie and James R. Hulbert, *A Dictionary of American English*, 4 vols. (Chicago, 1938–44).

[35] For a discussion and citations, see the section on linguistic geography, below.

[36] H. L. Mencken, *The American Language, Supplement I* (New York, 1945); *Supplement II* (New York, 1948).

(lone calf), *dog irons* (andirons), *eaves troughs* (gutters), *evener* (doubletree), *fatcake* (doughnut or cruller), *firedogs* (andirons), *hogshead cheese* (pork mixture), *hoosegow* (jail), *jackleg* (untrained person), *lead horse* (horse on the left), *llano* (prairie), *lumber room* (store room), *mesa* (plateau), *middling(s)* (salt pork), *milk gap* (cow pen), *mosquito hawk* (dragonfly), *nigger shooter* (boy's weapon), *olla* (water jar), *pilón* (something extra), *pirogue* (canoe), *rainworm* (earthworm), *redbug* (chigger), *snake feeder* (dragonfly), *toot* (paper bag), and *worm fence* (rail fence). That these are common usages is attested by the fact that 31 of them are entered in the *Dictionary of American English*, while no less than 38 of them are treated in *Webster's Third New International Dictionary*[37], usually with some indication of their geographical distribution.

It is clear that there has never been assembled an American dialect lexicon to compare with that of England[38]. In fact, it is hardly possible that such a collection can ever be made, since "dialect" in the European sense is much less common in America than in England. The American population has always been more fluid than that of Europe, both geographically and socially. Conditions were simply not right for the development of extensive local patois. There is often little distinction between dialect and standard speech; regional terms are frequently found in the usage of the educated, and even "illiterate" features are common in the works of novelists who deal with "local color". Most general dictionaries have taken cognizance of these facts and have included a great many terms of regional and even local currency. The *Century Dictionary*, first published in 1889[39], in successive editions entered and documented large numbers of American words of a "dialectal" nature[40]. The same may be said of the *Dictionary of American English* (as exemplified on the preceding page), as well as of Mathew's *Dictionary of Americanisms*[41]. *Webster's Third New International* includes most of the words that are mapped in the *Linguistic Atlas of New England* and in Hans Kurath's *Word Geography*—even down to such Northern localisms as *belly bump(er)*, *belly bunt*, *belly bust(er)*, *belly flop(per)*, *belly gut(ter)*, and *belly whop(per)*, all of which denote the act of coasting down a hill on one's belly.

In spite of the limitations that are apparent, and in spite of the overlapping that must of necessity take place, most members of the ADS, including myself, are hopeful that a truly systematic and comprehensive dictionary of American dialect terms may be prepared. It is, however, only realistic to recognize that such a project must have a single leading spirit as director, who must have

[37] Philip B. Gove, ed., *Webster's Third New International Dictionary* (Springfield, Mass., 1961).

[38] Wentworth's dictionary contains a little over 15,000 entries; Wright's includes 19,767 in the letters A to C only. Wright, Vol. I, p. vii.

[39] William D. Whitney, *The Century Dictionary*, 6 vols. (New York, 1889–91).

[40] For example, the edition in my possession (that of 1906) includes *devil's darning needle*, *snake feeder*, *snake doctor*, and *mosquito hawk*, as well as the literary equivalent *dragon fly*.

[41] M. M. Mathews, *A Dictionary of Americanisms on Historical Principles* (Chicago, 1951).

adequate time, adequate financing, and an adequate organization to carry the task to completion. No dictionary has ever compiled itself.

Since 1944 the ADS has evidenced a considerable broadening of interests; its new series of *Publications*[42] has by no means restricted itself to the amassing of a dialect lexicon, but has on the other hand served as a medium for the circulation of important monographs on many subjects[43].

As has been mentioned, new sources of lexical usage are now available. Moreover, more systematic methods are being developed for the collection of vocabulary. One such method, devised largely by Frederick G. Cassidy, involves the circulation of extensive questionnaires to individual informants so that at least a nucleus of items may be compared on a nationwide scale[44]. The similarity of this procedure to that of many linguistic atlases is apparent, and other methods of the same sort will be discussed later.

In summary we may say that, although American words of a "dialectal" nature have been rather fully treated in separate studies and in general dictionaries, we still lack a comprehensive and fully documented dialect dictionary for the country as a whole.

1.2 LINGUISTIC GEOGRAPHY

Atlases of the Atlantic States

The idea of preparing a linguistic atlas of the United States must have been current for a good many years before any actual work was undertaken[45]. It was, however, in the years 1928 and 1929 that concrete proposals and plans were made. In December of 1928 the Present-Day English Group of the Modern Language Association approved the appointment of a committee to study the possibility of preparing an American atlas. At about the same time (independently, it seems), Edgar H. Sturtevant of Yale University, Director of the Linguistic Institute, had arranged for a conference of linguistic scholars to

[42] After a brief lapse during the Second World War, *Dialect Notes* was discontinued and the official series became *Publication of the American Dialect Society (PADS)* beginning in 1944.

[43] For example, D. W. Maurer, "White Mob," No. 24 (1955); Einar Haugen, "Bilingualism in the Americas," No. 26 (1956); Dwight I. Bolinger, "Interrogative Structures of American English," No. 28 (1957)—in addition to works on linguistic geography, some of which will be mentioned later.

[44] Cassidy is now "Custodian of Collections" for the ADS. His distinguished dialect studies, in the United States as well as in Jamaica, qualify him superbly to be the "leading spirit" in a nationwide lexical survey. [With the joint support of the University of Wisconsin and the U.S. Office of Education Cassidy is now engaged in collecting and editing data for the Dictionary of American Regional English, which will realize the American Dialect Society's long-cherished hope of a comprehensive lexicon of American dialects. Eds.]

[45] The project of George Hempl has already been described. Many others had shown a keen interest in a speech survey: for example, Harry M. Ayres, Charles C. Fries, W. Cabell Greet, John S. Kenyon, and George P. Krapp. See Hans Kurath and others, *Handbook of the Linguistic Geography of New England* (Providence, R. I., 1939), pp. x–xi.

consider the same project[46]. The two groups were very shortly acting jointly, and proposals were soon submitted to the American Council of Learned Societies with a view to financial support. In August of 1929 the Executive Committee of this body authorized the appointment of a committee, headed by Hans Kurath, to prepare a somewhat detailed plan and an estimated budget. In view of the magnitude of the project, it was agreed that a relatively small area should first be surveyed, and the choice of the New England States[47] seemed the most feasible one.

The methodology of the American *Atlas* has been essentially that of Gilliéron[48], as refined and modified for Italy by Karl Jaberg and Jakob Jud[49]. During the summer of 1930, Kurath engaged in extended conferences with these scholars, as well as with Paul Scheuermeier, the leading fieldworker for the Italian *Atlas*[50].

The staff for the New England *Atlas* was shortly set up with Kurath as Director, Miles L. Hanley as Associate Director, and Marcus L. Hansen as Historian. Since it was desirable to complete the survey in a minimum of time, several fieldworkers were employed; the number was ultimately augmented to nine. Headquarters were established at Yale University, which also provided a Sterling Fellowship for one of the fieldworkers as well as half the salary of the Associate Director[51]. Other universities and colleges likewise shared in financial support of the *Atlas*; these included Dartmouth, Brown, Mt. Holyoke, and the University of Vermont.

The staff of the *Atlas* underwent a short but concentrated training period during the summer of 1931, when Jakob Jud and Paul Scheuermeier were present as instructors and advisers. There followed the actual fieldwork, which occupied a period of 25 months, ending in September of 1933.

The editing of the New England materials required several years, during which Kurath, with the able collaboration of Bernard and Julia Bloch, prepared 713 maps for publication. Between 1939 and 1943 the three volumes (bound in six parts)[52] were off the press, along with a *Handbook*[53] which explained the

[46] *Ibid.*, p. xi. See also "Plans for a Survey of the Dialects of New England," *DN* VI, Part II (1930), 65–66, and "The Conference on a Linguistic Atlas of the United States and Canada," *Bulletin No. 4* of the Linguistic Society of America (Baltimore, Md., 1929), pp. 20–47.

[47] These states are Maine, New Hampshire, Vermont, Massachusetts, Rhode Island, and Connecticut.

[48] Jules Gilliéron and Edmond Edmont, *Atlas linguistique de la France* (Paris, 1902–12).

[49] Karl Jaberg and Jakob Jud, *Sprach und Sachatlas Italiens und der Südschweiz*, 8 vols. (Zofingen, 1928–40).

[50] Hans Kurath, "Report of Interviews with European Scholars . . .," *DN*, VI, Part II (1930), 73–74.

[51] "Progress of the Linguistic Atlas" ("Progress"—a series of reports), *DN*, VI, Part III (1931), 91–92.

[52] Hans Kurath, Miles L. Hanley, Bernard Bloch, and others, *Linguistic Atlas of New England*, 3 vols. in 6 parts (Providence, R.I., 1939–43).

[53] Hans Kurath and others, *Handbook of the Linguistic Geography of New England* (*Handbook*) (Providence, R.I., 1939).

methodology, provided historical data, and summarized some of the most important dialectal features of the area.

Beginning in 1933, fieldwork was continued in the Middle Atlantic and South Atlantic States[54]. Guy S. Lowman, the ablest of the New England field-workers, gathered material more or less continuously until his death in an automobile accident in 1941. By this time he had completed work in all of the Atlantic States[55] except South Carolina, Georgia, and New York. In the years following the Second World War, this work was brought to completion by Raven I. McDavid, Jr. As yet these raw materials have not been prepared for publication.

The procedures which were used in the New England survey, and which were essentially followed in the other Atlantic states, may be described under a number of headings.

Communities. Ultimately 213 New England communities[56] were chosen for investigation. Of these a considerable majority were small towns or semi-rural communities; but the principal cities of the area were also included. The oldest settlements were given preference, and most of them were investigated; however, a fair selection was also made of secondary settlements and even of newer industrial areas. A brief history of each community was compiled, including its original settlement, subsequent changes in population, principal industries, and other pertinent characteristics[57]. Communities tended to be more or less equidistant save in northern Maine, where population was sparse. In the Middle Atlantic and South Atlantic States the same principles were followed, with possibly greater attention given to the larger cities. There are, for example, 22 records from the adjoining boroughs of Manhattan and Brooklyn, and McDavid gathered at least 10 in Charleston, South Carolina.

Informants. It is in the choice of informants that the American *Atlas* differs most strikingly from its European predecessors. Rather than restrict the investigation to rustic, or "folk", speech, Kurath required the inclusion of three principal types, which he describes as follows:

Type I: Little formal education, little reading, and restricted social contacts.
Type II: Better formal education (usually high school) and/or wider reading and social contacts.

[54] The Middle Atlantic States consist of New York, New Jersey, Pennsylvania, and West Virginia. The South Atlantic States are made up of Delaware, Maryland, Virginia, North Carolina, South Carolina, Georgia, and Florida.

[55] Only portions of Georgia and Florida were surveyed. In addition to the states mentioned above, several field records were made in the easternmost section of Ohio. A few were also made in parts of Canada that adjoin the United States—chiefly in New Brunswick and Ontario.

[56] "Communities" as here used means points, or numbers, on the map. Occasionally two adjoining towns are treated as the same community.

[57] For a full account of the New England communities, see *Handbook*, pp. 159–240.

Type III: Superior education (usually college), cultured background, wide reading, and/or extensive social contacts.

Each of these types is divided into two sub-classes: A, aged or old-fashioned, and B, middle-aged or younger, hence presumably more modern in usage[58]. The idea of the divisions, of course, is to provide a means of determining the extent to which "dialect" characteristics appear in the speech of better-educated members of the various communities. Of the 413 informants actually represented in the New England *Atlas*, 148 fall in Type I, 214 in Type II, and 51 in Type III[59]. In the remainder of the Atlantic States the proportions were about the same, except that in some areas Type I informants were proportionally more numerous than in New England. This would depend, of course, on the nature of the areas themselves. For example, during the 1930s in the Southern mountains it was not difficult to find illiterate or semi-literate informants of sufficient intelligence to answer the questions. In the whole of the Atlantic States there are 157 informants designated as "cultured[60]."

Actual choice of the informants was left to the individual fieldworkers, but certain general requirements were laid down. Every effort was made to secure truly native representatives, usually those born and reared in the area and descended from local families. No informant should have spent an extended period away from the area which he represented. Both men and women were accepted on equal terms and in about equal numbers. Fieldworkers were expected to provide material for a brief biography and character sketch of each informant.

Fieldworkers. The fieldworkers who did the interviewing in the Atlantic States are as follows: Hans Kurath, Bernard Bloch, Martin Joos, Guy S. Lowman, Miles L. Hanley, Lee S. Hultzén, Rachel S. Harris, Cassil Reynard, Marguerite Chapallaz, and Raven I. McDavid, Jr. All of these worked in New England except McDavid; in the other Atlantic states, as has been mentioned, Lowman and McDavid made all of the field records. All of the *Atlas* fieldworkers were highly trained. Several of them held the doctor's degree and were well grounded in the type of linguistic discipline that was current at that time. Moreover, they all underwent intensive training in phonetic transcription as part of their preparation for *Atlas* work. The idea of using several fieldworkers in New England has been justified by the relatively rapid completion of the *Atlas*. There are, however, certain unavoidable disadvantages. For one thing, most of the pronunciation features must be interpreted by someone who is thoroughly familiar with the materials[61]. Moreover, some fieldworkers were

[58] *Ibid.*, p. 44.
[59] *Ibid.*, pp. 42–43.
[60] H. Kurath and Raven I. McDavid, Jr., *The Pronunciation of English in the Atlantic States* (Ann Arbor, Michigan, 1961), pp. 23–27.
[61] For example, as Kurath points out, the symbols [ɒ] and [ɔ] might represent the same sound in the transcriptions of different fieldworkers. *Handbook*, pp. 126–127.

more inclined than others to elicit archaisms in vocabulary and grammar. It is my opinion that where multiple fieldworkers are used their work should be spread over the same areas rather than confined to respective "territories". Otherwise there will appear what seem to be geographical cleavages in usage which must be discounted as merely fieldworker differences.

The Work Sheets. The actual questions that were posed to the informants were chosen after much research in previously published materials[62]. Actually, the final form was not determined until after a certain amount of preliminary fieldwork had been completed. In general, the items on the list represented everyday concepts, and sought to elicit usages that would ordinarily be transmitted orally within the family rather than in schools. Questions were arranged topically in order to avoid incoherence and to provide a more conversational atmosphere for the informant. Some of the topics were: the weather. the dwelling, utensils and implements, topography, domestic animals, and foods. The work sheets contained a sampling of pronunciation features, lexical peculiarities, morphological variants, and occasionally syntactic characteristics. Some pronunciation items sought to determine whether a phonemic distinction existed or not, or whether it existed in a certain environment (*mourning* as against *morning*); others were concerned with the incidence of a given phoneme (/s/ as against /z/ in *greasy*) or with the exact phonetic quality of a phoneme or sequence of phonemes (e.g., the vowel nucleus in *five*). Vocabulary items were concerned mainly with the currency of various synonyms for the same concept (*angleworm, angledog, eaceworm, mudworm, earthworm*). Very few, if any, were directly aimed at the recording of variant meanings, although most fieldworkers took note of deviant ideas or reactions on the part of the informants. The greater number of morphological items were concerned with verb forms, such as *clum* for *climbed*, *sot* for *sat*, or *hain't* for *haven't*. The total number of items (of all categories) used in New England was 711[63]; this was augmented to 772 in the South Atlantic States. An interview was expected to occupy from eight hours to a good many more, depending on the personality of the informant.

Conducting the interviews. Gilliéron's method of merely asking the informant to translate a term into his dialect would have little value in the United States, since no one wants to admit that he speaks a dialect. The desired response had to be elicited indirectly, if possible without using a word or phrase that might be part of the answer. No standard form was ever adopted for the questions themselves[64]; each fieldworker was expected to use his ingenuity in producing

[62] McDavid cites in particular the following: C. S. Grandgent, J. S. Kenyon, G. P. Krapp, and George Hempl. See "The Linguistic Atlas of New England," *Orbis*, I (1952), 95–103; esp. p. 98. [Centre International de Dialectologie Générale, Louvain.]

[63] *Handbook*, pp. 147–158.

[64] By contrast, The Linguistic Atlas of England requires that all fieldworkers ask the same question in the same words. See Harold Orton, "An English Dialect Survey: Linguistic Atlas of England," *Orbis*, IX (1960), 331–348. [See p. 230 in this book.]

a response. In the case of a concrete object, a brief description might be given. For example, Bloch would usually secure a term for *seesaw* by asking: "What do you call a plank laid across a trestle for children to play on[65]"? McDavid's form for this question was somewhat fuller: ". . . you'd have a plank laying across—maybe a section of rail fence or a sawhorse or something like that, and a kid gets on one end and another gets on the other and they go up and down, what do you call that[66]"? Sometimes, particularly in the case of a verb form or a phrase, a question might be of the completion type. McDavid builds up this imaginary situation in order to bring out *new suit*: "Say somebody's about to get married, and his mother or his sister will look him over and say, 'You can't get married in those old clothes—you better go round to the store and get you a . . .' ". Sometimes, in order to encourage the use of a synonym, a question might take the form: "Do you ever call it anything else"? Actual suggestion— that is, using what might be the response and asking the informant whether or not it is his usage—might be resorted to occasionally, but usually only if all other means of securing an answer had failed[67].

Fieldworkers were instructed to keep careful notations regarding the types of responses. Besides occurring normally in answer to a question, a word or phrase might come out in conversation without a question having been asked at all; or it might have been directly suggested; or it might have been "forced" by undue insistence on the part of the fieldworker. The informant might label the usage as old-fashioned or obsolescent; or he might obviously be using a term humorously; or he might (rightly or wrongly) state that a feature is often heard in the community but that he himself never employs it. It is doubtful that fieldworkers' practice in these matters was uniform, particularly with regard to old-fashioned usage. Indeed, McDavid often asked his original question in the form: "What did you call so-and-so in the old days[68]"?

Phonetic transcription. The system of phonetic notation used in the American *Atlas* must be regarded as highly complicated by any standard. The editors take 20 pages in the *Handbook*[69] to explain it, and it seems to me that the reader would need a rather good grounding in phonetics in order to understand the explanation. Thirty-two basic vowel symbols are provided, and each of these may be modified by "shift signs" to indicate intermediate vowel positions. Other diacritics may be used to indicate length or shortness, nasalization, labialization, retroflection, or devoicing. Over 50 consonant symbols are given,

[65] Bernard Bloch, "Interviewing for the Linguistic Atlas," *American Speech*, X (1935), 3–9; p. 7. [Columbia University Press, New York.]

[66] From a tape recording of a sample interview made by McDavid.

[67] Clearly this method would be less objectionable if several alternate terms were suggested together, as *fish worm, fishing worm, angleworm, mud worm, red worm*, etc., from which the informant might make a choice.

[68] Lowman left behind a considerable number of abbreviated labels for different types of usage; for example, *asuch*, meaning used as a child; *snat*, suggested, and regarded by the informant as natural, and so on.

[69] *Handbook*, pp. 122–143.

and many of these may also be marked so as to indicate special qualities such as aspiration, palatalization, velarization, dentalization, labialization, voicing, devoicing, retroflection, length, or syllabic quality. Stress marks were supposed to be used in polysyllabic words, and in some instances indications of intonation were required. The most skilled of the fieldworkers could manipulate the entire system accurately only in rather short utterances, and even then phonetic features were often overlooked or taken for granted[70]. Different practices by the individual fieldworkers can frequently be detected; these are most noticeable in the case of the low back vowels[71]. In view of the complexity of the system of transcription, we must say that the American *Atlas* is firmly committed to the idea of using "professional", or highly trained, fieldworkers; others can make little contribution, at least in the field of pronunciation.

Mechanical recording. Although the desirability of a permanent aural record was recognized early[72], none of the actual *Atlas* interviews were mechanically recorded. In the early days this was partially attributable to the awkwardness of the mechanisms themselves. However, shortly after the completion of the New England fieldwork, arrangements were made which permitted Miles L. Hanley to begin a collection of phonograph records in the area. In the years 1933 and 1934 he completed 657 double-faced 12-inch records which contained natural conversation and narrative materials from a variety of informants and communities. Many of the speakers were the same informants who had previously been interviewed for the *Atlas*[73].

In the Middle and South Atlantic States no financial provision was made for the making of discs or tapes of informants' speech; hence mechanical recording in these areas has been very sporadic. I know of no comprehensive collection covering any large portion of the Atlantic States outside of New England.

Editing and Publication. The New England *Atlas* was prepared for publication according to Gilliéron's idea of entering each response in phonetic notation at its appropriate point on the face of a map. The mechanics of editing, important as they are, need be sketched only briefly. The first step was to stamp a positive identification on every page of every "work book" or field record. Then the books were disassembled so that all the page 1's, all the page 2's, and so on might be placed together. After this all the responses to a single "item", or question, were copied in the form of a list, with each response given the number which had been assigned to the informant who uttered it and to his community. The entering of the data on the faces of the maps required a good deal of

[70] For example, the aspiration of the initial consonant in *two* and *twice* is marked only sporadically (Map 53); the same may be said of the nasalization of the vowel in *broom* (Map 155) and *mumps* (Map 507).

[71] *Handbook*, pp. 126–127.

[72] "Progress," *DN*, VI, Part V (1932), 281.

[73] "Progress," *DN*, VI, Part IX (1934), 419.

Figure 1.1: Portion of a map (Map 236) from the *Linguistic Atlas of New England*, showing variant terms for the earthworm. Reprinted by permission.

planning and experimentation. Kurath's original hope was that a font of phonetic type might be cast, but various practical difficulties led to the decision to have the transcriptions drafted by hand[74]. The drafting was done (under the close supervision of Bernard Bloch) on a transparent overlay, and the base map was photographed through the overlay. The result was that the community numbers and the important geographical features (rivers, mountains, State boundaries, etc.) appeared in a light brown shade whereas the linguistic data came out in a clearcut black. A portion of one of the maps is reproduced (in black and white) in Figure 1.1.

The size chosen for the maps was 20 by 24 inches (about 51 by 62 centimeters). This permitted the entering of all actual responses at the proper point—even responses that were suggested, or heard from others, or regarded as obsolete, or used humorously, and so on. Entries of the latter types are preceded by an arbitrary symbol. However, a good deal of non-linguistic or semi-linguistic material usually remained: deviant meanings, expressions of attitude toward a word and/or its referent, and similar data. The most important

[74] "Progress," *DN*, VI, Part X (1935), 449–450; *DN*, VI, Part XI (1935), 481.

portion of this material was entered in the "commentaries" which appeared by the side of the maps. Some of these commentaries are very full, and contain observations of great interest to folklorists as well as to linguists[75].

The method used in publishing the New England records was obviously an expensive one and would be much more expensive at the present time. The published price of the New England *Atlas* was $180—a price which severely limited its circulation, yet one which today would cover only a fraction of the cost. We can hardly hope that the field records of the Middle and South Atlantic States will see publication in such a sumptuous format. If the complete raw materials of these areas are to appear, the most likely presentation seems to be in the form of lists or columns of responses, from which individual researchers may prepare maps to suit their purposes.

Interpretive presentations. Both the published and the unpublished field records have been scanned by the *Atlas* staff and others, and various methods have been used for the cartographic presentation of linguistic data in summary form. In the case of lexical variation, it is usually sufficient to assign a symbol to each "word"[76] and to enter this symbol at its appropriate point on a much reduced map. The New England *Handbook* (pp. 27 ff.) contains a number of such presentations, where the principal lexical variants are entered on maps measuring only $3\frac{3}{4}$ by $4\frac{3}{4}$ inches ($9\frac{1}{2}$ by 12 centimeters). This type of cartography was used by Kurath in his *Word Geography of the Eastern United States*[77], which was based on the *Atlas* field records of all of the Atlantic States. The maps on which the data is entered measure about $7\frac{1}{2}$ by 9 inches (19 by $22\frac{1}{2}$ centimeters); the portion occupied by New England is only about $2\frac{3}{4}$ by 3 inches, a space only one-eighth the diameter of the *Atlas* maps. In order to avoid overcrowding, Kurath sometimes used more than one map to present all the responses to a particular question. Another device which he developed was that of using oversized symbols at intervals in order to indicate universality of usage within a given area. (See Figure 1.2.)

The method of *isoglosses* has also been used for the cartographic presentation of lexical features. What must be realized is that an isogloss based on the American materials can seldom, if ever, be more than approximate, since usages do not as a rule terminate abruptly. Moreover, since responses from more than one informant are normally entered at each "point", an isogloss should never be regarded as a dividing line between two usages; rather it is an indication of the approximate outer limit of a single feature. Many usages are not amenable to presentation by this method, since they appear in such scattered fashion

[75] For example, details in the observance of the mockserenade (charivari, Katzenmusik) after a wedding (Map 409).

[76] Obviously, *word* is immensely difficult to define; yet practical problems in the American materials are not extremely serious. Usually phonological variants (such as *troughs* and *troths*) can be grouped together as the same "word."

[77] Hans Kurath, *A Word Geography of the Eastern United States* (Ann Arbor, Michigan, 1949).

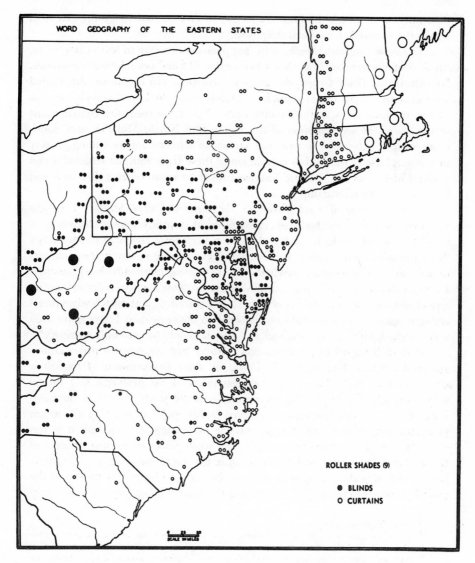

Figure 1.2: Map showing lexical variants by means of symbols, from Hans Kurath, *A Word Geography of the Eastern United States*. Dots indicate the currency of *blinds* and *curtains*, for roller shades. Reprinted by permission.

that a large number of lines would have to be drawn in order to encircle them accurately. No presentation by isoglosses is very convincing unless these are drawn by a competent scholar, and even then we need to know the individual distributions on which the lines are based, so that we may judge the extent to which the materials have been simplified.

The New England *Handbook* (p. 29) presents one map of lexical isoglosses, but it contains so many lines that it has a maze-like and bewildering appearance. Kurath, in his *Word Geography*, gives no less than 119 isoglosses, distributed over 41 maps[78]. His use of these lines to determine the lexical speech areas, as well as the focal areas, of the Atlantic States[79] is one of the major contributions of his book; his segmentation of the region into North, Midland, and South (with various sub-areas) is now well known to scholars and is finding its way into general use as well[80]. His correlation of these areas with the settlement and cultural history of the Atlantic Seaboard must be regarded as a thorough and brilliant work of scholarship.

In my *Survey of Verb Forms in the Eastern United States*[81] I largely followed Kurath's methods of cartographical representation. Ordinarily a separate symbol would be assigned to each verb form that was phonemically distinguishable from another. Problems of decision were relatively few, and pertained mainly to such matters as whether or not to group *taken* and *takened* together. I also experimented with the use of shading on some maps in order to indicate universality or near-universality of usage (see Figure 1.3), particularly when interesting minority usages needed to be entered on the same map. I have never been very satisfied with this device, and feel that it should be used only sparingly[82].

It is with regard to pronunciation features that interpretive presentations are most difficult. Kurath and McDavid, in their *Pronunciation of English in the Atlantic States*[83], have solved a great many of the problems in a logical way, although not within the framework used by many structural linguists. First of all, the idea (sometimes followed in Europe)[84] of entering all variant pronunciations of the same "word" on the same map was rejected, if it was ever considered. To take an example, the word *father* in various dialects of England and America may show variation in the initial consonant ([f] as against [v]); it may also show a considerable number of vowel qualities for the *a*; the medial consonant may be [ð] or [d]; and the final syllable may show not only

---

[78] *Ibid.*, Figures 4–43.

[79] Kurath's methods of counting lines have never been explained in print. Presumably he estimated the numbers of lines in the larger and smaller bundles.

[80] *Webster's Third New International Dictionary* frequently assigns a term to one or another of Kurath's divisions; for example, *snake feeder* is labeled as *Midland*, *lightwood* as *Southern*.

[81] E. Bagby Atwood, *A Survey of Verb Forms in the Eastern United States* (Ann Arbor, Michigan, 1953).

[82] Others, however, have used shading quite freely. See, for example, Raven I. McDavid, Jr., and Virginia G. McDavid, "Regional Linguistic Atlases in the United States," *Orbis*, V (1956), 349–386; and Sumner Ives, "Pronunciation of 'Can't' in the Eastern States," *American Speech*, XXVIII (1953), 149–157. [See p. 169 in this book.]

[83] For citation see above.

[84] For example, in the Walloon *Atlas*, twenty-one pronunciations of the word *maison* are entered on the same map by means of symbols. See Louis Remacle, *Atlas linguistique de la Wallonie*, Vol. I (Liège, 1953), Map 56.

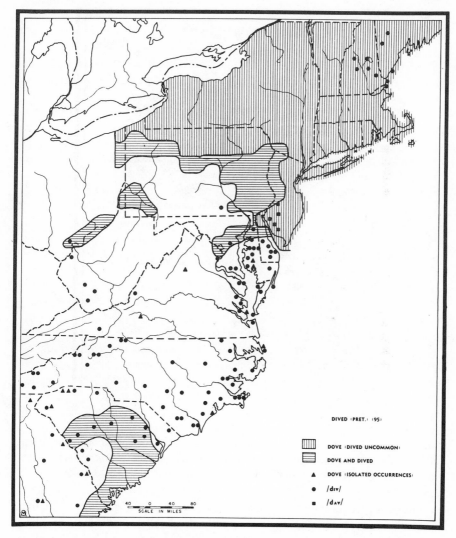

Figure 1.3: Map showing morphological variation by the use of shading and symbols, from E. Bagby Atwood, *A Survey of Verb Forms in the Eastern United States*. Shading and dots indicate the currency of variant preterite forms of the verb *dive*. Reprinted by permission.

variant vowel qualities but also different types of /r/: retroflex, tongue-tap, tongue-trill, and even uvular. At least 100 combinations of these features are possible, and the chances are that most of them would actually be used somewhere in the English-speaking world. The Kurath–McDavid principle, which is rigidly adhered to, is to observe one feature at a time, and to map only that

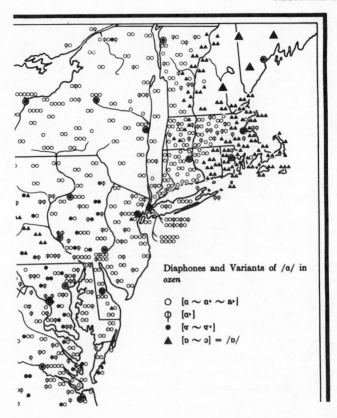

Figure 1.4: Map showing pronunciation variants by means of symbols, from Kurath and McDavid, *The Pronunciation of English in the Atlantic States*. Dots indicate the vowel variants in the word *oxen*. Reprinted by permission.

feature on a particular map. Thus, in the case of *father*, the qualities of the first vowel are plotted on Map 32, those of the final syllable on Map 151. This method demands an early decision as to what features are to be observed. It also requires an understanding of what types of variation are possible; that is, whether we are dealing with a phonemic distinction (in certain environments), as in *four* and *forty* (Map 44), or with the incidence of a phoneme, as the /v/ in *nephew* (Map 169), or with the phonetic quality of a phoneme, as in the first vowel of *oxen* (Map 15—a portion of which is reproduced in Figure 1.4). With regard to the last type of variation, Kurath has revived the term *diaphone*, but with a meaning somewhat different from that assigned to it by Daniel Jones[85]. As I understand Kurath's use of the term, it would denote the sort of variation that occurs in the word *nine* (Map 26), where most informants have the same

[85] Daniel Jones, *An Outline of English Phonetics*, 6th ed. (New York, 1940), pp. 52–53.

phonemic arrangement, but where readily observable differences in quality exist. That is, *diaphones* are sub-phonemic differences that occur between one speaker and another, or between one area and another, as opposed to *allophones*, which occur in the speech of a single individual and which are determined by the environment of the phoneme. Kurath and McDavid have adopted the "unitary" system of interpreting English vowels; that is, for example, everything that comes between the /t/ and the /k/ in *take* is interpreted as a single entity /e/, as opposed to the two entities /ey/ required by the "binary" system of Trager and Smith[86]. Thus, maps in *The Pronunciation of English* present a great many vowel diaphones, since both monophthongal and diphthongal pronunciations may often be grouped together.

An interesting feature of Kurath and McDavid's presentation is the inclusion of a series of 70 vowel "synopses" indicating the differences in vowel quality observed in the records of cultured informants. From these tabular chartings one can usually perceive at a glance the phonemic and sub-phonemic variations that occur in educated speech as one moves from region to region.

Obviously the Kurath–McDavid presentation could not be complete[87]. Moreover, the huge mass and infinite variety of phonetic transcriptions had to be greatly simplified, so that sometimes a single symbol on a map covers a multitude of phonetic sins[88]. Useful as the work is as a summary, it is not a substitute for the raw material itself, which we can only hope will soon be made available.

It is not possible in the present paper to do justice to the numerous doctoral dissertations that have been based on the *Atlas* field records[89]. One of the earliest of these was Bernard Bloch's study of the post-vocalic /r/[90]. Others have been prepared by Rachel S. H. Kilpatrick[91], Yakira H. Frank[92], Sumner Ives[93], T. H. Wetmore, Jr.[94], Walter S. Avis[95], and several others[96]. Most of these are

[86] George L. Trager and Henry L. Smith, Jr., *An Outline of English Structure* (Norman, Oklahoma, 1951).

[87] Very little material is found on variation in consonants.

[88] For example, on the map showing the vowel diaphones in *nine* (Map 26), diphthongs with their beginnings in low front, low central, and low back position are all represented by the same symbol.

[89] That is, some dissertations have not been mentioned at all; moreover, some of those that are mentioned are familiar to me only through *Dissertation Abstracts* (University Microfilms, Inc., Ann Arbor, Michigan).

[90] The Treatment of Middle English Final and Preconsonantal *R* in the Present-Day Speech of New England (Brown University, 1935).

[91] The Speech of Rhode Island: the Stressed Vowels and Diphthongs (Brown University, 1937).

[92] The Speech of New York City (University of Michigan, 1949).

[93] The Negro Dialect of the Uncle Remus Stories (University of Texas, 1950). Revised as "The Phonology of the Uncle Remus Stories," *PADS*, No. 22 (1954).

[94] The Low-Central and Low-Back Vowels of the Eastern United States (University of Michigan, 1957). *Diss. Abstracts*, XVIII, 1423. Revised as "The Low-Central and Low-Back Vowels in the English of the Eastern United States," *PADS*, No. 32 (1959).

[95] The Mid-Back Vowels in the English of the Eastern United States (University of Michigan, 1956). *Diss. Abstracts*, XVII, 140.

[96] For a further listing see Raven I. McDavid, Jr., and Virginia G. McDavid, "Regional Linguistic Atlases in the United States," *Orbis*, V (1956), 353.

detailed studies of individual problems of pronunciation or of small areas, and the methodology is too complex and varied for compact summary.

Extensions of Atlas Work

The originally planned "Linguistic Atlas of the United States and Canada", directed by Kurath and at least partially sponsored by the American Council of Learned Societies, will, it seems certain, be confined to the States of the Atlantic Seaboard. For some time, however, a framework has existed within which scholars in other areas could gather material comparable with that collected in the original *Atlas* survey, whether or not such material might result in a published atlas. An abridgement of the *Atlas* questionnaire consisting of about 500 items was prepared by Kurath in 1939; this has been the basis of most investigations to the westward. The "Short Work Sheets", as they are called, have usually been augmented by items which might elicit usages of a regional nature not current in the Atlantic States. A compilation of the regional work sheets was prepared by David W. Reed and David DeCamp[97].

The progress of linguistic geography in the United States as a whole since the Second World War has been slow and uneven. This fact is usually attributable to lack of financial support rather than to lack of scholarly interest. Since the 1940s, particularly since the emergence of the Cold War, both Federal and foundation support, as well as that of the American Council of Learned Societies, has gone chiefly to such "strategic" fields as the study of exotic languages and the teaching of English as a foreign language. Most dialect scholars have not been good beggars for private funds to carry on their research. Along with lack of money has gone lack of manpower, which, of course, is only another way of saying that times have changed. The fieldwork for the Atlantic States was mostly done in a time of depression and unemployment, when the services of competent and even brilliant young scholars could be obtained for a bare living, if that. The stipend of Lowman's fellowship for the academic year 1935–36 was $533[98]. If he were available at the present time, there is not the slightest doubt that he would receive many offers of over 10 times that amount to teach in one of our swollen colleges or universities.

In view of these difficulties, the use of multiple fieldworkers has become the rule rather than the exception. Most people engaged for this work can, or will, spend only a limited period of time at the task, usually as part of their work for an advanced degree. The use of tape recorders has varied from none at all to the taping of every interview complete. Publication of results will probably take many forms; and the various collections of data, particularly in the field of pronunciation, are not likely to be fully comparable.

I believe that (aside from the Atlantic States) the regional atlas that has

[97] This is, I believe, still available in mimeographed form. See also Sever Pop, *Bibliographie des Questionnaires Linguistiques* (Louvain, 1955).
[98] "Progress," *DN*, VI, Part XI (1935), 482.

been longest in progress is that of the North Central States[99], directed by Albert H. Marckwardt of the University of Michigan[100]. Some records in this area were gathered as early as 1933[101], but it was in 1938 that the main body of the work was begun. The "Short Work Sheets", with a few modifications, were used, and interviewing practices were essentially the same as those used in the Atlantic States. Up to the present time, with the interviewing almost complete, work has been done by 15 different fieldworkers, whose abilities have varied considerably[102]. Among them they have gathered something like 460

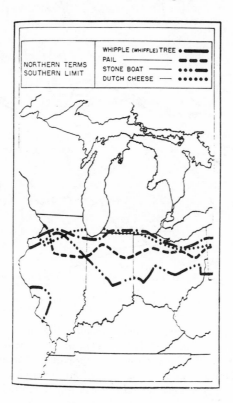

Figure 1.5: Map showing lexical limits by means of simplified isoglosses, from A. H. Marckwardt, *Principal and Subsidiary Dialect Areas in the North-Central States.* The lines show the southward extent of certain Northern words. Reprinted by permission.

[99] These are the states of Ohio, Indiana, Illinois, Michigan, Wisconsin, and Kentucky.
[100] Marckwardt has recently accepted a position at Princeton University (New Jersey). I do not know what effect this will have on the progress of the Atlas.
[101] "Progress," *DN*, VI, Part VII (1933), 365.
[102] We would expect the best results to have been achieved by Guy S. Lowman, Raven I. McDavid, Jr., Cassil Reynard, Harold Allen, and Frederick G. Cassidy, all of whom have made field records in the area.

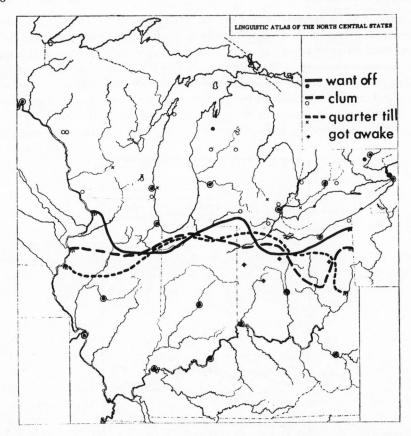

Figure 1.6: Map showing grammatical variations by the use of isoglosses and symbols, from Raven I. and Virginia G. McDavid, *Grammatical Differences in the North Central States*. The lines show the approximate northward extent of the preterites *clum* (climbed) and *got awake* (woke up), as well as of the idioms *want off* (want to get off) and *quarter till* (quarter to). Reprinted by permission.

field records. Tape recordings were sometimes made during the later years of the survey; in some cases the entire interview was recorded and transcribed later from the tapes. No concrete arrangements have been made for the publication of the raw materials themselves; and presentations of results have so far been of the interpretive sort. Toward the beginning of the survey, Marckwardt mapped a number of distributions by the use of symbols on maps[103]; more recently he had published some isoglosses (both lexical and phonological)

[103] "Folk Speech in Indiana and Adjacent States," *Indiana History Bulletin*, XVII (1940), 120–140. [Department of Education, Indianapolis.]

based on a fuller coverage of the area[104]. These isoglosses are apparently only approximate, and are not accompanied by indications of exceptional usages[105] (see Figure 1.5). Nevertheless, Marckwardt's publications provide reasonably convincing evidence that Kurath's previously demonstrated cleavage between Northern and Midland continues through the North Central States. Raven I. and Virginia G. McDavid have published grammatical materials from the same area[106]. Their maps provide both isoglosses and symbols for individual occurrences. It is doubtful that some of the lines should have been drawn; for example, one can see on the map which is reproduced (Figure 1.6) some 13 occurrences of the form *clum* that lie beyond the isogloss that purports to indicate its limits.

In the North Central States we were given our first convincing demonstration that lexical (as against phonological) features may be collected separately by quicker and less costly methods than the employment of trained fieldworkers. Toward the end of the 1940s Alva L. Davis prepared a lexical questionnaire (now called a "checklist") of 100 items and sent copies of it by mail to various more-or-less academic people (usually teachers of history or some subject other than English) at many points in the area. These checklists were to be placed directly in the hands of suitable informants and ultimately mailed back. The items on the list were in the form of brief definitions followed by a number of synonyms; the informants were supposed to encircle the usage which they regarded as natural to them, or to write it down if they did not find it listed. A typical example would be Item 45: "BEANS EATEN IN PODS: green beans, string beans, snap beans". The results of this survey were presented in Davis's doctoral dissertation[107]. The maps which Davis prepared indicated the actual incidence of the lexical variants in the different localities; but he was also able to draw isoglosses which corresponded remarkably well to those based on fieldwork for the North Central Atlas. Other uses of checklists have been made in the area, but they are in the hands of different investigators, and I believe that they have not been incorporated into the atlas.

Another regional atlas in the northern part of the country is that of the Upper Midwest[108], directed by Harold B. Allen of the University of Minnesota. Allen's basic procedure was very similar to Marckwardt's with regard to questionnaire, methods of interviewing, and so on; and he seems to have chosen about the same proportion of the different types of informants[109]. Allen himself

[104] "Principal and Subsidiary Dialect Areas in the North-Central States," *PADS*, No. 27 (1957), 3–15. [See p. 74 in this book.]

[105] For example, Kurath's *Word Geography* (cited above) shows several occurrences of both *stone boat* and *Dutch cheese* to the southward of Marckwardt's lines. Kurath, Figures 78 and 125.

[106] "Grammatical Differences in the North Central States," *American Speech*, XXXV (1960), 5–19.

[107] A Word Atlas of the Great Lakes Region (University of Michigan, 1949).

[108] These are the States of Minnesota, Iowa, North Dakota, South Dakota, and Nebraska.

[109] The approximate proportions are 45 percent Type I, 45 percent Type II, and 10 percent Type III.

did a large part of the interviewing, working mainly in the summers with the support of the University of Minnesota. Six other fieldworkers contributed records from time to time. All together, 208 field records are on file, and I believe that the survey is regarded as complete. In addition to conventional fieldwork, Allen made use of a checklist of 137 items; he was the first to definitely incorporate such materials into a regional atlas. Over 1000 of the checklists have been returned and are in the files. Since both field interviews and checklists were used through the same geographical areas, and since the latter were confined to vocabulary, there will be no possibility of methodological isoglosses[110] to mislead a user of the atlas.

As in other areas, it is hoped that the raw materials from this region may be published, although no definite arrangements have been made. A presentation of the Gilliéron type (all transcriptions entered on maps) does not seem feasible, and Allen's present plan is the listing of responses in tables, with some of the distributions indicated by means of symbols on maps. Allen has already published some of his findings in the form of isoglosses of a simplified type[111].

Students in the Midwestern states (North Central and Upper Midwest) have produced a number of doctoral dissertations dealing with a variety of topics. Two of these, by Virginia G. McDavid[112] and Jean Malmstrom[113], have dealt with grammatical usage throughout the area. Dissertations by Edward E. Potter[114], Robert R. Howren[115], and several others have embodied complete studies of small areas or individual communities.

Investigators in the westerly portions of the country are faced with extremely serious problems arising chiefly from settlement history. In many of these areas, original settlement came relatively late, and population is still very sparse in many places. Recent sizable increases in population have come about largely through wholesale migration from many portions of the country. The most striking illustration of this state of affairs is California, which has been doubling its population about every 20 years. Between 1900 and 1960 the population of the United States as a whole increased by a proportion of about 2.4 to 1. Not many Eastern states have exceeded that rate, and the states of the Upper Midwest have fallen short of it. The population of California,

[110] This is my own phrase, by which I mean that in some instances different methods might produce different results. In a field interview there might be elicited certain "illiterate" usages which would seldom if ever be written by an informant in answer to a question.

[111] "Minor Dialect Areas of the Upper Midwest", *PADS*, No. 30 (1958), 3–16. [See p. 94 in this book.]

[112] Verb Forms of the North Central States and Upper Midwest (University of Minnesota, 1956). *Diss. Abstracts*, XVII, 1594.

[113] A Study of the Validity of Textbook Statements About Certain Controversial Grammatical Items in the Light of Evidence from the Linguistic Atlas (University of Minnesota, 1958). *Diss. Abstracts*, XIX, 1306.

[114] The Dialect of Northwestern Ohio: A Study of a Transition Area (University of Michigan, 1955).

[115] The Speech of Louisville, Kentucky (Indiana University, 1958). *Diss. Abstracts*, XIX, 527.

however, has increased by a proportion of about 10.5 to 1[116], and the influx is continuing with phenomenal rapidity.

Fully aware of the difficulties, David W. Reed has nevertheless undertaken an atlas-type investigation of California and Nevada. Eleven fieldworkers have gathered some 300 records, and this phase of the work is regarded as complete. About 1500 checklists, of the type previously described, have also been returned and are now in the files. All geographical areas have been covered, but obviously many more records were collected in the centers of population than in the mountainous and semi-desert areas. Tape recordings were not used as a regular feature of the survey.

Reed hopes ultimately to publish his raw materials in the form of lists. However, as yet the only publications based on the California–Nevada survey have largely taken the form of statistical summaries. Reed's study of Eastern dialect words in the region provides percentages of occurrence of various lexical features characteristic of the North, the Midland, the South, and various subdivisions and combinations of these areas[117]. In David DeCamp's dissertation on the speech of San Francisco[118], mathematical methods were devised to compare usage with that of the Atlantic States in matters of pronunciation as well. It seems to me that mathematical analysis will be a highly important tool in the presentation of material from such newly settled and linguistically mixed regions as the Pacific Coast. Moreover, although Reed's survey will determine some of the older and newer layers of usage, it would be highly desirable that similar work should be repeated a generation later, in order to bring to light the processes of selection and change that operate in such a situation.

Another atlas-type survey being conducted on the West Coast is that of the Pacific Northwest[119], directed by Carroll E. Reed of the University of Washington. This project has made use of the "Short Work Sheets", with a good many additions; six fieldworkers have collected something like 50 records. Over 1000 checklists are also on file. Both tape and disc recordings have been made in connection with many of the interviews. As in the case of California, a great deal of attention was paid to urban areas, and records from such communities outnumber those from rural districts.

It is the hope of Carroll Reed that his materials may be published in map form, although probably not in the large format of the New England *Atlas*. He has already published a short "Word Geography" based very largely on the

[116] The proportions have been worked out from raw population figures given in *The World Almanac* for 1961 (New York, 1961), pp. 80–81; 463.

[117] David W. Reed, "Eastern Dialect Words in California", *PADS*, No. 21 (1954), 3–15. [See p. 105.]

[118] The Pronunciation of English in San Francisco (University of California, Berkeley, 1954). Summarized under the same title in *Orbis*, VII (1958), 372–391; VIII (1959), 54–77.

[119] This includes the states of Washington, Oregon, and Idaho. [Before Carroll Reed joined the faculty of the University of Massachusetts in 1969 he merged his atlas project with the California study directed by David Reed, who since then has become a member of the faculty at Northwestern University.—Eds.]

lexical checklists[120]. In addition to tabulations of the relative frequency of Eastern usages, he includes a series of maps on which individual usages are entered by means of symbols. He has used the half-serious term "scattergram" to describe this type of presentation. Although no clearcut isoglosses are likely to emerge, he feels (rightly, I think) that individual usages should be presented cartographically, regardless of whether or not they show concentrations or cleavages.

Another westerly area for which atlas plans have been made is the Rocky Mountain region, in which two statewide surveys have so far been made. One of these, by T. M. Pearce, covers the state of New Mexico, in which 50 interviews have been conducted. In addition to Pearce himself, who did about half the interviews, some 19 graduate students contributed from one to seven field records each. Some use was made of disc recordings. Informants were more highly educated than in other areas; something over half of them are of Type III (with college education). About 500 lexical checklists are also on hand. Pearce's plan for publication envisages small maps with symbols for individual usages[121].

In the state of Colorado, a survey has been undertaken by Marjorie Kimmerle of the University of Colorado. Besides Miss Kimmerle, five field-workers were used, including McDavid, who conducted a summer course in field methods at the University of Colorado in 1950. Sixty-eight field records have been collected from 29 communities; the majority of these were made by Miss Kimmerle herself. The "Short Work Sheets" were used and it is clear that these had been augmented by items peculiarly adapted to the regional culture and topography[122]. Tape recordings were made of brief passages (5 to 20 minutes) of connected material from about half the informants. Checklists were used in a preliminary survey, but it is my impression that these will not be incorporated into the atlas.

A survey of the Colorado lexical materials has been published by Clyde T. Hankey[123], who used a variety of methods in presenting the results. Tables of relative frequencies of the Eastern words are, of course, indispensable. These indicate, for the state as a whole, a Northern–Midland mixture, with a rather low proportion of Southern usages. Clearcut isoglosses, as might be expected, are not numerous, and cannot be grouped in a convincing way. A more fruitful approach is the setting off of areas within which specific numbers of regional terms occur[124]; from this presentation, for example, it can be observed that Southern usages as a group are largely limited to the eastern and southeastern

[120] "Word Geography of the Pacific Northwest", *Orbis*, VI (1957), 86–93. See also, by the same author, "Washington Words", *PADS*, No. 25 (1956), 3–11.

[121] Pearce believes that scholars might well adopt symbols of a specific shape or appearance to designate words from specific dialect areas of the East. He terms these symbols *grapholexes*.

[122] See Marjorie M. Kimmerle, "The Influence of Locale and Human Activity on Some Words in Colorado", *American Speech*, XXV (1950), 161–167.

[123] "A Colorado Word Geography", *PADS*, No. 34 (1960).

[124] *Ibid.*, pp. 20–23.

extremities of the state, although any one individual usage might seem to show a scattered distribution. Another similar device is that of demarcating "participation areas"; that is, subdivisions of the state which share relatively high proportions of usages that are less frequent in other areas[125]. It is unfortunate that individual word distributions are not given by the use of symbols on maps rather than by a presentation that involves somewhat wandering lines[126] and shaded areas. Chaotic as they might seem on the surface, the "scattergrams" would have been welcome, if only as a means of judging the nature and validity of the isoglosses.

Another statewide survey which is well under way is that of Oklahoma, directed by W. R. Van Riper. Work sheets are rather full (over 900 questions) and include items of regional and local interest with regard to both pronunciation and vocabulary. Van Riper himself has done all the fieldwork, and he has now completed about 40 records. His interviewing of informants has been largely by means of "directed conversation", with specific questions only if necessary. Every interview has been recorded in its entirety on magnetic tape. In addition to this type of fieldwork, Van Riper has used special vocabulary questionnaires or checklists[127].

Undoubtedly a great deal of valuable material has been collected in other portions of the Western and Midwestern states, but, because of my lack of direct information on these projects, I am unable to describe them in any detail. McDavid[128] reports fieldwork in progress in Utah, Wyoming, and Montana; and certainly there have been other dialect studies that have received little publicity or recognition.

In the states of the Gulf Coast and adjoining portions of the South[129], the preparation of linguistic atlases in the traditional sense has not progressed rapidly, chiefly because of the lack of financial support. This is unfortunate, since these states offer an excellent field for investigation. With the exception of Texas, they have had a relatively slow population growth; and the lack of extensive industrialization has tended to preserve a greater stability of population and hence, presumably, of dialect features.

The oldest collection of atlas materials in the South Central part of the country is that of C. M. Wise of Louisiana State University. Between 1935

[125] *Ibid.*, pp. 36–50.

[126] Some of the lines seem to be improperly drawn, in that they connect two communities that are not adjacent by actual measurement; for example, Figure 4 (Walden and Mecker), Figure 8 (Castle Rock and Akron), Figure 14 (Salida and Lake City), Figure 18 (Salida and Silverton), and Figure 19 (Saguache and Lamar).

[127] Some of these were of the same type as those used in Texas (see below). For a preliminary report on Oklahoma, see W. R. Van Riper, "Oklahoma Words", *The Round Table of the South-Central College English Association*, Vol. 2 (May, 1961), p. [3].

[128] "Regional Linguistic Atlases", pp. 377–378.

[129] These are the states of Georgia, Alabama, Mississippi, Tennessee, Louisiana, Arkansas, and Texas. [In May, 1968, with the support of the Southeastern Regional Educational Laboratory, Lee Pederson of Emory University held in Atlanta, Georgia, a conference of nine dialect specialists for considering plans for a proposed dialect atlas of the Gulf States and Inner South.—Eds.]

and 1945, Wise's advanced students gathered 68 field records from various parts of Louisiana[130], and work of this sort has been continuing to the present time. The "Short Work Sheets" have been augmented by a rather large number of lexical items of regional interest. In recent years tape recordings of the interviews have been made. Under Wise's direction, a very considerable number of dissertations and theses have been prepared[131]. Most of these pertain to pronunciation features, often those observed in a single community.

In other portions of the South and Southwest, there have developed certain departures from traditional atlas methodology. In my own investigations, which have centered in Texas, I have been able to assemble only a very limited number of satisfactory atlas field records of the conventional type; the best of these were collected by Arthur M. Z. Norman[132] and Janet B. Sawyer[133]. I came to the decision some time ago that fieldwork in vocabulary and in pronunciation might well be conducted separately. This idea developed from a number of considerations. In the first place, I was highly dissatisfied with the practice of using considerable numbers of partially trained fieldworkers for the making of phonetic transcriptions. I could hardly believe that in regions where this procedure was used the results would be satisfactory; yet there seemed to be no possibility of financing the work of a real expert for two or three years. On the other hand, experimental investigations had shown that it was relatively easy to teach advanced students to collect vocabulary features, especially if they worked in communities where they had friends or relatives. Accordingly I extracted from the *Atlas* work sheets those vocabulary items which had proved to be most productive in the Atlantic States, and added to them a fairly large number of items designed to elicit words of Southwestern origin or currency[134]. The total number of vocabulary questions was about 270. Being addicted to the idea of field investigation *sur place*, I placed the vocabulary work sheets in the hands of fieldworkers rather than mail them out to be filled in by informants. Most of the interviewing was done by advanced students, originally those in my own classes, but later also students from other institutions under the direction of colleagues who were interested in linguistics[135]. This type of work went on for several years; at the present time there are on hand about 470 vocabulary field records gathered in Texas and portions of adjoining states.

[130] C. M. Wise, "The Dialect Atlas of Louisiana—A Report of Progress", *Studies in Linguistics*, III (1945), 37–42. (University of Buffalo, New York.)

[131] For a list of these see *ibid.*, pp. 41–42.

[132] A Southeast Texas Dialect Study (diss., University of Texas, 1955). A summary, under the same title, is found in *Orbis*, V (1956), 61–79. [See p. 135 in this book.]

[133] A Dialect Study of San Antonio, Texas: A Bilingual Community (diss., University of Texas, 1957). A partial summary is found in the article "Aloofness from Spanish Influence in Texas English", *Word*, XV (1959), 270–281.

[134] For example, items that were used to demonstrate the currency of *burro* (donkey), *mott* (clump of trees), *draw* (dry creek), *remuda* (band of horses), *pilón* (extra gift), and many others.

[135] These included Robert N. Burrows, N. M. Caffee, Ernest Clifton, J. L. Dillard, Rudolph Fiehler, Alan M. F. Gunn, Sumner Ives, Charles B. Martin, Elton Miles, Ray Past, W. R. Van Riper, Harold White, and L. N. Wright.

In order to expedite editing and publication of the vocabulary materials, I made use of mechanical sorting and listing processes[136]. Every occurrence of every word was punched on a separate IBM card, together with coded data on the locality of its use and the characteristics of its user—age, education, sex, and so on. The tabulating machine was thus able to provide a running count not only of the total occurrences of a given usage, but also the occurrences in each geographical sub-area and each age and education group.

These lexical materials have recently been published in my volume entitled *The Regional Vocabulary of Texas*[137]. As might be supposed, I gave considerable attention to actual frequencies of occurrence, not only of individual words, but also of groups of words from the different dialect areas of the East, before ultimately concluding that the region is basically Southern. The editing methods also permitted a fairly precise examination of social distributions, as well as such matters as obsolescence and replacement. Geographical data was presented mainly in the form of individual "scattergrams"; but a fair number of isoglosses also emerged, notably a bundle separating Texas from Southern Louisiana[138].

Other lexical studies based on similar methods have been made in both Texas and Louisiana. These include doctoral dissertations by Fred A. Tarpley[139] and Lucille P. Folk[140], both of whom made use of mechanical processing methods under the direction of Nathan M. Caffee of Louisiana State University. Another lexical survey was that of the late Mima Babington, whose materials on southern Louisiana were to have been presented as a doctoral dissertation at The University of Texas[141].

In other states of the Gulf Coast and interior South, a strictly lexical survey is being conducted by Gordon R. Wood of the University of Chattanooga (Tennessee). This is based on a postal checklist of 147 items, which is placed directly in the hands of informants. Out of a considerably larger number, Wood has selected about 1000 of the checklists for processing[142]. His methods of mechanical sorting and editing would seem to be similar to those used in Texas, although I am sure that he has made some significant advances. His reports have indicated an extensive use of arithmetical frequencies for terms used in the different portions of his territory. It seems that there will also emerge some

[136] I claim no credit for having originated this idea, and I have no certain knowledge that I was the first to put it into practice. The Texas materials were processed between the years 1957 and 1959.

[137] University of Texas Press, 1962.

[138] *The Regional Vocabulary of Texas*, pp. 95–98.

[139] A Word Atlas of Northeast Texas (Louisiana State University, 1960). *Diss. Abstracts*, XXI, 2289.

[140] A Word Atlas of North Louisiana (Louisiana State University, 1961). *Diss. Abstracts*, XXII, 3653.

[141] For a summary of this work, see Mima Babington and E. Bagby Atwood, "Lexical Usage in Southern Louisiana", *PADS*, No. 36 (1961), 1–24.

[142] For non-linguistic reasons, a good many of the returned checklists were rejected. The most common reason for rejection was insufficient length of residence in a specific locality. See Gordon R. Wood, "Word Distribution in the Interior South", *PADS*, No. 35 (1961), 1–16.

very interesting concentrations and cleavages in lexical usage. It is to be strongly hoped that the cartographical presentation of these features will take some form other than the simplified lines and shaded areas that have appeared so far[143].

The concentration on vocabulary study in some of the major areas should not be interpreted to mean that the hope of recording pronunciation features has been abandoned. On the contrary, it is my own feeling that such work will be facilitated, in that the work sheets for pronunciation may be disencumbered of many items of purely lexical interest. Thus more samples may be taken in the same amount of time. Possibly in the future more attention may be paid to such features of suprasegmental structure as stress, intonation, and juncture[144]. It seems clear that tape recording will be almost obligatory in future pronunciation surveys. Earlier difficulties, such as poor fidelity of the mechanisms and the lack of rural electrification, have been so nearly eliminated that there remain no reasons other than financial for neglecting the permanent preservation of speech itself. The newly developed science of sound spectrography[145] will almost certainly prove to be of use in the examination of speech differences; for such an application to be made we will need high fidelity recordings of actual utterances.

The present paper has so far omitted mention of a great deal of important dialect work, particularly that which does not fit readily into the usual categories. For example, John S. Kenyon's observations of American pronunciation through the years have resulted in his very useful *Pronouncing Dictionary*[146], which takes full account of differences in standards from one region to another. Charles K. Thomas had also assembled a great deal of recorded data on pronunciation, which forms the basis of several publications on regional and social variation[147]. His studies have been based to some extent on the reading and recording of standard texts by literate informants. Other investigators—for example Katherine E. Wheatley and Oma Stanley[148]—have applied this method in studies of particular areas.

In other English-speaking areas of the Western Hemisphere there has also been progress in dialectology. Fieldwork in Canada, although not extensive, has been conducted by competent scholars[149]. In Jamaica, extremely sound work

[143] *Ibid.*, pp. 7–12.

[144] The problem of the application of structural linguistics to dialectology is a rather vexed one and has not been completely solved. For a recent discussion, see Pavle Ivić, "On the Structure of Dialectal Differentiation", *Word*, XVIII (1962), 33–53. (Linguistic Circle of New York.)

[145] For general discussions of this type of research, see Martin Joos, *Acoustic Phonetics*, Supplement to *Language* (Baltimore, 1948); and Ernest Pulgram, *Introduction to the Spectography of Speech*, *Janua Linguarum*, No. 7 (The Hague, 1959).

[146] John S. Kenyon and Thomas A. Knott, *A Pronouncing Dictionary of American English* (Springfield, Mass., 1944).

[147] A summary of Thomas's work is found in his *Introduction to the Phonetics of American English*, 2nd ed. (New York, 1958).

[148] The latest of their publications is "Three Generations of East Texas Speech", *American Speech*, XXXIV (1959), 83–94.

[149] For a summary of this work, see McDavid, "Regional Linguistic Atlases", pp. 380–381.

in lexicography has been accomplished by Frederick G. Cassidy; his forth-
coming dialect dictionary is a model of thoroughness. Robert B. Le Page and
David DeCamp have examined other aspects of usage by the use of atlas
methodology[150]. DeCamp's successful application of the word-and-thing
method[151] in his fieldwork should result in important publications concerning
the relations of language and culture.

In summary we may say that dialect investigations of one sort or another
have been carried on in almost all parts of the United States. The multiplicity
of fieldworkers, the unevenness of their training, and the variations in their
methodology will make much of their work very difficult to analyze and evaluate.
This is particularly true of the recording of pronunciation, some of which in
the long run may have to be done over again. We seem closest to achieving an
overall picture of dialect vocabulary, and indeed this accomplishment will not
be a trifling one. What is needed in all aspects of the work is support, financial
and moral; for a full measure of this we may need to await a change in climate.
The history of scholarship is to a considerable degree a history of patience, and
of this quality the dialect scholar has need of more than his share[152].

[150] See Le Page, "General Outlines of Creole English Dialects in the British
Caribbean", *Orbis*, VI (1957), 373–391, and VII (1958), 54–64; also Le Page and DeCamp,
Jamaican Creole (London, 1960).

[151] For example, he gathered data on many styles of baskets, machetes, and other
artifacts.

[152] I am much indebted to colleagues in various parts of the country for having
supplied me with recent information regarding their work, in personal conversations and
in correspondence.

2

Sense and Nonsense about American Dialects

RAVEN I. McDAVID, JR.

IN MY BOYHOOD—more years ago than I care to remember—we used to define an expert as "a damned fool a thousand miles from home." Since I am considerably less than 1000 miles from where I grew up, and stand but a few minutes from my residence in Hyde Park, it behooves me to avoid any claim to expertness about the problems faced in practical situations where the dialect of the school child is sharply divergent from what is expected of him in the classroom. For many of these situations, neither I nor any other working dialectologist knows what the local patterns actually are; for some, there has been no attempt, or at best a partial and belated one, to find out the patterns. Nevertheless, the implications of dialectology for the more rational teaching of English in the schools—and not only in the schools attended by those we currently euphemize as the culturally disadvantaged—are so tremendous that I am flattered to have John Fisher ask for my observations. The problems are not limited to Americans of any race or creed or color, nor indeed to Americans; they are being faced in England today, as immigrants from Pakistan and the West Indies compete in the Midlands for the same kinds of jobs that have drawn Negro Americans to Harlem and the South Side, and Appalachian whites to the airplane factories of Dayton. In fact, such problems are faced everywhere in the world as industrialization and urbanization take place, on every occasion when people, mostly but not exclusively the young, leave the farm and the village in search of the better pay and more glamorous life of the cities. In all parts of the world, educators and politicians are suddenly realizing that language differences can create major obstacles to the educational, economic, and social advancement of those whose true integration into the framework of society is necessary if that society is to be healthy; they are realizing that social dialects—that is, social differences in the way language is used in a given community—both reflect and perpetuate differences in the social order. In turn, the practicing

Professor of English at the University of Chicago, Dr. McDavid is also director and editor of *The Linguistic Atlas of the Middle and South Atlantic States*. This address was given at the English general meeting of the Modern Language Association in Chicago, December 28, 1965. Reprinted by permission from *Publications of The Modern Language Association*, 81.7–17 (1966).

linguist is being called on with increasing frequency to devise programs for the needs of specific groups—most often for the Negroes dwelling in the festering slums of our Northern and Western cities; and generous government and private subsidies have drawn into the act many teachers and administrators—most of them, I trust, well meaning—who not only have made no studies of dialect differences, but have ignored the studies and archives that are available, even those dealing with their own cities.

Perhaps a data-oriented dialectologist may here be pardoned an excursion into the metaphors of siegecraft, recalled from the time when under the tutelage of Allan Gilbert I learned something of the arts of war and gunnery, if not all their Byronic applications. In confronting our massive ignorance of social dialects, the professional students of the past generation have been a forlorn hope—burrowing into a problem here, clawing their way to a precarious foot-hold of understanding there, seizing an outwork yonder. Like many forlorn hopes, they have been inadequately supported, sometimes ignored, even decried —not only by their literary colleagues, with the usual patronizing attitude toward anything smacking of affiliation with the social sciences, but also by their fellow linguists who are interested in international programs for teaching English as a second language, in machine translation, in formulaic syntax, or in missionating to convert the National Council of Teachers of English. It is small wonder that some students of dialects have withdrawn from the assault to participate in these better-heeled campaigns; it is a tribute to the simple-minded stubbornness of the survivors that they have not only persisted but advanced. Today their work, their aims, are embarrassingly respectable, as legions spring from the earth in response to the golden trumpet sounding on the banks of the Pedernales. It is inevitable, perhaps even fitting, that the practical work in social dialects should be directed by others than the pioneers in research. But it is alarming that many of those now most vocally concerned with social dialect problems not only know nothing about the systematic work that has been done, about the massive evidence (even if all too little) that is available, but even have a complete misconception about the nature and signi-ficance of dialects. At the risk of drawing the fire of the House Un-American Activities Committee, I would agree with my sometime neighbor James H. Sledd that our missionaries should at least know what they are talking about before they set out to missionate.

I have a particular advantage when I talk on this subject: I am one of those who speak English without any perceptible accent. I learned to talk in an upper-middle-class neighborhood of Greenville, South Carolina, among corporation lawyers, bankers, textile magnates, and college presidents, among families with a long tradition of education and general culture. Many of my playmates, like myself, represented the sixth generation of their families in the same county. It never occurred to any of us to tamper with our language; our only intimate acquaintance with non-standard grammatical forms in writing came from stories in literary dialect or from the quaint and curious exercises that infested our textbooks—though we knew that less privileged forms of speech than ours were found in our community, and were not above imitating them for rhetorical effect. Not a single English teacher of an excellent faculty—our superintendent had his doctorate, not from Peabody or from Teachers College, Columbia, but from the University of Berlin in 1910—made a gesture of tampering. Nor have I ever heard anything in the exotic dialects of the Northeast or the Middle West that would make me feel less content with a way of speaking that any educated person might want to emulate. And yet, a few years ago, my younger sister, who has remained in the South Carolina upland, told me over the telephone: "Brucker, you've been North so long that you talk just like a Yankee." Even though I doubt if I would fool many real Yankees, I know that something has rubbed off from my travels and teaching to make me talk a little different from the boys I grew up with. Still, whenever I go back and start talking with them again, I find myself slipping into the old ways; it is natural for us to shift our way of talking, according to the people we are talking with. In fact, it is the people we talk with habitually who give us our way of talking. Here, in essence, is the way dialects originate. And until everybody lives in a sterile, homogenized, dehumanized environment, as just a number on the books of an all-powerful state, we can expect differences in environment to be reflected in those differences in speech that we call dialects.

An appreciation of this fact would avoid a lot of nonsense expressed in categorical statements in educational literature. Two amusing if distressing examples are found in *Language Programs for the Disadvantaged: Report of the NCTE Task Force*, a booklet released at the 1965 convention of the NCTE. These statements, the more distressing because so much of the report is magnificently phrased, probably arose from the inevitable wastefulness of haste (the Task Force was in the field only last summer) and from the imbalance of the Task Force itself: there was only one linguist and not a single sociologist or anthropologist or historian in a group heavily loaded with supervisors and (to coin a term, which is probably already embalmed in educationese) curriculologists:

Most disadvantaged children come from homes in which nonstandard English dialect is spoken. It may be pidgin, Cajun, Midland, or any one of a large number of regional or cultural dialects. Many preschool teachers are concerned about the dialect of their children and take measures to encourage standard pronunciation and usage. (p. 70)

. . . the general feeling is that some work in standard English is necessary for greater social and job mobility by disadvantaged students with a strong regional or racial dialect. (p. 89)

Among the bits of nonsense to be found in these two statements we may notice:

1. A belief that there is some mystical "standard," devoid of all regional association. Yet the variety that we can find in cultivated American English, as used by identifiable informants with impeccable educational and social creden-

tials, has been repeatedly shown in works based on the American *Linguistic Atlas*, most recently and in greatest detail in Kurath's and my *Pronunciation of English in the Atlantic States* (Ann Arbor: University of Michigan Press, 1961).

2. A belief that there are "racial" dialects, independent of social and cultural experiences.

3. A snobbishness toward "strong" dialect differences from one's own way of speaking. Would Bobby Kennedy, politically disadvantaged after the Atlantic City convention, have run a better race in New York had he learned to talk Bronx instead of his strong Bostonian?

4. A glib juggling of terms, without understanding, as in the parallelism of "pidgin, Cajun, Midland." *Pidgin* denotes a minimal contact language used for communication between groups whose native languages are mutually unintelligible and generally have markedly different linguistic structures; typical examples are the Neo-Melanesian of New Guinea and the Taki-taki of Surinam. However scholars may debate the existence of an American Negro pidgin in colonial days, speakers of pidgin constitute a problem in no Continental American classroom, though it would be encountered in Hawaii and the smaller Pacific islands. *Cajun* properly describes the colonial varieties of French spoken in southwestern Louisiana and in the parts of the Maritime Provinces of Canada from which the Louisiana Acadians were transported; even if by extension we use the term to describe the varieties of English developing in the French-speaking areas of Louisiana and the Maritimes, the problems of teaching English in these areas are really those of teaching English as a second language. *Midland* is a geographical designation for those dialects stemming from the settlement of Pennsylvania and embracing a broad spectrum of cultural levels. At one extreme, we may concede, are the impoverished sub-marginal farmers and displaced coal miners of Appalachia; at the other are some of the proudest dynasties of America—the Biddles of Philadelphia, the Mellons of Pittsburgh, the Tafts of Cincinnati, and their counterparts in Louisville and in St. Louis, in Memphis, and in Dallas—people it were stupid as well as impractical to stigmatize in language like that of the Task Force Report. So long as such glib generalities are used about social dialects, we must conclude that our educators, however well intentioned, are talking nonsense.

And regrettably, such nonsense is no new phenomenon in American culture; it has long been with us. Much of it, fortunately, runs off us like raindrops off a mallard's back. But enough lingers in the schoolroom to do positive harm. My friend Bob Thomas, the anthropologist—a Cherokee Indian and proud of it, though with his blond hair and blue eyes he looks far less like the traditional Cherokee than I do—tells of his traumata when he moved to Detroit from Oklahoma at the age of fourteen. Although Cherokee was his first language, he had picked up a native command of Oklahoma English. Since he had always lived in a good neighborhood, and his family had used standard English at home, he had no problems in grammar; through wide reading and a variety of experiences he had acquired a large and rich vocabulary.

But his vowels were Oklahoma vowels; and some benevolent despot in Detroit soon pushed him into a class in "corrective speech." The first day the class met, he looked around the classroom and noticed everybody else doing the same. As eyes met eyes, it became apparent that the class in "corrective speech" contained no cleft palates, no stammerers, no lispers, no foreign accents, not even any speakers of sub-standard English—for again, the school was in a good neighborhood. The only thing wrong with the boys and girls in the class was that they had not learned English in Michigan, but in Oklahoma, Arkansas, Missouri, Kentucky, Tennessee, West Virginia, Mississippi, and Alabama. "We all realized immediately," Bob told me years afterward, "that they were planning to brainwash us out of our natural way of speaking; and it became a point of honor among us to sabotage the program." To this day, Bob flaunts his Oklahoma accent belligerently; if the teachers had let him alone, he might have adapted his pronunciation to that of the Detroit boys he played with, but once he felt that the school considered his home language inferior, nothing could make him change. The first principle of any language program is that, whatever the target, it must respect the language that the students bring with them to the classroom.

Another kind of nonsense was demonstrated by the head of the speech department at the University of Michigan during my first Linguistic Institute. Impelled by the kind of *force majeur* that only a four-star general can exert, I had compromised with my scientific interest in linguistics to the extent of enrolling in a course in "stage and radio diction," only to find myself bewildered, frustrated, and enraged from the outset. Typical of the petty irritations was the panjandrous insistence on the pronunciation /'pradjus/, though all my friends who raised fruits and vegetables for market, many of them gentlemen with impeccable academic credentials, said /'prodjus/. But far more distressing were the pronunciations advocated in the name of elegance. We were advised to reject the Middle Western and Southern /æ/, not only in *calf* and *dance* and *command*, but even in *hat* and *ham* and *sand*, for an imitation of the Boston /a/ in environments where Bostonians would never use it, so that we would say /hat/ and /ham/ and /sand/, pronunciations legitimate in no American dialect except that of the Gullah Negroes of the South Carolina and Georgia coast. A few departmental underlings even went all out for an equally phony British [ɑ], again in the wrong places, yielding [hɑt] and [hɑm] and [sɑnd], and all of them plumped for replacing the Midwestern [ɑ] of *cot* and *lot* with an exaggerated [ɔ]. Of course, Midwesterners ordering [hɔt hɑm 'sɑndwɪčɪz] are as suspect as counterfeit Confederate $3 bills. It is possible that some compulsive aspirants to social elegance docilely lapped up this pap; but those of us who were seriously concerned with English structure and usage laughed the program out of court and left the course, never to return. A second principle can be deduced from this experience: to imitate a dialect sharply different from one's own is a tricky and difficult assignment. A partial imitation is worse than none, since the change seems an affectation to one's neighbors, and the imperfect acquisition seems ridiculous to those whose speech is being imitated. Any attempts at teaching a standard dialect to those who speak a non-standard one should be directed toward an attainable goal, toward one of the varieties of cultivated speech which the student might hear, day after day, in his own community.

At this point, perhaps, some of you may be muttering, "But what do these experiences have to do with dialects? I always thought that a dialect was something strange and old-fashioned." Many will share your opinion, especially in such countries as France and Italy, where an academy accepts one variety of the language as standard and casts the rest into outer darkness. In such countries the word *dialect* implies a variety of the language spoken by the rustic, the uneducated, the culturally isolated. To say that someone "speaks a dialect"—as one Italian professor patronizingly described one of the best soldiers working with me on our Italian military dictionary—is to exclude him forever from the company of educated men. For a dialect, to such intellectuals, is a form of the language they had rather be found dead than speaking.

True, there are other attitudes, Germans and Austrians make a distinction between the standard language—literary High German—and the dialects, local and predominantly rural forms of speech. But educated Germans do not always avoid dialect speech forms; in some areas, such as the Austrian Tyrol, an educated person will take particular pains to use some local forms in his speech, so as to identify himself with his home. The attitude may be a bit sentimental, but it does help to maintain one's individual dignity in a homogenizing world.

A more extreme attitude was prevalent in the Romantic Era. If the Augustans of the seventeenth and eighteenth centuries looked upon dialects as corruptions of an originally perfect language, the Romantics often alleged, in Wordsworth's terms, that people in humble and rustic life used "a purer and more emphatic language" than that to be met with in the cities. In this viewpoint, the dialects represent the pure, natural, unchanging language, unencumbered by the baggage of civilization. This attitude has long prevailed in Britain; even today the English Dialect Survey is heavily slanted toward archaic forms and relics and ignores modern innovations.

Nor are Americans wholly free from this attitude that a dialect is something archaic and strange. Time and again, a fieldworker for our Linguistic Atlas is told, "We don't speak no dialect around hyur; if you want *rale* dialect you gotta go down into Hellhole Swamp"—or up into Table Rock Cove, or at least across the nearest big river. To many of us, as my student Roger Shuy put it, a dialect is something spoken by little old people in queer out-of-the-way places.

When we become a little more sophisticated—as we must become on a cosmopolitan campus—we realize that cities as well as rural areas may differ in the ways in which their inhabitants talk. Thus we next conclude that a dialect is simply the way everybody talks but us and the people we grew up with; then, by force of circumstance, we realize that we speak a dialect ourselves. But at this point we still feel that a dialect is something regional or local. When we notice that people of our own community speak varieties of English markedly different from our own, we dismiss them as ignorant, or simply as making mistakes. After all, we live in a democratic society and are not supposed to have class markers in our speech. It is a very sophisticated stage that lets us recognize social dialects as well as regional ones—dialects just as natural, arising out of normal, everyday contacts.

By this time we have elaborated our definition of a dialect. It is simply a habitual variety of a language, regional or social. It is set off from all other such habitual varieties by a unique combination of language features: words and meanings, grammatical forms, phrase structures, pronunciations, patterns of stress and intonation. No dialect is simply good or bad in itself; its prestige comes from the prestige of those who use it. But every dialect is in itself a legitimate form of the language, a valid instrument of human communication, and something worthy of serious study.

But even as we define what a dialect is, we must say what it is not. It is different from slang, which is determined by vogue and largely distinguished by transient novelties in the vocabulary. Yet it is possible that slang may show regional or social differences, or that some regional and social varieties of a language may be particularly receptive to slang.

A dialect is also different from an argot, a variety of the language used by people who share a common interest, whether in work or in play. Everyone knows many groups of this kind, with their own peculiar ways of speaking and writing. Baptist preachers, biophysicists, stamp collectors, model railroad fans, Chicago critics, narcotic addicts, jazz musicians, safe-crackers. But in the normal course of events a person adopts the language of such sub-cultures, for whatever part of his life it may function in, because he has adopted a particular way of life; he uses a dialect because he grows up in a situation where it is spoken. Again, some argots may show regional or social variations; the term *mugging*, to choose one example, is largely found on the Atlantic Seaboard; the sport has different designations in the Great Lakes region and on the Pacific Coast.

Nor are dialect differences confined to the older, pre-industrial segments of the vocabulary. Here European and American attitudes differ sharply. The late Eugen Dieth chided the editors of the *Linguistic Atlas of New England* for including such vocabulary items as window shades, the razor strop, and the automobile, such pronunciation items as *library* and *post-office* and *hotel*, on the ground that these are not genuine dialect items. Yet if they have regional and social variants, as all of these have in North American English, they warrant inclusion. In my lifetime I have seen the *traffic circle* of the Middle Atlantic States become the *rotary* of Eastern New England; the *service plaza* of the Pennsylvania *Turnpike* become the *oasis* of the Illinois *Tollway*; the *poor boy* of New Orleans—a generous sandwich once confined to the Creole Gomorrah and its gastronautic satellites—appearing as a *grinder* in upstate New York, a *hoagy* in Philadelphia, a *hero* in New York City, a *submarine* in Boston. Nor will dialect terms be used only by the older and less sophisticated: a Middle Western academician transplanted to MIT quickly learns to order *tonic* for his children, not *soda pop*, and to send his clothes to a *cleanser*. And though some would consider dialect a matter of speech and not of writing, one can find regional and local commercial terms on billboards and television as well as in the advertising sections of local newspapers.

Finally, dialect terms are not restricted to sloppy, irresponsible usage—a matter of personality type rather than of specific vocabulary items. And though regional and local terms and usages are likely to appear most frequently in Joos's casual and intimate styles, the example of William Faulkner is sufficient evidence that they may be transmuted into the idiom of the greatest literature.

All of these comments are the fruit of centuries of observation, at first casual and anecdotal, later more serious and systematic. The grim test of the pronunciation *shibboleth*, applied by Jephthah's men to the Ephraimites seeking to ford the Jordan, the comic representations of Spartan and Theban speech by Aristophanes, the aspiration of the Roman cockney Arrius-Harrius, immortalized by Horace, the Northern English forms in the Reeve's Tale—these typify early interest. With the Romantic search for the true language in the dialects came the growth of comparative linguistics, and the search for comparative dialect evidence in translations of the Lord's Prayer and the proverb of the prodigal son. The search for comparable evidence led, in the 1870s, to the monumental collections for Georg Wenker's *Deutscher Sprachatlas*, later edited by Ferdinand Wrede and Walther Mitzka—44,251 responses, by German village schoolmasters, to an official request for local dialect translations of 44 sentences of standard German. Designed to elicit fine phonetic data, the collections proved notably refractory for that purpose, but the sheer mass of evidence corrected the unevenness of individual transcriptions. More important, the discovery that questions designed for one purpose may yield a different but interesting kind of evidence—as *Pferd* proved useless for the /p: pf/ consonant alternation in dialects where the horse is *Roß* or *Gaul*—was reflected in greater sophistication in the design and use of later questionnaires. Less happy was the effect on German dialectology, with later investigations, such as Mitzka's *Wortatlas*, sticking to correspondence techniques, a short questionnaire, an immense number of communities, and an expensive cartographic presentation of the data. But the *Sprachatlas* and *Wortatlas*, and the Dutch investigations modeled upon them, provided us with the evidence on which to determine their own defects.

A valuable innovation was made at the turn of the century in the *Atlas linguistique de la France*, directed by Jules Gilliéron. Correspondence questionnaires gave way to field interviews on the spot, in a smaller number of selected communities (some 600 in this instance) with a longer questionnaire; a trained investigator interviewed a native of the community in a conversational situation and recorded his responses in a finely graded phonetic alphabet. As with the German atlas, however, the communities chosen were villages; larger places were first investigated in the Atlas of Italy and Southern Switzerland, under the direction of the Swiss scholars Karl Jaberg and Jakob Jud, who also introduced the practice of interviewing more than one informant in the larger communities. With certain refinements, then, the basic principles of traditional dialect study were established by the First World War. Some subsequent investigations have followed Wenker, others Gilliéron; some, like the current Czech investigations, have combined both methods, relying primarily on field interviews but using correspondence surveys in the early stages, so that the selection of communities can be made most effectively. Only the British Isles have lagged, perhaps because Joseph Wright's *English Dialect Dictionary*, with its claim to have recorded ALL the dialect words of English, has erected a Chinese Wall worthy of Mr. Eliot's scorn. Not till the 1950s did any kind of fieldwork get under way in either England or Scotland; in both countries it was handicapped by a shortage of funds and fieldworkers, and in England by an antiquarian bias that over-emphasized relics, shunned innovations, and neglected opportunities to provide data comparable to that obtained in the American surveys. Yet both Harold Orton in England and Angus McIntosh in Scotland have enriched our knowledge of English.

Perhaps because American linguists have kept in touch with European developments, the *Linguistic Atlas of New England*, launched in 1930, drew on the lessons of the French and Italian atlases. Although the transition from casual collecting to systematic study was not welcomed by all students, never-theless—even with the Hoover Depression, the Second World War, the Korean intervention, and the tensions of the Cold War—a respectable amount of progress has been made toward a first survey of American English. *The Linguistic Atlas of New England* was published in 1939–43; scholars are now probing for the changes that a generation has brought. For four other regional surveys, fieldwork has been completed and editing is under way: (1) the Middle and South Atlantic States, New York to central Georgia, with outposts in Ontario and northeastern Florida; (2) the North-Central States: Wisconsin, Michigan, southwestern Ontario, and the Ohio Valley; (3) the Upper Midwest: Minnesota, Iowa, Nebraska, and the Dakotas; (4) the Pacific Southwest: California and Nevada. Elsewhere, fieldwork has been completed in Colorado, Oklahoma, Washington, and eastern Montana; respectable portions have been done in several other states, Newfoundland, Nova Scotia, and British Columbia; with a slightly different method the late E. Bagby Atwood produced his memorable *Regional Vocabulary of Texas*. In all of these surveys the principles of European dialect investigations have been adapted to the peculiarities of the American scene. Settlement history has been studied more carefully before fieldwork, since English-speaking settlement in North America is recent, and its patterns are still changing. At least three levels of usage are investigated—partly because cultivated American speech has regional varieties, just like uneducated speech, and the cultivated speech of the future may be foreshadowed in the speech of the intermediate group; partly because until very recently general education has been a more important linguistic and cultural force in the United States than in most of the countries of Europe. Urban speech as well as rural has been investigated in each survey, and intensive local investigations have been encouraged. The questionnaires have included both relics and innovations. All of these modifications were suggested by Hans Kurath, first Director of the Atlas project, who is currently drawing on his experience in developing a new theory for the interpretation of dialect differences.

Just as warfare is still decided ultimately by infantrymen who can take and hold territory, so dialect study still depends on competent investigators who can elicit and record natural responses in the field. The tape recorder preserves free conversation for later transcription and analysis, and permits the investigator to listen repeatedly to a response about whose phonetic quality he is in doubt; but the investigator must still ask the right questions to elicit pertinent data. He must remember, for instance, that *chicken coop* is both a vocabulary and a pronunciation item—that the pronunciation in the American North and North Midland is /kup/, in the South and South Midland /kʌp/, that *coop* in the North designates the permanent shelter for the whole flock, in the South a crate under which a mother hen can scratch without an opportunity to lead the little ones off and lose them in the brush. The full record for such an item may require three or four questions, which only a human interviewer can provide.

But if the fieldworker remains essential, the objects of his investigation may change. Recent studies have turned increasingly to urban areas, urbanizing areas, and minority groups. To a long list of impressive early investigations one can now add such contributions as Lee Pederson's study of Chicago pronunciation and Gerald Udell's analysis of the changes in Akron speech resulting from the growth of the rubber industry and the consequent heavy migration from West Virginia. Among special groups investigated in detail are the Spanish-American bilinguals in San Antonio by Mrs. Janet Sawyer, the American Norwegians by Einar Haugen, the New York City Greeks by James Macris, the New England Portuguese by Leo Pap, the Chicago Slovaks by Mrs. Goldie Meyerstein, the Gullah Negroes by Lorenzo Turner, and the Memphis Negroes by Miss Juanita Williamson. In all of these studies the emphasis has been on the correlation between linguistic and social forces.

Another significant development has been the investigation of the way language attitudes are revealed by the choice among linguistic variants under different conditions. The most impressive work of this kind has been done by William Labov of Columbia University, in his study of the speech of the Lower East Side of New York. Limiting himself to a small number of items—the vowels of *bad* and *law*, the initial consonants of *think* and *then*, the /r/ in *barn* and *beard*—phonological details that can be counted on to appear frequently and in a large number of contexts during a short interview, Labov gathers specimens of linguistic behavior under a wide range of conditions. At one end of the spectrum is the reading of such putatively minimal pairs as *bed* and *bad*; at the other is the description of children's games or the recounting an incident when the informant thought he was going to be killed. The difference between pronunciations in the relaxed situation and those when the informant is on what he considers his best linguistic behavior is an index of his social insecurity. Almost as revealing is the work of Rufus Baehr with high-school students in the Negro slums of the Chicago West Side. It is no surprise that in formal situations the students with greater drive to break out of their ghetto reveal striking shifts of their speech in the direction of the Chicago middle-class norm. This kind of discovery should give heart to all who believe that a directed program of second-dialect teaching can make at least a small dent in our problem of providing a wider range of economic and educational opportunities for the aspiring young Negro.

Out of all these investigations two patterns emerge: (1) a better under-standing of the origin and nature of dialect differences; (2) a set of implications for those who are interested in providing every American child with a command of the standard language adequate for him to go as far as his ability and ambition impel him.

No dialect differences can, as yet, be attributed to physiology or to climate. Perhaps anatomists will discover that some minor speech differences arise from differences in the vocal organs; but so far there is no evidence for any correlation between anatomy and dialect, and the burden of proof is on those who propose such a correlation. As for climate: it is unlikely that nasality could have arisen (as often asserted) both from the dusty climate of Australia and the dampness of the Tennessee Valley. And though it is a favorite sport among Northerners to attribute the so-called "Southern drawl" to laziness induced by a hot climate, many Southerners speak with a more rapid tempo than most Middle Westerners, and the Bengali, in one of the most enervating tropical climates, speak still more rapidly. For an explanation of dialect differences we are driven back, inevitably, to social and cultural forces.

The most obvious force is the speech of the original settlers. We should expect that a part of the United States settled by Ulster Scots would show differences in vocabulary, pronunciation, even in grammar from those parts settled by East Anglians. We should expect to find Algonkian loans most common in those regions where settlers met Algonkian Indians, French loans most frequent in Louisiana and in the counties adjacent to French Canada, Spanish loans most widespread in the Southwest, German loans clustering in cities and in the Great Valley of Pennsylvania, and indubitable Africanisms most striking in the Gullah country.

Speech forms are also spread along routes of migration and communication. The Rhine has carried High German forms northward; the Rhone has taken Parisian forms to the Mediterranean; in the United States, the same kind of dissemination has been found in the valleys of the Mississippi, the Ohio, and the Shenandoah.

If speech forms may spread along an avenue of communication, they may be restricted by a physical barrier. As Kurath has observed, there is no sharper linguistic boundary in the English-speaking world than the Virginia Blue Ridge between the Potomac and the James. The tidal rivers of the Carolinas, the swamps of the Georgia coastal plain, have contributed to making the Old South the most varied region, dialectally, in the English settlements of the New World.

The economic pattern of an area may be reflected in distinctive dialect features. *Fatwood*, for resin-rich kindling, is confined to the turpentine belt of the Southern tidewater; *lightwood*, with a similar referent, to the Southern coastal plain and lower Piedmont. *Case weather*, for a kind of cool dampness in which is is safe to cut tobacco, occurs over a wide area, but only where tobacco is a money crop. *To run afoul of*, a maritime phrase in the metaphorical sense of "to meet," seems to be restricted to the New England coast.

Political boundaries, when long established, may become dialect boundaries in the Rhineland, pronunciation differences coincide strikingly with the boundaries of the petty states of pre-Napoleonic Germany. In the New World, on the other hand, political boundaries have seldom delimited culture areas. Yet *county site*, for the more usual *county seat*, is common in Georgia but unknown in South Carolina, and Ontario Canadians speak of the *reeve* as chief officer of a township, the *warden* as chief officer of a county, and a *serviette* instead of a table napkin—terms unfamiliar in the United States.

Each city of consequence may have its distinctive speech forms. The grass strip between the sidewalk and the curb, undesignated in South Carolina, is a *tree belt* locally in Springfield, Massachusetts (and hence unlabeled in *Webster's Third New International Dictionary*), a *tree lawn* in Cleveland, a *devil strip* in Akron, and a *boulevard* in Minneapolis and St. Paul. And only Chicagoans naturally refer to political influence as *clout*, or to a reliable dispenser of such influence as a *Chinaman*.

Nor are differences in the educational system without their effect. Where separate and unequal education is provided to particular social groups, we can be sure that a high-school diploma or even a college degree will be no indication by itself of proficiency in the standard language. That this problem is not confined to any single racial or cultural group has been shown by institutions such as West Virginia State College, which have undergone the process of reverse integration. This particular school, which once drew an elite Negro student body, is now 80 percent white, with the white students mostly from the disadvantaged mountain areas along the Kanawha. Since the teachers in the mountain schools are not only predominantly local in origin, but often have had little education beyond what the local schools offer, and then, since most of them habitually use many non-standard forms, it has been difficult for the college to maintain its academic standards in the face of increasing white enrollment, however desirable integration may be.

Most important, perhaps, is the traditional class structure of a community. In a Midwestern small town, it is still possible for one brother to stay home and run a filling station, and another to go off and become a judge—and nobody mind. But in parts of the South there is a social hierarchy of families and occupations, so that it is more respectable for a woman of good family to teach

in an impoverished small college than to do professional work for the government at twice the salary. Here, too, an aristocratic ideal of language survives,
and the most cultivated still look upon *ain't* as something less reprehensible
than incest—but use it only in intimate conversation with those whom they
consider their social equals. Here too we find the cultural self-assurance that
leads an intelligent lawyer to ask the linguistically naive qusetion: "Why is it
that the educated Northerner talks so much like the uneducated Southerner?"

If social differences among the WASP population are reflected in linguistic
differences, we should not be surprised if similar differences among later
immigrants are reflected in the extent of linguistic borrowing from particular
foreign-language groups, or even from the same foreign-language group at
different times. Our longest continuous tradition of borrowing, with probably
the largest and most varied kinds of words, is that from various kinds of German.
Even the bitterness of two world wars cannot prevent us from seeing that of all
foreign-language groups the Germans have been most widely distributed,
geographically and socially, throughout the United States—as prosperous
farmers, vaudeville comedians, skilled craftsmen, merchants, intellectuals. In
contrast, the hundreds of thousands of Italian- and Slavic-speaking immigrants
of the last two generations have left few marks on the American vocabulary;
most of them were of peasant stock, often illiterate, and settled in centers of
heavy industry as basic labor.

Even more striking is the change in the incidence of Texas borrowings
from Mexican Spanish. In her study of the bilingual situation in San Antonio,
Mrs. Sawyer has shown that although early Spanish loans were numerous,
quickly assimilated, and widely spread—*canyon, burro, ranch, lariat, broncho,
silo* are characteristic examples—there have been few such loans in the last 70
years. The explanation is the drastic change in the relationships between Anglos
and Latins. When English-speaking settlers first moved into Texas, they
found the hacienda culture already established, and eagerly took over culture
and vocabulary from the Latins who constituted the local elite. Anglo and
Latin, side by side, died in the Alamo 4 March 1836 and conquered at San
Jacinto seven weeks later. But since 1890 the Texan has encountered Mexican
Spanish most often in the speech of unskilled laborers, including imported
braceros and illegally entered wetbacks; derogatory labels for Latins have
increased in Texas English, and loans from Spanish have declined. We borrow
few words from those we consider our inferiors.

We can now make a few clear statements about the facts of American
dialects, and their significance:

1. Even though much work remains to be done, we can describe in some
detail most of the principal regional varieties of American English and many
of the important sub-varieties; we can indicate, further, some of the kinds of
social differences that are to be found in various dialect areas, and many of
the kinds that are to be found in some of the most important cities.

2. We can be sure that in many situations there are tensions between

external norms and the expectations of one's associates. These tensions, most probably, are strongest in the lower middle class—a group anxious to forget humbler backgrounds but not sure of their command of the prestige patterns. Since the teaching profession, on all levels, is heavily drawn from the lower middle class, we can expect—as Marjorie Daunt found years ago—that anxiety is the characteristic attitude of the English teacher toward variations in usage. There is a strong urge to make changes, for the sake of making changes and demonstrating one's authority, without stopping to sort out the significance of differences in usage. This attitude is reflected in the two most widely known programs for teaching better English to the disadvantaged: a socially insignificant problem, such as the distinction between *Wales* and *whales*, is given the same value as the use of the marker for the third singular in the present indicative. Future programs should use the resources of the dialect archives, at least as a start, even though more detailed and more recent information may be necessary before one can develop teaching materials. The inevitable prescription in a pedagogical situation can be no better than the underlying description.

3. There is evidence that ambitious students in slum areas intuitively shift their speech patterns in the direction of the prestigious local pattern, in situations where they feel such a shift will be to their advantage. Some actually achieve, on their own, a high degree of functional bidialectalism, switching codes as the situation demands. In any teaching program it would seem intelligent to make use of this human facility.

4. The surest social markers in American English are grammatical forms, and any teaching program should aim, first of all, at developing a habitual productive command of the grammar of standard English—with due allowance for the possibility that the use of this grammar may be confined to formal situations in which the speaker comes in contact with the dominant culture.

5. Relatively few pronunciation features are clear social markers, though in many Northern cities there is a tendency to identify all Southern and South Midland pronunciations as those of uneducated rural Negroes. How much one should attempt to substitute local pronunciations for those which are standard in regions from which migrants come would probably depend on the extent to which variations in standard English are recognized and accepted in the community: Washington, for instance, may be more tolerant than New York City. In any event, programs to alter pronunciation patterns should concentrate on those pronunciations that are most widely recognized as sub-standard.

6. Few people can really identify the race of a speaker by pronunciation and voice quality. In experiments in Chicago, middle-class Middle Westerners consistently identified the voice of an educated urban white Southerner as that of an uneducated rural Negro, and many identified as Negro the voice of an educated white Chicagoan. Similar experiments in New York have yielded similar results. And many white Southerners can testify to personal difficulties arising from this confusion in the minds of Northerners. In Ithaca, New York, I could not get to see any apartment advertised as vacant until I paid a personal

visit; over the telephone I was always told that the apartments had just been rented; James Marchand, a Middle Tennessean now on the Cornell faculty, must carefully identify himself as "Professor Marchand," if he wants a garage-man to come and pick up his car. And the telephone voice of my Mississippi-born chairman, Gwin Kolb, is racially misidentified with alarming regularity.

7. There can be no single standard in programs for the disadvantaged; the target dialect must vary according to the local situation. In Mississippi, the same program can be used for Negroes and whites, because they share most of the same grammatical deviations from the local standard, and share phonological patterns with that standard; in Cleveland, grammatical features in writing are sufficient to distinguish Negro college applicants from white better than 90 percent of the time, and deviations from local standard pronunciation are far more striking and numerous among Negroes than among locally-born dis-advantaged whites.

8. To the suggestion that Southern Negroes should not be taught local standard pronunciation, but some external standard—the hypothetical variety some call "network English"—there is a simple answer in the form of a question: "Do you want integration in the South?" The Southern patterns of race relations have suffered too long from too many separate standards for Negro and white; it would be ironical if those speaking most loudly in behalf of the aspirations of the Southern Negro should create new obstacles to those aspirations. The language problems of the uneducated Southern Negro are the language problems, even to fine detail, of the uneducated Southern white in the same community; the South may well solve the language problems in its schools before Detroit does. Once the races are brought into the same classroom, a community will need only one intelligent program based on a solid body of dialect evidence.

9. While we are planning language programs for our disadvantaged, we must educate the dominant culture in the causes and significance of dialect differences; it is particularly urgent that we educate teachers on all levels, from kindergarten through graduate school. The disadvantaged will have enough to do in learning new patterns of language behavior; the dominant culture must meet them part way, with greater understanding, with a realization that dialect differences do not reflect intellectual or moral differences, but only differences in experience. Granted that this reeducation of the dominant culture is bound to be difficult, we should not be so cynical as to reject it, on the ground that it cannot take place. In an age when we are turning the heat off under the melting pot and accepting the cultural contributions of Americans with ancestral languages other than English, in an age when we are learning the art of peaceful coexistence with a variety of economic and political and cultural systems, it should not be difficult to extend this acceptance to fellow Americans of different cultural backgrounds and linguistic habits, and especially to recognize that cultured American English may be found in many regional and local varieties. It is a poor cultural tolerance that would accept all cultivated speech except that in other parts of our own country.

With my deep-ingrained horror of patent medicine salesmen, I would not leave you with the impression that we already have all the answers, or even all the evidence we need to arrive at those answers. We need many more kinds of investigation, and we should like to think that John Fisher, with his unlimited license to stalk money-bearing animals, might help us conduct some of them. We are still to do even the preliminary surveys in such parts of the country as Tennessee and Arkansas; we need many more studies of the actual patterns of social dialects in most American cities. We really have no serious evidence on regional and social differences in such prosodic features as stress and pitch and juncture. The recognition of paralanguage—the non-linguistic modulation of the stream of speech—is so recent that we have no idea as to the kinds of regional and social differences that may be found in tempo and rhythm, in range of pitch and stress, in drawl and clipping, in rasp and nasality and mellifluousness. We have not even begun to study regional and social variations in gesture and other kinds of body movement. But we do have a framework which we can fill in detail, continually building our teaching programs on solid research into the ways in which Americans communicate in various localities, and into the attitudes of specific speakers toward those whose usage differs from their own. In comparison with the immensity of our social problems, our linguistic knowledge is as a little candle in the forest darkness at midnight; let us not hide that candle under a basket, but put it in a lantern and use it to find our way.

BIBLIOGRAPHICAL NOTE

The significance of dialect differences has been often discussed, notably in Leonard Bloomfield, *Language* (New York, 1933), chapter xix. The most detailed summary of dialect investigations to the mid-century is Sever Pop, *La Dialectologie*, 2 vols. (Louvain, 1950). Kurath's *Areal Linguistics: Problems, Methods, Results* (Bloomington, Indiana, 1970), will be shorter but more up to date.

The most widely known summary of American dialects is to be found in chapter ix of W. Nelson Francis, *The Structure of American English* (New York, 1958); the most accessible bibliographical summary is in the footnotes of chapter vii of the one-volume 1963 edition of H. L. Mencken, *The American Language*. Annual summaries of research will be found in the reports of the Committee on Regional Speech and Dialectology, in *Publications of the American Dialect Society*; recent research is reported in the quarterly bibliographies in *American Speech*, less extensively in the supplement to *PMLA*. The method of the American atlases is discussed in detail in Kurath's *Handbook of the Linguistic Geography of New England* (Providence, R.I., 1939). For summaries of particular dialect features along the Atlantic seaboard, see Kurath, *A Word Geography of the Eastern United States* (Ann Arbor, Michigan, 1949); Atwood, *A Survey of*

Verb Forms in the Eastern United States (Ann Arbor, Michigan, 1952); Kurath and McDavid, *The Pronunication of English in the Atlantic States* (Ann Arbor, Michigan, 1961). Atwood's *The Regional Vocabulary of Texas* was published by the University of Texas Press, Austin, in 1962. For particular regions see articles by A. H. Marckwardt for the Great Lakes, Harold B. Allen for the Upper Midwest, Marjorie M. Kimmerle and Clyde Hankey for Colorado, David W. Reed and David DeCamp for California. *A Dictionary of American Regional English*, directed by Frederic G. Cassidy, is currently under way at the University of Wisconsin.

The first direct attention to American social dialects is McDavid, "Dialect Geography and Social Science Problems," *Social Forces*, xxv, 168–172; basic for the problems of Negro speech is Raven I. and Virginia McDavid, "The Relationship of the Speech of American Negroes to the Speech of Whites," *American Speech*, xxvi, 3–17. A 1964 conference on social dialects, held at Bloomington, Indiana, is reported in *Social Dialects and Language Learning*, a publication of the NCTE, edited by A. L. Davis and Roger Shuy (Champaign, Illinois, 1965); in 1965 the NCTE also published *Language Programs for the Disadvantaged: A Report of the NCTE Task Force*, and reprinted two of McDavid's articles as a monograph, *American Social Dialects*. A teachers' manual on the subject has been requested by the U.S. Office of Education. [It was published in 1970 by the National Council of Teachers of English.—Eds.]

The most familiar American analysis of stress, pitch, and juncture was first sketched in G. L. Trager and H. L. Smith, Jr., *Outline of English Structure*, *Studies in Linguistics*: Occ. Paper 3 (Norman, Oklahoma, 1951); a more detailed exposition is found in A. A. Hill, *Introduction to Linguistic Structures* (New York, 1958). A different analysis is that of Kenneth L. Pike, *The Intonation of American English* (Ann Arbor, Michigan, 1945). The importance of paralanguage, previously discussed by Trager and Smith, is shown in Robert E. Pittenger, Charles F. Hockett, and John J. Danehy, *The First Five Minutes* (Ithaca, N.Y., 1960); the most detailed treatment of gesture is in Ray Birdwhistell, *Introduction to Kinesics* (Washington, 1952), later reprinted by the University of Louisville. A good popular treatment of communication in culture is Edward T. Hall, *The Silent Language* (New York, 1959), now available in paperback. Martin Joos's theories of style are summed up in *The Five Clocks* (Bloomington, Indiana, 1962).

Area Studies

INTRODUCTION

The nine articles in this section concern language characteristics of various regions in the United States. Each article, except those by Thomas, Wood, and Norman, is directly related to some one of the established atlas projects.

The reader should have access, if not to the *Linguistic Atlas of New England*, at least to Hans Kurath's *Word Geography of the Eastern United States* and Kurath and McDavid's *Pronunciation of English in the Atlantic States*. Also useful for its wide coverage is the specialized monograph by Atwood, *A Survey of Verb Forms in the Eastern United States*. All these are based upon the fieldwork for the atlases of New England and of the Middle and South Atlantic states under the direction of Professor Kurath.

An alternative approach to the speech of New England is that of the late Charles K. Thomas, who devoted many years to collecting tape recordings of cultivated speakers throughout the country. For New England Thomas's group is younger and more recent than the Type III speakers interviewed for the atlas project; hence possible trends of phonetic change may be inferred from comparing descriptions of the speech of the two groups. Although Thomas defines his transcription as phonetic and not phonemic, it should be observed, however, that his allophonic discriminations are not so fine and precise as those reported in the New England *Atlas* and in the volume by Kurath and McDavid.

Dialect geographers generally hold that an atlas survey should be repeated at least every half-century. Already, in accord with this principle, the great atlas of France is now being completely redone. In anticipation of the imminent need to reassess the area covered in the first finished American atlas and with the desire to provide a continuing check on regional speech, Miss Audrey R. Duckert reports on her undertaking a preliminary second survey in New England.

Although editing of the collected data for the North–Central atlas has

been long deferred, an examination of the distribution of some critical items soon after the completion of fieldwork enabled the director, Albert H. Marckwardt, to make a substantial contribution to our knowledge about regional patterns. His article reveals that Kurath's recognition of Midland as distinct from Northern is effectively supported by the analysis of the responses of Ohio, Indiana, and Illinois informants, whose residence reflected the earlier western migration from the Eastern Seaboard. But at the same time he reports that his preliminary study indicates secondary regional patterns attributable to population shifts other than the basic western movement.

For the Upper Midwest, as Harold B. Allen's two articles reveal, the data further substantiate the Northern–Midland division, although with noticeable recession of key Northern features. They likewise signal the effect of secondary population movement such as that of Midland speakers up the Mississippi and that of South Midland speakers into lower Iowa and Nebraska. Since both Allen and Marckwardt drew their conclusions from a restricted sample of data, some revision in the area isoglosses may be required when the publication of their atlases provides more information.

In the vast expanse between the Midwest and the Pacific Coast only Colorado is as yet represented in dialect publications. Until the future appearance of the edited material based upon the atlas collections of the late Marjorie Kimmerle, the most significant publication must be the dissertation of Clyde Hankey, *A Colorado Word Geography*, published in 1960 by the American Dialect Society and too long for inclusion in this book. Colorado settlement patterns, he found, materially altered the simple Northern–Midland contrast, an effect reflected as well in the situation reported by David W. Reed and Carroll Reed on the Pacific Coast.

After an initial study of the materials collected in California David Reed finds in his article that Northern and Midland terms dominate in that state but that clearcut isoglosses between the two dialects cannot be drawn. Carroll Reed similarly reports that although Northern and North Midland pronunciations are in the majority in the Northwest, their distribution correlates with local settlement concentration rather than with a putative extension of the Northern–Midland boundary.

Gordon R. Wood's article is derived from a quite different set of data from that obtained by atlas fieldwork. Despairing of realization of the dream of a linguistic atlas of the Inner South, Wood assumed the responsibility of carrying on a major survey through mailed checklists. What he discovered turned out to be of extraordinary importance and suggestive of the great value of that future atlas when field investigation can be undertaken. Wood's revelation of Midland features that occur in a huge downward dip from Tennessee into Alabama and Mississippi rather drastically alters previous notions of the make-up of southern speech.

Although Atwood's volume on the regional vocabulary of Texas, already mentioned, offers a clear conspectus for the entire state, Arthur M. Z. Norman's

dissertation, summarized in his article here, provides additional insights for that dialectal area of East Texas set off from the remainder of the state by a number of distinctive language characteristics.

Influences upon the speech of New Mexico, not included in this collection, appear in the articles by T. M. Pearce listed in the bibliography. In making vocabulary studies Pearce learned that Northern and Midland features are found in northern New Mexico as a result of migration over the Santa Fe trail from Kansas and the east and over the Raton Pass from Colorado, and that Southern and South Midland features occur in southern New Mexico because of the population influx through El Paso and up the Rio Grande Valley.

3

The Phonology of New England English

C. K. THOMAS

This article, based on the speech of over a thousand New Englanders, mostly college students, is an inquiry into the normal usages of present-day pronunciation in the six New England states. It has two main purposes: (1) to determinate the predominant forms in words of divided usage, and (2) to determine the geographical areas in which the predominance of certain forms differs from the predominance in other areas within the region. It offers, incidentally, an opportunity to compare present-day usages with the traditional usages of a changing New England.

THE STUDY OF ENGLISH PRONUNCIATION in the six New England states has attracted investigators for several generations. In the early days of the American Dialect Society, E. S. Sheldon, a native of Waterville, Maine, published "A New Englander's English and the English of London."[1] Nearly a decade later, C. H. Grandgent published his important article "From Franklin to Lowell. A Century of New England Pronunciation."[2] Other writers followed; a more or less complete listing would turn this article into a bibliography.

The largest and most complete study of New England speech is the *Linguistic Atlas of New England*,[3] a cooperative venture under the able editorship of Hans Kurath. In the preparation of the material, nine fieldworkers investigated the speech of 415 typical speakers, or "informants," of various ages and types. In every community investigated, the fieldworkers selected one elderly old-fashioned and relatively unschooled informant in an effort to "establish the regionalism of the pre-industrial era of New England in considerable detail."[4] The second informant in each community was normally middle-aged, with an education extending through secondary school, though in a fifth of the com-

After his retirement from Cornell University the author became Professor of Speech at the University of Florida, a position he held at the time of his death. His article is reprinted by permission of the Speech Association of America from *Speech Monographs* 28.223–32 (1961).

[1] *Dialect Notes*, I (1890), 33.

[2] *PMLA*, XIV (1899), 207.

[3] The *Atlas* consists of a *Handbook of the Linguistic Geography of New England* and six large volumes of maps, all published by Brown University in 1939.

[4] *Handbook*, p. 41.

munities a more educated and cultured informant was selected.[5] It will be noticed that the summary table in the *Handbook* includes only 51 informants of this cultured type.[6]

The *Atlas* is thus most valuable in its preservation of the styles of speech that represent an age which is passing, if, indeed, it has not already passed. It is no fault of the *Atlas* that many subsequent commentators have ignored the distinctions in age and education spelled out so carefully in the *Handbook*.[7]

The present study represents a different approach. It is based on the speech of 1226 speakers, most of them college students, and therefore roughly comparable to the educated informants of the *Atlas*. Because they are college students, it has been possible to reduce the ranges of both age and education to a minimum, thereby bringing the regional variations into as sharp a focus as possible. I have listened to every one of these 1226 speakers, at Cornell and at New England colleges and universities, either in person or on tape recordings.[8] The speakers grew up, in every instance, in the counties to which they have been accredited. They represent every county in the six states, and their distribution is roughly in proportion to the populations of those counties. The tape recordings consist of readings of a series of standardized passages designed for the purpose of collecting large numbers of pronunciations of the same words. From the students whom I interviewed personally I was able to add notes based on their general conversation. This study, then, is an attempt to investigate the speech of the young educated adult, roughly comparable to *Atlas* Type III informants,[9] with a minimum range in age and cultural levels.

In investigating the individual sounds of New England speech, my approach has necessarily been phonetic rather than phonemic. Where a phonemic reference is intended, the symbol is enclosed in diagonal bars, thus /t/. Where a phonetic reference is intended, the symbol is enclosed in square brackets, thus [t]. Some phonemes are obvious and have been identified from the outset; some are less obvious, and will be enclosed in square brackets until the evidence of their phonemic character has been accumulated.

3.1   Vowels

/i/: the high-front tense syllabic phoneme usually found in *beet*. Principal

    [5] *Ibid.*   [6] *Handbook*, p. 43.

    [7] For example, C. M. Wise, in his *Applied Phonetics* (Englewood Cliffs, N. J., 1957), Chapter IX, refers to map after *Atlas* map in his section labeled "Standard Eastern Speech," with no reference whatever to the types of informants represented on those maps.

    [8] Special thanks are due the following persons, who have sent me recordings: Wofford Gardner, University of Maine; Ryland Hewitt, then of Bates College; Edmund Cortez, University of New Hampshire; John V. Neale, Dartmouth College; Eleanor Luse, University of Vermont; S. J. Savereid, University of Massachusetts; Joan Bernitz, then of the University of Connecticut; and Brobury P. Ellis, New Britain State Teachers College, Connecticut.

    [9] *Handbook*, p. 44.

allophones: [i], [ɪi], and occasional high-central variants. /ɪ/: the high-front lax syllabic phoneme usually found in *bit*. Principal allophones: [ɪ], a slightly lengthened [ɪ] before [r] or [ə], and occasional high-central variants.

Variations: in 9109 instances in the final unstressed syllables of *chimney, coffee, country, donkey, February, foggy, greasy, heavy, hurry, laundry, luxury, mahogany, many, Mary, noisily, quarry, rainy, sandy, slowly, sorry, suddenly,* and *worry,* between 96 and 97 percent use [i], the remainder [ɪ]; [ɪi] does not occur.

Variations: in 2519 instances of the inflectional ending *-ed* in *crowded, decided, haunted, knitted, lighted, mended, needed, noted, painted, persisted, regulated, rented, seated, sounded, started, visited, waited,* and *wanted,* [ɪ] ranges from 57 percent in Massachusetts to 82 percent in Vermont. In 654 instances of the inflectional ending *-es* in *courses, dishes, horses, houses, matches, noises, oranges, packages, pages, pieces, reaches,* and *sausages,* [ɪ] ranges from 64 percent in Massachusetts to 89 percent in New Hampshire. In 500 instances before [-t] in *basket, blanket, chocolate, pulpit, quiet,* and *secret,* [ɪ] ranges from 30 percent in Connecticut to 56 percent in New Hampshire; the latter is the only state in which [-ɪt] is the majority form. *Forest* shows 202 instances of [-ɪst] as against 699 of [-əst], despite almost universal dictionary recording of the less frequent pronunciation.

Variations in unstressed medial syllables, as in *animal, authority, correspond, corridor, Florida, horrible, medicine, military, noisily, oranges, packages, physical, political, sausages,* and *visited,* are not clearly patterned, but [ə] is more frequent than [ɪ]. In unaccented prefixes, as in *because, before, began, beside, decide, demand, regard, respect, return,* and *revolve,* [i] is most frequent, [ɪ] moderately frequent, and [ə] least frequent. In *details,* the predominant pronunciation is ['ditelz]; in *enough,* [ɪ'nʌf].

/e/: the mid-front tense syllabic phoneme usually found in *bait.* Principal allophones: [e] and [eɪ]; [ɛɪ] is extremely rare. /ɛ/: the mid-front lax syllabic phoneme usually found in *bet.* Principal allophone: [ɛ] plus a relatively infrequent centralized variety. In *syrup,* for example, the most frequent vowel of the stressed syllable is [ɪ], followed, in order, by [ɜ], centralized [ɪ], [ɛ], [ʌ], and centralized [ɛ], the last two variations confined to Maine and New Hampshire. In *general* and *get,* [ɛ] predominates; [ɪ] is extremely rare on this educational level. In *rinse, since,* and *until,* [ɪ] predominates; [ɛ] is rare; centralized [ɪ] occurs occasionally in *until.* In *edge,* [ɛ] predominates; [e] and [eɪ] are rare. In *vase,* [e] and [eɪ] predominate. In *various,* [ɛ] predominates; [e] occurs about 10 percent of the time; [æ], about 5 percent. In *catch* and *January,* [æ] predominates over [ɛ]; only in Vermont does *catch* show more instances of [ɛ] than of [æ].

[æ], [a], and [ɑ]. For the present it seems desirable to leave phonemic considerations in abeyance and treat these sounds as allophones until sufficient evidence has been shown to permit phonemic analysis. [æ] is usually located in the high low-front area, but variable in the degree of muscular tension, as in *cat* and *man.* [a] varies between low-front and low-central, and usually involves lax muscles; it is most likely to occur in such words as *aunt* and *barn.* [ɑ] varies from low-back almost to low-central and involves lax muscles and unrounded lips. It, too, may occur in such words as *aunt* and *barn*, and sometimes in such words as *not* and *lock*.

In *barrel, barren, carrots, carry, kerosene, narrow,* and *parrot,* [æ] predominates over [ɛ], more strongly in Rhode Island than in the other states. Frequent use of [ɛ] occurs, as might be expected, in western Vermont and western Massachusetts, but unexpectedly in Aroostook County in northern Maine. This series includes a few instances of [a], but nothing like the high concentration found in Pennsylvania.

In *barn, car, dark, farmer, father, garage, large, march, part, sharp, started,* and *yard,* with a total of 4271 instances, [a] accounts for over 60 percent, [ɑ] for over 30 percent, with only about 5 percent for [æ], almost all the last from Maine. There are two instances of [ɒ] in southwestern Connecticut. The heaviest concentrations of [ɑ] come in western and southern Vermont, Massachusetts west of the Connecticut River, and Connecticut.

In the so-called broad-*a* words, *after, answer, ask, aunt, basket, baths, blast, glass, pass,* and *past,* there are 2397 instances of [æ], 343 of [a], and 82 of [ɑ], a confirmation of the decline of the so-called broad-*a* which Mrs. Miller noted several years ago.[10] Of the words noted above, *aunt* shows the highest incidence of [ɑ].

Other words involved in this variation: *calendar* has over 700 instances of [æ], 5 of [a]. *Colorado* shows about 60 percent for [ɑ], 25 percent for [æ], 15 percent for [a]. *Garage* shows about 60 percent for [a], 40 percent for [ɑ]. *Khaki:* about 50 percent [ɑ], 30 percent [æ], 20 percent [a]. *Nevada:* about 70 percent [ɑ], 20 percent [æ], 10 percent [a]. *Rather,* the most variable of the lot, has 33 instances of [ɛ], 390 of [æ], 148 of [a], 104 of [ɑ], and 44 of [ʌ]; restressing, of course, accounts for [ɛ] and [ʌ]. In *scallops,* [a] predominates over [æ]. Throughout the area, [a] occurs most frequently in words in the *aunt* type and the miscellaneous group just discussed. In western Vermont and western Massachusetts, [a] may occur occasionally in such words as *not* and *odd*, as in upstate New York and the Great Lakes Basin. It is noteworthy that [a] does not occur in words of the type of *man*, as it often does in New York City.

[ɑ], [ɒ], and [ɔ]. Again phonemic considerations will be deferred. [ɑ] varies as previously noted. [ɒ] is low-back and lax, with slight lip rounding. [ɔ] ranges from low-back to higher low-back, but has tenser muscles and stronger lip rounding than [ɒ]. One of the most characteristic variations in this area is illustrated by *authority, borrow, coral, correspond, corridor, Florida, foreign, forest, horrible, horrid, horror, moral, orange, Oregon, quarry, sorry, tomorrow, torrents,* and *warrant.* Here, with slightly over 12,000 instances, we find clear isophonic lines. In the north, Aroostook County, Maine, with a 73 percent preponderance of [ɔ], gives further evidence of being a speech island. In the southwest, Fairfield County, Connecticut, with a 58 percent preponderance of [ɑ], is not a speech island, but an extension of the downstate New York area.

---

[10] Virginia R. Miller, "Present-Day Use of the Broad A in Eastern Massachusetts," *SM,* XX (1953), 235.

Elsewhere, the counties which show a preponderance of [ɔ] are Addison, Bennington, Chittenden, Franklin, Grand Island, and Rutland in western Vermont, and Lamoille and Washington in north-central Vermont; Berkshire, Hampden, and Hampshire in Massachusetts; Hartford, Litchfield, and New Haven in Connecticut. The eastern boundary of this block of counties marks the most important boundary between eastern and western New England.[11] In every county in Rhode Island and New Hampshire, [ɑ] is the most frequent variant.

Before velar consonants, [ɑ] predominates in *catalog, clogged, donkey, fog, foggy, frogs, gong* (except in Maine and Vermont, where (gɒŋ] is more frequent), *hogs, honk, log*, and *mahogany*. In *dog* and *long*, [ɔ] predominates, but [ɒ] is frequent. *Chocolate* is highly variable; [ɔ] predominates only in Connecticut.

Before voiceless fricatives, [ɔ] predominates in *across*. In *cloth, coffee, cough, cross, lost*, and *sausages*, [ɔ] predominates in Connecticut and Rhode Island; [ɒ], in the other States. In *offer* and *office*, [ɒ] predominates in Maine and New Hampshire; [ɔ], elsewhere. Before voiced fricatives, *because* divides about evenly between [ɔ] and the restressed [ʌ]. In *bothered*, [ɒ] predominates in Maine, [ɒ] and [ɑ] are about equal in New Hampshire, and [ɑ] predominates elsewhere.

Before *r* and a consonant, [ɔ] predominates in *absorb* (except in Maine), *corner* (except in Maine and New Hampshire), *morning, order, sort, warm*, and *wharf*; in the exceptions cited, [ɒ] predominates. Before [l], [ɑ] predominates in *doll, involve, resolve*, and *solve*, though [ɒ] occurs frequently. In *dissolve*, [ɔ] predominates in Maine, [ɔ] and [ɑ] are equal in New Hampshire, [ɒ] predominates in Vermont, and [ɑ] in the other three states.

Miscellaneous variations: in *brought*, [ɒ] predominates in Maine and New Hampshire, [ɔ] in the other states. In *daughter*, [ɒ] predominates in Maine and Vermont, [ɔ] and [ɒ] are about equal in Massachusetts, and [ɔ] predominates elsewhere. In *odd*, [ɒ] predominates in Maine and New Hampshire; [ɑ], elsewhere; a few instances of [a] occur in western Vermont and northwestern Connecticut. *On* and *onto* regularly have [ɑ]; Maine, New Hampshire, and Massachusetts use [ɒ] in about 10 percent of the occurrences, and there are a few instances of [a] in western Vermont and western Massachusetts. In Maine, New Hampshire, and Vermont, [-rənt] predominates in *restaurant*; in the three southern states, [-rɑnt]. In *want, wash*, and *watch*, [ɑ] predominates everywhere but in Rhode Island, where [ɒ] is slightly more frequent. In *laundry*, [ɑ] shows a slight preponderance everywhere except in Connecticut, where there is a heavy preponderance of [ɔ]. In *swamp*, [ɑ] predominates everywhere, with the combined total of [ɒ] and [ɔ] ranging from about 20 in Maine and Massachusetts down to about 10 in Connecticut, and with scattered instances of [a] in the western areas. *Talk, walk*, and *walls* vary between [ɒ] and [ɔ], with [ɒ] more frequent in the northern states, [ɔ] in the southern, and with the heaviest concentration of [ɔ] in Rhode Island.

[11] Cf. C. K. Thomas, "The Dialectal Significance of the Non-Phonemic Low-Back Vowel Variants Before R," *Studies in Speech and Drama in Honor of Alexander M. Drummond* (Ithaca, 1944), p. 244.

/o/: the mid-back tense rounded vowel commonly found in *boat* and *go*. Principal allophones: [o] and [oʊ]; the traditional "New England short *o*," a monophthongal allophone intermediate between [o] and [ʌ], occurs, on this educational level, only in a scattering of instances in *road* and *whole* in Maine, Vermont, and western Massachusetts; in western New England and in upstate New York, the allophone becomes virtually indistinguishable from [ʌ].

The historical distinction between [ɔr] and [or] remains in Northeastern New England, but has been lost in the west. In southeastern New England the distinction seems to be breaking up. Franklin County, Massachussets, eastern in most other respects, has largely lost the distinction. Newport and Washington Counties, Rhode Island, are divided. Connecticut has largely lost the distinction except in Windham County, in the northeast corner. In 4865 instances of *before, board, course, court, door, floor, four, more, porch, shore, store*, and *story*, the total for the six States shows 2483 for [o] and 2382 for [ɔ]; thus about half the population has substituted, for the historical [o] of these words, the historical [ɔ] of *border* and *form*. Maine has 90 percent [o]; New Hampshire, 80 percent; Massachusetts and Rhode Island, 53 percent, Vermont has 64 percent [ɔ]; Connecticut, 84 percent. /o/ in these words is [o], not [oʊ].

In *borrow, follow, narrow, tomorrow*, and *window*, the preponderant vowel of the unstressed final syllable is [o], except that Maine and Vermont have [ə] more frequently in *borrow*, and all States have a scattering of [u] in *window*.

/ʌ/, /ʊ/, and /u/: These are all formed well back in the mouth, with only minor allophonic variations. /ʌ/ is the mid-back lax unrounded vowel usually heard in *butt*; the centralized allophones often heard in the Southern mountains and in the coastal South are virtually unknown. /ʊ/ is the high-back lax vowel with moderate lip rounding usually heard in *book* and *poor*. /u/ is the high-back tense vowel with stronger lip rounding usually heard in *boot*. Principal allophones for /u/ are [u] and [ʊu], but the centralized allophones common in other areas do not normally occur here.

In *pulpit*, the stressed vowel is usually [ʊ], but scattered instances of the newer [ʌ] occur in Vermont and the three southern states. Similarly, in *soot* the vowel is usually [ʊ], but Massachusetts and the three northern states have a few scattered instances of [ʌ], and all but Rhode Island have a somewhat larger scattering of [u]. The first vowel of *cuckoo* and the vowels of *roof, room*, and *soon* are usually [u]; in *hoof*, [ʊ]. The stressed vowels of *during, poor*, and *tourist* are usually [ʊ], though [ɔ] and [ɜ] occur occasionally in *tourist*. In *due, duty, new*, and *tune*, [u] and [ʊu] are almost universal; there are almost no instances of either [ɪu] or [ju].

[ɝ] and [ɜ]. These symbols represent the syllabics in *Bert* and *bird*, the first including [r]-coloring and formed in a higher mid-central position, with or without retraction of the tongue tip; the second, lower mid-central, without [r]-coloring. Both vowels are tense, and serve as allophones of each other. Both are produced slightly farther forward in the central position than the [ɝ] of upstate New York or the [ɜ] of New York City.

Presence or absence of [r]-coloring is the principal regional variation. In 3252 instances of *absurd, burn, church, first, girl, heard, perch, percolator, return, word*, and *work*, Maine shows 91 percent [ɜ]; New Hampshire, 88 percent; Rhode Island, 87 percent; Massachusetts, 66 percent. On the other hand, Vermont shows 72 percent [ɝ]; Connecticut, 85 percent. Connecticut also shows a few instances of [ɜɪ] in these words: in Fairfield County, where the pronunciation may be regarded as an extension of the New York City type; and in New London, where it is still to be found among a decreasing number of old families.

Other variations in this general category are uncommon. *Hurry* is predominantly ['hʌri] everywhere except in Vermont, which has ['hɜri] or ['hɜ˙i] 53 percent of the time. Incomplete information on *courage, flourish, nourish, turret*, and *worry*, and similar words suggests that [ɜ] is more frequent than [ʌ].

In unstressed syllables, [ɚ] and [ə] divide in much the same way as [ɝ] and [ɜ]. In 7116 instances of *after, answer, better, bothered, calendar, corridor, counters, daughter, dinner, eastern, farmer, father, flowers, horror, offered, orator, overheard, percolator, perhaps, persist, picture, rather, surprise, water*, and *weather*, Maine shows 95 percent [ə]; Rhode Island, 95 percent; New Hampshire, 92 percent; Massachusetts, 73 percent. On the other hand, Vermont shows 70 percent [ɚ]; Connecticut, 71 percent.

3.2 Diphthongs

/aɪ/: allophones: [aɪ] and [ɑɪ]. [ɑɪ] is rare except before voiced continuants, as in *line, miles*, and *surprise*. /ɔɪ/ is almost wholly stable as [ɔɪ]; the old-fashioned [aɪ] of *join* and *poison* seems not to occur on this educational level.

/aʊ/: allophones: [ɑʊ], [aʊ], [æʊ], and [ɜʊ]. [ɜʊ] is almost completely limited to the position before a voiceless consonant, and largely confined to the northern states. In Maine, for instance, [ɜʊ] is more frequent than [ɑʊ] in *about, doubt, house, out*, and *without*, but slightly less frequent in *outside* and *south*. Though it is nowhere else the majority form, [ɜʊ] is nevertheless frequent in New Hampshire, Vermont, and Massachusetts.

[æʊ] is the least frequent, limited largely to the neighborhood of nasals, as in *down, found, now*, and *town*. Although the boundaries of the allophones are not sharp, [aʊ] seems to be considerably more frequent than [æʊ], and [ɑʊ] most frequent of all. *Route* (a numbered highway) is overwhelmingly [rut], with scattered instances of [ɑʊ] throughout the area, and of [ɜʊ] in the four northern states.

3.3 Consonants

Assimilation and dissimilation account for most of the variations among /p/ and /b/. *Principle* frequently changes the second /p/ to /b/, partly through dissimilation, partly in response to wakening stress. The first /b/ of *absorb* occasionally dissimilates and drops out. /d/ of *absurd* frequently changes to /b/, perhaps by remote assimilation, perhaps by analogy with *absorb*.

/hw/ and /w/ balance about evenly, with /hw/ somewhat more frequent in New Hampshire and Vermont, /w/ somewhat more frequent in the four other States. These findings are based on *somewhat, whale, wharf*, and *wheat*; a larger selection might well show a more definite pattern.

With has been tested in a large variety of contexts. Though some areas show a variation related to the nature of the initial sound of the word immediately following *with*, New England shows a heavy preponderance of [ð] over [θ]. In *garage*, the forms with [-dʒ] everywhere predominate over those with [-ʒ]. In *pancakes*, [-nk-] everywhere predominates over [-ŋk-]. *Luxury* predominantly has [-kʃ-]. *Luxurious* has [-gʒ-], [-kʃ-], and [-kʒ-], in that order.

Variations between [s] and [z]: in *absorb*, [s] outnumbers [z] in Maine and New Hampshire, but is less frequent than [z] in the other four states. In *absurd, blouse, desolate, greased, greasy, persist, rinse*, and *vase*, [s] outnumbers [z] throughout the area. In a few instances, *rinse* is [rɪntʃ], a pronunciation reminiscent of the South. *Baths, moths*, and *paths* most frequently have [-ðz], less frequently [-θs]. *Grocery* shows some survival of [-ʃ-], especially in New Hampshire and Vermont. In *peninsula*, [-s-] predominates, but there are occasional instances of [-ʃ-] and [-sj-].

Variations involving [j]: *beyond* loses [j] from 15 to 20 percent of the time; *January*, only occasionally in Maine and New Hampshire. *Percolator* adds [j] from 20 to 30 percent of the time, except in Rhode Island. *February* acquires [j] through dissimilation of [r], which will be discussed later.

The treatment of /r/ before a consonant or a pause is one of the traditional characteristics of New England speech, the western area retaining [r], the eastern replacing it with added vowel length or, in some contexts, with [ə]. Generally the traditional view is true, but the boundary between east and west is somewhat farther east than for some of the other east–west distinctions. In 11,295 instances of /r/ in *absorb, barn, before, board, car, cheerful, cleared, course, court, dark, fire, floor, fork, forty, four, horse, large, march, more, morning, near, porch, queer, sharp, shore, sort, started, store, warm, wharf*, and *yard*, we find 4721 instances of [r] and 6574 of its loss or change to [ə]. In Maine we find [r] retained in Aroostook County 58 times as against 32 losses. The rest of Maine and every county in New Hampshire and Rhode Island are consistently without [r] predominance. In Vermont, Caledonia, Essex, and Orange Counties consistently lose [r]; the other counties retain it. Massachusetts retains [r] west of Worcester County. In Connecticut, only New London and Windham Counties, in the extreme east, lose [r]. Despite variations throughout central New England, predominant usage is as indicated.

Loss of /r/ is, of course, aided by dissimilation when more than one /r/ occurs in the same word. Thus various patterns of loss occur in such words as *corner, February, library, order, surprise*, and *thermometer*. In *corner, order*, and *thermometer*, either /r/ or both may be eliminated; in *February*, the first /r/ may be replaced by [j] or eliminated completely.

Other losses: /g/ may be occasionally lost from *distinguish*, *England*, or *English*. /h/ may occasionally be lost from *huge*, *human*, *humor*, etc. These minor losses are probably general, rather than regional, characteristics.

3.4 The Patterns

The consonants of New England are substantially those of the Northern area which extends westward into upper New York and the Great Lakes Basin. Limitations on their use are, except for /r/, substantially the same. In fact, most of the area stretching westward from the lower Connecticut Valley and the summits of the Green Mountains is very closely related to upper New York State, both phonologically and historically, more closely so than to Eastern New England. In respect to /r/, as well as in respect to some of the vowel variations, Aroostook County, Maine, goes with the west.

Vowels and, less noticeably, diphthongs give us the clues to the regional patterns. There can be no doubt that the syllabics of *beet*, *bit*, *bait*, *bet*, *bat*, *boat*, *butt*, *book*, *Bert*, *bite*, *bout*, and *boy* represent either simple or compound phonemes. The debatable sounds are the weak central vowels, such as those in *soda* and *odor*, which need not be discussed in this connection, since the variations can be satisfactorily handled on the phonetic level.

The syllabics in such words as *ask*, *barn*, *box*, *boss*, and *bought*, however, need to be examined. The first thing to notice is the tremendous variation in the idiolects, or patterns of individual speakers, in the range between *bat* and *bought*, or even between *bat* and *boat*. Second, despite the decline in the use of [a] in words of the *ask* type, the New Englander does not extend this class to include words like *bad* and *land*, as New York City sometimes does. There, [a] may be regarded as an allophone of /æ/; in New England it is kept separate. For words like *barn*, on the other hand, [a] is probably the most favored allophone in the larger part of eastern New England, and it seems fair, therefore, to group the syllabics of the *ask* and *barn* categories, for many New Englanders, in the single category of /a/.

To the extent that New Englanders distinguish between *barn* and *born*, and that some of them distinguish between *cot* and *caught*, it seems necessary to set up additional categories. *Barn* and *born* contrast, but /a/ takes care of *barn*. *Cot* and *caught* overlap, but *cot* varies in the direction of [ɑ], and *caught* in the direction of [ɔ]. It seems fair, therefore, to set up the phonemes /ɒ/ for *cot*, *box*, and *boss*, and /ɔ/ for *caught*, *bought*, and *born*. Granted that *bought* and *caught* may, in some idiolects, fall in the /ɒ/ category, we cannot deny the contrast in other idiolects, nor can we put *born* in the /o/ category because of the contrast between [-ɔr-] and [-or-] already noted. Although the speech of eastern New England carries its own special flavor, it is a flavor compounded of many elements. . . .

In western New England, on the other hand, we can set up the same pattern of /æ/ in *cat*, /ɑ/ in *cot* and *cart*, and /ɔ/ in *caught* as we can in upper New York, where the characteristic phonology was, in large part, derived from that of Western New England.

4

The *Linguistic Atlas of New England* Revisited

AUDREY R. DUCKERT

THE FIELDWORK FOR THE *Linguistic Atlas of New England* (*LANE*) was completed in September, 1933—now a generation ago as the years of man are customarily counted. The plan to survey the entire United States and Canada has been carried out over most of these two countries; the fieldwork has been completed in many areas and preliminary surveys have been made in those areas yet to be studied.[1] Only *LANE* has been published in its entirety, but numerous articles and other publications based on the findings of the fieldworkers are available elsewhere.[2] The Kurath *Word Geography of the Eastern United States* and the Kurath–McDavid *Pronunciation of English in the Atlantic States* (*PEAS*) are based in part on *Atlas*-collected materials beyond New England. The cost of editing and publishing will almost certainly preclude a uniform series of Linguistic Atlas volumes to match *LANE*[3] though photo offset and microfilm may make some unpublished materials available.

Had it been possible to survey the entire area of English-speaking North America during the two years (1931–33) in which the *LANE* fieldwork was done, we should have had materials for a nearly perfect synchronic description of the language. That linguists have been denied this Empyrean is perhaps just as well. For one thing, work sheets and questionnaires used later contained additions and modifications that resulted from critical scrutiny of the New England work sheets and their results. Certain obvious regional adjustments were necessary—no use asking about the sea in Kansas or about quahogs in

Miss Duckert is an associate professor of the department of English at the University of Massachusetts. Her article is reprinted from *Publications of the American Dialect Society* 39.8–15 (1963) by permission of the University of Alabama Press.

[1] For a progress summary, see the preliminary transcript of the proceedings of the 1961 Conference on Dialectology held during the MLA meetings in Chicago under the chairmanship of Raven I. McDavid, Jr.

[2] For a convenient listing of many of these, see Vernon S. Larsen, *A Working Bibliography of English Dialect Geography in America*, Chicago, 1961. (Mimeo edition by Science Research Associates, Inc.)

[3] The pros and cons of publication were discussed at the 1961 conference. More recently, David W. Reed (University of California at Berkeley) has been considering ways of reproducing the actual worksheets for distribution prior to editing.

Wisconsin, and no field worker would press an urban informant for calls to sheep and hogs.

Without absolutely identical questionnaires, the antiseptic data so prized by today's laboratory linguists could not be gathered anyway; there are too many human variables, no control group, no way of feeding the data into a computer.[4] But it is the availability of so much carefully collected, well organized data in *LANE* that is the major motivation for the *Linguistic Atlas of New England* Revisited (LANER). A serious problem in diachronic linguistics is the lack of sufficient longitudinal data that can be used to determine the nature and rate of lexical and phonological changes and to assess the influence of changes in communication and socio-economic structure on the speech of a community. It is the aim of LANER to provide an additional set of data for use in conjunction with *LANE* findings in the continuing study of New England speech. LANER is, for now, a far less ambitious undertaking than *LANE*; its hope is to reinvestigate some of the old areas and to study some new ones as well.

LANE had three major objectives: (1) to define the dialect areas of New England; (2) to discover innovations; and (3) to find relics in speech.

LANER will also be concerned with these; but to repeat *LANE* work on a *quid pro quo* basis would be productive of comparisons only, and this is not enough in view of the possibilities. Some questions that proved valuable in fieldwork done after *LANE* will be added; in addition, many useful suggestions have been offered by Professors Kurath and McDavid, e.g., specific inquiry into the influence of the technical terms of major occupations on the general vocabulary of a region.[5] Further helpful suggestions have come from Professors Cassidy and Avis.

The heart of LANER will be a questionnaire including items from *LANE* work sheets and from the Cassidy–Duckert *Method for Collecting Dialect*.[6] This questionnaire can also be used for another much needed line of inquiry—saturation studies. In no way can the validity of a sampling technique be so well tested. Particularly desirable would be saturation studies of urban districts —a South Boston parish, for instance—and of conservative rural communities that appear to have undergone a minimum of change.

Marcus Hansen's *LANE* bibliography is being brought up to date, with census figures for 1940, 1950, and 1960 added also. A portable tape recorder of reasonably high fidelity can help to control subjectivity in the recording of data, but it will be used with discretion, since some good informants may be

---

[4] This human factor, compounded by the old-fashioned kind of scholarly analysis performed in the minds of the men who had most to do with collecting the data, seems to irritate the more ardent engineers in linguistics; apparently it is what prompts the scolding given Kurath and McDavid by Dr. Samuel Keyser of MIT in his review of PEAS (*Language*, XXXIX, No. 2, Part 1 (April–June 1963), pp. 303 ff.)

[5] A senior honors project at the University of Massachusetts now in progress is a study of scalloping and fishing terms and their influence on the general vocabulary in the Dartmouth-New Bedford area of Bristol County.

[6] Published as *PADS*, No. 20 (1953).

more intimidated by the gadget than by the fieldworker's pencil and paper.

The selection of informants will necessitate a reconsideration of the three types sought by *LANE*. Type I, the descendant of an old family who is unspoiled by a great deal of education or wide social contacts outside the community, is even rarer now than in 1930. The old families are still there, but the isolation that once went with life in a Berkshire hilltown has now largely vanished. Type II, with more formal education and more social contacts, will be easy to find. This classification will be extended beyond *LANE*'s limits so that it takes in some college graduates, for a college degree has proved to be no guarantee of great verbal sophistication. Type III—cultured informants—will probably be even more active and widely traveled than their *LANE* counterparts; they will also include some holders of graduate degrees.

Data gathered by this entire survey, or complex of surveys, may be used to study phonology, vocabulary, and—to a certain extent—syntax. At present, the main focus is on lexical items. This decision is based on two considerations: (1) the possibility of doing at least part of the survey through the mail, a technique that worked well on the Wisconsin Survey once the right informants were located; and (2) the immediate contribution of the results to the files from which the Society's Dictionary of American Regional English will be edited.[7] LANER, then, is not intended to be a mere repetition of *LANE*, or a sort of bear-went-over-the-mountain piece of work; the results of the re-survey, used in conjunction with the findings of *LANE*, will help put the Dictionary on a sound diachronic basis that will enable it to take its deserved place with the *DAE* and the *DA* in American historical lexicography.

4.1   Preliminary Indications

Time, personnel, and funds have not yet come available to launch the re-survey on a full scale; yet it has advanced at least one step beyond the scholar's dream, thanks largely to a group of willing students in the History of the English Language class at the University of Massachusetts in the spring of 1962.[8] Student work cannot be taken uncritically or *in toto* into the files, but much of it has been valuable. Over 90 percent of the student body are natives of Massachusetts, and they take an unusually keen interest in their home communities; also, they have a good deal of knowledge and insight not available from books or records. The changes that have affected the language have also affected their lives—this includes everything from the modernization of farms to the south-

---

[7] See F. G. Cassidy's paper, read at the American Dialect Society's Washington meeting in December, 1962, published elsewhere in this issue of *PADS*.

[8] It is a pleasure to recognize these students personally. They are: Richard Burns, Richard Bush, Jacqueline Carmel, Joyce Champion, Kathryn Connolly, Mary Patricia Daley, Raymond Dion, Claire Duclos, Carol Eastman, Alice Eldridge, Michael Feer, Sandra Goddard, Carolyn Goyer, Carol Hajjar, Hilda Jennings, Suzanne LaCroix, Janice Lundgren, Claudine Madec, Martin Mould, David Perry, Joan Rubenstein, Ruth Schell, Miriam Shamey, John Urban, and Nancy West.

TABLE 4.1: COMPARISON OF LINGUISTIC ATLAS FINDINGS WITH RESULTS OF PRELIMINARY RE-SURVEY (1962)

HARDWICK, MASSACHUSETTS (*LANE*, 218) A rural community in western Worcester County, once a mill and mining center. Many old Yankee families, but Polish and French populations steadily increasing. Population 1930:2460; 1962 ca. 3500, nearly the same as 1910, reversing decrease noted in *LANE*.

INFORMANTS (all of old Yankee stock)

LANE 1: Farmer, 63; a few weeks high school; some notions on correctness.

LANE 2: Retired dress-maker, 64; one year high school; fairly narrow social circle; wanted to speak correctly.

R-1: Farmwife, 72; high school graduate; gregarious; correspondent for two weekly newspapers; prefers reading to television; has notions on correctness.

R-2: Farmwife, 83; one year high school; still runs farm; limited social contacts, no travel except trip to New York World's Fair in 1938.

LANE map	Item sought	218.1	218.2	R-1	R-2
296	egg yolk	yelk	yolk	yolk	yolk
295	poached/dropped egg	poached	dropped	poached; "porched" is wrong	dropped
312	tonic/soda	sody water	soda water	soda	grape juice
344	pantry/buttry	pantry	pantry †buttry	†buttry (f.'s term) (room reported no longer found)	†buttry
342	quilt/comforter	quilt sug. comforter	quilt comfortable	quilt comfortable	comfortable
125	second crop of hay	rowen	rowen	rowen	rowen
238	lightning bug/firefly	lightning bug	fireflies sug. lt. bug	lightning bug	lightning bug
654	past tense of *plead*, vb.	plead	plead	pleaded	plead
450	rustic	hayseed country bumpkin	hayseed	†hick †rube †wayback	hayseed
576	belly-flop (on sled)	belly bunt	belly bunt	belly bump	belly bump
409	shivaree/serenade	serenade	serenade (never among the "best class")	†serenade (not done now)	? housewarming

ward movement of textile mills and the increasing summer resort business in what the *LANE Handbook* called "quiescent coast towns."

Briefly, the plan for the class project was this: the material on dialect geography was taken up just before spring vacation, and the students were given a 35-item questionnaire containing items from the *LANE* work sheets and from the Cassidy–Duckert questionnaire as it appeared in *PADS*, No. 20. Instructions were to find and interview an elderly, old-family resident of their own hometowns—the closest they could come to *LANE* Type IA. A number of students used their own grandparents or other elderly relatives; there were few problems in rapport since they usually chose people they had known all their lives. Comments on differences in usages among the generations were frequent, and there were occasional shrewd comments on responses the field-worker knew to be guarded or hypercorrected. A student from Cape Cod observed that her 78-year-old grandfather, member of an old family there, prided himself on knowing both Cape English [tɔnɪk] and Florida English [sodə]. The class had been drilled on using the IPA since the beginning of the term, and though some of the transcriptions were excellent, they were not an unqualified success. For this reason, this preliminary discussion deals chiefly with lexical matter.

The first class to try this 35-item questionnaire had 25 students who made 33 records from 23 communities in Massachusetts. Six of these localities had been studied by *LANE* and three more were close enough to allow a degree of comparison.[9]

A stroke of good fortune brought two records from Hardwick, a small town in central Massachusetts which was *LANE* community 218. Following is a comparison of the 1962 re-survey interviews with what Bernard Bloch, the *LANE* fieldworker there, found in the early 1930s. All four informants are of

TABLE 4.2: COMMUNITIES FOR COMPARISON

Section of State	LANE Number	Community	1962 Comparison
East	102	Westport	Dartmouth
East	116	Barnstable ⎫	Brewster
East	119	Eastham ⎭	
East	104	Rehoboth	Seekonk
East	150	Boston	Boston, Revere
Central	205	Worcester	Worcester
Central	218	Hardwick	Hardwick
West	224	Springfield	Springfield, Longmeadow
West	225	Southampton ⎫	Easthampton
West	226	Northampton ⎭	
West	242	Pittsfield	Pittsfield

[9] Since this first experiment, a hundred additional records have been made by students taking the course. They appear to yield more of the same kind of information, but they are not cited here because analysis is incomplete.

similar backgrounds, though R-1 has more education and social contacts than the others.

Comparison of these responses to eleven items reveals:

1. Consistency and homogeneity (*rowen, lightning bug*);
2. Retention of divergent forms in one small community (*poached/dropped*);
3. Retention, possibly sentimental, of a relic (*buttry*);
4. Disappearance of an older term (egg *yelk, serenade*);
5. Introduction—unlikely by innovation—(*belly-bump*).

Following is a comparison of terms recorded by *LANE* with those recorded in 1962 in the same or adjacent communities.

4.2   Summary and Comment

LANE, Map 125 (second crop of hay): *rowen* (pronounced [rɑu-] or [raᵒ-], occasionally [roʷ-]) remains the general term among those who know the concept. Boston had *rowen, second crop, aftermath* in *LANE*; four blanks in 1962. The term appears to be going out of memory in urban areas.

Map 238 (lightning bug): *lightning bug* and *firefly* about even. Seekonk 1962 *firefly* (cf. Rehoboth *lightning bug*); *glow-worm* in Springfield 1962 as in *LANE*, but missing from Boston, where *LANE* found it.

Map 576 (belly-flop on a sled): *belly-bump, -s, -er,* and *belly-bunt* remain dominant in communities compared; *-bump* has replaced *-bunt* with both informants in Hardwick; *-flop* seems to be gaining at the expense of *-gut*, which it replaced in Springfield and Pittsfield. Easthampton 1962 reported *belly-flopper* (cf. *LANE -gut* in Southampton and *-guts* Northampton, where *LANE* informant was a cultured lady).

Map 231 (frogs): For the bullfrog, *jug-o-rum* and *jig-a-rum* appear to be innovations in Easthampton and Worcester, areas where *frog* was recorded by *LANE*; *patty-go-round* appeared in Seekonk (cf. Rehoboth *bullfrog*).

For the spring frog, *peeper* and related terms remain firm. Caveat to those who would rely solely on local newspapers for authentic dialect: Student from old Brewster family reports that the *Cape Cod Standard-Times* always announces that *spring peepers* are back, but "natives think this term too classy; they say *pinkwink*."

Map 312 (tonic/soda): *tonic* strong and possibly even spreading. Immediate response from four informants in Boston area, 1962; (?) innovation in Seekonk (Rehoboth *summer drink*, s. *soft drink*), Worcester (*LANE pop*), and Pittsfield (*LANE sody water, soda*)—though students from Berkshire County report *tonic* an exception in Western Massachusetts. *LANE* recorded *soft drink* and *tonic* in Westport; Dartmouth 1962 only *soda*, confirmed by native students as common term.

Map 344 (pantry): *pantry* still used and known, though few houses now have them; *buttry* (not recorded with more than two syllables) still well remembered, occasionally as having been used only for storing dairy products. Seekonk recorded *pantry*, *kitchen closet*, and *buttry*, with functional distinctions, in 1962, cf. Rehoboth *closet*. *LANE Handbook* (p. 14) says *buttry* remembered everywhere but in Narragansett Bay area where it "does not occur at all"—yet here it is, and from an informant of *LANE* type IA.

Map 409 (shivaree/serenade): *serenade*, reported by *LANE* in all comparison communities, recorded only in Seekonk in 1962, though recalled in Hardwick. Suggested response *shivaree* in Easthampton; question frequently drew blank. Terminology apparently disappearing with custom, unlike *buttry*, a term still cited as old-fashioned for a room now virtually non-existent.

These, then, are some beginnings. The next step, already underway, is to complete the basic questionnaire and begin the fieldwork. The time is now right to make the re-survey, and its results, studied in the context of *LANE*, should contribute significantly to our knowledge of spoken English and its history as well as to the making of the Dictionary of American Regional English.

5

Principal and Subsidiary Dialect Areas in the North–Central States

ALBERT H. MARCKWARDT

WITH THE PUBLICATION OF Kurath's *Word Geography of the Eastern United States*,[1] students of American English were provided for the first time with a sound and solidly based concept of the dialect areas to be recognized in this country. There is no need to go into details of his study. It will suffice to say that Kurath disposed once and for all of such negatively conceived catch-all categories as General American. On the positive side he must be credited with the concept of Midland as a specific speech area and type, and with recognizing the essential unity of Northern. This is brief, but it establishes a basis for the present discussion.

It will be recalled that each of Kurath's major dialect regions is divided into a number of sub-areas. Those which are significant for the present purpose are shown in Map 5.1. The largest single subdivision in the Northern speech area is Kurath's Number 4, consisting of upstate New York and western Vermont. It leads directly into the Western Reserve of Ohio and into the portion of Ontario which is included in the territory covered by the Linguistic Atlas of the North–Central States. The three subdivisions of the Midland area adjacent to the territory included in the North–Central atlas are numbered 10, 11, and 12 by Kurath. He calls these areas the Upper Ohio Valley, Northern West Virginia, and Southern West Virginia, respectively. In general the boundary between areas 10 and 11 follows the northern watershed of the Monongahela; that between areas 11 and 12 is the line of the Kanawha Valley.

Except for a few scattered places in Kentucky and Indiana, the field records of the Linguistic Atlas of the North–Central States have been completed. They

Reprinted, by permission of the University of Alabama Press, from *Publications of the American Dialect Society* 27.3–15 (1957). The author, professor of English and linguistics at Princeton University, is director of the Linguistic Atlas of the North–Central States. For greater significance to the reader the liberty has been taken of extending Professor Marckwardt's isoglosses into the Upper Midwest region upon the basis of corresponding data in the Upper Midwest atlas files.

[1] Hans Kurath, *A Word Geography of the Eastern United States* (Ann Arbor, 1949).

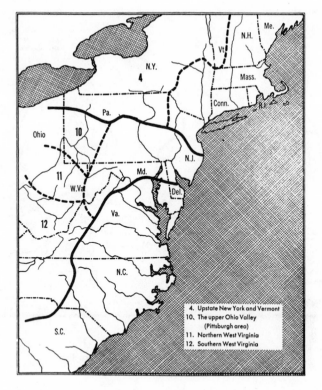

Map 5.1: Speech areas of the Eastern United States (according to Kurath).

are approximately 350 in number, representing some 175 communities in the
six states and the portion of Ontario indicated on Map 5.2 and those which
follow. Preliminary chartings made soon after the beginning of the project
indicated that in general the principal boundary between the Northern and
Midland speech types would continue westward in such a way that most of
Indiana would be included within the Midland area, but that the upper third
of Ohio and Illinois would be Northern.[2] All subsequent studies, notably by
Davis[3] and Potter,[4] and numerous incidental observations by McDavid have
confirmed this early prognostication.

Now, with virtually all the material necessary for the atlas in hand, it is
time to subject this early conclusion to a somewhat more detailed scrutiny and

[2] Hans Kurath, "Dialect Areas, Settlement Areas, and Culture Areas in the United
States," in *The Cultural Approach to History*, ed. Caroline F. Ware (New York, 1940).

[3] Alva L. Davis, "A word atlas of the Great Lakes region," unpubl. diss. (University
of Michigan, 1948).

[4] Edward E. Potter, "The dialect of northwestern Ohio: a study of a transition area,"
unpubl. diss. (University of Michigan, 1955).

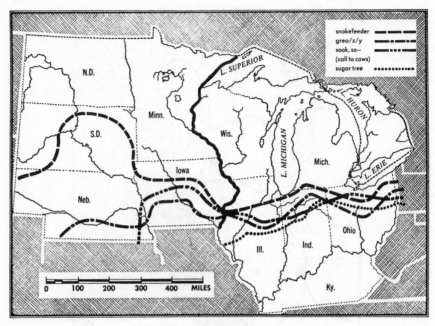

Map 5.2: Midland terms—northern limit.

to begin to outline the minor or subsidiary dialect areas on the basis of more complete evidence than Davis had at his disposal. Since the boundaries which Kurath drew between his areas 10 and 11, and between 11 and 12, as they are presented on Map 5.1, lead directly into the North–Central region, this naturally raises the question as to how they are to be projected. The present study is at least a beginning of an examination of these questions.

Maps 5.2 and 5.3 serve to reaffirm the major boundary between the Northern and Midland areas. Map 5.2 in particular reflects the kind of isogloss that has generally been employed to establish this line: namely, the northernmost extension of typical Midland features. The isoglosses of the four items here represented all have several common characteristics. Three of the four go around the Western Reserve, and even the fourth, though penetrating the Reserve proper, dips below the adjacent Fire Lands. All four cut across the northwestern corner of Ohio, the transition area studied in detail by Potter. Most of Indiana falls below these isoglosses; in one instance, virtually all of it. In three of the four cases, the Illinois boundary terminates in Henderson County, just across the Mississippi River from Burlington, Iowa.

Less frequently have the southern limits of distinctly Northern terms been employed to establish the Northern–Midland boundary. Four of these are indicated on Map 5.3. It will readily be observed that some of these are some-

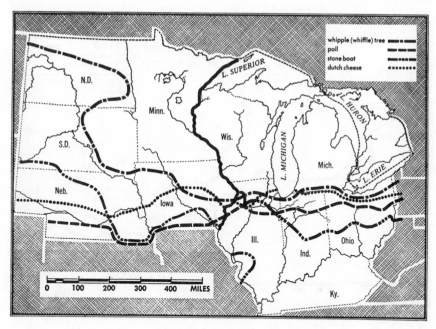

Map 5.3: Northern terms—southern limit.

what to the south of those items charted on Map 5.2, the net effect being to create a transition belt, varying in its width but particularly broad in Indiana and the adjacent portions of Illinois and Ohio. In one instance, that of *stone boat*, there is an additional speech island along the Mississippi, opposite St. Louis.

What we see indicated here is symptomatic of the overlapping spread in the North–Central territory of a number of individual items which maintain a well defined regional distribution to the east. For example, Kurath's *Word Geography* shows a clearcut line of demarcation between *sweet corn* and *roasting ear*, following the general direction of the isoglosses separating the North and the Midland.[5] In the North–Central territory, *sweet corn*, though concentrated in the North, is found throughout the area. No state is without an instance of it, and even as far south as Kentucky there were seven occurrences. *Roasting ear* has a complementary distribution, heavy in the south but thinning out as one goes northward. It was not recorded in Ontario, only twice in Wisconsin and once in the Upper Peninsula of Michigan, but it turned up no less than thirteen times in the Michigan Lower Peninsula. Although space does not permit the presentation of additional examples, we now know that many items, between which the line of cleavage was sharp in the East, have invaded each other's

[5] Kurath, *Word Geography*, Figure 41.

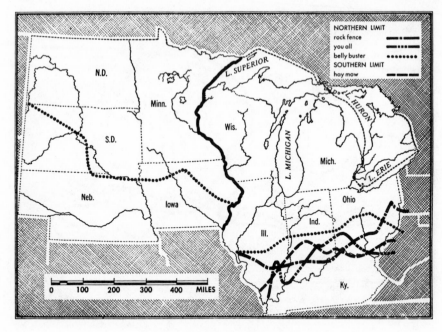

Map 5.4: Extension of boundaries between Areas 11 and 12.

territories in the North–Central states, resulting in broad belts of multiple usage. The nature of these items, their general cultural patterning, the extent to which they may have developed distinctions in meaning, are all matters for future investigation.

We shall find it convenient to consider next certain of the features whose boundaries in the Eastern United States generally follow the line separating the eleventh and twelfth of Kurath's divisions. Map 5.4 shows four of these; one is the southern limit of a Northern and North Midland term, *hay mow*. The remaining three isoglosses represent the northern limits of South Midland features. In general the lines follow the Ohio River. On occasion they veer upward, but rarely do they penetrate north of the line of the Old National Road, which connected Wheeling, Columbus, Indianapolis, Vandalia, and St. Louis.

Judging from the general configuration of these isoglosses, we are led to the conclusion that the New England speech island consisting of the area around Marietta, namely the Ohio Company lands, offered an initial obstacle to the introduction of South Midland features. The dips in two of the isoglosses reflect this, and in them there are no significant bulges to the north until they cross Indiana and Illinois. The remaining two items apparently did gain acceptance in the Marietta area, but their spread north of that was prevented by the

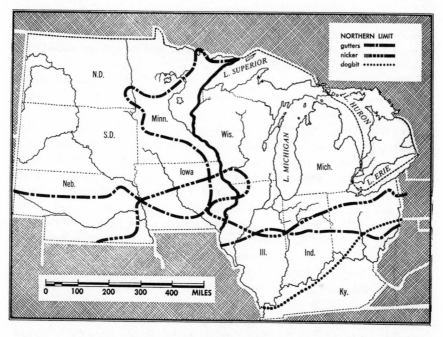

NORTHERN LIMIT
gutters ■■■■■■
nicker ■■■■■■■
dogbit •••••••••

Map 5.5: Extension of boundaries between Areas 10 and 11.

prior establishment of terms current in Pennsylvania. Nevertheless, they did spread north as far as the line of the Old National Road. At all events, these extensions of the boundary between what Kurath calls the Northern and Southern West Virginia areas do present a fairly clearcut picture, one which is repeated in other items which have not been charted here.

Much less predictable is the behavior of the features which constitute the boundary between the tenth and eleventh of Kurath's subdivisions. A glance at Map 5.5 will indicate that their behavior is not such as to warrant any general conclusion. The isogloss of *nicker*, though entering Ohio just a little north of Wheeling, quickly rises toward the Western Reserve and follows generally the major boundary between the Northern and Midland speech areas. In addition, we find the term current in the Galena Lead Region, which though mixed in settlement history was originally developed by a Kentuckian. The northern limit of *gutters* follows the Old National Road in Ohio, but upon reaching Indiana again jumps northward almost to the principal Northern–Midland boundary. *Dogbit* as a participial form behaves in a decidedly different fashion. Though not charted by Kurath, this item does appear in Atwood's analysis of verb forms in the Eastern United States.[6] He shows it to be current throughout

[6] E. Bagby Atwood, *A Survey of Verb Forms in the Eastern United States* (Ann Arbor, 1953), Figure 3.

all of West Virginia and extending into Pennsylvania up to the Monongahela. This isogloss, after following the Old National Road two-thirds of the way across Ohio, suddenly dips toward the Ohio River, and in fact veers considerably below it over a large part of Kentucky.

This raises a question. How are we to account for the erratic behavior of these items? Any explanation undoubtedly can be little more than conjectural, but up to the present there is little ground even for conjecture. It is true, of course, that between the Old National Road and the principal dialect boundary separating the Northern and Midland areas there were no natural barriers, no important pathways of communication and travel, nor patterns of settlement which might have helped to create a second east–west line continuing the division between the tenth and eleventh of Kurath's areas. Moreover, a glance at the last map in the series will suggest that whatever items current in the area between the Monongahela and the Kanawha might have entered Ohio at this point, they would have been in competition with the Northern features of the Western Reserve and the Ohio Company lands and also with the Southern or extreme South–Midland features of the Virginia Military District. Consequently, a deflection of these isoglosses either upward or downward is not too surprising.

More important still, perhaps, is the fact that features of the language spreading westward from the West Virginia panhandle and along the Monongahela were thrown into competition with others current throughout Pennsylvania, which were also penetrating the Ohio territory. The general path of this penetration is shown on Map 5.6. *Spouting*, as the term for gutters or eavestroughs, is now found in a band running all the way across central Ohio, crossing slightly into Indiana. *Run*, as the term for a small stream tributary, covers somewhat more territory, with one point heading into southeastern Michigan as well. *Serenade*, as an alternate for *belling*, *horning*, or *chivaree*, has an even larger radius; it does not go quite as far north as the others but includes the Kentucky bluegrass and part of the hill country. *Fishing worm*, not shown on the map, is more extensive in its coverage than any of those charted.

This points to the fact that in the North–Central area we must reckon with three major population movements and corresponding transmissions of speech features. Heretofore much of our thinking has been primarily in terms of two: the migration from New York and New England into the northern part of the territory, and that from Virginia and the Carolinas into Kentucky and then northward across the Ohio River into southern Ohio and Illinois and most of Indiana. In fact, the census figures for 1870 do explain very satisfactorily the predominance of Northern items in Michigan and Wisconsin, of Midland terms in Indiana, and the division between Northern and Midland in Ohio and Illinois. Convincing and helpful as all of this is, as far as explaining the Hoosier apex is concerned, it does not take into account the migration from Pennsylvania as a third factor, which suggests an historical reason for what may be called an Ohio wedge.

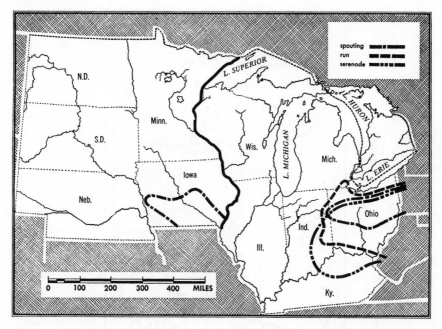

Map 5.6: Westward expansion from Pennsylvania and West Virginia.

This brief account does not exhaust the possibilities of subsidiary dialect areas which a further examination of our records will enable us to chart. The Northern items entering the area were not all of one piece, and we may confidently expect to find belts or islands in which coastal New England terms are current. We have seen that with respect to at least one feature, the Galena Lead Region constitutes a distinct island. There are others as well, and indeed I am confident that we shall find the movement of settlers up and down the Mississippi River reflected in the distribution of a number of items.

Thus far our analyses do seem to verify the existence of a bundle of isoglosses cutting through our three central states in an apical line, thus constituting the principal dialect boundary between Northern and Midland speech. In general these isoglosses form a relatively broad band, and in many instances they must be interpreted as representing the limits of areas of concentration rather than of actual occurrence. For many terms there is considerable spreading throughout much of the area.

Another band, bounded on the north by the Old National Road and on the south by the Ohio River, constitutes a second transition belt, north of which Southern and South–Midland features fail to penetrate. A third group of South–Midland items, entering the area slightly to the north, have failed to establish a well defined boundary of their own but have either spread as far as

Map 5.7: Areas of settlement.

the Northern–Midland boundary or have been squeezed behind the subsidiary belt to the south. Finally, a wedge-like intrusion of Pennsylvania terms into and across Ohio has immensely complicated the dialect picture in the latter state.

At this point it is clear that we are dealing with a challenging and highly complex dialect situation: one which will require our drawing upon every available facet of cultural and settlement history to give it meaning and to make it understandable.

6

The Primary Dialect Areas of the Upper Midwest

HAROLD B. ALLEN

IN 1949 HANS KURATH, drawing upon the materials of the three Atlantic coast atlases for his *Word Geography of the Eastern United States*, made obsolete the traditional tripartite division of American English into Eastern, Southern, and General American. Four years later his overwhelming lexical evidence for the existence of what is now called the Midland dialect between the Northern and the Southern areas was supplemented by E. Bagby Atwood's *Survey of Verb Forms in the Eastern United States* with its showing that many non-standard forms are distributed according to the dialect divisions outlined in Kurath's study.

By implication both works raised the question: How far do the principal Atlantic coast dialect boundaries extend west of the Appalachians? For the immediately contiguous area in the northern part of the country an answer has now appeared in a preliminary review of the data collected under the direction of Albert H. Marckwardt for the Linguistic Atlas of the North Central States [see p. 74 in this book]. These data suggest that the principal dialect areas in the North Central States are reflexes of the Midland–Northern areas along the Atlantic coast. The major bundle of Midland–Northern isoglosses stretches west to the Mississippi so that roughly the northern third of Ohio, the northern fourth of Indiana, and the northern third of Illinois lie north of the bundle, that is, in a territory settled largely by people who had moved westward from the Northern speech areas of northern Pennsylvania, New York State, and western New England. South of the bundle lies derivative Midland and South Midland speech territory.

The recent completion of fieldwork for the Linguistic Atlas of the Upper Midwest now makes possible for the first time a definitive demonstration of the Midland–Northern relationship in the region immediately west of the North Central States. It is the function of this paper to delineate that relationship

Reprinted, by permission of the English Language Institute of the University of Michigan, from *Studies in Language and Linguistics in Honor of Charles C. Fries*. Ann Arbor, Michigan, 1964. The author, professor of English and linguistics at the University of Minnesota, is director of the Linguistic Atlas of the Upper Midwest.

rather than to establish a correlation between dialect patterns and population history, but a brief covering statement may provide a framework for the language information.

Settlement in the five states designated as the Upper Midwest—Minnesota, Iowa, North and South Dakota, and Nebraska[1]—began with the first inrush of English-speaking families shortly before the Civil War. Into northern Iowa and southeastern Minnesota came settlers from western New England and New York State and from their secondary settlements in Ohio, Michigan and northern Illinois, and even Wisconsin. Into central and southern Iowa—but with a large overflow into Minnesota—came settlers from the mid-Atlantic area, principally Pennsylvania, and from the derivative settlements in Ohio, Indiana, and Illinois. And also into southern Iowa came a third group, smaller but distinctive, with its source in the earlier movement westward through the Cumberland Gap into Kentucky and thence into southern Indiana and southern Illinois. Gradually, though with waves roughly corresponding to economic cycles, population spread after the Civil War into western and northern Minnesota, the Dakotas, and Nebraska, reaching some parts of the extreme western sections as late as 1910[2]. This later spreading was caused by an influx of newcomers having the same three origins, by a second westward move on the part of families who already had settled in Minnesota or Iowa, and to a very large measure by the massive advent of thousands of immigrants directly from non-English-speaking countries in western and, later, in eastern Europe. For all these except the last, the following delineation of the principal Upper Midwest dialect divisions will permit reasonable inferences about the population distribution even though fully detailed treatment of the settlement history must await the future publication of the Upper Midwest Atlas. That in this area such inferences can be drawn safely without regard for any influence of the non-English-speaking immigrants has already been ascertained.[3]

Evidence for the dialect divisions described here is almost entirely that provided in the field records of 208 informants interviewed by fieldworkers between 1947 and 1956. Of this number, 103 are classed as Type I (older and uneducated or old-fashioned), 89 as Type II (middle-aged with high school education), and 16 as Type III (younger with college education). Except for about 25 additions the questionnaire used is essentially that of the short work sheets of the New England Atlas and of the work sheets of the North Central Atlas. The additions were of some general items thought to be productive, such

[1] These states have an area of 365,297 square miles and, in the 1950 census, a population of 7,931,298.
[2] The region adjacent to the extreme western boundary between the Dakotas had no significant permanent settlement, for example, until the Milwaukee railroad extended its line west to the Pacific coast in the late 1900s. Previously, of course, a sparse handful of cattle ranchers had occupied the region for three or four decades.
[3] Support for this statement was offered by the writer in a paper, "The validity of the use of informants with non-English-speaking parentage," read before the Linguistic Society of America in Chicago, December 29, 1955.

as *slick* and *boulevard*, and of other items intended to probe lexical differences in the vocabulary of the cattle-country west of the Missouri River. Besides the general body of data there is available a supplementary resource in the marking of 137 lexical items on checklists returned by 1069 mail informants in the five states. For these particular 136 items, therefore, there actually is evidence from 1275 informants. Although it is statistically unsound to add the returns from the two groups together in light of the lower validity of the mailed responses, the latter often turn out to have a strong confirming value.

Even though full analysis of the data is only now underway, the preliminary analysis of replies to more than 125 items in the full questionnaire offers clear evidence for the establishment of the primary isogloss patterns shown on the accompanying map. Replies to some two dozen others indicate a gradual dialect variation corresponding to these primary divisions, one so gradual that it can more effectively be shown by percentage comparisons. By "primary" is meant "reflecting Midland–Northern differentiation as carried west by population movement." Secondary patterns, those reflecting ecological, commercial, or other influences peculiar to the Upper Midwest, will be treated in another article for publication elsewhere. [See p. 94 in this book.]

Of the primary patterns revealing Midland–Northern differentiation the major isogloss bundle is shown on the map by the 1–1 line, with certain deviations represented by the a–1 line. (All references to the symbols on the map will read from right to left in conformity with population movement.)

The 1–1 boundary represents generally the northern limit of the following lexical items: *rick*, *scum* (of ice), *fire dogs*, *bucket* (of metal), *slop* (*-pail* or *-bucket*), *coal oil*, *nicker*, *piece* (a distance), *piece* (a lunch), (*died*) *with*, *slick* (of a pavement), and *taw* of *taw-line*. Of these items *fire dogs*, *bucket*, *slop-*, *coal oil*, *nicker*, *piece* (distance), and *piece* (lunch) are shown in the *Word Geography* (*WG*) as typical Midland or South Midland forms. Inferentially, the other items may be considered as having at least a typical Midland distribution pattern in the Upper Midwest, although *slick* cannot be checked with materials of the other atlases since it is one of the added items.

Phonological matters occurring largely in this Midland area are [mɪniz] *minnows*, [ɛ] in *since*, and [k] in *spigot*.

The a–1 boundary, which presumably indicates the presence of a strong Northern population element in the Iowa triangle set off by Davenport, Cedar Rapids, and Dubuque, is the northern limit for Midland *draw* "shallow valley," *light bread*, *snake feeder*, and *belly-buster*, as well as for the non-standard morphological item *clum*, the preterit of *climb*. Of these *light bread*, *snake-feeder*, and *belly-buster* are attested as Midland in the *WG*; and *clum* is similarly classified by Atwood.

The 1–1 boundary is also the southern limit in the Upper Midwest for the common *slough* [slu] "swamp," *griddle cake*, and the infrequent *quite* (*cold*), and for the phonological items [ɑn] *on* stressed, [ɛ] in *scarce*, [ɔ] in *caught*, [hj] in *humor*, and [ɑ] in *nothing*. Of these *griddle cake* is dominantly Northern in the *WG*, and [ɑ] for *o* in *on* is revealed as Northern (though not Eastern New England) in the Linguistic Atlas of New England and in an unpublished summary by Atwood.

The a–1 boundary appears as the southern limit of Northern lexical features such as *devil's darning-needle* "dragonfly" and *belly-flop*, but of no phonological items. Both of these are of frequent occurrence despite competition with a considerable number of other Northern regionalisms.

Study of the lesser areas within the principal Midland zone reveals at least three isogloss bundles which may represent successive waves of Northern and Midland population, although the first bundle may well indicate also the extension of South Midland features into this area.

The Midland lesser area included within a–1–b or 1–b, southern Iowa, is marked by the occurrence of *spouting* "eavestrough," *branch* "stream," *dogbit*, *pullybone* "wishbone," *sook!* "call to cows," *corn pone, sick in* and *sick on* (*one's stomach*), *drying cloth, -towel*, or *-rag* "dishtowel," *french harp* "harmonica," and *rack* "sawbuck," within the lexical evidence, and by fronted beginning of the [au] diphthong as in [kæu] *cow* and by the [e] in *Mary*, within the phonological evidence. South Midland origins are likely for the infrequent *dogbit* and *pullybone*; the others presumably are Midland.

The second Midland lesser area includes southern Iowa and the eastern half of Nebraska below the isogloss line 1–c. Like the first lesser area, it is marked by the appearance of exclusively Midland forms, although the boundary marks also the southern extension of two Northern pronunciation features. Lexical inclusions are *weather-boarding, barn)lot, plumb across, fice(t* "small dog," [pui] and [hoi] as calls to pigs, *chickie!, clabber cheese* and *smearcase, barn owl, polecat*, and *babycab*. Phonological matters include [rɛnts] for *rinse*, [kæg] *keg*, *tushes* for *tusks*. [ʌ] in *rather*, and [u] in *Cooper*. At the same time the 1–c bundle includes one isophone and one isomorph limiting two expanding Northern forms, [æ] in *married* and *dove* as the preterit of *dive*. *Dove*, incidentally, is significantly dominant with all types of speakers despite repeated pedagogical injunctions against it.

The third Midland lesser area, 1–d, includes the southern two-thirds of Iowa and all of Nebraska. Its main lexical features are *till* (in time expressions), *blinds, dust up* (a room), *comfort* "bedcovering," *pallet, paving* "rural concrete highway," *dip* "sauce for pudding," *hull* (of a walnut), *butter beans, snake-feeder*, and *sick at* (*one's stomach*). *Sick at*, which competes with two other Midland regionalisms, interestingly enough is often listed in textbooks as standard in contrast to the dominant Northern form *sick to*. A conspicuous non-standard phonological characteristic in this area is the excrescent [-t] on *trough* and *eavestrough*.

At the same time the 1–d bundle serves to set off a fourth area between 1–d and 1–1, southwestern South Dakota, in which is found the maximum extension of a few Northern forms, *parlor match, haycock*, and *tarvy* or *tarvia* for a macadamized road. Of these only *parlor match* was reported as used in

Iowa. The *tarvy* item may require further study, as its incidence could be related to variables not related to population distribution.

Although detailed investigation of the Type distribution of each of the terms in these three lesser areas would be needed before accurate classification of each as expanding or receding, a reasonable inference would seem to be that, in general, Midland forms limited to these areas are receding or at least checked and that Northern forms found here are expanding.

The converse, then, may with equal reason be inferred with respect to the Midland and Northern forms whose distribution is marked by the isogloss bundles setting off the lesser areas north of the main dialect boundary, 1–1. There appear to be four such lesser isogloss bundles, 1–e, 1–f, 1–g, and 1–h, designating the limits of expanding Midland or checked or receding Northern forms.

Isogloss bundle 1–e, for example, clearly represents the northern limits of the Midland *armload* and *seed* (as in both *cherry-seed* and *peach-seed*), which are found in nearly all of South Dakota. They compete with Northern *armful* and *stone*. On the other hand, it appears to represent also the limit of the rather infrequent Northern expression *pothole*. This last term was not recorded in Minnesota or Iowa during fieldwork, but checklist returns show a spotty frequency in Minnesota in addition to the recorded uses in North Dakota.

Similarly, the boundary 1–f is chiefly comprised of isoglosses showing the northern expansion of Midland terms. Here in northwestern South Dakota and western North Dakota the Midland *hayshock* and *haydoodle* have successfully competed with the receding Northern *haycock*. Midland *mouth harp* likewise is found here as far north as the Canadian border; so are Midland *bottoms* or *bottomland, roasting-ears, firebug* (firefly), and the locution *want off/in*. Only one apparently Northern word has so far been found to be limited by 1–f, *boulevard*. This term was not included in any eastern atlas study, so that no comparative data are available except some isolated occurrences reported in private correspondence from northern and central Ohio. However, in the sense "strip of grass between sidewalk and street," this term patterns exactly like a typical Northern word, and strong confirmation of this patterning is found in the responses on the checklists.

Although the line 1–e,g, setting off the eastern Dakotas, does indicate the full northern expansion of several Midland terms, it largely denotes the limited western extension of Northern forms which probably are receding or checked. Midland forms which have spread widely, if sparsely, as far as Canada are: *evening* "time before supper," *cling peach, took sick, come back* and *come back again,* and *the baby) crawls.* Northern words rarely found beyond this boundary are *the wind) is calming (down* (mostly in Minnesota), *curtains* (on rollers), *red up* and *rid up, whipple-* or *whiffle-tree, cluck(hen* "brooding hen," *fried cakes* "doughnuts," and *skip school.* Even in the North Central States the Midland *singletree* was unaccountably well on its way to supplant *whippletree* before the advent of the tractor. The Northern term now appears on the road to obsolescence. In addition several Northern pronunciation items are seldom recorded beyond this boundary: [ɑ] in *fog* and *foggy*, [gul] *goal*, [draut] "drouth," [sut] *soot*, and [bɑrəl] "*barrel*." The last three of these apparently are old-fashioned, used almost exclusively by Type I speakers. The receding and infrequent Northern [klɪm], non-standard preterit of *climb*, also occurs only within this lesser area. [ɑ] in *fog*, it is curious, is obviously receding while the [ɑ] in stressed *on*, contrariwise, is expanding with vigor.

Boundary 1–e,h, enclosing principally northern Iowa and southern Minnesota with a small margin of South Dakota, chiefly sets off the extreme extension of receding Northern forms. Among them appear to be *spider* "frying pan," *fills* or *thills*, *brook* "fishing stream" (only in Minnesota), *feeding time*, [ho] "call to a horse," [kə'de] "call to sheep," *lobbered milk*, and *sugar bush*. Also apparently receding Northern forms are the pronunciations with [θs] or [ðz] in *troughs* and *eavestroughs* and [e] in *dairy*, and the morphological feature *see* as the preterit of *see*. This limited area also represents a last-ditch stand against at least two Midland forms which have spread throughout the rest of the Upper Midwest, possibly because of reinforcement by Midland population influx through Duluth. One is *rock*, as in *He threw a rock at the dog*; the other is *bawl*, to describe the noise made by a cow.

The regional patterns which have been outlined above are slightly complicated by the presence of at least one enclave and perhaps another. The area marked X on the map contains a number of Northern forms not reported generally in Southern Iowa or elsewhere in Nebraska. Its existence probably is to be correlated with the migration of a number of New York and Ohio families into the Eastern Platte River Valley after the Civil War. Within or marginal to this enclave, for example, both parents of each of two informants came from New York and the mother of another was born there. One informant reported both parents born in Ohio; another reported his mother's birthplace in that state. Besides, one informant's father came from Illinois and both parents of another came from Wisconsin. All other informants are of foreign-born parentage. Among the hence presumably Northern forms which appear in the Platte River Valley are *parlor match*, *haycock*, [ho], [kə'de], *fried cake*, *boulevard* and *quite* (*cold*), in addition to the pronunciations [ɑ] in *fog* and *foggy*, [ɔ] in *caught*, and [hj] in *humor*.

The putative second enclave is designated by Y on the map. It includes Duluth, Minnesota, and the communities along the Mesabi Iron Range. Considerable investigation is called for by the appearance in this area of a number of Midland forms. Although no one informant has consistent Midland speech (not one of them has a Midland background), the frequency with which Midland items occur points to a possible Midland influence because of the contacts between Duluth, a major port, and the Lake Erie ports of Sandusky, Cleveland, and Erie, which are not far from the Midland territory of southern Ohio and Pennsylvania. Lexical items with usual Midland distribution which turn up in this enclave are *cling* (*peach*, *blinds*, *lot*, *bucket* (of metal), *spigot* "faucet," *bag* (of cloth), *armload, coalbucket, bawl, chickie!, dip* "sauce," *hull* (of walnut), *butter bean, come back again, died with,* and *took sick.* Phonological forms recorded here include [e] in *chair* and *Mary,* [u] in *spoons,* [ɔ] in *on,* [u] in *Cooper,* and [wo] "call to horse."

But the description of the Midland–Northern differentiation in the Upper Midwest is by no means complete in terms of isogloss boundaries. As the existence of the various "lesser areas" reveals, a number of Northern terms have been recorded in various parts of that principal Midland-speaking territory which is set off by the main isogloss bundle 1–1; and, correspondingly, a number of Midland terms have been recorded north of that bundle. Clearly the Midland–Northern distinction becomes less sharp as the dialect boundary is followed westward. The distinction is clearest in Iowa; it has so far broken down in South Dakota that that State might as well be designated a transition area. Actually the degree of the breakdown is much greater than the map would suggest, for the diffusion of many a dialect feature is so gradual that an isogloss cannot be drawn for it. Rather, recourse must be had to percentage of frequency.

For nearly all forms already cited the distribution patterns are so clear that isoglosses may be drawn with some certainty. For example, a quick glance at a map bearing symbols marking the occurrence of *comfort, comforter,* and *comfortable* is adequate for one to be able to draw the isogloss of *comfort,* which is clearly limited to the Midland 1–d area. To establish its distribution pattern there is no need to resort to a study of the percentages. The statistics merely confirm the obvious. How percentages are related to a clear pattern may be seen in the figures for *comfort*:

$$
\begin{array}{cc}
\text{o} & 2 \\
\text{o} & \\
25 & 35
\end{array}
$$

This table, in which the figures are arranged so as to correspond spatially with the relative positions of the Upper Midwest states, is to be read like this: 2 percent of the Minnesota field informants replying to this particular question use the lexical variant *comfort,* 35 percent of those in Iowa, none in either of the two Dakotas, and 25 percent of those in Nebraska.

Such a table should now be compared with the following, which shows the percentage of frequency of occurrence of *poison* in the locution "Some berries are poison" (in which it contrasts with *poisonous*):

$$
\begin{array}{cc}
31 & 29.5 \\
50 & \\
54 & 39
\end{array}
$$

Reference to a map bearing symbols for the occurrences of *poison* would indicate no possibility of drawing an isogloss. Even the slight differences in percentage at first appear to be insignificant, easily due to the variables that operate when informants are interviewed by different fieldworkers. But when a corresponding differential appears with item after item, and when each variation correlates consistently with the Midland–Northern contrast, then the gradation must be recognized as significant and not accidental. Examination of numerous tabulations now makes clear that, regularly, some attested Midland forms not susceptible of delimitation by isoglosses occur with greatest frequency in Iowa and Nebraska, less in South Dakota, still less in Minnesota, and, usually, least in North Dakota. Conversely, some attested Northern forms appear regularly with highest percentages in Minnesota and North Dakota, less in Iowa and South Dakota, and least in Nebraska. Since the percentages have been calculated on the artificial basis of the political boundaries, actually the figures are more significant than at first sight, for the Midland percentage for Iowa would be still higher if the informants in the Northern-speech territory of the two upper tiers of counties had been counted in Minnesota rather than in Iowa. The reverse, of course, would hold true for a Northern form, which would have a lower frequency in Iowa if the northern third had been counted in with Minnesota.

Now even though the spread in the percentages for *poison* is not great— between 29.5 and 54—the spread clearly indicates a higher rate of occurrence in Midland territory. Similar spread appears in the percentages ascertained for these words:

the sun)	came up		skillet	paper)	sack
11.5	10.5	27	49.5	70	55
27		65		85	
40.5	22	81	90	81	73

Of these, *skillet* is shown in the *WG* to be the dominant Midland term, with only a scattered handful of instances reported along Long Island Sound. It would seem to be expanding with some vigor in the Upper Midwest, and the checklist replies confirm this expansion. The figures for *sack* may be questioned, but they conversely match those for *paper bag*, which appears to have a slight Northern dominance.

With the phonological items recourse to percentage analysis is particularly productive, for matters of pronunciation seem much less likely than vocabulary items to be characterized by fairly distinct regional patterns. Yet regional variation on a graduated scale appears when the statistics are examined for such as these:

[sʌt] *soot*		[æ] in *razor-strap*		[ɑ] in *wheelbarrow*	
19	25	46	37	10	22
24		48		8	
30	31	47	49	22	39
[-o] final in *wheelbarrow*		[-wain] in *genuine*		[θ] in *with milk*	
19	22	56	66	36	34
27		59		42	
30	50	62	73	41	52
		[u] in *root*			
		38	23		
		25			
		40	46		

A Midland emphasis appears also in the distribution of a few morphological items which do not have sharp isoglossal patterning. With each of these items variation is heard from only Type I and Type II informants:

bushel (pl. after numeral)		who-all?		begun (pret.)		drownded	
36	40	51	57	0	6	19	19
52		57		0		43	
50	72	78	66	11	19.4	14	35

At least two lexical items exhibit Northern weighting in their distribution:

paper) bag		warmed up	
73	74	62.5	62.5
56		61.5	
40	58	38	28

Phonological responses revealing Northern emphasis are:

[bɑb] wire		[ɑ] in harrow		[ɪŋ] in plurals and gerunds	
23	16	16	33	59	82
19		7		47	
11	10	6	12	48	46

Two morphological items may have Northern weighting also, the non-standard adverbial genitive *anywheres* (contrasting with *anywhere* and *anyplace*) and the preterit *fitted*:

anywheres		fitted	
23	19	28.5	22
16		17	
13	11.7	8	14

Although certainly most of the Upper Midwest worksheet items classed in the eastern atlases as either Midland or Northern reveal, to some extent at least, the same correlation, there are a few for which the evidence is puzzling and will require some special investigation if not supplementary collecting. *Clean across*, for instance, is reported in the *WG* as a "regional phrase" current along the South Atlantic Coast; but in the Upper Midwest it turns up only twice in Midland Iowa and Nebraska, four times in South Dakota, and five times in North Dakota. *Mosquito hawk* "dragonfly" is reported in the *WG* only along the South Atlantic Coast from southern New Jersey to South Carolina (although Raven I. McDavid, Jr., has additionally recorded a few scattered occurrences in Upper New York); in the Upper Midwest this variant shows distinct Northern distribution with its seven occurrences in Minnesota and four in North Dakota but none in either Iowa or Nebraska. *Buttery*, according to Kurath, "is unknown in the Hudson Valley and in the entire Midland and South." Yet as a relic term it appears not only in Minnesota but also in the Midland speech area of Iowa and Nebraska. *Lead-horse*, according to the *WG*, is limited to Midland and South Midland areas; as a relic in the Upper Midwest it has fairly even distribution in the five states. *Fishworm* was recorded frequently in both New England

and New York as well as in South Midland territory; in the Upper Midwest it
is exclusively Midland. Both the field records and the checklists show that
angleworm is the overwhelmingly dominant form in the Northern speech regions
of the Upper Midwest. *Firebug* is reported in the *WG* as Pennsylvania vocabulary
variant for *firefly*, with only a solitary instance in New York. But in the Upper
Midwest the percentage distribution surely is not Midland:

15.4   9.5

16

2.7   1

Furthermore, the checklist responses number 45 in Minnesota and North
Dakota with only 10 in Iowa and 9 in Nebraska. *Raised* in "The sun raised at
six o'clock" Atwood calls Middle Atlantic, but in the Upper Midwest it occurs
as a rare non-standard form seven times north of the 1–1 boundary and only
four times in Midland territory south of it.

In summary:

1   The primary Midland–Northern dialect contrast of the Atlantic coast
States is maintained in the Upper Midwest.

2   The distinction is particularly clear in the eastern half of the Upper
Midwest, that is, between the lower two-thirds of Iowa and the upper third of
Iowa.

3   The distinction is less clear in the western half, that is, west of the

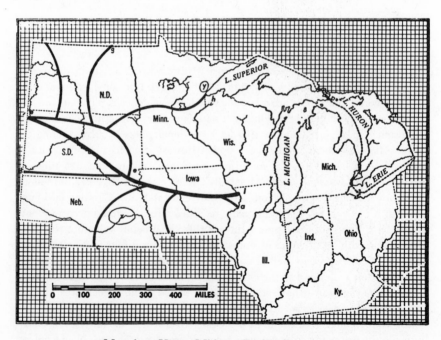

Map 6.1—Upper Midwest Dialect Patterns.

Missouri River, where splitting of the major isogloss bundle reveals several lesser dialect areas delimiting expanding or receding forms.

4 In general, Northern speech forms seem to be yielding to Midland.
   a. The principal isoglosses bend northward, even to the point of indicating a complete blocking of some Northern terms.
   b. Most of the expanding forms are Midland; most of the receding forms are Northern.
   c. Diffusion appears to be more intensive for Midland forms in Northern territory, especially in Minnesota, than for Northern forms in Midland territory, especially southern Iowa.

5 One Northern enclave occurs in Midland territory; a probable Midland enclave occurs in Northern territory.

7

Minor Dialect Areas of the Upper Midwest

HAROLD B. ALLEN

YEAR BY YEAR new data from the regional linguistic atlases expand the outline of the great panorama of the westward extension of the principal eastern seaboard dialect patterns. Recent analyses of the field records of both the North Central[1] and the Upper Midwest[2] atlases clearly reveal that the major isogloss bundles are projections of the same basic Northern–Midland contrast first made specific by Hans Kurath in 1949 in his *Word Geography of the Eastern United States*. But the study of the Upper Midwest records reveals also the presence of significant independent minor dialect areas within this five-state region of Minnesota, Iowa, the two Dakotas, and Nebraska.

The major division in this region is indicated in Map 7.1 in terms of the items chosen by Marckwardt to illustrate his article on the North Central states.[3] Here the isoglosses marking the southern limit of the Northern *stone boat* and the northern limit of the Midland *belly buster* and *snake feeder* suggest that Northern speech may be receding in the Upper Midwest. Other evidence is confirmatory. Although some Northern terms have expanded into Nebraska, the general spread is only into the northeastern diagonal half of South Dakota.

Reprinted by permission of the University of Alabama Press from *Publications of the American Dialect Society* 30.3–16 (1958).

[1] Albert H. Marckwardt, "Principal and Subsidiary Dialect Areas in the North-Central States," *Publication of the American Dialect Society*, No. 27 (Apr. 1957), pp. 3–16. [See p. 74 in this book.] Part of Map 7.1 is based upon this article.

[2] Harold B. Allen, "Primary Dialect Areas of the Upper Midwest," pp. 303–14 in *Studies in Languages and Linguistics in Honor of Charles C. Fries*, Ann Arbor, Michigan, 1964. [See p. 83 in this book.]

[3] It is hardly necessary to review here the methodology of dialect geography in the United States, as several recent articles in various journals have described it in some detail. The 208 informants interviewed in their Upper Midwest homes are of the accepted three types: I, oldest and least educated lifelong resident; II, middle-aged high school graduate; III, younger graduate of regional college or university, also a lifelong resident. Data from these persons have been supplemented in the Upper Midwest by replies to 137 checklist or questionnaire items returned by mail from 1069 informants representing all but two of the 400 counties.

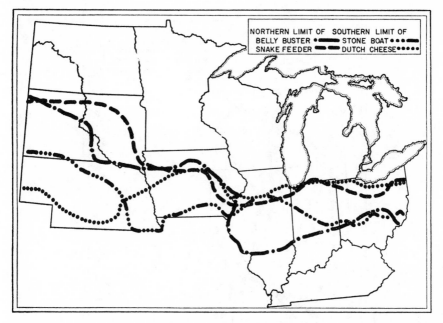

NORTHERN LIMIT OF SOUTHERN LIMIT OF
BELLY BUSTER ●━━━ STONE BOAT ●●●━━
SNAKE FEEDER ━━ ━ DUTCH CHEESE●●●●●

Map 7.1.

Stone boat, for example, has an incidence of 95 percent in Minnesota, 92 percent in North Dakota, 85 percent in South Dakota, and only 16 percent in Nebraska. Midland features, on the other hand, often extend north of the main dialect division and even in Minnesota may occur with statistically significant frequency. *Belly buster*, with a frequency of 58 percent in Iowa, has an incidence of 4 percent in Minnesota and 6 percent in North Dakota (12 percent and 21 percent, respectively, by the less reliable checklists), in contrast with zero frequency for *snake feeder* in these two Northern speech states.

But a number of lexical terms do not occur in geographical patterns corresponding to the isogloss divisions for known Northern and Midland features. Most of these aberrant terms, on the contrary, reveal an East–West contrast which correlates rather with the differences between the farm lands and occupations of the Midwest and the ecology of the dry western prairies.

In Map 7.2 appear isoglosses illustrating this important sub-dialect split. *Flat*, or *hayflat*, when a specific use is to be indicated, is a term applied to a topographical feature common in this region, level bottomland near a lake or prairie stream, or a somewhat higher area such as a shelf of land between a stream and a plateau. Although *flat(s* is not infrequent in New York and Pennsylvania, the term does not appear in Minnesota or Iowa, where a feature roughly similar would have one of the more common eastern designations *meadow*, *bottoms* or *bottomland*, or perhaps *swale*.

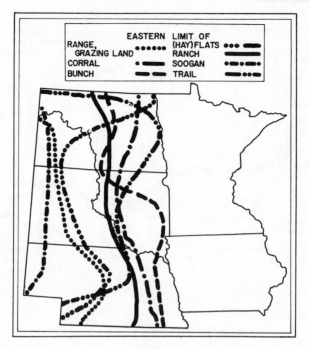

RANGE, GRAZING LAND ••••••
CORRAL • ━━━
BUNCH ━━ ━━

EASTERN LIMIT OF
(HAY) FLATS ••• ━━
RANCH ━━━━
SOOGAN •━•━•━•
TRAIL ━━•••━━

Map 7.2.

Map 7.2 shows also the eastern limit of *range*, signifying open grazing land. Although much of the range country is now fenced, open expanses of thousands of acres still occur in such cattle-producing areas as Cherry County, Nebraska; and elsewhere the word infrequently is still heard with application to very large pastures. But it does not occur in Minnesota or Iowa.

Ranch, denoting an establishment for cattle-raising and not for tilling the soil, is distributed pretty much as is *range*, although the somewhat prestigious nature of the word has spread it eastward through its adoption by farmers who have large wheat-farms or who both farm and also raise beef-cattle. A man with such a dual establishment in central Nebraska or South Dakota is more likely to identify himself as a rancher rather than as a farmer. Areal statistics for *ranch* are not available, since the item was added to the work sheets after the completion of fieldwork in Minnesota and Iowa.

With its referent a man-made feature found on a ranch, the term *corral* has almost the same distribution and frequency. It is absent in Iowa, occurs with only 1.7 percent of the Minnesota informants, but appears with a frequency of 73 percent in North Dakota, 53 percent in South Dakota, and 62 percent in Nebraska—and most of the instances are in the western two-thirds of each state. Semantically this term is peculiar in the ambiguity of the referent.

Many informants use the term indifferently to apply to the enclosure itself and also to the wooden fence which forms the enclosure. The context ordinarily prevents misunderstanding. One rancher in Nebraska admitted to me in some surprise, "I guess I could say that Jim was sittin' on the corral watchin' the horses in the corral, but I sure never thought of it that way before."

Two other western terms appear now only as relics; like their referents they have become archaic and may well disappear with this generation. One is *soogan*, of Irish origin, the name for the wool-filled comforter in a cow-puncher's bedroll. The word was reported only in the extreme western fringe of the area, and then only by informants with memories of round-up days of a generation and more ago. The other term is *jerky*, folk-etymologized from Mexican Spanish *charqui*, and sometimes further transformed into *jerked-beef*, a designation for beef (or venison cr, formerly, buffalo meat) sun-dried in strips. Mostly it is older Type I speakers who recall the expression, but even then only 25 percent in South Dakota and 20 percent in Nebraska.[4] In Iowa only one old-timer remembered the word; it did not turn up at all in North Dakota or Minnesota. The distribution suggests the spreading influence of the northward-traveling cattlemen from the Spanish-speaking southwest, the source also of *lasso*, *lariat*, *rodeo*, *remuda*, and *canyon*, terms having their own but related distribution patterns in the plains country.

What soon may be another archaism is *trail* as the name for the meandering way over the prairie to a distant ranch. Although in most of the area the early trails have been replaced by surveyed roads that generally can follow section-lines, the older term is still known to 30 percent of the informants in the three western states. But a third of even this group consider it old-fashioned.

When cattle-raising became an enterprise of fenced-in ranches, many ranchers were compelled to supplement the natural feed supply by raising hay, but on such a large scale and under such climatic conditions that the eastern *haycock* and *hayshock* seemed unsuitable terms. Lack of summer soaking rains required the "hay-waddies" only to "buck up" the hay with huge horse- or tractor-drawn haysweeps into loose bunches instead of smaller hand-prepared "cocks," "shocks," or "doodles." So *bunch* is a common word in this part of the country, with the specific variant *sweep-bunch*. The term has zero occurrence in Iowa, 3.7 percent in Minnesota, but 29 percent in North Dakota, 16 percent in South Dakota, and 15 percent in Nebraska. Confirmation appears in the checklist data, where the proportions are: Iowa 0, Minnesota 2 percent, North Dakota 11 percent, South Dakota 23 percent, and Nebraska 15 percent.

This western section is itself divided by a few terms into a northern and a southern half. Map 7.3 indicates the southern limits of *coulee* and *honyock(er* and the tentative invasion of the Canadianism *bluff*. *Coulee*, indeed, occurs elsewhere in the Upper Midwest—in a narrow strip north and south of Winona,

[4] One South Dakotan living not far from the Pine Ridge Indian reservation said that while he had used the term *jerky* the usual designation when he was a young man was the Sioux equivalent ['tado].

SOUTHERN LIMIT OF
COULEE ●●●●●●● HONYOCK(ER ●●━━●● BLUFF ━● ●●━

Map 7.3.

Minnesota, where it is applied to the narrow ravines and valleys leading to the Mississippi River. But its chief spread is in North Dakota, where it means not only a ravine but also a longer and shallower valley through which a watercourse passes (although the valley may be quite dry in summer). In South Dakota and Nebraska a similar valley is likely to be called by the westwardborne Midland designation *draw*. Instances of *coulee* around Winona and in the northwestern corner of the state raise the frequency to 43 percent in Minnesota. Of the North Dakota informants 96 percent report its use. But in sharp contrast no citations at all occur in the three other states. A fairly similar picture is that shown by the returns from the checklists: Minnesota 28 percent, Iowa 3 percent, North Dakota 80 percent, South Dakota 4 percent, and Nebraska 1 percent.

Also occurring in this area but with an even more limited range—only the western Dakotas—is the invidious term *honyocker* applied some 70 years ago to the incoming homesteaders by the resentful cattle-ranchers. It is probably related to *honyock*, a pejorative found also in the eastern United States but here in the Upper Midwest apparently restricted to the district of Czech and German settlement in eastern Nebraska, where it designates a boorish and uncouth farmer of foreign background. *Honyocker* (rarely *honyock*) was applied, on the contrary, to anyone who fenced in the open range. The New Englanders who homesteaded in southwestern North Dakota, for example, were so called by the cattlemen. Though many of the resentments of the early days of settlement have been softened by passing years, the designation is still a fighting word among the old-timers. "Them damned honyockers," growled my old Black Hills informant between tobacco ejections, "was always a-runnin' off our mavericks." Of the South Dakota informants 31 percent report it—all in the western half; in North Dakota 12.5 percent—again all in the western half.

Bluff, peculiar only to the extreme northern border area, is a Canadian immigrant. Reported by correspondents as common in Saskatchewan and Alberta with reference to a clump of trees on the level open prairie, this term has understandably eased itself into North Dakota over the easily crossed boundary. In this sense *bluff* is, incidentally, a neologism still unnoticed by commercial dictionaries. The semantic development may be guessed. Cottonwood trees may grow by a stream on a flat opposite an eroded bank or bluff (in the general sense of the latter). Where wood is scarce the important feature of this topographical melange is not the bank but the trees, hence the sense-transference. None of my Canadian informants had any notion of the word's history; perhaps the hoped-for Dictionary of Canadian English on Historical Principles will someday provide the answer.[5]

Like the northern half, the southern half of the western section stands apart because of the appearance of several distinctive terms. Here occur *gulch* and *canyon* for the short and deep valleys peculiar to the eroded hills along many streams. The 28 percent of the Nebraska informants reporting the words are all residents of the western plateau, as is suggested by Map 7.4.

Prairie owl and *prairie dog owl*, equally frequent names for the burrowing owl (*Speotyto cunicularia hypugaea*), are expressions used by 23 percent of the Nebraska informants and by 16 percent of the South Dakotans, all in the western part of each state. The second name is derived from the owl's practice of making its home in a prairie dog's burrow if one is convenient.

In the same general area is found *thicket* as a designation not of shrubbery but of a clump or small grove of trees. This semantic shift has not turned up elsewhere in the Upper Midwest, but it is not a surprising one in an area where the few trees may be so small that no easy demarcation can be drawn between them and shrubs and bushes.

In this semi-arid region the eastern *stone boat* is so far from navigable water that lexical tradition has become too ironical to be maintained. To 7 percent of the South Dakota informants and to 32 percent of the Nebraskans the device is more descriptively known as a *sled*, specific varieties being

---

[5] Since this was written, Charles J. Lovell, in offering a series of sample entries for such a dictionary in *Journal of the Canadian Linguistic Association*, IV (Spring 1958), 13, has actually included a tentative treatment of *bluff*. In his first two citations, of c1752 and 1821 respectively, its occurrence is only in the expression *bluff of wood*. Without the descriptive modifying phrase it appears first in 1889 in the Regina, Saskatchewan, *Journal*. [Eds.—The term is treated in *The Dictionary of Canadian English*, now published.]

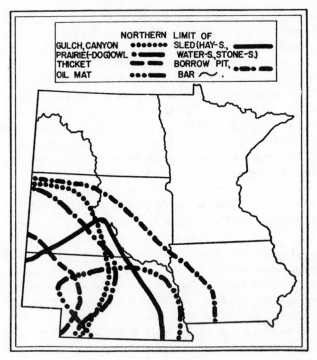

Map 7.4.

designated a *hay-sled*, a *water-sled*, or a *stone-sled*. A current development, reported by northern Nebraska residents other than Atlas informants, is the extension of the term *hay-sled* to a low, wide, small-wheeled vehicle upon which an entire haystack is loaded for transfer to some other place.

Not on the map but includable as terms marking off a smaller subsection of the southwestern area are the localisms of the great sandhill region of north central Nebraska. Residents here are known as *sandhillers* or *Kincaiders*.[6] It may be observed also that western ranch nomenclature occurs normally in this major cattle-raising area (an area, enthusiastic local citizens affirm, which preserves much of the "Old West").[7]

Bar-pit and its variants are distributed within the limits shown on Map 7.4 as setting off the southern half of the western area. In Iowa, it is true, rail-

[6] The latter term comes from the Kincaid Act of 1904, by which homesteaders in this wellnigh rainless region were entitled to "prove up" on an entire square mile, a section of 640 acres, instead of the previously allowed quarter-section. Experience proved that not enough forage could be raised upon 160 acres to feed a herd of cattle large enough to support one family.

[7] An excellent list of local words is provided by Melvin Van den Bark in his article, "Nebraska Sandhill Talk," *American Speech*, IV (1928–29), 125–133.

road construction workers use the variants *borrow-pit*, folk-etymologized *barrow-pit*, and shortened *bar-pit* to refer to an excavation from which gravel is taken to build up the roadbed. This excavation is not necessarily near to the roadbed. But 10 percent of the South Dakotans and 26 percent of the Nebraskans use this group of terms—though principally *bar-pit*—in a related but specifically different sense. To them the referent is the ditch beside a graded road. Checklist returns suggest that actually this meaning may have an even wider distribution than the field records show: Minnesota 26 percent, Iowa 3 percent, North Dakota 6 percent, South Dakota 19 percent, and Nebraska 26 percent again. But these terms are clearly a feature of the southwestern quarter of the Upper Midwest.[8]

Within the more sharply delineated and smaller area of the eastern two-thirds of Nebraska the familiar *blacktop* and *tarvia* (or *tarvy*) of other parts of the Upper Midwest are frequently replaced by the distinctive *oil mat*. This term is reported by 17 percent of the Nebraska informants, all of them in the east. "If you drive a mile north, you can take the mat back into town," one farmer told me when I mentioned that I had come out to his place over a pretty dusty road.

Map 7.5 displays the tentative boundaries of several terms heard in the central north-to-south region. The distribution is not always yet explicable. A Pennsylvania word, *handstack*, for instance, here turns up between the *hayshock* and *haybunch* regions, but no informant indicates a difference in construction between a hayshock (or haycock) and a handstack. Here, too, the burrowing owl, which farther west is associated with the prairie itself or with the prairie dog, is called simply *ground owl*. In the same region, though preponderantly in North Dakota (25 percent of the informants there), the first wave of homesteaders three-quarters of a century ago has left its watermark in the persistence of *sodbuster* and *soddy* as not necessarily opprobrious designations of the new settlers who came with their plows to cut through the tough buffalo grass of the virgin prairies.[9] In a different context *soddy* is also used to refer to the sod-house, the homesteaders' frequent first dwelling in the treeless plains.

This lack of trees led Congress in 1873 to supplement the original 1862 Homestead Act by the Timber Culture Act which, with subsequent amendments, enabled homesteaders to obtain an additional allotment by planting 40 acres of trees. The groves thus originated are still often called *tree claims*, especially (see Map 7.5) in the Red River Valley.

Another term shown on Map 7.5 as peculiar to this mid-belt is explained in the light of the economics of raising beef-cattle. Many stockmen of the semi-

---

[8] Marjorie Kimmerle of the University of Colorado reports by letter that in this sense *barrow-pit* is common in that state, so common that she added the term to the worksheets used in fieldwork for the Colorado unit of the Rocky Mountain Linguistic Atlas. Whether a still wider spread exists west of Nebraska can be determined upon the completion of the other state units in that atlas project.

[9] See *Sodbusters, Tales of Southeast South Dakota*, Federal Works Progress Administration, Mitchell, S.D., 1938.

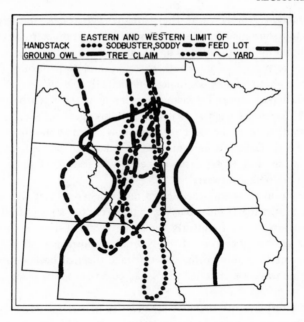

Map 7.5.

arid country in western Nebraska and South Dakota ship or truck their cattle to "feeders" in the mid-belt. Here the cattle are pastured in "feed-lots" or in "feed-yards" to be fattened before final shipment to stockyards and packing-houses in St. Paul, Omaha, Des Moines, or Chicago. (The distinction between *yard* and *lot* reflects the complex contrast between Northern and Midland speech patterns in the Upper Midwest. See note 2.)

Map 7.6, finally, illustrates the range of several terms having almost unique distribution patterns. One is *tote*, with its compounds. Not yet proved positively to be etymologically related to the more familiar South Midland *tote* "carry," which occurs sporadically in southeastern Iowa, this term is peculiar to the lumbering region of northern Minnesota and adjacent Canada. Here the reference is rather to transportation by horse-drawn vehicles. Supplies were toted to a logging-camp by a tote-wagon or a tote-sled over a tote-road. In the same area, as the map suggests, occurs the expression *go-devil* with the specific meaning, "a U-shaped rig for skidding logs." This rig might be so crude as to be simply the fork of a tree; or it might be constructed of two or three pieces of timber. Occasionally an "outfit" would add two wheels and still call the device a *go-devil*. It may be added that one farmer north of Minnea-polis said that he used a go-devil in clearing land; what he used was, he said, "a platform on two poles." Of the Minnesota informants 17.5 percent re-ported *go-devil*; all are in the less-populated northern half of the state. One

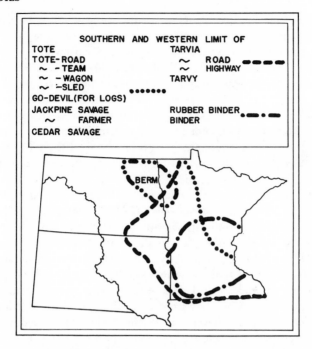

SOUTHERN AND WESTERN LIMIT OF

TOTE — TARVIA
TOTE-ROAD — ~ ROAD
~ -TEAM — ~ HIGHWAY
~ -WAGON — TARVY
~ -SLED
GO-DEVIL (FOR LOGS)
JACKPINE SAVAGE — RUBBER BINDER
~ FARMER — BINDER
CEDAR SAVAGE

Map 7.6.

occurrence was noted in the logging area of the Black Hills in South Dakota.

A rather curious distribution shown on Map 7.6 is that of the variants *tarvia road*, *tarvia*, and *tarvy*, designating a rural macadamized highway. They occur almost exclusively in Minnesota (27 percent, with *tarvy* especially in the eastern half) and in South Dakota (30 percent), while only a sprinkling occurs in North Dakota (8 percent) and a stray 3 percent in Nebraska. It may be suspected that the fairly close correspondence with distribution of known Northern forms is more than accidental; but further study is needed. Checklist returns, incidentally, are mildly confirmatory: 22 percent in Minnesota and 7 percent in South Dakota, and none elsewhere.

Even more striking as a subject for further investigation is the word *berm* (Map 7.6) when used to designate the strip of grass between the sidewalk and street in a town or city. Although this item was added to Atlas worksheets for the first time in the Upper Midwest and hence no statistical comparison with eastern practice is now possible, some correspondents have suggested that some of the more than two dozen other variants (*boulevard*, *parking*, *tree-lawn*, *terrace*, *curb strip*, etc.) do reflect scattered eastern usage. In the Upper Midwest the term *boulevard*, for example, is numerically the most common; its distribution coincides precisely with that of most Northern language features, and it seems to have at least sporadic occurrence in Ohio. *Berm* likewise is in use in Ohio, but with a different meaning. There, correspondents report, it is a technical term employed by the state highway department for the unpaved strip beside a rural highway.[10] The Upper Midwest use with reference to town and city streets apparently is a specialized new development. Its focal center is Grand Forks, North Dakota. In Minnesota it is known only in a small area contiguous to Grand Forks; it appears as far west as Devils Lake, and as far south as Mayville. It was not reported in Pembina, the next community to the north. Checklist returns support the field records with an 8 percent return in North Dakota, all in this eastern segment, but with two isolated examples also in Iowa.

A final unexplained feature having its own distribution pattern is the term *rubber-binder* as a synonym for *rubber-band*. Also added to worksheets for the first time in the Upper Midwest, this word is shown by Map 7.6 to have the Twin Cities as a focal center. The only South Dakotan reporting it once worked in Minneapolis. The frequency of distribution increases sharply around the urban area. That the term is dynamic is obvious from the type distribution. Type I informants who know it declare that it was new to them only a few years ago; they have learned it from their children or from other younger persons in the community. Several informants said that they first heard it from clerical and secretarial workers. Aside from the field records it may be remarked that *binder* is the common term of local students at the University of Minnesota.

It is true that among the limited lexical list of the Atlas worksheets there is only a small group of words pointing to the existence of minor dialect areas in the Upper Midwest. But these words constitute persuasive evidence against the assumption that leveling of earlier dialect features will produce colorless uniformity. As older variants become fewer, new ones appear—to make for continuance of diversity in our speechways.

[10] But cf. Oliver F. Emerson, "A New Word and a New Meaning," *Modern Language Notes*, XLI (Feb. 1926), 125–127. Emerson said that in northern Ohio a highway engineer defined *berm* both as the ledge at the side of a city street, on which are usually a sidewalk and often a strip of sod in between the sidewalk and the curb, and also as the ledge at the side of a road, from the top of the ditch to the boundary of the highway. The Upper Midwest meaning does not include the sidewalk. Only the rural application is recognized in *Webster's New International Dictionary* (3 ed.) and in the *Dictionary of Americanisms*.

8

Eastern Dialect Words in California

DAVID W. REED

THE STUDENT OF CALIFORNIA DIALECTS must take into careful account the unusual, often unique, patterns of California settlement history. The most striking fact about that history is the unparalleled rate of growth of the population. In the 1850 census, the first in which California participated, the population of the state was found to be over 92,000,[1] and a large share of that number had entered during the Gold Rush of the preceding year. In 1860 the population was found to have increased at the phenomenal rate of 360 percent to a figure of almost 380,000. Although this rate of increase was never again attained, the proportion of increase by decades has never fallen below 20 percent. The percentage increase in the depression years of the 1930s was 21, and in the 1890s it was 22. On the other hand it reached 60 between 1900 and 1910, 65 between 1920 and 1930, and 53 between 1940 and 1950. In the 93 years since 1860, the population of California has doubled, on an average, every 18 years; and the rate of growth shows no sign of slacking. With the 1950 census, California surpassed Pennsylvania, to become the second most populous state in the Union.

Even more startling than the growth of the state as a whole is the rate of increase of California urban population. Between 1850 and 1860 the urban population grew from 6820 to over 78,000—an increase of 1053 percent! The proportion of the state's population that was urban in 1860 amounted to less than 21 percent. By 1950, four out of five of the state's $10\frac{1}{2}$ million people lived in cities of more than 5000 inhabitants. At the same time, vast areas of California mountains and desert were among the most sparsely settled regions in the country.

Reprinted by permission of the University of Alabama Press from *Publications of the American Dialect Society* 21.3–15 (1954). Professor Reed, former chairman of the department of linguistics at the University of California, Berkeley, and director of the Linguistic Atlas of the Pacific Coast, in 1970 joined the linguistics faculty of Northwestern University.

[1] The population statistics here and in what follows are taken from the following publications of the U. S. Bureau of the Census: *Seventh Census of the United States* (1850), through *Seventeenth Census of the United States* (1950). The titles of the specially pertinent volumes vary, but ordinarily mention "Census of Population" and "Characteristics of the Population."

Coincident with the growth of cities has been a shift in the population center from the San Francisco Bay area to Southern California. Although Los Angeles began its spurt with the land boom of the 1880s, only with the 1920 census did its population surpass that of San Francisco. In the 30 years from 1920 to 1950, however, the southern city came to be almost three times as large as the northern. The 1950 census showed Los Angeles to rank as fourth largest in the nation, with just less than 2 million inhabitants. By 1952 it was officially estimated to have attained third rank by outgrowing Philadelphia. According to the 1950 census, the eight southernmost counties of California, which even with vast tracts of desert and mountains comprise only 29 percent of the state's total area, have over 53 percent of the total population. Entirely apart from the construction that chambers of commerce may place on these figures, they are obviously of great importance in dialect development.

The composition of California's population has been equally interesting. The proportion of foreign-born has always been high, usually falling between 25 and 40 percent of the total population, although there has been some slacking off in the last three decades. The city of San Francisco, for example, in 1870 had 49 percent foreign-born population, and this proportion had dropped only to 22 percent by 1940. Although roughly one-third to one-fourth of the foreign-born white population in California have usually come from English-speaking areas like the British Isles and Canada, there has always been a large segment of the citizenry whose mother tongue was not English. Among the most important foreign languages spoken in California have been Spanish, German, Italian, Chinese, Japanese, French, and Swedish.

In the nineteenth century, of Californians born in the United States but outside California itself, natives of New York State formed consistently the largest single element. By 1930 New Yorkers had dropped to fourth place behind natives of Illinois, Missouri, and Iowa. Natives of Illinois were not numerous in California before the turn of the century, but from 1910 to the present they have constituted the largest single element. Missourians have been second or third in frequency from the earliest settlement to the present. They ranked second to New Yorkers from 1850 to 1880, third to New Yorkers and Illinoisans from 1890 to 1910, and second to Illinoisans from 1920 to the present. New Englanders, notably those from Massachusetts and Maine, were an important element in California, especially in the San Francisco Bay area, until about 1880. Natives of Pennsylvania and Ohio have come to California in significant numbers throughout the settlement period, but have never approached top rank in frequency. Since 1930 Oklahomans and Texans have migrated to California in large numbers and have presumably formed part of the great increase in Southern California population during recent years.

What dialect significance can the linguistic geographer find in these facts and figures of settlement history? First, it seems to me, he can recognize a number of factors in California favoring the establishment of language forms with widespread distributions in the East, and working against the more local-

ized expressions from whatever Eastern area. The rapid growth of the population, its increased confinement to urban areas, the presence of large numbers
of foreign-language speakers who are dialectally neutral toward English, the
relative heterogeneity of provenience of the native population with all Eastern
areas except the deep South well represented—all these factors point to a
dialect situation still largely in a state of flux, perhaps, but one in which forms
in general use in the East stand the best chance of becoming established.
Second, the dialectologist might assume from the settlement history that where
a more local variant comes to prevail over the generally distributed Eastern
word, it is likely to be of North Atlantic or North Central states origin, since
natives of those areas have tended to predominate in all but the most recent
periods of the state's settlement. Third, he might expect to find some dialect
differentiation between Northern and Southern California, since their patterns
of settlement by Easterners differ considerably.

It is not the point of this report to attempt to substantiate this third
expectation, since in general the collection and analysis of data by the Linguistic
Atlas of the Pacific Coast have not proceeded far enough to enable me to come
to really valid conclusions on dialect differentiations within the state. I cannot
resist, however, remarking on one clear Northern California dialect characteristic, which was discovered in our data more or less by accident. The word
chesterfield, meaning "davenport, couch, or sofa," and found elsewhere on this
continent principally in Canadian English, occurs in three-quarters of the
questionnaires filled out in the area north of the 10 southernmost counties of
California and west of the Sierra Nevada. East of the Sierra in Northern
California it appears in only one-quarter of the individual responses, and in
Southern California it is known to only 1 person in 20. I suspect that it will be
found west of the mountains in Washington and Oregon, but as yet have no
proof of this.

The data to be presented here have a bearing on the first two matters
mentioned above—the establishment in California of language forms with
widespread distributions in the East, and the prevalence of an occasional more
local variant at the expense of a more generally used Eastern term.

Following standard Linguistic Atlas procedures, the Atlas of the Pacific
Coast began in 1949 to distribute vocabulary check lists in California and in
1952 to make field interviews. The California and Nevada section of the project
calls for the collection by 1957 of 1500 completed checklists and 300 interviews.
At the present time about 600 checklists have been filled out and 85 interviews
have been made. The material being reported on here is contained in the first
506 vocabulary checklists. Because the checklists are filled out directly by
informants, usually without actual contact with an interviewer for the Linguistic
Atlas, there are some difficulties in assessing their validity—the informant
himself may not have all the requisite qualifications as to residence, age, and
education; he may fill in what he thinks to be the "correct" word rather than
the one he normally uses; or he may misinterpret the directions and mark only

one word in each item rather than his full range of usage, as desired. Whatever flaws in validity may arise in occasional checklists, however, the large numbers of them that are filled out almost certainly give them greater reliability than the field interviews. Application of the statistical method of standard error[2] to the sample of 506 checklists now being reported on, reveals that the odds are 2 to 1 that the percentage frequencies found in the sample are within $2\frac{1}{4}$ percent of the actual frequencies of usage in the population which the sample represents, and reveals further that the odds are 1000 to 1 that the sample frequencies are within $7\frac{1}{2}$ percent of the actual frequencies of the whole population. It is expected that by the end of the project the comparison of highly valid data from field interviews with highly reliable data from vocabulary checklists will make possible quite accurate statements about California dialect usage.

A word of caution should be given regarding the population represented by the sample of 506 checklists. This population is not the same as the population of California, in that the sample undoubtedly contains larger proportions of people from certain areas and with certain social characteristics than would be found in the total population of the state. For example, it is known that Northern California and rural California are more heavily represented than their share of the total population would warrant. Furthermore, the sample is unavoidably biased in representing only those people who are willing to take time to fill out a checklist, and intentionally biased in including more long-time residents of single communities than one would find in the population as a whole. With these cautions in mind, it would be unwise to place too much reliance on the exact figures about to be presented, although they are certainly reliable enough to give a general indication of the fate of Eastern words in California.

The long table giving these percentages has been classified according to the Eastern distributions of the words in Kurath's *Word Geography of the Eastern United States*.[3] The first 14 headings classify distributions in an order largely from the most general to the most localized. Localized words which, contrary to expectations, have prevailed in California over words of more general distribution appear separately in section 15, which also includes a few words that have come into much more general use in California than have most other words with similar Eastern distributions. In sub-classifying the words and expressions in category 15, I have also indicated their distribution in the Great Lakes region, according to A. L. Davis's *Word Atlas of the Great Lakes Region*,[4] since the behavior of a dialect term in the North Central states often foreshadows its fate in California.

Proceeding to a detailed consideration of the table, we note that words in

[2] See David W. Reed, "A Statistical Approach to Quantitative Linguistic Analysis," *Word*, V (1949), 235–247.

[3] Ann Arbor: University of Michigan Press, 1949. I have not thought it necessary to cite page references for the discussion of each individual dialect term in Kurath, since the book is carefully indexed.

[4] Microfilm diss. Ann Arbor: University of Michigan, 1949.

sections 1 and 2, those of general and almost general distribution in the East, have tended to become majority usage in California. Exceptions to this rule are explained partially by the cross references to competing words in section 15. *Barnyard*, for example, is no more frequent than 53 percent, because of the competition of the Western word *corral* (section 15.4) which occurs in 51 percent of the checklists. Use of the general word *bread* to refer to a loaf made with white flour appears in a deceptively low 44 percent of the checklists, largely because the expanded form *white bread* also appears in 44 percent of the questionnaires. Kurath reports principally three expanded forms in the East: *white bread* in Eastern New England, *wheat bread* in the remainder of the North and North Midlands, and *light bread* in the South and South Midlands. Davis reports *wheat bread* no further west than Ohio, and gives *white bread* and *light bread* as the usual Northern and Midland expanded forms, respectively, in the Great Lakes region. If *wheat bread* was ever common in California, it has apparently died out because of confusion with *wheat bread* as an abbreviated form of *wholewheat bread*. There is no actual conflict between *bread* and *white bread* in California usage. *White bread* is merely the normal expanded form of the general word.

Seesaw is used in California only to about the same extent as *teeter-totter* (15.2) in spite of a more general distribution in the Atlantic coast states. The generally distributed *pancake* is a poor second to *hot cake*, unfortunately not included in Davis's study, but limited according to Kurath to eastern Pennsylvania. The limited use of *hot cake* as a folk term in the East may obscure a fact of general use in formal English. In parts of the Middle West where I have lived, one is likely to make *pancakes* at home, but to order *hot cakes* in a restaurant. It would seem much more likely that California preference for the term *hot cake* derives from formal usage rather than from the popular speech of eastern Pennsylvania. Another Western word, *flapjack* (15.4), occurs with a frequency of 7 percent. It seems to be limited in application to a pancake made over a campfire rather than in a kitchen.

(Sick) at his stomach, the general Eastern expression, is slightly less frequent than *to his stomach* (15.1), a phrase limited to the Northern dialect in the Atlantic coast and Great Lakes states. *Lightning bug*, the general Eastern term, is considerably less frequent than *firefly* (15.2), a Northern term on the Atlantic coast, which becomes distributed more generally in the Great Lakes region. This development may be due in part to the fact that there are no lightning bugs in California. Confusion as to the nature of the beast is apparent in section 15.5 with the occurrence of *glow-worm* in this meaning at a frequency of 11 percent.

Burlap (*bag* or *sack*), terms of almost general distribution in the East, fare badly in competition with *gunny* (*sack* or *bag*) (15.2), terms which first appear in the upper Ohio valley, but become general in the Great Lakes region. There may be in the prevalence of *gunny sack* a reflection of the fact that California's rural population, which has primarily to deal with the article, derives more from the North Central than the North Atlantic states. A Western expression, *barley sack* (15.4), also occurs with this meaning in 6 percent of the checklists. Finally, in section 2, the almost general Eastern expression, *a bite* (*to eat*), fares badly in competition with the equally general *snack*. The development of *snack bars* may have had something to do with the favoring of the latter.

Looking next at sections 3, 5, and 7, we observe that expressions occurring throughout two of the three major speech areas tend to predominate in California usage if not in competition with even more generally distributed Eastern terms. Exceptions to this rule are *clingstone* (*peach*) (3), *baby carriage* (5), and *comfort* (7). The competitors of the first two, *cling* (*peach*) (15.3) and *baby buggy* (15.2) begin as Western Pennsylvania words and hold their own or become more general in the Great Lakes region. The rival that is displacing the third in California, *comforter* (15.1), is an exclusively Northern term in the Atlantic coast and Great Lakes states. It may have become so general in California as a result of mail-order catalogue usage. The occurrence in section 15.5 of the term *quilt* with this same meaning in 35 percent of the checklists reveals a confusion on the item, since it was described in the question as "tied *not* quilted."

Turning now to sections 4.1 and 6.1, we note that words used throughout the North and in any additional area tend to predominate in California usage if not in competition with more generally distributed terms. The only clear exception is (*hay*) *cock* (4.1), which finishes a poor second to (*hay*) *shock* (15.3), the Southernmost of the terms which occur with unexpected frequency in California. One may perhaps question whether the popularity of (*hay*) *shock* has not been considerably promoted by a euphemistic disfavoring of (*hay*) *cock*.

In the remaining sections of the table, except 15—that is 4.2, 6.2, and 8 through 14—we observe that words which occur in restricted parts of two major dialect areas or wholly within one major dialect area tend to be in minority usage or non-existent in California. Most of the words in section 15 are exceptions to this rule, and in addition we may note *clabber*(*ed*) (*milk*) (8.1), a term in use everywhere south of the Mason-Dixon Line, which seems to predominate in California largely because most of its Eastern rivals are of extremely localized occurrence. In fact, its principal competitor is *sour*(*ed*) *milk* (15.5), an expression which I ascribe to the lack of need for discrimination of the varying degrees of sourness in the typical urban environment.

The sub-classification of words in section 15 demonstrates that most of the terms which have attained to frequent use in California in the face of competition from more generally distributed words in the Atlantic coast states are Northern, Midland, or both. They are, moreover, all words of fairly general distribution in the Great Lakes region. *Chivaree* (15.2) has, after a nationwide study,[5] been found to occur throughout the area of French settlement of the United States and everywhere west of that settlement area.

[5] A. L. Davis and R. I. McDavid, "*Shivaree*: An Example of Cultural Diffusion," *American Speech*, XXIV (1949), 249–255. [See p. 178 in this book.]

In section 15.4 the only Western word that has not already come up for discussion is *grate*, which occurs in 20 percent of the checklists as an alternate or substitute for *andirons*. The device in a California fireplace often consists of both two large supports for logs and a metal basket for paper, kindling, or coal. In this case *andirons* or *grate* is applied indiscriminately to the entire device, and the original distinction is forgotten.

While some of the terms in section 15.5—*eaves* and *drainpipes* meaning *gutters* or *eaves troughs*, *breastbone* meaning *wishbone* or *pulley bone*, *worm* meaning *angleworm* or *fish(ing) worm*, and *haystack* meaning *hay shock* or *hay cock*—may ultimately prove characteristic of California folk speech, the best guess at present is that their frequency is due largely to urban unfamiliarity with the item in question.

In rapid final summary, the popularity of a word in California tends to reflect the generality of its distribution in Eastern dialects. Words that occur everywhere in the East or in parts of the three major dialect areas or throughout two major dialect areas or throughout the North and in parts of another area, usually predominate in California. Words that occur in parts of two major areas or exclusively in a single major area tend to be in minority usage or non-existent in California. Words which in spite of this last kind of distribution in the East are unexpectedly frequent in California are usually Northern, Midland, or partly both in the Atlantic coast states and at least moderately frequent in the Great Lakes region. It is hoped that more detailed analysis of the California materials, including especially the field interviews, will reveal other dialect lines within the state like that noted in the case of the word *chesterfield*.

PERCENTAGE FREQUENCY OF EASTERN WORDS IN CALIFORNIA CHECK LISTS

1. Words of general distribution, Atlantic coast states.

Merry Christmas	99	to shell	72
(clothes) closet	98	hauling	69
faucet	96	andirons	68
(just) a (little) way(s)	95	dragon fly	61
hay stack	94	moo	59
picket fence	92	barnyard [cf. 15.4]	53
corn bread	92	bread [cf. 15.1]	44
midwife	90	seesaw [cf. 15.2]	44
wishbone	81	pancake [cf. 15.3]	43
cottage cheese	79	at his stomach [cf. 15.1]	41
frying pan	72	lightning bug [cf. 15.2]	29

2. Words occurring in parts of North, Midlands, and South (almost general).

(window) shades	86	(Hudson Valley, South, and urban)
(hay or barn) loft	81	(North, South Midlands, South)
string beans	80	(North, Eastern Penna., Chesapeake Bay)
(wooden or well) bucket	76	(Eastern New England, Midlands, South)
a snack	63	(South, South Midlands, and urban)

gutters   46   (E. New England, New York City, E. Pa.,
                                                     South)
so (boss) (ie)   42   (General exc. Virginia)
burlap (bag or sack) [cf. 15.2] 26   (North, North Midlands, Virginia)
a bite [see *snack* above]   16   (New England, Hudson Valley, E. Pa.,
                                                     Ches. Bay)

3. Words occurring throughout the North and Midlands.
   clingstone (peach) [cf. 15.3]   50   clothes press [cf. 1]   0

4. Words occurring in parts of the North and Midlands.
   4.1 Throughout the North and North Midlands
   skunk   93   (hay) mow [cf. 2]   21
   (corn) husks   81   (hay) cock [cf. 15.3]   18
   whinny   43   wheat bread [cf. 1 and 15.1]   3
   quarter of [cf. 5]   27

   4.2 Parts of New England and Midlands
   fish worm [cf. 15.1]   21   (New England, Hudson Val., E. Pa.,
                                          West Va.)
   heap (of hay) [cf. 4.1, 15.3]   0   (Eastern New England and Pennsyl-
                                          vania)
   bonny clabber [cf. 8.1]   0   (Eastern New England and E. Pennsyl-
                                          vania)

5. Words occurring throughout the North and South.
   quarter to   66   (wooden) pail [cf. 2]   18
   baby carriage [cf. 15.2]   23

6. Words occurring in parts of the North and South.
   6.1 Throughout the North and part of the South
   kerosene   64   (Carolinas)
   curtains [cf. 2, 11]   5   (Virginia and Coastal North Carolina)
   6.2 Parts of New England and the South
   low [cf. 1]   11   (South and scattered in New England)
   serenade [cf. 15.2]   11   (E. New England and South, scat. else-
                                          where)
   yeast bread [cf. 1, 15.1]   3   (E. New England and Chesapeake Bay)
   lucky bone [cf. 1]   0   (NE. New England and Virginia)
   whicker [cf. 4.1, 8.2]   0   (E. New England and South exc. Virginia)

7. Words occurring throughout the Midlands and South.
   (milk or water) bucket   75   pulley bone [cf. 1]   4
   coal oil [M. & Ches. B.]   53   spicket [cf. 1]   2
   skillet [cf. 1]   34   paling fence [cf. 1]   2
   comfort [cf. 15.1]   21   corn pone [cf. 1]   2
   saw (boss) [cf. 2]   12

8. Words occurring in parts of the Midlands and South.
   8.1 Everywhere south of the Mason-Dixon Line
   clabber(ed) (milk)   57   barn lot [exc. Md.; cf. 1, 15.4]   2
   (corn) shucks [cf. 4.1]   17   dog irons [exc. Md.; cf. 1]   2
   light bread [cf. 1, 15.1]   16   granny [also W. Pa.; cf. 1]   1
   Christmas Gift! [cf. 1]   3   fire dogs [cf. 1]   0
   8.2 Virginia and West Midland
   nicker [cf. 4.1]   26   lamp oil [cf. 6.1, 7]   2
   snake doctor [cf. 1]   9   plum peach [cf. 3, 15.3]   0
   fishing worm [cf. 15.1]   4

8.3 Restricted parts of the Midlands and South

smearcase [cf. 1]	12	(North Midland and Chesapeake Bay)
in his stomach [cf. 1, 15.1]	11	(S. Penna., Chesapeake Bay, Coastal N. Car.)
pile (of hay) [cf. 4.1, 15.3]	8	(E. Pennsylvania and South)
quarter till [cf. 4.1, 5]	4	(West Midland and North Carolina)
a (little) piece [cf. 1]	4	(Midland and North Carolina)
(hay) rick [cf. 1]	2	(E. Pennsylvania and Virginia)
granny woman [cf. 1]	0	(West Virginia, Ches. Bay, and N. Car.)

9. Words occurring throughout the North.

(milk or water) pail [cf. 7]	34	johnny cake [cf. 1]	7
eaves troughs [cf. 2]	18	spider [cf. 1]	4
darning needle [cf. 1]	13		

10. Words occurring in part of the North.

10.1 Throughout New England and in some other Northern areas

teeter(ing) (board) [cf. 1, 15.2]	26	(New York)
Dutch cheese [cf. 1]	6	(All of North but the Hudson Valley)
loo [cf. 1]	4	(New York)
carting [cf. 1]	2	(New York, New Jersey)
drawing [cf. 1]	0	(Hudson Valley)

10.2 Restricted parts of the North

eaves spouts [cf. 2]	1	(Northern New England and Western Reserve)
lobbered milk [cf. 8.1]	0	(Western New England and New York)
comfortable [cf. 7, 15.1]	0	(SW. New England and Hudson Valley)
raised bread [cf. 1, 15.1]	0	(Eastern New England)
teaming [cf. 1]	0	(Eastern Massachusetts)
fritter [cf. 1, 15.3]	0	(Northeastern New England)
cow yard [cf. 1, 15.4]	0	(Eastern New England)
ground mow [cf. 2]	0	(Eastern New England)
high beams [cf. 2]	0	(Northeastern New England)
(hay) tumble [cf. 4.1, 15.3]	0	(Northeastern New England)
great beams [cf. 2]	0	(Central Massachusetts)
Dutch cap [cf. 4.1, 15.3]	0	(Southeastern New England)
pot cheese [cf. 1]	0	(Hudson Valley)
(hay) barrack [cf. 1]	0	(Hudson Valley)

11. Words occurring throughout the Midlands.

(window) blinds [cf. 2]	27	spouts, spouting [cf. 2]	1
to hull [cf. 1]	13	spigot [cf. 1]	1
snake feeder [cf. 1]	6		

12. Words occurring in part of the Midlands.

green beans [cf. 2]	17	(Western Pennsylvania and South Midlands)
fire bug [cf. 1, 15.2]	7	(Pennsylvania)
piece [food] [cf. 2]	6	(Pennsylvania)
cruddled milk [cf. 8.1]	3	(Pennsylvania)
hand stack [cf. 4.1, 15.3]	3	(Pennsylvania)
thick milk [cf. 8.1]	2	(Pennsylvania)
overhead, overden [cf. 2]	0	(Pennsylvania)
paled fence [cf. 1]	0	(Eastern Pennsylvania)
(hay) doodle [cf. 4.1, 15.3]	0	(Western Pennsylvania and Ohio Valley)

carbon oil [cf. 6.1, 7]   o   (Western Pennsylvania)
hap [cf. 7, 15.1]   o   (Western Pennsylvania)

13. Words occurring throughout the South.
    carrying [cf. 1]   29   batter cakes [cf. 1, 15.3]   o
    snap beans [cf. 2]   4

14. Words occurring in part of the South.
    mosquito hawk [cf. 1]   9   (South except Virginia)
    earthworm [cf. 15.1]   8   (North Carolina, learned elsewhere)
    hand irons [cf. 1]   2   (Chesapeake Bay)
    tow sack [cf. 2, 15.2]   1   (North Carolina)
    guano sack [cf. 2, 15.2]   o   (Virginia and Maryland)
    croker sack [cf. 2, 15.2]   o   (Virginia and South Carolina)
    press peach [cf. 3, 15.3]   o   (South except Virginia)
    (sea) grass sack [cf. 2, 15.2] o   (Chesapeake Bay)
    pale yard [cf. 1]   o   (North Carolina)
    walling [cf. 1]   o   (Eastern North Carolina)

15. Words of "unexpected" frequency.
    15.1 Primarily Northern
    comforter   94   (New England, New York, Northern
                                      Great Lakes)
    angleworm   53   (Northern, including Northern Great
                                      Lakes)
    to his stomach   46   (Northern, including Northern Great
                                      Lakes)
    white bread   44   (Eastern New England, Michigan, Ohio)
    15.2 North and Midland
    baby buggy   85   (Western Pennsylvania, Ohio Valley,
                                      Great Lakes)
    chivaree   78   (Northern New England, S. Midland,
                                      Gr. Lakes exc. Ohio)
    gunny (sack or bag)   66   (Ohio Valley, Great Lakes)
    firefly   54   (New England, New York, Penna., Great
                                      Lakes)
    teeter totter   43   (New York, New Jersey, Great Lakes)
    15.3 Primarily Midland
    hot cakes   65   (Eastern Penna., [no inform. from Great
                                      Lakes])
    cling (peach)   55   (Western Penna., South Midland, Mid-
                                      land Gt. Lakes)
    (hay) shocks   55   (South of Mason-Dixon, Midland Great
                                      Lakes)
    15.4 Western
    corral   51
    grate   20
    flapjacks   7
    barley sack   6
    15.5 Due to urban unfamiliarity with item?
    sour(ed) milk   46   breast bone   19
    quilt   35   worm   19
    eaves   21   hay stack [meaning *shock*] 12
    drain pipes   20   glow worm   11

9

The Pronunciation of English in the Pacific Northwest

CARROLL E. REED

AS HAS BEEN POINTED OUT on several occasions,[1] varieties of American English spoken in the Pacific Northwest are largely derived from eastern sources. A good deal of information is already available on the geographical distribution of vocabulary throughout the United States, so that dialectologists now have a fairly clear idea of lexical continuity in the vast areas of western settlement. For this reason it has become standard procedure to identify dialectal types within these areas in accordance with the criteria presented by Hans Kurath in his *Word Geography of the Eastern United States* (Ann Arbor, 1949). A monumental work by Kurath and McDavid on the pronunciation of English in the Atlantic States has now been published,[2] and new comparisons of dialect distribution east and west are therefore in order.

In the matter of pronunciation it is possible to examine not only the incidence of certain phonetic types among the items furnished by the Atlas questionnaire,[3] but also the basic aspects of phonemic structure in various idiolects. In this way, a kind of typology can be developed synoptically for extended areas of transition. For the purpose of describing and epitomizing "regional dialects" on a given speech level, therefore, Kurath and McDavid have devised a large number of "synopses" showing vocalic incidence among

Reprinted by permission from *Language* 37.559–64 (1961). Professor Reed is a member of the department of German at the University of Massachusetts, and until 1967 was director of the Linguistic Atlas of the Northwest Pacific Coast.

[1] Carroll E. Reed, "The Pronunciation of English in the State of Washington," *American speech* 1.186–9 (1952); id., "Word Geography of the Pacific Northwest," *Orbis* 6.86–93 (1957); David W. Reed, "Eastern Dialect Words in California," *Publication of the American Dialect Society* 21.3–15 (1954). [See p. 105 in this book.]

[2] Hans Kurath and Raven I. McDavid Jr., *The pronunciation of English in the Atlantic States* (Ann Arbor, 1961).

[3] *Worksheets of the Linguistic Atlas of the Pacific Coast*, selected and adapted by David W. Reed and David DeCamp (1952) from *A compilation of the worksheets of the Linguistic Atlas of the United States and Canada*, by Raven I. and Virginia McDavid (Hans Kurath, ed.), (1951).

cultivated speakers in the Atlantic States. Individual deviations around such norms have then been dealt with chiefly from the standpoint of their function as representatives of a phonemic structure.

The amazing complexity of variations thus revealed is especially striking when the relatively clearcut distribution of lexical items in the *Word Geography* is recalled. If pronunciation remains so variegated in older, longer established colonial areas, what are the linguistic results of their proliferation in areas of eventual resettlement? The files of the Linguistic Atlas of the Pacific Northwest, incomplete though they are, give an answer to this question.

In general, it seems reasonable to expect that the proportions of regional representation already observed in connection with vocabulary will also hold good for pronunciation. Synoptic examination of phonemic patterns, moreover, represents a new approach to the study of dialect variation. It is at least the first step toward the establishment of a structural dialectology, in the light of which, it may be hoped, some of the fundamental facts about language change will eventually be brought to light.

The following treatment of Northwest pronunciation will be concerned with the reflection of eastern variants in Washington, Idaho, and adjacent sections of Oregon and Montana. Foremost among the things to be investigated here are the elements of phonemic structure and the distribution of phonetic data in selected sets of examples.

9.1   Vowels

Most native speakers in the Pacific Northwest have the following vocalic nuclei or slight variations of the same:

[i] *three, grease*	[u] *two, tooth*
[ɪ] *six, crib, ear, beard*	[ʊ] *wood, pull, (poor)*
[e] *eight, April*	[o] *ago, coat, road, home, know*
[ɛ] *ten, egg, head, Mary, stairs, care,*	
(*married*)	
[ɚ] *thirty, sermon, furrow*	[ʌ] *sun, brush*
[æ] *bag, glass, half, aunt,* (*married*)	[ɔ] *forty, morning, corn, horse,* (*poor*)
[a] *father, crop, palm, barn, garden, borrow*	[aᵁ] *down, out, flower*
[aᴵ] *five, twice, wire*	[ɔᴵ] *joint, boil, oil*

A partial list of vowel phonemes can be given as follows: /i ɪ e ɛ æ a ɔ o ʊ u ai oi au/.[4] There seems to be no reason why [ɚ] cannot be analyzed as /ər/, and, so far, at least, why [ɔ] in *forty* cannot be classed as a variety of /o/ before /r/. In the examples given, furthermore, it should be noted that distribution occasionally varies: /ɛ/ ~ /e/ in *egg* and *Mary*, /ɛ/ ~ /æ/ in *married*, /æ/ ~ /a/ in *half, glass, aunt,* and /u/ ~ /o/ in *poor*.

A low-back rounded vowel is widely represented in *chocolate, moth, coffee,*

---

[4] Without wishing to criticize either the "binary" or the "unitary" analysis of vocalic segments, I am adopting the unitary system here, because it facilitates comparison of dialect data.

office, frost, sausage, costs, daughter, caught, law, saw, haunted, long, strong, log, fog, dog, launch, haunches, walnut, wash, always, warmed, on, watch, water, swallow, and *wasps.* With some speakers this may be regarded as an allophone of /a/. Wherever an opposition such as *cot ≠ caught,* [a] ≠ [ɒ], is maintained, another vowel phoneme must be posited.

In the speech of some people, the words *forty, horse,* and *morning* contain a low-back rounded vowel which is distinguished from the higher-back vowel in *four, pour, hoarse,* and *mourning.* The latter can, in such instances, be regarded as an allophone of /o/, and the vowel of *forty,* etc. can be assigned to /ɔ/; the [ɒ] of *caught, log,* etc. and the [ɔ] of *forty, horse,* etc. can be defined as positional variants of /ɔ/. The maximum list of vowel phonemes thus analyzable is /i ɪ e ɛ æ a ɔ ə o ʊ u ai oi au/. For speakers who have neither of the oppositions /o/ ≠ /ɔ/ and /a/ ≠ /ɔ/, a phoneme /ɔ/ is, of course, not pertinent. Further mention of such cases will be made below.

A few speakers also have the vowel [θ] in *home, coat,* and *road.* While it is theoretically possible to recognize a phoneme /θ/ in this case, it seems more reasonable to regard this [θ] as a free variant of /o/. Because of the weak opposition of [a] and [ɒ] in such pairs as *cot ≠ caught,* the same argument might be suggested for /ɔ/; here, however, the more widespread use and function of /ɔ/ would seem to militate in its favor, particularly with respect to its occurrence before /r/.

9.2 Consonants

The inventory of consonants used in the Northwest is almost identical with that given by Kurath and McDavid for the Atlantic States: /p t č k b d ǰ g f θ s š v ð z ž m n l r ŋ w j h/. There is no lack of pre-consonantal or post-vocalic [r] in this area, and the "linking [r]" is non-existent. Other matters pertaining to consonant distribution will be dealt with below.

9.3 Dialect Variation

The incidence of alternate phonemes or allophones in Northwest English may be considered in three ways, with reference to: (1) relative frequency; (2) geographical occurrence; and (3) social correlation. The following outline of linguistic data is divided first according to the relative frequency of the items examined, after which comments are added on geographical or social factors wherever the facts permit.

The first form predominates; the second is infrequent to rare:

[æ] in *glass, half, aunt, can't*	[a] used by a small number of cultured speakers.
[o] in *coat, road, home*	[θ] used by a few older people around Port Townsend.
[ɔ¹] in *oil, boil, joint*	[ɑ¹] used by an older speaker in the Port Townsend area.

[ʊ] in *pull*

[ʊ] in *butcher*

[u] in *blew, suit, two, tube, Tuesday, new, chew, due*

[i] in *negro*

[ɪ] in *ear, beard*

[ɪ] in *crib*

[ɪ] in *bristles*

[ɛ] in *again*

[ɛ] in *chair*

[ɛ] ~ [æ] in *wheelbarrow*

[ɛ ¹] [ɛ] in *egg, keg*

[ɛ] [ɛᵊ] in *deaf*

[ɛ] in *Mary*

[ɛ] in *married*

[ɑɚ] in *hearth*

[a] in *garden, barn, borrow, tomorrow*

[a] in *on, calm, haunches, water, watch, swallow, wasps, warmed*

[ɒ] in *chocolate, moth, coffee, office, frost, costs, sausage, law, saw, daughter, caught, long, strong, fog, dog, log, haunted, launch, walnut, always, wash*

[ɔ] in *oranges*

[ʌ] in *bulk, bulge*

[ʌ] in *brush*

[ʌ] in *guns*

[ʊ] in *put*

[ʊ] in *soot*

[ʊ] in *hoofs*, especially on the west side of Puget Sound

[u] in *coop*

[ɑᵁ] in *mountain, house, drought*

[ʉ] sporadic in the Port Townsend area, also in southeastern Washington.

[u] used by an older speaker in the Port Townsend area.

[iu] commonly a prestige form, occurring most often on the east side of Puget Sound.

[ɪ] infrequent.

[i] used by a few older speakers.

[ɪᵊ] occurs in eastern Washington, Oregon, and Idaho.

[ɨ] rare.

[ɪ] occasionally around Puget Sound.

[ɛ¹] sporadically in eastern Washington.

[ɑ] rare.

[e¹] [e] infrequent.

[i] used by a few older speakers.

[e] used by some older speakers.

[æ] used by some older speakers.

[ɚ·] used by some speakers in the Puget Sound area.

[ɒ] generally infrequent, concentrated in the Puget Sound area.

[ɒ] generally infrequent, concentrated in the Puget Sound area.

[a] used in all of these to some extent, especially in eastern Washington, Oregon, and Idaho.

[a] ~ [ɒ] rare.

[ʊ] rare.

[ʌ¹] ~ [ɛ] occasionally in southeastern Washington and in Idaho.

[u] used occasionally in the Port Townsend area.

[ʌ] rare.

[u] used by cultivated speakers.

[u] infrequent, concentrated in eastern Washington.

[ʊ] rare.

[aᵒ] used by some speakers in southeastern Washington, Oregon and Idaho.

Stressed vowels are generally the same in the pairs *hoarse–horse, mourning–morning, four–forty*; they are opposed in the speech of some speakers in southeastern Washington and adjacent sections of Oregon and Idaho, occasionally also in the Port Townsend area.

[o] in *yolk*

[ɚ] in *stirrups*

[ol] and [ɛl] rare, the latter restricted to a few older speakers.

[ɪɚ·] and [ɛɚ·] rare.

[i] in the final syllable of
   Missouri

[ə] used by some speakers in southeastern Washington and a few in the Puget Sound area.

[hj] in *humor*

[j] rare.

[hw] in *whinny, whip,*
   wheelbarrow

[w] in *wheat, wharf*

[w] infrequent.

[a/ɒ] in *wash*

[hw] infrequent.

[ð] in *without*

[aʳ/ɒʳ] used only around Puget Sound.

[s] in *greasy*

[θ] infrequent.

[f] in *trough*

[z] rare.

[θ] used by a few older people.

Items of nearly evenly divided usage follow; the more frequent form is given first.

[ɛ] in *catch*	[æ]	[ʊʹ] in *push*	[ʊ]	
[ɛ] in *wheelbarrow*	[æ]	[ʊ] in *roof*	[u]	
[ɛ] in *parents*	[æ]	[ʊ] in *roots*	[u]	
[æʹ] in *bag*	[æ]	[ʊ] in *hoops*	[u] in cultivated speech.	

[t] in *drought*, used by cultivated speakers. [θ]

9.4 Relation of Eastern to Northwestern Dialect Variants

A quantitative examination of like variants in the Atlantic States and the Pacific Northwest shows the following general correlations:

   1   Items of widespread occurrence in the Atlantic States are also common in the Pacific Northwest, e.g. [æ] in *half*, [u] in *due*, [a] in *tomorrow*, [u] in *roof*, [ʊ] in *soot*, [ɪ] in *crib*, [ʌ] in *brush*, [ɛ] in *egg, deaf*, and *again*, [aɚ] in *hearth*.

   2   Northern and North Midland forms are strongly represented in the Pacific Northwest, e.g. [ɪ] in *creek*, [ɛ] in *chair*, [ɛ] in *Mary* and *married*, [ʌ] in *bulk* and *brush*, [ɔ] in *oranges*, [o] in *negro*, [ʊ] in *roots* and *hoops*, [aᵁ] in *house* and *drought*.

   3   Midland forms are in a minority generally, but they are more prominent in eastern Washington, Oregon, and Idaho, e.g. [ɪᵊ] in *crib*, [ʌʹ] ~ [ɛ] in *brush*, [θ] in *without*, [i] in *creek*, [ʉ] in *pull*, [ʊ] in *bulk* and *bulge*, [aº] in *house* and *drought*. Such forms are especially prevalent when they are matched in some Northern areas, e.g. [a] in *water*, [u] in *roots*, and [ʊʹ] in *push*.

   4   Northern forms are particularly frequent in the Puget Sound area, notably on the west side of the Sound; Midland forms are concentrated in and around Seattle.

   5   The old New England settlement area at the northwest entrance to Puget Sound (here called "the Port Townsend area") preserves a number of New England relic forms, e.g. [θ] in *home, coat*, and *road*, [a] occasionally in *glass, aunt*, and *can't*, [e] in *Mary*, initial [j] in *humor*, [a] in *sausage, haunted*, and *long*, [aʹ] in *oil*, [u] in *butcher* and *gums*.

   Some of the forms in this area are found in both New England and the South Atlantic States, but settlement history would indicate that they are probably to be connected only with the former, e.g. [ʊʹ] in *push*, [ʉ] in *pull*, [e¹] ~ [e] in *egg* and *keg*, and [ɒ] in *fog*. A few speakers around Port Townsend, as well as some others in southeastern Washington, also distinguish opposing vowels in the pairs *hoarse–horse*, *mourning–morning*, and *four–forty*. It seems highly probable that the two areas inherit this peculiarity from two different eastern sources, that is, from the North and from the South Midland respectively.

6 Minor folk forms of the Atlantic states also occur sporadically in the Northwest, e.g. [ɪ] in *again*, and [i] in *deaf*.

7 Prestige forms, occasionally adopted by educated speakers, include [iu] in *Tuesday* and *suit*, [a] in *aunt* and *can't*, [u] in *soot*, and [hw] in *wheat*.

9.5 Comparative Structures

There seems to be no significant difference in the vocalic structure of cultured and uncultured speakers in the Pacific Northwest. The basic set of phonemic oppositions here involved equals generally those designated by Kurath and McDavid as belonging to Type I, which is peculiar to speakers in upstate New York, Eastern Pennsylvania, and the South Midland.[5] A total of 14 vowel phonemes is thus to be posited: /i ɪ e ɛ æ a ɔ ə o ʊ u ai oi au/. A considerable proportion of speakers, however, have only 13 vowel phonemes, lacking a separate /ɔ/. This system corresponds to Type IV, characteristic of speakers in western Pennsylvania. A notable difference, however, can be observed on the sub-phonemic level: in the Northwest, /a/ is a low-central unround vowel with slight retraction before /l/ and in some other positions, whereas the Pennsylvania phoneme seems to be more frequently low-back rounded. Northwest speakers using this system are predominantly younger and better educated, living chiefly in eastern Washington and Idaho, where Midland characteristics are relatively more common.

From the arrangements of examples in Kurath and McDavid's synopses, it may be noted that the incidence of vocalic phonemes varies appreciably, even among cultured speakers, in the Atlantic states. Similar checking of individual speakers in the Northwest also reveals great variability, but within a more limited range of difference; that is to say, the impositions of dialect provenience very largely restrict the range of possible deviation, while the treatment of any extensive set of examples is characterized by a number of unique combinations.

It is, of course, difficult to estimate the extent to which given dialect variants, phonemic or allophonic, have been influenced in their distribution by successive irregular mixtures of settlers coming to the Northwest. In addition to the substantial influx of people from the upper Middle West and from New England, various other groups of immigrants must be taken into account. Contributions of Scottish and Irish speakers to Northwest English (the Irish particularly in Idaho) are difficult to assess, and the effect of Scandinavian and German speak-

[5] *Op. cit.* 6–7.

ers throughout the Pacific Northwest can hardly be measured at the present time.

Conclusions based on lexical analysis tend to be confirmed by the observations subsequently made in regard to pronunciation. The residual effects of Northern and North Midland speech forms are readily demonstrable in the Pacific Northwest, and a proportionate distribution of dialect variants is clearly in evidence. Especially notable in this regard are the elements of phonemic structure.

Dialect Contours in the Southern States

GORDON R. WOOD

THE CONTINUING STUDY of American English dialects has clarified some of our ideas about the true nature of our language. It used to be thought that the tangled pattern of migration and settlement has produced a "general American" dialect west of the Appalachians. Now, because of the work of many linguistic geographers, we know that southern limits of the Northern dialect can be traced from the Atlantic states west to Nebraska and the Dakotas.[1] Furthermore, we know that Midland words occur in parts of the former Confederate States and that these words can be found as far west as the Oklahoma panhandle.

This article deals with the presence of Midland and Southern words in those parts of the South which were settled after 1800. Its main purpose is to show the diversity of regional vocabulary found in Alabama, Arkansas, Florida, Georgia, Louisiana, Mississippi, Oklahoma, and Tennessee, a vocabulary investigated by means of postal questionnaires.[2] For convenience in explaining this diversity, we will say that the events of the nineteenth century have three phases in this region: first, the advancing frontier; second, the growth of towns and permanent settlements; and, third, the increase of regional communication. Each of these can be associated with certain aspects of twentieth-century regional vocabulary in the South.

The first stages of advance into the interior South were by way of the Appalachian mountain valleys and gaps. By 1820 Daniel Boone and his contemporaries had pushed the frontier into Tennessee and Kentucky, south to the Gulf of Mexico, and northwest along the rivers of Louisiana and Arkansas. The general direction of this advance, then, is from Pennsylvania southwest

Reprinted by permission from *American Speech* 38.243–56 (1963). Professor Wood is a member of the department of English of Southern Illinois University at Edwardsville.

[1] Maps showing the westward advance of Northern and Midland words are in Harold B. Allen, *Minor Dialect Areas of the Upper Midwest*, PADS, No. 30 (November, 1958), particularly Map 1, p. 4. [See p. 94 in this book.]

[2] Details of preparation, distribution, and analysis of the findings were published by the American Philosophical Society. See Gordon R. Wood, "A Word Geography of the Interior South," *Year Book 1961* (Philadelphia, 1962), pp. 602–604.

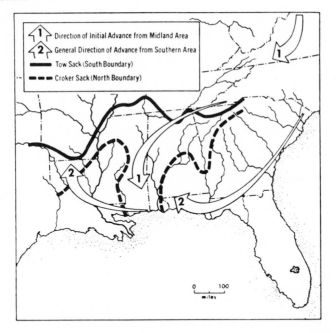

Map 10.1.

along the Virginia mountain corridors into Tennessee and Kentucky, and then south or west again; it was soon joined by movement down the Ohio River. Travel directly west from settled parts of South Carolina and Georgia was blocked by mountain barriers and by hostile Indians.[3]

Thus, at this stage, the migrant from Pennyslvania had a series of ways to reach the interior, while the South Carolina or Georgia migrant was blocked. In short, the first stage favored the introduction of Midland or Northern dialect words at the expense of coastal Southern words. The term *tow sack* has served to illustrate this point before and will serve here. It is a North Carolina term for "burlap bag" and obviously went with North Carolinians when they moved west to settle Tennessee. When we superimpose the southern isoglosses of *tow sack* on a map of the first lines of migration into the interior of the South, we see (on Map 10.1) that the present regional occurrence follows those lines southward; its occurrence in Louisiana and Arkansas is complicated by later migrations of Tennesseeans across the Mississippi River.

Of course, *tow sack* might have come into this region later. Its occurrence along the line of pioneer advance into the region could be merely a coincidence. But, whether my explanation of the presence of *tow sack* as a consequence of

---

[3] A fuller discussion of the geographical and human influences is in Gordon R. Wood, *Word Distribution in the Interior South, PADS*, No. 35 (April, 1961), 1–16.

early migration is valid or not, the present distribution shows how far south and west one word has gone which entered the region along the same corridors that the Midland vocabulary entered. It can stand for the regional introduction of Midland words by 1820.

At the time that Midland words were being brought southwest, the invention of the cotton gin caused Southerners to become interested in raising upland cotton. The Virginian, Carolinian, or Georgian living east of the Blue Ridge Mountains left his rice or tobacco plantation and secured for himself new lands in the wilderness. And thus the Southern vocabulary was brought into the interior of the South, an event which presents a very real difficulty for those who would discuss the regional language of the interior states. In this article I shall use "coastal Southern" as the technical term for that vocabulary which Kurath, McDavid, and others call "Southern."

The general advance of coastal Southern was west and north, though in far too erratic a fashion to describe here. The extent and direction of this advance is across and into the Midland region which we have already discussed. It can be illustrated by the current distribution of *croker sack*, *crocus sack*, a coastal synonym of *tow sack*. The arrows marked 2 on Map 10.1 show in a schematic way how *croker sack* and some other coastal Southern words commingle with *tow sack* and the Midland influences moving south (arrows numbered 1).

In discussing the second phase, the period in which towns, villages, and plantations were established, we cannot say how the forces of stability acted upon a particular element in the regional vocabularies. But we can delimit those regions in which Midland or Southern became the distinctive vocabulary.

Let us begin with Midland again. The mountain dialect of colonial Virginia and of the Carolinas was Midland, or more narrowly South Midland. After the American Revolution, migrants from these states moved to the uplands of eastern Tennessee and Kentucky, of northern Georgia, Alabama, and Mississippi; later they settled in Arkansas, Oklahoma, and Texas.

The area in which this Midland dialect is prominent can be delimited by drawing the combined isoglosses of *French harp*, *pack* "to carry," *clabber milk*, *red worm*, *sugar tree*, and *fireboard*, "mantelpiece." The resulting boundary (see Map 10.2 below) places this aspect of Midland in eastern Kentucky, east and middle Tennessee, north Georgia and Alabama, northeast Mississippi, and, west of the Mississippi River, in northwest Arkansas. The southern point of origin for this line is at that terminus which Kurath established when he drew the main boundary between Midland and Southern along the crest of the Blue Ridge Mountains until it entered the upland counties of South Carolina. From that point the evidence enables us to extend the boundary west in the hill country of Georgia, Alabama, and Mississippi, turning it north and east in Tennessee along the Cumberland Plateau. West of the Mississippi River, this evidence points to no specific part of the southern Arkansas uplands as being significantly South Midland in dialect traits; in northwest Arkansas, however, we can delimit an area which has these specific Midland features already mentioned.

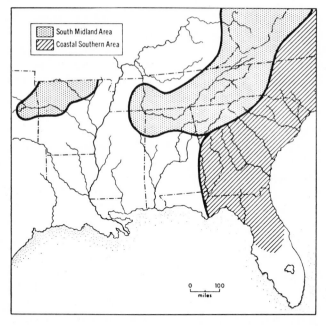

Map 10.2.

With Midland restricted to the mountain regions, we could hope that the vocabulary of the rest of the South is entirely Southern. But the evidence tends to dash that hope.

The combined isoglosses of eight coastal Southern words will enable us to draw a second significant boundary in the South. These words are *lightwood* "kindling," *low* "the sound made by contented cows," *tote* "to carry," *co-wench* "a call to cattle," *snap beans* or *snaps, harp* or *mouth harp* "harmonica," *turn of wood* "an armload," and *fritters*. These isoglosses form a wide band in north Georgia, its outer edge touching the Midland isogloss which I constructed earlier; for convenience, the band is drawn as a single line. As the isoglosses move westward, they converge and then turn south. Generally the boundary follows the valley of the Chattahoochee River as it flows west and south. This river line and part of the political boundary of Georgia coincide with the boundary of coastal Southern (see Map 10.2). A small island of coastal words in south Mississippi will interest us later in this article. At the moment, however, we can say that Southern comes to an end along the Chattahoochee River in much the same way that Midland comes to an end along the Cumberland Plateau. The main boundary which divided the two in the Blue Ridge splits in north Georgia, the Midland half continuing west and the Southern half turning abruptly south.

While some events served to stabilize the pattern of word distribution, other events introduced change. During the nineteenth and twentieth centuries, movement from place to place became easier. To cite but one factor that disturbed the elements of linguistic stability in the interior South, steamboats, trains, automobiles, and airplanes increased the degree of movement from one region to another. Backwoodsmen came to town; city slickers went into the country; mail-order catalogs appeared everywhere. Increasing ease of communication introduced abrupt shifts in the standing of regional words. The terms *tote sack* and *shelly beans* suddenly became commercial names to be used nationally; *fireboard*, on the other hand, gave way to the mail-order catalog choice of the regional words *mantel* or *mantelpiece*.

There are evidences that these more startling events are accompanied by quieter but probably more significant linguistic movements, our third phase in this study. To describe this third linguistic development, we need to use a different kind of map, one that stresses the frequency with which particular groups of words occur within a region. This sort of density map is initially drawn in the same way that our earlier maps of Midland and Southern distribution were drawn. But, instead of trying to establish a general outer boundary from the isoglosses, we seek to generalize and delimit the areas of increasing overlap among the words mapped. An example may help clarify this procedure. If we put one coin on top of another so that the edge of one covers about half of the other, we could draw a line around the two which would resemble a figure eight, the isogloss of the region covered by both coins. If we draw only the area of overlap, however, our figure would resemble a pair of parentheses, the density map of the region covered by parts of both coins. We would put the numeral 2 in the center of these parentheses to show that the density at that point is composed of two elements.

Now to the evidence from the regional vocabulary. In an earlier paragraph I wrote that the coastal Southern vocabulary formed a broad band in north Georgia. Such a band comes into being when isoglosses do not occur close together. Or to put it another way, as we move from north Georgia southward we find an increasing number of Southern isoglosses. The increasing density of coastal Southern words can be demonstrated from the maps of *mosquito hawk* "dragon fly," *press peach, fatwood* "kindling," *spider* "skillet," *whicker* "a sound which horses make," and the cattle call *co-wench*. The resulting pattern of densities (Map 10.3) shows that all six of these words occur within a limited area and that adjacent to it is a wide zone in which four of the six words occur; these densities are shown by the numerals 6 and 4, respectively. Outside that area the numbers decrease rapidly, the degree of rapidity depending on the direction in which one moves.

From this map we learn that the heaviest current concentration of coastal Southern words is several hundred miles south of the boundary which we first established between Southern and Midland in Georgia. We can draw other conclusions from the map. To do so, however, we must assume that these six

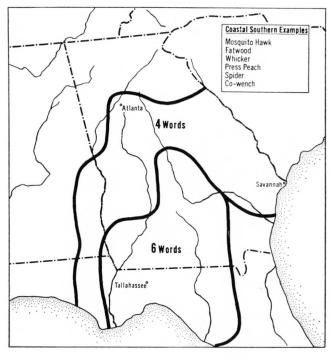

Map 10.3.

words were a part of the colonial vocabulary in the English settlements along the Savannah River. With that agreed on, we then notice that Savannah and its adjacent counties are in the zone of lesser density. To rephrase the matter, the center of coastal Southern vocabulary has shifted west of its colonial origins and is now located between Albany, Georgia, and Tallahassee, Florida. Its chances for expansion are severely limited by the geography of the region and because it is far removed from newer centers of activity such as Atlanta.

The continuity of coastal Southern even in this region is threatened by Midland influences. We noted earlier that the main Midland boundary passed through the mountains of north Georgia. This boundary now becomes a kind of line of departure for a southward penetration. The evidence for this advance comes from the density map of the Midland *Jew's harp* or *juice harp, comforter, fatback* "a kind of bacon," *dog irons, middling(s)*, and *ash cake*, and from a composite formed by the responses *cock, hay cock, rick, hay rick*, and *hand stack*. One edge of this density map (Map 10.4) touches the Savannah River in east Georgia; the other edge lies in eastern Alabama. The zone of greatest density, however, has its axis in Georgia along the valleys of the Flint, Ocmulgee, and Suwannee rivers. All seven of the mapped terms have followed the river and

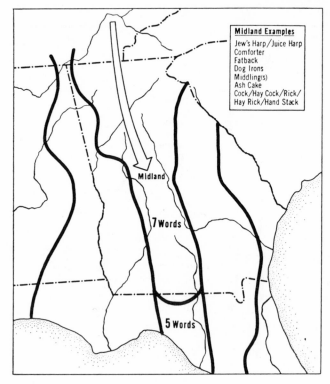

Map 10.4.

valley complex southward through Georgia to its southern political boundary; five of the same terms have gone on into Florida; a smaller number of the terms have come south on either side of this main corridor.

We will understand the significance of this penetration a little better if we superimpose the map of Midland densities on that which we have drawn of coastal Southern densities. When we have done this (see Map 10.5), we find that the zone of greatest Midland density has split the Southern zones.

As we follow *Jew's harp* and the other Midland words southward on Map 10.5, we see that in the vicinity of Atlanta all seven of the examples enter and cross the zone in which four coastal words such as *mosquito hawk* are located, and that the same seven words then enter and cross the zone in which all six coastal words are concentrated. The words form zones of concentration with 11 and 13 words of a composite Midland–Southern dialect. On either side of this corridor of greatest density, the Midland–Southern pattern changes, decreasing in variable ways. The relative densities of these adjacent zones have been omitted in order to emphasize the conditions along the main corridor.

The significance of this development for Georgians living within the

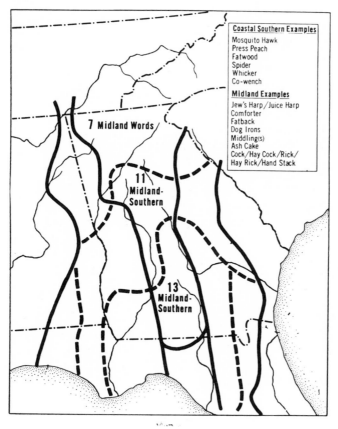

Coastal Southern Examples
Mosquito Hawk
Press Peach
Fatwood
Spider
Whicker
Co-wench

Midland Examples
Jew's Harp/Juice Harp
Comforter
Fatback
Dog Irons
Middling(s)
Ash Cake
Cock/Hay Cock/Rick/
Hay Rick/Hand Stack

7 Midland Words

11 Midland-Southern

13 Midland-Southern

Map 10.5.

bounds of the main corridor is that north of Atlanta the Midland vocabulary predominates, from Atlanta for 100 miles or so south the Midland is evident more frequently than is the Southern, and chiefly in the extreme south central part of the state the two dialects are approximately equal in frequency of use. The areas of lesser Midland density east and west of this central corridor do indicate that Midland influences are spreading in both directions, so that natives of Georgia and Alabama have used and are using an increasing number of words from this regional dialect.

No other linguistic corridor appears in Alabama until we reach its western political boundary. But there, in Alabama and Mississippi, we find a similar pattern of Southern and Midland densities. Coastal Southern appears to have been established in Mississippi when the first planters occupied lands south of the thirty-second meridian; Alabama was settled later and thus does not pro-vide the events which would link the coastal Southern dialect of Georgia with

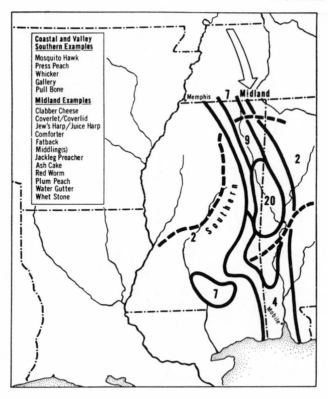

Map 10.6.

that of Mississippi.

The density pattern in Alabama–Mississippi is made up of the coastal words *mosquito hawk*, *press peach*, and *whicker* combined with *gallery* "porch," and *pull bone*. For lack of better labels we can call the last two "Mississippi Valley words." They occur in densities of two or more and are shown on Map 10.6 between the broken lines. Midland words enter this region along the Tennessee state line and generally advance south, following the trace of the Tombigbee River. This is a surprising development when we notice that no similar advance can be discovered along the Mississippi River. My explanation, a guess, is that travel and commerce from Memphis to Mobile was easier along the Tombigbee than it was on the more violent Mississippi; the ease of movement up and down river is thus reflected by the linguistic corridor which developed in the Tombig-bee Valley.

The evidence for this corridor is derived from the density patterns of the Midland words *clabber cheese*, *coverlet* or *coverlid*, *Jew's harp* or *juice harp*, *comforter*, *fatback*, *middling(s)*, *jackleg preacher*, *ash cake*, *red worm*, *plum peach*, *water gutter*, and *whet stone*. On Map 10.6, we see that the density pattern of seven of these words forms a narrow corridor extending south from the Tennessee border and that four of them form a somewhat wider corridor extending in the same direction and reaching Mobile. In northeast Mississippi they form a composite Midland–Southern density pattern of nine words along the main corridor. Near the confluence of the Tombigbee and Black Warrior Rivers they become a Midland–Southern zone of 20 words, and to the south-west a second zone of seven words.

From this evidence we can draw almost the same conclusions that we drew from the evidence in Georgia. The only real problem is to explain the difference in relative width of the two linguistic corridors if we compare the distances between their respective outer edges. The difference may be explained simply as the consequence of the geography of rivers: in Georgia there are many avenues southward; in Mississippi proper there is the one key river leading in the same direction. On the other hand, the differences in width of the two linguistic corridors may be explained as history: the Midland vocabulary entered Georgia earlier and thus has had time to penetrate south and to expand east and west; it entered Mississippi later and, having advanced along a main avenue of communication, has not had time to expand laterally to the same extent that it has in Georgia. Whatever the explanation may be, we have evidence that Midland densities have been superimposed on Southern densities in this region. Where the Midland densities are greatest, the native speaker has the widest range of choice between competing dialectal vocabularies.

We have seen that the zones of Midland density have taken linear or tubular shapes east of the Mississippi River; west of that river, the density pattern has corpuscular shapes—free forms with boundaries advancing irregularly south and west. Words found in northwest Arkansas will serve to introduce us to the new shapes.

The South Midland dialect has already been reported for Arkansas (Map 10.2). In the same general region we find a few coastal words also, but mainly Midland words. A concentration map of *mosquito hawk, spider, big house* "living room," *tin panning, blinds* "window shades," *worm fence, jerked beef, pressed meat, coal hod, snake feeder, tied quilt, coverlet* or *coverlid, ridy horse, breaking off* "clearing skies," *sow belly* and *fatback, head cheese* or *hog's head cheese, sallet* or *salad, corn dodger, smearcase,* and the complex formed of *cock, hay cock, rick, hay rick,* and *hand stack* shows that all these items are reported from Washington County (see Map 10.7). There all twenty items are known. Ten are reported from the counties immediately to the north and 14 from the counties to the east. To the west the count is zero. This gradual increase from four to 20 items as we move west or from ten to 20 as we move south seems to present no great difficulty. These are signs of movement into the area by speakers who were able to travel either overland or along the river. The abrupt southern and western loss of density is another matter. The southern edge is in the Ozark Mountains, a linguistic and physical barrier to entrance into the valley of the

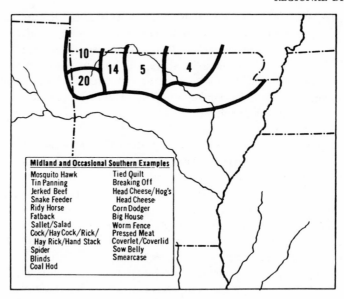

Map 10.7.

Arkansas River. The western edge may be as it is because of the reservation of Oklahoma lands for the Indians until the end of the past century.

A larger configuration comes from the density patterns of *dog irons, snake doctor, flying jenny* "merry-go-round," *red worm, tow sack, fairing off, side meat,* and the composite maps of *wheel horse* and *line horse* (see Map 10.8). These eight words have a center of density near Little Rock, Arkansas. One axis extends along the Arkansas River and presumably is advancing along that historic travel route; the other axis extends south or southwest across five counties. Six of the words form a second density zone which covers most of Arkansas and enters eastern Oklahoma, with an island forming in the south central part of the same state. Zones of lesser density form outer arcs in Louisiana, Arkansas, and Oklahoma. The recent publication of Atwood's *The Regional Vocabulary of Texas*[4] will enable readers to extend the density patterns into Texas itself. If and when a study of local words in Missouri appears, we will be able to trace the same patterns in that state too.

West of the Mississippi the Midland vocabulary is widespread in Arkansas, Oklahoma, and Louisiana. In some localities the density of Midland words in use is greater than in others, but the shape of the contours suggests that this vocabulary is moving steadily south and west. Of course, there are words from other regional vocabularies scattered here and there—witness the occurrence of

[4] E. Bagby Atwood, *The Regional Vocabulary of Texas* (Austin, 1962).

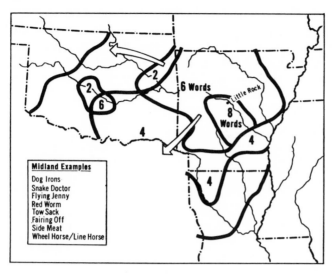

Map 10.8.

mosquito hawk. But, from the evidence thus far examined, I have not found indications that Midland has penetrated another dialect in the way that it penetrated coastal Southern in Georgia.

In considering these aspects of regional vocabulary in some of the states of the former Confederacy, we have seen that change and dialect mingling have been common in those parts of the land settled after 1800. The earliest migrations from the Atlantic states brought Midland into the deep South and then superimposed coastal Southern on it at some points but not at others. In time the interior settlements developed distinctly Midland traits in the uplands of Georgia, Alabama, Mississippi, Tennessee, and northwest Arkansas. (Kentucky and West Virginia have these same traits, but they are not a part of this study.) Coastal Southern has a western boundary along the Chattahoochee River in Georgia and a few isolated outposts further west. It is convenient to say that the forming of the South Midland and Southern dialect areas is the second stage of linguistic history in the interior; obviously, however, this development is simply a part of an ongoing process. While some activities or events serve to establish the boundaries of Southern and Midland in the states west and south of the Appalachians, other events introduce change. Among these events is the increasing ease of movement from place to place. East of the Mississippi River, the avenues of travel and communication led southward in Georgia and Mississippi; along these avenues Midland words moved into areas where coastal Southern had already been used. The density maps show this change in the available vocabulary, a kind of tubular thrust into the coastal plains. West of the Mississippi, the Midland vocabulary, with an occasional

Southern term included, appears to be steadily expanding west and south in wide zones. If we consider that these density patterns mark the third and latest stage of development, then we must say they show that in the interior regions of the South dialectal patterns have not stabilized themselves. Further more, the density patterns indicate that Midland is actively intruding on other dialectal traits that may have been in the region earlier.

A Southeast Texas Dialect Study

ARTHUR M. Z. NORMAN

11.1 The Area of Investigation

THIS STUDY REPRESENTS a detailed investigation of the speech of Jefferson County, Texas, with attention to the speech of Chambers, Hardin, and Orange Counties.[1] These four counties are located in the southeasternmost tip of the state.

Jefferson, the largest of the four counties in this study, had in 1950 a population of 195,083 persons, 147,633 of whom were native-born whites and 44,122 colored. There were 3225 foreign-born whites in the county, and 103 persons of other races. Jefferson is the most urban of the counties in this

Reprinted by permission from *Orbis* 5.61–79 (1956). Professor Norman, a member of the Department of English of the University of Texas at Austin and a member of the Daedalus Research Institute, has made some corrections and minor changes in this article.

[1] This paper attempts to summarize the most important findings of the writer's doctoral thesis, which was supervised by Professor E. Bagby Atwood, the University of Texas, 1955.

Previous investigations of Texas dialect have been limited to pronunciation or vocabulary studies, usually at the county level. These investigations include Oma Stanley's "The Speech of East Texas," a study of the phonology of Smith County with attention to a number of neighboring counties, which was serialized in *American Speech*, XI (1936), 1–36, 145–166, 232–255, and 327–355; Carmelita Klipple, "The Speech of Spicewood, Texas," *American Speech*, XX (1945), 187–191; Zelma Boyd Hardy, "A Vocabulary Study of Kerr County, Texas," (M.A. thesis, University of Texas, 1950); and Randolph A. Haynes, Jr., "A Vocabulary Study of Travis County, Texas," (M.A. thesis, University of Texas, 1954). E. Bagby Atwood's "A Preliminary Report on Texas Word Geography," *Orbis*, II (1953), 61–66, contains an important presentation of the Spanish, French, and Southwestern influences in the state.

In 1962, less than a year before his untimely death, Professor Atwood's last book, *The Regional Vocabulary of Texas*, was copyrighted and later released for publication by the University of Texas Press in Austin. In Chapter IV, "Geographical Aspects of Usage," Atwood shows "that a major dialect boundary exists," one that tends "to set off southern Louisiana from the remainder of the territory that has been surveyed." Many of the isoglosses, in fact, "pass just to the eastward of Jefferson and Hardin Counties, setting these off from Orange County and the Louisiana parishes of Calcasieu, Acadia, and St. Martin, as well as from all the other points lying closer to New Orleans." Still, the "presence of a good many of the Louisiana terms in southeastern Texas" leads Professor Atwood "to consider this corner of Texas as being a transition zone" (pp. 97–98).

investigation, being only 1.5 percent farm rural, 8.1 percent non-farm rural, and 90.4 percent urban.

Chambers County had in 1950 a population of 7871 persons, 6291 of whom were native-born whites and 1526 of whom were colored. Twenty-six were foreign-born whites and 28 of other races. Chambers County is entirely non-urban, being 14.1 percent farm rural and 85.9 percent non-farm rural.

Hardin County in 1950 had a population of 19,535, of whom 16,361 were native-born whites and 3079 colored. Eighty-nine were foreign-born whites and six belonged to other races. Hardin is 16.3 percent urban, 64.0 percent non-farm rural, and 19.7 percent rural in composition.

In 1950, the population of Orange County was 40,567, of which 35,797 persons were native-born whites and 4387 were colored. There were 335 foreign-born whites and 48 of other races. For the most part, Orange is an urban county. Its population is 5.0 percent farm rural, 36.5 percent non-farm rural, and 58.5 percent urban.[2]

Chambers County contains the oldest settlement in the area, dating from 1821 when the Spanish placed a fortress at Anahuac and invited American colonists.[3] Three years later, in 1824, the first settlement in Jefferson County was made on the Neches River by Noah Tevis and was called Tevis Bluff. By 1835, for no convincing reason, the Tevis settlement became known as Beaumont, the city which is now the county seat of Jefferson. Here at Spindle-top, in 1901, the American oil industry was revolutionized by the appearance of the Lucus Gusher, which spouted oil two hundred feet into the air and could not be controlled for nine days.[4]

In order to show how this area was settled, I have constructed nativity tables based on microfilm copies of the Census returns for Jefferson County in 1850 (at which time Hardin and Orange Counties were largely a part of Jefferson County and Chambers County was a part of both Liberty and Jefferson Counties).[5] My figures show that as early as 1850, 35.7 percent—more than a third—of the 1567 inhabitants were Texas-born (and presumably born in the Southeast Texas area). The main source of migration was from Louisiana, which contributed 33.6 percent of the settlers. The other important sources of migration were from Mississippi (5.8 percent), Georgia (3.4 percent), Alabama (2.0 percent), and Tennessee (2.1 percent). Migration from New York, Ohio, and Pennsylvania—which are outside the speech area known as Southern—is limited to 4.2 percent. The only large foreign-born element is German (1.7 percent).

[2] *Texas Almanac, 1954–55*, (Dallas, 1953), pp. 100–102; 529; 559–560; 570; and 593.

[3] *Handbook of Texas*, ed. Walter Prescott Webb (Austin, 1952), I, 327.

[4] Federal Writers Project, *Beaumont* (Houston [no publisher or date]), pp. 36; 39–40; 97–104.

[5] Manuscript returns of the United States Seventh Census, 1850, Schedule No. 1, Free Inhabitants, for all counties of Texas. The originals are in the National Archives, Washington 25, D.C. Microfilm copies are in the Library of the University of Texas in Austin.

If we assume that the chief influence upon a child's speech habits is the mother, it is possible to suggest even more precisely which states exerted greatest influence upon the dialect of these earliest settlers. By re-examining the 1850 Census returns and tabulating all informants according to the birthplace of the mother, we discover that 49.4 percent, or almost half, of the 1567 inhabitants were born in Louisiana or had mothers from Louisiana. Some 9.6 percent were born in Mississippi or their mothers were born in Mississippi. Some 3.8 percent were of Tennessee extraction; 3.5 percent were of South Carolina matriarchy; and 3.4 percent were second generation Texans of Texas-born mothers.

The nativity tables printed for the Tenth Census provide us with information concerning the settlement of the area in 1880.[6] We find that by 1880, the entire area was two-thirds populated by native-born Texans. We also note that Louisiana contributes considerably less to the population than in 1850, but is still the greatest source of settlers in all counties except Hardin. Migration from Louisiana has evidently slackened, and the Louisiana-born settlers are being diluted in the increasingly Texas-born population. The next largest contributions are from Alabama, Mississippi, and Georgia.

	Chambers	Hardin	Jefferson	Orange
Total Population	2102	1858	3353	2789
Percentage Alabama	3.7	8.8	3.0	3.0
Percentage Foreign-born	4.1	0.1	4.1	5.3
Percentage Georgia	0.9	6.2	3.9	1.7
Percentage Louisiana	7.3	6.2	10.9	16.3
Percentage Mississippi	1.8	8.6	2.6	2.5
Percentage Texas-born	77.2	65.2	67.5	66.2

11.2 Worksheets and Informants

The worksheets used for this study are based on Hans Kurath's "short" worksheets of 1939, revised for the North Central States in 1949 by A. L. Davis and Raven I. McDavid, Jr. In May, 1951, E. Bagby Atwood re-edited these worksheets for the Southwest, adding a number of expressions illustrative of the Spanish, French, and ranching influences of the area.

The worksheets' format differed somewhat in construction from the format hitherto in use in the United States. Instead of writing down an informant's response on a tablet of blank paper, "books" were used upon which the questions were actually mimeographed at suitably spaced intervals. The technique proved successful in the field and helpful in the process of editing.

Among the additions to the worksheets made by Professor Atwood are the following items. (Items printed within virgules were included chiefly for pronunciation):

[6] *Statistics of the Population of the United States at the Tenth Census* (Washington, 1883), pp. 528–530. The reports of the Ninth Census and the Tenth are the only ones that give nativity tables for counties.

Acadian French
Acequia (main irrigation ditch)
Arroyo (dry creek bed)
/Bar/
Brioche (small cake)
Buck (to try to throw the rider)
Burro (small donkey)
Canyon
/Car/
Chaparral (place where mesquite grows thick)
Chaps (leather leggings for riding)
Chigger
Cinch (band that holds the saddle on)
Corral (place where horses or cows are enclosed on a ranch)
Cush (a kind of mush)
Dogie (a motherless calf)
Feedbag (bag attached to horse's head to feed him)
Gate (place to let cars or trains through a fence)
Gumbo (soup made with okra)
Hackamore (rope halter to control a wild horse)
Haunches
/Hem/
Horned toad (small, flat lizard with horns on head and back)
Hunker down (to squat)
Junk room
Lagniappe (bonus or gift given with purchase or when bill is paid)
/Lamp cord/
Lasso (rope with a loop)
/M and N/
Maverick (an unbranded calf)
Mesa (high, flat land)
Mexican
Mexican brown beans
Mustang
Name for a band or herd of saddle horses
Name for workers on a ranch
Niggershooter (boy's weapon made of forked stick with rubber strips)
Olla (large jar to hold drinking water)
Paint (mottled Indian pony)
/Partner/
/Pecan/
Pillow slip
/Playing card/
Prairie (flat grassy country)
Praline (sugar candy made with pecans)
Racket store (store where all kinds of cheap things are sold)
Rawhide rope
/Safety pin/
Shinnery (land where scrubby oak grows)
Sidewalk
/Strength/
Tacky (slovenly)
Tank (artificial pool to water livestock)

/Tar/
Texan of Mexican ancestry
/Tin can/
Town square
Wasteland

The informants were chosen to represent as broad a distribution as possible with regard to social, educational, and age levels. Three age groups were set up: (1) Group A, of people 60 and over; (2) Group B, of informants 40 to 59 years old; (3) Group C, representing a younger generation 39 years and less. Group C is something of an innovation in American dialect studies, since heretofore this younger generation has been ignored in favor of the speech of the older generations. Three educational levels are considered: (1) Type I, informants with as little formal schooling as possible; (2) Type II, informants with a fair education (approximately high school level); (3) Type III, informants with two years of college or more.

Twelve informants were interviewed, including four of Group A, five of Group B, and three of Group C. Four informants, moreover, are of Type I, four of Type II, and four of Type III. Two of the informants are Negroes; one is Acadian French. One is a farmer by profession, but eight of the others have farmed or have a rural background. Nine of the informants are from Jefferson County and one each is from Chambers, Hardin, and Orange Counties.

The informants, who will be identified by Arabic numerals, may be classified according to age and educational levels and by sex:

Informant 1. Type IA. Male.
Informant 2. Type IA. Female.
Informant 3. Type IA. Male (Acadian French.)
Informant 4. Type IIIA. Female.
Informant 5. Type IB. Female (Negro.)
Informant 6. Type IIIB. Male (Negro.)
Informant 7. Type IIIB. Female.
Informant 8. Type IIB. Female.
Informant 9. Type IIB. Female.
Informant 10. Type IIC. Female.
Informant 11. Type IIIC. Male.
Informant 12. Type IIC. Male.

11.3 Vocabulary: Incidence of Eastern Dialect Words

Since the publication of *A Word Geography of the Eastern United States*, it has become possible to compare the vocabulary of an inland area with the vocabulary features of the principal dialect areas of the Eastern seaboard.[7] These Eastern dialect areas have been succinctly defined by Raven I. McDavid, Jr.:

[7] Hans Kurath, *A Word Geography of the Eastern United States* (Ann Arbor, 1949). Comparisons of this type have been done a number of times, for example by Mrs. Hardy in her study of Kerr County and by Randolph Haynes in his investigation of Travis County.

... the term *North* designates New England, the Hudson Valley and their derivative settlements; *North Midland*, Pennsylvania and Northern West Virginia; *South Midland*, the Shenandoah Valley and the Southern Appalachians; *Southern*, the plantation settlements from Chesapeake Bay to northern Florida, plus their immediate derivatives.[8]

In order to estimate the influence of Eastern dialect vocabulary upon the four Texas counties of this investigation, we must examine Kurath's key words for the North, the Midland, and the South with the South Midland, listing the number of times each word was elicited from the Southeast Texas informants:

NORTH

Key Word	Occurrences
Pail (a bucket)	8.00
Whiffletree *or*	1.00
Whippletree (a singletree)	0.00
Boss! (a call to cows)	0.00
Johnnycake (cornbread)	0.33
Darning Needle (a dragonfly)	0.00
Angleworm (an earthworm)	2.00
Stone Wall (a wall made with rocks)	0.00
Nigh-horse (horse on the left)	0.00
Total	11.33
Frequency	11.8%

MIDLAND

Key Word	Occurrences
Blinds (roller shades)	3.00
Skillet (frying pan)	12.00
Spouting *or*	0.00
Spouts (eaves troughs)	0.00
[Little Piece] (a short distance)	3.33
To Hull (to shell beans)	0.00
[Arm] Load (an armful)	7.00
Snake Feeder (a dragonfly)	0.00
Sook! *or*	1.00
Sookie! (a call to calves)	0.00
Bawl (cry of a calf being weaned)	4.33
I Want Off	5.00
Quarter Till [Eleven]	2.00
Total	37.66
Frequency	28.5%

SOUTH AND SOUTH MIDLAND

Key Word	Occurrences
Light Bread (wheat bread in loaves)	7.66
Clabber (curdled milk)	8.00
Snack (food taken between meals)	10.33
Middlins (salt pork)	2.00

[8] Raven I. McDavid, Jr., "The Position of the Charleston Dialect," *Publication of the American Dialect Society*, No. 23 (1955), p. 41.

Ash Cake (a type of corn cake)	0.00
[Hay] Shock (a small heap of hay)	5.33
[Corn] Shuck (corn husk)	11.00
You-all (you)	12.00
Waiter (best man)	0.00
Pallet (a makeshift bed)	12.00
Gutters (eaves troughs)	10.66
[Barn] Lot (barnyard)	3.00
Rock Fence (a wall made with rocks)	3.00

Total 85.00

Frequency 54.5%[9]

A number of the various expressions listed by Kurath as characteristic of the sub-areas of the North, Midland, and South may also be pointed out as very common in the Southeast Texas area. *Coal oil* (kerosene), for example, which is found in eastern Pennsylvania and the Chesapeake Bay area, is used by ten of the Texas informants. *Baby buggy* (a baby carriage), a term common throughout western Pennsylvania and northern West Virginia, is given by eight of the Texas informants. Of the expressions listed by Kurath as typical of the southern coast, *curtains* (roller shades) is used by five of the Southeast Texas informants, *mosquito hawk* (a dragonfly) by twelve, and *earthworm* (a worm) by five of the informants.

Kurath also provides lists of words quite common throughout the North and the Midland; the Midland and the South; and the North and the South.[10] Of these expressions, the following were used by one-half or more of the Southeast Texas informants:

NORTH AND MIDLAND

Key Word	*Occurrences*
Moo (noise made by a cow)	7.33
Wishbone (clavicle of a chicken)	9.00
Sheaf (of grain)	6.00
Bacon (smoked bacon)	7.00
Cling [-stone Peach] (a type of peach)	8.66
Freestone [Peach] (a type of peach)	9.00
Stringbeans (a type of bean)	6.00

MIDLAND AND SOUTH

Key Word	*Occurrences*
Singletree (on a one-horse rig)	7.00

[9] See Kurath, pp. 12, 28–29, and 38. From Kurath's list of typical words, the expressions *roll the baby* (wheel the baby) and *salad* (garden greens) were not asked for in these interviews and are therefore omitted from consideration.

The percentages for the three speech areas are derived from:

$$\frac{\text{(Number of responses from Texas informants)} \times 100}{\text{(Number of key words given by Kurath)} \times (12 \text{ informants})}$$

Suggested responses (responses recorded when, in the opinion of the fieldworker, the informant accepted the suggested word enthusiastically, used it in an illustrative sentence, or amplified the word's definition) are here valued at one-third the weight of a spontaneous response.

[10] Kurath, pp. 28–29, 38, and 48–49.

Seesaw (children's game)	11.00
Comfort (a quilted blanket)	8.00
Polecat (a skunk)	9.33

NORTH AND SOUTH

Key Word	Occurrences
Quarter to Eleven (ten forty-five)	6.00
Gutters (eaves troughs)	10.66

It will be noted that the frequency with which dialect terms from the North were used was 11.8; 28.5 for the Midland; and 54.5 for the South and South Midland. These frequencies stand in a proportion of 1:2.2:4.9. In other words—if we may run the risk of oversimplification—in the dialect vocabulary of Southeast Texas Southern words are used twice as much as Midland expressions, which in turn are used twice as much as Northern terms.

11.4   Vocabulary: Old Versus New

The Southeast Texas counties illustrate quite well the changing usages of all living vocabulary. Though these changes follow no logical pattern, it is demonstrable that formally schooled informants do not keep their folk words to the extent that elderly and/or rural informants do.[11] The words chosen to demonstrate this changing Texas vocabulary deal chiefly with foods, artifacts, and customs.

The expressions used for an ear of corn cooked on the cob show an interesting variation between older and younger informants. The distinctly modern term is *corn on the cob*, reported by informants 7, 9, 11, and 12. *Sugar corn* is used by only one informant, number 5. The term *sweet corn* (informants 2, 6, 8, 9, and 12s) and *roasting ears* (informants 1, 3, 4, 7, and 12s) are characteristic of the elderly and middle-aged informants,[12] *sweet corn* appearing more among the middle-aged and *roasting ears* more among the elderly; neither expression is in active use among the youngest informants.

The word *cracklins*—fried pieces of pork rind from which the fat has been cooked out—is known to informants 1, 2, 3, 4, 5, 6, 7, 9, 10, and 12s, leading us to think that perhaps the increasing urbanization may account for the younger generation's relative unfamiliarity with the term. This view is supported by the informants' acquaintance with *chittlins* (informants 1, 2, 4, 6, 7, 9s, and 12s) and *chittlings* (informants 3, 5, and 8)—the fried small intestine of swine—which is a term almost unknown to the youngest informants.

The usual term for the cheese made from milk curds is *cottage cheese* (informants 1, 2, 3, 4, 7, 8, 9s, 10, 11, and 12s), which one informant (number 1) characterizes as a modernism. The older folk-name for this home-made curd cheese is *cream cheese* (informants 2, 4, 5, 6s, 7, 8, 9, and 12s), which informant

---

[11] See Kurath, p. 8.
[12] The letter *s* appended to an informant's code number is used to designate a suggested response in contrast to the spontaneous responses of other informants.

7 labels old-fashioned. Another informant (number 3) reports having heard the term *clean cheese*, obviously a folk variant of *cream cheese*. From a comparison of these two expressions, the first current among all three generations of informants, the second used only by the elderly and middle-aged groups, we may infer that *cottage cheese* has been encouraged in recent years by the commercial use of the name while the term *cream cheese* has been displaced by *Philadelphia Cream Cheese*, a sweet cheese spread altogether different from curd cheese.

An interesting distinction showing the preference of the more modern speakers for grammatically "correct" usage is illustrated by *hog head cheese* (informants 1s, 3, 5, and 6) versus *hog's head cheese* (informants 4, 7, 8, 9, 10, and 11). This latter expression is for the food made from the head meat of swine (possibly under the influence of the word *hogshead*). If we remember that informant 4, a well-educated lady, often tends to give very modern expressions, while the colored informants 5 and 6 are considerably more conservative, we see a clearcut dichotomy in the use by the older informants of *hog head cheese* and by the younger informants of *hog's head cheese*.

A striking example of a word that has been made old-fashioned by the advent of the automobile is *singletree* (known to informants 1, 2, 3, 4, 5, 6, and 8). The fact that a term for the swivel to which the traces of a horse are connected is unknown to the informants under 50 can be used rather exactly to date the automobile. On the other hand, words for the prominent and less intricate parts of a wagon—the *tongue* for example—are still known to all informants.

Gallery is a word which has gone out of fashion even to the two groups of informants who report it. It is used by informants 1, 2, 3, 4, 5, 6, 7, 8, and 9 (the elderly and middle-aged groups) and is characterized as old-fashioned by all these informants except 1, 3, and 7. *Porch*, the standard term, is used by informants 2, 3, 4, 5, 6, 7, 8, 9, 10, and 11; informant 1 also mentions the word, calling it an expression heard from others.

For the portable device to protect against rain, *umbrella* is the universal word among the Southeast Texas informants. Its cousin, *parasol* (in the sense of a sunshade), is reported by informants 3, 4, 5, 6, 8, and 9; called old-fashioned by informant 2; and noted as heard from others by informant 10. We note in *parasol*, therefore, a type of apparel that has gone into disuse, taking the word with it.

Dishrag and *dish cloth* offer us a contrast between old and new based on fashion and gracious living. *Dishrag*, a name for the cloth with which dishes are soaped and washed, is used by informants 1, 2, 4, 5, 7s, 8, 9, 10, and 12. *Dish cloth* is a young word (as contrasted with words which, though known to the older folk, attain their real currency among the younger), just beginning to make inroads in the *dishrag* province. If we consider how inappropriate the *rag* element of *dishrag* must seem to urban, well-educated Southern ladies (and gentlemen), *dish cloth* appears to be a well-considered substitute and one destined to replace *dishrag* eventually.

For the group of trees growing in an open meadow or prairie, the elderly and middle-aged informants use the word *island*. *Island* was elicited from informants 1, 2, 4, 6, 8, 11s, and 12s. It is known to the modern informants chiefly as a place-name element. *Pine Island Bayou*, for example, was mentioned by informants 4, 6, 8, 9, and 12 as the name of one of the local streams.

Terms of address to one's father show a marked distinction between the use of *papa* by the elderly and middle-aged informants (including 1, 2, 3, 4, 6, 7, 8, 12, and 5, who terms it old-fashioned), and *dad* or *daddy* (words known to informants in all age levels, but almost the exclusive term of the younger informants). *Dad* is given by informants 5 and 12. *Daddy* is used by informants 1, 8, 10, and 11.

The word *niggershooter*, a child's weapon for shooting birds, is reported by informants 1, 2, 3, 4, 6, 7, 8, 9, 12, and called an old-fashioned expression by informants 10 and 11. The variant *slingshot* is used by informants 1, 2, 4, 5, 7, 8, 9s, 12, and by 10 and 11 (who term it a modernism). Informant 6 uses *sling*, and the word *beanshooter* was given by informants 3 and 9. It may be noted that the mention of *niggershooter* by informant 6, who is colored, indicates a certain currency among Negro speakers. Likewise, informant 9, who states that she would never use the word *nigger*, does use the compound *niggershooter*, along with its variant *beanshooter*.

The burlesque serenade accorded newly-wedded couples is called a *shivaree* by informants 1, 2, 3, 4, 7, and 8, and (by a process of folk etymology) a *chivalry* by informant 9. Inasmuch as the younger informants do not recognize the custom, the demise of the *shivaree* would seem to have occurred in the first decade or so in this century.

The custom of *lagniappe*—any small gratuity given, for instance, with a purchase or with the payment of a bill—is limited to the elderly and middle-aged groups. The word is reported by informants 1s, 2, 3, 4, 5s, 6, 7, 8, 9, and 10s (who calls it a word heard from others). No synonym for *lagniappe* exists among the younger informants; it is a bit of the old South displaced forever by the more business-like practices of the chain stores and urban civilization.

Another expression which is vanishing from Southeast Texas is the greeting *Christmas gift!* Originally, the expression was a Christmas-day game in which children tried to be nrst in surprising one another with the greeting, the loser being obliged to present a gift to the winner. As a greeting, it is used by informants 1, 2, 5, 7, and 8, and upon suggestion by informants 4 and 6 (who terms the expression old-fashioned). The more prevalent greeting, *merry Christmas*, is used by all informants.

11.5   Vocabulary: French, Spanish, and other Southwestern Influences

Since the Old Spanish Trail cuts through the four Southeast Texas counties that make up this study, we might expect to find in the area Spanish words brought from the west as well as French words imported from Louisiana. In addition we should look for ordinary English and American expressions which take on new meanings under the influence of a ranching, farming, or rice-growing culture.

Of the group of Louisiana French expressions which E. Bagby Atwood suggested might be found in East Texas,[13] *bayou, cush,* and *lagniappe* are the only ones having any real currency in Southeast Texas, although many others, such as *banquette* (a sidewalk), *armoire* (a wardrobe), *batteau* (a boat), *boudin* (a sausage), and *piroque* (a boat), are to be found.

Bayou was used by informants 1, 2, 3, 4, 5s, 6, 7, 8, 9s, 10, 11s, and 12 as a name for a small stream. The word is an Acadian French derivative of the Choctaw Indian *bayuk*.[14] *Cush* or *cush cush* is the Texas version of the Acadian *couche-couche*, a fried preparation of cornmeal dough and sugar.[15] *Cush* was reported by informants 5 and 6 as a name for *mush* and by informants 2s, 4, 5, 6, 8, and 11s as the name for a preparation made of seasoned corn-meal dough fried with onions. *Cush cush* was used spontaneously only by informant 3, who is Acadian French, but upon suggestion by informants 1 and 9. *Lagniappe*, a combination of the French definite article *la* with Spanish *ñapa* (ultimately from Kechuan), is used by most of the elderly and middle-aged informants, as discussed above.[16]

In addition to these expressions, two other words borrowed from the Acadian dialect are current among most informants. These are *gumbo*, a word obtained by the Acadian French from an African term for the okra plant,[17] and *Cajun*, an aphetic form of *Acadian* which is in use among the Acadian French themselves. *Gumbo* is reported by informants 1, 2, 3s, 4, 7, 8, 9, 10, 11, and 12. *Cajun* was elicited from all informants except 3, who used it upon suggestion.

Of the various terms mentioned by Atwood as typically Southwestern,[18] only *norther, lariat,* and *corral* are in common use. *Norther* was given spontaneously by all informants except 2 and 3, both of whom used the word upon suggestion. *Lariat* was reported by informants 1, 2, 3, 4, 6, 8, 10, 11, and 12. *Corral* is a popular word, used by informants 2s, 4, 7, 8, 9, 10, 11, and 12s.

Two other expressions of local currency are *canal* and *bellyband*. *Canal* is the usual word for a drainage ditch, reported by informants 1, 2, 3, 4, 5s, 6, 8, 9s, 10, 11, and 12. Because Southeast Texas does a vast amount of rice farming, it is natural that the irrigation canals should become associated with drainage ditches. *Bellyband*, a saddle girth, is used by informants 2, 3, 6, 7, 8, 9, and 12s.

---

[13] E. Bagby Atwood, "A Preliminary Report on Texas Word Geography," *Orbis,* II (1953), 64.

[14] William A. Read, *Louisiana French,* Volume V of *Louisiana State University Studies* (1931), p. 82.

[15] Read, p. 122. Raven I. McDavid, Jr., in "Africanisms in the Eastern United States," an unpublished paper read to the Modern Language Association in 1952, points out that *cush* is also used in the areas of Chesapeake Bay, Albemarle Sound, the Neuse River, and the South Carolina low country. He does not find enough evidence to support the recent suggestions that *cush* is an Africanism.

[16] Read, p. 442.   [17] Read, p. 122.   [18] Atwood, pp. 65–66.

11.6 Pronunciation

A study of pronunciation must take into account three possible types of differences: (1) variations in the system of phonemes (such as the /ǝɪ/ phoneme of New York City speech); (2) sub-phonemic differences in the pronunciation of the same phoneme (for example, the mutually non-distinctive voiceless stops in *paper* [p'eɪpɚ]); (3) systematic and individual differences in the occurrence of phonemes (such as the use of /z/ or /s/ in *grease*).

With regard to (1), no differences in the phonemic system are posited for Southeast Texas. In order to survey (2), brief summaries will be made of the sub-phonemic differences of the vowels. Only two of the consonants, /l/ and /r/, show variations important enough for consideration in this abstract.

/i/ as in *grease*: regularly a high front vowel with either an upgliding element or lengthening. Its usual forms are [iiˆ, i·] and also [ii, i·ˆ, iˆi] in that order of frequency.

The phoneme /i/ is distinguished from /ɪ/ before tautosyllabic /r/ only in the word *ear* (by informants 1, 2, 4, 6, 7, 8, 9, and 11).

/ɪ/ as in *dish*: a mid-high front vowel whose usual forms are [ɪˈ, ɪ].

Before nasals, /ɪ/ is no longer distinct from /ɛ/ and appears phonetically as [ɪˈ, ɪ] with variants [ɪˠ, ɛˢ], which show lowering.[19] The variant [ɛˢ] is used chiefly by the oldest informants, 1 through 5, and possibly indicates the increased variation that may occur when two phonemes (/ɪ/ and /ɛ/) cease to be distinctive in a certain position (here, before nasals). The younger informants apparently tend to use a retracted /ɪ/ which is phonetically close to [ɛˢ] both for /ɪ/ and for /ɛ/ before nasals, as in *chimney, Cincinnati*, and *clingstone*; and in *hem, hen*, and *strength*.

/e/ as in *way*: regularly a high-mid front vowel with a high central glide. Its usual forms are [ei, eˇi].

Before inter-syllabic /r/, /e/ is irregularly distinguished from /ɛ/ by seven of the 12 informants in the words *dairy* and *Mary*. In *dairy*, /e/ is used by informants, 4, 8, 9, and 10; in *Mary*, by informants 3, 4, 5, and 9.

Before tauto-syllabic /r/, /e/ is distinguished from /ɛ/ in the word *chair* by informants 5, 7, 9, and 10, who use /e/.

/ɛ/ as in *seven*: a mid-front vowel with the usual form [ɛ].

Before nasals /ɛ/ is not often distinguished from /ɪ/. Before /m/ as in *hem*, [ɪˈ] and [ɛˢ, ɪ] are used by informants, 1, 2, 5, 6, 7, 8, 9, 10, 11, and 12. Before /ŋ/ as in *strength* [ɪˠ, ɪˈ] are used by informants 1, 4, 5, 8, 9, 10, 11, and 12; [ɛˢ] by informants 2 and 7; [ɛ, ɛˈ] only by informants 3 and 6.

Before /n/ as in *end*, [ɪˠ, ɪˈ] are used by informants 1, 2, 5, 6, 7, 8, 9, 10, and 11, while informants 3, 4, and 12 use /ɛ/. Pronunciations such as [ɪˠ] (which may be phonemicized here as /ɪ/), as in the words *cents, fence, hen, men, pen, ten, M*, and *N*, are most common among the Groups B and C informants, who use it 4½ times more often than the Group A informants.

[19] Diacritics showing nasalization are here omitted.

/æ/ as in *bath*: a higher low-front vowel with the usual phonetic forms [æ, æˆ].

Before the fricatives /f/ and /s/ and less frequently before / ʃ/, nasal clusters, and velar stops, /æ/ sometimes develops a mid-high central glide with the usual phonetic form [æᶦ], as in the words *answer, ashes, aunt, bag, basket, calf, chance, class, dance, glass, hamper,* and *lamp*. This diphthongization is to be found most often among the Groups A and B informants, although it is recessive even in their speech.

/ɑ/ as in *father*: a low-central vowel whose usual form is [ɑ] with the principal variants [ɑˈ, ɑ·, ɑ'].

Before tauto-syllabic /r/, /ɑ/ and /ɔ/ are no longer distinct (as in *card, cord*), and /ɑ/ shows a number of phonetic variants ranging from [ɑˈ, ɑ, ɑ·] through [ɒ, ɒˆ, ɔ], as in *armful, bar, barbed wire, barn, car, card, cartridge, garbage, garden, harmonica, hearth, Martha,* and *tar*. For the 12 informants, the overall ratio of [ɑ] to [ɔ] before /r/ in this group of words is 2:1. The well-educated informants 4, 6, and 7 rarely use [ɔ] at all in these words. Informants 1, 2, and 3 (Group A) prefer [ɑ] to [ɔ] in a ratio of 5:1, while informants 5, 8, and 9 (Group B) use it in a ratio of 3:1. With informants 10, 11, and 12 (Group C), the ratio is reversed, and these informants are found to use [ɔ] to [ɑ] with a frequency of 2:1.

/ʌ/ as in *judge*: a retracted and stressed low-mid central vowel whose usual phonetic quality is [ʌ]. The form [ʌ̞] with lip-rounding occurs as a free variant, but is used most frequently in the word *onion*.

Before inter-syllabic /r/, /ʌ/ combines to produce [ʌr] and also [ʌ-r, ɜ-r] as in *furrow* and *worry*. The variant [ɜ-r] is limited to informants 4 and 7 (Type III).

Before /rC/, /ʌ/ usually becomes [ʌr] with the variants [ɜᶦ, ərᶦ, ɜ, ß], as in *first, girl,* and *worm*. The latter variants are limited to the Negro informants 5 and 6 (with whom they are quite frequent) and to informant 1 (who uses them occasionally).

/ə/ as in *sofa*: a weakly stressed mid-central vowel whose phonetic quality is [ə] or [əˀ].

/u/ as in *tooth*: a high-back vowel with lip-rounding which appears either as a diphthong with an advanced first element or as an advanced lengthened monophthong [uˈu, u··].

/ʊ/ as in *foot*: a mid-high back vowel with moderate lip-rounding, the usual phonetic forms of which are [ʊ, ˈʉ].

/o/ as in *boat*: a high-mid back vowel with lip-rounding, which appears fronted with a mid-high central rounded glide [oˈʉ].

Before tauto-syllabic /r/, all informants distinguish /o/ from /ɔ/ (as in *hoarse, horse*); /o/ takes the phonetic form [o].

/ɔ/ as *caught*: a mid back vowel with lip-rounding which, as a monophthong, is usually [ɔ, ɔˆ]. The phoneme diphthongizes in all positions except before /r/ to [ɒˈ, ɒᴰˆ]—that is, the vowel becomes higher and more rounded during its utterance. The diphthong is used in a ratio of 1:1 with the mono-phthong of this phoneme in the words *all, brought, caught, costs, cough, daughter, dog, fought, law, loft, moth, saw, trough,* and *water.* The diphthong appears twice as frequently among the younger six informants than among the older six.

/aɪ/ as in *five*: a diphthong composed of a low-front element and a mid-front glide, somewhat retracted. It usually appears as [aɛ] with the variants [aɪ, aɛ!, a·]. In all positions, [aɛ] is used four times as much as the fuller diph-thong [aɪ]. Before /r/, as in *barbed wire* and *andirons*, the monophthongal [a] is usual.

/aʊ/ as in *drouth*: a diphthong composed of a low or higher low front element and a high central glide with lip-rounding. Its usual forms are [æʉ] and [aʉ]. The variant [æʉ] is used in a ratio of 1:1 with [aʉ] for all informants. The well-educated informants (4, 6, 7, and 11) use [æʉ] in a ratio of 1:3 with [aʉ]. The Type IA informants (1, 2, 3) use [æʉ] in the proportion 3:5 with regard to [aʉ]. The younger informants of Types IB, IIB, and IIC (5, 8, 9, 10, and 12) use [æʉ] considerably more than anyone else, in a ratio of 5:1 with regard to [aʉ].

/ɔɪ/ as in *boy*: a diphthong composed of a mid-back vowel with lip-rounding followed, usually after a slight "pause," or drop in breath pressure, by a mid-high central glide. Its usual phonetic form is [ɔ-ɪ].

/l/ as in *Billy*: inter-vocalically before mid-high or high-front and central vowels, a "bright *l*" [ʮ] or a non-velarized [l] regularly appears, as in the words *Dallas, Illinois, jelly, Nelly,* and *pallet.*

Before /j/, as in *stallion*, /l/ usually appears as the palatalized [ʮ].

/r/ as in *father*: post-vocalically, /r/ is usually a retroflex or "constricted" vowel [ɚ]. Informants 1, 3, 4, 5, 6, and 7, however, substitute /ə/ freely. In-formants 4, 5, and 6, in whose speech this feature is more noted than in the other informants, nevertheless use the constricted vowel twice as frequently as the vowel without *r*-coloring. Of those who use only the constricted vowel, informants 2, 10, and 12 occasionally give pronunciations with only weak retroflexion.

In the words *oyster, wash, washing,* and *Washington,* an intrusive /r/ is used by all informants except 4, 7, 8, and 12 about three times out of every eight occurrences. The /r/ always appears in the form of a mildly retroflex vowel.

11.7 Pronunciation: Systematic Differences in the Patterning and Occurrence of Phonemes

Before /w/, /h/ is regularly pronounced by all informants, as in the words *wheat* and *whip.* Before /j/, /h/ is frequently pronounced by all informants, as in *humor* and *Houston.*

After the alveolar consonants /t, d, n/, /u/ is frequently preceded by /j/ in one of two forms. In the word *Tuesday*, for example, informants 2, 3, 4, 5, 6, 7, 8, 9, 10, and 12 use either a palatalized /t/ plus a diphthong: [ɪʉ], or a palatalized /t/ with /j/ glide and vowel: [tʃɪu]. In the word *tube*, palatalization is restricted to informants 3, 4, 6, and 7, while in *student* it is limited to informants 4 and 7. Informant 1 uses /t/ and a diphthong without palatalization: [tɪu] in *Tuesday* and *tube*; in *student* he employs [tu].

After /d/ in *due*, palatalization before /u/ occurs in the responses of informants 1, 2, 3, 5, 6, and 7. In *dues*, however, palatalization is limited to informants 3, 4, 5, and 6. The unpalatalized consonant plus diphthong, [dɪu], is given by informants 9 and 12 in *due* and by informants 1 and 2 in *dues*. The use of [du] is apparently typical of the younger Group C informants.

After /n/, as in *new* and *New Year*, palatalization before /u/ occurs in the responses of informants 1, 2, 3, 4, 6, 7, 8, 10, and 12. Informants 9 and also 12 (in other responses) use the diphthong [nɪu] without preceding palatalization, and informants 5 and 11 (and also 8 and 10 in other responses) use a monophthong without palatalization: [nu].

In final unstressed syllables, as in *evening*, *laughing*, *lightning*, *nothing*, *singing*, *something*, and *thinking*, /n/ alternates with [ŋ]. This substitution is random, appearing about once in every three occurrences of these words in the speech of all informants except 4, 8, and 11.

Before /g/, Middle English "short *o*" is regularly pronounced /ɔ/, except in the speech of several of the well-educated and female informants. In *fog* and *foggy*, for example, /ɑ/ is employed by informants 4, 7, 8, and 10. Informants 7 and 8 use /ɑ/ in *log*. In *hog*, /ɑ/ is used by informants 4 and 8, and in *frog* by informants 4 and 7.

In words with inter-syllabic /r/, as in *borrow*, *Florida*, *orange*, and *tomorrow*, the Middle English "short *o*" category (into which *orange* and *Florida* have fallen) regularly becomes /ɔ/ in the speech of all but some of the well-educated and female informants. *Borrow* is pronounced with /ɑ/ by informants 4, 6, and 7. In *Florida*, informants 4, 7, and 8 use /ɑ/. In *orange*, /ɑ/ is given by informant 4, and in *tomorrow* by informant 6.

In words in which Middle English /ɑ/ follows /w/, as in *swamp*, *wash*, *washing*, *Washington*, and *wasp*, /ɔ/ appears twice in every three occurrences. With the exception of the word *swamp*, in which informants 10 and 12 use /ɑ/, the use of the /ɑ/ phoneme in these words is restricted to informants of Groups A and B. Informants 4, 6, and 7, moreover, who are of Type III, account for one-half of all occurrences of /ɑ/.

Before alveolar consonants in weakly stressed syllables, both "short *e*" and "short *i*" regularly become [ɪ], as in *basket* and *dishes*.

When final in weakly stressed syllables, as in *borrow* and *yellow*, /o/ is replaced by /ə/ once in every two occurrences.

11.8   Verb Forms and Syntactical Peculiarities

Urbanization (and with it, better education) makes itself most apparent in the "correctness" of grammar in use throughout the area of investigation, where it is difficult to elicit a double negative, the word *ain't*, or a non-standard verb form even from the least educated of the informants. But as Atwood has pointed out, this is to be expected in an urban area,[20] and does not mean that non-standard verb forms are not in use. Notwithstanding this apparent purity of Southeast Texas grammar, a number of idiosyncrasies may be pointed out.

Dive. For the preterit of *dive*, *dove* and *dived* are used about equally. Such a mixture is typical of a "belt" along the upper Ohio in north–central and eastern Pennsylvania.

Drink. Among the Texas informants, *drank* is the regular preterit of *drink*. Usage is divided between *drunk* (informants 3, 4, 6, 7, 8, 9, and 10) and *drank* (informants 1, 2, 5, 10, 11, and 12) for the past participle. It will be noted that *drank* is favored by all three of the Group C informants (10, 11, and 12). This usage may be compared with Atwood's findings for the East, which show that the standard *drink–drank–drunk* forms are not usual, being rejected by one-half of the "cultured" New England informants and two-thirds of the well-educated informants in the Middle Atlantic States, but finding acceptance among the well-educated informants of the South Atlantic States.

Lie. *Lie* and *lay*, as present tense forms, show an interesting division in usage between the older and younger informants. *Lay*, used by informants 1, 2, 3, 4, 5, and 8, is the distinctly older usage; *lie*, given by informants 6, 7, 9, 10, 11, and 12, is the schoolroom expression of all the younger informants with the exception of 8. This contrast in usage is lost in the preterit, where *lay* is used by informants 1, 3, 4, 8, 9, and 10, and *laid* by informants 5, 6, 11, and 12. Throughout the East, *lie* predominates in the present tense and, except for a few small areas and in cultivated speech, *laid* predominates in the preterit.

Sweat. *Sweated* is used as the preterit of *sweat* by all informants except 2, 3, and 4, who employ the uninflected form *sweat*. *Sweat* is characteristic of the North, although used equally with *sweated* in some parts of the South, including Virginia and South Carolina.[21]

Cain't. A pronunciation of *can't* rhyming with *ain't*, *cain't* probably represents a diphthongization of *can't* to [kæɪnt] with subsequent raising to [eɪ]. It is limited in use to informants 1, 2, 4, 5, and 8 (Types I and II informants except for 4).

Sick at the Stomach. Informants 1, 2, 4, 5, 6, 7, 8, 9, 10, 11, and 12s use the Midland and Southern construction *sick at the stomach*. Informants 8, 9, and 10 report the expression *sick to the stomach*, but informant 8 terms it old-fashioned and informant 10 characterizes it as heard from others. This construction is typical of the New England settlement. Informants 3 and 4 (who reports it as heard from others) mention *sick in the stomach*, an expression found in southeastern Pennsylvania and in the South from southern Maryland as far as the Neuse in North Carolina.[22]

---

[20] E. Bagby Atwood, *A Survey of Verb Forms in the Eastern United States* (Ann Arbor, 1953), p. 37.

[21] See Atwood, *Verb Forms*, pp. 9, 11, 18, and 22.   [22] See Kurath, p. 78.

It is not likely that any of the speech features of the four Southeast Texas counties are unique when compared with the rest of East Texas. Since it is the combination of typical speech patterns which gives individuality to an area, the probability is that no other four counties in Texas will produce the same configuration of vocabulary, pronunciation, and verb usages which has been shown to characterize this area.

Single-Feature Studies

Single-feature studies, which may cut across dialect boundaries, illustrate some of the interpretive applications of the analysis of the raw data collected by fieldworkers or from mailed questionnaires. Such detailed studies often throw light upon various linguistic processes as well as add substance to our knowledge about the ways in which language matters are correlated with the non-linguistic environment.

The first significant single-feature study in this country was that of the *greasy–greazy* contrast, undertaken by the late George Hempl nearly three-quarters of a century ago. His report is included here not only because it is an important historical document but also because a subsequent study of the same contrast by E. Bagby Atwood makes possible a useful comparison of both methodology and results. Even a relatively unsystematic sampling such as Hempl's provided him with the information upon which boundary divisions, still generally acceptable, could be drawn. Hempl, for example, was able to distinguish an area intermediate between Northern and Southern that he called "Midlands." He thus anticipated by more than 50 years the definition of the "Midland" dialect area proposed by Hans Kurath in 1949 upon the basis of lexical distribution. Kurath, however, did not follow Hempl in assigning New York City to Midland; nor did he put into one Southern category the speech of the entire eastern United States south of the Mason–Dixon Line. Other evidence besides that of *greasy* led Kurath to recognize an intermediate area, with its own complex of speech features, between plantation Southern and Midland, an area he has called South Midland.

Atwood's recent study does not strikingly refute the major assumptions of Hempl, but rather adds the dimension provided by data from three different social classes. He thus is able to prove what is perhaps only implicit in Hempl's results, that the *greasy* distinctions are purely geographical and are not social. It also demonstrates the greater degree of accuracy with which statements upon speech variation can be made if they are based upon a carefully selected sample cross section of the population.

The same corpus of material is used by Sumner Ives in his study of what, at least in some of its variations, is a highly controversial matter of social usage —the pronunciation of *can't*. For the first time we have in this article a factual presentation of the distribution of the so-called "broad a" form in eastern New England, and of the "long a" in parts of the South. The evidence is not comforting to those who would insist upon the "broad a" everywhere as the cultivated pronunciation nor to those who would stigmatize the "long a" as a sure sign of lower-class membership.

In the next article Alva Davis and Raven I. McDavid, Jr., are likewise concerned with contrast in social usage but link their concern with their study of the diffusion of a term taken into American English from Canadian French too far west to become part of Atlantic coast speech. Their information is particularly timely because of the rapid shift in marriage customs and the corresponding decline of the old practice, sometimes friendly and sometimes not, of serenading a newly-wedded couple.

How Atlas records can provide a plausible solution for a hitherto puzzling etymological problem is Walter S. Avis's contribution to this volume. Previous speculation based upon the lexical form *crocus sack* can now be replaced by the evidence of phonological variants, with inferences that make the history of this term an interesting part of the story of the relationships between the colonies and the mother country.

One of the first full-length studies derived from atlas files was the doctoral dissertation of the late Bernard Bloch. In his article here Bloch draws upon his complete study to indicate not only the diverse spread of post-vocalic /r/ in New England but also the direction of inferred change. Like Ives, Bloch is not very helpful to those teachers who in the Middle West and West have sought to have their students imitate r-less "broad a" speech on the ground that it has generally greater prestige.

A quite different sound-feature in New England, one that is rather rapidly becoming obsolete, is the subject of this next paper by Avis. A procedural model, the paper indicates how interviews with people of different ages offer data that, carefully analyzed, make possible a diachronic statement and hence a prediction. A number of other items in the atlas field work sheets are probably sufficiently affected by recent change to constitute material for further studies of this kind.

George B. Pace deals with a subtler phonological problem, that historical complex behind the situation queried in "Why do you say Missoura when it's spelled with *i*?" Evidence as to the eastern distribution of this pronunciation for Missouri and a number of other words ending in *-i* Pace interprets in the light of additional historical evidence. His explanation cannot be accepted as indisputable, but it is certainly most plausible; and his study ably indicates how atlas-discovered linguistic facts can be correlated with historical data in an effort to solve a linguistic mystery.

12

Grease and Greasy

GEORGE HEMPL

IN THIS MY FIRST REPORT on the distribution of American dialect I would from the start emphasize two things: First, the report is in part based upon insufficient data, and is therefore tentative. Where the number of replies is very small, the percents based upon them will be given in fainter type. Secondly, the attempt to define the limits of diversity of usage in this country is a larger and more difficult task than I thought when I began it. And this means that my personal effort at collecting answers to the test questions is quite insufficient; I must have all the assistance that those interested in such things can give me.

I now have some 1600 sets of answers to my list of questions, but these are quite unevenly distributed, there being a much larger proportion from the North than from other parts, for example, as many from Michigan as from the whole South. A preliminary examination of the replies to several of the questions makes it certain that the following *general* division of the country into four sections can be but little out of the way.

NORTH: New England, New York State, and the country west that was settled from them (Mich., Wis., Minn., the settled portions of the Dakotas; together with the adjoining northern part of Iowa, Ill., Ind., Ohio, and Penn.).

SOUTH: the states below the Mason–Dixon line (except Del.) and the country settled from them (including southern Ind., southern Ill., most of Mo., Texas, and all the country to the southeast).

MIDLAND: a belt separating the North from the South and extending from the Atlantic to the Mississippi (including Long Island, New York City and the adjoining counties, New Jersey, Del., all but the northern strip of Penn., the upper prong of West Virginia, southern Ohio, middle Ind., middle Ill., and St. Louis County, Mo.).

WEST: the territory west of the North, the Midland, and the South. It begins with southern Iowa and northern Missouri as an extension of the Midland, but soon flanges to the northwest and the southwest.

The late Professor Hempl of the English department of the University of Michigan was one of the earliest members of the American Dialect Society and served as its president from 1901 to 1905. His article is reprinted from *Dialect Notes* 1.438–44 (1896).

The District of Columbia is peculiarly national; for this report I have taken the liberty of incorporating it, like Delaware, with the Midland.

In some matters Canada (especially Lower Canada) goes with the North, in others with the Midland and the South. It will probably turn out that in the majority of original differences it affiliates with the Midland and the South, but with the North in more recent matters—due to mutual contact and to similarity of climate and social conditions; this theory, however, presents some difficulties. In parts of Canada the influence of Irish English, in others of London English, is marked.

In this report the attempt is made to apply this division of the country (as determined by the replies to several other questions) to the answers so far received as to the pronunciation of 'to grease' and 'greasy.' It will be seen from the accompanying table that the general justice of the division is abundantly verified. The numbers indicate the percent favoring voiceless *s* (as in 'sin'); the first number in each case is the percent for the verb 'to grease,' the second for the adjective 'greasy.'

The dictionaries until recently recognized the voiceless *s* in the noun only, and prescribed the sound of *z* in the verb and the adjective. But in the 1870s *s* began to gain recognition in the two latter also. In 1874 Donald's edition of Chamber's Dictionary gave the adjective as having *z* or *s*, and of the verb said, "sometimes *z*." The Imperial (I have access only to the edition of 1883) assigns the adjective *z*, and the verb *z* or *s*. The Webster of 1884 admitted *s* by the side of *z* for the verb and adjective. The Century even prefers *s* to *z* for both verb and adjective, as does also the so-called Standard in the case of the verb, while for the adjective and for 'greaser,' it gives only *s*. None of the dictionaries suggest the use of *z* in the noun.

We have numerous singular nouns that end in a voiceless fricative like *s* or *þ*, while the plural, a related verb, or a derivative, has the corresponding voiced fricative: 'the house,' but 'houzez,' and 'to houze'; 'louse,' but 'louzy,' etc. As is well known, this is due to the fact that in the singular of the noun the fricative was from the start a final consonant; while in the plural, in the verb, and in the derivative, it is or once was followed by a vowel or other voiced sound, and hence was itself voiced. It *may* be that the word *grease* (ME. *gres(s)e*, riming with the infinitive *encrese* in 'The Phisiciens Tale,' OF. *gresse, graisse*) at an early day quite conformed to this category; that is, it is possible that at one time all English-speaking persons gave the noun *s* and the verb and adjective *z*. If so, the present frequent use of *s* in the verb and adjective would be due to later influence of the noun. It is much more likely, however, that in the larger part of the English-speaking territory the group never thoroughly conformed to the category: "*s* in noun; *z* in verb and adjective," and that the use of *s* in the verb and adjective is original, arising out of the older *ss*, and being retained just as it has in other such words: 'release' (ME. *relas(s)en*, OF. *relesser, relaisser*), lease, 'increase,' 'cease,' etc.[1] But Walker, probably guided by local usage, regarded

[1] Words like 'ease,' 'please,' 'tease,' go back to single *s*.

Brit. Columbia.
100–100
Wash.   Mont.
60–40   67–50

Idaho.
100–100
Oregon.   Wyo.
50–38

Nev.
Cal.   100–33
46–52
Utah.
95–90

Ariz.   N. Mex.   Okla.
75–38

Quebec.   N. Br.
60–80   100–75
Vt.   N. H.   Me.
87–84   80–80   93–81

Mass.
91–79
Conn.   R. I.
88–82   88–100

N. Dak.
100–80
Minn.
92–88
N. Y. State.   N. Pa.
82–84   80–100
S. Dak.   Wis.
100–86   84–86
Ontario.
N. Ia.   Mich.   88–88
88–85   91–85
N. Ill.   N. Ind.   N. O.
83–86   77–70   83–80

S. Ia.
57–51
Nebr.   N.-W.Mo.
55–53   23–16
Colo.   Kans.
75–68   41–31

S. Pa.   N. J.   N. Y. City, etc.
47–47   55–41   50–31
S. O. (&N. W. Va.)   D. C.   Del.
30–27   50–38   33–33

St. Louis.   M. Ill.   M. Ind.
54–31   37–37   31–17
S. Ill.   S. Ind.   Ky.   W. Va.   Va.   Md.
0–0   0–0   4–23   0–0   0–0   0–0

S. Mo.   Tenn.   N. C.
11–11   37–35   44–0

Ark.   Miss.   Ala.   Ga.   S. C.
11–11   7–3   0–0   12–15   25–25

Texas.   La.   Fl.
10–21   14–14   25–0

The numbers indicate the percent favoring voiceless *s* (as in 'sin'); the first number in each case is the percent for 'to grease,' the second for 'greasy.' Where the percents are based upon but few replies, fainter type is used.

156

'grease' as belonging to the category; in fact, gave it as the first word in the list. In this he was slavishly followed by his successors and their various worshippers, who taught, or still teach, that *s* in the verb and adjective is "wrong." This is of importance, for it introduces a disturbing element in the natural development of usage. For example, while Massachusetts, like New England and the North generally, strongly favors *s* in the adjective and the verb, the influence of the schoolteacher and the dictionary in and about Boston has materially reduced the percentage of the *s*-sound. Outside of Suffolk County, 94 percent of Massachusetts people favor *s* in the verb, and 81 percent of them favor it in the adjective; but in Suffolk County the figures are, respectively, 80 and 74 percent. Similarly, in England, exclusive of London, it would seem that 84 and 74 percent, respectively, favor the *s*-sound in 'to grease' and 'greasy'; while in London, only 25 and 33 percent do so, if the reports received are fairly representative. But this great difference between London usage and that of England generally is doubtless in part due to other causes than teaching.

Aside from this, the diversity of usage will be found to be largely geographical. In this country the North and the South present the two extremes: 88[2] and 83 percent on the one hand, and 12 and 12 percent on the other. In the Midland Belt the figures are 42 and 34 percent; in the West, 56 and 45 percent. In each district the usage is fairly uniform. Of course, that part of the North that was most exposed to immigration from the Midland shows a somewhat lower percent than the states north of it; this is most pronounced in northern Indiana, where the two currents of migration got badly mixed. While the percents from the South are often based upon insufficient material, little inconsistency is betrayed except in the cases of Tennessee and North Carolina; in the case of the latter, I believe an element of inaccuracy was introduced by the fact that several of the reports were by Northerners who reside there, and kindly offered to observe and report the local usage, but may possibly have been misguided in a case like this.

In the West the usage is naturally not so uniform. Utah stands out as remarkably Northern. The West is a compromise between the North and the South, and so in many things resembles the Midland, which, too, has contributed largely toward it. But there is a difference that I shall be able to make plain in my reports on other questions: the earlier usage of the West was largely that of the South and the Midland; to a very large extent this later yielded to, or compromised with, that of the North, *but to a different extent in different parts of the language complex*. Of course, in time, the West will break up into sections, and it may be that more replies would reveal such a state of things now; at present I can only speak of certain counties and towns as more Northern or Southern.

From the following table, it will be seen that in the matter of the pronunciation of 'grease' and its kin there is practically no difference between New England and the North as a whole, and that Connecticut is the average New

---

[2] These percents are obtained directly from the replies, not by averaging the percents of the states.

England as well as Northern state. For the Middle North (that is excluding
New England and the British Possessions), northern Iowa occupies a similar
position, as does southern Iowa for the West, and middle Illinois for the
Midland belt. The territory covered by Arkansas and most of Missouri is in a
similar way representative of the South.

North	88–82 ⎞		
New England	89–82 ⎠	Conn.	88–82
Middle North	87–84	N. Iowa	88–85
West	56–47	S. Iowa	57–51
Midland	42–34	M. Ill.	37–37
South	12–12	Ark. and S. Mo.	11–11

Although my replies for the Old Country are all too meagre, they are so
interesting that they must not be omitted. If their inaccuracy should lead our
friends across the water to send me more reports, they will serve a good purpose.

England, exclusive of London	84–74
Ireland	75–75
London	25–33
Scotland	14–14

This, like many of the other questions, shows the interesting fact that our
North harmonizes fairly with the larger part of England, while our Midland
and even more our South show distinct traces of the Scotch and Scotch–Irish
ancestry of a large part of their population.

Aside from the geographical question, the replies have brought to light
various interesting matters. In those parts where z prevails, it occasionally
appears in the noun, too, and this in the Old Country as well as over here. There
are various reasons why we might expect the z-sound to be favored in the adjective more than in the verb. In the first place, most adjectives in -*sy* have the
z-sound, while many verbs end in the *s*-sound. Where the analogy of 'the grease'
is felt as affecting the verb and the adjective, it is evident that the verb 'grease'
would be more likely to accord in pronunciation with the noun than the adjective
'greasy' would. Verb and noun are both monosyllables, and the verb as well as
the noun is now often followed by voiceless sounds beginning the next word,
whereas the *s* of 'greasy' is always in voiced neighborhood. This is substantiated
by the fact that some speakers give the verb the *s*-sound, except in the form
'greasing.' in which they use z. Moreover, where natural usage is influenced by
the school and the dictionary (until recently advocating z in verb and adjective),
this influence is the more apt to prevail the oftener the word occurs in general
conversation where it may be "corrected." Now, 'greasy' may be heard often
enough at school and in general intercourse, but 'to grease' is rarely heard except
in the barnyard—of greasing wagon wheels—and in the kitchen—of greasing
pans. These things naturally reduce the percent of *s* in 'greasy,' cf. the table of
states. On the other hand, where the tendency is to yield to the category: "noun

s, verb and adjective *z*." this will prevail the more in the case of the verb, because there are more verbs with *z* corresponding to nouns with *s* (for example, 'advise,' 'use,' 'house,' 'mouse,' espouse,' etc.) than there are adjectives with *z* corresponding to such nouns (I know of none but 'lousy'); and thus in a few districts the percent of *s* in the adjective is higher. An interesting psychological problem is presented by the fact that some people who normally say 'greasy' with *s*, pronounce the word with *z* when speaking of a disagreeable greasiness.

I shall close this report as I began it by saying that I am well aware of its imperfectness, and that I appeal to all who have the matter at heart to aid me in securing sufficient material to make future reports better. Strange to say, I have thus far received very little assistance from my colleagues in the various philological societies. I should have at least one set of replies from every county; in states with large counties even this would be far too few. I shall always send copies of the questions[3] to those who ask for them; but I would especially urge teachers of English in colleges, normal schools, and young ladies' seminaries to use the questions as an exercise in English, requiring each student in the class to write out answers to the dictated questions and to hand in the paper in lieu of an impromptu essay. Wherever the experiment has been tried it has not only been found very profitable to the students as well as to "the cause," but it has also in a healthy way aroused an unusual interest in English work.

[3] Cf. also *Dialect Notes*, p. 316.

13

Grease and Greasy: A Study of Geographical Variation

E. BAGBY ATWOOD

THE FACT THAT THE VERB *to grease* and the adjective *greasy* are pronounced by some Americans with [s] and by others with [z] has long been well known even to amateur observers of speech.[1] It has also been pretty well accepted that the incidence of [s] or [z] in the words in question is primarily dependent on the geographical location of the speaker rather than on his social or educational level—that [s] is, in general, "Northern," [z] "Southern."

As early as 1896, George Hempl published a study[2] of these two words, based on a rather widely circulated written questionnaire. His returns enabled him to divide the country into four major areas, according to the percentages of [s] in *to grease* and *greasy*, respectively. The "North"[3]—extending from New England to the Dakotas—showed 88 and 82 percent of [s] pronunciations; the "Midland," comprising a fairly narrow strip extending from New York City to

Reprinted by permission of Mrs. Atwood and the University of Texas Press from *Studies in English* (University of Texas) 29.249–60 (1950). Before his death in 1963 the author was Professor of English at The University of Texas and director of the Texas dialect project.

[1] Webster's *New International Dictionary* states that [z] in *grease* is found "esp. Brit. and Southern U.S."; [z] in *greasy* is "perhaps more general in England and the southern U.S. than in the North and East." Kenyon and Knott, *Pronouncing Dictionary* (Springfield, Mass., 1944), give [s] and [z] for the country as a whole, only [z] for the South. *The Century, Funk and Wagnalls New Standard*, and the *American College Dictionary* merely give [s] or [z] for both words. Kenyon and Knott state that "['grizɪ] and [tə griz] are phonetically normal; ['grisɪ] and [tə gris] imitate the noun *grease* [gris]." Certainly many verbs since Middle English times have been distinguished from the corresponding nouns by voicing the final fricative; cf. *house: to house, proof: to prove, wreath: to wreathe, abuse: to abuse*—and with vowel change—*bath: to bathe, breath: to breathe, grass: to graze*, etc. This paper will not be concerned with the origin or history of the feature.

The pronunciation of the vowels is of no significance in our study. For convenience I am using the sumbol [i] for both the stressed and unstressed vowels in *greasy*.

[2] "*Grease* and *Greasy*," *Dialect Notes*, I (1896), 438–44. [See p. 154 in this book.]

[3] In addition to New England, this area includes New Brunswick, Quebec, Ontario, New York, Michigan, Wisconsin, North Dakota, South Dakota, Minnesota, and the northern portions of Pennsylvania, Ohio, Indiana, Illinois, and Iowa.

St. Louis,[4] 42 and 34 percent; the "South,"[5] 12 and 12 percent; and the "West"
—an ever-widening area extending westward from St. Louis—56 and 47 percent.
The material which Hempl was able to collect was admittedly "insufficient";[6]
moreover, he had no means of selecting strictly representative informants;[7] and
the answers may not always have been correct, since, it seems to me, an understanding of the questions would have required a certain degree of linguistic
sophistication.[8] Still, in spite of these handicaps, Hempl's study has not been
greatly improved upon by later writers. Most authorities content themselves by
stating that [z] in *to grease* and *greasy* is predominantly Southern, and that either
[s] or [z] may occur elsewhere.[9] Few investigators have gathered material that
would enable them to draw clearer lines between [s] and [z] than Hempl was
able to do.[10]

The field records that have been gathered for the *Linguistic Atlas of the
United States and Canada*[11] provide us with an excellent basis for delimiting
the geographical and social spread of speech forms in the eastern United States.

[4] This includes New York City, New Jersey, Delaware, the District of Columbia,
southern Pennsylvania, southern Ohio, northern West Virginia, middle Indiana,
middle Illinois, and St. Louis, Missouri.

[5] This includes everything to the south of the Midland, as far west as Texas.

[6] *Op. cit.*, p. 438.

[7] For example, he urged his colleagues, especially "teachers of English in colleges,
normal schools, and young ladies' seminaries" to use the questions as an exercise in
English. (*Ibid.*, p. 444.)

[8] Question 45 reads: "In which (if any) of the following does *s* have the sound of *z*:
'*the grease*,' '*to grease*,' '*greasy*'?" (Hempl, "American Speech Maps," *Dialect Notes*,
I [1896], 317.) Judging from my experience in teaching phonetic transcription to college
seniors and graduate students, a considerable proportion of a class would simply not
know whether [s] or [z] was used in such words; certainly many students unhesitatingly
write [s] in words like *rose* and *has* simply because the *letter s* is used in standard spelling.

[9] See footnote [1]. It is sometimes pointed out that the same speaker may use both
['grisi] and ['grizi] with a distinction in meaning. This point will be discussed below.

[10] A. H. Marckwardt was able to draw a fairly clear line through Ohio, Indiana, and
Illinois, though on the basis of relatively little data. See "Folk Speech in Indiana and
Adjacent States," *Indiana History Bulletin*, XVII (1940), 120–140. Henry L. Smith has
long been using the word *greasy* as a test word in his demonstrations of regional variation
and to determine the origins of speakers, though he has not published his material. I
presume that Dr. Smith's observations are the source of Mario Pei's statement: " 'greazy'
... would place the speaker south of Philadelphia, while "greassy" would place him
north of Trenton." (*The Story of Language* [Philadelphia and New York, 1949], p. 51.)
C. K. Thomas considers the word *greasy* in his survey of the regional speech types, but
comes to the strange conclusion that "the choice between [s] and [z] in words like *discern*,
desolate, *absorb*, *absurd*, and *greasy* seems to be more personal than regional." (*An Introduction to the Phonetics of American English* [New York, 1947], p. 154.) G. P. Krapp is
likewise at fault when he states that, in *greasy*, "popular usage and, in general, standard
speech have only the form with [z]." (*The Pronunciation of Standard English in America*
[New York, 1919], p. 119.)

[11] The New England materials have been published as the *Linguistic Atlas of New
England*, ed. Hans Kurath and Bernard Bloch, 3 vols. (Providence, R.I., 1939–43). Field
records for most of the Middle Atlantic and South Atlantic states were gathered by the
late Guy S. Lowman; recently (summer, 1949) Dr. Raven I. McDavid, Jr., completed
the work for the eastern seaboard. The records, in an unedited but usable state, are filed
at the University of Michigan, where they were made available to me through the courtesy
of Professor Kurath. [Now at the University of Chicago.—Eds.]

A number of features of the *Atlas* methodology[12] are conducive to an accurate picture of native and normal speech. The informants, though relatively few,[13] were carefully chosen, each being both native to and representative of his community. The answers to questions were elicited, so far as possible, in a conversational atmosphere, and thus the occurrence of ungenuine forms was minimized. Finally, the forms were recorded by trained phoneticians, who would be very unlikely to make such errors as to write [s] when the informant actually uttered [z].

A few words should be said regarding the cartographical representation of linguistic atlas data. In such works as the *Atlas Linguistique de la France*,[14] in which each community, or "point" on the map, is represented by a single speaker, it is usually possible to draw lines, or *isoglosses*, separating those communities where a form occurs from those where it does not occur. Often these isoglosses set off a large block of "points," forming a solid area—as, for example, the southern French territory marked by initial [k] in the word *chandelle*.[15] A more complex presentation is sometimes required, as in the case of the northern French occurrences of [k] in this same word: after setting off our solid area we find outside it a number of scattered communities where the feature in question occurs; there must be indicated by additional lines encircling the "points" where the form is found.[16] In still other cases, the communities where a given speech form occurs (for example, *conin* for "rabbit") are so scattered that it is impossible to connect them; in such cases our isoglosses must consist merely of scattered circles here and there on the map.[17] When this situation obtains we would probably do better to assign a symbol (say, a cross, a dot, or a triangle) to the scattered form in question, lest the labyrinth of lines becomes too much for the reader to cope with.

Now, in presenting data from the American *Atlas*, we are faced with all these complications, plus others arising from the fact that more than one informant was chosen to represent each community. That is, at nearly every "point" the American fieldworkers recorded the usage of one elderly, poorly educated informant and one younger, more modern informant. In certain key communities, a third type was included—a well educated, or "cultured," speaker who presumably represented the cultivated usage of the area. Thus, at the same point on the map we often find such variants as *sot down* (preterite), representing rustic usage, *set* or *sit down*, representing more modern popular usage, and *sat down*, representing cultivated usage.[18] It is obviously impossible

[12] See *Handbook of the Linguistic Geography of New England*, ed. H. Kurath and others (Providence, R.I., 1939), for a complete account of the *Atlas* methodology.

[13] Something like 1600 informants have been interviewed, representing communities from New Brunswick to northern Florida, approximately as far west as Lake Erie.

[14] Ed. J. Gilliéron and E. Edmont, 7 vols. (Paris, 1902–10).

[15] See Karl Jaberg, "Sprachgeographie," *Siebenunddreissigstes Jahresheft des Vereins Schweiz. Gymnasiallehrer* (Aarau, 1908,) pp. 16–42; also Plate III.

[16] *Ibid.*, Plate III.   [17] *Ibid.*, Plate X.

[18] In addition, the same informant often uses more than one form; all of these are of

to draw isoglosses separating *sot* from *set* or *sat*; it is even impractical to set off the *sot* areas, since the form occurs in about every other community through considerable areas. In other cases, of course, it is quite easy to mark off an area where a certain form is current. *Holp* (for *helped*), for example, occupies a very clearcut area south of the Potomac.[19] Yet a line marking off this area would by no means constitute a dividing line between *holp* and *helped*, since most of the younger informants within the *holp* area use the standard form *helped*. My point is that an isogloss based on American *Atlas* materials *should in all cases be regarded as an outer limit, not as a dividing line between two speech forms.*

The examples hitherto adduced have, of course, illustrated the incidence of "non-standard" as against "standard" speech forms. What of those instances of two forms which are equally "standard," each within its area? Kurath's map of *pail* and *bucket* provides an example.[20] Here too we must follow the same principle: we must first draw the outer limit of one form, then that of the other. The two lines will lap over each other at some points, enclosing certain communities of mixed usage.[21] Thus, *a dividing line is a double isogloss*, each being the outer limit of one of the two speech forms in question. The areas of overlapping between the two lines may be wide or narrow, depending on many social, geographical, and historical considerations.

Let us return to *grease* and *greazy*. The variation between [s] and [z] in these words furnishes an almost ideal example of geographical (as against social) distribution. Consider first the verb *grease*. It is unnecessary to describe in detail the incidence of [s] and [z], since the accompanying map tells its own story. The northern line of the [z]-form, it may be observed, takes in the southwestern corner of Connecticut (west of the Housatonic); from there it passes westward just to the north of New Jersey; then it dips sharply southward to Philadelphia, to the west of which it again rises gradually northward to the northwestern corner of Pennsylvania. The transition area (where both [s] and [z] are used), is relatively narrow to the west of Philadelphia; to the northeast, however, it widens considerably so as to include most of northern New Jersey, as well as New York City and eastern Long Island.

Outside our pair of isoglosses there is a surprisingly small number of "stray" forms. All together, there are only six occurrences of [z] in the [s] area and only

---

course entered at that point on the map. On at least one occasion McDavid picked up from the same informant, as the preterite of *see*, *I seen*, *I seed*, *I see*, and *I saw*.

[19] This verb, as well as the others mentioned, is treated in my *Survey of Verb Forms in the Eastern United States*. [Ann Arbor, Mich., 1953.]

[20] *A Word Geography of the Eastern United States* (Ann Arbor, Mich., 1949), Figure 66.

[21] Even after drawing the lines we would find a good many scattered, or "stray," occurrences of *pail* within the *bucket* area and vice versa. Kurath's lines, which are all outer limits, do not attempt to indicate the presence of stray forms or small patches which occur outside the main area; however, since he also publishes maps on which each occurrence of each word is recorded by a symbol, the reader can easily check and interpret his isoglosses.

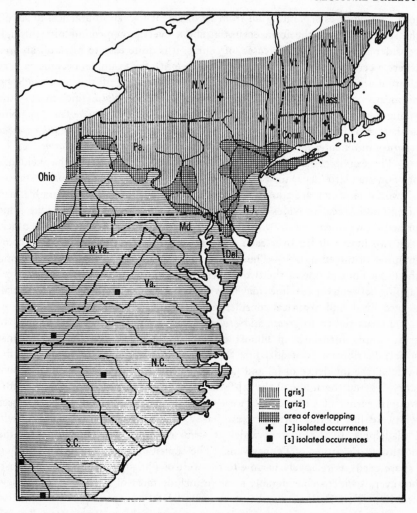

Map showing the distribution of [s] and [z] in grease (verb). Northern Maine and Eastern Georgia (not shown on the map) show the same usage as the adjoining areas. At the time of this study, no field records were available for Northern New York.

six of [s] in the [z] area.[22] (It will be observed, of course, that there is a second area, or island, of [s] along the Ohio River extending northeastward from the

[22] This amounts to less than one percent of the informants. Most of the informants who show exceptional usage also give the "normal" form; that is, they use both [s] and [z] forms.

vicinity of Marietta, Ohio.) There is no sign whatever of social variation within the solid [s] and [z] areas; cultivated usage is in strict agreement with popular usage.[23] Within the areas of overlapping there is naturally some variation between older and more modern informants—yet the general trend is not at all clear. In the communities of divided usage to the west of Philadelphia the more modern informant uses [s] in six out of eight instances; in such communities to the northeast of Philadelphia the modern preference is for [s] in six instances, for [z] in six others. As for cultured informants within the areas of overlapping, 10 use [griz], five use [gris], and one offers both [s] and [z] forms. One might state, very tentatively, that cultivated usage has tended to favor [griz], particularly in New York City and northern New Jersey.

For the adjective *greasy*, the pronunciations [grisi] and [grizi] show almost precisely the same isoglosses as those for [gris] and [griz]. The northern limit of [z] pushes further northward at three points in Pennsylvania;[24] correspondingly, the southern limit of [s] retreats northward at one point in Ohio, three in Pennsylvania, and two in northern New Jersey.[25] Within the [s] area, there are 10 stray forms with [z], scattered through New England and the Hudson Valley; six of these occur in the cultured type of informant. Within the [z] area, we again find six stray occurrences of [s]; and precisely the same island of [s] occurs along the Ohio River. In short, a few more eastern informants use [z] in *greasy* than in *grease*, though the difference is not great. Within the areas of overlapping we find almost exactly the same social distribution as in the case of *grease*. Cultured informants prefer [grizi] by 11 to 4; this fact, together with the six "stray" northern uses of [z] in the cultured type, inclines us to believe that [z] in *greasy* has penetrated into northeastern cultivated speech a little more palpably than in the case of *grease*—though still to a very slight extent.

After describing the incidence of the speech forms in question, we are still faced with a number of questions, to which our data can provide only partial answers.

What becomes of our isoglosses in the areas west of Pennsylvania? The materials being gathered for the Great Lakes atlas (under the direction of Professor A. H. Marckwardt) will undoubtedly provide an answer. I have not been able to examine the latest of these materials; but judging from preliminary information, as well as from a map already published by Professor Marckwardt,[26] the northern limit of [z] in *greasy* passes through central Ohio, then swings northward so as to take in almost the whole of Indiana, then bends southward

---

[23] Although the preterite form of the verb was not called for in the work sheets, Lowman picked up some five instances of *grez* [grɛz] in the [z] area; and a number of other informants reported having heard this form.

[24] Lehigh, Columbia, and Lancaster counties.

[25] Columbia, Armstrong, Blair, Cumberland, Hunterdon, and Morris counties.

[26] "Folk Speech of Indiana and Adjacent States," *op. cit.*, p. 128. [Editors' note: for a later statement based upon the completed study involving all three types of informants see A. H. Marckwardt: "Principal and Subsidiary Dialect Areas in the North-Central States," *Publication of the American Dialect Society*, No. 27 (April, 1957), reprinted in this book p. 74.]

through central Illinois in the direction of St. Louis. Whether the areas of transition are wide or narrow we can probably not determine with accuracy, since, in general, only one social type (the elderly, or rustic) is included in the Great Lakes survey.

Why should the isoglosses run where they do? The answer, in part, is relatively simple. Of the two sets of variants, the [s] forms were evidently generalized in the New England colonies, the [z] forms in the Middle and South Atlantic colonies. The westward migrations and settlements of the New Englanders covered New York (State), northern Pennsylvania, Michigan, Wisconsin, and the northern portions of Ohio, Indiana, and Illinois.[27] Many speech features mark off this Northern area from the "Midland"—the area occupied primarily by Pennsylvania.[28] Most of the northern lines, to be sure, pass further to the north in Pennsylvania than do those of the [s] in *grease* and *greasy*. Yet the penetration of northern forms to the area of Philadelphia is occasionally to be observed in other instances; for example, the line of Northern *clapboards* (as against Midland and Southern *weatherboards*) dips sharply southward so as to take in Philadelphia and northern Delaware. Another explanation for the prevalence of [gris] and ['grisi] in east central Pennsylvania might be the fact that much of the area was occupied in the early eighteenth century by Palatine Germans, whose native dialect had no [z] phoneme at all[29] and who may, for this reason, have favored [s] in any English words where variation between [s] and [z] occurred.

What is the British practice with regard to the pronunciation of *grease* and *greasy*? No complete survey has been made; but there seems no doubt that London usage, as well as "Received Standard" usage throughout Southern England, is mixed.[30] The questionnaires which Hempl circulated in England (for his study cited above) showed that in London only 25 and 33 percent of the informants used [s] in *grease* and *greasy*; but that in England exclusive of London the percentages of [s] were 84 and 74.[31] We have no ground, even yet, for rejecting these figures; but it should be pointed out that folk speech in England, just as in the United States, shows its isoglosses. A survey of the

[27] Kurath, *Word Geography*, pp. 1–7; see also Lois K. M. Rosenberry, *The Expansion of New England* (Boston and New York, 1909). Even the island of [s] forms around Marietta, Ohio, is to be explained on the basis of early settlement; this area was first settled by New Englanders as early as the 1780's. See Rosenberry, pp. 175 ff.

[28] Examples of Northern words (from Kurath) are *whiffletree, pail, darning needle* ("dragonfly"), and *co, boss!* (cow call). Verb forms which I have found to have similar distributions are *hadn't ought* ("oughtn't"), *how be you?*, *clim* ("climbed"), and *see* as a preterite of *to see*. Note that Kurath's definition of "Midland" does not coincide with that of Hempl; the area, according to the former, extends much farther to the south-westward of Pennsylvania than Hempl indicated. (See *Word Geography*, pp. 27–37.) [Editors' Note: see also Atwood's own later study, *A Survey of Verb Forms in the Eastern United States* (University of Michigan Press, Ann Arbor, 1953), and, in this book (p. 76), Allen's and Marckwardt's western extension of the s/z isogloss.]

[29] See Carroll E. Reed, *The Pennsylvania German Dialect Spoken in the Counties of Lehigh and Berks: Phonology and Morphology* (Seattle, Wash., 1949), pp. 20 and 29.

[30] See Daniel Jones, *An English Pronouncing Dictionary*, 9th ed. (London, 1948).

[31] Hempl, *op. cit.*, pp. 442–443.

linguistic atlas type conducted by Guy S. Lowman in 1934[32] shows that the [z] in *grease* (I have no information on *greasy*) occupies East Anglia and a small adjoining area; that [s] is universal in the remainder of southern England (we are speaking strictly of the rustic type of speaker). Since the line passes through (or very near) London, it is easy to see why the metropolitan area should show a mixture of usage.

Is there any evidence of a differentiation in meaning between ['grisi] and ['grizi]? The *Atlas* provides no answer to this question, since, in the interest of obtaining comparable data, the words were always called for in the same context ("grease the car, axle, etc." and "my hands are greasy"). In general, such differentiations in meaning are characteristics of areas of mixed usage, not of those where one pronunciation or another is definitely established. The distinction usually given in dictionaries is that ['grisi] may mean literally "covered with grease," while ['grizi] may be used with less literal, and sometimes unpleasant, connotations.[33] What we can say with confidence is that speakers to the south of our isoglosses do not follow this practice: ['grizi] is universal with the meaning "covered with grease"; whether or not speakers in the area of overlapping, and to the north of it, would have used ['grizi] had the context been different we are unable to determine.

How should we evaluate the *Atlas* data as a picture of reality? What is most important to realize is that the *Atlas* makes no attempt whatever to record the usage of non-native speakers, or even of those natives who have resided for long periods outside their home communities. Such speakers are rather uncommon in some communities, fairly numerous in others; in a few of the latter, the *Atlas* may even reflect the usage of a minority of old-timers. In view of this, we might be inclined to wonder whether the percentage method might not give a truer picture of prevalent usage than the isogloss method. The proportion of non-native speech forms in a community would, of course, roughly correspond to the proportion of non-native residents; such data would certainly be valuable, though to collect it on a large enough scale (say, 100 or so informants from each county) would be so difficult as to be practially impossible. Few investigators are qualified to make extensive phonetic observations and those few must take their informants from such captive groups as college classes whose usage may or

[32] Lowman's British field records are filed in an unedited state at the University of Michigan. [Now at the University of Chicago.—Eds.]

[33] Daniel Jones, *English Pronouncing Dictionary*: "Some speakers use the forms ... with a difference of meaning, ['gri:si] having reference merely to the presence of grease and ['gri:zi] having reference to the slipperiness caused by grease." *Webster's NID* states; "... many people in all sections use ['grisi] in some connotations and ['grizi] in others, the first esp. in the literal sense, covered with grease." Cf. Kenyon and Knott: "Some distinguish ['grisi] 'covered with grease' from ['grizi] 'slimy' " (*op. cit.*). G. P. Krapp states: "A distinction is sometimes made in the meaning of ['gri:si] and ['gri:zi], the latter being regarded as a word of unpleasant connotation" (*op. cit.*, p. 119). Webster's implies that this distinction is fairly general throughout the country—a very dubious proposition. T. Larsen and F. C. Walker simply prescribe [s] for the meaning "sticky" and [z] for the meaning "slippery"—as though this feature were standard and universal. (See *Pronunciation*, Oxford Press, 1931, p. 92.)

may not be spontaneous or representative. Another feature of the *Atlas* that must be considered is the preponderance of rather old informants. Since the interviews were conducted several years ago, many of the forms shown to be current among the aged may now be rare or even obsolete; moreover, the *Atlas* records would not reflect the most recent trends, fads, and innovations—some of which are extremely rapid, others extremely slow. It seems unlikely to me that the lines on *grease* and *greasy* have shifted radically in the last few years, yet I have no doubt that usage may have shifted in certain individual communities.[34] All things considered, the *Linguistic Atlas* offers the most reliable body of data as yet assembled, or likely to be assembled in the near future, on American speech; isoglosses based on it reflect the usage of a highly important segment of our population, and they are, moreover, of the highest value in a study of our cultural and settlement history.

[34] Dr. Smith expresses the opinion that the younger generation in New York City has gone over almost entirely to the [s] in *greasy*.

14

Pronunciation of 'can't' in the Eastern States

SUMNER IVES

THAT THE NEGATIVE CONTRACTION *can't* is pronounced in different ways in different parts of the country is well known; and most people know that it has, in some areas, the vowel of *father*, in others the vowel of *paint*,[1] and in the country at large some variations of what is called "short *a*." The first pronunciation is associated with New England and is sometimes considered to be more elegant than the others. The second pronunciation is usually associated with the South. Opinions regarding its distribution and status vary in accordance with opinions concerning the extent of that speech region and with attitudes toward its individual characteristics. The approximately 1400 field records of the *Linguistic Atlas of the United States and Canada* which have been gathered in the Atlantic states allow more precise statements concerning the pronunciation of the stressed vowel in *can't*. This is a report, on the phonetic level, of the vowel types and their distribution as revealed by these records.[2]

In interpreting the information which will be given, certain facts about the *Atlas* survey should be kept in mind. First, although the number of informants is considerable, there are not enough in proportion to the total population for conclusive decisions as to the exact frequencies of speech traits in the general population, considered locally or regionally. Secondly, the informants generally were older than the population average, and they represented the most stable elements among the local residents. It is possible, therefore, that the *Atlas*

Reprinted by permission from *American Speech* 28.149–57 (1953). The author is Professor of English at New York University.

[1] This pronunciation is not listed in the standard desk dictionaries, nor in the Kenyon–Knott *Pronouncing Dictionary of American English* (Springfield, Mass., 1944). It is, however, found in Harold Wentworth, *American Dialect Dictionary* (New York, 1944), in H. L. Mencken, *The American Language; Supplement II* (New York, 1948), p. 122, and in several studies on the speech of the Southern states.

[2] These records were examined during the summer of 1951 through the courtesy of Hans Kurath. For details of the *Atlas* procedure and the phonetic symbols used see his *Handbook of the Linguistic Geography of New England* (Providence, R. I., 1939). On the use of *Atlas* material see E. Bagby Atwood, "*Grease* and *Greasy*—a Study of Geographical Variation," *Texas Studies in English*, XXIX (1950), 249–260. [See p. 160 in this book.]

information is not definitive for younger individuals and more transient elements in some communities, for the speech of one generation is never in all particulars that of another. Thirdly, the fieldwork was done by different people. Hence, such matters as differences in transcription practice and in the selection of informants must be considered in the evaluation of the data. The fieldwork for the area between South Carolina and upper New York State, and some other regions, was done by Guy Lowman. In seeking out older and less educated informants (Type I), he normally reached less accessible places and sought out more primitive types than the other fieldworkers. Some differences in transcription practices can be found in very detailed studies of some features; however, those which are found in the stressed vowel of *can't* do not, I think, seriously affect the general conclusions which will be given.

An additional factor in using the *Atlas* evidence is the nature of the informants. Three types were interviewed. Type I consisted of older, less educated, and more isolated persons, whose usage could be expected to show the highest contemporary retention of archaic features and the least influence of school instruction. These constituted approximately one-half of the informants, although persons of this type certainly are not that common in the population as a whole. Type II consisted of persons with the average schooling for the locality. These were generally somewhat older than the population average but younger than Type I informants. The usage of these two groups, when it agrees, can probably be regarded as representative of the popular speech of a region, although somewhat old-fashioned. Type III represented those whose education was clearly superior and whose social contacts were primarily with others of educational and social advantage. Their speech traits can be regarded as broadly typical of usage among the older generation of educated people. This group constituted approximately 10 percent of the total number of informants.

The material for New England has already been published, and the pronunciation of *can't* appears on Map 695.[3] The other material has been neither edited nor published. It was gathered by two fieldworkers, Lowman, whose area has already been given, and Raven I. McDavid, Jr., who covered the rest of the area outside New England, namely, South Carolina and parts of New York, Georgia, and Florida. Since these field records have not been reviewed, evaluated, and classified, conclusions based on them are subject to later verification. However, I consider it unlikely that the generalizations here will be seriously modified, for I have limited them to what is sufficiently clear even in the present state of the evidence.

The pronunciation of *can't* was secured in the statement "I can't," and the fieldworkers were to record it as spoken with full stress.

In describing the distribution of vowel types in *can't*, I have organized the discussion according to three major differences: (1) transcriptions with [a] and

[3] In Hans Kurath and Bernard Bloch, *Linguistic Atlas of New England*, 3 vols. (Providence, R. I., 1938–42).

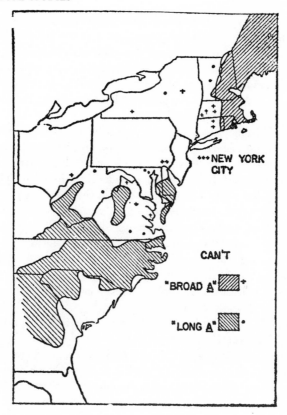

Figure 14.1.

[ɑ], regardless of diacritics, are treated as one type, called "broad *a*."[4] Evidence for doing this is the fact that records which indicated broad *a* in *can't* almost without exception had the same transcription for the stressed vowel of *father*; (2) transcriptions with an upgliding diphthong having [e] or [ɛ] as the first element are regarded as another type, called "long *a*." In verifying this grouping, I checked against transcriptions in the same records for the vowel of *strain*; (3) occurrences of [e], monophthongal or ingliding, would also have been considered as this type, but none was found.

For temporary identification, occurrences of [æ], regardless of diphthongization or other modification, are referred to as varieties of short *a*. It is reasonably clear that the broad *a* type and the long *a* type are phonemically distinct, both from each other and from the varieties of short *a*.

In the pronunciation of *can't* there is no significant difference between the

---

[4] See also Herbert Penzl, "Vowel Phonemes in *Father, Man, Dance* in Dictionaries and New England Speech," *Journal of English and Germanic Philology*, XXXIX (1940), 31.

usage of Type I and Type II informants; however, there are some local differences between the usage of Type III informants and that of others which should be noted. In the region where broad *a* is found, shown on Figure 14.1, it appears in approximately two-thirds of the records, regardless of type, but elsewhere occurrences of broad *a* are almost exclusively limited to Type III records. Only two occurrences, and these are in upstate and western New York, are found in other than Type III records. On the other hand, it appears in three of four Type III records from New York City, in two of three from Philadelphia, in three of twelve from eastern Virginia, and in one of one from southeast Ohio, originally settled from New England. At the same time, this is less than 10 percent of the Type III records from outside New England. This does not mean, of course, that broad *a* would be heard in this word only in these places or from educated people, for there is evidence apart from the *Linguistic Atlas* that it has at least some currency among older and less educated people in eastern Virginia and elsewhere.[5] However, the frequency was apparently not great enough for the *Atlas* sampling to reveal it in the speech of these people. One can, I think, conclude that this pronunciation of *can't* is regarded as elegant among at least some people in New York, Philadelphia, and eastern Virginia.

The pronunciation with long *a*, however, seems to have a different status, even where it is the most common usage in popular speech. From the region where this pronunciation is found, shown on Figure 14.1, there are 25 records which the fieldworkers classified as Type III. Only 4 of these 25 have long *a* in *can't*. In interpreting this evidence, one should realize that educated people in this region, as in other places, often use forms which they regard as incorrect in everyday, familiar speech, although they know and use those they regard as correct when they wish.[6] This evidence, therefore, does not prove that the pronunciation with long *a* is as limited in currency among educated people as the figures suggest. It does, however, suggest that the use of long *a* is regarded as incorrect or careless among most educated people of the region. As a former resident of the long *a* region, I think one is likely to hear both this pronunciation and some other from most native educated people, depending on the circumstances.

The most noticeable differences in the occurrence of vowel types are geographical. Figure 14.1 shows the distribution of broad *a*. The shaded area in New England limits the region in which this pronunciation is indicated for adjoining communities; hence there are a few occurrences, represented by crosses, west of the boundary, indicating less common usage. This boundary agrees with several other speech boundaries which mark off eastern New England as a distinct dialect region. One should note, however, that there is a small

    [5] The speech of this state has been much discussed. For a fairly complete list of studies see Mencken, *op. cit.*, pp. 223–224.
    [6] Allen Tate, *The Fathers* (New York, 1938), p. 17, has an interesting footnote describing levels of usage in the speech of the last generation.

unshaded area which includes the coast of New Hampshire. The pronunciation here is some variety of short *a*.

Within this broad *a* region, some differences in distribution between [a] and [ɑ] can be observed. In general, [ɑ] is limited to the Boston vicinity and to Maine; but [a] is very common alongside [ɑ] except along the western half of the Maine coast and along the eastern boundary of the state adjoining Canada, where occurrences of [a] are relatively rare. It should be noted, however, that in and near areas where [ɑ] predominates, [a] is often written with a shift sign for retraction and [ɑ] with a sign for fronting. In the western part of the broad *a* region, [a] is often fronted. Nevertheless, the phonemic separation from forms written with [æ], even when lowered, can be assumed, pending a more careful study of phonemic patterns in this region, for a retracted vowel is consistently written for *father* in records which have lowered [æ] for *can't*.

Occurrences of long *a* are also shown on Figure 14.1. The shaded area indicates occurrences of this vowel type in adjacent communities, and isolated occurrences are shown by a black dot. The boundary of this region is particularly interesting. In West Virginia, it corresponds generally with the northern limit of some other features of Southern speech. In Virginia, it does not include, except in the interior, the area for the typical eastern Virginia traits.[7] In South Carolina and Georgia it does not include the area of low country speech, nor does it include Florida. This distribution, together with the population history, indicates dissemination from the mountain country. But the occurrence of the islands in central Virginia and the Delmarva Peninsula and the relative infrequency of occurrence in Type III records indicate that this is a recessive feature, although this evidence is not, of course, conclusive.

The frequency of occurrence is greatest in the mountain portion of North Carolina, long *a* being almost universal in Type I and II records. North and south of there, in the adjoining states, it is found in about half the Type I and II records. Toward the coast of North Carolina, it becomes progressively less frequent, although it remains common except along the coast near Wilmington.

Varieties with both [e] and [ɛ] are found, but all have a distinct upglide, generally written with [ɪ], superior or level. Those with the open beginning are predominant in Delaware, along the North Carolina coast north of Wilmington and in a narrow band inland, and in the western tip of Virginia and a narrow band southward. A few occurrences with the open beginning are also found in South Carolina and Georgia. Elsewhere, a close beginning [e] is indicated. The distribution of open and close beginnings in *can't* is quite similar to the distribution of these forms in *strain*.

The incidence of varieties written with some modification of [æ] is extremely complicated, and several maps or charts would be required to show these varieties in detail. The distribution of a type characterized by having a

[7] E. Bagby Atwood, "Some Eastern Virginia Pronunciation Features," *English Studies in Honor of James Southall Wilson* (University of Virginia Studies, Charlottesville, 1951), pp. 111–124.

following upglide is, however, quite clear and probably of dialectal significance. The distribution of a lengthened type is sufficiently clear for representation on a map, although it is not so clear as that of the diphthongal type. In order, therefore, to make the best use of the map, only these are shown on Figure 14.2.

Although the phonemic status of the long *a* and broad *a* types seems to be clear, that of the various varieties of short *a* cannot be satisfactorily determined from the study of a single word in which these varieties appear. Nor would it be advisable to draw conclusions from a comparison with any other single word. The existence of two phonemes in short *a* has been proved for some types of American English;[8] however, the exact distribution, both geographically and socially, of each phoneme and the phonetic characteristics of each for the various regions where it may occur is not sufficiently clear for present decision without phonemic analyses of individual records. And whether phonemic analyses of individual *Atlas* field records would be definitive is open to question.

For convenience in discussion, the type with the upglide is written here as [æy]. In this writing, the first symbol represents any modification of [æ], raised or lowered, short or long, and the second symbol represents any upglide, whether written with [ɪ] or with [ɛ] and whether written superior or level. For the same reason, the lengthened type is here written [æ·]. This symbolization includes all transcriptions with length, whether raised or lowered, and whether or not an inglide release is indicated by a superior schwa.

In Figure 14.2, the distribution of [æy] is shown. The indicated area includes all but quite isolated occurrences of this type, which are shown by solid triangles. An interesting feature of this distribution is the fact that [æy] occurs in Virginia in an area which has several other distinguishing features and is generally regarded as a distinct dialect region. In the northern part of this dialect region, it occurs alongside other pronunciations, especially [æ·], but in the southern portion, it is clearly the predominant usage. In the other Southern states, its area generally overlaps the area of long *a* and popular usage seems to be about equally divided between the two forms; however, all Type III records in this area of mixed usage show [æy], and in northeast Florida all records of any type, except one, show [æy].

It should be noted that upper South Carolina and most of Georgia have a mixture of the Virginia and mountain types, but that lower South Carolina and coastal Georgia are clearly outlined. This distribution agrees with what is known of the settlement history, especially of Georgia.[9] That this diphthongal type is not entirely a Southern feature, however, is shown by the number of occurrences, in all types of records, in the Genesee Valley of western New York.

In most transcriptions which are generalized under this vowel type, the first element [æ] is written as raised and lengthened, although other modifications

[8] George L. Trager, "One Phonemic Entity Becomes Two: the Case of 'Short A,' " *American Speech*, XV (1940), 256.

[9] J. E. Callaway, *The Early Settlement of Georgia* (Athens, Ga., 1948).

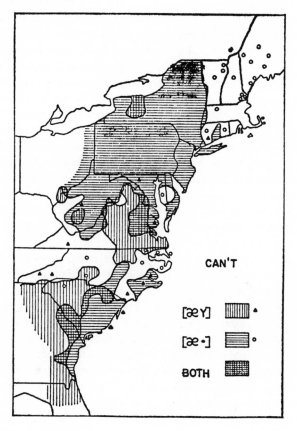

Figure 14.2.

except lowering and centering are sometimes found. The raised and lengthened transcriptions are particularly common in the records made by McDavid. His records also show a great preponderance of [ε] as the second element, but both Lowman and McDavid recorded the first element with and without raising, with and without length, and with both types of upglide. It is likely, therefore, that the upglide characteristic is less prominent outside the Virginia region than within it, although such a question cannot be answered conclusively on present evidence.

The distribution of [æ·] is likewise shown on Figure 14.2. This vowel type is found in nearly half of the over 1400 field records examined for this study, and it is the predominant type in the very populous Middle Atlantic region. Its distribution clearly sets off an area which begins with the eastern boundary of New York, extends south nearly to Norfolk, and extends west as far as the *Atlas* records which were used in this study. It includes the area which has been given for a contrast between two phonemes in short *a*; in fact, its northeast and south boundaries are approximately the same as this region. However, its western extent goes beyond it, for the western limit of the contrast is reported as a line roughly between Pittsburgh, Pennsylvania, and Albany, New York.[10] The next largest area where [æ·] is predominant is the coast of South Carolina and Georgia. Other small areas are in Connecticut and North Carolina, and there are many isolated occurrences, especially in eastern New England.

Within the main [æ·] region there are quite a few isolated occurrences of [æ] without length, and they are particularly common in central New Jersey, eastern and northern Pennsylvania, western New York, and along the North Carolina coast, although they are more common than [æ·] (in the [æ·] region) only in the Pennsylvania German locality. The type with unlengthened [æ] is, however, by far the predominant type in western New England, and it is more common than [æ·] in the rest of New England, where the predominant type is, of course, broad *a*.

There are two further distributions of phonetic types which may have importance in the study of American English. The first of these is the incidence of lengthened [æ] with inglide release. This form is almost universal in the low country of South Carolina and Georgia. The importance of this is the fact that it is surrounded by areas in which some type of upgliding diphthong is found, and further that it is the area which has an ingliding release in long *a* and long *o*, which are upgliding diphthongs in the surrounding regions. That is, the vowels of *late*, *road*, and *can't* are ingliding in this region and upgliding around it. This ingliding type of [æ·] is likewise the almost universal type in extreme western Pennsylvania, eastern Ohio, and northern West Virginia, and it is extremely common in New Jersey and eastern Maryland and Virginia. In New York state and the rest of Pennsylvania, ingliding types occur, but transcriptions without inglide are more common.

Another vowel type which is important in American English is that written with [æ] raised and lengthened, for this is the description given the short *a* phoneme which is written /eh/ in the Trager–Smith system.[11] This is the vowel of *can* (metal container) when it contrasts with the vowel of *can* (be able). In the *Atlas* records, a few, widely scattered occurrences of raised [æ·] were recorded in many places, but there are some concentrations which may have significance. Seven occurrences are found in the South Carolina low country dialect region, six of these at the boundaries of the region. Nine are in eastern Virginia, with four in or near Richmond. Eleven are in central Maryland north and east of Washington, which is rather heavy concentration, and occurrences are fairly common in a northeast band which extends into the lower Hudson Valley and includes New York City. There are also concentrations of this type in upstate

---

[10] Henry Lee Smith, Jr., in review of Hans Kurath, *A Word Geography of the Eastern United States*, in *Studies in Linguistics*, IX (1951), 11.

[11] *Ibid.* also George L. Trager and Henry Lee Smith, Jr., *Outline of English Structure* (Studies in Linguistics: Occasional Papers No. 3, 1951).

New York,[12] and occurrences are fairly common in most of western New York State. There are none recorded in New England, although [æ·] without raising is found sporadically.

The information which has been given concerning varieties of short *a* in *can't* neither confirms nor denies the existence of phonemic contrast between one variety and another. It does, however, reveal a condition in which phonemic change is a distinct possibility. A raised and lengthened, presumably more tense, allophone is potentially a separate phoneme, especially if there is pattern pressure by analogy with other front vowel contrasts and/or if this allophone is eliminated by teaching from some words in which it would normally occur. By the same reasoning, an ingliding allophone, especially with a raised, tense, or lengthened beginning, is likewise potentially a separate phoneme. This is, of course, extrapolation, but there seems to be enough evidence to indicate that an extended study of the problem, supplementing the *Atlas* material, would be a worthwhile project.

A review of the distributions of the various vowel types in *can't* shows that some of the already recognized dialect regions of American English are further marked by pronunciations of this word. Thus eastern New England, Eastern Virginia, and the South Carolina–Georgia low country are clearly set off.[13] The usual line bounding Southern and South Midland as one area agrees closely with the southern boundary of [æ·], unmixed with either long *a* or [æy], the distribution of long *a* gives a general Southern exclusive of Florida and the sub-regions mentioned above, and the distribution of [æy] gives a general Southern exclusive of North Carolina and the South Carolina–Georgia low country. These divisions all agree with some facts of regional settlement.[14] The distribution of [æ·], in the main, sets off a central Atlantic region with some common cultural traits, although it includes certain areas which are clearly set off as separate by other criteria. The pronunciation of *can't* is also confirming evidence that the geographical South is far from homogeneous as a dialect region.

---

[12] C. K. Thomas, "Pronunciation in Up-State New York," *American Speech*, X (1935), 290, finds no [ɑ] or [a] in *can't* but some occurrences of raised [æ].

[13] For regional demarcations which, as far as they go, agree with these see Kurath, *A Word Geography of the Eastern United States* (Studies in American English I, Ann Arbor, Mich., 1949), and C. K. Thomas, *An Introduction to the Phonetics of American English* (New York, 1947), p. 145.

[14] Callaway, *op. cit.*; T. J. Wertenbacker, *The Old South* ("The Founding of American Civilization," Vol. II, New York, 1942).

15

'*Shivaree*': An Example of Cultural Diffusion

ALVA L. DAVIS
RAVEN I. McDAVID, JR.

AS ONE OF THE YOUNGER BRANCHES of linguistic science, dialect geography has provided valuable evidence by which the student of languages can explain the apparent exceptions to phonetic laws or indicate the directions in which phonetic, grammatical, or lexical innovations have spread. To the social scientist, for whom linguistics is properly a branch of cultural anthropology, dialect geography is potentially a very useful tool for examining the cultural configurations and prestige-values operating in a speech community.[1] Both of these functions of dialect geography may be suggested by the study of the distribution of the form *shivaree* [ˌʃɪvəˈriː], "a noisy burlesque serenade, used chiefly as a means of teasing newly married couples" in the North American English speech community.

The term is of interest to the student of dialect geography for several reasons. Its occurrence was noted early in several areas by many students of American dialects, and it has continued to draw attention.[2] Its pattern of distribution is peculiar, with the isogloss setting off its area of prevalence generally running from north to south.[3] Without any commercial or social prestige to aid in its

Reprinted by permission from *American Speech* 24.249–55 (1949). Professor Davis is a member of the department of English at Illinois Institute of Technology and director of the American Language Center there; Professor McDavid is in the department of English at the University of Chicago and is the director of the Linguistic Atlas of the Middle and South Atlantic States.

[1] See, for example, Raven I. McDavid, Jr., "Dialect Geography and Social Science Problems," *Social Forces*, XXV (December, 1946–47), 168–72; [see p. 375 in this book.] "Postvocalic /-r/ in South Carolina: a Social Analysis," *American Speech*, XXIII (October–December, 1948), 194–203.

[2] For example, "Charivaria": I. Mamie J. Meredith, " 'Belling the Bridal Couple' in Pioneer Days"; II. Miles Hanley, " 'Serenade' in New England," *American Speech*, VIII (April, 1933), 22–26; John T. Flanagan, "A Note on 'Shivaree,' " *ibid.*, XV (February, 1940), 109–110.

[3] Both phonologically and lexically, American dialects seem to be divided into three main types—Northern, Midland, and Southern—with the isoglosses (lines setting off the zones of occurrence of forms characteristic of each area) running roughly east and west. For instance, in the Northern area, the vessel in which water is carried is generally

dissemination—such as undoubtedly helped the spread of *sauerkraut* or *spaghetti* —it has become one of the most widely distributed folk terms borrowed by American English from any European language.[4] Finally, the accent pattern [ˌʃɪvəˈriː], in the speech of many informants, is atypical for nouns in American folk speech, which predominantly have the primary stress on other than the final syllable.[5]

The etymology of *shivaree* has been satisfactorily established. It is derived from French *charivari* (compare Picard *caribari*) in turn a derivative of the Medieval Latin *c(h)arivarium*; its ultimate origin is unknown,[6] but its occurrence in French goes back at least to the fourteenth century. In some form the word occurs everywhere in France, generally designating a mock serenade following a wedding slightly divergent from the normal pattern in a community—such as that of an old maid, an old bachelor, a widow, or a widower.[7]

Although raucous celebrations are common in rural England following unpopular or atypical weddings or as a form of social censure,[8] the French term does not seem to be part of the British folk vocabulary. It was not recorded in the collections for Wright's *English Dialect Dictionary* nor in the field records

called a *pail*; in the Midland and Southern areas, a *bucket*. The conception of a division into Northern, Midland, and Southern dialect types—supplanting the older and less accurate division into Eastern, Southern, and so-called "General American"—has been enunciated and validated most clearly by Hans Kurath, Director of the *Linguistic Atlas of the United States and Canada*. See his *Word Geography of the Eastern United States* (Ann Arbor, 1949).

It is, of course, to be expected that dialect areas would be less sharply divided in the Mississippi Valley, a secondary settlement area, than along the Atlantic seaboard. Nevertheless, the isoglosses still generally follow an east–west direction, as for the areas of occurrence of *pail* and *bucket*, or for the pronunciations [ˈgriːsi] and [ˈgriːzi].

[4] The term *bateau*, "flat-bottomed rowboat," is practically universal in South Carolina and Georgia but is rare in the Middle West. *Clook*, "setting hen"; *rainworm*, "earthworm"; and *snits*, "dried sliced fruit," are normally found only in areas where the earliest settlers were predominantly German; *to cook coffee*, "make coffee," only in areas with a heavy Scandinavian settlement.

[5] On the basis of our present information, we are unable to make any definitive regional statements about the accent pattern; such a statement will not be possible until field records are available for the entire Mississippi Valley.

[6] E. Littré, *Dictionnaire de la langue française* (Paris, 1877).

[7] Marriage, as one of the critical acts in the life cycle indicating a change in social status, has always been a matter of public concern, through statute or mores or both. See William Graham Sumner, *Folkways* (Boston, 1940), pp. 370, 391–392, 409.

Even in our loosely organized industrialized urban society a marriage is an occasion for friends of the bridegroom and bride to harass them. For instance, the bacchanalian and priapic ribaldry of the stag supper for the bridegroom, deflating the tires of the bridegroom's automobile, decorating the bridegroom's car with tin cans and old shoes, and impeding the consummation of the marriage by telephoning the newlyweds' hotel room at frequent intervals. See Lael Tucker, "The Kiss, the Tree, and the Bullet," *Harper's Magazine*, CXCVIII, No. 1187 (April, 1949), 40–51. The importance of such outlets for the aggressive tendencies of a cultural group has been pointed out by many social scientists; see Clyde Kluckhohn, *Mirror for Man* (New York, 1949), pp. 277–278, and Stuart Chase, *The Proper Study of Mankind* (New York, 1948), p. 83.

[8] For example, the *skimmington, skimmington ride*, by which the citizens of Casterbridge expressed their disapproval of the behaviour of Lucetta. Thomas Hardy, *The Mayor of Casterbridge*, chapter 39.

from southern England made in 1938 by the late Dr. Guy S. Lowman, Jr.
Furthermore, all British citations in the *OED* indicate literary rather than folk
usage; the earliest occurrence given is 1745, in a translation of Bayle's dictionary
of French; the best known British occurrence is still in the sub-title of the
magazine *Punch; or, The London Charivari*, which began its career in 1841 as
a British analogue to the earlier *Charivari*, a humorous magazine in Paris.

In contrast with its literary occurrence in the British Isles, the word—
whether in the etymological orthography *charivari* or in something approxi-
mating a phonemic spelling—had been domesticated in (English-speaking)
North America as a folk word for a folk custom sometime before 1805. A
Pittsburgher transplanted to New Orleans, a city already considerably Ameri-
canized by the heavy river traffic, thus commented on the custom:

> Masquerades have ceased here since eight or nine years past; but *sherri-varries*
> are still practiced. They consist in mobbing the house of a *widow* when she marries;
> and they claim a public donation as a gift. When Madame Don Andre was married,
> she had to compromise by giving to the outdoor mass three thousand dollars in
> gold coin! On such occasions the mob are ludicrously disguised. In her case there
> were effigies of her late and present husband in the exhibition drawn in a cart:
> there her former husband lays in a coffin, and the widow is personated by a living
> person and sits near it. The house is mobbed by thousands of the people of the
> town, vociferating and shouting with loud acclaim; hundreds are seen on horse-
> back; many in disguises and masks; and all have some kind of discordant and
> noisy music, such as old kettles, and shovels, and tongs, and clanging metals can
> strike out. Every body looks waggish, merry, and pleased. Very genteel men can
> be recognized in such a melee. All civil authority and rule seems laid aside. This
> affair, as an extreme case, lasted *three entire days*, and brought in crowds from
> the country! It was made extreme because the second husband was an unpopular
> man, of humble name, and she was supposed to have done unworthily. Their
> *resistance* to yield *any homage* to the mob, caused the *exaction*, and the whole sum
> was honorably given to the orphans of the place. At a later period, Edward
> Livingston, esq., was *sherri-varried* here; on which occasion the parties came out
> promptly to the balcony and thanked the populace for their attention, and invited
> them to walk into the court-yard and partake of some of their prepared cheer.
> The compliment was recieved with acclamations and good wishes for many years
> of happiness, and the throng dispersed, none of the genteel partaking of the
> refreshment. When a *sherri-varrie* is announced, it is done by a running cry
> through the streets, as we cry, fire! fire! and then every man runs abroad, carrying
> with him any kind of clanging instrument, or any kind of grotesque mask or
> dress. All this comes from an indisposition to allow ladies *two chances* for husbands,
> in a society where so few single ladies find even one husband! a result, it is to be
> presumed, of the concubinage system so prevalent here.[9]

The present distribution of *shivaree* and other terms for the custom is
shown on the accompanying map. It is common to all of Canada and much of

---

[9] John F. Watson, "Notitia of Incidents at New Orleans in 1804 and 1805," *American
Pioneer*, II (1843), 229.

the United States. Only in the Eastern seaboard states and parts of the South is the word seldom encountered.[10]

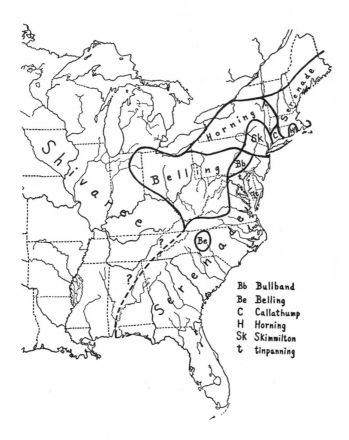

Bb Bullband
Be Belling
C   Callathump
H   Horning
Sk Skimmilton
t   tinpanning

[10] The data on which this study is based has been gathered from the files for the linguistic atlases of New England, the Middle Atlantic states, and the South Atlantic states; from records collected under the direction of Professor Albert H. Marckwardt (University of Michigan) for the North Central states, under the direction of Professor Harold B. Allen (University of Minnesota) for the Upper Midwest, and by Professor Henry M. Alexander (Queens University, Kingston, Ontario) for the Maritime Provinces; from field records made for local studies by Mrs. W. R. Barrett (University of North Carolina) in southeastern Alabama, by Professor James B. McMillan (University of Alabama) in east–central Alabama, by Professor C. M. Wise and graduate students under his direction (Louisiana State University) in Louisiana, and by Professor Lorenzo D. Turner (Roosevelt College, Chicago) in the Gullah Negro communities of the South Carolina and Georgia coast; from studies of regional vocabulary made by Professor A. L. Davis (*A Word Atlas of the Great Lakes Region*, University of Michigan dissertation, 1948), Professor E. Bagby Atwood (University of Texas) and Professor R. M. Lumiansky (Tulane University); from Harold Wentworth's *American Dialect Dictionary* (New York, 1941); and from additional information furnished by Professors McMillan, Wise, E. F. Haden (University of Texas), Louise Pound (University of Nebraska), Ben W. Black (University of Kentucky), R. L. Ramsay (University of Missouri), Carroll E. Reed

On the seaboard there is a multiplicity of words: *serenade*, which is general in the coastal South and in eastern New England; *tin-panning*, restricted to the Chesapeake Bay area and the neighborhood of Jacksonville, Florida; *bull-band(ing)* in the Pennsylvania German sector; *skimmilton* or *skimmerton* in the Hudson Valley; *belling* in most of Pennsylvania, West Virginia, Ohio, and the mountain districts of North Carolina; *salute* in eastern Nova Scotia; *callathump*, possibly a Yale College word, confined to Connecticut, with a few instances in the Yankee settlement area of New York; and *horning*, found in Rhode Island and in derivative settlements in western New England and upstate New York. *Shivaree* is extremely rare in these Eastern states, occurring only in those parts of New York and northern New England which are adjacent to Canada, where it is known from New Brunswick westward, and in the southwest corner of Virginia.[11]

In the secondary settlement areas—the Great Lakes region and the Mississippi Valley—*shivaree* is clearly the dominant term. Of the words which were brought to the interior by the westward movement, only *belling*, *horning*, and *callathump* seem to have survived. The first of these is common in Ohio and parts of Indiana, but rare elsewhere; *horning* has become established in most of the Yankee settlement area of New York State and Michigan—where it is used beside *shivaree*—and *callathump* is occasionally found in the expression *callathumpian band* or *callathumpian parade*, generally used of a children's procession with false faces, especially on the Fourth of July.[12] *Serenade* was occasionally given by Midwestern informants, but usually for a rather dignified celebration.

(University of Washington), David W. Reed (University of California), and Mr. John G. Mutziger, United States Board of Geographical Names.

[11] Whatever the local term, one may observe certain common features of the practice. It is now not confined to second marriages or to unpopular persons, but is a normal procedure in the community; in fact, the absence of such revelry may indicate that the couple is not fully accepted in the community. The celebration is no longer associated with consummation of the marriage, but is often deferred until the return of the couple from their honeymoon. Open resentment of the practice on the part of the newly married couple intensifies the noisemaking and other teasing. The noisemakers are customarily placated by an invitation to an informal supper, often prepared in advance, in anticipation of the revelry, gifts of beer and cigars, or a money contribution (usually the price of a keg of beer).

Noisemaking apparatus utilized for the celebration includes dishpans, cowbells, horns, and other bits of household and farm hardware, muskets and shotguns and other firearms (in the South, where rural houses usually lack basements and are built on pillars, the firearms are often emplaced and discharged at a position calculated by the revelers to be directly underneath the nuptial bed), suspended circular saws, homemade cannon (often fashioned of old anvils), and long strands of catgut stretched over barrel tops or between tree limbs and the house.

[12] The use of the term *callathump* for a procession with false faces may indicate that the wearing of masks was formerly a part of the merrymaking. The use of masks is noted only in the description of the New Orleans celebration.

George Phillips in his paper, "Ueber den Ursprung der Katzenmusiken" (1849), in *Vermischte Schriften* (Vienna, 1860), III, 26–92, gives an exhaustive treatment of the custom of medieval France, listing the following characteristics: (1) the participants wear masks; (2) the masked people make a great deal of noise; (3) the couple must pay for their release; (4) the custom was forbidden under threat of excommunication and fines.

In the entire Mississippi Valley from Minnesota and Wisconsin to the Louisiana Gulf *shivaree* is the ordinary term for the custom. Only in southeastern Alabama is the word rare, and this is adjacent to the Georgia *serenade* area. West of the Mississippi to the West Coast *shivaree* seems to be prevalent with only sporadic occurrences of any of the other terms. It is interesting to note that the term is more widely known in the northern part of the Pacific Coast than in California, possibly because the area was settled by a more homogeneous population, predominantly rural. Further evidence of the extent to which the term has been domesticated is the fact that *shivaree* has been borrowed into some of the American-Scandinavian dialects.[13]

Though the custom of wild horseplay to haze the bride and groom seems to have been common to all areas of the country so that we do not have to deal with any important change in the culture patterns of the settlers, the term *shivaree* has been borrowed on the folk level by all groups which moved west of the Appalachians. The reasons for this wholesale borrowing of a foreign word seem to be evident in the geographical extension of the native terms. In the secondary settlement areas those native words were in competition with each other as a result of the mixture of Easterners in the new lands, and the borrowing seems to have been a compromise. Furthermore, the most widely spread folk terms of the eastern United States, *horning* and *belling*, are of a makeshift nature; while *serenade* frequently has a more dignified and non-specialized meaning. *Skimmilton*, *bull-band*, and *callathump*, which might have had an appeal because of their distinctiveness, are highly localized in the East.

Other conditions favorable to borrowing were present. There were early settlements of French scattered throughout the area, especially along the waterways, which served as the avenues of approach for the English-speaking frontiersmen and remained the ordinary avenues of commerce until the building of the railroads. In addition, the area was buttressed to the north and to the south by large French communities. In the North the early lake trade with Canada, and the continuing migrations from Canada to the northern parts of the region, served as a constant reinforcement of French influence. In the South the port of New Orleans became the most important outlet for the products of the interior of the country. The flatboat laden with pork and lumber brought the Hoosier, the Sucker, and the Puke to that fascinating city; the river steamer plying the Mississippi, the Ohio, and the Missouri catered to those who could afford a more comfortable kind of transportation. The preceding account of the elaborateness of the New Orleans *sherri-varrie* indicates that it must have had a great appeal to the exuberant spirit of the woodsmen, rivermen, and early farmers; and the elite—or sedate—could not have failed to have been aware of it.

[13] Nils Flaten, "Notes on American–Norwegian with a Vocabulary," *Dialect Notes*, II (1900), 115–126; V. Stefansson, "English Loan-Nouns used in the Icelandic Colony of North Dakota," *Dialect Notes*, II (1903), 354–362; George T. Flom, "English Loanwords in American Norwegian, as Spoken in the Koshkonong Settlement [Dane County], Wisconsin," *American Speech*, I (July, 1926), 541–558.

Dialect geography with its careful techniques of investigation again bears out the shrewd guesses made by some of the earlier scholars who interested themselves in American English. One of these, John S. Farmer, supplies a fitting conclusion to this paper:

Chiravari, a noisy serenade to which the victims of popular dislike are subjected; a custom universally known but bearing different names according to locality. Discordant sound-producing instruments, such as tin pots, kettles, drums, etc., are employed. The custom is known under the name *chivaree* (pronounced chevaree) in all parts of Canada and the States originally colonized by the French.[14]

We would need only to augment the phrase "victims of popular dislike" to "wedding couples and occasionally victims of popular dislike."

[14] John S. Farmer, *Americanisms Old and New* (London, 1889), p. 140.

16

'Crocus Bag': A Problem in Areal Linguistics

WALTER S. AVIS

IN HIS *A Word Geography of the Eastern United States* Dr. Hans Kurath offers the following distributional statement:

> *Croker sack, crocus sack* is in common use (1) in the southern parts of the Virginia Piedmont, (2) in South Carolina and Georgia (also in Wilmington at the mouth of the Cape Fear), and (3) on Martha's Vineyard off Cape Cod.[1]

The fuller records now available in the *Linguistic Atlas* files lend overwhelming support to the statement for South Carolina and Georgia, and indicate that northeastern Florida should also be included. In fact, available data provide us with a full and accurate picture of the dissemination of this lexical item throughout the eastern United States. We can now do more than map the occurrence of *crocus sack* as a lexical variant of *burlap bag*; we can demonstrate how the *Atlas* records may be used in solving linguistic problems such as those posed by this dialect term.

Since *A Word Geography* was intended to deal only with lexical variants, in this case of the term *burlap bag*, little attempt appears to have been made to distinguish between such sub-variants as *croker sack* (*-bag*) and *crocus sack* (*-bag*).[2] Such distinctions would, of course, be of little importance in such a study. They are not, however, unimportant in themselves, for they point up an interesting and complex linguistic situation. Not only do the terms occur in the lexical variants represented orthographically above, they also occur in several phonetic shapes, the examination of which reveals a well substantiated

Reprinted by permission from *American Speech* 30.5–16 (1955). The author is Professor of English at the Royal Military College of Canada. He is also editor-in-chief of *The Dictionary of Canadianisms* and president of the Canadian Linguistic Association.

[1] Ann Arbor: University of Michigan Press, 1949, p. 57. Sporadic occurrences were also recorded in northern coastal Maine, a relic area.

[2] See Figure 71, where the entry reads "*croker sack* (also *crocus sack*)" and Figure 32, where the entry reads "*croker sack* 'burlap bag' "; on p. 41 of the text the same synonyms are given. I can find no reference whatever to the *-bag* variants, which are quite common in the field records for South Carolina.

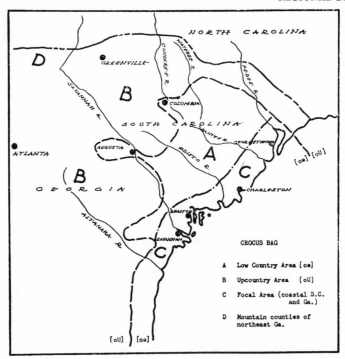

Figure 16.1.

process of linguistic change. At the same time, the results of this examination may throw some light on the historical origins of this curious term, the etymology of which, according to the *Dictionary of Americanisms*,[3] is "obscure."

The ideal region for this investigation is that represented in Figure 16.1— all of South Carolina and adjacent Georgia, as far west as Atlanta and including all the coastal counties. Several weighty reasons have dictated this choice: (1) the region contains two distinct dialect areas and therefore a transition area helpfully less stable than the flanking focal areas; (2) the region shows a high incidence of the terms in question; (3) the field records contain a wealth of evidence, simply because the fieldworker, Raven I. McDavid, Jr., consistently recorded as many variants as he could elicit, many of them observed in the informants' off-guard conversation. Moreover, Dr. McDavid has included in the work sheets many pertinent comments volunteered by informants.

For the purpose of this study, one of the most significant linguistic features

[3] Henceforth referred to simply as the *DA*. Other abbreviations used in this paper are: *OED*, the *Oxford English Dictionary*; *NID*, Webster's *New International Dictionary*; *DN*, *Dialect Notes*; *PADS*, *Publications of the American Dialect Society*.

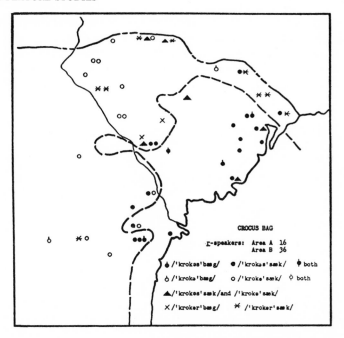

Figure 16.2.

of the region is the presence of speakers who pronounce a retroflexed (or constricted) *r* and speakers who do not. Another and more consistent feature is a
marked difference among the speakers of different areas in the actualization of
the /o/ phoneme. The isophone shown on Figure 16.1 sets off the speakers who
use an ingliding diphthong (Area A) in the word *stove* from those who use an
upgliding diphthong (Area B). This line probably constitutes a dialect boundary,
coinciding as it does with the lexically determined division between low
country and upstate South Carolina established by Dr. Kurath.[4] In a very
loose way this boundary approximates an *r*-isophone, inasmuch as the low-
country dialect area is predominantly *r*-less. Figure 16.2 shows the occurrence
of retroflection in all or any of the words *core, hoarse, mourning, porch,* and *croker,*
only those speakers being considered for whom some variant of *crocus bag* was
recorded. The symbols show the variant of *crocus bag* recorded for these speakers.
It should be added that very slight constriction is the rule for those low-country
speakers who are not completely *r*-less. Conversely, there are many *r*-less
speakers in the non-low-country dialect area. The importance of this dialect
boundary will become clear as the discussion proceeds.

[4] Kurath, *op. cit.,* Figs. 2 and 3. These two speech types are identified in some detail
by Raven I. McDavid, Jr., in "Application of the *Linguistic Atlas* Method to Dialect Study
in the South–Central Area," *Southern Speech Journal,* X (1949), 1–6.

Represented by distinctive symbols on Figure 16.3 are all the variants of *crocus bag* recorded for this region. Altogether, 220 responses were elicited from 180 informants. The discrepancy indicates that some informants (37) used more than one variant. The seven variants are distributed as shown in Table 16.1, where the occurrences in the low-country dialect area (Area A) are shown separately from those elsewhere (Area B):

TABLE 16.1: AREAL DISTRIBUTION OF VARIANTS

Variants	Area A	Area B	Total
/ˈkrokəs ˈsæk/	61	31	92
/ˈkrokəs ˈbæg/	46	4	50
/ˈkrokə ˈsæk/	16	45	61
/ˈkrokə ˈbæg/	1	4	5
/ˈkrokəsæk ˈbæg/	1	0	1
/ˈkrokər ˈsæk/	0	10	10
/ˈkrokər ˈbæg/	0	1	1
Total	125	95	220

If we consider the region as a whole, that is, without regard for the dialect boundary, these figures suggest an overwhelming preference for /ˈkrokəs ˈsæk/ and the obviously similar /ˈkrokə ˈsæk/ (154 of the 220 responses). If, however, we consider the distribution in terms of dialect areas, a significantly different situation presents itself. In the low country there is a relatively high incidence of /ˈkrokəs ˈbæg/, a term which appears but rarely outside this area. The four instances shown for Area B occur fairly close to the dialect boundary, that is, in the transition area. Again, there are no instances of /ˈkrokər ˈsæk/ or /ˈkrokər ˈbæg/ in the low-country area, even among the several speakers for whom constriction is recorded. On the other hand, Area B shows a high incidence of /ˈkrokə ˈsæk/, even among speakers for whom marked constriction is regularly recorded.

Since Table 16.1 does not take unsettled usage into account, being based on the total number of responses, the evidence is recast in Table 16.2 to show the number of speakers from whom more than one variant was elicited. All such cases are appropriately symbolized in Figure 16.3.

Table 16.2 reveals that the bulk of unsettled usage in the low-country area involves the variants /ˈkrokəs ˈsæk/ and /ˈkrokəs ˈbæg/. There is surprisingly little fluctuation between /ˈkrokəs ˈsæk/ and /ˈkrokə ˈsæk/ in this area. This fluctuation is most prominent on either side of the dialect boundary, while the former predominates in the coastal strip from Georgetown to Beaufort (Area C) in South Carolina. If we could assume that this Charleston focal area is that from which the expression spread, we might offer the hypothesis that an original form /ˈkrokəs ˈbæg/ passed through the following stages of development:[5]

[5] See McDavid, "Application of the *Linguistic Atlas* Method," *op. cit.*, p. 2 and n. 2, where the focal area of the low country is said to be "the strip within forty miles of tide-

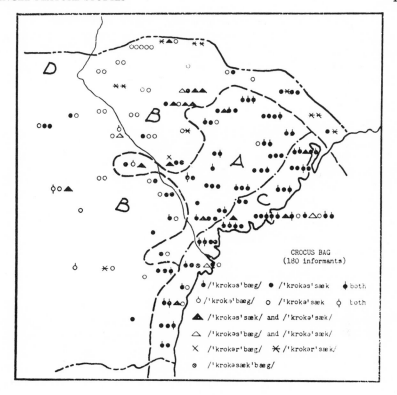

Figure 16.3

1 /'krokəs 'bæg/ became /'krokəs 'sæk/ (by substitution of a synonym for the second morpheme), which became /'krokə 'sæk/ (by the coalescence of adjacent and like consonants and the establishment of a new syllable boundary), which became /'krokə 'bæg/ (by substitution again). These steps account for the variants in Area A, except for /'krokəsæk 'bæg/, a rather striking hybrid.

2 In Area B, where the term seems to have become established in the third form of the above progression, /'krokə 'sæk/ became /'kroker 'sæk/ (among some r-speakers, by a commonplace analogy, namely, the "intrusive-r" process), which became /'krokər 'bæg/ (by substitution again).[6]

water, from the Waccamaw Neck to the Savannah River." A focal area is an area whose economical, political, or social prestige has led to the spread of its speech forms into surrounding areas.

[6] A native of Toronto, Canada, I had known the word *khaki* for years (for some of them I had been garbed in the material) before I learned that the dictionary pronunciation was /'kɑki/ and not /'karki/. In a spot check of 100 Canadians, most of them at the college level and coming from all parts of Canada, more than 95 percent used /'karki/, yet no dictionary that I can find recognizes such a pronunciation.

TABLE 16.2: SINGLE AND MULTIPLE RESPONSES

Variants	Area A	Area B	Total
Single responses			
/'krokəs 'sæk/	39	21	60
/'krokəs 'bæg/	28	1	29
/'krokə 'sæk/	7	33	40
/'krokə 'bæg/	1	2	3
/'krokər 'sæk/	0	10	10
/'krokər 'bæg/	0	0	0
/'krokəsæk 'bæg/	1	0	1
Subtotal	76	67	143
Multiple responses			
/'krokəs 'sæk/ or /'bæg/	15	1	16
/'krokəs 'sæk/ or /'krokə–/	6	8	14
/'krokə 'sæk/ or /–'bæg/	0	1	1
/'krokə 'sæk/ or /'krokəs 'bæg/	2	1	3
/'krokə 'sæk/ or /'krokəs 'sæk/ or /'krokəs 'bæg/	1	0	1
/'krokəs 'sæk/ or /'krokə–/ or /'krokər 'bæg/	0	1	1
/'krokə 'sæk/ or /'krokə 'bæg/ or /'krokəs 'bæg/	0	1	1
Sub-total	24	13	37
Total number of informants	100	80	180

This hypothesis looks like a neat proposition, coinciding as it does with the distribution of the variants in moving from the coast to Area B. A number of facts support the assumption that the term spread from the focal area: (1) the variant /'krokəs 'bæg/ occurs most commonly in the focal area, an area of primary settlement; (2) the assumed derivative /'krokəs 'sæk/ occurs both in the focal area and, more frequently, inland in Area A, often in free variation with /'krokəs 'bæg/; (3) the assimilated development /'krokə 'sæk/, which occurs but rarely in the focal area, is the most common form in the inland areas of secondary settlement.

As might be expected, the transition area between A and B in South Carolina reflects a great deal of unsettled and divided usage[7] between /'krokəs 'sæk/ and /'krokə 'sæk/.

Moreover, the term /'krokə 'sæk/ is usual and settled in those parts of Area B most distant from the focal area. One informant (in Atlanta, Georgia) insisted on /'krokə 'sæk/, refusing to accept /'krokəs 'sæk/ as a possible variant. It is also significant that there are only five cases of /'krokə 'bæg/, a development still further removed from the original form. The latter form occurs only once in Area A, and then on the very fringe of the dialect boundary (Augusta, Georgia).

Although there are 52 *r*-speakers in the region under discussion, only 10

---

[7] The term *divided usage* refers to variation within communities.

use /'krokər 'sæk/, all of them offering the term as a single response. The form furthest removed from the original, /'krokər 'bæg/, is recorded only once—as one of three responses from the same informant. It is significant, however, that the informant (Aiken Co., S.C.) used this form in his free conversation. None of the 16 r-speakers in Area A use /'krokər-/; in fact, only four of these use /'krokə 'sæk/, three of them in free variation with /'krokəs 'sæk/. Most significantly, 25 of the 36 r-speakers in Area B use other forms, 13 of them /'krokə-/ without constriction.

This analysis suggests that all variants of the term are relatively new in the area outside the low country. In fact, several informants in northwest South Carolina claimed that /'krokə 'sæk/ is a modern term for the older *tow sack*. Furthermore, the term is not recorded at all in the mountain counties of northeast Georgia (Area D) where dialectal influence from the coast is relatively slight.[8] On the other hand, the term *tow sack* is general only in northwest South Carolina and northeast Georgia, that is, in Area B. Only twice does it occur in Area A and then only as a variant of /'krokəs 'bæg/. Furthermore, two informants near the dialect boundary, in Area B, claim that *tow sack* is a modern term; these claims suggest that this term has spread southward from the north and northwest of the area under examination.[9]

Granting that the foregoing argument offers some support for the assumption that the direction of dissemination was from the coast inland, what evidence is there that the oldest form was /'krokəs 'bæg/? First, the comments of the informants might be considered, one of whom (McIntosh County, Georgia) responded with /'krokəs 'sæk/ but added, 'we used to call 'em *crocus bags*." A Beaufort County, South Carolina, informant, a Negro remarked that *crocus bag* was an old term, *crocus sack* a new one. Another informant, in Georgetown, South Carolina, stated that "the Negroes know 'em as *crocus bags*." If it is "likely that many relic forms ... are better preserved in the speech of some American Negro groups,"[10] then there may be some significance in the last two comments. But the responses of the 12 Negroes for whom the term is recorded seem to conform to the practice of the other informants in their respective communities. There is certainly no unanimity in their responses, nor should we expect that there would be.[11]

To these straws of "supporting evidence" may be added the fact that the earliest citation in the *DA*, 1699 (cited in the *OED* as well), refers to a "Crocus Ginger-bag." The *DA* also has "sew him up in a crocus bag" cited for 1790. On the other hand, there appears to be no citation for *crocus sack* earlier than

[8] See McDavid, "Application of the *Linguistic Atlas* Method," *op. cit.*, p. 2.

[9] See Kurath, *op. cit.*, Figure 71, for the distribution of *tow sack* and other synonyms (including *crocus sack*) in the eastern United States.

[10] Raven I. McDavid, Jr., and Virginia Glenn McDavid, "The Relationship of the Speech of American Negroes to the Speech of Whites," *American Speech*, XXVI (1951), 13.

[11] *Ibid.*, *passim*, and the writings of Lorenzo D. Turner referred to in this important article.

1926,[12] though *croker sack* is cited in the *DA* for 1908 (*DN*, III, 302), without phonetic indication of the pronunciation.

No doubt it is quite pointless to push the matter further, for it really matters very little whether *crocus bag* or *crocus sack* was the earlier form. Certainly the overwhelming weight of evidence establishes /ˈkrokəs-/ as the first element of the original compound. It remains to propose an etymology for this word.

There are two suggestions which ought to be dealt with at once. A colleague of mine, long resident in South Carolina, suggested that the term might come from the combination of *croaker* and *sack*. The croaker is a "small but important food fish of the gulf coast and the Atlantic south of Cape Cod" (*NID*). The first citation in the *OED* is 1637; the first U.S. citation in the *DAE* in 1676. It would seem that the habitat of this fish coincides with the range of distribution for *crocus sack* in the eastern United States and that the term *croaker* was current at an early enough date to become established in the areas of primary settlement. Against this etymology, however, are several arguments which make it extremely unlikely: (1) there is no record of this combination in the dictionaries; (2) the croaker is known along the entire coast, while the term *crocus sack* is used only in several well defined dialect areas; (3) the phonological development /ˈkrokə ˈsæk/ becomes /ˈkrokəs ˈsæk/ (a necessary step toward /ˈkrokəs ˈbæg/, be it noted) is much less probable than the reverse process. Moreover, the widespread incidence of /ˈkrokə ˈsæk/ in *r*-speaking areas would argue against association with *croaker*.[13]

The second suggestion appeared as a footnote to F. W. Bradley's "A Word List from South Carolina," and was offered by one of the contributors to his files.[14] According to this theory, *crocus sack* may come from

the croaker's sack of the ship surgeon into which dismembered portions of wounded men were dumped . . . for tossing overboard after a battle, to *croak*, in London slang, meaning to die, and the surgeon, or ship's doctor being known as the *croaker*. . . . EDD also gives *croaker*, a corpse, and *croak*, to kill.

Ingenious as this suggestion may be, the same arguments tell against it as told against the fish story, if anything with even more force. Apart from the fact that the context of *croaker's sack* was slangily technical and very much limited in distribution, the term does not lend itself easily to the process of linguistic change suggested by the evidence at the beginning of this discussion. Granting that *croaker's sack* became established in an *r*-less area, we are faced with the change process /ˈkrokəz ˈsæk/ becomes /ˈkrokəs ˈsæk/ becomes /ˈkrokə ˈsæk/.

---

[12] Harold Wentworth, *American Dialect Dictionary* (New York, 1944); Wentworth records as variants *cruckus bag* (B.W.I., *c.* 1880–1941) and *coker sack* (western Fla., 1895), neither of which were encountered in the *Atlas* records.

[13] The *NID* lists *crocus* as a local U.S. variant of *croaker*, but does not locate it. This form probably developed from the plural *croakers* as pronounced in *r*-less areas.

[14] *PADS*, No. 14 (1950), 23–24, n. 2. This word list includes *crocus-sack* and *croker sack* but no *bag* variants.

This sequence is more complex than the one suggested for *crocus sack*, since an assimilation of /z/ to /s/ rather than /s/ to /s/ is implied. Moreover, the high incidence of /'krokəs 'bæg/ is difficult to account for, unless we assume a universal change in the first step of the process and a substitution of *bag* for *sack* after the semantic content of the original term had been completely forgotten. Again, there is no record of /'krokəz 'sæk/ or /'krokərz 'sæk/, for that matter, in current use. Finally, there is no record of widespread general use of this term at any time.[15]

There seems no other course but to return to *crocus* /'krokəs/ as the original first element of the compound. The *OED*, the *DA*, and the *NID* all agree on this point. The first (sense 5), however, derives the word from *crocus*, an obsolete synonym of *saffron*; the American dictionaries state that the origin is obscure or uncertain. Certainly there is no evidence in the American citations to suggest any connection with saffron. Nor is there any evidence in the *Atlas* field records (at least for the area under discussion) to suggest that any of the informants recognize any such connection.

There were, nevertheless, a number of responses to the question: "What is a *crocus sack*?" Most attempted a definition by comparing it with similar articles, e.g. "Yankees call them *burlap bags*." Only two informants included a reference to the material in their definition. One said *crocus sacks* were made of "jute," the other, of "crocus stuff."

The identification of *crocus* with a kind of coarse, heavy cloth is well attested in America. The earliest citation in the *DA* is dated 1689, "Here is great want of . . . Crocos to make Straw beds" (*Maine Doc. Hist.* IV, 458). In addition, there are several citations of attributive uses of the word during the eighteenth century: *crocus-apron, -shirt, -breeches*. Even the earliest citation in which the element *bag* occurs suggests that *crocus* refers to the material: 1699, J. Dickenson, *God's Protecting Providence*, 35 "He gott some Canvass and Crocus ginger-baggs . . ."[16] We can only conclude that, so far as the recorded history of *crocus bag* in America is concerned, the first element refers to the material of the bag and not what it holds, or did hold when the term was first coined (cf. *paper bag* as against *sugar bag*).

Does it follow from the above evidence that the *OED* editors were in error in relating the first element of *crocus bag* to the *crocus* which is a synonym of *saffron*? The editors of the *DA* and those of the *NID* imply an affirmative answer to this question when they reclassify the term and label it "origin obscure."

[15] Oddly enough, the *OED* has a citation for *crocus*, "a quack doctor" (slang, 1877); and *crocus* or *crocus metallorum* (1785), "a nickname for the surgeons of the army and navy."

[16] The *OED* has a citation from J. Dickenson, *Journal of Travels*, p. 30: "[For clothing] I . . . had a Crocus Ginger-bag." The *DAE* cites *God's Protecting Providence*, p. 35: "I with others had each a Crocus Ginger-bagg." The two titles would appear to designate the same work. Dickenson appears to have been a traveller in America. His use of the term leaves in doubt the question whether *crocus* as the name for a material was native to America or whether it had been current in England. See Dr. Mathews' comments in the *DA*.

Nevertheless, a case can be made for the etymology offered by the *OED*, namely, that the *crocus* in *crocus bag* originally referred to saffron and not to any kind of material. Although the following argument is far from invulnerable, it is advanced in the hope that someone may have further evidence which will strengthen it or, failing this, that someone will have the kindness to put forward a more acceptable solution.

The term *crocus*, according to the *OED*, is from Latin *crocus* from Greek *krókos*, the crocus, and its product saffron: apparently of Semitic origin. *Crocus*, in its widest sense, is the generic name of a species of "hardy dwarf bulbous plants," indigenous to south and central Europe and the Near East. Since ancient times the word has also been used as a synonym for *saffron*, the product of one variety of the species. Saffron, or crocus, appears to have been an important commodity in ancient times and later, being widely used as a dyestuff and as an ingredient in early medicines and in cookery. That the commodity was known to the Anglo-Saxons is attested by the *OED* citation of OE *croh* (saffron) from the *Leechdoms* (*c.* 1000). The next *OED* citation, from Trevisa (1398), "saffron highte Crocus and is an herbe," suggests that *crocus* was not unknown as a synonym for saffron during the fourteenth century.

Although the *OED* states that *crocus* was "not known as an Eng. name to the 16th c. herbalists," the term *croker*, a cultivator or seller of saffron, is cited from Harrison's *England*, the date of which is 1577.[17] The *OED* has two later citations of *crocus* under the meaning "saffron": 1659, "Half a Crown in Crocus and Squills Wine"; and 1710, "Two Bales of Crocus" (London *Gazette*, No. 4658). Since the recorded usage in this sense ends here, the form has been duly marked "obsolete."[18]

If the term did become obsolete during the eighteenth century, the rapid decline and final extinction of saffron production in England may have been a contributing cause. According to the *Encyclopaedia Britannica* (14th ed.), following Hakluyt, saffron "was brought into England from Tripoli by a pilgrim, who hid a stolen corm in the hollow of his staff. It was especially cultivated near Histon in Cambridgeshire and in Essex at Saffron Walden, its cultivators being called 'crokers.' " It appears that saffron culture was dead by 1768 in England because of fungus growth.

Moreover, saffron was fast losing importance as a commodity. Since it has no therapeutic value, it was not in demand by pharmacists, and since cheaper, more easily produced dyes were being developed, its most important attraction for earlier traders was no longer significant. Thus with its referent no longer under cultivation in England and reduced to a relatively unimportant role in modern commerce (i.e. as an herb used in cooking), the term *crocus* in this sense appears to have been completely displaced by *saffron*.

[17] It should be pointed out that the *OED* has a 1578 citation, "Saffron is called . . . in latine *Crocus*," and another, dated 1599, of the same import.

[18] As the editor of the *DA* points out, the 1710 citation could refer to material, as in *crocus shirt*, for example.

Yet the term was not obsolete during the seventeenth and eighteenth centuries in England. It might well have been more common as a semi-technical "trade" term around the warehouses of such a port as London (cf. the London *Gazette* citation mentioned above). And the attributive use of the term in *crocus bag* might have developed in this environment.[19] If it did, we should not be surprised if it found its way to America at an early date, to become current in such long-established ports as Richmond, Virginia, Wilmington, North Carolina, Charleston, South Carolina, and Savannah, Georgia. These cities are the foci of the very dialect areas in which the term *crocus bag* (or its variants) is still flourishing. That the term was once known in New England is suggested by its occurrence on Martha's Vineyard, a repository of many relic forms once widespread in eastern New England.[20]

In spite of the many "if's" in the above explanation, the hypothesis seems neither impossible nor improbable. Once it is granted that *crocus bag* immigrated to early American colonial ports through trade channels, the proposed history of the term seems reasonable enough. Certainly the analysis of the *Atlas* evidence offered at the beginning of this discussion supports the contention that *crocus bag* reached Charleston early and that /'krokəs/, rather than any of the other forms discussed above, was the form in which it arrived. But, as in the first element of *gunny sack* (*gōn, gōni*, Hindi and Mahratti: Skt. *gōṇī*, "sack"), the original meaning of *crocus* has become obscured, with the result that both now refer to the coarse, woven material of which such bags are made.

[19] The *OED* has two citations of *saffron bag*, dated 1508 and 1540.

[20] And see n. 1 above. It will be recalled that the earliest U.S. citation of *crocus* for the material is localized in Maine, 1689. It is to be expected that these two meanings would exist side by side at some point in their history. It is of course possible that the first element in *crocus bag* had already come to refer to the material rather than to the onetime contents of the bag, that is, before the term reached America. Such a situation would not invalidate the present line of argument.

17

Postvocalic *r* in New England Speech, a Study in American Dialect Geography

BERNARD BLOCH

ONE OF THE FEATURES which distinguishes the so-called Eastern type of American English from the Western or General American type is the pronunciation of the *r* in words like *work, first, girl*. Such words are pronounced in most of the northern United States with an *r*-colored or retroflex vowel, but in a large part of New England without any retroflection. In this paper I shall sketch first the distribution of forms with and without *r* in present day New England speech, and then, as my chief point, the observable drifts in the local dialects of the region.[1] The material for this study is taken from the records of the Linguistic Atlas of New England, which will soon be ready for publication[2].

From the geographical distribution of the *r* in words like *work* (see Chart 17.1) three facts are obvious: (1) that New England cannot be regarded as a single homogeneous dialect area, since western New England, where the pronunciation with *r* is predominant, differs in at least this one important respect from eastern New England, where the *r* is usually silent; (2) that no clear boundary can be drawn between the two sections; (3) that in both sections,

Reprinted by permission of Walter Bloch and of Cercle Linguistique de Copenhague from *Actes du quartième Congrès internationale de linguistes*. Copenhagen: Munksgaard, 1939. Pp. 195–199. At the time of his death the author was Professor of Linguistics at Yale University and editor of *Language*. He had served as assistant editor of *The Linguistic Atlas of New England*.

[1] The sound in question is the reflex of Early ModE ər from ME *ir* (*er*), *ur*, *ür*. For a detailed treatment of the entire problem see my doctoral dissertation, Postvocalic *R* in New England Speech (Brown University 1935), to be published in the Language Dissertations series of the Linguistic Society of America. (The original form of the present paper, as read in Copenhagen, included separate treatment of the *r* in words like *work* and in words like *father*; a sketch of N.E. settlement history; a historical interpretation of the linguistic material; and a reconstruction of the dialects of the original N. E. colonies. The paper was illustrated by seven lantern slides, of which two are reproduced here.)

[2] Cf. Hans Kurath, The Linguistic Atlas of the United States and Canada, in Essai de Bibliographie de Géographie Linguistique Générale, edited by Jos. Schrijnen for the Comité International Permanent des Linguistes, Nimègue 1933; id., The Linguistic Atlas of New England, in Proceedings of the American Philosophical Society 74.3 (1934); Bernard Bloch, Interviewing for the Linguistic Atlas, in American Speech 10.1 (1935).

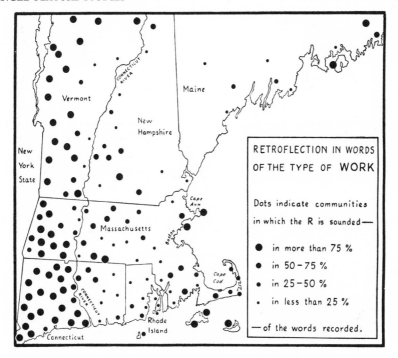

Chart 17.1.

but especially in central and southeastern New England, the usage of many individual speakers is inconsistent.

The area of predominant retroflection, where the pronunciation with *r* is the prevailing type, includes approximately the western third of the territory. Outside this area, in central and eastern New England, there are several "speech islands" where the treatment of *r* is at variance with the practice of the section as a whole. These are Martha's Vineyard and Nantucket, two islands off the coast of Cape Cod; Cape Cod itself, and Cape Ann, till recently two of the most self-contained corners of Massachusetts; a small section in the hill country of south–central New Hampshire; and a cluster of isolated villages along the sparsely settled coast of eastern Maine. In addition to these definite speech islands there is also a rather heavy scattering of exceptional or sporadic forms with *r* turning up in the speech of persons who usually pronounce words of this type without retroflection. Only in the immediate neighborhood of Boston and in the greater part of New Hampshire and Maine is the so-called Eastern pronunciation universal.

The surest guide to the drifts in the spoken language of a region is the difference between older and younger speakers. If we find that in a cluster of several communities or in a whole section the speech of most of the older people

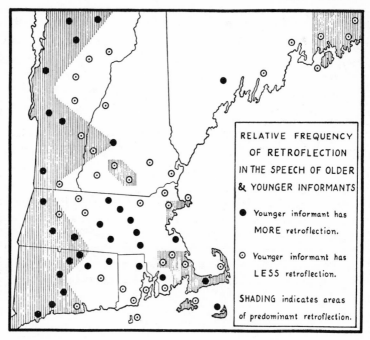

Chart 17.2.

differs in the same way from that of most of the younger ones, we may safely infer that the dialect of the region is in process of change. The Linguistic Atlas of New England provides a firm basis for such inferences. Nearly all the communities investigated for the Atlas are represented by two informants: one of 70 years or more, the other of middle age.

Mapping the distribution of communities where the two speakers disagree in their pronunciation of words like *work* (see Chart 17.2), we observe that in several distinct areas there is a constant difference between the speech of the two generations. (Isolated and exceptional cases cannot be considered here.) In the area of predominant retroflection the pronunciation with *r* is growing still more general; and at the same time it is gaining ground in a large part of the southern Connecticut Valley, which has always been a zone of divided usage.

The opposite type is also active. Throughout the northern Connecticut Valley there is a clustering of communities where the disagreement between older and younger speakers points to a gradual disappearance of the *r*. Similar clusters occur in eastern Maine, in northeastern Massachusetts and the adjoining part of New Hampshire, on Cape Cod and in southern Rhode Island. Note that in nearly all the speech islands along the New England coast where the pronunciation with *r* has been preserved until the present day, retroflection is now giving way to the prevailing type.

Two contrasting dialectal types, then, are spreading vigorously from opposite centers. The focal point for the spreading of the type with silent *r* is clearly the city of Boston and its neighborhood. This is not a new force in the shaping of New England speech; for since the dawn of American history the old Massachusetts Bay Colony and its chief city, Boston, have been the most important center of influence in New England.

The pronunciation with a retroflex vowel, on the other hand, seems to be spreading from the southwestern corner of our territory. Economically and socially, western Connecticut is intimately related to the Hudson Valley and to the vast and populous area beyond; and its speech agrees in many features (including the pronunciation of post vocalic *r*) with that spoken by the majority of Americans in the northern states. For this reason, western Connecticut has come to serve as a kind of "passage area" through which the speech forms of the north–central U.S. filter into the Connecticut Valley. We may say, therefore, that the eastward extension of the pronunciation with *r* reflects not merely the spreading of a single feature from southwestern New England but a gradual victory of the chief type of American English over a specifically provincial dialect.

There is no reason to suppose that these drifts will change their direction. The pronunciation with *r* will doubtless grow still more common in western and central New England; while in eastern New England the forces now at work will continue, finally effecting the complete loss of post vocalic *r* at least in the coastal area. If the spreading of the General American type should then continue as vigorously as at present, it is at least possible that some day the *r* in words like *work* will be reintroduced even in those parts of New England from which it is now disappearing.

18

The "New England Short *o*": a Recessive Phoneme

WALTER S. AVIS

THIS STUDY IS INTENDED TO ILLUMINATE the highly recessive nature of the "New England Short *o*." The varying stability of the feature from word to word and from region to region and the extent of divided and unsettled usage from community to community and speaker to speaker provide an unusual glimpse of a linguistic phenomenon long recognized but never adequately documented.[1]

The data used in this investigation are those of the Linguistic Atlas of the United States and Canada, housed at the University of Michigan; much of the relevant material has been published in the *Linguistic Atlas of New England*,[2] where the phonetic detail for most of the words referred to below may be found. It should be added that much of what follows is taken from my doctoral dissertation, which was written under the direction of Hans Kurath and which dealt primarily with the status of non-upgliding mid-back diaphones throughout the Eastern United States.[3]

One of the major areas of concentration for non-upgliding phonic types in words like *road* and *coat* is New England, where a highly complex situation exists, for here such diaphones occur only in a limited number of phonetic environments, and in a relatively small number of words, virtually none of which show these types exclusively. In view of this complexity, it is impracticable to present the results of the analysis for the area as a whole; the greater part of the discussion will, therefore, be based on the Atlas records for the northeastern region, specifically those of Guy S. Lowman, recorded in eastern Vermont,

Reprinted by permission of the Linguistic Society of America from its journal *Language* 37.544–58 (1961). The author is Professor of English at The Royal Military College of Canada.

[1] See Charles H. Grandgent, From Franklin to Lowell: A century of New England pronunciation, *PMLA* 14.207–39 (1899).

[2] Edited by Hans Kurath, Bernard Bloch, and others; 6 vols. (Providence, 1939).

[3] Walter S. Avis, The mid-back vowels in the English of the eastern United States: A detailed investigation of regional and social differences in phonic characteristics and in phonemic organization (University of Michigan, 1955: unpublished doctoral dissertation, available in microfilm).

New Hampshire, northeastern Massachusetts, Maine, and southwestern New Brunswick, Canada.[4]

This limitation, in addition to rendering the data manageable, has several advantages: (1) the area includes a large sample of evidence, some 137 informants in 85 communities; (2) it also includes most of the informants who use ingliding diaphones with a significant degree of regularity; (3) the data are uniform, having been recorded by one fieldworker, one of the most competent of those operating in New England;[5] (4) the problem of fieldworker differences in notation can be bypassed, a problem that is more troublesome at the phonetic than at the phonemic level;[6] (5) the findings for this area provide a reliable index for the incidence of similar diaphones throughout New England, although as one moves westward from the northeastern region and away from the east generally, the feature becomes progressively less common and less stable.

In Northeastern New England, then, a set of upgliding diphthongs is regularly found in words like *ago* and *know*, whereas in words like *road* and *smokestack* similar upglides are found together with a set of very different ingliding or monophthongal types, which do not have the same incidence from word to word and which do not necessarily occur in all words of similar phonetic environment. Thus, the ingliding diphthong occurs widely in *road* but not at all in *rode* and seldom in *Rhode Island*; the related monophthong occurs widely in *smokestack*, less widely in *yoke*, and very rarely in *woke*. Such evidence strongly implies the existence of two phonemes.

The phonetic norm for the stressed vowel in *ago* is a diphthong, beginning in a somewhat lowered mid-back position and ending with a prominent upglide, [oˑu]. It should be noted that neither ingliding diphthongs nor monophthongs occur in *ago* or any other word in which the phones occur word-finally.

A similar set of upgliding diphthongs occurs in *road*, and alongside these occurs a set of ingliding diphthongs and monophthongs. The phonetic norm for the latter set is a diphthong, beginning in a fronted and lowered mid-back position and ending with a prominent inglide, [θə]. The monophthongal types differ from the diphthongs only in the absence of the inglide. They occur rarely in *road*, more often in *back road*, *side road*, and similar compounds. The diphthongal types occur predominantly in *toad*, *stone*, *coat*, and *boat*, whereas the monophthongal types occur most often in *toadstool*, *stone wall*, *stone walk*, *smokestack*, *folks*, *most*, and *whole*. It should be noted that all such diaphones occur only in checked position.[7]

A study of the diaphones [θə] and [θ] in *road*, *coat*, and *whole* reveals clear

---

[4] The area referred to is substantially that shown as Area 1 among the speech areas of the Atlantic States in Hans Kurath and Raven I. McDavid Jr., *The pronunciation of English in the Atlantic States*, Map 2 (Ann Arbor, 1961). See the line of demarcation drawn on Figure 18.1 below.

[5] See Hans Kurath, Bernard Bloch, Marcus L. Hansen, and Julia Bloch, *Handbook of the linguistic geography of New England* 52–3 (Providence, 1939; second printing 1954).

[6] See Avis 106ff.

[7] For a full description of the diaphones recorded, see Avis 81ff. For a succinct discussion of free and checked vowels, see Kurath and McDavid 3–5.

contrast with the diaphones in *good, caught,* and *hull,* indicating that [θə/θ] do not belong to the phonetically similar and adjacent phonemes /ʊ/, /ɔ/, and /ʌ/. Furthermore, for most speakers the diaphones [θə/θ] are in contrast with [oʊ] diaphones in such identical or analogous environments as *road/rode, coat/shoat, most/coast, home/loam,* and *whole/knoll.* In these pairs the first member usually has [θə/θ]; the second member never has these phones.[8] It follows from the foregoing evidence that [θə/θ] and [oʊ] belong to different phonemes, which will henceforth be referred to as /θ/ and /o/, respectively.[9]

The phoneme /θ/ has two dominant positional allophones, an ingliding diphthong and a monophthong, though the alternation is not necessarily clearcut for every speaker. Probably because of varying prosodic conditions, both types occur to some extent in nearly all the words. Nevertheless, the tendencies are abundantly clear when the total number of responses is taken into consideration: ingliding diphthongs of the type [θə] predominate in monosyllabic words before the front stops /t/ and /d/ and before /n/; monophthongs of the type [θ] predominate before the back stop /k/, before the fricatives /s/ and /z/, and before /m/.[10] The predominance of one allophone or the other appears to vary according to the position of the morpheme containing the phone: if the morpheme is final, as in *wishbone, freestone, clingstone, grindstone, whetstone,* the usual allophone is that commonest in the simplex (e.g. *stone*), in all instances here listed an ingliding diphthong, though it should be observed that the proportion of monophthongs has in all cases increased; if the morpheme is not in utterance-final position the monophthong appears to predominate, as in *smokestack* (100 percent), *railroad station, Rhode Island, toadstool,* and *stone wall.* In the few instances where [θə] or [θ] occur in polysyllabic words, the monophthong also predominates, as in *soldiering, poultry, bonny clabber, harmonica,* and *suppose.* Two other allophones merit mention: a half-long vowel in *home* and, much less commonly, a markedly short vowel in compound words having the relevant morpheme as the first component, e.g. *smokestack, toadstool, stone wall,* and *Rhode Island.*

To make clear the incidence of the phoneme /θ/ in the Atlas materials for the northeastern region the following inventory is presented. It will be convenient to gather the words concerned, all of which have been fully charted for the entire New England area, into four groups: (1) those words of reasonably wide dissemination which often have /θ/, and a number of others which have a relatively low incidence of /θ/ but figure prominently in the discussion; (2) those words for which /θ/ was recorded but which for one reason or another are sparsely represented in the data (sporadically recorded compounds containing simplexes listed in Group 1 are shown in parenthesis after the relevant word in that group); (3) those words of reasonably wide dissemination in which /θ/

[8] See Avis 92 (Table 14) for a detailed listing of such contrasts.

[9] The unitary interpretation of syllabics adopted here has most recently been defended in Kurath and McDavid 3–5. See also Avis 7–8.

[10] See Avis 94 (Table 15) for a statement of the proportional occurrences of these allophones in 32 words, including compounds.

occurs rarely in the data; (4) those words in which /θ/ does not occur at all in the Lowman materials.

GROUP 1. These words form the basis for the greater part of the discussion concerning the status of /ø/: *boat*, (*stone-, motor-*), *coat* (*over-*), *smokestack* (*smoked meat*), *folks* (*home-, kin-*), *most*, '*most* "almost", *toad* (*hop-, tree-*, etc.), *toadstool*, *road* (*dirt-, side-*, etc.), *railroad station*, *Rhode Island*, *home*, *stone* "pit" (*cherry-, peach-*), *stone* "rock" (*-boat, -road*), *stonewall*, *grindstone*, *whetstone* (*soap-*), *wishbone* (*pully-, lucky-*), *holt* "hold", *soldiering* "loafing", *whole*, *yoke*.

GROUP 2. The number of occurrences with /θ/ in total occurrences follows each entry: *goat* 1/1, *open* 4/11, *broken* 1/1,[11] *cloak* 4/5, *kofe* 5/15 (a call to cows), *loads* 26/32, *pogey* 18/78 "menhaden", *scupogue* 1/1 "menhaden", *toast* 1/4, *close to* 36/46 (all instances of *close* /kloz/ have /o/), *suppose* 39/48, *none* 5/5, *colt* 1/1, *hold* 3/17, *poultry* 25/25, *swollen* /swθln/ 21/75, *yolk* 72/105 (/jθlk/; /jok/ without /l/ always has the upglide), *bonny clabber* 54/132, *harmonica* 25/113.[12]

GROUP 3. The number of occurrences with /θ/ in total occurrences follows each entry: *oats* 5/132, *cove* 2/102, *posts* 1/134, *post office* 3/133, *don't* 1/137, *doughnut* 4/137, *sofa* 3/138, *tuberculosis* 1/115.

GROUP 4. Words for which the data are scant are marked with an asterisk: *shoat*, *toted, *write*, *yolk* /jok/, *pokey "haunted", *loafing, *coast*, *ghosts, *wardrobe, *rode*, *blowed*, *growed*, *throwed, *dove*, *drove*, *grove*, *stone*, *close* /kloz/, *clothes*, *froze*, *rose*, *those*, *toes, *loam, *grown*, *coal*, *hole, *goal, *pole*, *rolls, *stole, *swollen* /swolǝn/, *cold*, *old*, *shoulder*, *crocus bag, *grocery*, *hotel*, *motor car*, *motorboat, *over*, *robust, *social*, *soda, *ago*, *blow*, *blowing*, *beau*, *below, *depot*, *doe, *ewe /jo/, *glow worm, *go*, *know*, *low* "moo", *low shoes*, *lowland*, *mowing*, *no, *show, *throw up, *crowbar.

It is obvious from the foregoing inventory that the phoneme /θ/ occurs in a limited number of words and in an even more limited number of environments, substantially those outlined in the statement concerning positional allophones. It is also obvious from Groups 3 and 4 that /θ/ does not occur in word-final position (that is, as a "free vowel") and occurs rarely in polysyllabic words where it precedes a morpheme boundary (*doughnut*) or in so-called open syllables (*sofa*). Even in checked position /θ/ occurs in a relatively small number of words, and its incidence varies strikingly from word to word. With respect to the words in Group 1, those for which there is a meaningful amount of evidence, no speaker uses /θ/ exclusively, and (in the northeastern region) very few use /o/ exclusively. In some of the words the former phoneme predominates throughout the region, in others the latter. In short, unsettled usage is everywhere the rule from word to word and often from utterance to utterance of the same word. Almost everywhere, moreover, the informants in whose speech the /θ/ phoneme is most stable are members of the older and/or the less educated social group, especially those in rural or relatively isolated communities.

[11] Informant 160.2 in Billerica "uses [θ] at home in such words as *coat, broken*, but avoids it in public speaking" (fieldworker's comment).

[12] It appears that /gθnǝ/ in the context *am I going to . . .* occurs surprisingly seldom among a wide variety of pronunciations.

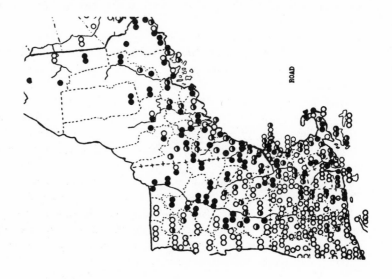

Figure 18.2

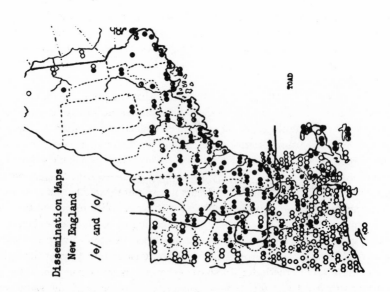

Dissemination Maps
New England
/e/ and /o/

Figure 18.1

204

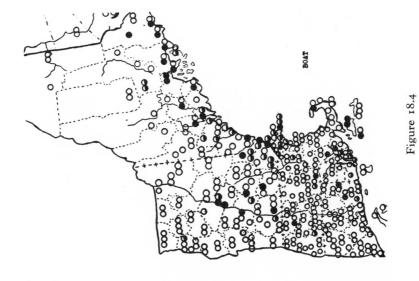

Figure 18.4

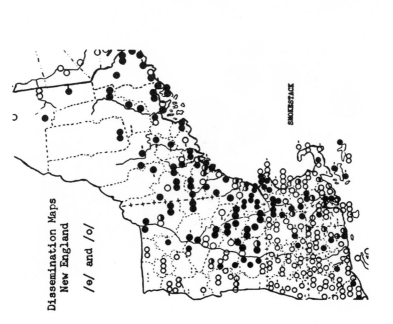

Dissemination Maps
New England

/ɵ/ and /o/

Figure 18.3

205

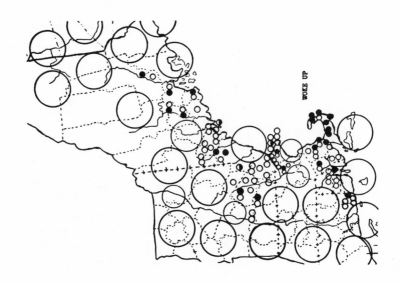

Figure 18.6

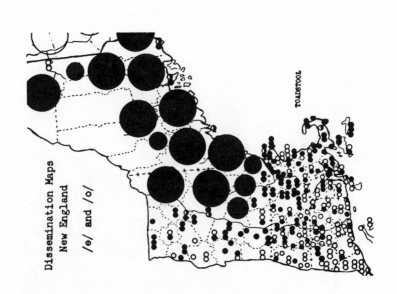

Dissemination Maps
New England

/e/ and /o/

Figure 18.5

206

The evidence for the northeastern region clearly indicates that /θ/ is to a considerable extent recessive and for this reason has a highly complex regional and social dissemination. This conclusion is reinforced when the evidence for the entire New England area is taken into consideration. Figures 18.1–6 show the overall distribution pattern for the words *toad* (Figure 18.1), *road* (18.2), *smokestack* (18.3), *boat* (18.4), *toadstool* (18.5), and *woke up* (18.6).[13] On the maps, a solid circle represents a pronunciation with /θ/, an open circle a pronunciation with /o/, and a half-solid circle pronunciations with both /θ/ and /o/ by the same speaker. The first four maps, showing words in which /θ/ is relatively unstable in the northeastern region, chart the usage of every informant; the last two, showing words in which either /θ/ or /o/ is relatively stable, chart separately only the instances of unsettled or divided usage, but represent the remaining instances by large circles which indicate uniform use of one phoneme or the other.

As appears from the maps, the incidence of /θ/ varies from word to word, often quite markedly even in northeastern New England. Thus /θ/ is much more commonly heard in *road* than in *boat*, in *smokestack* than in *woke up*, and so on. This variation can be grasped more readily by comparing the proportional-response figures in Table 18.1, which shows for the northeastern region the proportion of informants using /θ/, either alone or beside /o/, in each word, as opposed to the proportion using /o/, either alone or beside /θ/. By comparing the entries opposite each word, one can see both the degree of stability of /θ/ in that word and the tendency to recessiveness from word to word. In the table, the first column shows the relative incidence of /θ/, the second shows the proportion of speakers using only that phoneme; comparison of these two figures indicates the extent of unsettled usage in the word. Columns 3 and 4 give corresponding figures for /o/. Column 5 shows the proportion of all informants who used the word in question, with /θ/ or /o/ or both. All figures in the table are percentages.

Table 18.1 shows, for example, that in *toad* /θ/ was used by 90 percent of the informants, whereas in *road* it was used by 81 percent. Moreover, in *toad* /θ/ was used to the exclusion of /o/ by 69 percent of the informants, whereas in *road* the proportion using /θ/ exclusively was only 57 percent. The first comparison indicates that /θ/ is more common in *toad* and the second that the phoneme is also more stable. In both of these words, however, the "short o" is more common than in *Rhode Island* and less common and less stable than in *railroad*, in which 12 and 94 percent, respectively, of the informants responded with /θ/. Further comparisons using other words on the table which have roughly similar phonetic environments will reveal similar disparities, a fact which suggests that the phonetic environments, limited in range though they are, are not the only factor which determines the presence or absence of /θ/ in a given word.

---

[13] The following maps in Kurath and McDavid illustrate other words discussed in this article: 20 *ago*; 30 *coat*, *whole*, and *stone* (*wall*); 121 *ewe* /jo/; 123 *home*; 124 *loam*; 125 *won't*; 126–128 *yolk*.

TABLE 18.1

WORD	/θ/	/θ/ ONLY	/o/	/o/ ONLY	Proportion of informants
holt	97	97	3	3	62
whole	95	89	11	5	89
railroad station	94	94	6	6	60
yolk	93	93	7	7	51
toadstool	93	90	10	7	94
whetstone	93	90	10	7	96
toad	90	69	31	10	97
folks	90	86	14	10	78
grindstone	89	88	12	11	95.5
stone wall	89	86	14	11	98.5
freestone	85	83	17	15	58
stone "pit"	85	68	32	15	96
home	84	80	20	16	95
'most midnight	83	79	21	17	70
road	81	57	43	19	99.5
wishbone	79	72	28	21	94.5
smokestack	75	69	31	25	75.5
coat	74	36	64	26	99
most cheeses	71	61	39	29	88
yoke	62	57	43	38	87
soldiering	53	53	47	47	57
boat	31	15	85	69	81
swollen /swθln/	23	23	77	77	54.5
Rhode Island	12	12	88	88	88
woke up	9	8	92	91	85

The comparative figures on Table 18.1 suggest that prosodic factors also exert an influence on the incidence and stability of /θ/. It will be noticed that when the simplexes containing the phoneme appear as parts of compound words, the stability of /θ/ is regularly greater in the latter; cf. *stone wall, whetstone, grindstone, freestone, toadstool, railroad,* and *Rhode Island,* to which may be added *stoneboat, hoptoad,* and *post office.* The higher stability of /θ/ in such compounds is so regular that it seems reasonable to predict that in *smoke* and *bone,* simplexes not recorded for the Atlas, /θ/ would be both less common and less stable than in *smokestack* and *wishbone,* both of which appear on Table 18.1.

Sentence stress and speed of utterance, not clearly identifiable from Atlas evidence, appear also to have some connection with the stability of the /θ/ phoneme. The high stability of the phoneme in *whole,* taken in the frame *the whole of it,* seems to be a case in point; certainly the presence of /θ/ before final /l/ is most unusual, for *whole* regularly fails to rime with *pole, knoll,* and *hole,* although evidence for the last is scant. Probably the fairly frequent occurrence of /θ/ in *'most anywhere, I suppose so,* and *am I gonna go?* can be attributed to similar obscure influences.

But neither phonetic environment nor prosodic influences account for all of the variations in the stability of /θ/. Certain factors associated with what may be called "social context" seem to have an important bearing on the presence or absence of /θ/. Thus a word current largely in popular or dialectal speech is more likely to retain /θ/ than a word learned in school. Again, a word which occurs in a relatively limited social environment, for example on the farm, in the family circle, or as a variant peculiar to a certain limited speech area, will more probably have /θ/ than a word in wide general use. Finally, /θ/ will be retained longer in words with a relatively low frequency of use than in others which have a high frequency and which, consequently, are more affected by the movies and radio, to say nothing of outside influences of other kinds.

The significance of such factors as these is implied in Table 18.1, where the words with /θ/ are ranked according to the stability of the phoneme.

At the top of the list is *take* (*a*) *holt* (i.e. *hold*), in which 97 percent of the informants responding used /θ/, all of them exclusively. The high degree of stability for /θ/ in this word is undoubtedly due to the social context in which the expression occurs, for the expression itself is colloquial and the pronunciation /hθlt/ for *hold* popular or dialectal. Column 5 reveals that only 62 percent of the informants offered this response, a low yield due in part to the currency of competing variants, but more importantly to the fact that the pronunciation /hθlt/ is relatively uncommon among younger, better-educated informants, especially those in urban areas. It is significant that 20 informants, mostly of this class, offered the expression with the pronunciation /hold/, which like *old* and *cold* has /o/ almost exclusively; /hθld/ occurred only three times in the area.

The fact that /θ/ has a higher incidence and greater stability in *whetstone* than in the simplex *stone* is probably due in part to prosodic factors but also to the different social contexts in which the words are used. The former is strictly a farm word, that is, a word used in a relatively limited environment, whereas the latter has a much wider range and also a much greater frequency of use. Several of the words on the list fall into the same rustic category, as *toadstool*, *stonewall*, and *grindstone*. Moreover, the disparity between the incidence and stability of /θ/ in these words and in such words as *road* and *coat* seems attributable in part to similar influences.

It is illuminating in this regard to compare *toad* and *road* (Table 18.1), both simplexes in which the phoneme precedes the same final consonant. In *toad*, a word of relatively limited milieu and correspondingly low frequency of use, the incidence and stability of /θ/ are quite high; in *road*, which has a much broader milieu and a much higher frequency of use, the incidence and stability of /θ/ are both appreciably lower. Note, however, that certain less widely used terms— *side road*, *dirt road*, *tote road*—occur with /θ/ in the *road* component in the speech of many informants who use /o/ in *road*. Similarly, speakers who use /o/ in *stone* and/or *boat* often use /θ/ in less frequent compounds containing these words, as *stonewall*, *stoneboat*, *steamboat*, *boatlanding*. A speaker may use /o/ invariably in *coat*, but retain /θ/ in the word when it occurs in a particular context, as *coat of paint*.

The position of the preterit *woke* at the bottom of Table 18.1 is striking.

Occurring in the context *woke up* (Figure 18.6), under prosodic conditions making for stability of /θ/, the word has a far lower incidence of that phoneme than *yoke*, which occurs as a simplex and which, moreover, is a book word for many people, the referent having fallen into disuse. Certain facts in the evidence may explain this apparent anomaly.

Throughout the northeastern region the preterit *woke up* competes with the variant *waked*, for which there were 75 responses.[14] Of these, 28 were suggested by the fieldworker, and many of the informants designated the form as "older", "old-fashioned", or "rare"; on the other hand, several who offered *woke up* designated it "modern". *Waked* must have been formerly of much wider dissemination than at present.[15] It is not unlikely that *waked* was displaced relatively late, perhaps through the schools, by *woke up* /wok/. The evidence also shows that of /θ/ and /o/, the latter is the usual, almost invariable, phoneme in verb forms, as *rode, froze, drove,* and *dove,* a fact which again suggests school influence.

The word *boat* (Figure 18.4) is another striking example, ranked near the bottom of Table 18.1. /θ/ is common in this word only among the older, relatively uneducated informants along the Northeast Coast, the very region where the word is apt to have a relatively high frequency of use. Inland, where boats are not so intimately a part of everyday life, /θ/ has almost entirely been replaced by the innovating /o/.

In the northeastern region the /θ/ phoneme occurs to some extent in every community; there are, in fact, only three informants who do not use it at least once (180.2 Marblehead, 2A; 190.4 Haverhill, 2B; and 422.1 Fort Fairfield, 1A).[16] Regional dissemination in this area can be described as general, variations in the incidence of /θ/ being for the most part dependent on the word and on the age or social status of the informant. Nevertheless, there are several communities in which /θ/ appears to have a lower incidence than others in the same general locality. These atypical communities are of two kinds: (1) some have a settlement history distinct from that of neighboring communities; (2) some today are urban rather than rural centers.

Differences in settlement history are clearly responsible for the almost exclusive use of /o/ in 422 Fort Fairfield (see Figure 18.7), which lies on the

[14] See E. Bagby Atwood, *A survey of verb forms in the eastern United States* Figure 20 (Ann Arbor, 1953).   [15] Atwood 25.

[16] Informants for the *Linguistic atlas* are identified by a decimal number, in which the part before the decimal point denotes the community and the part after it the individual informant. They are characterized as follows: Type 1, persons with little or no formal education, little reading, and restricted social contacts; Type 2, persons with better education (usually through high school), wider reading, and more varied contacts; Type 3, persons of cultivated background with superior education (usually through college), wide reading, and extensive contacts; Type A, old, or regarded by the fieldworker as relatively old-fashioned; Type B, young, or regarded as relatively modern. Thus the designation 1A refers to an old man with little or no formal schooling, 3B to a relatively young man with considerable education, and so on. See Kurath, *Handbook* 41–42.

[17] See Kurath, *Handbook*, ch. 3, for an outline of New England settlement history; references to settlement history in this part of the discussion are based on that outline and on the detailed accounts of communities and informants in ch. 4.

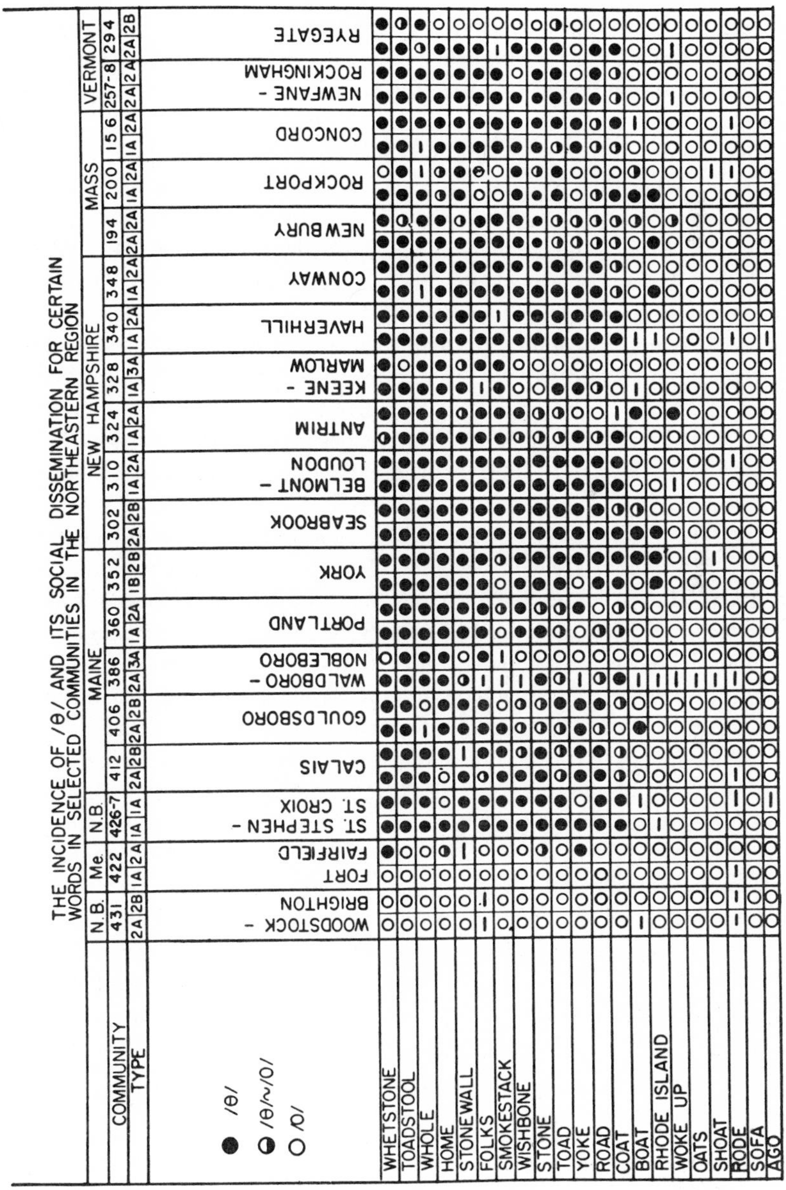
THE INCIDENCE OF /θ/ AND ITS SOCIAL DISSEMINATION FOR CERTAIN WORDS IN SELECTED COMMUNITIES IN THE NORTHEASTERN REGION
● /θ/
◐ /θ/~/o/
○ /o/
COMMUNITY
TYPE
N.B.
Me.
N.B.
MAINE
NEW HAMPSHIRE
MASS
VERMONT
431
422
426-7
412
406
386
360
352
302
310
324
328
340
348
194
200
156
257-8
294
WOODSTOCK - BRIGHTON
FORT FAIRFIELD
ST. STEPHEN - ST. CROIX
CALAIS
GOULDSBORO
WALDBORO - NOBLEBORO
PORTLAND
YORK
SEABROOK
BELMONT - LOUDON
ANTRIM
KEENE - MARLOW
HAVERHILL
CONWAY
NEWBURY
ROCKPORT
CONCORD
NEWFANE - ROCKINGHAM
RYEGATE
WHETSTONE
TOADSTOOL
WHOLE
HOME
STONEWALL
FOLKS
SMOKESTACK
WISHBONE
STONE
TOAD
YOKE
ROAD
COAT
BOAT
RHODE ISLAND
WOKE UP
OATS
SHOAT
RODE
SOFA
AGO

Figure 18.7

Canadian border in Northeastern Maine.[17] Like most of adjacent New Brunswick, where /o/ is generally current in the words under discussion, Fort Fairfield was settled by Loyalists who left the neighborhood of New Jersey and New York at the time of the Revolutionary War. Moreover, the town is both culturally and economically oriented toward New Brunswick rather than toward the more distant economic and cultural centers of New England. It is of interest that the people in Fort Fairfield prefer, according to the fieldworker, to call themselves Americans rather than Yankees.

Another Maine–New Brunswick border town, 424 Fort Kent, similarly reflects Canadian usage, though not as strongly as Fort Fairfield. This community has a mixed settlement history; it was first settled by Acadian French, who were later joined by English-speakers from Kennebec County and New Brunswick. The fieldworker reports that there are few English-speaking families in the community, adding that the informant, though of Yankee stock on both sides of the family, is bilingual, and that certain French traits are evident in his speech. No doubt as part of his Yankee heritage, this informant (Type 2B) retains the New England "short o" in several words in which it has high stability farther south.

In 384 Waldoboro–Nobleboro, Me. (Figure 18.7), a settlement largely German and Scotch–Irish in background, there appears to be another enclave with infrequent /θ/. The Type 3A informant uses the phoneme in only three words, *toadstool*, *home*, and *stonewall* (alongside /o/ in the last). The 2A informant, for whom the record is only partial, uses /θ/ much more commonly, often beside /o/ and often with an intermediate pronunciation. It might appear that the low incidence of /θ/ in the case of the educated speaker simply reflects a difference in social usage; yet in this part of Maine it is most unusual for educated speakers to have /θ/ so rarely. To this group also belong several Scotch–Irish communities: 318 Derry–Londonderry, 320 Bedford–Amherst, 322 Francistown, and 324 Antrim (Figure 18.7) in the Lower Merrimack Valley, and 294 Ryegate (Figure 18.7), on the Vermont side of the Upper Connecticut. In these communities /θ/ is common, especially among the older, less educated speakers; but /o/ is common also, more so than in nearby communities of New England English background. The communities with unstable /θ/ are among those that use post-vocalic /r/, a fact which is not surprising in view of the settlement history: both /o/ and post-

TABLE 18.2

	1	2	3	4	5	6	Total
coat	16	24	1	3	0	3	47
road	9	15	10	6	0	3	43
stone	12	19	5	3	1	0	40
yoke	16	1	3	0	10	5	35
toad	8	19	2	3	1	0	33
boat	12	6	8	1	3	1	31
Total	73	84	29	16	15	12	229

vocalic /r/ are characteristic of the speech both of the New Brunswick settlements and of Scotch–Irish settlements in the Eastern United States generally.

Especially interesting is 180 Marblehead, Mass., a relatively isolated, self-contained fishing community on the north shore of Boston Bay. Although originally planted from Salem, Marblehead seems to have taken an independent road in linguistic matters. On the one hand, perhaps because of its independence and isolation, it is one of the relic areas of the region, as in the retention of post-vocalic /r/;[18] on the other, perhaps because of its long association with the shipping industry, an activity which brought Marbleheaders in touch with many outsiders, it has been receptive to innovations, as in the adoption of the /o/ phoneme. It is possible, of course, that /θ/ was never common in Marblehead; but the facts of original settlement and the sporadic presence of the /θ/ in the speech of the 1A informant argues against this theory. Proximity to Boston, where /θ/ has largely disappeared, may help to account for the prevalence of /o/ in Marblehead.

A number of informants represent the several urban communities in the region: 190 Haverhill, 328 Keene–Marlow (Figure 18.7), 356 Biddeford, and 360 Portland (Figure 18.7). The responses of these informants make it clear that /θ/ has a relatively low incidence and stability as compared with the status of the phoneme in rural communities in the vicinity. Among the younger, better-educated social group the "short o" is common only in words where it is of especially high incidence throughout the area; among the older, less-educated speakers /θ/ is more frequently met with (even in Boston, where /θ/ is highly recessive). Nevertheless, it is markedly unstable in most words at all social and age levels.

On the maps (Figures 18.1–6), circles farthest to the right in any one row represent the younger and/or better-educated informants. Even a cursory examination of these maps will show that in most of the communities with divided usage the recessive /θ/ is used by the older and/or less-educated, the innovating /o/ by the younger and/or better-educated. Exceptions to this rule generally involve educated New Englanders of the Old School, among whom the "short o" has prestige value as a symbol identifying them with New England. But even these speakers frequently use /o/, often in free variation with /θ/.

All the evidence reinforces a generalization already indicated: if usage in a given community is divided for a particular word, the recessive phoneme /θ/ usually occurs, alone or beside /o/, in the speech of the older and the less-educated; and the innovating phoneme /o/ usually occurs, alone or beside /θ/, in the speech of the younger and better-educated.[19] Table 18.2 shows the incidence of /o/ and /θ/ in the speech of older and younger informants in the same communities. Italic numbers at the heads of the columns represent six types of distribution, as follows: *1* older has /θ/, younger /o/; *2* older /θ/,

[18] Kurath, *Handbook* 34 (Chart 16).
[19] See Avis 133–138 (Tables 20–23) for the data on the dissemination of /θ/ and /o/ by informant types in the northeastern region.

younger /o, θ/; *3* older /θ, o/, younger /o/; *4* older /o/, younger /o, θ/; *5* older /o, θ/, younger /θ/; *6* older /o/, younger /θ/. Older informants who use /θ/ total 201, younger informants who use /o/ total 202; older informants who do not use /θ/ total 28, younger informants who do not use /o/ total 27.

The generalization about the recessive nature of /θ/, though based on a detailed study of Northeastern New England only, holds good for New England as a whole. Any word in which /θ/ is widely disseminated and stable in the Northeast, as shown in Table 18.1, will have /θ/ fairly often elsewhere as well; any word in which /θ/ is rare and unstable in the Northeast will have /θ/ rarely or not at all elsewhere. In short, /θ/ is receding throughout New England, lingering longest among the older and the less-educated, especially in rural areas. Table 18.3 shows the approximate frequency of /θ/ throughout New England.[20] In this table the symbol x indicates that /θ/ is common; a slant line / that it is fairly common; a circle o that it is not common; and a dash — that it is rare or lacking.

Diaphones of /θ/ occur, though sparsely, in Upstate New York and in the adjacent counties of Pennsylvania, that is, in the New England settlement area

TABLE 18.3

	wVt.	*wConn.*	*wMass.*	*seConn.*	*Narragansett Bay*	*MV and Nantucket*	*Cape Cod*	*Plymouth Region*	*Boston Bay*	*cMass.*	*neMass.*	*Coastal Me. & NH*	*Inland Me. & NH*	*Upper Conn. Valley*	*swNH*
whole	x	x	x	x	x	—	x	x	x	x	x	x	x	x	x
stone wall	/	o	/	x	x	x	x	x	o	/	x	x	x	x	x
toadstool	/	o	/	/	/	x	x	x	/	x	x	x	x	x	x
grindstone	/	o	/	/	/	x	x	/	o	/	x	x	x	x	x
stone	o	—	o	/	o	x	x	o	o	/	x	x	x	x	/
coat	o	o	—	o	/	/	/	/	—	o	x	x	x	x	o
road	—	—	—	/	/	/	/	/	o	o	x	x	x	x	o
home	—	o	—	/	/	x	o	o	o	—	x	x	x	/	/
wishbone	—	—	—	/	/	x	o	o	o	o	x	x	x	x	/
folks	—	—	—	—	—	—	—	/	—	/	x	x	x	x	x
yolk	—	o	—	—	o	—	/	/	—	—	/	x	x	/	/
poultry	o	o	—	—	—	—	/	/	o	—	/	x	x	/	—
yoke	—	—	—	—	o	—	—	o	—	—	/	/	x	/	—
most	—	—	—	—	—	o	—	—	—	—	x	x	x	/	/
(al)most	—	—	—	o	—	—	—	—	—	—	/	x	x	/	/
boat	—	—	—	o	o	/	—	—	—	—	/	/	o	o	o
woke	—	—	—	—	—	—	x	/	—	—	o	o	—	—	—
Rhode Island	o	—	o	o	—	—	—	—	—	o	/	o	—	o	—
post office	—	—	—	—	o	—	—	—	—	—	o	—	—	—	—
oats	—	—	—	—	—	—	—	—	—	—	—	—	o	—	—

[20] For a detailed treatment of the evidence for New England outside the Northeastern region, see Avis 142–166.

north and west of the Hudson–Mohawk Valley.[21] The phoneme in this region is decidedly recessive, as in Western Vermont (Table 18.3), with which it combines to form a sub-area of the Northern Speech Area.[22] Finally, it occurs as a relic feature on the Canadian side of the border, in the St. Lawrence Valley, an area whose settlement history links it with Western New England and Upstate New York.[23]

[21] The maps referred to in fn. 13 above illustrate the dissemination of /θ/ in this settlement area. See also Avis, Figures 54–61 and Tables 33–35.

[22] Area 4, Map 2 in Kurath and McDavid.

[23] It must be remembered that the Atlas records here under examination were made almost thirty years ago; many of the informants are now dead. In view of the recessive character of /θ/ in the 1930s, it seems improbable that the feature is still common now. If someone were to record comparable data for /θ/ and /o/ today, the extent of drift in New England would almost certainly be even more remarkable than is shown by this study.

19

Linguistic Geography and Names Ending in ⟨i⟩

GEORGE B. PACE

THE FILES OF THE LINGUISTIC ATLAS of the United States and Canada contain a limited, but unique, body of material of interest to students of names. For example, items 86.5–87.1 of the New England work sheets offer boundless data on the pronunciation of *New England, Connecticut, Massachusetts, Rhode Island, New Hampshire, Vermont, New York, Virginia, North Carolina, Georgia, Florida, Tennessee, Missouri, Texas, California, Boston, New Haven, Springfield, Chicago, Cincinnati, Ireland, France, Russia,* and *Asia.* Occasionally, the work sheets have other material also, since it is the practice of most fieldworkers to jot down anything of possible sociological significance. Analyzed according to the methods of linguistic geography, this body of material—pronunciations plus notes—will often throw new light on old problems, this being one of the chief ways in which linguistic geography can make contributions.

The names *Missouri* and *Cincinnati*, on which this article[1] will focus, have attracted attention and discussion because of a peculiarity of pronunciation which they share with certain other words ending in the grapheme ⟨i⟩, e.g. *Miami, Ypsilanti, Naomi.* In addition to the grapheme, these words have enough morphophonemic features in common to justify regarding them as a group or class—what is called here, loosely, names ending in ⟨i⟩. The pronunciation peculiarity is, of course, the occurrence of /ə/ as the final vowel.

Attempts have been made to explain this phenomenon, and of these the best known is probably Edgar H. Sturtevant's:

In the dialect of Missouri and the neighbouring states, final *a* in such words as "America," "Arizona," "Nevada," becomes *y*—"Americy," "Arizony,"

Reprinted by permission from *American Speech* 35.175–87 (1960). The author is Professor of English at the University of Missouri.

[1] The writer would like to express gratitude to the American Council of Learned Societies, whose award made possible the basic research. He would also like to thank the authorities of the Linguistic Atlas for allowing him to study their collections. In an earlier form a part of the article was read at the December, 1954, meeting of the Modern Language Association.

"Nevady." All educated people in that region correct this vulgarism out of their speech; and many of them carry the correction too far and say "Missoura". . . .[2]

Other explanations have been offered, "phonetic ease," analogy, and regional dialect being the principal ones. None of these theories can be said to have general acceptance; in recognition of this fact, Allen Walker Read ends his lengthy article, "Pronunciation of the Word 'Missouri' ", thus: "Whatever its [the /ə/'s] origin . . ."[3]

To the writer, a notable objection to all the explanations is their failure to account for the virtual limitation of the phenomenon to words sharing certain distinct morphophonemic features (see below) and ending in the grapheme ⟨i⟩. The last half of this article will attempt to explain this limitation and thus to account for the phenomenon. It is also noteworthy that all the discussions suffer from a lack of precise data. This defect the first half of this article will attempt to remedy, by presenting the results of a study of 1286 pronunciations of *Missouri* and 1200 of *Cincinnati*. These 2486 pronunciations, taken down by the highly trained fieldworkers of the Linguistic Atlas and covering an area stretching from Maine through Georgia, constitute the largest and most trust-worthy body of data ever brought to bear on the problem, and perhaps ever likely to be.[4]

Before considering this material, however, its limitations should be noted. The pronunciations were recorded over a span of some 27 years; hence the material is only *relatively* suitable for synchronic study (the word *today*, when used below, needs to be interpreted in the light of this fact). The sampling, furthermore, is not exactly even; that is, the number of informants is not strictly proportionate to the total population, nor are all age and social groups represented equally. There is, for example, a tendency to use the older, rather "rustic" informant; it is quite possible that urban and cultured usages have somewhat inadequate representation. There will inevitably be divergent estimates of these limitations and of their importance, ranging all the way to the extreme position of Glenna R. Pickford.[5] To the writer, the limitations mean that the picture is probably as true as a sampling survey can give for those who speak the charac-teristic speech of an area, since the informants were carefully chosen as repre-sentative of their localities. It may well be out of focus, but not necessarily so, in areas where a characteristic speech no longer seems a significant concept.

---

[2] *Linguistic Change* (Chicago, 1917), pp. 79–80; a later statement occurs in his *An Introduction to Linguistic Science* (New Haven, 1947), pp. 81–82. John S. Kenyon (who formulated the theory independently) continues to give it as *the* explanation in the last edition of his *American Pronunciation* (Ann Arbor, 1950), p. 174.

[3] *American Speech*, VIII (1933), 35. On pp. 32–35 Read summarizes the major theories (W. A. Read, Grandgent, Sturtevant–Kenyon) and offers his own.

[4] *Missouri* was dropped in the reduced form of the questionnaire used in the Great Lakes states; material on *Missouri* from the Linguistic Atlas of the Upper Midwest is presented in Harold B. Allen, "Distribution Patterns of Place-Name Pronunciations," *Names*, VI (June, 1958), 76.

[5] "American Linguistic Geography: A Sociological Appraisal," *Word*, XII (1956), 211–233.

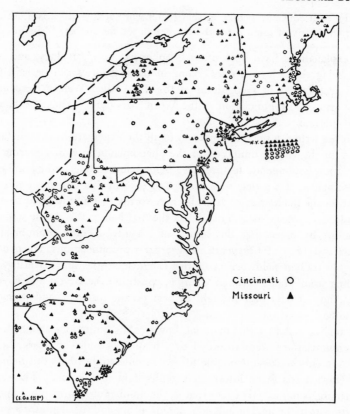

Map 19.1: [Iˆ, ɪˆ] or higher final nucleus.

Perhaps the wisest attitude is to regard the picture as a broad one, surest when it is confirmed by other information (like that from the settlement history discussed below) or when it confirms itself (the coincidence of pattern on Map 19.1).

It will be convenient to begin with the phonetic nature of the final vowel in *Missouri*. The 1286 pronunciations show vowels predominantly in the following ranges: high- and mid-front, and high-, mid-, and upper-low central. Because of the narrow, impressionistic technique of the Atlas fieldworkers, these vowels are rarely, of course, transcribed unmodified; the transcriptions very commonly include single- or multiple-shift markers, or superscript symbols indicating diphthongal offglides, or both. This whole set of symbols and combinations of symbols is analyzable into high and mid vowels horizontally and front and central vertically. It is probably impossible, however, to give more than a rough phonemic statement. This is all the writer will attempt to do.[6]

Disregarding the even half-dozen mid-front vowels /e/, hardly significant in a total of 1286, one finds mainly the following: /iy, i, ɨ, ə/. The first two of these, however, are decidedly less frequent than the last two; specifically, only 97 vowels in the front range /iy, i/ were transcribed (mostly in New England and New York State). Thus the variation, at least in the area covered by this study, is primarily between high- and mid-central, /ɨ/ and /ə/, and not, as is usually said, between high-front and mid-central.[7] The simple phonemic statement that one deals primarily with allophones of /ɨ/ and /ə/ is, however, slightly misleading; for it obscures what, since it has a geographical pattern, seems to be another distinct pronunciation—something neither *Missoury* nor *Missoura* but in between: a lowered [ɨ] or a raised [ə].

It will simplify the presentation, without appreciably distorting the picture, if these various pronunciations are sorted into three groups: (1) the clear *Missoury* type /iy,i,ɨy,ɨ/; (2) the intermediate pronunciation with lowered [ɨ] or raised [ə]; and (3) the clear *Missoura* type /ə/.

Approached purely quantitatively, *Missoura* is the favored pronunciation in all areas except the following: Kurath's Northern speech area, South Carolina, and Georgia. Furthermore, *Missoura* occurs in all areas of any size except Georgia (there is one instance in northern Georgia). The figures are these: *Missoura*, 655; intermediate type, 109; *Missoury*, 528. Hence, one may travel over nearly the whole of the Eastern United States and expect to hear *Missoura*, quite possibly more frequently than *Missoury*. This is true, however, only with the reservation that one does not restrict his contacts, for the figures above are, as stated, purely quantitative; that is, no account has been taken of the relative social status of the various informants. Because of the well known classification of the Atlas informants into types, however, their social status can be taken into consideration.

The word was recorded for 143 informants regarded as Type III (cultured). Of these, 85 said *Missoury*, 43 *Missoura*, a proportion of 2:1 for *Missoury*. (Eleven used an intermediate vowel; seven used more than one pronunciation —with awareness, it might be noted.) Geographically, the areas in which Type III informants tended to favor *Missoury* are New England (by a proportion of 21:8), New York State (12:4), New York City (5:1), Philadelphia (4:0), South Carolina (13:5), Georgia (8:0). A high-final vowel, hence, probably has some

---

[6] From time to time it is more convenient to use phonetic notation; throughout, the phonemicization is tentative, and is done mainly to avoid the clumsiness of such statements as "an [ɪ]-like vowel." On the problem of interpreting the data phonemically, see: Raven I. McDavid, Jr., "The Dialects of American English," in W. Nelson Francis, *The Structure of American English* (New York, 1958), p. 513; Allan F. Hubbell, "The Phonemic Analysis of Unstressed Vowels," *American Speech*, XXV (1950), 105–11; N. M. Caffee, "The Phonemic Structure of Unstressed Vowels in English," *American Speech*, XXVI (1951), 103–109.

[7] Cf., e.g., Read, *op. cit.*, p. 33. As Map 19.2 shows, however, the contrast is frequently with a nucleus higher than [ɪ].

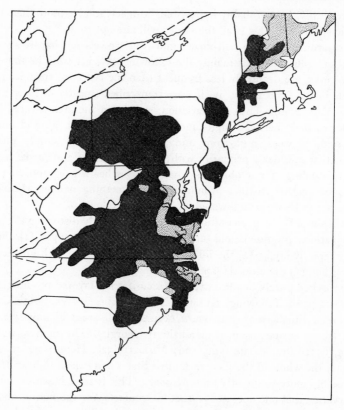

Map 19.2: *Missouri*. Overwhelming predominance of /-ə/ (light gray areas
represent predominance of [ɪˇ,əˆ]).

prestige in these areas, especially in the large urban centers. It is questionable,
however, that it does in, say, Georgia, for on down through Type I (rustic),
Missoury is seemingly what everyone says.

The last statement suggests what is certainly a fact: the pronunciations of
cultured speakers often depend upon where they live. This is strikingly true in
the large area in the Midland and South (see Map 19.2) where *Missoura* predominates. In this area seven cultured informants said *Missoury*, but 13 said
Missoura (see below, however, for a different situation in Virginia with
Cincinnati). Three said something in between. (Six informants of Types I and
II, incidentally, said *Missoury*.)

With *Cincinnati* the phonetic aspect is sufficiently similar to that of *Missouri*
to make separate discussion unnecessary. Quantitatively, however, the /-ə/ is
much in the ascendancy, *Cincinnata* occurring 903 times as opposed to 269 for

Cincinnaty and 39 for the intermediate type. The only areas of any size in which *Cincinnata* is not predominant are New York City, Philadelphia, the western fringe of West Virginia, and Charleston, South Carolina. Even in Georgia, a solid *Missoury* area, *Cincinnata* is twice as frequent as *Cincinnaty* (the latter is confined almost entirely to the cities).

Cincinnati was recorded for 129 Type III informants. Of these, 63 said *Cincinnaty* and 51, *Cincinnata*; 5 said both; 8 used an intermediate vowel. The areas in which the high vowel would seem to have prestige are New York State (12:3), Philadelphia (3:0), Virginia (7:1), South Carolina (11:2), Georgia (3:0). New York City shows an even split (3:3), although, when Types I and II are included, *Cincinnaty* has overwhelming predominance (16:6). In a few areas the /-ə/ *may* have prestige: West Virginia (6:0), Pennsylvania minus Philadelphia (10:4), and New England (17:11; both 5; intermediate type 4). Many New England informants termed *Cincinnata* the "older" pronunciation, a factor that often influences prestige in old, established areas. At this point, however, it may be well to observe that the two Cincinnati informants investigated for the Linguistic Atlas of the North Central States both said *Cincinnaty* (one only was Type III).[8]

The most significant charting for *Cincinnati* is obviously not the /-ə/; rather it is the distinctly high vowel which shows a meaningful distribution, corresponding closely with the same kind of final vowel in *Missouri*.[9]

The areas in the Midland and South (see Map 19.2) in which the /-ə/ is overwhelmingly predominant seem significant so far as the geographical spreading of *Missoura* is concerned. It is often fallacious to draw inferences as to the past from contemporary situations.[10] In this instance, however, it is known that Virginia and North Carolina furnished, ultimately, the bulk of Missouri's early settlement, and there is also evidence that the /-ə/ existed in the early nineteenth century.[11] In view of the dense concentration of *Missoura* in Virginia and North Carolina today—the word *today* is of course used loosely; more specifically the 1940s—it seems considerably more probable that the early Missourians took with them the pronunciation now characteristic of the state than that they sent it back.

This conclusion, that the diffusion was predominately westward (because

[8] Information on *Cincinnati* was kindly furnished by the director of the Atlas, Albert H. Marckwardt.

[9] Eight instances of *Cincinnati* with /-ər/ in North Carolina (six of them in a well-defined area on the coast south of the Neuse River) and three in South Carolina are worth recording; the pronunciation occurs only once elsewhere (in Maryland). *Missouri* with /-ər/ appears three times (once each in North Carolina and South Carolina and once also in Maryland, but not from the same informant as the *Cincinnater* one).

[10] Cf. Wilson D. Wallis, "Inference of Relative Age of Culture Traits from Magnitude of Distribution," *Southwestern Journal of Anthropology*, I (1945), 142–59; Charles F. Hockett, *A Course in Modern Linguistics* (New York, 1958), pp. 478ff.

[11] For the /-ə/ in *Missouri* see Read, *op. cit.*, p. 32. For the settlement of Missouri, see F. C. Shoemaker, *A History of Missouri and Missourians* (Columbia, Mo., 1927), p. 37; Jonas Viles, *A History of Missouri* (New York, 1933), pp. 85–86; see also note 13 below.

of family ties there would inevitably be some exchange both ways), in line with the population movement, is borne out by the statements of Missourians in the great controversy over the pronunciation of the state's name in the 1890s. Read quotes a St. Louisan, writing in 1897, "I call it Missoura. That is the Southern pronunciation and if we are an integral part of the South, it should be so called"; and comments, "It was the consensus of observation that the 'a' ending was most prevalent among those people whose speech background lay in Virginia, Kentucky, and the South."[12] Incidentally, the Linguistic Atlas evidence probably explains why the controversy occurred when it did, in the 1890s rather than earlier. After the Civil War the source of migration to Missouri shifted to the Northern states,[13] to include what are today the *Missoury* areas. The suggestion is that the high-final vowel was relatively uncommon in Missouri until it was brought in in increasing numbers by the post-Civil War settlers from the North.

Finally, we need to consider the phonetic origin of the /-ə/ in *Missouri* and *Cincinnati* and also in the other words in which the phenomenon has been observed. The evidence so far presented can hardly be seen as supporting Sturtevant's "overcorrection" theory, at least as a general explanation of the bulk of the /-ə/ forms. As Sturtevant stated the theory, he limited it to "Missouri and the neighboring states." It is of course possible that the pronunciation spread from this area throughout nearly the whole of the Eastern United States; it is also possible that the mistaken striving for elegance (overcorrection) operated independently in the various regions. The evidence, however, does not support these possibilities. Sturtevant's theory rests solely on its *a priori* probability. That this must be considerable is suggested by Kenyon's independent formulation of it, and its acceptance by Krapp and, with reservations, by Menner.[14] Nothing concrete, however, has been adduced in its support.[15]

Other suggestions are that the /-ə/ is related to some feature of regional dialect or to some phonetic process analogous to the /-o/ *vs.* /-ə/ variation in *Ohio* and similar words.[16] As for the regional dialect possibility, Map 19.2

[12] Read, *op. cit.*, p. 27.

[13] "The Anglo–American immigration to Missouri before the [Civil] War was mostly from the southern states; Kentucky, Tennessee, Virginia, and North Carolina supplying the greatest numbers. After the War the heaviest flow shifted to the North; Illinois, Indiana, Ohio, Pennsulvania, and New York being the largest contributors" (James Fernando Ellis, *The Influence on the Settlement of Missouri* [St. Louis, 1913], p. 150).

[14] John S. Kenyon, *American Pronunciation* (1st ed.; Ann Arbor, 1924), p. 110; George P. Krapp, *The Pronunciation of Standard English in America* (New York, 1919), pp. 80–81; Robert J. Menner, "Hypercorrect Forms in American English," *American Speech*, XII (1937), 171.

[15] In an effort to provide evidence for Sturtevant's theory, the writer has charted items like *Martha : Marthy, sofa : sofy*, but has found no coincidence in geographical distribution which would suggest that the two phenomena are related. (Many people in the areas where *Missoura* is predominant say *Marthy* and *sofy*, for example.) It almost goes without saying that complete disproof of Sturtevant's theory is impossible; only its unlikelihood can be shown.

[16] Other suggested solutions have been offered (e.g., analogy with such state names

shows that today there is a regional distribution of the overwhelming pre-dominance of the /-ə/ in *Missouri*; however, as noted, the /-ə/ occurs virtually everywhere. A map for *Cincinnati* would be made up almost entirely of /-ə/'s. The suggestion is that, if the explanation lies in some dialectal feature, it is too widespread a one to be termed regional.[17] The other explanation, for which the old-fashioned term "phonetic ease" may suffice, is not controverted by the evidence, so long as it is limited to the two words so far discussed. It makes the assumption implicit in the formula /-ɨ/ > /-ə/, that *Missoura* is a phonetic development of *Missoury*, and so on. This may seem self-evident, but it is not necessarily true. If it is, then the defining of the principal variation as between high-central and mid-central (see above) becomes important and the allophone which produced the /-ə/ is probably the intermediate type charted on Map 19.2. It is possibly significant that this allophone is found especially in the two relic areas (see note 17). To this extent, then, the evidence supports this explanation. As for other phonetic possibilities, the writer has charted the various segmentals in *Missouri* in the hope of finding a pattern which would explain the variation. The results, though negative, seem worth recording: no particular /r/ seems to accompany the /ə/, nor does the quality of the vowel in the second syllable seem involved; the /ə/ occurs with both /s/ and /z/;[18] there seems to be no relation-ship between /ə/ in the first syllable and /ə/ in the last.

Menner has perhaps pointed the way to the solution by observing that it may be a mistake to seek the same origin for all the words in which the variation occurs.[19] The /-ə/ has been recorded in the following: *Naomi, Missouri, Cincinnati, Miami, Ypsilanti, Potosi* (Mo.), *Okoboji* (Iowa), *Lamoni* (Iowa), *Mississippi, spaghetti, macaroni, ravioli, gladioli, prairie, Dorothy, doily.*[20] All but the last three exhibit a pattern: (1) they are of more than two syllables; (2) the last syllable is unstressed and is immediately preceded by primary stress in the most common pronunciation; (3) the final vowel varies between /ɨ/ and /ə/; (4) graphically, the final vowel is ⟨i⟩, not ⟨y⟩.

as *Alabama*, the undesirable diminutive effect of the /-ɨ/). The evidence presented here is obviously not applicable to theories of this type.

[17] It is impossible not to see a regional pattern on Map 19.2, especially in the close matching of the northern boundary of Kurath's Midland in Pennsylvania; there are also shadowings of his northeastern and southwestern New England areas, and a striking resemblance between the lightly shaded portions and two of the relic areas identified on McDavid's map in "Linguistic Geography and the Study of Folklore," *New York Folklore Quarterly*, XIV (1958), 259. The isolated patches on Map 19.2, incidentally, may suggest that the /-ə/ was once more prominent than now. Since Map 19.2 charts, however, only the overwhelming predominance of the /-ə/, inferences of this sort cannot have much validity.

[18] The /s/ pronunciation was also a feature of the late nineteenth-century controversy (Read, *op. cit.*, pp. 23ff.); today the /s/ seems virtually confined to New England (only one instance below Pennsylvania).

[19] Menner, *op. cit.*, p. 171.

[20] Most of these are familiar and occur in the various discussions mentioned; Read (*op. cit.*, p. 33) qualifies *Mississippi* with "seldom"; the /-ə/ in *gladioli* may actually be a confusion with the New Latin singular. Quite possibly there are other words in which the /-ə/ occurs (e.g., *Biloxi, Mexicali*).

In addition, an abnormally large number are names. Following Menner's suggestion, the writer will largely exclude *prairie*, *Dorothy*, and *doily* from consideration as probably being "something else" and will focus attention on the 13 which seem to be the "same thing."[21]

Any or all of the characteristics shared by these 13 may be significant. It is noteworthy that Kenyon and Knott's *A Pronouncing Dictionary of American English*[22] does not record the variation in dissyllabic words, although there are a number of United States place names in which the /-ə/ might be expected, such as, *Chili*, *Hayti*, *Delphi*; with such names the variation is seemingly always between /iy, i/ and /ay/. Further, a charting of the Atlas evidence for *pretty*, for the same area as *Missouri* and *Cincinnati*, revealed no /-ə/ although the word was often recorded in the phrase *pretty well*, an environment which might encourage the lowering of the vowel. Turning to trisyllabic words, it is striking that, except for *prairie* /pərérə/, Kenyon and Knott record the variation only in words ending in ⟨i⟩. It is also striking that a charting of *Kentucky* for New York State, Pennsylvania, Virginia, North Carolina, South Carolina, and Georgia, showing more than 600 pronunciations, reveals only one /-ə/.[23] It is again striking, as Read notes, that the variation never occurs in *Moberly* /mówbərli/, Missouri, even though many of the town's inhabitants say /mizúrə/. Seemingly, then, except as noted for *prairie*, *Dorothy*, and *doily*, in order for the variation to occur the word needs to be fairly long, have primary stress on the penult, weak on the last, and to end in the grapheme ⟨i⟩.

The possible significance of the spelling has not been investigated, although there is no reason why the problem should not have a graphic aspect as well as a phonetic one, since most of the words became common at a time when general literacy was rising (Cincinnati was named in 1790, Ypsilanti in 1823, the Missouri Territory dates from 1812, and so on). That when *Missouri*, *Miami*, *Cincinnati*, and the like began appearing in newspapers and letters the final grapheme would present a problem in oral interpretation to many people seems obvious. The choice, however, would seemingly not have lain between /i/ and /ə/ but between /i/ and /ay/ (more strictly speaking, between allophones of /iy,

[21] The exclusion of these three is not wholly because of the pattern. With *prairie* the /-ə/ seems confined to the trisyllabic form /pərérə/; here the problem is not merely the final vowel but also the extra syllable; the two may well be related. The writer's information on *Dorothy* is limited to Menner's statement (*loc. cit.*) that a Pennsylvania family called one of the girls *Dorotha*; his information on *doily*, to Sturtevant's statement that "many Americans speak final [ə] in *Cincinnati . . . doily . . .*" (*Introduction to Linguistic Science*, p. 82). The problem of examples which do not fit is a difficult one; it has not been handled lightly here. If they actually are a different matter, to include them will prevent a solution. Ideally, they should be shown to be something else and then explained. The writer has stated the grounds for considering them to be something else; he is unable to explain them. In view of the many attempts to solve this problem for *all* instances of the variation—none wholly successfully—Menner's suggestion seems worth following.

[22] John S. Kenyon and Thomas A. Knott, *A Pronouncing Dictionary of American English* (Springfield, 1944).

[23] In northern West Virginia; the informant paralleled his *Kentucka* with *Missoury*! (No data are given for New England, as *Kentucky* was not one of the items sought there.)

i, i̯/ and allophones of /əy/ and /ay/).[24] Such pronunciations as the following, all recorded with [aɪ] in Kenyon and Knott, indicate that at one time ⟨-i⟩ more commonly represented /ay/ than it does now: *Adelphi, a fortiori, alibi, alkali, alumni, anno Domini, a priori, casus belli, Chili* (N.Y.), *Delphi, Eli, Engedi, gladioli, Hayti* (United States places), *Lodi* (United States places), *Magi, Malachi, Manti, Mattaponi, Paoli* (United States places), *Naomi, Phillipi, Pulaski* (United States places), *quasi, rabbi.* This list, which can be amplified (e.g., *corpus delicti*), establishes that ⟨-i⟩ frequently represented /ay/, as it still does. It will be noted that only two of the words (*gladioli, Naomi*) which show the /i̯/:/ə/ variation appear here. The absence of the rest is not merely surprising but also suspicious. It suggests that *Missouri, Miami,* and *Cincinnati,* for example, may have once had an /-ay/ pronunciation, but that the /-ay/ has changed into something else, namely, /-ə/.

There is evidence, of varying weight, for five of the words. With the so-called "English" method of pronouncing Latin in nearly universal use in English-speaking countries until near the end of the nineteenth century, *Cincinnati* ends in /-ay/. John Walker's standard *A Key to the Classical Pronunciation of Greek, Latin, and Scripture Proper Names* states the rule thus: "Every final *i,* though unaccented, has the long open sound; thus the final *i* forming the genitive case, as in *Magistri . . .* has the long open sound, as in *vial.*"[25] There seems no question, then, that some people once pronounced *Cincinnati* with /-ay/. Walker also recommends the "full diphthongal sound" for *Naomi* (as noted earlier, the /-ay/ survives in this word today.)[26] *Ypsilanti* is not included

[24] On the possible allophones in early American English see George P. Krapp, *The English Language in America,* II (New York, 1925), 186–189. The choice today for many speakers is also, of course, between /i̯/ and /ay/, especially in dissyllabic words. (Within the past month the writer has heard /hówpày/ *Hopi* from two college students.)

[25] The writer's copy is the 4th ed (London, 1812), p. xix. Walker's rules underlie many of the Latin grammars of the nineteenth century and also the treatment of Latin entries in *Webster's New International Dictionary,* 2d ed. (see p. liv) and, somewhat oddly, the Latin entries in Kenyon and Knott's *Pronouncing Dictionary* (p. xlviii). Perhaps Noah Webster's preference for the Roman treatment accounts for the /iy, i̯/ in *Cincinnati,* though the influence of the wide-scale adoption of the Roman method is obvious everywhere. The following note from Walker seems of enough interest to warrant quoting: ". . . a most disgraceful affectation of foreign pronunciation has exchanged this full diphthongal sound [/ay/] for the meagre, squeezed sound of the French and Italian *i . . .* as *Faustina, Messalina,* &c. Nay, words from the Saxon have been equally perverted and we hear the *i* in *Elfreeda, Edweena,* &c. It is true this is the sound the Romans gave to their *i . . .*" (p. xx). (Map 19.1 here may well represent Walker's "meagre, squeezed sound.")

[26] Pages 173, 181, 209. The following letter (John Cleves Symmes to Joseph Dayton, Cincinnata [*sic*], 1791) is interesting in the present context: "Having mentioned Cincinnata [*sic*], I beg, Sir, you will enquire of the literati in Jersey whether Cincinnata or Cincinnati be most proper? . . . I have frequent combats in this county on the subject, because most men spell the place with *ti.* when I always do with *ta.* Please to set me right if I am wrong" (B. W. Bond, Jr., *The Correspondence of John Cleves Symmes* [New York, 1926], p. 142). In a way, this is evidence for the /-ə/ coexistent with the naming of the city, Symmes presumably pronouncing as the spelling suggests. He does not seem to be concerned, however, about the pronunciation; perhaps he has confused *Cincinnatus, -i* with *cincinnatus, -a, -um.* Symmes had changed his spelling to *ti* at least by January 20, 1796.

in Walker's Glossary, but his rule for Latin applies equally to Greek. With these three words, a pronunciation with /-ay/, probably on a fairly wide scale, would seem to be likely.

The evidence for the other two words is contemporary, and may have no historical bearing—though it should be stated that the writer has been unable to make a special search for such evidence (as, say, that afforded by rhymes). In New England *Missouri* was recorded once with what can be phonemicized as /-ay/ (informant 200.1), once with /-əy/ (informant 316.1), and once with a pronunciation which is possibly /-əy/ (informant 190.2). It is of interest that all three informants came from the relic area referred to earlier, that the speech of informant 200.1 is described as "extremely old-fashioned," and that informant 316.1 is said to use "naturally a great many archaic expressions."[27]

The fifth word is *ravioli*, probably the latest of the borrowings. The writer has heard /ræviówlày/ more than once in the local supermarket.

These last two are presumably instances of either analogical or spelling pronunciations, particularly that type of spelling pronunciation which pronounces according to the name of the latter. As Kenyon observes, "spelling pronunciation is especially apt to affect proper names—particularly names of places . . ."[28]. This presumably lies behind such pronunciations as /čáylày/ *Chili*, /héytày/ *Hayti*, /lówdày/ *Lodi*, /piówlày/ *Paoli*, and /pəlǽskày/ *Pulaski*, as well as many others which the reader can supply. It is hard to believe that *Missouri*, *Miami*,[29] *Potosi*, *Lamoni*, and *Okoboji* were immune to this process— or, for that matter, *Cincinnati* and *Ypsilanti*.

The writer regards the *a priori* probability as sufficient to justify grouping the words now showing the /-ɨ/ : /-ə/ variation together as once having had an /-ay/ pronunciation, whether or not it survives today, and seeking a phonetic explanation for the derivation of the /-ə/ from it. For this latter purpose, a three-stress system (such as that used by Kenyon and Knott) is inadequate. In a four-stress system the words, when they end in /ay/, will have tertiary stress on the final syllable; that is, /nèówmày/. Even in dialects which may employ a three-stress system, some sort of stress must be on the final syllable, *otherwise the diphthong will lose its second element and the first will be raised to /ə/*. A parallel case is the behavior of the pronouns *I* and *my* under weak stress. Phonetically, then, all that is necessary for, say, /nèówmày/ to become /nèówmə̆/ is to reduce the stress on the final syllable. If, then, at least tertiary stress is not maintained on the diphthong, the following development is bound to take place (some of the steps may be theoretical): /nèówmày/ > /nèówmăy/ > /nèówmă/ > /nèówmə̆/; /nèówmə̀y/ > /nèówmə̆y/ > /nèówmə̆/; /mɨzúrày/ > /mɨzúrăy/ > /mɨzúră/ > /mɨzúrə̆/, and so on. (In some dialects the allophone may have

---

[27] Hans Kurath *et al.*, *Handbook of the Linguistic Geography of New England* (Providence, R.I., 1939), pp. 189, 190, 216. Informant 200.1 also pronounced a similar diphthong in *Cincinnati*.

[28] *American Pronunciation* (10th ed.), p. 118.

[29] The first syllable seemingly shows an interpretation of the ⟨i⟩ as /ay/; cf. /miáhmì/ (*Webster's New International*, second pronunciation).

been [ɑ:]; in this case the loss of stress will remove the lengthening, with resultant raising to /ə/, as in *Cuba*.)[30]

Perhaps the strongest reason for believing this process actually occurred is the virtual limitation of the phenomenon to words ending in ⟨i⟩—and with a particular morphophonemic pattern.[31] It is certainly curious that words with only the morphophonemic pattern seem virtually immune to the phenomenon (for example, *Kentucky*). It is curious that words with only the graphic feature (the dissyllabic words ending in ⟨i⟩) seem also immune. It is also curious that a few of the words exhibiting the phenomenon almost certainly had an /-ay/ form at one time (*Cincinnati, Ypsilanti*); a similar problem exists with those which probably had /-ay/ as a spelling pronunciation (*Missouri, Miami*, and so on). *Naomi* shows the full range, /nèówmɨ/:/nèówmǯ/:/nèówmày/, and also shows that the /-ə/ could be derived from either direction. If the derivation is assumed to be from /-ɨ/, however, the puzzling discrepancies just mentioned remain unexplained.[32]

This article has attempted to handle a number of matters, not all closely related in kind. A summary focusing on the most significant aspects seems called for: (1) in *Missouri* the /-ə/ predominates in most of the Eastern states; in *Cincinnati* it greatly predominates. Even so, there is evidence that a higher vowel has prestige in some areas;[33] (2) atlas data are relevant for the question of the origin of the /-ə/: the geographical distribution indicates that the phenomenon began in the East and was carried westward in line with the movement of population (this is confirmed, for *Missouri*, by historical evidence); the remaining implications are largely negative; that is, they do not support the existing theories; (3) these theories, moreover, do not take into consideration that 13 of the 15 words showing the variation end in the same grapheme, an uncommon one in word-final position in English, and share distinct morphophonemic features. A theory which will account for these matters assumes that the final ⟨i⟩ was once widely pronounced /ǝy, ày/ but that this diphthong has developed, because of the morphophonemic features, to /ǯ/.

[30] Some of the respellings in the newspaper items quoted by Read suggest that this pronunciation existed in the 1890s: "M-i-z-z-o-o-r-a-h, with a soft accent on the r-a-h"; "Missourah" (seven examples); "Mizzouraw" (pp. 23–29). The writer has often heard a vowel lower than [ə] in the state today, particularly when the name is pronounced in isolation. Lowered [ə] and [ɐ] were recorded a number of times in New England, and by most fieldworkers.

[31] What caused the loss of the tertiary stress? The suggestion is that the number of syllables is involved (cf. the situation in dissyllabic words); the penult must also have maximum stress. The writer has observed a fluctuation between /-ay/ and /-ə/ in one Illinois speaker (*Illini* /iláynày/ but also /iláynǯ/).

[32] The derivation from /-ay/ explains, of course, why the /-ə/ never occurs in the Missouri towns noted by Read (*op. cit.*, p. 33): *Moberly, Bernie, Waverly*. They lack the necessary conditions.

[33] Nevertheless, it is surprising to find /mɨzúrə/ called a localism in *Webster's New World Dictionary*.

The Comparative Approach

Although dialect research is primarily descriptive and synchronic, articles in the preceding section indicate that it may also be diachronic. But the dialectologist, like the general linguist, can, in addition, turn to comparative study once the descriptive data have been provided. As, for example, more and more material becomes available from the English Dialect Survey, it is increasingly relevant for students of American dialect features to examine their correlations with the English of England.

The section opens with Harold Orton's statement about the founding and the procedures of the English Dialect Survey. Next is an article by W. Nelson Francis, an American, who discusses certain findings of the Survey and relates them to what is known about American speech.

Comparison of the methods used in English linguistic geography with those employed in the United States reveals certain important differences. The English Dialect Survey deals only with non-urban older and uneducated informants, equivalent to the Type I speakers in American dialect fieldwork. Hence no comparative studies of middle-aged and educated speakers are possible. Another difference is that the Survey insists upon rigid adherence to a prepared written question read by the fieldworker to the informant; the American interviewer uses simply a minimal lexical clue in improvising his question to suit the informant and the situation. The American records are thus more likely to include relevant but unanticipated information, while the English records are more likely to exclude ambiguous responses. What one gains in precision it sometimes loses in freedom; what the other gains in freedom it may lose in precision.

Orton, well known to most American dialectologists through several visits and visiting professorships in this country, has long sought American graduate students who would draw upon the resources of this country's atlas files and of his own materials for comparative and historical dissertations. Now that the publication of the final volumes of the English Dialect Survey is near, the value of such individual researches becomes even greater than when the Survey was only in process. Even before publication of the remaining volumes of the Survey, however, Orton is preparing to edit the maps that will constitute the *Linguistic Atlas of England*. The time of their publication cannot yet be determined.

Francis's familiarity with English field methods derives from his year as a Fulbright scholar at the University of Leeds, during which he himself interviewed a number of informants. In his first article he looks at the English Survey from an American linguist's viewpoint and draws certain comparisons based upon lexical items. In his second article he turns to morphology and treats the English distribution of various non-standard verb forms also familiar in the United States. Both articles suggest what future comparative studies might yield.

Hans Kurath similarly compares English and American features, this time in phonology. His data from England, however, are not from the Survey but rather are from field records made by the American fieldworker, the late Guy Lowman, nearly 30 years ago. Now that more recent and extensive phonological evidence is at hand, it will be useful to broaden the base of this comparison by drawing upon the Orton materials as well.

The final article in this section opens the door to another kind of comparative study in dialectology, the comparison of dialect distribution patterns of two different languages spoken in the same geographical region. The prime example for such comparison is found in the United States to be the relationship between English and German, which Carroll E. Reed describes in some detail upon the basis of his having been co-editor of the *Linguistic Atlas of Pennsylvania German*. The article is also important for the insight it provides to the process by which loan words move from one language to another when two languages overlap geographically. Both French and Spanish might serve for similar comparative studies in other parts of the United States.

An English Dialect Survey: Linguistic Atlas of England

HAROLD ORTON

THE ENGLISH DIALECT SURVEY described below dates from 1946. And last year 1959, the fieldwork in the entire network of 300 localities spread over the whole of England was completed. Further, preparations for the publication of the first volume containing the results of the Survey are well under way: it will contain in tabular form the material relating to the six Northern Counties and the Isle of Man. But first, a few words of a personal nature about the genesis of the Survey.

Early in 1946, after the Second World War was over, my old friend, Eugen Dieth, then Professor of English Language in the University of Zurich, resumed by letter our close relations of pre-war days. In it he suggested that we should collaborate on a linguistic atlas of English. We thereupon decided to go ahead together, at once, with a new survey of English dialects. It was no blind act of faith, but rather a perfectly rational step for us both to take together: for each of us had had over 20 years' activity in the practical study of English dialects, some of it, indeed, in collaboration.

That summer, still 1946, we started on our projected Linguistic Atlas during his brief stay in my home in Sheffield, where I was then on the staff of the University. We decided to undertake a systematic and comprehensive national investigation of the oldest existing forms of English used in this country and to collect enough representative and comparable material throughout a network of suitable localities to enable the production of a linguistic atlas of regional English spoken in England and elsewhere. However, when Professor Angus McIntosh's present Scottish Survey started from Edinburgh in 1949, our project became restricted to England. But many difficulties were expected to lie ahead; and not all of them would be financial and organisational. But the first question to be settled was the kind of dialect to be investigated.

Reprinted by permission from *Orbis* 9.331–48 (1960). The author is Emeritus Professor of the English Language at the University of Leeds and director of the English Dialect Survey.

Many grades of vernacular exist in England today. They vary from the oldest forms of regional dialect, localised in our rural communities, down through the numerous mixed dialects of our towns and cities, to the widely acceptable type of English often called Standard English: for example, that used by the B.B.C. news-reader on the General Home Service. All these diverse types have their special interest for phoneticians and philologists. Indeed, a historical analysis of their various elements would be a fascinating and worthwhile undertaking. Our target, however, was traditional vernacular, genuine and old; and we were fully determined to collect the essential material direct, and only through the medium of trained investigators working on the spot in each of the localities of a carefully chosen network. For this purpose we needed a special questionnaire. A postal questionnaire for indirect investigation, although it could provide certain advantages, attracted us but little. Already before the Second World War we had had some joint experience of this method, but without much success. Further, we knew that both A. J. Ellis and Joseph Wright had in their day utilised the postal questionnaire. But they had not, so it seemed to us, achieved the completely dependable results that we were anxious to secure from this new survey. So we agreed to spend the next long vacation—at Leeds University, whose staff I was soon to join—preparing the first version of our questionnaire, the fundamental instrument of our projected Atlas. This first version ultimately occupied almost 10 weeks of our time in the wonderfully fine summer of 1947, most of which we spent in the sunless basement of the Brotherton Library at Leeds University. But by the beginning of the new university session of 1947–48, our draft questionnaire was ready for testing in the field.

From 1946, and until his untimely death from a stroke on 24th May, 1956, Eugen Dieth and I collaborated very closely, especially at the beginning of our joint enterprise. During those 10 years, he had come to work with me in Leeds at least once a year, and sometimes twice. A tremendous enthusiast for English philology, he was truly an inspiring colleague. His most fruitful work on the Survey undoubtedly went into the organisation and compilation of our questionnaire. It was for him a challenging, captivating task, one that he delighted in doing and into which he put all of his almost limitless physical and mental energy.

Our questionnaire was ultimately printed and published in January 1952 under the title of *A Questionnaire for a Linguistic Atlas of England*.[1] Between that date and the summer of 1955, when we agreed to work independently on the Northern material—he to construct and publish phonological maps, and I to prepare and publish the basic material in list form—he more or less restricted himself to his own private study of these Northern field recordings. But he was destined never to realize his cherished ambition, namely the completion of the Atlas itself. He had only just started upon his Northern maps

[1] It was a reprint, with separate pagination, of Part IX of Vol. VI., *Literary and Historical Section, Proceedings of the Leeds Philosophical and Literary Society*, Leeds, 1952.

when he died. The loss to English dialectology was a disaster; and my own debt to him is incalculable and permanent.

The goal that Dieth and I had before us was a linguistic atlas of England. Our task, as it presented itself to us in 1946, fell into several stages: (1) there was the production of a comprehensive questionnaire, to reveal the distinctive lexical, phonological, morphological, and syntactical features of all the main English dialects; (2) the selection of an adequate network of rural localities with enough dialect-speaking informants of the right kind; (3) the selection and training of competent fieldworkers to use the *Questionnaire* for securing the responses wanted from informants; (4) the editing of all this material preparatory to publication; (5) the publication of the results of the Survey in a suitable form, whether maps, or lists, or both; (6) the provision of the necessary accommodation from which to carry on the Survey; lastly, the requisite money to finance the project had to be assured.

Our *Questionnaire* was printed in January 1952 after thorough testing in four separate versions in various parts of the country.[2] By now it had been extensively revised. Version I had been purely notional. In essence it simply listed the notions for which equivalent dialectal expressions were wanted, for example, *fields, cowhouse, trough*; and the fieldworker was instructed to obtain them from chosen informants in his own way. The method was basically unsound. It was wrong not to prevent entirely the phrasing of the question as asked of the informant from suggesting the actual words of his response. The essential thing was to put the wanted notion clearly into his mind without even hinting at the wording of the desired response, and then let him give his answer absolutely in his own way, the local way. For example, our *Questionnaire* asks *Where do you keep the birds that lay eggs for you?*, I.1.6.[3] *What do you call the man who looks after the animals that give us wool?*, I.2.1. The informant then finds his own expression out of his own linguistic experience; he pronounces it entirely in his own way, the way he is accustomed to in his own locality.

We abandoned the method of Version I with its lists of wanted notions, and thereafter set out all the questions in full. Version II and all three later Versions are thus drawn up in this way: actual questions, expressed in full. We purposely excluded any words, phrases or sentences for translation by the informant into his own vernacular speech. Further, the fieldworker was regularly instructed to keep rigidly to the question as set out in the *Questionnaire*. In this way we

---

[2] The first version (800 notions) was tested in the County of Durham by Mr. J. Lloyd Bailes in 1947–48, and again in 1948 by Dr. Paul Wettstein of Zurich, who used it experimentally in North Derbyshire; the second, in 1948, at one selected locality in Yorkshire (West Riding), Lancashire, Lincolnshire, Derbyshire, Warwickshire and Devon by a team comprising Mr. P. Wright, Dr. Fritz Rohrer of Zurich, and ourselves; the third in 1949 by Mr. P. Wright in Cumberland, Westmorland and Northumberland; and the fourth was used in 1949–50 by Mr. P. Wright for actual field-recording in Yorkshire (all three Ridings).

[3] The figures refer to question no. 6 on page 1 of Book I of the *Questionnaire*. We always refer to the questions in this manner.

expected to secure strictly comparable responses throughout the whole network of localities. And of course unless, as sometimes, the object varied according to region, we normally did so. Since publication, the *Questionnaire* has remained almost intact. One specimen page below exhibits its characteristic features.

Our *Questionnaire* contains 1095 numbered questions, though altogether there are some 1270. They are arranged in nine numbered Books, or sections, entitled respectively The Farmstead; Cultivation; Animals; Nature; The House and Housekeeping; The Human Body; Numbers, Time and Weather; Social Activities; and the ninth and last, States, Actions and Relations. In short, it concerns the farmer and his domestic and social life. Why the farmer? Because he and his family and the farming community in general, best preserve regional dialect in England today. We deliberately ignored all other industries, like mining, fishing, weaving. These are localised, whereas farming is universal. We also ignored the towns—though they should certainly be studied by somebody soon. In scope our *Questionnaire* is linguistically comprehensive. Of the questions, 365 are designed to throw light on any given dialect's sound system, 62 on its morphological features, 41 on its syntactical features, and at least 730 on its lexical features. Almost all the questions except the lexical ones are specially marked with signs, which are attached to the keywords, to show the fieldworker, and readers, at a glance why the questions have been included. Thus an asterisk marks a phonological question; a dagger, a morphological one, and a double dagger a syntactical question. Several examples occur on the specimen page; and see particularly TEETH*, VI.5.6, included for both its phonological and its morphological importance.

Drawing up each question in full was a strenuous task. It meant learning a new technique; and there eventually emerged five types of questions. We called them naming, completing, talking, converting, and reverse questions. Most are naming, with completing questions good runners-up. All are expressed in simple, brief, direct and colloquial language. A few words about each in turn.

First, the naming question, the simplest type. Here we merely point to an object, describe it, show a picture or diagram of it; or else imitate an action, or make an appropriate gesture; and then ask the informant to name it. For example:

VI.2.1   *What do you call this?* HAIR*.
III.13.5   *What do you call a dog with half a dozen breeds in it?* MONGREL.
I.1.1. □⁴ *What do you call these?* FIELDS.
V.8.1.   *What am I doing now* [imitate]? DRINKING.

Second, the completing question. Here the question is set out in the form of a statement, which the fieldworker, by using a suitable intonation, invites his informant to complete with his own expression.

⁴ Denotes: "Show a picture"—an instruction to the fieldworker.

For example:

IX.3.5.   *Never drop a tumbler on the floor, because it's bound to* . . . BREAK*.
VI.3.4.   *A man who cannot see at all is* . . . BLIND*.

Third, the talking question—admittedly a poor name.

V.5.4.   *What can you make from milk?* BUTTER*, CHEESE*.
IV.10.1.   *What trees have you round here?* BIRCH*, OAK*, ELM*, ELDER, WILLOW.

This type of question is very sparingly used; and we always go on to ask the appropriate specific question to ensure that the wanted response is secured.

The fourth kind is the conversion type. Two good examples occur on the specimen page.

VI.5.11.   *When I have an apple, I* [i.] . . . EAT* it.
           Then to convert, as instructed, we ask
           Yesterday when I had an apple, I [i.] . . . ATE* it.
           Whenever I've had an apple, I have always [i.] . . . EATEN* it.

See also VI.5.5. on the same page. We employ this type very infrequently, and only to obtain the forms of the irregular verbs.

Now the fifth and last type, the reverse question. Here we give the informant a particular word and ask him what he means by it. The question aims at ascertaining the range of meanings of a particular word—its local semantic variability. There are only 10 of these special questions. For example:

I.1.11. Rev.   *What's the* BARN *for and where is it?*
II.5.1. Rev.   *What do you mean by* CORN *here in these parts?*

So much for the form of the questions. As for the kinds of notions involved, the questions mostly concern concrete ideas (nouns) and less frequently actions (verbs), qualities (adjectives), and grammar (morphology and syntax). They occur, when possible, consequentially, thereby avoiding any needless racing of the informant from one semantic area to another. When used by competent fieldworkers, who must of course be taught how to handle it properly, the *Questionnaire* has proved wholly successful. The informants really enjoy the interviews and often equate the procedure, and their performance, with programmes they can hear on the radio. Each of the nine books of the *Questionnaire* takes about two hours to answer; and the whole book, when progress is good, about a week of the fieldworker's time. But this includes everything, getting there, finding accommodation, making contacts, securing the best informants, making tape recordings—the whole process from start to finish.

Our fieldworkers have all been specially trained for their task. We have had eight, namely Dr. Peter Wright, B.A., Ph.D. (North Country), Mr. Stanley Ellis, M.A. (the North and the Central and East Midlands), Mr. Peter Gibson, M.A. (Staffordshire), Mr. Donald Sykes, M.A. (West Midlands), Miss Averil Playford (now Mrs. G. Sanderson), M.A. (Leicestershire and Rutland), Dr. Nelson Francis, Professor of English, Franklin and Marshall College, Lancaster, Pennsylvania, U.S.A. (Norfolk), Mr. John T. Wright, M.A. (Western Counties south of the Thames), and Mr. Michael V. Barry, B.A. (Essex, and Eastern and Central Counties south of the Thames). All but one had received special phonetic training prior to acceptance as fieldworkers, some of it in the University's Phonetics Department under Mr. P. A. D. McCarthy. Five of them had previously written, for their first degrees, short dissertations on the results of their independent investigations into the phonology of current dialectal English. And five subsequently submitted post-graduate theses[5] on the linguistic geography of counties they had recorded with the *Questionnaire*. A sixth is about to do so. Professor Francis came over from the U.S.A. in 1955 especially to help with the fieldwork in Norfolk and we are most grateful to the Fulbright authorities who enabled him to come. Fieldworkers need careful training. But academic competence in phonetics and English philology will alone not make a good fieldworker. He must, in addition, have physical and mental toughness, energy and drive, sociability, cheerfulness, tact in seeking out and handling informants, a certain histrionic ability and obvious sincerity. Nor need the fieldworker always be a male: Miss Playford proved highly successful in Leicestershire and Rutland. Apart from her and Dr. Nelson Francis, the fieldworkers all took their first degrees in English at Leeds University.

Our informants were chosen by the fieldworkers themselves after direct inquiries on the spot. They (and preferably their parents too) had to be natives and natural dialect speakers; and small farmers, too, or else associated with the farming community. We never used professional dialect speakers, dialect reciters, or educated people, or people who practised cultivated vernacular for some private purpose. Informants had to be at least 60 years of age, and normally not above 75, although some were actually 80 and over. Besides being knowledgeable, they had to have good heads, good mouths, good hearing, and good eyesight. Further, they had to be people who were willing to spare the necessary time for the interviews—and this often meant disrupting their normal daily life. We preferred to interview them in their own homes. Here they could be at their ease, and comfortable enough to cope with the unfamiliar, indeed unique situation that had so suddenly developed out of the fieldworker's intrusion into their privacy. Here, if anywhere, the fieldworker could most easily induce that satisfying and, to them very agreeable, relationship of master and pupil, which is always so favourable to effective recording. The informant plays the rôle of the teacher; he is the authority; the fieldworker is the pupil, univer-

---

[5] S. Ellis, *A Study of the Living Dialects of Lincolnshire*, (1952); P. Gibson, *Studies in the Linguistic Geography of Staffordshire*, (1955); Averil H. Playford (now Mrs. G. Sanderson) *Studies in the Linguistic Geography of Leicestershire and Rutland*, (1957); D. R. Sykes, *The Linguistic Geography of Shropshire and Worcestershire* (1956); John T. Wright, *Studies in the Linguistic Geography of Somerset* (1957). These theses have all been deposited in the Brotherton Library of the University of Leeds; but all except the first mentioned are published on microcards and micro-films by Micro-Methods Ltd., East Ardsley, Wakefield, Yorks., to whom application for copies should be made.

sity man though he is. Short as their stay was, our fieldworkers made friends with their informants; and never offered to pay a single penny for their services. Our informants gave their help voluntarily, and were almost always happy and proud to do so.

In each locality the whole *Questionnaire* was asked once only; but we did not rely upon only one informant. Few informants can reasonably be expected to spare the time required to answer some 1270 questions—unless of course they are house-fast and therefore, perhaps, anxious for unusual and interesting company. Yet the use of several informants did not, we think, prove a drawback; it was often very advantageous. So we usually took two or three informants. At first, inexperience sometimes forced the fieldworkers to employ as many as five. Very occasionally they were able to use only one.

The fieldworkers transcribed the informants' responses phonetically, and impressionistically, in the phonetic alphabet of the International Phonetic Association. They wrote them down on the left-hand side of specially prepared sheets (subsequently bound in one book); and on the right-hand side, they noted down any words and expressions from the informant's conversation during the interviews that had some bearing upon the problems implicit in the *Questionnaire*. This incidental information is truly invaluable, for it is quite unconditioned by the essentially artificial circumstances of the interview. Being wholly unprompted and spontaneous, it is used for confirming, correcting and amplifying the evidence that the responses themselves provide. Selections from this material will, when relevant, be included in the proposed four volumes of basic material; but most of it is more suitable for separate publication as "Companion Volumes of Incidental Material".

Besides these written records, our fieldworkers also made tape recordings on portable recorders in most of the localities of the network. At the end of the week's interviews the fieldworker would invite his best informant to tell him about his daily life or work, about for example, ploughing, harvesting, stacking, hedging. This material was always informal, unscripted, unrehearsed, and un-prepared, for example a topic that cropped up naturally in the conversation and seemed to merit discussion there and then. The fieldworker had his recorder ready, and switched it on at his discretion. The fieldworkers soon became expert in handling informants before the microphone and quickly got them to talk uninhibitedly. Incidentally, the tape recordings were later sent to the British Broadcasting Corporation, who re-recorded from them what they wished for eventual deposit in their Permanent Record Library. These tape recordings should, of course, have been preserved, but the cost was prohibitive. Instead, the best specimens of each dialect are being dubbed (in duplicate) onto double-sided 12-inch gramophone records, one for preservation as a master record and the other for study. The task is being carried out in the University's Phonetics Department by Mr. Henry Ellis, an expert technician, to whom we are deeply indebted. These uninhibited, spontaneous records of dialectal English will be invaluable to future students of English Philology.

When eventually published—and transcribed, I hope, in both phonetic and ordinary spelling—they should interest English scholars all over the world. Up to the present, tape recordings have been made at 190 of the 300 localities in the network.

Our network of localities was provisionally decided at the beginning of the Survey by Mr. Peter Wright, my first Research Assistant, working under direction. In general geographical position and population figures determined the selection of the various places. They are mainly rural, with, preferably, some 400–500 inhabitants, and are suitably spaced, usually not more than about 15 miles apart. There has been no time, money, or enough trained field-workers to investigate more. Incidentally, the obligations of National (Military) Service took three of the fieldworkers away from the Survey just when they had reached the peak of their efficiency.

The cost of the Survey has been almost wholly covered by the University of Leeds. With the appointment of my first Research Assistant in July 1948 to undertake the fieldwork, the Survey became an integral part of the researches of the University's Department of English Language and Medieval English Literature. From here the investigations have been organised, administered and controlled. Among other things the University provided salaries for two specially engaged fieldworkers, and maintenance for a third, helped one of the married ones to buy a caravan for use in the field, bought us two motor cars, one motor cycle and several tape recorders, financed almost all the fieldwork and allowed us the clerical assistance of the Departmental Secretary, Miss Vera Cracknell, who has already given us enormous help; it also allotted the requisite accommodation, and has already made a handsome grant towards the cost of our proposed publications. Certain small contributions have also accrued from fees for lectures and broadcasts, one or two from anonymous donors, and some from the British Broadcasting Corporation in return for the use of our tape recordings. The Leverhulme Trust gave me two grants in 1954 and 1955 towards the cost of fieldwork in the West Midlands. Five of the fieldworkers, whose investigations were undertaken as part of their courses for higher degrees, were financed by University Scholarships or Research Grants. But Mr. Stanley Ellis nobly bore the expense of his own fieldwork in Lincolnshire. Further, Eugen Dieth's visits to this country for work on the Survey were partly paid for himself, and later subsidised from certain official Swiss sources. And last year Mrs. McGrigor Phillips, Dorothy Una Ratcliffe, whose munificent gifts have promoted so many excellent causes and projects, many within Leeds University, gave £500 towards the expense of our proposed publications; and the Philosophical and Literary Society of Leeds not only paid the whole cost of printing and publishing our *Questionnaire*, but recently made a grant of £150 towards our imminent publication expenses. For all this most generous financial support, we are deeply indebted to all our benefactors; and most especially to the University of Leeds. To my colleagues in the University, and in particular to the Vice-Chancellor, we owe an enormous permanent debt of gratitude for their confidence in us and for sympathetic, indulgent and practical interest and support.

Our publication programme is now under close consideration. It is intended to issue the whole work as *A Linguistic Atlas of England* over the names of Harold Orton and Eugen Dieth.

The undermentioned publications are proposed:

1   Four volumes of basic material in tabular form as follows:

    a. The Basic Material of the Six Northern Counties and the Isle of Man, ed. by H. Orton and W. J. Halliday. [In preparation.]

    b. The Basic Material of the East Midland Counties, ed. by H. Orton and S. Ellis.

    c. The Basic Material of the West Midland Counties, ed. by H. Orton and E. Kolb.

    d. The Basic Material of the Southern Counties, ed. by H. Orton and H. E. Kylstra.[6] [In preparation.]

At the time of writing we have not been able to make definite arrangements with a prospective publisher. Hence our proposals are purely tentative. But each of the above volumes might well be issued in 10 parts as the manuscript becomes available. Part I of Volume I would be introductory and would include a short account of the fieldwork, the fieldworkers, the phonetic transcriptions, the list of localities, the informants, as well as the final version of the *Questionnaire*. Parts II–X would contain the basic material corresponding to the nine parts (or "Books") of the *Questionnaire*. The other three Volumes would have the same form, except that the *Questionnaire* would not need to be reprinted again.[7]

2   Four companion volumes of selected incidental material.

They would correspond to the four volumes of "Basic Material" and would relate to the problems implicit in the *Questionnaire*, e.g. the treatment of certain Middle English historical sounds, and of morphological and syntactical features. This material is bound to be voluminous and should be invaluable.

3   The *Atlas* itself. This would show lexical, phonological, morphological and syntactical features over the whole network. We wish to start issuing maps,

[6] Dr. W. J. Halliday, a graduate, as well as an honorary graduate, of Leeds University, and Chairman of the Council of the Yorkshire Dialect Society, has in his retirement from school-mastering and University-Extension lecturing, been a voluntary member of our team during the last eight years. Mr. S. Ellis, who has carried out most of the fieldwork of the Survey, is an Assistant Lecturer in this Department. Dr. E. Kolb, Ph.D. (University of Zurich), is the late Eugen Dieth's former Research Assistant and is a Professor of English in the University of Basle. H. E. Kylstra is a former student of Professor P. Harting in the University of Amsterdam and a former Lecturer in Dutch in the University of Melbourne, Australia. He now holds a Research Fellowship in English Dialectology in this Department.

[7] [Eds.: The following have been published since the date of Professor Orton's article: H. Orton, *Survey of English Dialects: Introduction* (1962); H. Orton and W. J. Halliday, *Six Northern Counties and the Isle of Man, Part I* (1962), *Parts II and III* (1963); H. Orton and Martyn F. Wakelin, *Southern Counties*, Part I (1967). The publisher is E. J. Arnold & Son, Leeds.]

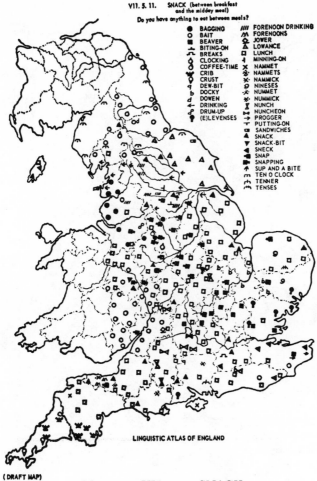

VII. 5. 11. SNACK (between breakfast
and the midday meal)

Do you have anything to eat between meals?

●	BAGGING	////	FORENOON DRINKING
○	BAIT	⋀	FORENOONS
■	BEAVER	⚎	JOWER
⌐	BITING-ON	▲	LOWANCE
⌣	BREAKS	▢	LUNCH
⦶	CLOCKING	⊣	MINNING-ON
⦵	COFFEE-TIME	✕	NAMMET
⦸	CRIB	⋇	NAMMETS
⦷	CRUST	⋇	NAMMICK
⊣	DEW-BIT	⦵	NINESES
⋒	DOCKY	⋇	NUMMET
⌂	DOWEN	✱	NUMMICK
⊢	DRINKING	⊻	NUNCH
⫝	DRUM-UP	⋈	NUNCHEON
⦂	(E)LEVENSES	→	PROGGER
		⊤	PUTTING-ON
		⊡	SANDWICHES
		▲	SNACK
		▼	SNACK-BIT
		◀	SNECK
		◀	SNAP
		▶	SNAPPING
		⊼	SUP AND A BITE
		⋔	TEN O CLOCK
		⋔	TENNER
		⋔	TENSES

LINGUISTIC ATLAS OF ENGLAND

(DRAFT MAP)

Map 21.1: VII. 5.11. SNACK.

perhaps in folders, as soon as possible. But since only the Northern material
has so far been fully edited, the maps could not be regarded as definitive. The
phonological maps could not, of course, be attempted on a national scale until
the editorial work has been completed for the whole country.

4 Phonetic transcriptions, in both narrow and broad systems, of the tape
recorded specimens of the unscripted speech of selected informants. Some 190
such recordings dubbed onto discs are now in possession.

It should be mentioned here that Dr. E. Kolb has continued to work on
Dieth's phonological maps relating to the Six Northern Counties and hopes to
publish a series of them from Zurich relatively soon.[8]

[8] [Eds.: Now published as: Edward Kolb, *Phonological Atlas of the Northern Region:
The Six Northern Counties, North Lincolnshire and the Isle of Man.* Bern: Francke, 1966.]

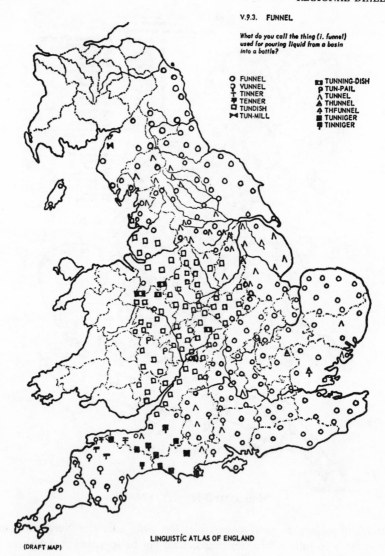

V.9.3.   FUNNEL

What do you call the thing (i. funnel) used for pouring liquid from a basin into a bottle?

O FUNNEL	▥ TUNNING-DISH
ϙ VUNNEL	ꝑ TUN-PAIL
T TINNER	∧ TUNNEL
⊤ TENNER	▲ THUNNEL
▢ TUNDISH	⟃ THFUNNEL
⋈ TUN-MILL	▪ TUNNIGER
	▮ TINNIGER

LINGUISTIC ATLAS OF ENGLAND

(DRAFT MAP)

Map 21.2: V. 9.3. FUNNEL.

We append a specimen from the proposed Volume I of the Basic Material. It concerns HAWS, the fruit of the wild rose, IV.11.6. At the head of the page are the *Questionnaire* reference and keyword; and underneath the question as asked, and the responses (in the modified orthography of J. Wright's *English Dialect Dictionary*) received in the six Northern Counties and the Isle of Man. On the left of the sheet are the numbers and abbreviations of the counties.

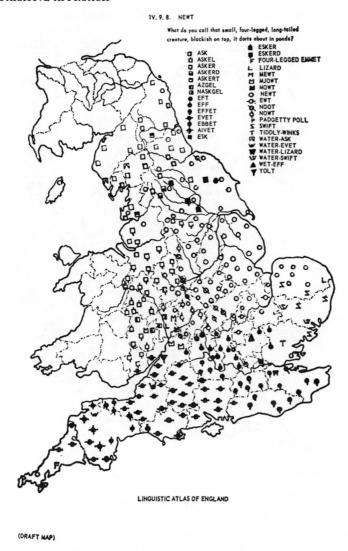

IV. 9. 8. NEWT

What do you call that small, four-legged, long-tailed creature, blackish on top, it darts about in ponds?

ASK
ASKEL
ASKER
ASKERD
ASKERT
AZGEL
NASKGEL
EFT
EFF
EFFET
EVET
EBBET
AIVET
ESK

ESKER
ESKERD
FOUR-LEGGED EMMET
LIZARD
MEWT
MJOWT
MOWT
NEWT
EWT
NOOT
NOWT
PADGETTY POLL
SWIFT
TIDDLY-WINKS
WATER-ASK
WATER-EVET
WATER-LIZARD
WATER-SWIFT
WET-EFF
YOLT

LINGUISTIC ATLAS OF ENGLAND

(DRAFT MAP)

Map 21.3: IV. 9.8. NEWT.

Then follow the phonetically transcribed responses, locality by locality. The identity of the locality and of the informant who has given the response would be ascertainable from Part I of the Volume. Any relevant incidental material noted in the recording books is prefixed by a superior circle and followed by the informant's number (attached as a superior letter). In square brackets is enclosed any supplementary information excerpted from the incidental material relating to the response given. The abbreviations *s.f.* and *s.w.* preceding a

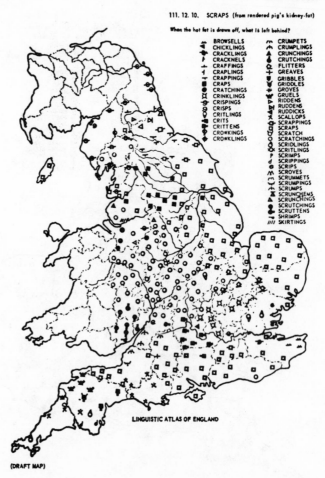

111. 12. 10.   SCRAPS (from rendered pig's kidney-fat)

When the hot fat is drawn off, what is left behind?

BROWSELLS
CHICKLINGS
CRACKLINGS
CRACKNELS
CRAFFINGS
CRAPLINGS
CRAPPINGS
CRAPS
CRATCHINGS
CRINKLINGS
CRISPINGS
CRISPS
CRITLINGS
CRITS
CRITTENS
CROWKINGS
CROWKLINGS

CRUMPETS
CRUMPLINGS
CRUNCHINGS
CRUTCHINGS
FLITTERS
GREAVES
GRIBBLES
GRIDDLES
GROVES
GRUELS
RIDDENS
RUDDENS
RUDDICKS
SCRAPPINGS
SCRAPS
SCRATCH
SCRATCHINGS
SCRIDLINGS
SCRITLINGS
SCRIMPS
SCRIPPINGS
SCRIPS
SCROVES
SCRUMMETS
SCRUMPINGS
SCRUMPS
SCRUNCHEMS
SCRUNCHINGS
SCRUTCHINGS
SCRUTTENS
SHRIMPS
SKIRTINGS

LINGUISTIC ATLAS OF ENGLAND

(DRAFT MAP)

Map III. 12.10. SCRAPS.

response mean that the form and the word, respectively, were suggested to the informant by the fieldworkers; *n.k.* means that the informant did not know the answer; and *obs.*, that the informant reported that the word concerned was obsolete.

To conclude this account of the new Survey, four (rough) lexical maps of the various words for *funnel, newt, scraps (from rendered pig's kidney fat)* and *snack (between breakfast and the midday meal)* are appended. Similar maps, professionally executed by the University Photographer, could be issued periodically during the next few years contained, unbound, in folders, say 50 at a time.

Lastly, fortunate circumstances have enabled us to start a fieldworker upon

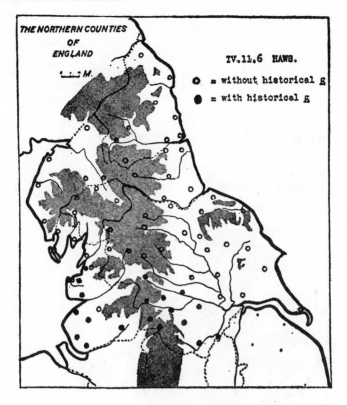

THE NORTHERN COUNTIES
OF
ENGLAND

IV.11.6 HAWS.

O = without historical g
● = with historical g

Map 21.5: IV.11.6. HAWS.

an investigation (by questionnaire) of the English dialects spoken in the Welsh Marches. It would be very gratifying to be able to turn this into a more extended and comprehensive project.

IV.11.6 HAWS

You know that bush which has white flowers in May and red berries in autumn and winter. What do you call its berries?

CAT-HAIGS (-HEGGS), CAT-HAWS, HAIGS (HEGGS, HIGGS), HAIGINS, HAWS, HAY-HEGGS, HEAGLES, SKEGS (sic)

1 Nb 1 hɔːəz, °hɔːəz[1] . 2 hæːz [haːθɔːn[2], haːθɔ́ːn[2] *hawthorn*]. 3 hæːz . 4 kathaːz [haːθɔ́ːn[1] *hawthorn*]. 5 haːz . 6 katæːˀz . 7 hɔːs . 8 kathaːz . 9 katɔːz, °—[1] .

2 Cu 1 haːz . 2–4 katɔːz . 5 katɔːʐ , °katɔːs . 6 ɔːz .

3 Du 1 haːz . 2 kataːz . 3 kathɔːz . 4–5 kataːz . 6 kataːz [haːθɔːn[2], θɔːn[2] *hawthorn*].

4 We 1–3 katɔːz . 4 kataːz .

5 La 1–2 kataːz . 3 kataːz [aːθɔːn[1] *hawthorn*]. 4 eːəgz, kataːz ["older"]. 5–6 eːgz . 7 eːɛgz . 8 eːgz . 9 ɔːz . 10 eː-ɛgz . 11 eːgzˀ . 12 igz . 13 iːglz [ɔːθɔ̹ːnboʃ[2] *hawthorn-bush*]. 14 eːgz .

6 Y   1 katɔːz . 2 katɔːz [ɔəθoːn³ *hawthorn*]. 3–4 katɔːz . 5 kataːz . 6 kataɹz [*sic*]
      7 katɔːz, s.f. kataːz [obs.]. 8–9 katɔːz . 10 katɑːz [ɔːθɔːn⁵ *hawthorn*]
      11 ɔːz . 12 kaːtɔːz [*sic*]. 13 katɔːz . 14 ɔːz . 15–16 katɔːz . 17 katɛgz,
      °katɛəgz . 18 katɔːz [ðɛ gɹɔo ɒn θɔːnz¹ *they grow on thorns (... hawthorns)*].
      19 katɔːz . 20 katɔːz [ɔːθɔːn³ *hawthorn*]. 21 eːgz . 22 p. eːgz, kateːgz
      [bɹɛdəntʃiːzboʃ³ *bread-and-cheese-bush* (= *hawthorn*)]. 23 eːgz [eːgtɹiː¹
      haig-tree (= *hawthorn*). 24–25 katɔːz . 26 eːginz . 27 eːˀgz [ɔːθɔːntɹiːz³
      hawthorn-trees]. 28 katɔːz . 29 p. eːgz . 30 eːgz . 31 ɛgz [wiːkɔːl əm ɛgz
      nɒt ɔːz¹ *we call them haigs not haws*]. 32–33 eːgz . 34 nːk.

Man   1 skɛg [hɔːtˀɔːˀn³ *hawthorn*]. 2 s.w. hɔːs .

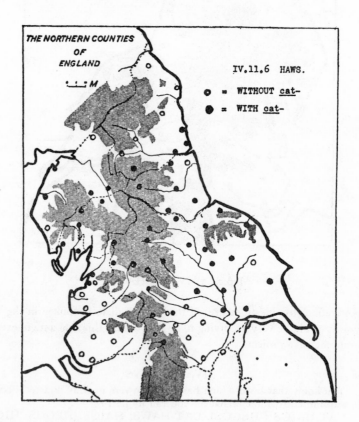

Map. 21.6 IV.11.6. HAWS.

21

Some Dialect Isoglosses in England

W. NELSON FRANCIS

EVER SINCE SYSTEMATIC STUDY of the regional dialects of America began, both linguists and laymen have been interested in the relationship of local dialects in America to the local dialects of Great Britain. The reasons for this interest are, I suppose, sufficiently obvious, ranging from rather naïve curiosity about the British origin of individual American localisms to a more sophisticated interest in the complex patterns established by the wholesale transfer of the English language from the Old World to the New. Until recently, however, investigation of this question has perforce been random and disorganized because of the lack on either side of the water of systematic data, procured under carefully controlled conditions. Today, as the collection of materials for the American and English linguistic atlases approaches completion, we are able to begin the kind of careful comparative study which must be the necessary preliminary to whatever general conclusions we may ultimately be able to draw. The purpose of this paper is to show examples of a few of the different kinds of relationships that exist. All the illustrations are drawn from lexicon, primarily because Kurath's *Word Geography of the Eastern United States*[1] has supplied us with a large number of lexical isoglosses of significance in America which challenge investigation of their British counterparts. All American data I have used are drawn from that book; the British materials are taken directly from the field records of the Linguistic Atlas of England at Leeds University.[2]

There is no need to describe the Linguistic Atlas of the United States and Canada. But since the Linguistic Atlas of England is presumably less well

Reprinted by permission from *American Speech* 34.243–57 (1959). The author is Professor of English and Linguistics and chairman of the department of linguistics at Brown University.

[1] Hans Kurath, *A Word Geography of the Eastern United States* (Ann Arbor, Mich., 1949).

[2] Most of the material I took directly from the field records during the winter of 1956–57, which I spent at Leeds as a Fulbright research scholar. For data from records made subsequent to June, 1957, I am indebted to Stanley Ellis, Lecturer in the English Language at Leeds University, who kindly transcribed them for me.

known, some information about its history and methods seems in order.[3] It grew out of the interest in dialect of two scholars, Harold Orton, of Leeds, and the late Eugen Dieth, of Zurich, both of whom had written monographs on local British dialects.[4] Beginning soon after the close of the Second World War, they had by the summer of 1951 produced a questionnaire that had gone through five successive versions and been extensively tried out in the field.[5] Fieldwork began that year, and has continued virtually without interruption until the present. Seven different fieldworkers have been at work at various times,[6] though one of them, Stanley Ellis, has done about half of the work. In January, 1959, the collection of data was more than four-fifths complete; about 240 of a projected 300 localities had been surveyed, and the fieldwork has been going forward steadily since.

The localities are spaced at intervals of 15 to 20 miles, with attention to such variable factors as population density, topographical features, and the history of population movements. Since the survey aims at recording the oldest surviving form of the most stable local dialects, the localities and informants have been chosen almost entirely from the most conservative element in English society—the small agricultural villages. With the exception of single partial recordings from London, Leeds, and Sheffield, the localities are villages and small towns of 300 to 2000 people, often going back in history to the Domesday Book, and as free as possible from recent immigration. Informants were almost all over 60 when interviewed, and many were in their 80s. They are all natives of the village where they now live or its immediate neighbourhood; most of them had no more than five or six years of schooling and have not traveled any great distance or for any long time away from home. A large number of them are agricultural laborers or, as we would say in America, "hired men."

In each locality a trained fieldworker completes a questionnaire of over 1300 items by interviews with from one to four informants. Unlike the American Atlas work sheets, the questions in the Dieth–Orton questionnaire are fixed in their phrasing, and the fieldworker is instructed not to depart from the printed wording unless he has to in order to get a response, in which case he makes an appropriate note in the recording. The recordings are written in International

---

[3] On the history of the English atlas, see the following: Harold Orton: "Dialectal English and the Student," *Transactions of the Yorkshire Dialect Society*, Part 47; VII (1947), 27–38; Harold Orton and Eugen Dieth, "The New Survey of Dialectal English," *English Studies Today*, ed. C. L. Wrenn and G. Bullough (London, 1951); Harold Orton, "A New Survey of Dialectal English," a paper read on February 16, 1952, at a meeting of the Lancashire Dialect Society (pamphlet, n.d.); Harold Orton, "Remarks upon Field Work for an English Linguistic Atlas of England," *English Studies*, XXXIV (1953), 274–278; Stanley Ellis, "Fieldwork for a Dialect Atlas of England," *Transactions of the Yorkshire Dialect Society*, Part 51; IX (1953), 9–21.

[4] Eugen Dieth, *A Grammar of the Buchan Dialect* (Aberdeenshire) (Cambridge, 1932); Harold Orton, *The Phonology of a South Durham Dialect* (London, 1933).

[5] Eugen Dieth and Harold Orton, *A Questionnaire for a Linguistic Atlas of England* (Leeds, 1952).

[6] The fieldworkers were Messrs. P. Wright, Ellis, Sykes, Gibson, J. T. Wright, and Francis, and Miss Playford.

Phonetic Alphabet script on special sheets which are later bound together by localities. Response to the questionnaire are recorded on the left-hand half of the sheet and conversational material on the right-hand half. After extensive editing, the work of Professor Orton and Dr. Wilfred Halliday, the material will be published in tabular form in four regional volumes. The volume for the six northern counties is well along, and should appear soon. Meanwhile, a collection of maps is being prepared at Zurich under the direction of Professor Kolb, successor to Professor Dieth. These will presumably be independently published.[6a] A tape recording of free talk is made at each locality, part of which is preserved on disks by the B.B.C.

Although there are as yet no recordings from Cornwall, Sussex, Berkshire, and Suffolk, and other parts of the southeast and East Anglia are only sketchily filled in, it is possible to draw a good many isoglosses that are accurate and a good many more that will need at most minor adjustment when the records are all in. But before turning to these, I should like to call attention to a few of the difficulties involved in making lexical comparisons between different regions, even in so small a country as England. These difficulties arise principally from the fact that in making such comparisons we are dealing with two variables, the lexical items and the referent. For significant comparison we must be sure that one of these variables is being held constant; that is, that we are comparing either different local words for the same thing, or different local referents for the same word. There may be, for instance, the disappearing referent. For example, one question in the Dieth–Orton questionnaire reads: "[What do you call] those dark blue berries the size of a pea, growing on a low plant on the moors? You make pies with them and the juice stains your teeth." (IV.11.3). The suggested answer is *bilberries*. This question invariably baffled my Norfolk informants, because, as I very soon learned, there are neither moors nor bilberries in Norfolk. But sometimes, perhaps just to be obliging, they produced answers such as "whortleberries," which are an entirely different kind of fruit.

Then there is the shifting referent. One question reads: "[What do you call] those insects with small thin bodies and thin legs, that fly up and down the window-pane?" The suggested answer, I discovered with some surprise, is "daddy-long-legs," which to me meant a long-legged spider with a small, round body. I discovered that it sometimes meant this to my Norfolk informants as well. Furthermore, many of them were also familiar with the term *harvestman*, and virtually every possible combination of the two terms with the two referents exists within the one county. It is obvious that we get a different picture if we consider the total distribution of a given lexical item from the one we get if we consider its distribution with a given referent. Since uneducated rustics do not have a taxonomist's precision of reference and terminology, we may have quite complex problems to deal with when investigating the vocabulary relating to plants, animals, and insects.

[6a] [For publication data see p. 238, footnote 7, and p. 239, footnote 8, in this book.— Eds.]

Likewise, even with the most careful questioning, the referent may be ambiguous. Some of the English recordings are unreliable on the very important item of the swingletree because some of the informants and fieldworkers apparently did not distinguish between it and the evener, or long beam to which two swingletrees are attached. Finally, we may have the problem of synonymous expressions, so interchangeable in the informant's vocabulary that it is a matter of chance which one comes out first. I became interested in the distribution of the Norfolk term *on the sosh*, meaning crooked or diagonal. The actual recordings, however, give a very imperfect picture of the spread of this term, since the informants often responded to the appropriate question with "slanting," "crooked," and other phrases or words, which went down in the recordings as the first and hence official responses and would have been the only ones if my particular interest has not led me to elicit others by further questions or even direct suggestions.

For these reasons, and others besides, our picture of lexical distributions based upon the broad and perforce hasty kind of survey that is made for a dialect atlas must be an inaccurate one. This fact must always be kept in mind as we look at lexical maps and isoglosses. It will help us to guard against the contrary errors of being enthralled by their symmetry or frustrated by their jumbled complexity. With these cautions in mind, let us now look briefly at some representative isoglosses. I have chosen five which illustrate five different types of relationship that may exist between American and English distribution patterns.

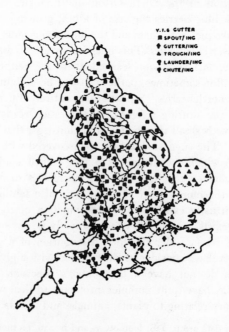

Map 21.1.

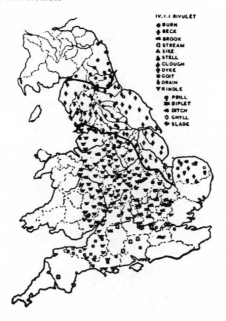

Map 21.2.

First, we may find broad regional distribution in America matching broad regional distribution in England. Kurath's Maps 53 and 54 show the principal terms for gutters to catch rain along the eaves of a roof. All along the Atlantic seaboard the word *gutters* itself is common, while further inland alternative words become more frequent. In general terms we can say that *eaves spouts* predominates in northern New England, *eaves troughs* and its variants in the rest of the Northern area, *spouting* and *spouts* through the North and South Midland, and *gutters* itself in the South. The more or less standard *gutters* is also strong in the urban areas along the coast, including Boston, New York, and Philadelphia. *Eaves troughs* appears to be recessive in New England, as well as in the South, where there are scattered instances in North Carolina and Virginia.

Map 21.1 shows a somewhat similar pattern in England. Here again *trough–troughing* is a recessive term, predominantly Midland, as can be seen by the relic areas in East Anglia and on the Welsh border, split by the dominant northern *spout–spouting*. This, in turn, encounters in the home counties the more or less standard *gutter*, which apparently extends throughout the South, though our lack of complete data is a handicap here. There is another recessive term, *chute–chuting*, either predominant or alternating with *gutter* through Somerset and Dorset and extending at least into northern Hampshire; until we have the data from Devon, Surrey, and Sussex we cannot be sure of its

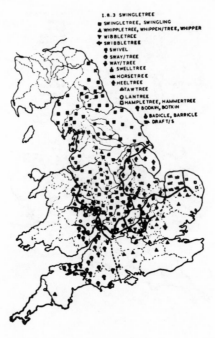

I.8.3 SWINGLETREE
■ SWINGLETREE, SWINGLING
▲ WHIPPLETREE, WHIPPEN/TREE, WHIPPER
▼ WIBBLETREE
◆ SWIBBLETREE
❡ SWIVEL
◒ SWAY/TREE
▲ WAY/TREE
▲ SWELLTREE
▬ HORSETREE
✦ HEELTREE
△TAWTREE
○ LANTREE
□ HAMPLETREE, HAMMERTREE
❡ BODKIN, BOTKIN
▲ BADICLE, BARRICLE
DRAFT/S

Map 21.3.

limits. The interesting thing to me about the distribution of these terms is the
fact that on both sides of the Atlantic *troughs* is recessive (note another relic
area in the Pennines in eastern Lancashire, western Yorkshire, and northern
Derbyshire), while *spouting* is a strong regional term, competing in urban areas
with a standard form, *gutter*, which also has a regional distribution (the south
of both countries).

In a second type of relationship we again see broad regional distribution in
both countries, but with a shift of terms. Kurath's Map 93 shows the Eastern
United States distribution of local alternatives to *creek* as terms for a small
running stream. The regional pattern is very clear, with *brook* universal in the
North, *run* in the Midland, and *branch* in the South. Turning to England (Map
21.2) we see the same kind of broad north–south stratification, though the only
term common to both countries is *brook*, dominant in spite of many local terms
throughout the Midlands and into the South. The competitors here are *burn*,
coming down from Scotland into the border counties of Cumberland, Northumberland, and northern Durham, and the Scandinavian *beck*, virtually universal
throughout the area of Danish settlement from Cumberland and northern
Lancashire, through Yorkshire and Lincolnshire, to Norfolk. Lacking records
from Suffolk and Essex, we cannot yet complete the southeastern end of this
historic isogloss, which has presumably remained virtually unchanged for 1000
years.

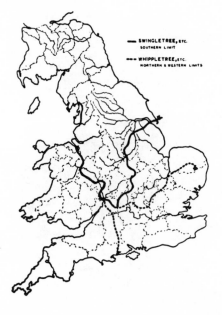

Map 21.4.

The significance of this map seems to me to be the fact that while *brook*, with strong regional distribution supported by Received Standard acceptance,[7] was carried across the ocean, its two strongest regional rivals were left behind, together with a host of localisms. Instead, two new terms, both apparently unknown in the mother country—*run*[8] and *branch*—developed as dominant regional forms.

In a third type of relationship we find a complex English situation, involving many local terms of relatively narrow range, matched by a much simpler regional pattern on this side of the ocean. One of the best known and most spectacular of Kurath's lines is the *whippletree–singletree* isogloss that lies along the border between the North and the Midlands. These terms, with their variants such as *whiffletree* and *swingletree*, dominated the whole area, except for *swiveltree*, which turns up in a little island between the two in central New Jersey. In England, on the other hand (Map 21.3), the situation is much more complex. The sources of the two dominant American forms are clearly apparent (Map

[7] If Tennyson had used his native Lincolnshire, he would have written "The Beck" instead of "The Brook."

[8] *OED*, s.v. Run *sb.*[1], lists this meaning as "Chiefly *U.S.* and *north. dial.*" The British quotations are all from Scots (except a single one from Charles Kingsley) and show the word qualified by a phrase—"the rin of the said loch" (1581), "a run from a sulphureous spring" (1768). The atlas materials do not report *run* from anywhere in England.

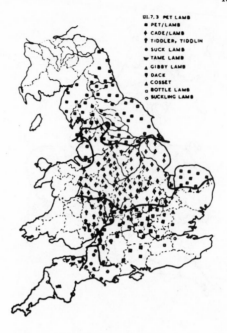

Map 21.5.

21.4). *Swingletree* and its variants pervade the North and the West Midlands except for the Welsh border, where the localisms *tawtree* and *lantree* appear; and *whippletree* and its variants seem to dominate the Southeast, from central Wiltshire and the Dorset–Hampshire line all the way across to Suffolk—though with more data from this region the picture may change in detail. But there are many local terms that apparently never crossed the ocean; or, if they did, they have succumbed to the dominant regional terms—note the Lincolnshire *heeltree*, Norfolk *horsetree* and *hampletree*, southwestern *bodkin*, and a very complicated pattern in the South Central Midlands and the home counties. Among the local terms in this area we find the New Jersey *swivel*, reported from two localities in eastern Gloucestershire and northern Oxfordshire. Here is the answer to the question posed by Kurath: "*Swiveltree* does not turn up anywhere else in the Eastern States and may well be a local descriptive term (cf. *swivel chair*)—or does it have a Dutch background?"[9] Our question now is whether this corner of New Jersey was settled from northern Oxfordshire.

One other matter of great interest here is the clear illustration of how phonemic variants of etymologically distinct forms may provide a series of easy transitional steps from one to the other across a border area. Beginning in eastern Gloucestershire and moving northeast through Oxfordshire into the

[9] Kurath, *op. cit.*, p. 13.

Map 12.6.

northwest corner of Bucks and then swinging southeast, we encounter in order the variants *swingletree, swivel, swibbletree, wibbletree, whippletree.* A little farther north are *swelltree* and *swaytree,* with a transitional *waytree* between *swaytree* and *whippletree,* similar to the transitional *wibbletree* between *swibbletree* and *whippletree.* The local distribution of these terms in this region is both complicated and intensely interesting, and should be made the subject of a much more intensive and fine-grained survey than that of the English atlas.

The remaining two types of relationship may be more briefly glanced at. On the one hand, a term of broad regional distribution in England may be a narrow localism in the U.S.A. Map 21.5 shows the English terms for an orphan lamb raised on the bottle. Note that *cade–cade lamb* is the dominant form throughout the Midlands. In this country, on the other hand, *cade* is a localism restricted to the Narragansett Bay area and Cape Cod.

On the other hand, a narrowly local term in England may show broad regional spread in this country. Map 21.6, for instance, shows the English terms for a second growth of grass in the meadow after the hay harvest. Note that there are several local terms, but the dominant forms are *fog* in the North, *eddish* in the North Midlands, and *aftermath–lattermath* in the South Midlands, with *second crop* prevalent south of the Thames and in East Anglia. But in a

small area in Hertfordshire and Essex—we lack detail to delimit it closely—
occurs the term *rowen*. As Kurath's Map 112 shows, this is the dominant
regional term throughout the Northern area of the United States, with only
scattered instances of *aftermath* in New England and upstate New York.

What has been shown here is, of course, sketchy and selective evidence,
but it permits us to make two general observations about what has happened
to lexical patterns in the course of the mass transfer from the homeland to the
New World. In the first place, our already fairly firm conviction that regional
patterns were not transferred intact is strengthened. There is some suggestion
in the maps for *brook*, *whippletree*, and *rowen* that Southern English terms tend
to show up in the northern United States, but the converse is not always true
and *gutter* actually reverses this pattern. Secondly, it is apparent that the mixing
of settlers from different parts of England produced a shaking up of lexical
patterns and a resulting competition for survival among local terms which
suddenly changed from settled regionalisms to competitive synonyms. We
need more research into local American speech of the seventeenth and early
eighteenth centuries in order to document this interesting phenomenon more
precisely.

22

Some Dialectal Verb Forms in England

W. NELSON FRANCIS

IN THE CHAPTER ON "CONCLUSIONS" in his *Survey of Verb Forms in the Eastern United States*, Bagby Atwood makes some cautious statements about the origin of the verb forms whose distribution he has discussed. He finds that very few forms seem to be of American origin, the great majority being recorded either in Early Modern English or in nineteenth and twentieth century British dialects. He abjures any attempt to trace particular forms to specific dialects of seventeenth century England, on the grounds judiciously stated in the following footnote:

> Our knowledge of the present-day distribution of dialect features in England is far from complete, and our knowledge of Early Modern English dialects is extremely limited. To argue from present-day distribution that a certain form must have been brought to an American colony from a certain area of England is risky and neglects the possibility that many forms may have become obsolete in certain areas in the course of two or three hundred years. Such a study should be undertaken only after many cautions and much historical research, and preferably only after a complete survey of England on Linguistic Atlas lines.[1]

Now that such a survey of England has been completed, it is possible to begin the process of cautious comparison which Atwood here suggests. On the basis of the field records for the Linguistic Atlas of England, which supply data for 300 localities in all areas of the country,[2] we can begin to see some suggestive patterns of distribution. This paper will deal with a few of these.

Reprinted by permission from *Orbis* 10.1–14 (1961). For the author see the preceding article.

[1] E. Bagby Atwood, *A Survey of Verb Forms in the Eastern United States* (University of Michigan Press, 1953), p. 42, n. 18.

[2] For information about the Linguistic Atlas of England, see H. Orton, "An English Dialect Survey: Linguistic Atlas of England" *Orbis* IX (1960), and my article "Some Dialect Isoglosses in England," *American Speech*, XXXIV (1959), 243–250, fn. 3 and 6. [See p. 245.] Some of the data from the field records used in this paper I took directly from the records; the rest were kindly transcribed for me by Messrs. Stanley Ellis and Robin Brown of Leeds University. I am indebted to Professor Harold Orton of Leeds, Director of the Atlas, for permission to use this material and for many other courtesies.

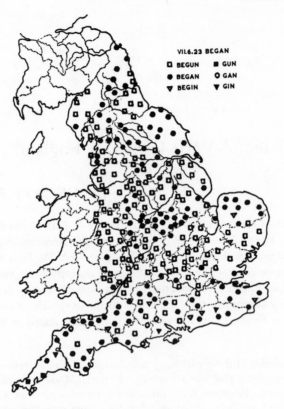

Map 22.1: VII.6.23 BEGAN.

Before coming to specific cases, however, two general points must be made. In the first place, since the two surveys used different questionnaires and somewhat different methods, the comparability of the results is only partial. Many of the verb forms which show interesting regional distribution in the United States were not included in the English survey. Nor were the contexts in which the forms were sought always comparable semantically and grammatically. Secondly, the English survey is confined almost entirely to the kind of informants classed in the American atlas as Type I or IA = older, old-fashioned, poorly educated, and rustic.

It is thus not possible with existing material to make for English speech the kind of comparisons of class dialects that the American survey makes possible and that Atwood has taken full advantage of. With the English materials we are confined to studying regional distribution in uneducated speech.

This is well illustrated when we look at the map for the preterit of *begin*

(Map 22.1), which was elicited in the frame "dark clouds gathered and soon it . . . to rain". Since this item is marked with a dagger in the questionnaire, fieldworkers pressed for this verb, though some informants preferred other verbs, especially *started*. As the map shows, responses are fairly evenly divided between *began* forms (125) and *begun* forms (142), with only a few widely separated instances of *begin*, which Atwood found to be fairly common in the South Atlantic States.[3] Except perhaps for some localized concentrations of *began*—as in the East Riding of Yorkshire, Leicestershire and Rutland, Norfolk, and Somerset—no meaningful regional pattern is perceptible here. Instead, the intermingling of forms indicates a competition in uneducated rural speech between the Standard English form *began* and the leveled form *begun*. It is to be noted that historically speaking *begun* may represent either a late Middle English leveling on the preterit plural instead of the preterit singular, or a later leveling of the preterit to the past participle, since *begun* is the modern reflex of both the Middle English preterit plural and past participle.

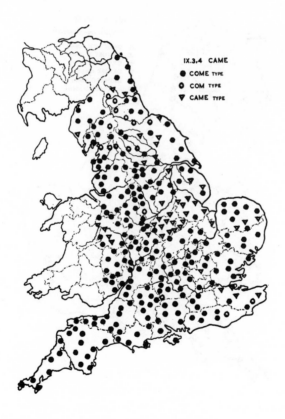

Map 22.2: IX.3.4 CAME.

[3] *Op. cit.*, p. 6.

Atwood finds the same kind of mixed usage in Type I speech everywhere in the Eastern United States. In the preterit of *come*, however, he finds the class distribution somewhat complicated by regional differences.[4] Thus *came* is standard in Type III (educated) speech everywhere and *come* is standard Type I speech everywhere except in the vicinity of New York City. But in the middle group—the Type II speakers—he finds the ratio of *come* to *came* varying from 1:2 in New York to 7:1 in North Carolina.

Once again the English map (Map 22.2) shows a pretty thorough mixing of forms. Greater phonological variety somewhat obscures the morphological distribution, since the reflex of a Middle English long ā may range all the way from Northern [ɪə] to Norfolk [æɪ], and there is a third form, [kɛm], descending from a Middle English (or Danish) form with a short low-back vowel, which appears in the North, especially along the Pennine Ridge and in the Yorkshire Dales. In general, however, it is possible to sort out the forms and

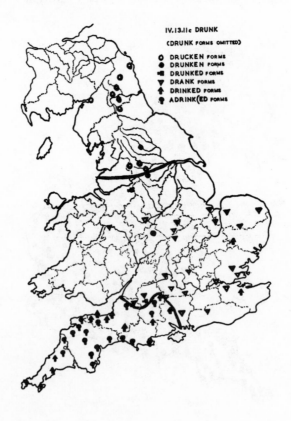

Map 22.3: IV.13.11c DRUNK.

⁴ *Ibid.*, p. 9.

observe that *come* forms predominate everywhere except in the Northeast Midland area of Leicestershire, Rutland, and Lincolnshire. The ratio of *come* to *came* is about 5:1, with 16 instances of [kɐm] and 3 of weak forms like *comed*.

More significant regional distribution on both sides of the water begins to appear when we turn to the past participle of *drink*. Since the American atlas recorded the preterit as well as the past participle, Atwood was able to observe that leveling of preterit and past participle is the prevalent practice among the large number of informants who do not use the standard form.[5] The usual non-standard forms for the past participle are the leveled preterit *drank*, which is common in New England, and the weak form *drinked*, which prevails in a sizable area of Virginia and North Carolina. The form *drunken*, which Atwood labels "archaic", is reported from only 15 informants, 9 of them cultured.

The English distribution of non-standard forms of the past participle (Map 22.3) is more clearcut. North of the Humber virtually the only form other than

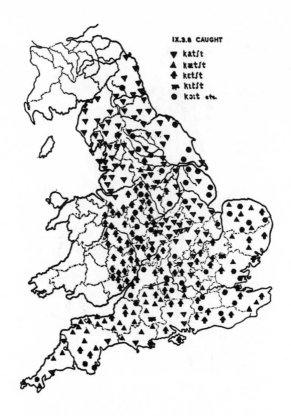

Map 22.4: IX.3.8 CAUGHT.

[5] *Ibid.*, pp. 10f.

standard *drunk* (commonly pronounced /drunk/) is *drucken*, which either did not go to America at all or has died out there. In the whole Midland area and in the South as far west as the middle of Hampshire, the only non-standard form (except for one instance of *drinked* from Suffolk and one from Kent) is *drank*, while *drinked* and its variants *adrinked* and *adrink* dominate the South-west.

A marked difference between the usage of uneducated informants on opposite sides of the water shows up in the past tense of *catch*. Atwood notes that "the standard *caught* /kɔt/ is dominant in all areas among all classes, though limited in Type I."[6] The weak preterit *catched*, usually pronounced /kečt/, he finds to be scattered rather sparsely over the whole area except for eastern Massachusetts, western Vermont, and central New York.

The situation among the Type I informants in England (Map 22.4) is just about the reverse: that is, weak forms outnumber *caught* forms in a ratio of

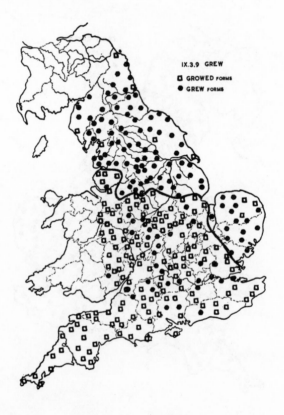

Map 22.5: IX.3.9 GREW.

[6] *Ibid.*, p. 8 and Figure 4.

about 5:1. As the map shows, the *caught* forms occur all over the country, from Northumberland to Cornwall and Kent, with more or less prominent concentrations in the Yorkshire Dales, northern Lincolnshire, and Norfolk. This is clearly an instance of greater conservatism in England, for while the two forms have existed together since the thirteenth century, the older *catched* was dominant even in educated speech until the nineteenth century.[7]

Though our concern here is with morphology rather than phonology, I cannot forbear commenting on the regional distribution of the pronunciation /kečt/ with the mid-front vowel. This pronunciation, which McDavid found to be used by more than three-fourths of the informants in all areas of the eastern United States except Ohio, central Pennsylvania, central Massachusetts, and the New York City area,[8] is confined in England to two well

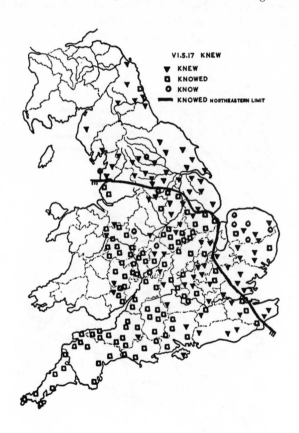

Map 22.6: VI.5.17 KNEW.

[7] *OED, s.v.* Catch, v.

[8] Raven I. McDavid, Jr., "Notes on the Pronunciation of *Catch.*" *College English*, XIV (1952–53), 290–291.

marked regions, one corresponding precisely to the West Midland area of Middle English and the other including the Home Counties, Kent, and Sussex, and extending into East Anglia on one side and Hampshire and northern Wiltshire on the other. A narrow corridor through Oxfordshire joins these two /kečt/ areas, which separate Northern [katʃt] from Southwestern [kætʃt]. The difference between these last two is best considered sub-phonemic (or diaphonic), since [a] is the customary Northern form of the low-front vowel. But [kɛtʃt] definitely represents a phonemic variant, since [ɛ] contrasts with [a] in the northern part of the West Midland and with [æ] in the southern part and the Home Counties.

A clearcut pattern of regional distribution appears in the preterit of *grow*. The strong form *grew*, which is also the standard form of cultivated speakers, is almost universal in the North, the Northeast Midland, and East Anglia, while in the West and Central Midland and the South, *growed* is heavily preponderant (Map 22.5). As might be expected, there are scattering *grew* forms,

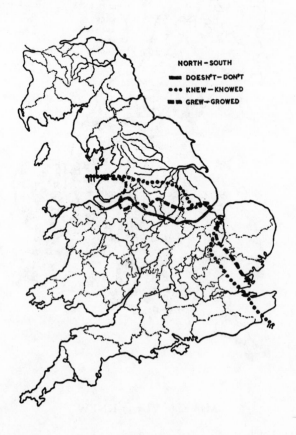

Map 22.7: North vs. South.

attributable to the influence of Standard English, in the *growed* area, but there are only six instances of *growed* northeast of a line running from the mouth of the Ribble southeast to the Isle of Ely and thence southward to the mouth of the Thames estuary. An almost similar line (Map 22.6) a bit farther north separates a northern and eastern *knew* area from one where *knowed* preponderates. This pair of isoglosses, which are plotted on Map 22.7 together with a third which marks the boundary between Northern *he doesn't* and a Midland and Southern *he don't*, are of great interest, because they correspond closely with a major bundle of lexical isoglosses. The dialect boundary thus established historically marks the southwesterly extent of strong Danish influence, though it lies some 50 to 75 miles northeast of the boundary of the Danelaw.

In America, *growed* is a form having general distribution in Type I speech, though varying in intensity from one region to another. Atwood finds that

It is used by about three fourths of Type IA informants in n. e. N. Eng. and by from one fourth to one third of the other non-cultured informants. Elsewhere *growed* occurs in Type I speech with a frequency varying from about one third (e. N. Y. and N. J.) to well over nine tenths (N. C.). In Type II it is rare in N. Y., N. J., and Del.; elsewhere it is used by from one fourth to nearly one half of this group.[9]

One final case, the preterit of *see* (Map 22.8), shows a clear case of well marked regional distribution on both sides of the Atlantic. In the United States, as Atwood points out and his map makes clear,[10] the predominant form throughout New England is *see*, identical with the present. Throughout the Midland area of New Jersey, Pennsylvania, Maryland, West Virginia, and the Shenandoah Valley of Virginia, the dominant form is *seen*, identical with the past participle. Tidewater Virginia again shows *see*, while in North Carolina and inland South Carolina, the dominant form among Type I informants is the weak *seed*.

As Map 22.8 shows, these three forms are in clearcut regional distributions i England. Standard *saw*, not entered on the map, is preferred by the uneducated rural informants only in the Scottish border counties of Northumberland, Cumberland, and Westmorland, and in a northeast Midland area comprising Leicestershire, Rutland, and southern Lincolnshire. Otherwise, *seed* is almost universal in the North and Northwest Midlands and in the Southwest, *see* in the East Midlands, East Anglia, and the Southeast (except Kent), and *seen* in the Southwest Midlands and in a corridor going through northern Wiltshire and Hampshire south to the Isle of Wight.

What has been here presented is only a very small series of samples of varying types of distribution of non-standard verb forms among the uneducated rural speakers of England. This evidence does not justify us in advancing very far beyond Atwood's caution about attempting to find the proto-

[9] Atwood, p. 15.
[10] *Ibid.*, p. 20 and Figure 17.

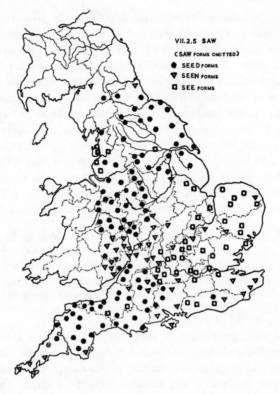

Map 22.8: VII.2.5 SAW.

type of a certain form in a specific area of England, though some examples
like *drinked*, *see*, /kečt/, and *growed* are tempting. They further point up the
need for study of seventeenth and eighteenth century speech in the colonies.
I should be surprised if we did not find that most regions were dialectal melting-
pots, in which individual lexical and morphological items were in more or less
open competition, so that each settlement area ultimately established its own
composite. But we must scrutinize all the available evidence before we can be
sure.

23

British Sources of Selected Features of American Pronunciation: Problems and Methods

HANS KURATH

1 THE PHONEMIC SYSTEMS of all regional types of cultivated American English (AE) correspond very closely to that of Standard British English (SBE).

There is no difference in the system of consonants, except that unsyllabic /ə/, as in *here, four*, etc. appears only in dialects that lack postvocalic /r/. Differences in the incidence of the consonants in the vocabulary, as of /r/ in *four, hard*, /s ~ z/ in *greasy*, /j/ in *due*, /h/ in *white*, are few. Phonic differences in the allophones, as of medial /p, t, k/ in *pepper, bitten, bucket*, of /r/ in *merry*, and of /l/ in *jelly*, are somewhat more numerous, but not very prominent.

In the vowel system the differences between the regional types of AE are greater, but all types have much in common with each other and with SBE, although the phonic character of most of the vowel phonemes varies markedly from dialect to dialect and differences in the lexical incidence of the vowels are rather numerous.

If we choose to interpret diphthongal as well as monophthongal vowels as phonemic units, the vowel phonemes shared by all dialects of AE and by SBE, as well as the phonemes peculiar to one or several dialects (the latter in parentheses), can be conveniently exhibited in a composite table, as shown in Table 23.1.

Free vowels are up-gliding, unless monophthongal; *checked* vowels are in-gliding, unless monophthongal. The phonemic contrast between free and checked vowels in the same phonic range (e.g. high-front, mid-back, etc.) thus rests either on phonic quality alone (if both are monophthongal) or on quality together with "drift" in quality (if one or both are diphthongal).

The substantial agreement in the phonemic systems of the several regional dialects of AE with that of SBE is a measure of the overwhelming importance of SBE in the development of all varieties of AE spoken in the Atlantic States,

Reprinted by permission from *In Honor of Daniel Jones* (Dennis B. Fry *et al.*, eds.). London: Longmans, Green & Co., Ltd., 1964. Pp. 146–155. The author is Emeritus Professor of English at the University of Michigan and editor of *The Linguistic Atlas of New England*.

TABLE 23.1: COMPOSITE TABLE OF VOWEL PHONEMES

Checked :	free	Checked :	free	Checked :	free
ɪ :	i			ʊ :	u
ɛ :	e	(ʌ)[1] :	3	(θ)[2] :	o
æ :	(a)[3]	(ɑ)[4] :	(ɑ)[5]	(ɒ)[6] :	ɔ
	ai		oi		au
crib :	three			wood :	two
ten :	day	(sun)[1] :	fur	(coat)[2] :	know
bag :	(car)[3]	(lot)[4] :	(car)[5]	(lot)[6] :	law
	pie		boy		now

[1] Checked /ʌ/, as in *sun*, is lacking in SBE (which has /ɑ/ in *sun*).

[2] Checked /θ/, as in *coat*, only in New England.

[3] Free /a/, as in *car*, only in eastern New England.

[4] Checked /ɑ/, as in *hot* (SBE *hut*) is lacking in eastern New England and in western Pennsylvania.

[5] Free /ɑ/, as in *car*, only in dialects that lack postvocalic /r/ except eastern New England, which has /a/).

[6] Checked /ɒ/, as in *hot*, only in SBE.

and, secondarily, of all regional dialects current in the Middle States and the Far West. Even if the vowel systems of the various regional folk dialects of England, Scotland, and Ireland should turn out to conform largely to that of SBE—which appears to be rather improbable—the dominant influence of SBE upon the systematic features of AE pronunciation could not be questioned.

In view of this unquestionable fact, supported by the practical identity of the systematic aspects of the morphology and syntax of AE and SBE, the chief task of the historian of AE is to account for the divergent features current in the regional dialects. Are they derived from different stages in the phonological development of SBE, or from regional variants of SBE? To what extent do they reflect regional differences in English folk speech, especially in the phonic (subphonemic) characteristics of shared phonemes and in their incidence in the vocabulary? Are they American innovations? Now that an adequate record of usage on the Atlantic seaboard is available, specific questions can be formulated, a procedure can be outlined, and some probable or possible answers can be suggested.

The following examples are intended to illustrate this approach.

2   The consonant /r/ survives in SBE only in prevocalic position. After the high vowel of *here* and the mid-vowels of *care* and *door*, /r/ has become the semivowel /ə/; after the low vowel of *car*, *Martha*, and the mid-central vowel of *fur*, *Thursday*, this derivative /ə/ is merged with the vowel to produce new vowel phonemes, /ɑ/ and /ɜ/, respectively. SBE shares the types of /hiə, kɛə, dɔə, kɑ, fɜ/ with the folk speech of the eastern counties of England to the north of the Thames. The folk dialects of the south and the west of England, on the other hand, preserve the postvocalic /r/, rather generally as a constricted [ɚ].

In the United States, several dialect areas on the Atlantic seaboard—eastern New England, Metropolitan New York, large parts of Virginia with adjoining sections of Maryland and North Carolina, and most of South Carolina, Georgia, and Florida—and all the states on the Gulf of Mexico as far west as eastern Texas—agree with SBE in lacking postvocalic /r/. Here the high and mid-vowels are normally followed by unsyllabic /ǝ/; car has the new phoneme /a ~ ɑ/, articulated regionally as [a· ~ ɑ·] or [ɑ· ~ ɑɒ]; fur has /ɜ/, pronounced regionally as [ɜ· ~ ß· ~ ɜɪ], with or without partial constriction of the tongue.

Each of the four geographically separated areas on the Atlantic seaboard now lacking postvocalic /r/ had in Colonial times one or more prominent seaports (notably Boston, New York, Richmond, Charleston) through which close contacts with England were maintained until the War of Independence, and gradually resumed thereafter. From the centres of these areas, this feature spread to the hinterland. It must have been rather firmly established in South Carolina and Virginia by c. 1800, since the cotton belt along the Gulf of Mexico, settled from these areas between 1810 and 1840, exhibits this feature.

It is well known that the loss of postvocalic /r/ in SBE, and the consequent emergence of the phoneme /ɑ/ of car, garden, and the unconstricted /ɜ/ of fur, Thursday, are of rather late date. They are not noted by orthoepists until the last quarter of the eighteenth century. The fact that landlocked Middle Atlantic States (Upstate New York and Pennsylvania) and the southern Upland universally preserve the postvocalic /r/ and a fully constricted /ɜ/ in fur, Thursday, supports this chronology. Today all the Inland and the West of the United States, settled by westward expansion between 1800 and 1850, preserve the /r/ after vowels. Approximately three-fourths of the American people use /r/ in all positions, but about 40 million living in the areas mentioned above do not.

The questions to be raised are these: (1) Did some early settlers on the Atlantic seaboard bring with them the postvocalic unsyllabic /ǝ/ from the folk dialects of the East Midland counties of England, where early loss of postvocalic /r/ is attested? (2) To what extent do the Middle Atlantic States owe the preservation of postvocalic /r/ to settlers from the South and West of England and from Scotland and Northern Ireland? (3) Did all American colonies originally have both /r/ and /ǝ/ after vowels, achieving uniformity in usage at a later date? (4) To what extent is the loss of postvocalic /r/ as such in certain coastal areas to be attributed to the cultural influence of SBE after the original settlement, especially also after the political separation of the American colonies from England?

To give realistic historical answers to these questions much work remains to be done on both sides of the Atlantic.

3 In SBE, the ME long low vowel /ā/ and the up-gliding diphthong /ai/ are merged in one phoneme, /e/, articulated as an up-gliding diphthong [eɪ ~ ɛɪ], so that tale rhymes with tail. Merging in an up-gliding [eɪ ~ ɛɪ ~

æɪ ~ aɪ] has also taken place in the folk speech of parts of eastern England (chiefly Middlesex, Essex, Hertfordshire, Bedford, Surrey, and western Kent) in which London is embedded.

In the dialects of western England, on the other hand, these two phonemes are kept apart, ME /ā/ is now represented by an in-gliding [eᵊ ~ ɛᵊ], as in *tale, lane, April*, ME /ai/ by up-gliding [ɛɪ ~ æɪ ~ aɪ], as in *tail, way*. They also kept apart in Norfolk and Suffolk as well as in coastal Sussex.

On the margin of the area in which coalescence in an up-gliding diphthong occurs, some speakers exhibit merging of the two phonemes in an in-gliding diphthong [eᵊ ~ ɛᵊ].

In conformity with SBE and the folk dialects of eastern England, ME /ā/ and /ai/ are regularly merged in the phoneme /e/ in American English. However, the articulation of this /e/, as in *tale, lane, April*, and *tail, way* varies regionally.

Over large areas /e/ is pronounced [eɪ ~ ɛɪ], as in SBE. Monophthongal [e· ~ e] alternating with in-gliding [eᵊ]—the latter in checked position—is widespread in South Carolina and Georgia. Relics of [e· ~ eᵊ] survive along Chesapeake Bay in Virginia and Maryland. Monophthongal [e·] is common in the German settlements of eastern Pennsylvania. Hence, though all dialects of AE share the merging of ME /ā/ and /ai/ with SBE, the phonic character of /e/ derives in part from the folk dialects of the West of England and of East Anglia, and in part from German.

4 Parallel to the coalescence of ME /ā/ and /ai/, SBE has merged ME /ǭ/ and /ou/ into one phoneme, /o/, articulated as an up-gliding diphthong [oʊ ~ ɔʊ ~ ßʊ], so that *stone* rhymes with *grown*. SBE shares this merging into an up-gliding /o/ with the folk dialects of the Home Counties.

In two widely separated areas, East Anglia, with the valley of the Welland, and the southwestern counties (Dorset, Somerset, Devon), ME /ǭ/ and /ou/ coalesce either in an in-gliding [oə ~ uə] or in a short monophthong [ʊ ~ ʌ ~ ɔ].

Elsewhere the two ME phonemes remain distinct in English folk speech: here *stone, road, clothes* have an in-gliding vowel [oə ~ uə] or monophthongal [ɔ ~ ʊ ~ ʌ], *grown, know* an up-gliding [oʊ ~ ɔʊ].

Except for New England, American English conforms to SBE and the folk dialects of the Home Counties, East Anglia, and the southwestern counties in merging the two ME phonemes completely.

In conformity with SBE, this /o/ is an up-gliding diphthong over large areas. Coalescence in a monophthongal [oᵊ ~ o], similar to that of the folk dialects of East Anglia and the southwestern counties, occurs chiefly in South Carolina and Georgia, whatever the actual historical connections may be.

Only New England preserves the original distinction, though to a limited extent. Here the old monophthong survives in checked position as a short and fronted mid-back vowel /θ/, as in *stone, road, coat* /stθn, rθd, kθt/, contrasting with up-gliding /o/, as in *know*, *grown* (but also, e.g. in *no*, *rode*). This so-called "New England short *o*" is sharply recessive. This feature of the New England dialect is somehow related to regional English folk speech, perhaps also the early SBE usage.

5 In the greater part of the Eastern States, *law*, *salt*, and *lot*, *crop* have contrasting vowels, the /ɔ/ of *law* ranging phonically from rounded [ɔ· ∼ ɔ] to [ɒɔ], the /ɑ/ of *lot* from unrounded low-central [ɑ ∼ ɑ·] to low-back [ɑ ∼ ɑ·]. This distinction corresponds to SBE /ɔ/ as in *law* vs. /ɒ/ as in *lot*. However, in AE the incidence of /ɔ/ is more extensive than in SBE: it is regular before voiceless fricatives, as in *cough*, *moth*, *frost*, and predominates before the /g/ of *dog*, *log*, etc.

In English folk speech, contrasting /ɔ/ and /ɒ ∼ ɑ/ are normal in the eastern counties north of the Thames and in large parts of the Midlands, though their incidence deviates regionally from SBE (e.g. /ɔ/ is usual in *dog*, *frost*, etc. in East Anglia). SBE obviously reflects the folk usage of this area.

South of the Thames and from Bucks westward, on the other hand, the two phonemes are merged in an unrounded [ɑ ∼ ɑ] sound. Merging of the two phonemes is found also in two sub-areas of the Atlantic States, eastern New England and western Pennsylvania. Here the resulting vowel, which I shall represent by the phonemic symbol /ɒ/, has a wide range of positional and prosodic allophones running from more or less rounded [ɒ· ∼ ɒ] to un-rounded [ɑ· ∼ ɑ ∼ ɑ].

How shall we interpret this coalescence in two widely separated sub-areas of the Atlantic States? Does western Pennsylvania reflect the usage of the Ulster Scots, since according to Joseph Wright (EDG) *law*, *all*, etc. have an unrounded vowel in Scotland and the northernmost counties of England? What shall we say about the merger in eastern New England? Is it somehow related to English folk usage current in the southern and the western counties, or is this simplification the result of the blending of two English dialectal types? Perhaps we shall see more clearly, when Harold Orton of Leeds publishes the findings of his dialect survey of England.

6 In AE the incidence of the free vowel /u/ of *do* and the checked vowel /ʊ/ of *full* in words like *room*, *coop*, *hoof*, *root*, *soot*, *food* varies regionally, socially, and from word to word. For instance, in *room*, *broom* checked /ʊ/ is common in the North and the South Atlantic States, but not in the Middle States and the southern Upland; in *Cooper*, /ʊ/ is regular south of Pennsylvania, but uncommon to rare farther north; in *roof* and *soot*, /ʊ/ is common outside the South; in *food* it is largely confined to Pennsylvania. Moreover, in *soot* the checked vowel /ʌ/ of *hut* occurs extensively in common and in folk speech in most parts of the Eastern States, but in *hoof* only in parts of the South.

This disconcertingly variable incidence of three different derivatives of ME /ọ̄/ (and of /ū/ before labials) in AE has its counterpart in English folk speech, and to some extent in SBE (cf. *food*, *good*, *blood*). Broadly speaking, the eastern counties of England have /ʊ/ in *room*, /ʊ ~ u/ in *hoop, soot*, /u ~ ʊ/ in *root, afternoon*, and /ʊ ~ ʌ/ in *hoof, soot*; the western counties have /u/ in *room*, /ʊ/ in *hoop, soot*, /u ~ ʊ/ in *root, afternoon*, /ʊ ~ u/ in *hoof, soot*; the "London Corridor" lying in between (widening out into the central Midlands, as so frequently) agrees either with the eastern or the western counties, but generally favours /u/, as does SBE.

It would seem obvious that the complexities in AE reflect the multiple regional variations in English folk speech and the resulting unsettled usage of SBE, especially of earlier times. To trace specific regional variants of AE to particular British sources will remain hazardous until we are better informed about the English dialects and the regional adaptations of SBE, about which we know so little. Nevertheless, it is highly probable that the /ʊ/ in *room, broom*, used primarily in New England, Virginia, and South Carolina, became established in these coastal areas under the influence of SBE of the eighteenth century. In earlier days both /ʊ/ and /u/ must have been current, because the settlers came from western as well as eastern England.

7   In all the Southern states, as far north as the southern boundary of Pennsylvania, the vast majority of speakers on all social levels use the vowel /o/ of *door, boar* also in *poor, sure*. From Pennsylvania northward, *poor, sure* have a high vowel, /u/ or /ʊ/, *door, boar* a mid-vowel, /o/ or /ɔ/, except that in northeastern New England the high vowel is merged with the mid-vowel /o/, as in the South.

Coalescence of earlier /u/ before a historical /r/ with /o/ (or the derivative /ɔ/), has taken place in SBE and in the folk speech of the eastern counties of England lying north of the Thames, coalescence in an [uᵊ]-like sound (here regular in *stone, road*, etc.) farther west. But distinct vowels are preserved in this position in the folk speech of Kent, Surrey, Hampshire, Oxfordshire, Wiltshire, and Dorset, though not consistently.

The regional differences in AE, therefore, reflect regional differences in the mother country. Shall we attribute them simply to the folk speech of England, or has SBE had some influence? If the latter, why should the Southern States follow the lead of SBE, and Philadelphia, Metropolitan New York, and Boston with their hinterland keep entirely aloof? Should we infer from this diversity in the behaviour of the seaports that SBE usage was as unsettled in the latter part of the eighteenth century as it is today?

8   The diphthongal vowel /au/, as in *cow, down, out*, has a wide range of phonic variations (diaphones) in the Eastern States. Some variants are regional, some social, others positional or prosodic.

Marked positional allophones are characteristic of Virginia and the Low Country of South Carolina. Before voiceless consonants, as in *house, out*, Virginia has a "fast" diphthong [əu], South Carolina [ɐu]; in other positions, as in *cow, down, loud*, the former area has a "slow" diphthong [æˑʊ], the latter [ɑu]. Elsewhere in the Atlantic States, positional variation is slight.

The phonic type [ɑʊ ~ aʊ], similar to that of SBE, is usual in Pennsylvania, Metropolitan New York, and much of the New England settlement area, where it is regularly used by the better educated. It is also common in the Lower South, especially in South Carolina.

The type of [æʊ ~ ɛʊ] occurs to some extent in all of the Atlantic States, but its social dissemination, hence also its social standing, varies sharply. Virginians of all social levels use it regularly before voiced consonants, and no stigma attaches to it here or in other parts of the South, even where it is not very common. From Pennsylvania northward, however, [æʊ] is rustic or old-fashioned, being avoided by the better educated. The type of [ǝu ~ ɐu], with centralized beginning, which appears in parts of the South as a positional allophone of /au/, occurs sporadically in old-fashioned speech of the North, especially in northeastern New England, but without positional restriction.

All of these variants of the phoneme /au/ are current in present-day British folk speech, but the marked positional allophones of Virginia appear to have no counterpart in England and may therefore be an American innovation.

9   In the eastern United States the diphthongal phoneme /ai/, as in *nine* and *twice*, exhibits a wide range of variants. Some of them are regional or social, others positional or prosodic.

Striking positional allophones of /ai/ are confined to two sub-areas of the South. Virginia, with adjoining parts of Maryland and North Carolina, has a "fast" diphthong [ǝi] before voiceless consonants, as in *twice*, *light*, and a "slow" diphthong [a·ᵉ ~ a·ᵊ] in other positions, as in *nine*, *high*. Correspondingly, the Low Country of South Carolina has [ɐi] and [a·ᵉ ~ aᶿ] in these positions.

Elsewhere in the Atlantic States positional variation of the phoneme /ai/ is slight, but regional differences in articulation are very marked. Thus the southern Upland has [a·ᵉ ~ a·ᵊ], Pennsylvania, Metropolitan New York, and southern New England have [aɪ ~ a·ɪ ~ ɑɪ], Upstate New York and northeastern New England not infrequently [ʌɪ ~ ǝɪ], though these variants are yielding ground to [aɪ].

The widely used American variants [aɪ ~ a·ɪ ~ ɑɪ ~ ɑ.ɪ] have their counterparts in SBE of today and in the folk speech of a corridor leading from Middlesex–Essex through Hertfordshire and Bedfordshire northward into the Midlands.

The variants [ɐɪ ~ ʌɪ ~ ǝɪ], current positionally in parts of the American South but without positional restriction in parts of the North, correspond rather closely to the variants rather generally used by the folk east, west, and south of the "London Corridor". Shall we say that this phonic type of American English is wholly derived from the English dialects of these areas, or should we assume that it was also current in SBE of an earlier day? The narrow corridor to which the phonic type of SBE is now confined in English folk speech makes one suspect that [ɑɪ ~ a] is fairly recent in SBE. Such an inference finds support in the observation that [əɪ ~ ɐɪ] is now current, though positionally restricted, in the cultivated speech of two sub-areas on the Atlantic Seaboard—Virginia and South Carolina—which had intimate contact with England throughout the Colonial Period and after. The positional restriction of these variants, however, may well be an American innovation.

10 My purpose has been to pose specific problems concerning the British sources of some features of American pronunciation restricted to certain sub-areas of the Atlantic States—that section of the United States from which all varieties of American English are ultimately derived—and to suggest probable or possible solutions. I am well aware of the tentative nature of my suggestions. I hope that they may stimulate others to follow them up and to gather further evidence that may lead to firm conclusions. We must learn more about earlier usage in the major focal areas on the Atlantic Seaboard by gathering and interpreting unconventional spellings in local records, so that our historical inferences from present-day usage may be corrected. We need a clearer view of the regional folk dialects of England, Scotland, and Ireland than we now have, before American peculiarities can safely be traced to particular types of English folk speech, if they cannot be reconciled with SBE. We must try to find out more about regional variants in the cultivated speech of England during our Colonial period, before we can decide whether an American regionalism derives from the folk speech or from the cultivated speech of England. It may well be that, in time, regionally restricted cultivated pronunciations current in America will throw light upon earlier SBE usage and on its regional variants, which otherwise must be largely inferred from the present-day regional folk dialects of England.

11 In accordance with American practice, I cite phonemic units between slants and phonic features in brackets. Since the vowel systems of the various English folk dialects are yet to be worked out, I refrain from phonemicizing the phonic entities of these dialects. For my immediate purpose this procedure is adequate, and in future studies devoted to the British sources of American pronunciation purely phonic data will continue to have considerable importance.[1]

---

[1] Fuller information concerning the data upon which my statements of usage are based will be found in Hans Kurath and Raven I. McDavid, Jr., *The Pronunciation of English in the Atlantic States*, Michigan, 1961. A considerable number of the 1450 field records from the Atlantic States were made by Dr. Guy S. Lowman, Jr., who did his doctoral work under Professor Daniel Jones. Dr. Lowman also furnished the 60 field records of English folk dialects from which my English data are taken, unless otherwise stated. Daniel Jones' contribution to this paper, though indirect, is therefore quite substantial.

24

Double Dialect Geography

CARROLL E. REED

IN THE WORDS of Professor Raven I. McDavid, Jr., "the principle upon which all linguistic geography is built is the simple one of observing differences in grammar, pronunciation, and vocabulary, determining the regional and social distribution of these differences, and seeking their historical and cultural explanations".[1] One might also emphasize two other points: (1) the importance of statistical cartography in the analysis of such differences; (2) the significance of subsequent interpretation for a study of general linguistics.[2]

Dialectology, complex as it is, enters an even more challenging domain, however, when the interpretations it fosters are combined with problems of bilingualism. In at least one area of the world—the southeastern section of Pennsylvania—a *double dialect geography* has been effected. That is to say, the speech of a colonial German population, which accepts the English language while retaining its original dialect, is recorded in the Atlas of American English and, at the same time, in the Linguistic Atlas of Pennsylvania German.[3] While the dialectology of this area has been treated independently from the point of view of both English and German, no over-all consideration has been given so far to the simultaneous relationship of the two atlases with respect to cultural and historical matters.

Do the isoglosses in the English atlas coincide, or may they be expected to coincide with those of the German atlas? What position does the bilingual area hold in relation to the surrounding sections of monolinguals? These and other intriguing questions come immediately to mind when we begin to consider the problems of double dialect geography. The answers to such questions might well provide us with a rich store of useful information, not only in refer-

Reprinted by permission from *Orbis* 10.308–19 (1961). The author is Professor of German and Linguistics at the University of Massachusetts. He founded and until 1967 was the director of the Linguistic Atlas of the Northwest Pacific Coast.

[1] In W. N. Francis, *The Structure of American English* (New York 1958), p. 486.
[2] Cf. Sever Pop, *Le Centre International de Dialectologie générale, Orbis* I (1952), pp. 7–9.
[3] Hans Kurath, *et al., Linguistic Atlas of the United States and Canada* [Archives]. C. E. Reed and L. W. Seifert, *A Linguistic Atlas of Pennsylvania German.* Marburg 1954.

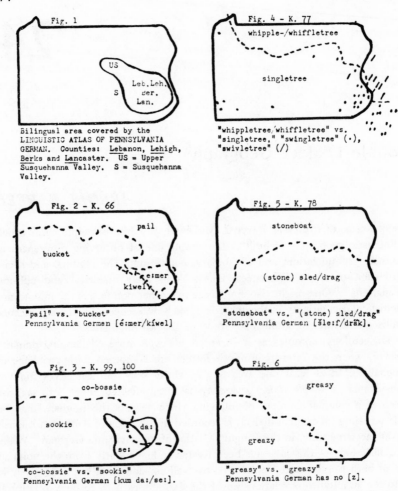

Fig. 1

Bilingual area covered by the
LINGUISTIC ATLAS OF PENNSYLVANIA
GERMAN. Counties: Lebanon, Lehigh,
Berks and Lancaster. US = Upper
Susquehanna Valley. S = Susquehanna
Valley.

Fig. 4 - K. 77
whipple-/whiffletree

singletree

"whippletree,/whiffletree" vs.
"singletree," "swingletree" (·),
"swivletree" (/)

Fig. 2 - K. 66

pail

bucket

e:mer
kiwe:

"pail" vs. "bucket"
Pennsylvania German [é:mer/kíwel]

Fig. 5 - K. 78

stoneboat

(stone) sled/drag

"stoneboat" vs. "(stone) sled/drag"
Pennsylvania German [šle:f/drãk].

Fig. 3 - K. 99, 100

co-bossie

sookie   da:

se:

"co-bossie" vs. "sookie"
Pennsylvania German [kum da:/se:].

Fig. 6

greasy

greazy

"greasy" vs. "greazy"
Pennsylvania German has no [z].

Figures 24. 1–6.

ence to this particular region, but also in areas of bilingual settlement—present
and past—in similar situations throughout the world.

The work of Professor Hans Kurath on the *Linguistic Atlas of the United
States* has revealed a number of important facts concerning the area in ques-
tion. In the first place, this part of Pennsylvania shares more or less the typical
dialect features of the Midland Area, and only occasionally those of the
Northern Area. Specifically, it is the most prominent part of the North Midland
Area.[4]

In the English of the entire Midland Area a number of German forms

[4] Hans Kurath, *A Word Geography of the Eastern United States*. Ann Arbor,
Michigan, 1949.

have been noted, although these are frequently restricted to smaller and smaller regions where bilingualism persisted over a long period of time.[5] In the German of this area, of course, English loan-forms have always been readily available; some which have remained in use reflect older stages of English and must, therefore, have been borrowed at an early time,[6] and many have been necessitated by cultural innovation after the time of the first settlements. English has also had a strong influence in the form of loan-creations.[7] Hence, it may be stated to begin with that the conditions arising from reciprocal relationships between English and German can best be interpreted in the light of the following general considerations: (1) through changing circumstances with respect to the development of American dialects, the texture of Pennsylvania German has changed variously and at different times; (2) the settlement history of Pennsylvania German, with its primary and secondary manifestations, created not only its own special patterns in the mother tongue, but also influenced the nature and development of the English in which it became enmeshed.

Let us consider the position of Pennsylvania German and English in reference to their role in the general dialect patterns of American English in the eastern United States. German forms in Pennsylvania English correspond regionally on the north to the maximum extent of the Midland Area. A typical isogloss in this instance is demonstrated by the distribution of the English terms "pail/bucket" (Figure 24.2). The original bilingual sector is located entirely within the "bucket" area, but in the German itself two terms are used which divide the area east and west into [é:mer] and [kíwel], respectively (the latter in the Susquehanna Valley). A container for carrying feed to hogs is known as a "slop-bucket" in English. The German uses a hybrid-form [šláp-è:mer], resp. [šláp-kìwel], which competes with [sái-è:mer/sái-kìwel]; the English Midland term "slop" (opposed to Northern "swill"), thus employed, enjoys the same regional domain as "bucket".

Similar division is made in the terms used for calling the cows. But in this case the English isogloss divides the German area in the center: Northern "co-boss(ie)" is opposed to Midland "sook(ie)". At the same time, a residue of German forms is used even in English, and the division for these—[kúm-dà:] on the east and [kúm-sè:] on the west—corresponds geographically to the [é:mer/kíwel] opposition cited above. Thus, alternative forms for addressing cows (who, presumably, are not bilingual) have a somewhat divergent distri-

---

[5] Hans Kurath, *German Relics in Pennsylvania English, Festschrift für M. Blakemore Evans* (Columbus, Ohio, 1945), pp. 96–102.

[6] C. E. Reed, *English Archaisms in Pennsylvania German, Publications of the American Dialect Society*, No. 19 (1953), pp. 3–7.

[7] Paul Schach, *Hybrid Compounds in Pennsylvania German, American Speech* XXIII (1948), pp. 121–134; *The Formation of Hybrid Derivatives in Pennsylvania German, Symposium*, III (1949), pp. 114–129; *Semantic Borrowing in Pennsylvania German, American Speech* XXVI (1951), pp. 257–267; *Types of Loan Translations in Pennsylvania German, Modern Language Quarterly* XIII (1952), pp. 268–276; *Die Lehnprägungen der pennsylvania-deutschen Mundart, Zeitschrift für Mundartforschung* XXII (1955), pp. 215–222.

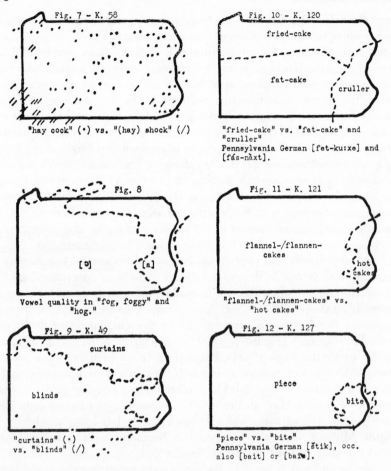

Fig. 7 - K. 58

"hay cock" (·) vs. "(hay) shock" (/)

Fig. 10 - K. 120

fried-cake

fat-cake

cruller

"fried-cake" vs. "fat-cake" and
"cruller"
Pennsylvania German [fet-kuːxe] and
[fás-nàxt].

Fig. 8

[ɔ]   [a]

Vowel quality in "fog, foggy" and
"hog."

Fig. 11 - K. 121

flannel-/flannen-
cakes

hot
cakes

"flannel-/flannen-cakes" vs.
"hot cakes"

Fig. 9 - K. 49

curtains

blinds

"curtains" (·)
vs. "blinds" (/)

Fig. 12 - K. 127

piece

bite

"piece" vs. "bite"
Pennsylvania German [štik], occ.
also [bait] or [baiᵂ].

Figures 24. 7–12.

bution in English and German within the same area, and the German forms
used in English follow a common German isogloss (Figure 24.3).

In relation to the English isogloss dividing Northern "whippletree/
whiffletree" from Midland "singletree/swingletree/swivletree", Pennsylvania
German has a single form [šílšàit], and stands well within the Midland Area,
although the English division between "singletree" and "swingletree" penetrates well into the eastern part of the bilingual area (Figure 24.4). Another
English isogloss, Northern "stoneboat" vs. Midland "(stone) sled/drag", enjoys
the support of a translatable German term, [šleːf], although the English itself
is not to be judged a loan-translation, since "drag" is widespread in eastern
New England, where German influence is nil (Figure 24.5).

Agreement between the German area and a Northernism in the matter of pronunciation is illustrated in Figure 24.6, where the voiceless [s] in "greasy" corresponds to the permissible allophone of dialect German /s/. In this instance, the English pattern may be directly influenced by the German. At least, their relations are compatible.

A more difficult problem, however, is presented in Figure 24.7, in which English (Northern) "hay cock" seems to predominate in the German area, while only a few instances of (Midland) "(hay) shock" are found there, restricted mainly to younger speakers. In the German, the loan-word [šak] is universal. Here a very interesting principle of bilingual geography is demonstrated: where competing lexical forms furnish the basis for loan-words in a bilingual area, the minor form tends to be accepted as "native" to the minority speech group. A striking instance of such nature is the twice-borrowed English word "pie" in Pennsylvania German; the English minor form [boi] is considered a German term, whereas [pai] is readily conceded to be a loan. The less common the minor form becomes, the more "foreign" it is in the donor language, and the more genuinely "native" it seems to the speaker of the recipient language.

The Pennsylvania German bilingual area thus not only represents a conservative enclave in the midst of the North Midland Area, but also one which participates in the competing fortunes of English dialect divergences. In its use of the vowel [a] in the words "fog, foggy" and "hog" (Figure 24.8), it reinforces the Northern forms, as opposed to Midland and Southern [a ∼ ɔ], even though the German phonemic system places no restriction on the choice. The area also maintains generally the Northern term "curtains" rather than the Midland "blinds" in referring to roller shades (Figure 24.9).

More intricate are the conditions under which certain linguistic forms used in the eastern part of Pennsylvania are shared, or partially shared by the bilingual area, in contradistinction to both the Northern and the Midland areas. In the German, for example, there are two terms for "doughnut", distinguished either according to shape or recipe, [fét-kù:xe] and [fás-nàxt]; they are translated generally as "cruller", the English (from Dutch) of the adjacent eastern area extending westward to the Susquehanna Valley. In the remaining part of the North Midland Area, however, the German term has been anglicized and there maintains itself as "fat-cake", opposed to the Northern term "fried-cake" (Figure 24.10).

Other such divisions of English within the bilingual area may be noted: the eastern sector, for example, has the term "hot-cakes", which competes on the west with the term "flannen-/flannel-cakes"—a folk-etymology based on the archaic German word [flám-kù:xe] (Figure 24.11); from the Philadelphia region, the word "bite" (for a light lunch, usually between meals) covers a part of the area in which the German has [štik] (occasionally also [bait] and [bais]), beyond which English again has a loan-translation, "piece", which is then widely distributed in the Midland Area (Figure 24.12).

Another feature of the Philadelphia region, the pronunciation of English

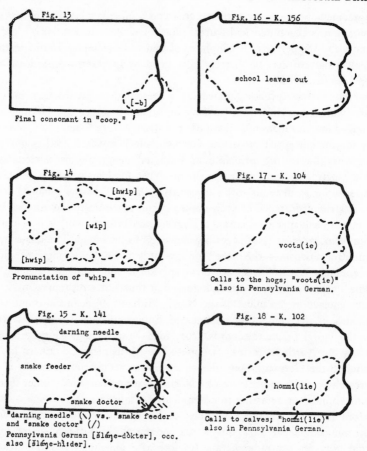

Figures 24. 13–18.

"coop" with final [-b], penetrates the bilingual sector, where German voiceless lenis [-ḅ] evidently supports it (Figure 24.13). Further evidence of phonetic reciprocity may be noted in the Pennsylvania pronunciation of "whip" with the initial [w-], rather than [hw-], concurrently with the Pennsylvania German (borrowed) type involving an initial bilabial voiced fricative [β-] (Figure 24.14).

A curious circumstance is to be noted in the relation of three words for the "dragon fly" which are found in the Midland Area. The term "snake feeder" is rare, and it occurs only within the bilingual sector. Much more common is the form "snake doctor" which is generally used in the English of the bilingual area and in nearby sections of Maryland and Virginia. By far the most extensive term, however, distributed throughout the entire Midland

Area, is "snake feeder". All of these terms, presumably, are of German provenience, although only *Schlangehüter* is attested in the *Deutscher Wortatlas*,[8]
and there it is Austrian rather than Palatine. The English terms of the competing Northern Area ("darning needle, devil's darning needle") are, indeed,
equally obscure. In Pennsylvania German the term [šláŋe-hì:der] is attested,
but the usual word is [šláŋe-dòkter]; the latter supports its English loan-form,
but as Figure 24.15 clearly shows, the Northern type, "darning needle",
impinges upon the bilingual area from an easterly direction.

The significance of this configuration is at once apparent when one observes
the superimposition of German loan-word isoglosses as furnished by Hans
Kurath.[9] The examples which he illustrates and describes may be seen to
coincide rather neatly on the eastern edge, but they diverge from one another
quite noticeably toward the west, where isogloss conformity is more the exception than the rule. In many instances, furthermore, the eastern isogloss-complex
does not cover the bilingual area at that point, but it tends to recede westward
as far as the Susquehanna Valley. Typical examples are presented in Figures
24.16–19: here it would seem that, while the German-speaking groups tend to
maintain distinctiveness because of their bilingual consciousness, the English
dialect features of eastern Pennsylvania (notably those sponsored by the
Philadelphia area) exercise an aggressive influence upon this region. The compact nature of loan-word isoglosses *in the midst of* the bilingual area emphasizes
especially this fact, corroboration of which will be found in the distributions
of "cruller" and "hot-cakes" treated above. The receding character of German
loan-words is aptly demonstrated in Figure 24.20, where the loan-translation
"overhead" is retained while the proto-type "overden" is increasingly restricted
to southwestern Pennsylvania. In the "overhead" area, however, German still
maintains the term [ò:wer-dèn]. A competitive struggle for bilingual variants
in such situations is epitomized in the remarks of one informant who observed
that, in calling hogs at a distance, he used the English term "poo-ie", but in
close proximity, he preferred the German "voots(ie)" (Figure 24.17).[10]

The most notable resistance to anglicization then—paradoxically enough—
is now to be found in the most concentrated bilingual area, i.e. east of the Susquehanna River. Indeed, the English of this area, in its eastern sector at least, is
remarkably less Germanized than the adjacent regions of the Upper Susquehanna Valley and of southwestern Pennsylvania in particular. (The converse
of this seems to be true of the German spoken in these same areas.) Figure
24.21 demonstrates the residual area in which German [tut] is accepted in

---

[8] Walther Mitzka, *Deutscher Wortatlas*, Vol. II.

[9] See notes ¹ and ² above p. 273.

[10] Another informant pointed out that there was really no need to call the hogs,
"they know when it's feeding time". The linguistic phenomena connected with this
activity therefore represent a kind of ritual, the functioning of which is confined to mere
speaking, rather than the response of the hogs. Nevertheless, such ritual behaviour
proves to be just as tenacious and culture-bound as that requiring communicative
efficaciousness.

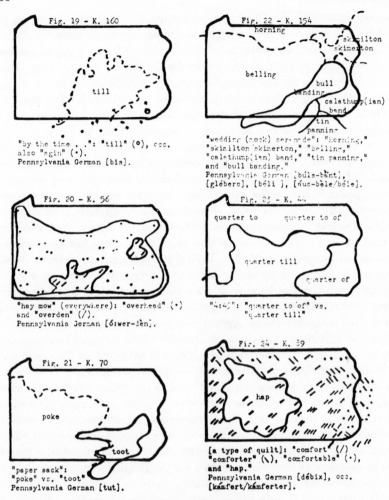

Figures 24. 19–24.

English. Immediately adjoining it to the west, the Midland form "poke" is widely current, a term which, of course, derives from another type of English than that represented along the eastern border of Pennsylvania. While the English [tut] area covers that portion of the German area having the same form, it does not include the southeastern sector in which German prefers the form [dut].

The core position of Pennsylvania German in relation to such isogloss patterns is strikingly illustrated by Figure 24.22, where German [búls-bànt] contributes to English "bull banding", equivalent to the Midland English word "belling", which in turn furnishes the basis of the German noun [béliŋ] and the verbs [áus-bèle/béle] in Upper Susquehanna Valley. In the English "calathum-pian" area, German has [glébere], and the essential instrument of a "bull band" is known as a [búls-gàik] or, more commonly, [sái-gàik] (i.e. "pig fiddle").

The position of "bull banding" with respect to competing English dialect forms presents us with a significant configuration. Northern "horning", Mid-land "belling", New York "skimerton/skimilton", and Mid-Coastal "cala-thump(ian band)" are thus separated by a linguistic redoubt which has its geographical center in the western part of the bilingual sector. The conservative effect of this area is no more clearly illustrated than here.

Regarding the residual area of loan-forms in Pennsylvania English, a summary of general observations may now be appropriate: the area may either be (1) an integral part of the Northern (and/or eastern) Area, (2) divided between the Northern and Midland Areas, (3) entirely contained in the Midland Area, or (4) a separate enclave between adjacent competing areas. Affinity with the South Midland Area is generally observable in the wider distribution of German loan-words, such as "snake doctor" (Figure 24.15), although a few items of pronunciation from the files of the Linguistic Atlas of the United States may also be cited. Southern [a] in "post-office", for example, is used in the English of this area. The word has long since found use in German as [pòst-àfis]—with the same vocalic characteristics. Likewise, the Southern pronunciation [kri:k] "creek" finds widespread acceptance in the English of this area, while German continues with its borrowed Northern form [krɪk].

On the western edge of the area, such (West) Midland forms as "poke" and "quarter till" (Figures 24.21, 24.23) seem to have little impact upon Penn-sylvania German; the substandard form "you'ns" (for "you", plural) is similarly restricted, giving way to the eastern term "yous" and checked at the Pennsyl-vania border by the Southern "you-all". Incidence of the type "belling" (Figure 24.22) in the German of the Upper Susquehanna Valley is matched there only by the Scottish term "hap", which is otherwise confined to the English of a small section of western Pennsylvania (Figure 24.24). The Pennsylvania German term is usually [débix], but [kámfert] is also used—a loan from the English Midland Area—and occasionally [kámferter], from the Northern and Eastern Areas.

The *Linguistic Atlas of Pennsylvania German* demonstrates certain notable dialect differences to be found within the area of early German settlement. Migration from this area, with subsequent spreading and mixing of dialect features, was treated in some detail in my article, entitled "Die Sprachgeographie des Pennsylvaniadeutschen" (*Zeitschrift für Mundartforschung* 25 (1957), pp. 29–39). The most significant division demonstrated there was the ethnolinguistic separation of Berks and Lehigh counties (on the east) from Lancaster and Lebanon counties (on the west, in the Susquehanna Valley). While this division had its primary impetus in the transplanting of several German dialects to the New World, political conditions of colonial Pennsylvania contributed heavily to its subsequent geographical distribution. The earliest settlers were, of course, almost exclusively German. But in a few decades a number of English settlers found their way among them, and the English language gained acceptance— first through commerce, and later by legislation. To the north, the westward movement of English settlement was politically determined by the boundaries representing the extension of Northern claims; the results are reflected plainly in many of the isoglosses mentioned above.

The Pennsylvania Germans had established themselves on the western frontier for some time before the Ulster Scots began to take up land to the west of them. But with these newcomers a different type of English speech was imported, part of which was assimilated in the German, as well as in the English of the Germans, and part of which, in turn, was to carry Germanisms with it as it spread further westward.

In my essay on English archaisms in Pennsylvania German, cited above, it was shown how English loan-words sometimes became imbedded, and were thus perpetuated, in the German of colonial Pennsylvania. It was also pointed out there that the directional flow of such loan-words could be traced to specific areas of English settlement concentrated on either side of the German area. From the discussion above it is now possible to perceive the dynamic nature of what may be called the westward pressure: English forms replace German loan-forms in the English, and the areas of replacement impinge upon the eastern part of the bilingual sector. The German area often stands as a solid unit, of resistance, and, as a consequence, isogloss bundles manifest themselves on its eastern edge. A dialect division within the Pennsylvania German area itself then furnishes a second line of resistance in the face of further inroads. It is a familiar axiom of dialectology that wherever there is maximum pressure and resistance in the use of competing speech forms, dialect divisions tend to become sharper and more concentrated.

Along with this obvious truism one must further consider the psychology of bilingualism itself. Where there is a clearcut division of the two languages, changes within the English seem to continue unimpaired; English loan-forms in German come to be regarded as part of the German itself and, thus, preserve a measure of integrity even independently of English. But in areas where bilingualism is less concentrated, the continuance of German loan-forms in English seems to be more tenacious. Part of the explanation for this, of course, pertains to the manner in which English settlers filtered westward through the German area. The rest can be ascribed to the refractive effects of the bilingual area itself, with its incumbent cultural peculiarities and ethnic awareness. Because of the gradual diffusion of German-speaking communities in peripheral sectors, and the bilingual nature of the core area itself, it may be readily observed that the distribution of German was here *internally* oriented, and the English around it *externally* oriented. It is no longer possible to distinguish a "German" and "English" population among older residents of the area itself, but the linguistic consequences of an earlier fusion of peoples may now be analyzed in a fascinating way by means of information to be gained through "double dialect geography". For, in this way, bilingual processes are not only amplified from the stand-point of structural compatibility, but also with respect to the pressures and adjustment of usage as affected by historical events.

Dialect Theory

INTRODUCTION

Gino Bottiglioni's article, which introduces the reader to the whole field of dialect geography, could well have been the first in this anthology. It seemed better, however, to place it here as a background for the following articles that seek to relate dialect research to recent developments in linguistic science. Indeed, Bottiglioni refers to American research only cursorily after he has presented the broad historical conspectus of modern scholarly concern with dialects. His general treatment shows how European scholars have found in dialect information profound implications for linguistic theory.

Uriel Weinreich's immediate research was directed toward establishing a Yiddish dialect atlas of Europe, but in this article he extends his interest to the relationship between dialect data and linguistic structuralism. The work of Kurath, and of George L. Trager and Henry Lee Smith, Jr., he considers as moving in the direction of what he has termed structural dialectology—but not far enough. Particularly in phonology does he see the need for this next step toward such a dialect theory.

Just how this step can be taken is described by Robert Stockwell, who during the past ten years has more than once asked American dialect geographers why they do not take this step. Until dialectologists do, he believes, the full linguistic importance of dialect studies cannot be realized. Kurath's *A Phonology and Prosody of Modern English* in 1964 may be looked upon as partly meeting Stockwell's demand, although he continues to ask the question.

Rudolph Troike moves Stockwell's question into the more recent sphere of generative grammar. He argues persuasively that the newer phonological approach, based upon distinctive features rather than upon phonemes and Weinreich's concept of the diaphoneme, can provide a more substantial foundation for a structural dialectology than can structuralism alone.

Finally, Trevor Hill, drawing not upon American dialect data but upon information collected by the Scottish Survey of Dialects, also proceeds to construct a theoretical phonological system. His method and conclusions may usefully be compared with those offered by Stockwell and Troike.

25

Linguistic Geography: Achievements, Methods, and Orientations

GINO BOTTIGLIONI

THE DEVELOPMENT OF SCIENCE includes both the discovery of new facts and the successive equalization of the methods of interpretation. As the methods increase in accuracy, it becomes possible to study other truths which, when they were first noted, seemed to darken that part of the horizon that had appeared clear to still earlier researchers. We have an unceasing contrast of shades and lights that, however, softens and composes itself harmonically to the eyes of those who observe the succession with serene minds while even the latest acquisitions of science get old in the course of time. The same may be said about linguistic geography, which is already half a century old. Now, with the fervor of the first neophytes calmed down and their comprehensible, but often too easy, enthusiasm moderated, linguistic geography can rightly fill the place it deserves among the methods of linguistic studies.

Linguistic geography owes its origin to the comparative method started by Bopp and his close successors who deduced the kinship of Indo-European languages from the observation of the corresponding linguistic phenomena, building their theory on the basis of those phonetic series that were improperly called laws and, in the wrong estimation of Schleicher and even more of the neogrammarians, were interpreted and applied as laws of the physical world.

But since H. Schuchardt[1] opposed naturalism and the strict neogrammarian uniformity with his spiritualistic interpretation of language, considered in the essence of its historical reality, new methodological needs appeared on the horizon of linguistics. And when Paul Meyer,[2] in conformity with the "Wellentheorie" of Schmidt[3] and in a polemic against Ascoli,[4] demonstrated that the

Reprinted by permission of the Linguistic Circle of New York from *Word* 10.375–87 (1954). At the time of his death the author, Professor Bottiglioni, was a member of the faculty of The Linguistic Institute of the University of Bologna.

[1] *Über die Lautgesetze. Gegen die Junggrammatiker*, Berlin, 1855.

[2] In *Romania*, 4.294–296.

[3] J. Schmidt, *Die Verwandtschaftsverhältnisse der indogermanischen Sprachen*, Weimar, 1872.   [4] See *Archivio Glottologico Italiano*, 2.385ff. (1876).

location of different isoglottic lines did not coincide in one linguistic area, it became necessary to represent and study each linguistic fact separately, abstracting oneself from those dialectical limits to which Meyer had denied any real objective existence. Among those who agreed with Meyer were also Antoine Thomas and Gaston Paris. The latter, in *Les parlers de France*,[5] showed the way later followed by his pupil Jules Gilliéron, the master of linguistic geography, a way which became an organic part of linguistics, improving and renewing the comparative method with a broader and more realistic view of developmental factors. As a matter of fact, after the first discoveries of Gilliéron, the grave deficiencies of traditional etymology became evident, particularly in the field of the Romance languages. It became clear that traditional etymology, confining itself to the relation between the starting-point of an evolution and its conclusion, ignored all intermediate phases, sometimes distorting the history of the word. With perhaps an excess of assurance and absolutism, Gilliéron proclaimed "the failure of phonetic etymology."

The new views of that multiform prism which is human language, illustrated by Gilliéron and his school, evoked a general echo of consent. When in 1919 his lecture on *La faillité*[6] appeared, the *Atlas linguistique de la France* (*ALF*)[7] had already been published, a "monumentum aere perennius"[8] which, as the first geographic representation of linguistic facts seen in a moment of their development, offered to historical-reconstructive research an effective means for the investigation of the complex reasons of their divergence. The principle and the procedure were obvious: just as the geologist moves from the morphological aspect of the ground to discover the sedimentary processes that have determined it, so the linguist needs a faithful representation of the linguistic area to reconstruct its history. Dictionaries were not and are not enough for this purpose. Though no atlas contains as much material as a dictionary, it can, with a limited number of grammatical and lexicological examples, offer a representation, even if synthetic and only sketchy, of a linguistic zone characterized in time and space. In addition, a careful observation and an ingenious comparison of the maps of the *ALF* revealed a series of developmental facts unnoticed by former linguists, and the processes through which innovation takes place appeared in all their complexity.

When Gilliéron undertook his task he may not have realized the consequences that would come from the study of the materials that Edmont, his wise and tireless cooperator, submitted to him, and that he was sketching in on outline maps of France. However, these consequences became evident soon

[5] Reprinted in *Mélanges linguistiques*, publiés par Mario Roques, Paris, 1909, 432ff.

[6] Jules Gilliéron, *Étude sur la défectivité des verbes. La faillité de l'étymologie phonétique;* résumé de conférences faites à l'École pratique des Hautes Études; Neuveville, Beerstecher, 1919.

[7] Paris, Champion, 1902–12; *ALF Corse*, 1914.

[8] This was defined by Meyer–Lübke himself (in *Litteraturblatt für germanische und romanische Philologie*, June, 1902), who in his sincere enthusiasm did not foresee the uncompromising struggle Gilliéron would wage against the neogrammarian school.

afterwards, upon the completion of the great work, in the studies of Gilliéron himself and of his most faithful disciples, Jean Mongines and Mario Roques.[9] These studies devoted particular attention to phenomena of a psychological nature which had not been considered significant before and stressed expressive peculiarities peculiar to the different social classes, the sexes, and the age groups of the speakers which had been submerged in the levelled neogrammarian studies.

Ethnic reactions and substratum phenomena brought out in Ascoli's learned work were subjected to stricter discipline through areal comparison. Thus for instance the occurrence of cacuminal sounds (such as $-\underline{d}(\underline{d})-$ < -LL-) in the amphizone of the Mediterranean and farther up to the Indian peninsula actually helps delimit the area of the peoples that were overpowered by Indo-European waves.[10]

The genesis and expansion of innovating currents crossing, interweaving, being superposed on one another, became evident. In an area of mixed languages like Corsica, areal comparison leads us to recognize the most ancient ethnic linguistic aspects (common to Sardinia and Sicily, too) which are partly obscured by the Tuscan stratum;[11] and we can follow the succeeding and more recent French penetration from the principal centers (Bastia, Aiaccio).[12] And if the Corsican sonorization of the voiceless intervocalic occlusives, originally intact, is to be attributed to Tuscan influence, as I think I have demonstrated, the *vexata quaestio* about the priority of Tuscan series like *ago* < ACU over the series *fuoco* < FOCU[13] is explained and settled.

The processes of Latin linguistic expansion could be traced in a new light through the successive strata of Romanized territory. In Sardinia we find derivations of Lat. JANUA, FORNU, ĪLEX and also of Lat. JENUA, FŬRNU and ĒLEX; the presence of the former in the central zone, the most conservative in the island, and of the latter in the peripheral zones, reveals two chronologically different moments of Sardinian Latinization.[14]

The phonetic decay that may bring about the destruction of the form of a word or create homonymies that are intolerable for the linguistic feeling of the speakers, now was ranked among the most important developmental factors in

[9] Among the many studies of linguistic analysis and reconstruction, we should mention here Gilliéron's *Généalogie des mots qui désignent l'abeille d'après l'Atlas linguistique de la France*, Paris, Champion, 1918.

[10] Bottiglioni, Indice fonetico per l'area di espansione ligure (Abstract from *Atti del 1º Congresso Internazionale di Studi Liguri*, 1950); L. Heilmann, Il problema delle cerebrali indiane, in *Scritti in onore di Alfredo Trombetti*, 287–304.

[11] Bottiglioni, La penetrazione toscana e le regioni di Pomonte nei parlari di Corsica, *L'Italia Dialettale* 2.156–210 and 3.1–69.

[12] Bottiglioni, Elementi costitutivi delle parlate còrse secondo l'Atlante Linguistico Etnografico Italiano della Corsica, *Memorie Accad. Bologna, Classe Sc. morali*, S. IV, V. ii (1939/41).

[13] Bottiglioni, Il còrso pretoscano nella classificazione delle lingue romanze, *Archivum romanicum* 21.524 (1937).

[14] See M. L. Wagner, La stratificazione del lessico sardo, *Revue de linguistique romane* 4(1928), num. 13–14.

lexical history. A language strengthens weakened words, abandons and replaces embarrassing homophones.[15] The reason why the Romance languages retain CAMBA and not CRUS is to be sought in the weak resistance of the Latin word. In the Gallo-Roman territory especially, where evolution is quicker and more destructive, many Latin monosyllables, dissyllables and trisyllables show a tendency to disappear if they are not strengthened by a suffix, so that SOLICULU > *soleil*, ACUCULA > *aiguille*, CORBICULA > *corbeille*, AETATICU > *âge* replace the doomed words SOLE, ACU, CORBE, AETATE. Against the few, marginal and weak survivals of APIS > *ef, es*, we have the flourishing of substitute designations which Gilliéron studied in their genetic relations with so much—perhaps too much—ingenuity.[16] Prov. *clavel* < CLAVELLUS replaces *claus* < CLAVUS which clashed with *claus* < CLAVIS;[17] *traire* < TRAHERE replaces *moudre* < MULGĒRE, which merged in the struggle with *moudre* < MOLĔRE;[18] in the Gascon area, the cock becomes a vicar (*bégey* < VICARIUM) or a pheasant (*hazan* < PHASIANUM) as GALLUS and GATTUS in the long run converge into the single ambiguous form *gat*;[19] the success of *viande* < VIVENDA is due to the Parisian pronunciation in which *char* < CARNE, pronounced *cher*, gets confused with *chère* < CARA.[20] The innovating effect of these phonetic and semantic conflicts may take place at any time and place; for instance—leaving the French sphere—we notice that in a part of the Italian territory bounded by Sillaro, Santerno and Senio (Emilia-Romagna) the "hedge" is referred to by derivations of Lat. SAEPE (> *sęva, sęve, siv, sęv*); in another part, these are replaced by derivatives of a deverbative of CLAUDĔRE (> *çǫda, kįǫda*). The reason for this substitution becomes evident if we observe that in the same territory, the derivations of Lat. SALVIA become *sęv* in the zone of *çǫda* (*kįǫda*), so that superposing the two areas of *çǫda* and *sęv* < SALVIA, we get perfect congruence.[21]

Besides the comparison of linguistic areas, we derive from linguistic geography the criteria for understanding not only the lexical evolution due to homonymy, but also to different aspects of monosemy and polysemy. If instead of starting from the *idea* reflected in its various denominations (onomasiology) we start from the *word*, we can construct semantic maps where different meanings of the same word characterize mutually exclusive areas (e.g. in Friuli *linda* < *LIMITA "eaves" and *linda* "lodge"), others where the two semantic values are superimposed on one another (e.g. in the north of Italy, *balcone* "window" and *balcone* "shutter"), and still others where the process of superposition is

[15] See J. Gilliéron, *Pathologie et thérapeutique verbales*, Paris, Champion, 1918.

[16] *Généalogie, cit.*, passim.

[17] Gilliéron, *L'aire "clavellus" d'après l' "Atlas linguistique de la France,"* Neuveville, 1912.

[18] Gilliéron–Mongin, Études de géographie linguistique III. Traire, mulgere et molere, *Revue de philologie française* 20.90–98 (1906).

[19] Gilliéron–Roques, Études de géographie linguistique XII. Mots en collision. A. Le coq et le chat, *Rev. phil. franç.* 24.278–288 (1910).

[20] Gilliéron, *Pathologie, cit.*, I, 2ff.

[21] See Antonio Quarneti, Un caso di omofonia nei dialetti delle alte valli del Síllaro, Santèrno e Sénio, *Memorie Accad. Bologna*, S. IV, V. iii (1939–41).

not completed but where it can be seen in action, or where semantic areas recede and lose contact with each other. The various reasons and conditions of polysemy may be seen in the comparison of semantic areas: thus the meanings have less stability and are weaker in the periphery of a zone, while in the middle they struggle more vigorously until they reach a definite order; the literary language avoids polysemy as much as possible; polysemy is frequent in dialectal speech especially when two ideas are included in the same sphere of human activity; and so forth.[22]

Areal comparison yields results not only in the field of lexicology, but is useful also in the fields of phonetics, morphology,[23] and syntax. Everywhere there is a ferment of studies aiming toward a biology of language, probing deeply into the analysis of thought and of its expression considered as the creative act of the individual in a socially determined environment.

Linguistic geography draws its origin from Gilliéron's *Atlas*; none of the earlier works of a similar nature[24] had a sufficient rigor or breadth of view to launch it. Considering the value of the first results of the new methods, one can easily understand the enthusiasm of the master and his disciples and their belief that they had overthrown the whole edifice built up in a century of work by the pioneers of linguistic science and by the neogrammarians. Gilliéron, an eminently critical and caustic mind, thought that the comparison of geographical areas could in itself resolve the most vexed linguistic problems, and thus worked almost exclusively with the materials of the *Atlas*. Notwithstanding the deficiencies pointed out by many people, he thought the *Atlas* to be essentially reliable and used it to destroy the myth of a phonetic law working, like a force of nature, blindly, rigorously, and inescapably. The Gilliéron critique nearly coincides with that of the linguists following Benedetto Croce's idealism;[25] they, too, in stressing correctly the spiritual value of the creative act of language, opposed the neogrammarian naturalism. But at bottom, Gilliéronians and Crocians followed fundamentally different principles and moved from different points of view. The former started from the system, considered in its arrangement, and from perturbations coming from expressive necessities incident to its equilibrium; the latter began with the word in the immediacy of its poetic creation.[26] In addition, both, though working together to throw down the last

---

[22] For this study of semantic areas, see K. Jaberg, *Aspects géographiques de langage*. Deuxième conférence (aires sémantiques), Paris, 1936, 43–77.

[23] See Jaberg, *Aspects géographiques, cit.* Troisiéme conférence (aires morphologiques), 79–106.

[24] Like the *Petit atlas phonétique du Valais roman* (sud du Rhône), Paris, Champion, 1880, also by Gilliéron; the *Sprachatlas von Nord- und Mitteldeutschland*, Strassburg, 1881 and the 28 maps added to the *Geographie der Schwäbischen Mundart*, Tübingen, 1895.

[25] B. Croce, *Estetica come scienza dell'espressione e linguistica generale*, Bari, 1922; La filosofia del linguaggio e le sue condizioni presenti in Italia, *La Critica* 39 (1941).

[26] See Karl Vossler, *Positivismus und Idealismus in der Sprachwissenschaft*, Heidelberg, 1904; *Sprache als Schöpfung und Entwickelung*, Heidelberg, 1905.

bulwarks of neogrammarian resistance and to clear the way of science toward new goals, had a one-sided view of the truth, which still escapes us. As we progress in our studies, we continue to discover the faults of our predecessors.

Gilliéron thought that he could discard the services of the historical-comparative method. But as the errors in some of his most daring constructions came to light,[27] the scope of geographical comparison was reducing itself to its proper limits.[28] For, if geographical comparison can point, for example, to homophony as the cause of a creative impulse, it can say nothing or very little about the reasons why the innovation becomes established in the mind of the speaker in one way rather than in another.[29]

"Quelle est," asks Millardet,[30] "la valeur primitive de l'image contenue dans *bégey* < VICARIUM 'coq'? Est-ce l'echo d'une satire anticléricale, nous reportant à l'inspiration des fabliaux? Ou bien le 'coq' est-il le vice-roi du poulailler, ou bien autre chose encore? Dans quel milieu social a pu se developper tout d'abord le sens nouveau? Le mot est-il savant ou héréditaire?" We cannot answer all these questions by means of linguistic geography alone. But we must also observe that the conception of the death of words due to phonetic decay was based on that very historical phonetics towards which Gilliéron and his first aides showed so much disdain; we can say that the phonetic law or, better, the phonetic series, which had been driven out through the door came in again through the window. The followers of Gilliéron have been speaking of super-seding the traditional method, but the work of those who discovered and studied the phonetic "laws" could not have been in vain if many of these "laws" have withstood the sharpest criticism and some of them have been allowed the reconstruction of forms which were subsequently confirmed by historical documents. The pronominal form EO (< EGO), resulting from Romance comparison (Sard, *eo*, Prov. Port. *eu*, It. *io*, Span. *yo*, etc.) found its confirmation in the manuscripts of the sixth century from which we may presume[31] the existence of that form in a former epoch. From the historical sources we derive the certainty which is missing in the results both of mere phonetic comparison and of areal comparison. Fethishists have made great claims for each of the latter

---

[27] E.g. in the *Abeille* (*cit.*) where, however, Gilliéron shows all the acuteness of his mind and his exquisite linguistic sensibility. For the criticism on this, see Dauzat, *La géographie linguistique*, Paris, Flammarion, 1922, 46ff.; Georges Millardet, *Linguistique et dialectologie romanes*, Paris, Champion, 1933, 42ff., 379ff., and passim.

[28] Karl Jaberg, *Aspects géographiques du langage*, Paris, Droz. 1936, 42: "La géographie linguistique n'a pas la prétention de créer un corps de doctrines particulières. Elle n'est pas, non plus, comme le feraient croire certaines travaux de nôtre maître Gilliéron, fier de la nouvelle voie qu'il avait ouverte, une sorte de "trobar clus". Elle peut cependant revendiquer quelques mérites. . . ." See also M. Grammont, *Rev. Lang. Rom.*, 63.319 (1926): "si le comparatisme historique a trop longtemps régné seul, il serait funeste que le comparatisme géographique régnât seul après l'avoir détrôné. On ne saurait faire œuvre utile et solide qu'en combinant ensemble toutes les informations fournies par l'un et l'autre, et en outre toutes les autres ressources dont on peut disposer."

[29] See Walther v. Wartburg, *Problèmes et méthodes de la linguistique*, translated from German by Pierre Maillard, Paris, 1946, 124ff.

[30] Millardet, *Linguistique et dialectologie, cit.*, 66.

[31] Schuchardt, *Vokalismus des Vulgärlateins*, Leipzig, I, 129.

methods, but it would be difficult to say which of them is farther from the truth when each of them sticks to positions which are not sustained by the facts. The numerous aspects of the phenomenon of language need different methods of study which must all contribute their best to its reasonable explanation. The facts which are beyond the scope of both phonetic comparison and geographic comparison are numerous. The latter cannot produce the reason for the semantic evolution of *pagus* "pale limiting a property" into *pagus* "village", of *paganus* "inhabitant of the pagus" into *paganus* "worshipper of the gods", of *vicus* "block of houses" into *vicus* "a street", of *aedes, -is* "fireplace, temple" into *aedes, -ium* "house of many stories". The innovations *casa* and *mansio*, preserved in the Romance languages instead of *domus* and *aedes*, are due to political and social causes and depend on factors of civilization[32] which explain also the vitality of *germanus* and the luck of *fratellus* against *frater*; and the reasons for the gradual abandonment of *patruus* and *matertera* and of the prevalence of the pair *avunculus—amita*, of the victory of the Graecism *zio, -a* < THIUS < *theîos* are of affective character.[33] The foreign elements, which often penetrate a language and become an integral part of it, are also discovered and arranged chronologically through phonetic and grammatical comparison[34] and through history, rather than through areal comparison. Moreover, we must not forget that homonyms and homophones are not always intolerable to the linguistic feeling of the speakers, and they can coexist conserving their different meaning, e.g. *riso* from "ridere" and *riso* "graminaceae", *rombo* from "rombare" and *rombo* "a sea fish", *canto* of the voice and *canto* "corner", *ratto* "rape" and *ratto* "rat", *mondo* "the earth, the universe" and *mondo* from "mondare", *fondo* from "fondare" and *fondo* from "fondere", *porto* from "portare" and *porto* "harbor"; *louer* < LAUDARE and *louer* < LOCARE; similarly, though they are spelled differently, *verre* "a glass", *vair* "various", *vert* "green", *vers* "towards"; *cou* "neck" and *coup* "stroke", etc., etc. It follows that homonymy and homophony considered as developmental factors should be used with great caution and not with the almost absolute faith in them which Gilliéron showed in his resourceful constructions.

On the other hand, the certainty of Gilliéron's reasonings and presumed conclusions is opposed at least by the poverty of the materials offered by each linguistic atlas, the richest of which can capture and represent in outline only the most general character of the linguistic territory, displaying it in broad strokes, while the most significant meanings escape it.[35] To this fundamental

[32] See Alfred Ernout, *Philologica*, Paris, Klincksieck, 1946, 103–118.

[33] See Paul Aebischer, *Annali della R. Scuola Normale Superiore di Pisa* 5.1–52 (1936); Vittorio Bertoldi, *Linguistica storica (Questioni di metodo)*, second edition, Roma, Soc. Dante Alighieri, s.a., 65–71.

[34] I cite, from among many, the now classic work of Alfred Ernout, *Les éléments dialectaux du vocabularie latin*, Paris, 1909.

[35] Wartburg, *Problèmes, cit.*, 133: "L'image qu'il donne du trésor linguistique ressemble à un paysage de collines dans une mer de nuages: seuls les sommets émergent; quant aux dépressions sur lesquelles s'élèvent ces hauteurs et forment le lien organique entre elles, elles restent dissimulées sous le voile opaque des nuages."

defect of all the works we are dealing with we should add the unavoidable mistakes made by the explorer of a zone, mistakes that are due, among others, to the way in which the plan of a linguistic atlas is organized and carried out. In so far as the *ALF* itself is concerned, the checks made in the course of time have subsequently revealed its grave deficiencies;[36] and since the atlas is the base on which the promoters of linguistic geography must build, we understand why in the works inspired afterwards by their masters, they have tried to re-examine the methodological standards in the light of the facts produced.

The importance of Gilliéron's teaching and the success of the *ALF* appear also from the considerable number of linguistic atlases that were published in Europe and elsewhere from 1910 to 1950 or are still in the process of study or completion.[37] They are all interesting, and some are indicative of new orientations and recent advances in the geographic sector of linguistic study.

It would be useful to deal here in particular with the later atlases, keeping an eye on the methodological criteria follow by Gilliéron, and comparing them with those which have been adopted since. Such criteria concern chiefly: (1) the choice of the points of inquiry; (2) the compilation of the work sheets; (3) the character of the fieldworker; (4) the character of informants; (5) the method of questioning.

1   As is known, Gilliéron chose the points of inquiry of the *ALF* quite mechanically, in a geometrical pattern, as it were. Consequently, Edmont was compelled to modify the plan as he went along.[38] This is obviously prejudicial to the objectivity which is required of a fieldworker, for it involves him in the analysis of the materials he is collecting and a comparison of the different zones— jobs which are the duty rather of the future user of the atlas. That is why I have long maintained[39] that the network of points must be made in advance, chiefly on ethno-linguistic principles derived from previous reliable knowledge of the

[36] See e.g. Dauzat, *cit.*, 11ff., 127ff.; Louis Remacle, Présentation de l'Atlas linguistique de la Wallonie (the first volume of which was published 1953) in *Essais de philologie moderne* (1951); Bibliothèque de la Faculté de Philosophie et Lettres de l'Université de Liège, fasc. CXXIX, Paris, 1953, p. 245. For the maps of Corsica, P. E. Guarnerio, *Rendiconti Istituto Lombardo* 48.517ff.; C. Salvioni, *ibid.*, 49.705ff.; V. Bertoldi, Vocabolari e atlanti dialettali, *Riv. della Soc. Filol. friul. G. I. Ascoli*, Anno V, fasc. II; Bottiglioni, La penetrazione toscana e le regioni di Pomonte, *cit.*, passim.

[37] They are listed, with satisfactory descriptions of their structure, but with judgments of methodological order which are not always reliable, in the weighty and highly meritorious work of Sever Pop (*La Dialectologie. Aperçu historique et méthodes d'enquêtes linguistiques*. Parties I (*Dialectologie romane*), II (*Dialectologie non romane*), i–xxi, 1–1334, Louvain, 1950), as supplemented by Albert Dauzat's remarks and additions, *Le français moderne*, 19° année, num. 3, 1951, 225ff. See also my own remarks in *Rendiconti dell'Istituto di Glottologia dell'Università di Bologna* (IV, 1952), Bologna, S.T.E.B., 1953, pp. 3–4, and in Questioni di metodo nella preparazione degli atlanti linguistici, *Cultura Neolatina* 12.144ff. (1952). For other interesting reports of the latest plans of linguistic Atlases see *Orbis. Bulletin intern. de documentation ling.* 1.87ff. (1952); 2.49ff. (1953).

[38] "De fait il n'est guère de département où nous ayons maintenu le nombre de points d'enquête qui avait fait été fixé primitivement" (*Atlas linguistique de la France, Notice*, Paris, 1902, p. 4).

[39] In Le inchieste dialettali e gli Atlanti Linguistici, *Atti della XX riunione* (settembre, *1931) della Società per il progresso delle Scienze (SIPS)*, Milano, 1932, Vol. I, 413–492.

area under study. This is now done in practice by most people, even by those who do not acknowledge it formally.

2 The drawing up of work sheets, or questionnaires, has also proceeded quite differently since Gilliéron. He had said that "le questionnaire . . . pour être sensiblement meilleur, aurait dû être fait après l'enquête";[40] hence the best work sheets are those which fit the specific character of the area under study and which result from previous studies of that very area. This is what most people have been doing since the *ALF*.

3 Another of Gilliéron's standards that we may now consider quite surpassed concerns the fieldworker. According to the Master, he should not be a linguist in order that a maximum of objectivity may prevail and lest he criticize while he collects.[41] Now it is a fact that the field workers of all linguistic atlases since the *ALF* have almost all been linguists: Oscar Bloch, Griera, Gauchat, Tappolet, Scheuermeier, Rohlfs, Wagner, Pop, Kurath and his assistants, etc. etc. This is because we now realize that the autosuggestion and the prejudice feared by Gilliéron cannot influence the man who, linguist or not, is devoted with all his mind to the difficult task of selecting an informant, establishing rapport, and transcribing so smoothly and so quickly as not to interrupt the contact which has been forming and binds the questioner to the questioned. The field worker, even if he is a specialist in linguistics, is so absorbed with this exhausting work that he could not, though he would, think of rules, phonetic laws, linguistic schemes.

The advantages that a native fieldworker may have over a foreigner in the area under study have also been discussed; but since it is now agreed that the area should be well known by those who work in it, it is plain that a native collector, with training and other necessary qualifications, will always produce better results. Hence a large territory which is linguistically diverse, like Italy or France, should be explored by a staff of fieldworkers, each of them able to get deeply into the specifics of the area in his charge. Gilliéron was not of this opinion, and his skepticism is shared by those who think it is impossible to get among the various fieldworkers that uniformity of procedure which is necessary to get methodologically uniform materials. I will not try to resume here my discussion of this problem of over twenty years ago.[42] I think that my arguments have since been proved correct by my colleagues, Hans Kurath and his nine able assistants who together compiled the New England Atlas,[43] and by Tomàs Navarro Tomàs who entrusted to eight explorers the collection of the materials for the Atlas of the Iberian Peninsula (*ALPI*), which is to be published soon.[44]

---

[40] *Etudes de géographie linguistique. I. Pathologie et thérapeutique verbales*, Neuveville, 1915, p. 45.

[41] *Abeille, cit.*, p. 3.

[42] In *Atti della XX riunione della SIPS, cit.*, (footnote 39).

[43] *Linguistic Atlas of New England*, Providence, Rhode Island, Brown University, 1939–43.

[44] *Atlas lingüistico de la Península Ibérica;* see M. Sanchiz Guarner, *La cartografía lingüistica en la actualidad y el Atlas de la Península Ibérica*, Instituto Miguel de Cervantes, Palma de Mallorca, 1953.

4   Concerning the criteria of a good informant (sex, age, familiarity with surroundings, amount of education, etc.), we can see both extremes. On the one hand, the authors of the Italian–Swiss Atlas (*AIS*),[45] which marked a considerable advance in methodology, think that "the fieldworker's rule must be not to stick to any rule."[46] Scheuermeier, one of the able fieldworkers, confirms this: "il n'y a pas de règle infallible pour le choix d'un bon sujet."[47] On the other hand, Pop requires a rigorous method[48] and enumerates as many as sixteen criteria[49] followed by him in the choice of his subjects for the Rumanian Atlas (*ALR*).[50] No one else, as far as I known, before or after Pop, has felt it necessary to stick to these or similar rules. We may conclude, I think, that except for certain irreducible requirements (certain knowledge of local speech, good pronunciation, intelligence, etc.), the choice of a good informant is entrusted to the intuition and experience of the fieldworker.

What remains to be ascertained is whether a single informant is superior to a group of two or more. Most linguistic atlases record the answer of one informant; but even Edmont sometimes had to question two or three persons, and the same happened to Griera for his Catalan Atlas (*ALC*),[51] to Scheuermeier and to other fieldworkers for the Italian–Swiss Atlas,[52] and to Pellis for the Italian Linguistic Atlas (*ALI*).[53] Pop distinguishes an inquiry made in a whole country, for which he allows the necessity of several informants, from that made in a given territory, where a single informant is preferable, though the possibility of parallel inquiries remains even here[54]; Bloch, for his Vosges Atlas[55] questioned, besides the principal informant, from two to six secondary ones.[56] For my Atlas of Corsica (*ALEIC*)[57] I used a single informant who was, as it were, responsible, but I admitted the help or corrections of other informants. Thus, even those who accepted the rule of the single informant (authors of the *ALF, ALC, AIS*, etc.) were often forced to resort to different informants,

---

[45] K. Jaberg und J. Jud, *Sprach- und Sachatlas Italiens und der Südschweiz*, Bände I–VIII, Zofingen, 1928–40. Among the great merits of this atlas is the addition of the study and comparison of ethnographic data to those of linguistic facts.

[46] Jaberg–Jud, *Der Sprachatlas als Forschungsinstrument*, Halle (Saale), 1928, p. 191.

[47] P. Scheuermeier, Observations et expériences personnelles faites au cours de mon enquête pour l'Atlas linguistique et ethnographique de l'Italie et de la Suisse méridionale, *Bulletin de la Société de linguistique de Paris*, 23.104 (1932).

[48] Pop, *La Dialectologie*, cit., p. 1156.

[49] *Ibid.*, pp. 723ff.

[50] *Atlasul linguistic român*, sub conducerea lui Sextil Puscariu, part I (by Sever Pop), II (by Emil Petrovici), Cluj, 1938–40.

[51] A. Griera, *Atlas lingüistic de Catalunya*, Montserrat, 1923–39. Interrupted at the 5th volume. See Pop, *La Dialectologie*, cit., p. 372.

[52] See Pop, *La Dialectologie*, cit., p. 579.

[53] Promoted by the Società Filologica Friulana G. I. Ascoli, directed by the late Professor Matteo Bartoli; Ugo Pellis, also deceased, collected almost all the materials now at the University of Turin. See Pop, *La Dialectologie*, cit., 598ff.

[54] *La Dialectologie*, cit., p. 726.

[55] *Atlas linguistique des Vosges méridionales*, Paris, Champion, 1917.

[56] See Pop, *La Dialectologie*, cit., p. 96.

[57] G. Bottiglioni, *Atlante Linguistico Etnografico della Corsica*, Pisa, 1933–41–42.

so that even this principle of the Gilliéron procedure may now be considered superseded once and for all.

5   Let us deal at somewhat greater length with the use of the work sheets, that is, of the questioning method, for on this point there has been an inclination to carry to the limit a procedure hinted at by Gilliéron, but which is to be attributed particularly to the directors of the *AIS*, followed by Pop and a few others.

I have discussed this subject on several occasions[58] and will briefly recapitulate here. It is a fact that Gilliéron's scheme has no strict rules,[59] so that Edmont, in using, for instance, his herbarium, added certain supplementary explanations which he did not report.[60] We may conclude that neither Gilliéron nor Edmont cared about the strict uniformity of questioning. The same goes for O. Bloch,[61] Le Roux[62] (when he thought he was not well understood, he made an additional interview[63]), and Gardette,[64] whose work sheets were changed several times during the inquiry.[65] On the contrary, the uniformity of questioning is an essential rule of the linguistic collection in the Italian–Swiss Atlas, and it was strictly observed by Pop and Pellis, the late lamented collector of the Italian Linguistic Atlas. This group thought that the answers of different informants are not comparable if they are not elicited in the same way; they lost sight of the true aim of this research, namely, to discover and record for each place the most exact expression of the idea proposed in the work sheets, an expression which will really be useful for comparative purposes.

Is it possible that informants of different character, habits, and culture when questioned in a uniform way, should reveal that objective truth which we are looking for? A hunter, well versed in the form and life of birds, will react properly when faced with a good picture or drawing, but a worker chosen at random will need detailed, circumstantial oral explanations; moreover, the opportunities which keep arising during the interview for pointing out to the informant an object for whose name we are looking are numberless, and to disregard them seems naïve, to say the least.

The conviction that the best answer is the first, given by the informant as a reaction to the first stimulus of the question itself, goes hand in hand with the belief that the uniformity of the question is essential to the comparative goal. And those who adhere to this method strictly know and admit that the materials

[58] Inchieste dialettali, *cit.*; Questioni di metodo; *cit.*; Il valore unitario e quello obiettivo degli Atlanti Linguistici, *Annali della R. Scuola Normale Superiore di Pisa*, S. II, Vol. i (1932), 167ff.; Come si preparano e come si studiano gli Atlanti linguistici, *ibid.*, S. II, Vol. ii (1933), 126ff.

[59] *Notice, cit.*, p. 4.

[60] Pop, *La Dialectologie, cit.*, p. 118.

[61] *Ibid.*, p. 94.

[62] In the *Atlas linguistique de la Basse-Bretagne*, Paris, 1924–43.

[63] See Pop, *La Dialectologie, cit.*, p. 949.

[64] In the *Atlas linguistique et ethnographique du Lyonnais* (ALL), Institut de Linguistique Romane, Facultés Catholiques de Lyon.

[65] See *Bulletin de l'Institut de Linguistique Romane de Lyon* I, 1953; Pop, *La Dialectologie, cit.*, p. 224.

they collect do not represent the maximum degree of objective truth, but only the effects that a uniform stimulus produces on different subjects. But this is a subjective truth which does not interest a future user of the atlas; he would like to be able to consider the material offered as a true image of the linguistic conditions in a given territory. For my own part, I have got rid of what I consider as prejudices and, as I have written several times, it is my opinion that the work sheet represents not the *means*, but the *aim* of the inquiry. By a series of words, it sets forth the impressions we want to produce in the informants; the expressions we may want of him may be stimulated and directed by any suitable means and at any occasion that arises during the interview. It follows that those who study an atlas compiled by the so-called impressionistic method (uniformity of question, answer at one stroke) may be comparing mistakes, too, while those who use an atlas made without the handicap of any such rules will be comparing the materials that synthesize the real average speech, checked by the one responsible informant. And it will be granted that everybody aims at this, even the adherents of the impressionistic method, so that for instance Sever Pop, who is among the latter, takes care to avoid the danger of "présenter des cartes linguistiques qui ne reflètent pas le parler de la majorité des individus employant encore le patois dans leur entourage."[66]

All agree, then, on the aim: both those whom we should call *rigorists*, that is adherents of a rigorous and mechanical method, like Pop, and the *free collectors*, like the writer himself, who follow a method corresponding to reality and free from the handicap of strict and tyrannic rules. We could continue this discussion, but the remarkable progress of linguistic geography, from the year when the *ALF* appeared to the atlases that now are being planned or completed, can be easily inferred from the preceding discussion. These atlases show that the method of the free collectors is being improved and the number of its followers is growing as the checking of the already published atlases proceeds and experience increases. In fact, the analysis of the deficiencies of the *ALF* has prompted the work of the regional atlases of France, inspired and directed by Albert Dauzat[67] in conjunction, and in full agreement on purpose and

---

[66] Pop, *La Dialectologie, cit.*, p. 1156.

[67] *Nouvel atlas linguistique de la France par régions* (*NALF*). To round out the information in *Le français moderne*, April, 1939, pp. 97–101 and January 1941, pp. 1ff. (see also Pop, *La Dialectologie, cit.*, 136ff.), I can add here the latest reports according to a personal communication from Dauzat. The first volume of 220 maps of the Gascon Atlas entrusted to Jean Séguy, Professor at the University of Toulouse, is going to be published; the Atlas Poitu-Charente is almost finished, Miss Massignon having completed the fourth part of the definitive inquiries; M. Loriot has done the field work for the Atlas of the North and Picardy in the whole South of the zone; Dauzat himself is doing with youthful vigor (in spite of his 76 years) the fieldwork for the Arvernian and Limousin Atlas; intensive work is also going on for the Atlas of Provence, entrusted to Ch. Rostaing, who will do the fieldwork at Bouches du Rhônes, his native town; M. Camproux, Luis Michel and Alibert are working on the Atlas of Languedoc; R. Sincou is busy with Quercy, the center of an Atlas Guyenne-Albigeois; the Atlas of the West will be directed by Abbé Guillaume; the Atlas of Normandy has been entrusted to F. Lechanteur who

method, with the well known Mgr. Gardette, who after the Lyons Atlas is now working on that of the Massif Central. Similarly, work is proceeding on regional atlases in the framework of the impressive Linguistic Atlas of the United States and Canada, as reported by Harold B. Allen in *Orbis* 1.89–94 (1952); the inquiries of R. Hotzenköcherle[68] for the *Linguistic and Ethnographic Atlas of German Switzerland*[69] are also in progress. Spain, too, is working hard: the materials of the *ALPI* should be published soon, while Luis Cortés Vasquez of Salamanca University is at work on the *Atlas lingüistico de Sanabria*—an interesting region in which four linguistic currents join and influence one another. In Italy the publication of the materials collected by the late Ugo Pellis for the *ALI* is now eagerly awaited; while the standards of the field work are not those demanded today, the collection itself is valuable.

There is, then, everywhere intense research and study[70] which shows that linguistic geography has become an essential part of linguistic science. We may say that there is no longer any scholar of historical-reconstructive linguistics who does not feel the need of recourse to areal comparison; such comparison may not be decisive as often as Gilliéron and his first pupils thought, but is always informative on problems not only of modern languages but even of the most ancient ones.[71] It is enough to recall, for the latter, how the theory of the marginal areas started and promoted, after the discovery of Tokharian,[72] a new conception of the original Indo-European guttural in the contrast of the *kentum* and *satem* languages, and illustrated the Basque-Caucasian connections in the frame of Mediterranean languages. Finally, it is likely that further achievements of linguistic geography may contribute enormously to reconcile the Saussurian dualism[73] in the modern orientation of structural linguistics that studies heterogenesis and endogenesis in the perpetual development of different systems. Linguistic geography may yet open to science those new fields outlined more than twenty years ago by N. S. Troubetzkoy when he called for the geographical-phonological description of the languages of the world.[74]

---

has almost completed his fieldwork on Cotentin and Bocage; Loriot will explore the Seine Inférieure. Further reports will appear in *Le français moderne*. The enthusiasm of my colleague Dauzat is obviously spreading among his able aides and the grand task to which they are devoting themselves will be completed.

[68] See *Bulletin de Lyon, cit.*

[69] See the report on it in *Essais de philologie moderne, cit.*, pp. 115ff.

[70] For the various Atlases which are being issued and drawn or planned, see Pop, *La Dialectologie, cit.*, cont. vol. II, pp. 1197–1198.

[71] The set of rules of spatial linguistics Matteo Bartoli dictated in 1925 (*Introduzione alla neolinguistica*, Biblioteca dell'*Archivum Romanicum*, S. II, Vol. xii, Genève) and applied during all his active life devoted to study (see *Saggi di linguistica spaziale*, Torino, 1945) is still very useful in this connection.

[72] See G. Campus, *Due note sulla questione delle velari arioeuropee*, Torino, 1916.

[73] See F. de Saussure, *Cours de linguistique générale*, Paris, 1931.

[74] Cf. *Travaux du Cercle Linguistique de Prague*, 6.228ff. (1931).

26

Is a Structural Dialectology Possible?

URIEL WEINREICH

I IN LINGUISTICS TODAY the abyss between structural and dialectological studies appears greater than it ever was. The state of disunity is not repaired if "phoneme" and "isogloss" occasionally do turn up in the same piece of research. Students continue to be trained in one domain at the expense of the other. Fieldwork is inspired by one, and only rarely by both, interests. The stauncher adherents of each discipline claim priority for their own method and charge the others with "impressionism" and "metaphysics," as the case may be; the more pliant are prepared to concede that they are simply studying different aspects of the same reality.

This might seem like a welcome truce in an old controversy, but is it an honorable truce? A compromise induced by fatigue cannot in the long run be satisfactory to either party. The controversy could be resolved only if the structuralists as well as the dialectologists found a reasoned place for the other discipline in their theory of language. But for the disciplines to legitimate each other is tantamount to establishing a unified theory of language on which both of them could operate. This has not yet been done.

While the obstacles are formidable, the writer of this paper believes that they are far from insurmountable. The present article is designed to suggest a few of the difficulties which should be ironed out if the theories of two very much disunited varieties of linguistics, structural and dialectological, are to be brought closer together. A certain amount of oversimplification is inevitable, for the "sides" in the controversy are populous and themselves far from unified. The author would not presume to function as an arbitrator. He simply hopes, without a needless multiplication of terms, to stimulate discussion with others who have also experienced the conflict of interests—within themselves.

If phonological problems dominate in this paper, this is the result of the fact that in the domain of sounds structural and non-structural approaches differ

Reprinted by permission of the Linguistic Circle of New York from *Word* 10.388–400 (1954). The late Professor Weinreich held the Atran chair of linguistics and Yiddish studies at Columbia University.

most;[1] semantic study has (so far, at least) not equalled sound study in precision, while in the domain of grammar, specifically structural points of view have had far less to contribute.

2   Regardless of all its heterogeneity, structural linguistics defines a language as an organized system. It was one of the liberating effects of structural linguistics that it made possible the treatment of a language as a unique and closed system whose members are defined by opposition to each other and by their functions with respect to each other, not by anything outside of the system. But since organization must have a finite scope, one of the major problems in a structural linguistic description is the delimitation of its object, the particular system described. Only in ideal cases can the linguist claim to be describing a whole "language" in the non-technical sense of the word. In practice he must delimit his object to something less. One of the steps he takes is to classify certain items in his data as intercalations from other systems, i.e. as "synchronically foreign" elements (e.g. *bon mot* in an otherwise English sentence). Another step is to make certain that only one variety of the aggregate of systems which the layman calls a "language" is described. These steps are taken in order to insure that the material described is uniform. This seems to be a fundamental requirement of structural description.

To designate the object of the description which is in fact a subdivision of the aggregate of systems which laymen call a single language, the term "dialect" is often used. But if "dialect" is defined as the speech of a community, a region, a social class, etc. the concept does not seem to fit into narrowly structural linguistics because it is endowed with spatial or temporal attributes which do not properly belong to a linguistic system as such. "Dialects" can be adjacent or distant, contemporary or non-contemporary, prestigious or lowly; linguistic systems in a strictly structural view can only be identical or different. It is proposed that the term "dialect" be held in reserve for the time being and that, for purposes of structural analysis as set forth here, it be replaced by "variety."

In deference to the non-structural sense of "dialect" as a type of speech which may itself be heterogeneous, some linguists have broken down the object of description even further to the "idiolect" level. This term has been used in the United States to denote "the total set of speech habits of a single individual at a given time." The term has been seriously criticized on two grounds: (1) constancy of speech patterns may be more easily stated for two persons in a dialogic situation (a kind of *dialecte à deux*) than for a single individual; (2) there are differences even within an "idiolect" which require that it be broken down further (e.g. into "styles").

"Idiolect" is the homogeneous object of description reduced to its logical extreme, and, in a sense, to absurdity. If we agree with de Saussure that the task of general linguistics is to describe all the linguistic systems of the world,[2]

---

[1] Some of the phonological points made here were inspired by N. S. Troubetzkoy's article on linguistic geography, "Phonologie et géographie linguistique," *TCLP* 4.228–34 (1931); reprinted in his *Principes de phonologie*, Paris, 1949, pp. 343–50.

[2] Ferdinand de Saussure, *Cours de linguistique générale*, Paris, 1949, p. 20.

and if description could proceed only one idiolect at a time, then the task of structural linguistics would not only be inexhaustible (which might be sad but true), but its results would be trivial and hardly worth the effort.

The restriction of descriptive work to homogeneous material has led to a paradox not quite unlike that proposed by Zeno about motion. A moving arrow is located at some point at every moment of time; at intermediate moments, it is at intermediate positions. Therefore it never moves. Rigidly applied, the typical elements of structural description—"opposition" and "function of units with respect to other units of the same system"—have come close to incapacitating structural analysis for the consideration of several partly similar varieties at a time. Fortunately, the progress of research no longer requires absolute uniformity as a working hypothesis.[3]

Structural linguistic theory now needs procedures for constructing systems of a higher level out of the discrete and homogeneous systems that are derived from description and that represent each a unique formal organization of the substance of expression and content. Let us dub these constructions "diasystems," with the proviso that people allergic to such coinages might safely speak of supersystems or simply of systems of a higher level. A "diasystem" can be constructed by the linguistic analyst out of any two systems which have partial similarities (it is these similarities which make it something different from the mere sum of two systems). But this does not mean that it is always a scientist's construction only: a "diasystem" is experienced in a very real way by bilingual (including "bidialectal") speakers and corresponds to what students of language contact have called "merged system."[4] Thus, we might construct a "diasystem" out of several types of Yiddish in which a variety possessing the opposition $/i \sim \mathrm{I}/$ is itself opposed to another variety with a single $/i/$ phoneme. Be it noted that a Yiddish speaker in a situation of dialect contact might find information in the confusion of $/i/$ and $/\mathrm{I}/$ of his interlocutor, which is opposed, on the diasystem level, to his own corresponding distinction. It might tell him (in a "symptomatic" rather than a "symbolic" way) where, approximately, his interlocutor is from.

It may be feasible, without defining "dialect" for the time being, to set up "dialectological" as the adjective corresponding to "diasystem," and to speak of dialectological research as the study of diasystems. Dialectology would be the investigation of problems arising when different systems are treated together because of their partial similarity. A specifically structural dialectology would look for the structural consequences of partial differences within a framework of partial similarity.

It is safe to say that a good deal of dialectology is actually of this type and contains no necessary references to geography, ethnography, political and cultural history, or other extra-structural factors. In Gilliéron's classic studies, the

---

[3] André Martinet, in preface to Uriel Weinreich, *Languages in Contact*, Linguistic Circle of New York, Publication no. 1, 1953, xii + 148 pages, p. vii.

[4] *Languages in Contact*, pp. 8f.

typical (if not exclusive) interest is structural rather than "external." In the diasystem "French," we may very well contrast the fate of *gallus* in one variety where *-ll-* > *-d-* with its fate in another variety where this phonological change did not take place, without knowing anything about the absolute or even relative geography or chronology of these varieties. Non-geographic, structural dialectology does exist; it is legitimate and even promising. Its special concern is the study of partial similarities and differences between systems and of the structural consequences thereof. The preceding is not to say, of course, that "external" dialectology has been surpassed; this subject will be referred to below (section 7).

Dialectological studies in the structural sense are, of course, nothing new. Binomial formulas like "Yiddish *fus/fis* 'foot'," which are often condensed to *f^u_is*, etc. have always been the mainstay of historical phonology. But it should be noted that structural dialectology need not be restricted to historical problems to the extent to which it has been in the past. Consequences of partial differences between varieties can be synchronic as well as diachronic. The following is an example of a "synchronic consequence." In one variety of Yiddish (we stick to Yiddish examples for the sake of consistency), the singular and plural of "foot" are distinguished as *(der) fus* vs. *(di) fis*, while in another variety, both numbers are *fis*. Now, in the number-distinguishing variety, the singular, *fus*, occurs also as a feminine (with *di*); even so, the distinction between singular and plural can still be made in terms of the vowel: *di fus* "sg."—*di fis* "pl." In the other dialect, *fis* is invariably masculine, perhaps as a consequence of, or at least in relation to, the fact that there only a masculine could distinguish between sg. *der fis* and pl. *di fis*.[5]

If structuralism were carried to its logical extreme, it would not allow for the type of comparisons suggested here: it could only study relations within systems; and since in a perfect system all parts are interrelated ("tout se tient"), it is hard to see how systems could even be conceived of as partially similar or different; one would think that they could only be wholly identical or different. Considerations of this nature prevented orthodox Saussureanism of the Geneva school from undertaking the study of gradually changing systems, since it was felt that languages could only be compared, if at all, at discrete "stages."[6] But a more flexible structuralism has overcome this hurdle by abandoning the illusion of a perfect system, and is producing notable results in the diachronic field.[7] We should now take the further step of asserting the possibility of a

---

[5] For an example of synchronic consequences in phonemics, see Anton Pfalz, "Zur Phonologie der bairisch-österreichischen Mundart," *Lebendiges Erbe; Festschrift . . . Ernst Reclam*, Leipzig, 1936, pp. 1–19, which is at the same time one of the rare instances of German phonemics and of structural dialectology.

[6] Albert Sechehaye, "Les trois linguistiques saussuriennes," *Vox romanica* 5.1–48 (1940), pp. 30f.; H[enri] Frei, "Lois de passage," *Zeitschrift für romanische Philologie* 64.557–68 (1944).

[7] Cf. the bibliography of diachronic phonemics by Alphonse G. Juilland in *Word* 9.198–208 (1953).

synchronic or diachronic dialectology based on a combined study of several partially similar systems.

This step in structural linguistic theory would, it seems, do much to bring it closer to dialectology as it is actually carried on.

3   We come next to dialectology's share in the proposed rapprochement. The main objection raised by structuralists against dialectology as usually practised might be formulated thus: in constructing "diasystems" it ignores the structures of the constituent varieties. In other words, existing dialectology usually compares elements belonging to different systems without sufficiently stressing their intimate membership in those systems.

In the domain of sounds, this amounts to a non-phonemic approach. A traditional dialectologist will have no scruples about listening to several dialect informants pronounce their equivalents of a certain word and proclaiming that these forms are "the same" or "different." Let us assume four speakers of a language who, when asked for the word for "man," utter (1) [man], (2) [man], (3) [mån], and (4) [mån], respectively. On an impressionistic basis, we would adjudge (1) and (2) as "the same," (3) and (4) as "the same," but (1) and (2) as "different" from (3) and (4). Yet suppose that informant (1) speaks a variety in which vowel length is significant; phonemically his form is $_1$/măn/. Informant (2) does not distinguish vowel length, and has given us $_2$/man/. We can further visualize a variety represented by informant (3) where a vowel with maximum degree of opening has the positional variant [å] between /m/ and /n/; phonemically, then, we have $_3$/man/. In the fourth variety, no such positional variation exists; that form is perhaps $_4$/mon/. The structural analysis is thus different from the non-structural one: (2) and (3) now turn out to be possibly "the same" (but only, of course, if the systems are otherwise also identical), while (1) and (4) appear to be different. Structural linguistics requires that the forms of the constituent systems be understood first and foremost in terms of those systems, since the formal units of two non-identical systems are, strictly speaking, incommensurable.[8]

A similar requirement could be made about the units of content, or "semantemes." It would not do to say, for instance, that the word *taykh* in one variety of Yiddish is "the same" as *taykh* in another if, in the one, it is opposed to *ózere* "lake," and hence means only "river," while in the other it is not so opposed and stands for any sizable "body of water." Similar structural cautions would be required with respect to "synonyms" in the diasystem. In the diasystem "Yiddish," *baytn*, *shtékheven*, and *toyshn* all signify approximately "to exchange," but they cannot be synonyms on the variety level if they do not all exist in any one variety.

A grammatical example might also be cited. In terms of function within the system, it would not be justified to identify the feminine *vaysl* "Vistula

[8] *Languages in Contact*, pp. 7f.

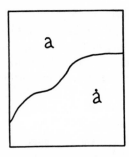

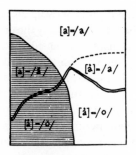

Map 26.1: Traditional   Map 26.2: Structural

THE VOWEL IN "MAN" IN LANGUAGE X

On Map 26.2, a continuous single line divides areas with different phonemic inventories (shaded area distinguishing vowel length, unshaded area not distinguishing it). The double line separates areas using different phonemes in this word (difference of distribution). The dotted line separates allophonic differences.

River" of two Yiddish varieties if in the one it is opposed to a neuter *vaysl* "eggwhite," while in the other it is completely homonymous with the (also feminine) word for "eggwhite." It is even doubtful whether any two feminines in these two varieties could be legitimately identified in view of the fact that one of the varieties does not possess a neuter gender altogether.

The dialectologist is used to comparing directly the "substance" of different varieties. The demand of the structural linguist that he consider the train of associations, oppositions, and functions that define linguistic forms seems to the dialectologist complicating, unreasonable, and unnecessary ("metaphysical"). To show up the disagreement most clearly, let us represent the phonic problem just discussed on a map and compare the traditional and the proposed structural treatments of it. Obviously the structural approach involves complications, but the dialectologist will become convinced of their necessity when he realizes that phonemics, like structural linguistics generally, represents not a special technique for studying certain problems, but a basic discovery about the way language functions to which structural linguists are completely committed.

Since, in the structural view, allophonic differences between sounds are in a sense less important than phonemic differences, the "substantial" isogloss (Map 26.2) which separates [a] from [å] in the overall /a/ area is structurally somehow less important than the purely formal isogloss which separates pronunciations of [mån] = /man/ from those of [mån] = /mon/; the latter isogloss may not reflect any difference in "substance" at all; it would not show up on the non-structural map (Map 26.1). The traditional dialectologist naturally wonders what he stands to gain by the drawing of such "metaphysical" lines. But if dialectological maps are considered diachronically as snapshots of change, and if it can be shown that the difference between phonemes and allophones can be material in determining sound change, it may be possible to convince the dialectologist that the structural map is after all more true to the reality of functioning language. Similar arguments, perhaps, could also be persuasive insofar as they are pertinent to grammatical and lexical matters.

If dialectologists would consider the functions of the elements which they use in their comparisons, their conception of a "diasystem" would come close to that proposed here for structural linguistics and might lead to the unified theory which is so badly needed.

4 The partial differences which are proposed as the specific subject matter of dialectologic study may be of two kinds: differences of inventory and differences of distribution. While the latter are the standard material of comparative study, the former have not received their due stress.

As an example of a difference in inventory, let us take a simple phonemic case first. In the following discussion, single slashes enclose sets of phonemes and single tildes designate phonemic oppositions in a variety identified by a preceding subscript number; oppositions in the constructed diasystem are characterized by double tildes, and the formulas for the diasystems are surrounded by double slashes. Given two varieties with identical five-vowel systems, we might construct the following diasystem: $_{1,2}//\text{i} \approx \text{e} \approx \text{a} \approx \text{o} \approx \text{u}//$. Now let us assume that in one of the varieties, the front vowel of the intermediate degree of openness is more open than in the other; choosing a phonemic transcription which would reflect this fact, we might indicate the difference in the diasystem thus:

$$_{1,2}//\text{i} \approx \frac{_1\text{e}}{_2\text{ɛ}} \approx \text{a} \approx \text{o} \approx \text{u}//.$$

Given two varieties, one of which (1) distinguishes three front vowels, the other (2) distinguishing four, we might formulate the corresponding part of the vowel diasystem thus:

$$_{1,2}//\frac{_1/\text{i}\sim\text{e}\sim\text{æ}/}{_2/\text{i}\sim\text{e}\sim\text{ɛ}\sim\text{æ}/} \approx \text{a} \approx \text{o}\ldots//.$$

Here is the actual vowel inventory of Yiddish considered as a diasystem of three dialects, 1. Central ("Polish"), 2. Southwestern ("Ukrainian"), and 3. Northwestern ("Lithuanian"):

$$\Big/\!\!\Big/_{1,2,3}\Big/\!\!\Big/ \frac{\dfrac{_1/\text{i}:\sim\text{i}/}{_2/\text{i}\sim\text{ı}/}}{_3\text{i}} \approx \text{e} \approx \frac{_1/\text{a}:\sim\text{a}/}{_{2,3}\text{a}} \approx \text{o} \approx \text{u}\ \Big/\!\!\Big/\ .$$

Similarly differences in inventory of grammatical categories might be stated, e.g. between varieties having two against three genders, three as against four conjugational types, and the like. All examples here are tentative and schematic; the possibilities of a more analytical statement of the diasystem, based e.g. on relevant features, remain to be investigated.

One thing is certain: In the study of language contact and interference (see section 5), a clear picture of differences in inventory is a prerequisite.[9]

Differences in distribution cannot be directly inferred from a comparison of the differences in inventory, although the two ordinarily stand in a definite historical relationship. For example, in the diasystem "Yiddish" described above, the phoneme $_3$/i/ in variety 3 usually corresponds to either $_2$/i/ or $_2$/ı/ in cognates of variety 2, and to either $_1$/i:/ or $_1$/i/ in cognates of variety 1 ($_3$/sine/: $_2$/sıne/: $_1$/sĩne/ "enmity"). This is, as it were, a correspondence between the nearest equivalents. But many $_3$/o/'s correspond to /u/'s in variety 1 and 2, even though all three varieties today possess both /o/ and /u/ phonemes. Thus, /futer/ means "father" in varieties 1 and 2, but "fur" in variety 3; /meluxe/ means $_{1,2}$"craft" and $_3$"state"; /hun/ means $_{1,2}$"rooster" and $_3$"hen." For the tens of thousands of speakers for whom the contact of these varieties is an everyday experience, these "Yiddish" sound sequences are not fully identified until the particular variety of Yiddish to which they belong is itself determined. Now no one would deny that a form like Yiddish [fi‹l] ($_{1,2}$"full," "many") is identified fully only in conjunction with its meaning in one of the varieties, i.e. when account is taken of the differences in distribution of sounds in cognates occurring in the several varieties. The less obvious point made here is that the form is not fully identified, either, if relevant differences in *inventory* are not accounted for, i.e. if it is not rendered in terms of the phonemes of one of the concrete varieties: [fil] = $_1$/fil/, $_2$/fıl/, $_3$/fil/.

Recent descriptive work on American English phonemics has come close to treating the language as a "diasystem" without, however, satisfying the requirements set forth here. The widely adopted analysis of Trager and Smith[10] provides a set of symbols by which forms of all varieties of American English can be described. It makes it possible, for example, to transcribe Southeastern /pæys/ *pass* in terms of some of the same symbols used in /pæt/ *pat* of the same dialect or in /pæs/, /bəyd/ *bird*, etc. of other varieties. This violates the principle advo-

---

[9] *Ibid.*, pp. 1f.

[10] George L. Trager and Henry Lee Smith, Jr., *An Outline of English Structure* (= *Studies in Linguistics, Occasional Papers* 3), Norman (Okla.), 1951, esp. pp. 27–29.

cated here that the phonemic systems of the varieties should be fully established before the diasystem is constructed. We are not told whether in the phoneme inventory of Southeastern American English, the /æy/ of *pass* does or does not correspond as an inventory item to the /æ/ of other varieties. We cannot tell if the [o] of *home* of Coastal New England is the same phoneme, or a different phoneme, from the [ow] in *go* in the same variety. For reasons of this type, the system has been criticized as providing not a phonemic description or a set of descriptions, but a "transcriptional arsenal."[11] Yet the remaining step toward the establishment of a phonemic diasystem is not difficult to visualize.

5   We might now restate and specify the suggested position of structural dialectology in linguistics as a whole. SYNCHRONIC DIALECTOLOGY compares systems that are partially different and analyzes the "synchronic consequences" of these differences within the similarities. DIACHRONIC DIALECTOLOGY deals (a) with DIVERGENCE, i.e. it studies the growth of partial differences at the expense of similarities and possibly reconstructs earlier stages of greater similarity (traditionally, comparative linguistics); (b) with CONVERGENCE, i.e. it studies partial similarities increasing at the expense of differences (traditionally, substratum and adstratum studies, "bilingual dialectology,"[12] and the like).

The opposite of dialectology, which hardly needs a special name, is the study of languages as discrete systems, one at a time. It involves straight description of uniform systems, typological comparisons of such systems, and diachronically, the study of change in systems considered one at a time.

6   It was stated previously that diasystems can be constructed *ad hoc* out of any number of varieties for a given analytic purpose. Constructing a diasystem means placing discrete varieties in a kind of continuum determined by their partial similarities. However, in passing from a traditional to a structural dialectology, the more pressing and more troublesome problem is the opposite one, viz. how to break down a continuum into discrete varieties. What criteria should be used for divisions of various kinds? Can non-technical divisions of a "language" into "dialects," "patois," and the like be utilized for technical purposes?[13]

Before these questions can be answered, it is necessary to distinguish between standardized and non-standardized language. This set of terms is proposed to avoid the use of the ambiguous word, "standard," which among

---

[11] Einar Haugen, "Problems of Bilingual Description," *Report of the Fifth Annual Round Table Meeting on Linguistics and Language Teaching* (= [Georgetown University] *Monograph Series on Languages and Linguistics* no. 7), in press.

[12] For an essay in bilingual dialectology, see Uriel Weinreich, "*Sábesdiker losn* in Yiddish: a Problem of Linguistic Affinity," *Word* 8.360–77 (1952).

[13] The possibility of introducing some scientific rigor into existing loose terminology has been explored by André Martinet, "Dialect," *Romance Philology* (1953/54), in press. The article by Václav Polák, "Contributions á l'étude de la notion de langue et de dialecte," *Orbis* 3.89–98 (1954), which arrived too late to be utilized here as fully as it deserves, suggests that we call "language" a diasystem whose partial similarities are grammatical while its partial differences are phonologic and lexical.

others has to serve for "socially acceptable," "average," "typical," and so on. On the contrary, STANDARDIZATION could easily be used to denote a process of more or less conscious, planned, and centralized regulation of language.[14] Many European languages have had standardized varieties for centuries; a number of formerly "colonial" tongues are undergoing the process only now. Not all leveling is equivalent to standardization. In the standardization process, there is a division of functions between regulators and followers, a constitution of more or less clearcut authorities (academies, ministries of education, *Sprachvereine*, etc.) and of channels of control (schools, special publications, etc.). For example, some dialectal leveling and a good deal of Anglicization has taken place in the immigrant languages of the United States, and we might say that a word like *plenty* has become a part of the American Norwegian koinê.[15] But in the sense proposed here, there is no "standardized" American Norwegian which is different from Old-World Norwegian, and from the point of view of the standardized language, *plenty* is nothing but a regional slang term.

Now it is part of the process of standardization itself to affirm the identity of a language, to set it off discretely from other languages and to strive continually for a reduction of differences within it. Informants of standardized languages react in a peculiar way; moreover, it is much easier to deal with samples of a standardized language, to make generalizations about it and to know the limits of their applicability. On the level of non-standardized or FOLK LANGUAGE,[16] a discrete difference between one variety and others is NOT a part of the experience of its speakers, and is much more difficult to supply. For example, it is easy to formulate where standardized Dutch ends and standardized German begins, but it is a completely different matter to utilize for technical purposes the transition between folk Dutch and folk German.

On the whole dialectologists have avoided dealing with standardized languages and have restricted themselves to folk language.[17] Consequently, in practice as well as in theory the problem of dividing and ordering the continuum of language is especially serious with respect to the folk level and not the standardized level. Time was when the continuum of folk language used to be divided on the basis of (usually diachronic) structural features, e.g. the geographic limits of a certain phonological development. Either one isogloss which the linguist considered important was selected (e.g. k/x as the line between Low and

---

[14] Cf. *Languages in Contact*, pp. 99–103. An interesting book about standardization is Heinz Kloss, *Die Entwicklung neuer germanischer Kultursprachen von 1800 bis 1950*, Munich, 1952.

[15] Einar Haugen, *The Norwegian Language in America*, Philadelphia, 1953, p. 588.

[16] Interesting parallels could be developed between the sociolinguistic opposition "standardized"—"folk" and the social anthropologist's opposition between the cultures of complex (industrialized) and folk societies or strata of society; cf. e.g. George M. Foster, "What Is Folk Culture?" *American Anthropologist* 55.159–73 (1953).

[17] Some people are not averse to calling modern standardized languages "Indo-European dialects," or speaking of "literary dialects." Dialectology in the sense proposed in this paper need not restrict itself to the folk level, but such usage is one more reason why the term "dialect" ought to be held in abeyance.

High German), or a bundle of isoglosses of sufficient thickness was used as a dividing line. In either case, the resulting divisions were not, of course, all of the same degree; they were major, minor, and intermediate, depending on the thickness of the bundle or the relative importance of the key isogloss. It is evident that no unambiguous concept of dialect could emerge even from this optimistic methodology any more than a society can be exhaustively and uniquely divided into "groups."

Classificatory procedures of this type are today virtually passé. Dialectologists have generally switched to extra-structural criteria for dividing the folk-language continuum. The concept of language area (*Sprachlandschaft*) has practically replaced that of "dialect" (*Mundart*) as the central interest in most geographic work,[18] and ever more impressive results are being obtained in correlating the borders, centers, and overall dynamics of language areas with "culture areas" in a broader sense. Instead of speaking, for instance, of the *helpe/helfe* and *Lucht/Luft* isoglosses as the border between the Ripuarian and Moselle-Franconian "dialects" of the German Rhineland, linguistic geographers now speak of the Eifel Barrier between the Cologne and Trier areas. This Eifel mountain range happens to be the locus not only of those two random isoglosses, but, among others, also the dividing line between *kend* and *keŋk* "child," *haus* and *hus* "house," *grumper* and *erpel* "potato," *heis* and *gramm* "hoarse"; between short-bladed and long-bladed scythes, grey bread in oval loaves and black bread in rectangular loaves, New Year's twists and New Year's pretzels, St. Quirin as the patron saint of cattle and the same as the patron of horses, two different types of ditty addressed to the ladybug, etc.[19] The line is meaningful as a reflex of a medieval boundary which can in turn be accounted for by more permanent climatic, orological, hydrographic, and other geographic factors.[20]

The search for ways to divide the folk-language continuum has also led to statistical correlation methods.[21] Rather than plotting the border lines of single selected structural features, which may be impossible in areas of amorphous transition, the following procedure is used. Inquiries are made at various points concerning the presence or absence of a whole list of test features; then the correlation between the results at some reference point and at all other points is computed, and may be represented cartographically, points with similar correlation coefficients being surrounded by lines which have variously been

[18] This is particularly evident in the methodologically most advanced German Swiss work; cf. the publications series *Beiträge zur schweizerdeutschen Mundartforschung* edited by Rudolf Hotzenköcherle.

[19] Linguistic data from Adolf Bach, *Deutsche Mundartforschung*, Heidelberg, 1950, pp. 123ff.; ethnographic data from Adolf Bach, *Deutsche Volkskunde*, Leipzig, 1937, p. 228.

[20] In the United States, Hans Kurath (*A Word Geography of the Eastern United States*, Ann Arbor, 1949), has successfully combined strictly linguistic with "external" criteria in breaking down the relatively undifferentiated American folk-language area.

[21] See David W. Reed and John L. Spicer, "Correlation Methods of Comparing Idiolects in a Transition Area," *Language* 28.348-60 (1952).

called "isopleths" or "isogrades." Theoretically related to this procedure are the tests of mutual intelligibility between dialects.[22] All these procedures must depend on an arbitrary critical constant (or constants) for the drawing of a dividing line (or lines, of various degrees of importance), but they do yield an insight into the makeup of a continuously varying language area which supplements, if it does not supersede, the results derived by other methods.

In the domain of dialect sociology, where transitions are perhaps even more continuous and fluid than in dialect geography, the use of extra-linguistic correlations and statistical sampling techniques offers promising possibilities of research in an almost untrodden field.[23]

The use of the social-science tools of "external dialectology" can do much to supplement the procedures outlined for a structural dialectology. One problem for combined structural and "external" linguistic investigation is to determine what structural and non-structural features of language have in fact helped to break up the folk-language continuum into the non-technical units of "dialects," "patois," etc. This combined research might get to the heart of the question of diasystems as empirical realities rather than as mere constructs. One of its byproducts might be the formulation of a technical concept of "dialect" as a variety or diasystem with certain explicit defining features.

7   Finally a word might be said about the interrelationship of structural and "external" points of view applied to a specific dialectological problem. Given a map showing an isogloss, the "external" dialectologist's curiosity is likely to concentrate on the locus of that isogloss. Why is it where it is? What determines the details of its course? What other isoglosses bundle with it? What communication obstacle does it reflect?

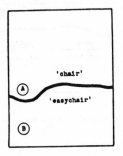

Map 26.3: Meaning of *shtul* in East European Yiddish (Schematized).

[22] Cf. for example C. F. Voegelin and Zellig S. Harris, "Methods for Determining Intelligibility Among Dialects of Natural Languages," *Proceedings of the American Philosophical Society* 95.322–29 (1951).

[23] See the interesting paper by Stanley M. Sapon, "A Methodology for the Study of Socio-Economic Differentials in Linguistic Phenomena," *Studies in Linguistics* 11.57–68 (1953). A scheme for the classification of varieties of a language according to their function (ecclesiastic, poetic, scientific, etc.) to replace the unsatisfactory terminology of "styles" has been proposed by Yury Šerech, "Toward a Historical Dialectology," *Orbis* 3.43–56 (1954), esp. pp. 47ff.

The structural dialectologist has another set of questions, stemming from his interest in partial differences within a framework of partial similarity. To take up the semasiological example of Map 26.3 (which is schematized but based on real data), if *shtul* means "chair" in zone A, but "easychair" in zone B, then what is the designation of "easychair" in A and of "chair" in B? Every semasiological map, due to the two-faceted nature of linguistic signs, gives rise to as many onomasiological questions as the number of zones it contains, and vice versa. If we were to supply the information that in zone A, "easychair" is *fotél'*, while in zone B "chair" is *benkl*, a new set of questions would arise: what, then, does *fotél'* mean in B and *benkl* in A?[24] This implicational chain of questions could be continued further. The resulting answers, when entered on a map, would produce a picture of an isogloss dividing two lexical systems, rather than two isolated items (see Map 26.4). This would be the "structural corrective" to a traditional dialect map.

It is easy to think of dialectological field problems for the solution of which "external" and structural considerations must be combined in the most intimate manner. Such problems would arise particularly if the cartographic plotting of systems should produce a set of narrowly diverging isoglosses. Assume that an isogloss is drawn between a variety of a language which distinguishes short /u/ from long /u:/ and another variety which makes no such quantitative distinction. The structuralist's curiosity is immediately aroused about length distinc-

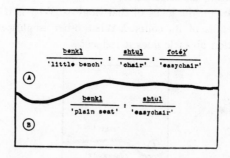

Map 26.4: Designations of Seats in East European Yiddish (Schematized).

tions in other vowels. Suppose now that the variety that distinguishes the length of /u/ does so also for /i/; but that the isoglosses, plotted independently, are not exactly congruent (Map 26.5). Some intriguing questions now arise concerning the dynamics of the vowel pattern of the discrepant zone. Nothing but an on-the-spot field study closely combining structural analysis and an examination of the "external" communication conditions in the area could deal adequately with a problem of this kind.

---

[24] The actual answer is that *fotél'* is not current in zone B, while *benkl* means "little bench" in zone A.

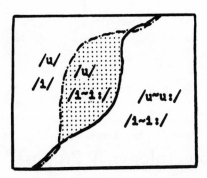

Map 26.5: Non-Congruent Vowel-Length
Isoglosses in Language *Y*.

8   In answer to the question posed in the title of this paper, it is submitted that a structural dialectology is possible. Its results promise to be most fruitful if it is combined with "external" dialectology without its own conceptual framework being abandoned.

27

Structural Dialectology: A Proposal[1]

ROBERT P. STOCKWELL

THE ANALYSIS OF ENGLISH PHONOLOGY proposed, in its present form,[2] by George L. Trager and Henry Lee Smith, Jr., in 1951 has had a curious history in the past eight years.

Reprinted by permission from *American Speech* 34.258–68 (1959). The author is Professor of Linguistics and chairman of the department of linguistics at the University of California at Los Angeles.

[1] The notions outlined here were developed in a graduate seminar at the University of California, Los Angeles, in the spring of 1958. The members of the class were Tommy R. Anderson, Ralph Goodman, Julianne Hitt, Robert Nussbaum, Jane Robinson, and Paul Schachter. This article is the result of collaboration with them. Professors A. A. Hill, Martin Joos, Noam Chomsky, and Sumner Ives were kind enough to read this paper in a prepublication version and to make critical suggestions, which we acknowledge with appreciation. I owe to Chomsky my awareness that the notion of "over-all pattern" for English is no more than a subpattern of some general phonetics grid that must be assumed to be reflected in the capacity of children to learn any language equally well.

[2] Brief remarks may be made about the prehistory of the analysis itself. The terminal junctures are the contributions of Trager and Smith, as well as the integration of the whole system, in *An Outline of English Structure, Studies in Linguistics*, OP 3 (1951). The nine vowels were proposed by Morris Swadesh, "On the Analysis of English Syllabics," *Language*, XXIII (1947), 137–51. The four pitches go back to Rulon S. Wells, "The Pitch Phonemes of English," *Language*, XXI (1945), 27–39, and to Kenneth L. Pike, *The Intonation of American English* (Ann Arbor, Mich., 1945). The four stresses date at least from Trager and Bernard Bloch, "The Syllabic Phonemes of English," *Language*, XVII (1941), 223–46, where the plus juncture also first appeared in its present form. The concept of the superfix, a phrase-binding combination of stress elements, is derived (with important modifications by Trager) from Wells, "Immediate Constituents," *Language*, XXIII (1947), 81–117. The distribution of stress phonemes in polysyllabic words and constructs was clarified by Stanley S. Newman, "On the Stress System of English," *Word*, II (1946), 171–87, though he worked with only three phonemic stresses. The postvocalic /h/ is Trager and Bloch, *loc. cit.*; the analysis of postvocalic front and back glides as glide phonemes different from the high-front and high-back vowels goes back, in recent times, through Bloomfield, *Language* (New York, 1933) and "Stressed Vowels of American English," *Language*, XI (1935), 97–116, at least to Henry Sweet, *A History of English Sounds* (Oxford, 1888). A major contribution to understanding the problems in the analysis of complex nuclei was Hockett's "Short and Long Syllabic Nuclei," *International Journal of American Linguistics*, XIX (1953), 165–71. The breakdown of the nine vowels into distinctive features is A. A. Hill's *Introduction to Linguistic Structures* (New York, 1958), as well as the full analysis of English phonotactics within this frame of reference. Details on the analysis of suprasegmental features have been

On the one hand, the analysis has provided the basis for an extraordinary surge of creative activity in applied linguistics (in the preparation of materials for teaching English as a second language,[3] of composition texts for native speakers,[4] of basic linguistics texts,[5] and in the application of linguistics to literary criticism[6]), in historical linguistics,[7] and in descriptive activity above

contributed from time to time by William E. Welmers, *Spoken English as a Foreign Language* (1953), James Sledd, "Superfixes and Intonation Patterns," *Litera*, III (1956), 35–41, Charles F. Hockett, *Manual of Phonology* (Baltimore, 1955), Hill, *loc. cit.*, Stockwell, "On the Analysis of English Intonation" (Texas Conference, 1957, [published 1962]), and Martin Joos (also at the 1957 Texas Conference). Problems in the analysis of vowels have been raised recently by Sledd in a review of Trager and Smith, *Language*, XXXI (1955), 312–46, and by Raven McDavid and Sumner Ives, along with Sledd, at the 1956 Texas Conference [papers published 1962]. McDavid, in a chapter of W. Nelson Francis's *The Structure of American English* (New York, 1958), has called attention to the same problems again in passing. Earlier, Haugen and Twaddell brought up similar problems ("Facts and Phonemics," *Language*, XVIII [1942], 228–37) with the six-vowel analysis of Trager and Bloch, but Twaddell, if not Haugen, has subsequently seemed to find that the Trager–Smith nine met his objections to the earlier Trager–Bloch. Problems in the analysis of stress and juncture have been raised by Chomsky, Halle, and Lukoff, "On Accent and Juncture in English," in *For Roman Jakobson* (The Hague, 1956), and by Dwight L. Bolinger in several recent articles but specially in "Disjuncture as a Cue to Constructs," with Louis J. Gerstman, *Word*, XIII (1957), 246–55. The whole vocalic analysis, but especially postvocalic /h/, has recently been attacked by Hans Kurath, "The Binary Interpretation of English Vowels: a Critique," *Language*, XXXIII (1957), 111–23, answered by Sledd in *Language*, XXXIV (1958), 252–58.

[3] Especially the American Council of Learned Societies series of texts, of which there are eleven (for Turks, Indonesians, Burmese, Iranians, Greeks, Chinese, Koreans, Siamese, Vietnamese, Yugoslavs, and Spanish speakers); a substantial body of material put out in various forms by scholars associated with the American Language Center of American University, the Georgetown Institute of Languages and Linguistics Turkish program, and others. Reasonably complete displays of such materials regularly appear at the annual meetings of the National Association of Foreign Student Advisors.

[4] Paul Roberts, *Patterns of English* (New York, 1956); Roberts, *Understanding English* (New York, 1958); Harold Whitehall, *Structural Essentials of English* (New York, 1956); D. J. Lloyd and H. R. Warfel, *American English in Its Cultural Setting* (New York, 1956). Several similar texts are due to appear in the next year or two.

[5] H. A. Gleason, *An Introduction to Descriptive Linguistics* (New York, 1955) (the phonology of English, occupying large sections of the text, is almost entirely based on Trager and Smith); Hill, *op. cit.*, (structure of English, including Trager–Smith phonology and utilizing the phonology to arrive at structure on higher levels); C. F. Hockett, *A Course in Modern Linguistics* (New York, 1958) (Trager–Smith phonology, with modifications); and Francis, *op. cit.* One is tempted to include even Z. A. Harris, *Methods in Structural Linguistics* (Chicago, 1954), where the English examples are cited in Trager–Smith conventions, and Hockett's *Manual of Phonology*, where many of Hockett's most telling points are made by taking issue with details of the same phonology, if not indeed accepting it largely unmodified.

[6] S. B. Chatman, "Robert Frost's Mowing: an Inquiry into Prosodic Structure," *Kenyon Review*, XVIII (1956), 421–38; Chatman, "Comparing Poetic Styles" (mimeographed, 1958); Hill, "English Metrics: a Restatement" (mimeographed, 1958). These three articles, at least, clearly utilize purely linguistic information for a direct and frontal attack on meter, rhythm, style, and other problems that obviously lend themselves to linguistic formulation. Hill has tried to utilize linguistic models to press further into literary analysis ("Towards a Literary Analysis," *English Studies in Honor of James Southall Wilson* [Charlottesville, Va., 1951]; "A Sample Literary Analysis," *Report of the 4th Annual Roundtable Meeting on Linguistics and Language Teaching* [Washington, D.C., 1953]; "An Analysis of the Windhover: an Experiment in Structural Method,"

the level of phonology.[8] On the other hand, the analysis has been the focus of violent partisan controversy,[9] of casual disdain,[10] and of total rejection[11] entirely or in part by several linguists of great competence.

One area in which it has not been significantly tested is that of dialectology, though Smith has suggested that here is precisely the area where it might be especially fruitful; Hill has taken the suggestion at full face value and has made useful dialect observations through the over-all pattern of Trager and Smith, concluding that it "constitutes the best basis yet devised for a systematic and structural approach to dialectology."[12] This paper is a proposal about

---

PMLA, LXX (1955), 968–78; "Pippa's Song: Two Attempts at Structural Criticism," University of Texas *Studies in English* [Austin, Texas, 1956]), but it is less obvious in the latter kinds of analysis that there is anything that is uniquely linguistic in the point of view.

[7] Stockwell and C. W. Barritt, "Some Old English Graphemic-phonemic Correspondences: *æ, ea,* and *a,*" *Studies in Linguistics,* OP 4 (1951); answered by S. M. Kuhn and R. Quirk, "Some Recent Interpretations of Old English Diagraph Spellings," *Language,* XXIX (1953), 143–56; reply by Stockwell and Barritt, with counterreply by Kuhn and Quirk, *Language,* XXXI (1955), 372–401; Stockwell, "Old English Phonology: a Structural Sketch," *Studies in Linguistics,* XIII (1958), 13–24; Trager and Smith, "An Indo-Hittite Chronology," *Studies in Linguistics,* VIII (1950), 61–70.

[8] Here we have in mind especially Hill's attempt to make his morphemic cuts on a phonological basis ("The First Step in English Morphemic Analysis," read before the annual meeting of the Linguistic Society of America in December, 1957) and such presentations of a phonologically based syntax as that by Smith in 1956, "Superfixes and Syntactic Markers," *Report of the 7th Annual Roundtable Meeting on Linguistics and Language Study* (Washington, D.C., 1957), presented in a somewhat different form at the Texas Conference on Syntax in May, 1958. While it is probably too early to evaluate these, at the conference there was no little indication that such attempts may have to be modified, supplemented, or (conceivably) abandoned in favor of the transformational approach advocated most narrowly by Chomsky, *Syntactic Structures* (The Hague, 1957), and somewhat more broadly by Harris, "Co-occurrence and Transformation in Linguistic Structure," *Language,* XXXIII (1957), 283–300. To say that changes will have to be made in them is not to suggest that they have been unfruitful; on the contrary, they had to be tried. What is more important, the operational tests that must be developed to arrive at valid answers to Chomsky's most crucial question ("Is *X* a grammatical sentence or not?") will be partially based on precisely the kind of phonological information that Hill and Smith have been examining. That there are phonologically signaled boundaries in utterances is beyond question; the nature of the relation of these signals to grammatical structure is still very much in question, but that there is a relation no one seems to doubt.

[9] Pike, "On the Phonemic Status of English Diphthongs," *Language,* XXIII (1947), 151–59; Kurath, *op. cit.*; Haugen and Twaddell, *op. cit.*; Ralph B. Long, who has vigorously opposed Trager–Smith phonologically based syntax in print, though he has not entered into controversy over the phonology itself, e.g. "Paradigms for English Verbs," *PMLA,* LXXII (1957), 359–72, and "Words, Meanings, Literacy, and Grammar," *English Journal,* XLVII (1958), 195–99.

[10] E. Stankiewicz, "On Discretenes[s] and Continuity in Structural Dialectology," *Word,* XIII (1957), 44–59, esp. p. 53; U. Weinreich, "Is a Structural Dialectology Possible?" *Word,* X (1954), 388–400, esp. p. 395. [See p. 300.]

[11] The papers cited under fn. 9 above rejected the analysis after controversy. Jakobson, Fant, and Halle, *Preliminaries to Speech Analysis* (Cambridge, Mass., 1952), Weinreich, "Stress and Word Structure in Yiddish," in *The Field of Yiddish* (New York, 1954), pp. 1–27, Chomsky, Halle and Lukoff, *op. cit.,* and Kemp Malone, "Transcribing English for Turks" (mimeographed, 1957), all rejected the Trager–Smith analysis completely, but without anything that might be called partisan controversy.

[12] Hill, *Introduction to Linguistic Structures,* p. 59. Smith's recommendations appeared in his review of Jones, *The Pronunciation of English, Language,* XXVIII (1952), 144–49.

how the analysis by Trager and Smith might be tested and utilized in a dialect survey. It goes beyond the suggestions offered by Smith and Hill because we found it necessary to do more than apply this analysis unmodified if we were to make of it the most useful tool for phonemically oriented dialectology. We suggest a frame of reference within which the analysis, or at least the general understanding of the analysis, may become meaningful to a large segment of the linguistic audience who have found it wanting. Our remarks are restricted to the analysis of vowels, but they may easily be extended throughout.

The analysis has in large measure deserved both the praise and the criticism that it has received. It deserves the former because it has a rightness about it that has satisfied the *sprachgefühl* of many linguists who were also native speakers. There is no other way to account for its enormous popularity. It deserves three kinds of criticism: (1) because in its first presentation, and in all subsequent presentations by the original authors or by others, it has been unsupported by any argument from a mass of fully analyzed individual dialect samples, available for others to hear or to check at least from close phonetic transcription;[13] (2) because its authors have claimed a degree of coverage for it ("structure of the English language as a whole," *Outline of English Structure*, p. 9) that has invited other competent scholars to look into their own speech and find a tenth vowel, a fourth semivowel, an unaccountable intonation pattern, and so on; and (3) because no one seems to be quite sure what the status of the concept "phoneme" is within this analysis.

The notion that generalizations like this analysis are exceptionless (or any others in science) is unfortunate: a good generalization is one with a short list of exceptions and a long list of coverages. But to show that the Trager–Smith phonological generalizations are good ones in this sense requires more data than they have supplied, and—more important from a theoretical point of view—it requires that we reexamine phonological systems of various kinds (involving phonological units of different degrees of generalization) to determine what their relation to this analysis is.

There are three kinds of inventories of phonological units. These are the phonetic inventory, the contrastive inventory, and the phonemic inventory.

    1   *Phonetic inventory.*—Phones that are subsequently assigned to phonemes as allophones: data are filtered through a screen or grid and sorted by procedures discussed below.

    2   *Contrastive inventory*
        a. *Idiolectal inventories.*—Contrasts within idiolects A_1, A_2, A_3, A_4 ... A_x making up dialect A; contrasts within idiolects B_1, B_2, B_3, B_4 ... B_x making up dialect B; i.e. by eliminating all noncontrastive

---

[13] Trager and Smith were aware of this weakness: "It is explicitly asserted . . . that the procedure with omission of much phonetic data is a practical one for the immediate purpose, and not the theoretically most desirable one that would be followed in a full discussion" (*Outline*, p. 8).

phonetic components in each idiolect (dialect), one arrives at *idio-
phonemes* (= pre-Trager–Smith *phonemes*).

b. *Diaphonemic inventory.*—All contrasts in all dialects; i.e. by super-
imposing A on B on C ... X so that all contrasts made in all
dialects are included, one arrives at *diaphonemes*.[14] A diaphonemic
system incorporates all the contrasts that *any* speaker makes.

c. *Core inventory.*—Contrasts shared by all dialects; i.e. by eliminating
contrasts that are unique to dialect A or B ... X, one arrives at
core phonemes (Hockett's *common core*[15]). A common core includes
only the contrasts that *every* speaker of the language makes.

3 *Phonemic inventory.*—The most parsimonious system of oppositions
necessary to describe almost all dialects with maximum internal congruence
and patterning; i.e. contrasts of the diaphonemic inventory are matched up
(by phonetic skewing) in such a way as to retain only the minimum inventory,
the *over-all pattern*, needed to account for the oppositions within the dialect
samples that are to be included without listing.[16]

The notion of pure phonetics is valid only, if anywhere, in the laboratory
of the acoustic phonetician. All other phoneticians listen and record through
a grid which permits them to ignore differences that exist at a level of greater

[14] The term has been used in many senses, but it is used by Weinreich in "Is a
Structural Dialectology Possible?" in precisely this sense. Hill uses the term (*Introduction
to Linguistic Structures*, p. 59), but in a way which does not distinguish *diaphonemes* from
phonemes in the over-all pattern.

[15] *Manual of Phonology*, pp. 18–22.

[16] Haugen and Twaddell (*op. cit.*) long ago remarked that "to us, in all sobriety, the
processes whereby Trager and Bloch combine sound-types into phonemes appear more
akin to artistic composition than to scientific classification; and the pleasure of watching
their operations with the material is rather esthetic satisfaction than scholarly conviction"
(p. 232). We suggest that phonemic assignments are capable of being made *only* by
"artistic composition," in a sense very close to what Haugen and Twaddell meant:
"maximum internal congruence and patterning" are certainly artistic criteria, and parsi-
mony is hardly more measurable objectively. It is possible, however, that Haugen and
Twaddell have reversed the statement one might wish to make. The principles of phonemic
analysis are pretty much those of all analytical work that aims at a coherent theory about
the structure of something. The resemblance to artistic construction is therefore neither
casual nor accidental. In perceiving artistic elegance in the procedures of phonemic
composition that they objected to, they saw corruption where we see mainly virtue. The
scholarly (=scientific?) conviction that we all desire to have after reading a phonemic
analysis derives from the adequacy of the phonetic and contrastive inventories, and no
phonemic inventory can do violence to them beyond a certain point. The limits of violence
to the phonetic inventory are set by the mono-uniqueness criterion (*not* bi-uniqueness):
from a transcription the phonetic facts must be recoverable by rule. (We do not require
that the one-to-one uniqueness apply in reverse, "once a phoneme always a phoneme,"
etc.) There are two kinds of these rules: one general (e.g. longer allophones before voiced
consonants than before voiceless); the other specific (e.g. in transcriptions of idiolect A,
read /ɑ/ as [Æ] in environment X; in transcriptions of idiolect B, read /ɑ/ as [a], etc.).
The limits of violence to the contrastive inventory are less easily fixed: some things can
be listed, and one must decide how long a list he will allow. The familiar Kenyon–Knott
transcription is essentially a common core. To make it complete requires a longer list
than we desire. But we, on the other hand, would list Sledd's tenth vowel on the grounds
that for most speakers of his type it can be assigned to /ay/ (or in some instances /æh/).

refinement than their particular grid discriminates.[17] To get a phonetic inventory of American English vowels, a phonetic grid is needed which is sufficiently refined to discriminate among all of the phonetic differences that might be described as "interesting differences" by the criterion that someone has bothered to comment about them in print or at public meetings, but no more refined than is required to meet this minimal specification. The consonants and suprasegments deserve the same kind of grid, but most of the controversy has focused on the vowels. The grid below allows for the transcription of all the differences which have been discussed as being possibly phonemic: it contains slots for every contrasting phonetic set that is possibly phonemic in some dialect of American English, or that is a difference of sufficient articulatory or acoustic magnitude to have received comment. This grid may quite properly be viewed as a subset of an unspecified universal grid, one which in some formal and general way represents the phonetic capacities of human beings.

Simple Nuclei

i				u
	ɪ	ï	ʊ	
e				o
	ɛ	ə	ʌ	
æ				ɔ
	Æ	a	ɑ	

Note: The symbol [ï] is used in place of "barred i."

Complex Nuclei
Each of the above combined with:

h   (glide toward mid and/or high central)
y   (glide toward higher front)
w   (glide toward higher back rounded)
:   (sustained vowel quality)
ɹ   (retroflection or retraction [*r*-color]
     simultaneous with vowel)

It is the nature of this (or any other) grid that it forces decisions: every observed syllabic nucleus must be assigned to one of the ninety slots in this "transcriptional arsenal" (Haugen's phrase). The grid may be expanded to suit the observer. This one was arrived at to meet the following requirements:

1   Six front vowels are needed to account, for instance, for differences between such items as: *leash* [liyš] vs. *fish* (fɪyš); *Hague* (*Haig*) [heyg] vs. *leg* [lɛyg]; *air* [æh] vs. *ire* [Æh].

2   No more than three central vowels are needed to account for differences that have been discussed.

[17] While we do not really believe that even acoustic phonetics can claim immunity from this limitation, the discussion of what grid limitations it has is away from the present discussion.

3 Six back vowels are needed to account for differences between such sets as: *buoy* [buy] vs. *bush* [bʊyš]; variant pronunciations of *no* [nʌw], [now]; and of *law* [lɑh], [lɔh], [loh].

4 Length to account for Sledd's *lavish* [læ:vɪš] vs. *salving* [sæhvɪŋ] (in his review of Trager and Smith, *Language, XXXI* [1955], 322).

5 *r*-color, apart from a spirant or continuant /r/, to account for such differences as that between two variants of *hurry* [hə́ɹi], [hə́ɹ], or *hurry* [hə́ɹi] vs. *furry* [fəˑɹi].

This inventory must expand if there are significant vocalic differences it will not transcribe in a way that reflects the articulatory and acoustic facts of American English with reasonable accuracy. It is much more refined than "broad" IPA phonetic transcription (which is not-entirely-digested phonemic transcription), considerably less refined than the Atlas phonetic arsenal, and thereby much easier to use in getting convergence from among several observers.

Among the several kinds of contrastive inventories the idiolectal one is central: regardless of what particular methodology is used to isolate (idio-) phonemes, the test which the isolation must stand is the pair test[18] to determine whether morphemically distinct utterances are differentiated by audible features. In a language being investigated for the first time, the inventory of contrasts in all positions will not lead in any direct way to the phonemicization that will be most useful later in the study. The investigator expects to rephonemicize several times. In working with a well known language like English, the investigator will not prejudice his results if even at this early stage he allows his knowledge of the morphophonemics, of dialectal variation, or of previous analyses to influence his phonemicization of the contrasts.

We will not presume to list the conditions one might require the "best" phonemicization to meet, since Hockett[19] and others[20] have made it clear that "best" is measurable only for specific aims. Most linguists would presumably agree that the phonemic solution of an idiolect requires that those segments be set up as minimal which have in their acoustic composition at least one feature that cannot be predicted by a rule written in terms of the phonological environment. But what features are treated as simultaneous components of a single segment and what features are abstracted and treated as successive segments can probably be determined only by the general simplicity of one solution as

[18] In its purest form the informant is asked to record in random order a series of minimally contrasting pairs of utterances. Then, on later listening, he must identify the morphemic differences between the pairs with consistent accuracy under testing conditions which eliminate the possibility that any clues remain in the material beyond the segments that the investigator seeks to isolate as minimally different.

[19] *Manual of Phonology*, especially the discussion of IC structure on the phonological level (pp. 150–75).

[20] Many scholars, beginning with Y. R. Chao's famous article, "The Non-uniqueness of Phonemic Solutions of Phonetic Systems," *Bulletin of the Institute of History and Philology*, Academia Sinica, IV, No. 4 (1934), 363–97, reprinted in *Readings in Linguistics*, ed. Martin Joos (Washington, D.C., 1957). The latest, and one of the best, that we have noted is Einar Haugen, "The Phonemes of Modern Icelandic," *Language*, XXXIV (1958), 55–88, which makes use of Hockett's IC principles and terminology.

compared with another. The requirement that prevents a given solution from being uniquely better than others is that while the inventory of phonemes must be such as to account for every phonemic contrast in every permitted environment, it should at the same time permit the generalizations of greater power about the allophone-predicting environment. There are many kinds of fruitful generalizations, not all of which are possible within the limits of any single phonemicization that has yet been proposed for any English dialect. It follows that if the generalizing power of an over-all pattern is useful to an analyst, he will decide between alternate solutions in favor of the one which integrates most easily into the inventory of the over-all pattern.

The diaphonemic inventory is a composite of all the idiophonemic inventories.[21] It can be reached, however, without passing through them, if one assumes that a partial phonemicization of idiolects is sufficient grounds to eliminate from the phonetic inventory all those slots which cannot be shown to contrast in any dialect. Such an assumption is certainly dangerous, and yet in practice most linguists operate as though it were quite safe. It is not uncommon, for example, to read that a dialect has such and such contrasts among the front vowels, without evidence that these also contrast with back vowels. Quite certainly, it was by some such procedure that Trager and Smith arrived at their analysis, since they acknowledge that they did not have full phonetic details for every dialect they proposed to include; but theirs is not, as Weinreich has pointed out,[22] a diaphonemic inventory because it includes only oppositions without regard for their relative phonetic position in any pair of dialects.

An example will serve to clarify this difference.[23] Many Southern dialects have, in the items *ear*, *heir* or *air*, *ire*, and *are*, the phonetic shapes [ɪh], [æh], [ɛh], and [ah]. Diaphonemically, the phonetic integrity of these contrasts must be respected in their assignment, since other dialects have [ɛh] instead of [æh]. There are, then, *five* diaphonemic slots. But such dialects have only a three-way high to low opposition among the front vowels, such that [ɪh] is assigned to /ih/, [æh] to /eh/, [ɛh] to /æh/, and [ah] to /ah/, giving only *four* slots in the phonemic system (over-all pattern). The crucial difference between a diaphonemic transcription and an over-all pattern phonemic transcription is that for the former only a set of *general* rules (see footnote 16) is needed to recover the phonetic data, whereas for the latter a set of specific rules about skewing is also needed. The former gives priority to phonetic integrity; the latter, to contrastive relevance.

[21] A sample phonemic *vs.* diaphonemic analysis of Yiddish is given by Weinreich, "Is a Structural Dialectology Possible?," p. 394. [See p. 306 in this book.]

[22] *Ibid.*, p. 395.

[23] Data from Ives, McDavid, and Sledd at the Texas Conference on English Phonology, April, 1956. Ives especially made it clear that such dialects have only a three-way high to low opposition among the front vowels, as elaborated in this paragraph. To Ives also belongs the credit for first attempting to distinguish clearly between a diaphonemic description and an over-all pattern (paper given at the 1956 Texas Conference, to be published).

The core inventory is the area of English phonology around which there is no serious controversy. The core contrasts have, language-wise, the highest functional load, are easiest to demonstrate by pair test, and are most important to teach to foreigners. They are reached by elimination of those contrasts in the over-all pattern that someone lacks. They can also be reached by way of the diaphonemic pattern, but a smaller set will emerge because of the phonetic integrity that is built into the diaphoneme.

The criterion for assigning diaphonemically different entities to a single slot in the phonemic inventory is dialectal complementation among the contrasts. Given four diaphonemically different contrasts, only three of which occur in any covered[24] dialect, two of the four must be complementary so that they can be phonemically merged. There must be limits, however, to the amount and extent of skewing that is allowable in an over-all pattern of phonemes. On the analogy of Austin's observations,[25] we suggest that skewing of idiophonemic contrasts into an over-all pattern is not likely to exceed one notch horizontally or vertically plus or minus a semivowel.

It appears to us that it would be feasible to accomplish a survey of English phonology in American dialects in the following steps:

1   Prepare a list of items, preferably buried, though under major stress, in nonridiculous contexts, which when read into a tape recorder would furnish data for screening through a phonetic inventory like the one suggested above.[26]

2   Ask linguistically interested scholars in universities all over the country to furnish tapes of interviews including responses obtained from such a list. They would also supply all the usual pertinent information about the informant.

3   File the tapes in central storage with some such organization as the recently formed American Library of Recorded Dialect Studies at Ohio State University, thus making them available for full analysis by any scholar with the time and inclination.

[24] Borrowing a metaphor from Chomsky, we assume that the purpose of description is to produce statements which will account for the facts both in a closed corpus and in an extended corpus that can be generated by rules abstracted from the closed corpus. If some of the statements or categories needed to cover a closed corpus are nonproductive in an extended corpus, it is better merely to list them. For this reason the over-all pattern will not necessarily coincide with the phonemic pattern of the maximum idiolect. Congruity within an over-all pattern justifies listing items from a closed corpus that break the congruity if, in extending the corpus, one finds that the congruity is not repeatedly broken in the same way. It is for this reason that our use of the term *over-all pattern* is different from Hockett's, both in his *Manual* (pp. 18–22) and in his *Course in Modern Linguistics*. He is talking about a *diaphonemic pattern*, not an *over-all pattern*, as we use the terms. One should note that Hill (see fn. 14 above) reverses Hockett: he is talking about an over-all pattern when he uses the term "diaphoneme." Conflicts like these were what first led us to see if two different kinds of realities lurked behind the terminology.

[25] William M. Austin, "Criteria for Phonetic Similarity," *Language*, XXXIII (1957), 538–43.

[26] Edith Crowell Trager and A. L. Davis at the American Language Center of American University prepared one such list which we have seen in dittographed form. Sumner Ives prepared another, also still in ditto. We do not know what plans the authors of the lists have for them, but perhaps they would agree to collaborate on a list of the type here suggested.

4 Perhaps it would be possible to ask that the original interviewer submit with the tape a phonetic inventory and an idiophonemic inventory of the material contained in the interview. While he could not arrive at a diaphonemic inventory, he could test the assignment of that particular idiophonemic pattern to the over-all pattern.

The ultimate goal of such collaborative activity would be to arrive at an over-all pattern including all the details of dialect distribution that are now missing. The activity could only supplement the continuing work of the Atlas, since it would be directed at any and all varieties of phonology found in American English, whereas the former is aimed at close phonetic and lexical work on older and primarily rural American speech. Before such a project can be formally undertaken, three things are needed:

1 For all parts of the phonology a phonetic inventory that a large number of scholars can agree is adequate in the sense suggested here.

2 A published sample of the procedure carried out in detail for a small set of interviews.

3 A questionnaire that will require no more than half an hour of actual recording time (1200 ft. at $7\frac{1}{2}$ i.p.s.) but still include data for making all the crucial decisions.

Besides its obvious practical advantage, that it would lead to the rapid collection of a vast body of contemporary speech by uniform procedures which would yield data that could be phonemicized easily (as, for instance, the Atlas records cannot), this proposal has considerable theoretical interest. We cannot expect to achieve a satisfactory universal phonetic grid if we have not gathered empirical evidence to reveal what subset of it is relevant to American dialects (as merely one instance). We cannot stop arguing about unimportant phonetic issues until we have agreed about the meaning and utility of the various kinds of phonological inventories, and have habituated ourselves to stating precisely which kind of phonological entity we are dealing with in any given discussion.

28

Overall Pattern and Generative Phonology[1]

RUDOLPH C. TROIKE

THE PAST DECADE has witnessed a great deal of discussion surrounding the question of an overall phonemic pattern for English dialects. In particular, dispute has centered about the familiar "three by three by three" system of notation devised by Bloch, Trager, and Smith to accommodate all the known vocalic contrasts in American English.[2] Sledd and others have pointed out that their system constituted little more than a "diaphonic" transcription which, as Sledd has convincingly demonstrated, was unable to represent the distinction between certain contrasting vowel nuclei found in his Southern dialect. Others have criticized the distortion of phonetic data implicit in the system, its extreme use of distributional complementation to reduce the inventory of phonemic symbols, and even the theoretical status of an overall pattern in phonology. Even among the detractors of the Trager–Smith system, however, the desirability of a uniform system for representing phonemic similarities and differences among dialects has often been expressed.

Criticism of another sort has come from the generative-transformational grammarians, notably Noam Chomsky,[3] who in the late fifties attacked the

This article was contributed to this volume by Professor Troike, who is a member of the department of English at The University of Texas, Austin.

[1] This paper was originally written in 1965, and was slightly revised and expanded for inclusion in the present volume. I wish to thank Emmon Bach, Archibald A. Hill, and James Sledd for reading and commenting on the original draft of the paper. Appreciation is also due to Emmon Bach for commenting on the present version.

[2] The so-called "Trager–Smith system," which had its rarely acknowledged roots in the work of Henry Sweet, was set forth in 1951 in a 92-page publication by George L. Trager and Henry Lee Smith, Jr., *An Outline of English Structure*, Studies in Linguistics: Occasional Papers 3, Norman, Oklahoma. The most important critical discussions of the system are to be found in James H. Sledd's review of the work in *Language* 31: 312–45 (1955) and A. A. Hill (ed.), *First Texas Conference on Problems of Linguistic Analysis in English* (1956), Austin, Texas, 1962.

[3] Chomsky and others have discussed the matter in a number of places; for a relatively early discussion see A. A. Hill (ed.), *Third Texas Conference on Problems of Linguistic Analysis in English* (1958), Austin, Texas, 1962. For more recent discussion, see N. Chomsky and M. Halle, "Some Controversial Questions in Phonological Theory," *Journal of Linguistics* 1: 97–138 (1965) and Paul M. Postal, *Aspects of Phonological Theory*, New York, Harper & Row, 1968.

use of what he termed the "biunique principle" in American phonemic theory generally, i.e. the insistence that a notation should provide symbols for the phonemic contrasts found in a language in such a way that, given the phonetic data, they could be uniquely represented phonemically, and given the phonemic transcription, it could be uniquely interpreted (through a set of rules involving distributional complementarity) into a phonetic representation. The force of this criticism has cast considerable doubt on the phonemic assumptions shared by most of the disputants in the earlier discussions, and has reduced their arguments, in many points, to triviality.

One of the points of phonemic theory which long plagued linguists, and led to differences of practice between linguistic "schools," was the question of representing phonetic entities in positions where phonemic contrasts recognized elsewhere did not occur. The "European" position was formulated in the concept of the "archiphoneme," represented by a special symbol in phonotactic positions where a particular contrast was "neutralized." Implicit in the use of the archiphoneme was the idea that the phones involved in its realization might potentially fluctuate throughout a range comprehending that of all the phonemes neutralized in that position. The "American" position, which came to be represented by the catch-phrase "once a phoneme, always a phoneme," held that a particular range of phones should always and everywhere be identified uniquely with a particular phoneme, and should be so represented in all positions,[4] even where random fluctuation or intermediate phonetic norms seemed to be permitted by certain phonotactic rules.

This rigid view of the relationship between a phonetic and phonemic record was, in fact, of rather recent growth in American linguistics, and coincided with a shift in viewpoint—so well chronicled in Joos's *Readings in Linguistics*[5]— from the morpheme as the central linguistic unit *represented* by phonemes, to the phoneme as the linguistic prime of which morphemes were *composed*. The shift in viewpoint was in fact more radical than might first appear from such a characterization, for along with it came the methodological concept of an analysis which proceeded through a series of "levels" beginning with the phonetic and progressing upward through morphology to syntax.

Chomsky's proposal for a "generative" approach to phonology, while new in many respects, was nevertheless clearly implicit in many of the ideas and writings of Bloomfield, Sapir, and even Boas.[6] All of these older linguists, in their thinking about linguistic form, had taken the morpheme as central and its phonemic–phonetic representation as secondary. Consequently, many of the pseudo-problems which plagued post-Bloomfieldian structuralist phonology had

---

[4] One result of this insistence in the Trager–Smith system was that elements which were phonetically predictable in certain positions (and in certain dialects) had to be represented phonemically because they were elsewhere in significant contrast.

[5] Martin Joos, *Readings in Linguistics*, 2nd ed., New York, American Council of Learned Societies, 1958.

[6] And of course in Jakobson's view of phonology, which has proven highly congenial to a generative reformulation.

their source in the rejection of the primacy of the morpheme. Bloomfield presents some very clear examples of a generative approach to phonology, though perhaps not formalized so completely or in such a compartmentalized fashion as recent generativists have attempted.

Several works on the generative phonology of English have appeared during the past several years, dealing with the nature of the phoneme-phone chain.[7] Most of these writers have assumed a basic underlying system of highly abstract phonological units sometimes called "systematic phonemes" which serve to "spell" extant lexical units (morphemes). These systematic phonemes are defined in terms of a set of binarily-opposed "features" (such as ± consonantal, ± vocalic, ± nasal, ± tense, and ± strident) and are connected to their phonetic actualization through a series of ordered rules. These rules serve to "map" the abstract, or "deep" phonological representation of morphemes into their actual, or "surface" phonetic realization. In this approach, phonemes, at least as American linguists have known them in the recent past, practically disappear.

The present paper attempts to demonstrate the utility of a generative approach in the description and comparison of dialects, and seeks to re-open and re-examine the question of an overall pattern for the phonology of a language and its dialects. Some few hints of this matter have appeared in scattered papers thus far,[8] but there has been little explicit discussion of the problems involved or the issues to be faced in formulating an overall pattern within a generative framework.

I

The value of a generative approach in dialectology may be illustrated by several examples from Kurath and McDavid's summary work on *The Pronunciation of English in the Atlantic States*,[9] in which they wrestle with the problem of a

[7] The principal articles dealing with English to appear to date are two by Morris Halle, "On the Bases of Phonology" and "Phonology in Generative Grammar," both reprinted in Jerry A. Fodor and Jerrold J. Katz, *The Structure of Language*, Englewood Cliffs, N.J., Prentice–Hall, Inc., 1964. The single most important and comprehensive work on the subject is Noam Chomsky and Morris Halle, *The Sound Pattern of English*, New York, Harper & Row, 1968. A useful introduction to methodology is Robert T. Harms, *An Introduction to Phonological Theory*, Englewood Cliffs, N.J., Prentice–Hall, Inc., 1968.

[8] E.g. Sol Saporta, "Ordered Rules, Dialect Differences, and Historical Processes," *Language* 41: 218–24 (1965), James H. Sledd, "Breaking, Umlaut, and the Southern Drawl," *Language* 42: 18–41 (1966), Samuel J. Keyser, review of Hans Kurath and Raven I. McDavid, Jr., *The Pronunciation of English in the Atlantic States*, *Language* 39: 303–16 (1963), and Paul Kiparsky, "Linguistic Universals and Linguistic Change," *in* Emmon W. Bach and Robert T. Harms (eds.), *Universals in Linguistic Theory*, New York: Holt, Rinehart, & Winston, 1968. Two additional important works (though they do not give specific attention to this question) are: E. Vasiliu, "Towards a Generative Phonology of Daco–Rumanian Dialects,": *Journal of Linguistics* 2.79–98 (1966), and Donald A. Becker, *Generative Phonology and Dialect Study: An Investigation of Three Modern German Dialects*, University of Texas Ph.D. dissertation (1967).

[9] Hans Kurath and Raven I. McDavid, Jr., *The Pronunciation of English in the Atlantic States*, Ann Arbor, 1961.

dialectal phonemics, or a phonemic dialectology. In dealing with the contrasts among the low back vowels in the dialect of Western Pennsylvania, they set up a "phoneme" which they transcribe as /ɒ/, to distinguish it from /ɑ/ and /ɔ/, which in many environments do not contrast in this dialect. Elsewhere they set up the same phoneme for Eastern New England, while noting some differences in its systemic status. This New England vowel will be discussed further below. The choice of a symbol for the /ɒ/ was made both to reflect the compromise phonetic norm in such words as *cot* and *caught* and to show the lack of contrast between the vowels of such words, which in other dialects contain /ɑ/ and /ɔ/, respectively. Their /ɒ/ phoneme is, then, in other terminology, an archiphoneme, representing a neutralization of /ɑ/ and /ɔ/.

The matter is not quite so simple, however. The authors further go on to point out one of the characteristics for which this dialect is famous, namely, the fact that it also lacks a contrast between *hoarse* and *horse*, *mourning* and *morning*, etc., i.e. between /o/ and /ɔ/ before /r/. Although Kurath and McDavid find that the phones involved in this particular neutralization are usually raised lower-mid back [ɔˑ], they assign the phonemic symbol /o/ to the representation of these words on the phonetic grounds that the allophones of /o/ are usually lowered before /r/.[10] Their use of /ɒ/ makes for difficulties in dialectal comparison, for this "phoneme" is incommensurable with the /ɑ/ and /ɔ/ of other dialects. If *on* is /ɑn/ in some Northern dialects and /ɔn/ in some Midland ones, what is it here? Can it be construed as /ɑ/, or as /ɔ/? Where does one draw the isogloss for the vowel in this word?

But the purpose here is not to criticize Kurath and McDavid, who have adopted a logical solution to the problem of neutralization, but simply to show how a generative approach avoids some of the difficulties which a biunique approach creates. As indicated above, there is a double neutralization in this dialect affecting words which in other dialects contain [ɔ] = /ɔ/. The direction which this neutralization takes is affected by the phonological environment of the phoneme in question; as seen from the examples, /ɔ/ before /r/ falls together with /o/ in the same environment. However, in all other positions, /ɔ/ is merged with what in other dialects would ordinarily be a low mid vowel, conventionally /ɑ/. Both come to be realized in Western Pennsylvania speech by [ɒ].

Now a phonetically-based biunique phonemics is forced to recognize this difference, and to assign the nuclei of *hoarse*/*horse* and *caller*/*collar* to two different phonemes. However, a generative approach can avoid these difficulties by moving to a plane which is at once more abstract and more general in order to represent the phonological entities contained in these words, and to account for their phonetic realization. This move involves the formulation of contrasting *diaphonemic units* which underlie the actual phonetic realization found in the dialect.

---

[10] As a purely incidental observation, it may be noted that their assignment of [ɔˑ] to /o/ in this dialect leaves the symbol /ɔ/ unused, so that it could just as well serve to transcribe words such as *log*, *law*, and the like, as well as *collar*, *rock*, etc.

With regard to our example, a very simple generative statement can be made for these diaphonemic units, taking into account the phonetic differences which have been observed. This can be done in the form of a few simple rules which will serve to make the phonetic entities predictable from the diaphonemic ones. The rules follow; diaphonemic symbols are enclosed in vertical lines:[11]

WESTERN PENNSYLVANIA

	Diaphonemic Form		Phonetic Form
1.	|o| + |r|	⟶	[ɔˆ]
2.	|o|	⟶	[o] ~ [oː] ~ [ow] etc.
3.	|ɔ| + |r|	⟶	[ɔˆ]
4.	|ɔ|	⟶	[ɒ]
5.	|a|	⟶	[ɒ]

Such a set of rules[12] makes possible a direct "reading" of a diaphonemic transcription in its appropriate phonetic form, while at the same time it characterizes succinctly the nature of the difference between this dialect and others in the matter of realizing these phonemic distinctions. In applying these rules to the representation of words in this dialect, we see that words which were *pronounced alike* would nevertheless remain *diaphonemically distinct*:

hoarse	|hors|	⟶	[hɔˆrs]
horse	|hɔrs|	⟶	[hɔˆrs]
caller	|kɔlər|[13]	⟶	[kɒlər]
collar	|kalər|[14]	⟶	[kɒlər]

Thus on a diaphonemic level of representation, three different vowels are found, and at this level the morphemes which they spell are distinct, but on the level of speech, the three diaphonemes are converted into only two ranges of pronunciation.

The difference between the phonetic realization of these diaphonemes in Western Pennsylvania and in Eastern New England can readily be seen by

[11] Although a fully adequate description would necessarily make use of a feature notation, unitary phonological symbols are employed here for ease of exposition.

[12] Rules 1 and 2 and rules 3 and 4 can be conflated as follows:

$$1\text{–}2\colon |o| \to \left\{ \begin{matrix} [ɔˆ]/\text{—}|r| \\ [o] \end{matrix} \right\}$$

$$3\text{–}4\colon |ɔ| \to \left\{ \begin{matrix} [ɔˆ]/\text{—}|r| \\ [ɒ] \end{matrix} \right\}$$

Braces indicate a choice between two or more alternatives; the notation /—X or /X— means "in the environment preceding or following X," the position being indicated by the blank.

[13] No attempt is made here to refine the system of representation for dealing with the vocalization of resonants by rules; that this is feasible, however, has been shown by W. Nelson Francis (*The English Language: An Introduction*, New York, W. W. Norton, 1965) and by Chomsky and Halle (1968).

[14] It will be observed here that these rules, as formulated to deal with American dialects, are clearly unhistorical. If morphophonemic considerations, together with British dialects, are taken into account, definite differences in content and order of the rules would result. This matter is discussed further below.

comparing the treatment of the same words in the two dialects. Kurath and McDavid note (page 120) that *hoarse* in ENE is usually heard as [hoə̯s], while *horse* is [hɒs], and *caller* and *collar* are both presumably [kɒlə(r] (they do not cite these as examples). The rules for the phonetic representation of the dia-phonemes are therefore somewhat simpler for ENE than for WPa:

EASTERN NEW ENGLAND

6.	$\begin{vmatrix}o\end{vmatrix}$	$\longrightarrow$	[o]
7.	$\begin{vmatrix}ɔ\end{vmatrix}$	$\longrightarrow$	[ɒ]
8.	$\begin{vmatrix}a\end{vmatrix} + \begin{vmatrix}r\end{vmatrix}^{15}$	$\longrightarrow$	[a]
9.	$\begin{vmatrix}a\end{vmatrix}$	$\longrightarrow$	[ɒ]

As a result, our words would appear as follows:

hoarse	$\begin{vmatrix}hors\end{vmatrix}$	$\longrightarrow$	[hoə̯s]^{16}
horse	$\begin{vmatrix}hɔrs\end{vmatrix}$	$\longrightarrow$	[hɒs]
caller	$\begin{vmatrix}kɔlər\end{vmatrix}$	$\longrightarrow$	[kɒlə(r]
collar	$\begin{vmatrix}kalər\end{vmatrix}$	$\longrightarrow$	[kɒlə(r]
car	$\begin{vmatrix}kar\end{vmatrix}$	$\longrightarrow$	[ka:]

The treatment of these same diaphonemes in certain Southern and South Midland dialects also merits comparison. In direct contrast to WPa, $\begin{vmatrix}o\end{vmatrix}$ and $\begin{vmatrix}or\end{vmatrix}$ are here kept distinct,[17] as are $\begin{vmatrix}a\end{vmatrix}$ and $\begin{vmatrix}ɔ\end{vmatrix}$ except before $\begin{vmatrix}r\end{vmatrix}$, where they have merged as [ɑr] or [ɒr]. The rules therefore would have the following form:[18]

SOUTH MIDLAND

10.	$\begin{vmatrix}o\end{vmatrix}$	$\longrightarrow$	[o]
11.	$\begin{vmatrix}ɔ\end{vmatrix}$	$\longrightarrow$	$[ɒ]/\text{---}\begin{vmatrix}r\end{vmatrix}$
12.	$\begin{vmatrix}ɔ\end{vmatrix}$	$\longrightarrow$	[ɔ] (or [o]; see footnote 17)
13.	$\begin{vmatrix}a\end{vmatrix}$	$\longrightarrow$	$[ɒ]/\text{---}\begin{vmatrix}r\end{vmatrix}$
14.	$\begin{vmatrix}a\end{vmatrix}$	$\longrightarrow$	[a]

A comparison of the three dialects can now be made directly on the basis of these rules, rather than, as traditionally, on the basis of the products of the

[15] Rules 8 and 9 may be conflated to form one rule:

$$8\text{-}9: |a| \rightarrow \left\{\begin{matrix}[a]/\text{---}|r| \\ [ɒ]\end{matrix}\right\}$$

[16] Rules for the realization of $|r|$ are not formulated here, but these would be easy to specify.

[17] In many Southern and South Midland dialects, $|ɔ|$ diphthongizes to $|ɔw|$ and for some speakers undergoes a further raising to [ow], so that $|o|$ and $|ɔ|$ come to merge, at least in certain environments. The merger could be expressed either by a single rule 12' (replacing rule 12):

$$12'.\ |ɔ| \rightarrow [o]$$

or by a sequence of rules having the effect $|ɔ| \rightarrow [ɔ] \rightarrow [ɔw] \rightarrow [ow]$. For many speakers, a further rule would operate to lower the beginning point of the diphthong to [aw] (this applies both to words containing underlying $|o|$ and to words containing underlying $|ɔ|$).

[18] Rules 11–12 and 13–14 can of course again be conflated, but are kept separate here to facilitate comparison.

rules. More significant results can be obtained thereby, as for example, we can see that the *direction* of change in SM (merger of |o| and |ɔ| *except* before |r|, merger of |ɔ| and |a| *only* before |r|) is almost exactly the converse of that in WPa. Such a generalization would be lost, however, in any comparison which attempted to work directly from the phonetic record, or on the basis of "phonemic" analyses made independently for each dialect, since all that could be shown would be charts of phone-distributions for each dialect without indication of the morphemes in which the phones occurred, or mere lists of morphemes tabulated separately for each dialect showing the phones which they contained. As an illustration, the observation that the phone sequence [ɒr] occurs in both WPa and SM is meaningless by itself, but not much less so than the statement that [fɒrm] represents either *farm* or *form* in SM, but only *farm* in WPa. A generative approach avoids such atomistic results, and by utilizing rules to derive surface phonetic forms from underlying diaphonemes, allows us to state generalizations about dialect characteristics or differences in a maximally revealing and useful way.

The examples given above have been intended to show that comparison of the dialects of a language can be sharpened considerably by the adoption of a generative approach to the formulation of the phonological structure. Not only can comparison be made more systematic, but the distinction between *systemic differences* in the phonological rules, and *individual* (incidental) *differences* in rules for lexical items, can be made readily apparent. (It should be noted that Kurath and McDavid have been careful to differentiate these in their work.)

Given a generative model, the strategy of dialect comparison can shift from a fixation on superficial phonetic differences to an examination of the underlying, "deeper" structural unity which ties the dialects together into a single overall phonemic pattern. The nature of dialect differences can also be assessed in a more significant way, e.g. by asking whether certain dialects do indeed possess a different phonological system on a deep level, or whether differences between them are merely in the number, form, or ordering of realization rules. In short, with the use of a generative model for dialect description, a structural dialectology is indeed possible.

II

A generative approach can also serve to resolve some of the questions raised by James Sledd in his review[19] of *An Outline of English Structure* by George Trager and Henry Lee Smith. A number of the difficulties which he recognized in the application of the Trager–Smith transcription to his (Atlanta) idiolect were a direct consequence of the then unquestioned assumption regarding phonemic overlapping. For it was generally held by American linguists at that

---

[19] See now Sledd's important paper "Breaking, Umlaut, and the Southern Drawl," in which he has adopted a generative approach to many of the same problems discussed here.

time that phonetically identical elements could not have different representations on the phonemic level. Such a condition is, as Halle and others have shown, unnecessary and unmotivated.

Assuming now, in a generative framework, some determinate relationship between the syntactic, morphological, and phonemic representations of a sentence, we may remove some of Sledd's examples from consideration within the context in which he treated them. The "reading rules" for *Will ya* and *we're* must certainly be of a different order from those for *veer* and *via*, if for no other reason than that the former sequences contain word boundaries; the reduction of their post-initial components so that they rhyme with the latter pair is therefore a product of sandhi rules. It is clear from this set, however, that any rule providing for the neutralization of [i]:[ɪ] before |r| in this dialect must apply *before* the deletion of word boundary and the prosodic deletion of the vowel of *are*, if Sledd's examples of *veer* [vɪ̯ə vs. *we're* [wɪ̯ə] are to be accounted for. In other dialects, however, this ordering would not apply, and the two items just cited would rhyme as [vɪə ~ vɪ̯ə] and [wɪə ~ wɪ̯ə], and the last would be homophonous with *weir* (similarly *there* = *they're*).

The answer to Sledd's famous "tenth vowel" was recognized in his review, when he suggested the possibility of simultaneous phonetic components to account for his low front vowel intermediate between [æ] and [ɑ] (Jones' cardinal vowel [a]). In many areas of the South and South Midland, a minimal triplet can easily be demonstrated to prove the (biunique) phonemic status of this vowel:

[tæm]	*tam*
[tam]	*time*
[tɑm]	*Tom*

An inductive analysis of such a dialect in isolation perhaps would force the recognition of a vowel phoneme /a/ in contrast to /ɑ/; however, any analysis in terms of an overall pattern would require an equivalence statement between this /a/ and the nucleus /ay/ found in other dialects. In generative terms, this would simply be formulated as a rule,[20]

15. |ay| ⟶   [a(:)]

so that even these Southern dialects would be considered to possess |ay| on the diaphonemic level. Even in many dialects which preserve the front glide, a contextual rule would be required to adjust the allophonic quality of the vowel,

---

[20] Southern dialects vary in the applicability of this rule in different environments It is most widely applicable before voiced consonants or in final position; in some it operates also before voiceless fricatives. The interdialectal confusion predictable from rules 8 and 15 was amusingly confirmed by a Southern speaker from Beaumont, Texas, named *Kaiser*, who upon moving to eastern New England found that the natives invariably interpreted her pronunciation of her name as *Carser*, and spelled it accordingly.

16. $|a|$ $\longrightarrow$ $[a]/\!\!-\!\!-\!\!-|y|$

17. $|y|$ $\longrightarrow$ $[\iota]$, $[\iota]$, etc.

Perhaps a more economical statement for Southern dialects lacking the glide component would be the substitution of a different rule for 17:

18. $|y|$ $\longrightarrow$ ø (null)/[a]$-\!\!-\!\!-$

Sledd's speech, however, according to his report contains a contrast between [a²] and [a¹], the second of which he assigns to /ay/, thus leaving the first unassignable to any known cell in the Trager–Smith matrix. His first two pairs of examples, *fire/fie* and *fired/defied* could probably be explained by rules such as the following (the period indicates syllable boundary; V = vowel):

19. $|a|$ $\longrightarrow$ $\left|\begin{matrix}[a]/\!-\!-|y|\,| \\ [\alpha] \end{matrix}\right|$

20. $|y|$ $\longrightarrow$ $\left|\begin{matrix}ø/[a]\!-\!-|r|\,| \\ [^1]/[a]\!-\!- \end{matrix}\right|$

21. $|r|$ $\longrightarrow$ $\left|\begin{matrix}[:]/[a]\!-\!-\!. \\ [^2]/V\!-\!-\!. \end{matrix}\right|$

His further example of *vial/vile* and *giant/pint* suggest the possibility of dialect mixture and the consequent use of coexistent sets of rules for these words, with special rules or alternative diaphonemic representations perhaps associated with particular lexical items. If, however, they are representative of a larger class, they may be accounted for by assuming that *giant* and *vial* are in fact bisyllables which have been monophthongized. A slight modification of rule 20 (rule 22 below) and the addition of one extra rule, whereby weakly-stressed $|ə|$ loses its syllabicity, will handle these examples adequately ($-$ = morpheme boundary; $\#$ = word boundary; C = consonant):

22. $|y|$ $\longrightarrow$ $\left\{\begin{matrix}ø/[a]\!\!-\!\!\left\{\left|\begin{matrix}ə \\ r\end{matrix}\right|\right\} \\ [^1]/[a]\!\!-\!\!-\end{matrix}\right\}$

23. $|ə|$ $\longrightarrow$ $[^2]/V\!\!-\!\!\left\{\begin{matrix}C \\ \#\end{matrix}\right\}$

Thus *vial* $|váyəl|$ → $|v[á]yəl|$ → $|v[á]əl|$ → $['va^2l]$

     vile $|vayl|$ → $|v[á]yl|$ → $|v[á^1]l|$ → $|'va^1l]^{21}$

More data would be required to formulate such rules with greater precision, and to determine to what extent they can be combined and simplified. Some economy in the treatment of rules 19–21 might be achieved by an ordering which places $|r|$ → [ə] first, after which the environmental statement in rule 20 could be simplified; rule 23 would then apply uniformly to all cases of [ə],

[21] It is striking that Sledd (1966, page 39) came to an almost identical conclusion with respect to these two forms; these rules and examples were completed in their present form before Sledd kindly showed the writer the manuscript of his paper.

from whatever source.[22] On the other hand, such treatment would obscure the origin of [ˀ] in |r|, and might well prove unmotivated in a larger context.

The problem of devising rules to handle situations where dialect borrowing creates apparent phonemic contrasts in one or more idiolects is complex. In the speech of one East Texas informant, this process has produced such contrasts as

[pæˆⁱnts] pants "trousers"   [pæˆⁱs] pass (v.)
[pænts] pants (v.)   [mæs] mass

These contrasts represent two strata in the informant's speech development, the first one (the earliest) involving a rule[23]

$$24. \quad |æ| \quad \longrightarrow \quad [æˆⁱ]/\!\!-\!\!-\!\!- \left| \begin{array}{l} \text{Vl. Fricative} \\ \text{Nasal + Vl. Stop} \end{array} \right|$$

which was absent from the later stratum. The relation of such rules to the lexicon, whether the range of their application can be restricted to portions of the total vocabulary or whether lexical entries are best keyed to applicable rules, is a matter for future consideration.

III

The choice of a generative model inevitably revives the question of whether it is possible to construct a uniform underlying phonological system for all the dialects of a language. It also raises in an interesting way the question of how the difference between *language* and *dialect* can be defined. The distinction has usually been made on highly subjective grounds, but the formalization inherent in a generative approach to linguistic description offers some hope that a more definitive criterion, intrinsic to the language itself, can be found.

It should be noted that the abstract underlying phonological units set up in a generative diaphonemic system, along with their realization rules, are not unlike the reconstructed phonemic units of a proto-linguistic state, and their corresponding derivational rules. Nor should this be surprising, since the differences between the dialects of a language are the product of historical changes, including "regular sound-changes", which are precisely the differences that must be accounted for in setting up both diaphonemic units and historical reconstructions. However, it does not follow that their results will always be

---

[22] Other sources would include |ɪ|, which commonly becomes a centering glide ([ə], [ɜ]) or length following vowels, as in *help* [hɛəp], *bulb* [bəɜb] or [bəːb]. See now Sledd (1966) for a detailed discussion of these.

[23] It is interesting to note the close parallel between the environments in this rule and those involved in the rule which converts |æ| to [aˀ] in standard British (and Eastern New England) speech (or, alternatively, which prevents the fronting of |a| to [æ]; see the discussion in the next section). The rule diphthongizing |æ| here can probably be taken together with the general South Midland rule (referred to in fn. 17) that diphthongizes |ɔ| to [ɔw], as being a result of tensing, since generally all tense vowels are diphthongized.

exactly the same, since synchronic generative description is concerned with internal questions of economy and simplicity, whereas the comparative method utilizes external information, when available, on geographical distribution and historical documentation.

Nevertheless, a generative-diaphonemic system must reflect many of the historical changes which have taken place in the dialects. We have suggested that most of the major phonological differences among American dialects can be accounted for by a few fairly simple rules. As we bring together dialects having greater time-depth and more extensive phonological differences, however, the problem of constructing a single uniform system becomes more complex. There is, of course, no difficulty in positing underlying lax vowel diaphonemes |ɪ|, |ɛ|, |a|, |ʊ| in such words as *ship*, *bed*, *that*, and *bush*, which are almost universally [šɪp], [bɛd], [ðæt], [bŭš], and presumably have been ever since Old English times.[24] But the extension of the overall pattern to include even Southern British English would require some changes in the diaphonemes and rules formulated earlier for American dialects, if the British [ɒ] in *cot*, rather than the American [ɑ], is taken as primary. In this case, no merging rule |a| → [ɒ] would be required for a form such as *collar*, as this would already be entered in the lexicon as |kɒlər|. However, the converse rule |ɒ| → [ɑ] would be required for all other American dialects in which this would emerge as [kɑlər]. The homophonization of *caught* and *cot* would then involve a coalescence of |ɒ| and |ɔ| rather than |ɔ| and |a|. Some dialects, however, such as New York City or Atlanta, where *father* is [fɒðə(r)], would still have the additional rule |a| → [ɒ].

Many of the dialects of Northern England and Scotland still preserve features of Old English or Middle English phonology unchanged, or have undergone independent innovations, so that a diaphonemic system which includes these will differ considerably from one which covers only American and Southern British dialects.[25] The extent of the phonetic differences is enough to raise the question as to whether these Northern dialects (including Scots) should be considered as belonging to the same language. For example, situations in which OE /ɪ/ was lengthened and raised during Middle English and became [ay] in Southern British English pose certain problems, as they are apt to correspond still to [ɪ] in certain modern dialects (e.g. *bind* [bɪnd] in Northern England). Similarly, Southern British [aw] will often be found to correspond

---

[24] There is no evidence of a comparative dialectal nature for positing a distinction between lax *a* and lax *æ* on the diaphonemic level. |a| has therefore been chosen as the symbol for this diaphoneme, i.e. a low central vowel. In addition, it is not necessary to include [ə] (=[ʌ]) as a diaphoneme, since Northern British dialects very clearly show it to be derived from |ʊ| by a rule

$$|ʊ| → [ə]$$

Thus Northern dialects still have [mʊk], [gʊl], where Southern dialects have [mʌk], [gʌl] for *muck*, *gull*.

[25] Most of the data on Northern British dialects cited in the following discussion are based on Harold Orton and Wilfred J. Halliday (eds.), *Survey of English Dialects*, Leeds, 1962–

to unshifted [u:] or [uw] in Scots and North of England dialects, as in *house*
or *out* (Old English *hūs*, *ūt*). It is evident, therefore, that if Southern British
(and American) [baynd] and [haws] are to be derived from |bɪnd| and |hus|
(which must be assumed to underlie the Northern forms), the phonological
rules applying to these dialects will have to reflect the change of |ɪ| to |i| in
certain "lengthening" environments, as well as such portions of the Great
Vowel Shift as |iy| → [ay] and |uw| → [aw]. We therefore formulate these
rules informally as follows (' represents stress; it will be assumed that all vowels
discussed herein are stressed unless otherwise indicated):

25.	|ɪ|	⟶	|i|——/nd#
26.	|i|	⟶	|iy|
27.	|iy|	⟶	[ay]
28.	|u|	⟶	|uw|[26]
29.	|uw|	⟶	[aw]

One of the apparent difficulties in the way of constructing a unified phonological system for Scottish and English dialects involves the OE velar fricative
phoneme /x/, which still survives in Scotland but has disappeared as such
from all other English-speaking areas. Despite its relatively low frequency, it
would have to be included in the system to account for such Scottish forms as
bright [brɪxt] and *enough* [inɪwx].[27] Because of the disparity of its development
in individual words (partly as a result of dialect mixture), few general rules
can be formulated to determine its actualization in other dialects; in most
instances it will probably have to be handled on the lexical level, though some
subregularities can be found. The correspondence of Scottish [brɪxt], Northumbrian [bri:t], and Southern British [brayt], for example, suggests the possibility
of a limited rule

30. |x| ⟶ |y|/|ɪ|——|t|

which would yield the derived form |brɪyt| underlying the Northumbrian
pronunciation. By rule 27, this will become Southern British [brayt], so that
the sequence is a "natural" one, with only the Great Vowel Shift standing
between them.[28]

Standard Irish English (and to a lesser extent some Northern British
dialects) still preserves the three-way contrast between *meet* [mi:t], *meat* [me:t],
and *mate* [mɛ:t] which prevailed in London English prior to the seventeenth
century. As a result, words such as these must continue to be represented on
the diaphonemic level by the tense diaphonemes |e|, |æ|, and |ā|, respec-

[26] A more general diphthongization rule would provide for the introduction of a
matching front or back glide after both high tense vowels.

[27] Since the [h] occurs only pre-vocalically and the [x] only post-vocalically, they
may be considered positional variants of a single diaphoneme |x|.

[28] Modern English spelling, precisely because of its anachronistic character, will
often be found to correspond closely to the correct representation of the diaphonemic
form underlying modern pronunciations.

tively, and the following merging rule must be applied for all dialects in which $|e|$ and $|æ|$ have coalesced:

31. $|æ|$ $\longrightarrow$ $|e|$

A second rule would then raise $|e|$, both original and that derived from $|æ|$, to [i]:

32. $|e|$ $\longrightarrow$ [i]

(Note that this must apply *after* rule 26 so that the product of rule 32 will not undergo rule 27—though it appears that a partial replica of rule 27 is now being applied to the output of rule 32 in many dialects.)

This is the simplest formulation, but a possible alternative would be

32a. $\begin{vmatrix} e \end{vmatrix}$ $\longrightarrow$ [i]
31a. $\begin{vmatrix} æ \end{vmatrix}$ $\longrightarrow$ $|e|$
32b. $\begin{vmatrix} e \end{vmatrix}$ $\longrightarrow$ [i]

with the raising of $|e|$ to [i] applying both before and after the shift of $|æ|$ to $|e|$. This latter ordering of rules 32a–31a is in fact what must be assumed for the dialect of Irish English referred to here; the Irish dialect, however, would lack rule 32b, so that the vowels in *meet* and *meat* still remain distinct. The difference between Irish and other English dialects could then be expressed as involving either a difference in rule order (31–32 vs. 32a–31a) or the presence or absence of a particular rule (32b).

Irish English would also have a rule shifting $|ā|$ to $|æ|$ in such words as *mate*:

33. $|ā|$ $\longrightarrow$ $|æ|$ (= [ε:])

Other dialects of English could be accounted for in one of two ways. Either they could be assumed to undergo an alternative rule (33a) shifting $|ā|$ directly to $|e|$:

33a. $|ā|$ $\longrightarrow$ $|e|$

or else they could be assumed to share rule 33 with Irish English, and undergo in addition the following rule, which would be a replica of rule 31:

34. $|æ|$ $\longrightarrow$ $|e|$

Again the difference between the dialects could be expressed as a difference in the form of a rule (33 vs. 33a) or as a difference in the number and order of rules required to derive the phonetic form of the respective dialects from the common underlying diaphonemic base.

A somewhat different problem is posed by the correspondence of Scottish [e:] and American [ow] (Southern British [əw]) in such words as *stane* [ste:n], *stone* [stown], or *nae* [ne:], *no* [now]. Here neither dialect represents the actual historical source, and the solution for positing a common underlying diaphonemic representation is not immediately obvious. We cannot use |e|, since rule 32 specifies that this is shifted to [i], nor can we use |æ| or |ā| as sources of the Scottish vowel, since the choice of these diaphonemes would yield the wrong output for other dialects. One possibility would be to select a compromise vowel, such as |ø|. This choice, in fact, is greatly strengthened by the occurrence of [stø:n] and [nø:] in Northumberland.

A somewhat different conclusion is suggested, however, if we view the decision in the context of the rest of the diaphonemic system our comparisons have led us to set up to this point. Thus far we have the following diaphonemes:

	Lax			*Tense*	
I		U		i	u
ε		ɒ		e	
	a			æ	ā

We can probably best approach the problem of the diaphoneme underlying *stone/stane* by considering another matter first. Since |u| is shifted by rules 28–29 to [aw], it is not available as the underlying source of the [u] ~ [u:] ~ [uw] found in such words as *goose* or *food*. On analogy with |e| as the diaphoneme underlying [i], we might posit |o| as the diaphoneme underlying phonetic [u] of Southern British and American dialects. This of course accords with the historical facts, though the presumed original [o:] apparently nowhere survives among existing dialects, so that our major justification for positing |o| must be analogy and simplicity in our description. (Note that this assignment of |o| in the diaphonemic system underlying the broader spectrum of English dialects will require us to revise the value assumed for the |o| in Part I in the discussion of American dialects; the change will not affect the substance of that discussion in any significant way, however, since its import was primarily methodological.) We may express this shift by a rule (35), which must follow rule 28:

35. |o| ⟶   [u]

Our chart of tense vowel diaphonemes may now be revised accordingly:

i		u
e		o
æ	ā	

Returning now to the question of the diaphoneme underlying Scottish [e] and American [o], we may note that positing |ø| would produce a considerable asymmetry among the tense vowels. A more symmetrical arrangement would be attained by positing |ɔ| as the underlying diaphoneme for *stone*, but more importantly, doing so would enable us to exploit certain additional parallels between shifts in the front and back vowels, which might otherwise be obscured. These may be represented roughly as follows:

i.a)   i(y)   u(w)   (mice)   (mouse)
         ↘   ↙
               ay   aw
i.b)   i   u   (feet)   (food)
         ↑   ↑
         e   o
i.c)   e   o   (meat)   (stone)
         ↑   ↑
         æ   ɔ

We can express these shifts by such generalizations as the following:

ii.a)   high vowel diaphonemes diphthongize and shift their first com-
         ponent to a low central vowel
ii.b)   mid vowels shift to high vowels
ii.c)   low vowels shift to mid vowels

Alternatively, if we adopt the following feature matrix for these vowels, the
same generalizations can be expressed even more economically by reference to
features (unless otherwise indicated, the vowels shown here are [+ vocalic],
[− consonantal], and [+ tense]):

	i	e	æ	ā	ɔ	o	u
High	+	−	−	−	−	−	+
Low	−	−	+	+	+	−	−
Back	−	−	−	+	+	+	+
Rounded	−	−	−	−	+	+	+

Omitting here for purposes of simplification the formulation of the diphthongization rule and the formal statement of the environment (before a matching front or back glide) in which the first shift occurs, we may express these
shifts as follows:

i/u   *a*

iii.a)   [+ high]   ⟶ $\begin{bmatrix} - \text{ high} \\ + \text{ low} \\ + \text{ back} \\ - \text{ round} \end{bmatrix}$ /——[y/w]

e/o   *i/u*

iii.b) $\begin{bmatrix} - \text{ high} \\ - \text{ low} \end{bmatrix}$ ⟶   [+ high]

æ/ɔ   *e/o*

iii.c)   [+ low]   ⟶   [− low]

Rules iii.a–c are thus an equivalent expression of the generalizations stated
verbally in ii.a–c.

Rule iii.c yields [ston] from |stɔn|; additional rules can very easily be
devised to derive the Northumbrian [stø:n] and Scottish [ste:n] from this:

$$
\text{iv.)} \quad \text{Northumbrian:} \quad \overset{o}{\begin{bmatrix} - \text{ high} \\ - \text{ low} \\ + \text{ back} \\ + \text{ round} \end{bmatrix}} \quad \longrightarrow \quad \overset{\o}{[- \text{ back}]}
$$

$$
\text{v.)} \quad \text{Scottish:} \quad \overset{\o}{\begin{bmatrix} - \text{ high} \\ - \text{ low} \\ - \text{ back} \\ + \text{ round} \end{bmatrix}} \quad \longrightarrow \quad \overset{o}{[- \text{ round}]}
$$

Rule v assumes that the vowel has first been fronted by rule iv, and then un-rounds it to [e]. However, the Scottish development need not be supposed to go through this intermediate state, and might instead be formulated[29]

$$
\text{v'.)} \quad \overset{o}{\begin{bmatrix} - \text{ high} \\ - \text{ low} \\ + \text{ back} \\ + \text{ round} \end{bmatrix}} \quad \longrightarrow \quad \overset{e}{\begin{bmatrix} - \text{ back} \\ - \text{ round} \end{bmatrix}}
$$

Other rules discussed previously could similarly be reformulated in feature terms, and further refinement of their use would undoubtedly reveal additional regularities among the phonetic realization rules of various dialects, but enough has been discussed here to indicate the direction such work might profitably take. There is no question that a feature notation is more useful than are unitary diaphonemic and phonetic symbols, since it allows us to express directly generalizations about phonological developments which can only be stated very awkwardly otherwise. The symbols will continue to have their use as a convenient shorthand for sets of features, which of course is what they have always been.

We may now quite justifiably ask what relationship a generative dia-phonemics has to current work in generative morphophonemics. Given rather

---

[29] This can be generalized further for some Scottish dialects, which also have [i] corresponding to southern British [u]. To cover both cases, the rule could be amended to read

$$
\text{v''.} \quad \overset{o/u}{\begin{bmatrix} - \text{low} \\ + \text{back} \\ + \text{round} \end{bmatrix}} \rightarrow \overset{e/i}{\begin{bmatrix} - \text{back} \\ - \text{round} \end{bmatrix}}
$$

From the fact that other Scottish dialects have [ü] corresponding to Southern British and American [u], however, it appears that a fronting rule

$$
\text{vi.} \quad \begin{bmatrix} - \text{low} \\ + \text{back} \\ + \text{round} \end{bmatrix} \rightarrow [- \text{back}] \text{ must have operated first, and that unrounding followed, but}
$$

has more widely affected [ø] than [ü]. Thus some dialects would have only rule v, while others would have the simpler and more general rule vii. $\begin{bmatrix} - \text{low} \\ - \text{back} \\ + \text{round} \end{bmatrix} \rightarrow [- \text{round}].$

similar methods, it should but be expected that their results will converge to a great extent. But if work on the morphophonemics of a language, with its inherently more intimate relation to the whole grammatical system, must take theoretical precedence, as it does, what remains for a diaphonemic analysis to contribute?

For one, it provides an approach to some of the same data from a different point of view, and can thereby sometimes produce insights which might be missed, or gained only with great difficulty, in the course of morphophonemic analysis. It would not be out of place here to compare the results of our quite skeletal analysis with those recently published by Chomsky and Halle in *The Sound Pattern of English*. Except for some vowel nuclei which we did not consider, the systematic vowel phonemes Chomsky and Halle propose for their variety of English are substantially identical to the diaphonemes which we posited, both tense and lax, on an entirely independent basis. Using very refined methods of internal reconstruction, they find strong grounds for assuming a /x/ in such a word as *right* (page 233), with a lax /ɪ/ preceding it; their conclusion coincides exactly with the results we had obtained by comparing Scottish with other dialects, and attempting to relate Scottish [brɪxt] to Southern British [brayt].

Constructing a diaphonemic system for a language essentially involves developing an algorithm for interrelating the dialects of that language. The emphasis in such an approach is on formalizing the specification of dialect differences in such a way that a more meaningful and systematic comparison of dialects may be made. Such a comparison can help us to reconstruct the historical order of changes, especially in languages where no historical records exist, so that we will be able to compare the historical and synchronic ordering of rules to determine what restructurings have occurred in the phonological grammars of the respective dialects. It should also contribute to the formulation of objective measures of dialect differentiation which will be based on features intrinsic to the dialects themselves rather than on the highly subjective reactions of informants to the intelligibility of a text. (Given such measures, in fact, it would be possible to test their correlations with informant reactions to dialect differences.) Since it has been possible for us to incorporate all English dialects within a single diaphonemic system, none of our examples within English have proven crucial for defining a language/dialect dichotomy. Nevertheless, the possibility still exists of finding objective criteria for characterizing this distinction in situations where dialect differentiation has exceeded that found within English.

Since as we have seen, a generative diaphonemics partakes of the comparative method, while a generative morphophonemics utilizes the methods of internal reconstruction, it is evident that the two approaches complement, rather than completely overlap, one another, and it is therefore not surprising if a diaphonemic analysis provides information which might be beyond recovery in the morphophonemics of a single dialect, or which might be overlooked in the process of constructing a morphophonemic description. Thus, even if a morphophonemic analysis of an American dialect had overlooked |x| in *bright*, *night*, etc. it would eventually have had to be posited in base forms in order to explain the morphophonemics of Scottish dialects.

Several brief examples will suffice to show how information which would form part of a diaphonemic description of English can contribute to a morphophonemic description of the language. Chomsky and Halle (page 172) suggest that such forms as *pint, count, plaint*, for which they assume underlying tense vowels, provide evidence that vowels in monosyllabic stems before an [nt] cluster are exceptions to the general laxing rule of vowels before consonant clusters. But it happens that *pint* and *count* are the only examples of [ay] and [aw] before [nt] in monosyllables (except for the clipped forms *fount* and *mount*), whereas forms such as *tint, mint, sprint*, and *hunt, brunt, stunt* are relatively common. Conversely, except for *wind* (n.) and *fund* (and a few proper names and loanwords), [nd] is preceded in monosyllables *only* by [ay] and [aw], never by [ɪ] and [ə] (< |ʊ|). Clearly, [nt] cannot be taken as regularly blocking a "laxing rule", whereas [nd] must be assumed to do so. An alternative solution, suggested by our earlier examination of *bind*, to which we assigned the base form |bɪnd|, is that a tensing rule similar to our rule 25, but generalized to cover |ɪ| and |ʊ|, should be added to their morphophonemic rules:

36.
$$\begin{bmatrix} + \text{high} \\ - \text{tense} \end{bmatrix} \longrightarrow [+ \text{tense}]/\begin{bmatrix} \\ + \text{stress} \end{bmatrix} \text{nd} \#$$

This would avoid having to specify [nd] as an exception to the laxing rule, and would permit *bind* and *bound* to be entered with underlying lax vowels (it will be noted that on page 209 Chomsky and Halle enter both forms with underlying tense vowels).[30]

A similar situation obtains with such words as *wild, child*, for which Chomsky and Halle assume an underlying tense vowel (pages 172, 176). In both instances they find it necessary to assume a laxing of the vowel in the forms of *wilderness* and *children*. However, if the base forms were assumed to have a lax vowel, as is suggested by the British dialect form [čɪld], and the grammar contained a tensing rule,

37. |ɪ| $\longrightarrow$ [+ tense]/——ld #

then the lax vowels in the derived forms would offer no problem, since they would not meet the conditions of the rule (i.e. preceding #). Similarly, the development of *hold* and *told* might be explained more simply if these were assumed to have the underlying lax vowel |ɒ|, which is tensed to |ɔ| before -ld, and subsequently raised to |o| and diphthongized.

As a final example, Chomsky and Halle present (page 224) a "velar soften-

---

[30] There would be reasons, therefore, for assuming that the stressed vowel of *profundity* remains lax since it does not meet the conditions of rule 36, while *profound* does, and is accordingly tensed.

ing rule", which changes underlying /g/ and /k/ to [j] and [ts], respectively, with the latter ultimately shifting to [s]. The first part of the rule (affecting /g/), is also motivated within a diaphonemic framework by such forms as Northumbrian [brɪg] for *bridge*. Some modification is suggested in the part of the rule affecting /k/, however, by the dialectal evidence of such forms as Northumbrian [θak] for *thatch*, and Scottish [kɪrk] for *church*, in which the original Old English /k/ has been preserved from palatalization, and so must be posited in the base diaphonemic forms underlying these words. This fact suggests the need for a broader re-examination of the assumption of /č/ as a systematic phoneme in the language, and of the morphophonemic rules which have been developed on the basis of this assumption.

IV

The adoption of a generative model for dialect comparison has numerous implications for dialectology, long the step-child of both descriptive and historical linguistics. This type of model is far from new in linguistics, of course, but its use as a major tool in dialect geography has yet to be exploited. It has a distinct advantage over static structural comparisons of phonemic and allophonic inventories in that it relates all dialects directly to a single underlying diaphonemic system, on the basis of which they may be compared as to number, scope, order, and form of the rules needed to derive their distinctive phonological characteristics. In addition, the use of such a model raises interesting new questions regarding the nature of phonetic differences among dialects and opens the way to more penetrating and significant answers to these and other questions of linguistic differentiation.

29

Phonemic and Prosodic Analysis in Linguistic Geography

TREVOR HILL

IT IS FREQUENTLY ASSUMED that a structural description of a tongue, for dialectological or other purposes, is necessarily to be made in terms of phonemes; a terminological index of this is the use of *phonemics*, among American linguists, as a synonym for *phonology* (in the synchronic sense). Recent fieldwork on the dialects of Lowland Scots spoken in the north and east of Scotland has however revealed phenomena that seem better adapted to a prosodic treatment; and in this paper I wish to present some of the material and outline the approach we have in mind. I will first state, as a basis for discussion, some principles that underlie contemporary analyses of the phoneme type. The form of my statement is admittedly conditioned by the viewpoint from which I wish to consider it; however, I think it is a fair representation of the approach.

i) It is postulated that the word (or other piece to be analysed) shall undergo a thorough division into segments, usually corresponding to what in the terms of articulatory phonetics are its vowels and consonants. Thus Postulate 11 in B. Bloch, *A Set of Postulates for Phonemic Analysis* (*Language* 24, 1948). The Scots word **drix**[1] will consist of four segments, **kwəini**[2] of six (or five?), and so on. In the word thus divided, significant alternances of vowel or consonant are seen to occur at various points, thus **drix/drip/drim, drix/brix/skrix**, etc[3]

Now at this stage, we have not yet produced a *phoneme* analysis: this was clearly seen by F. Twaddell, who on pp. 24-25 of *On Defining the Phoneme* (*Language Monographs*, NO. XVI, 1935), pointed out (I condense):

Reprinted by permission from *Orbis* 12.449–54 (1963). The author, formerly associated with the Linguistic Survey of Scotland, is now a member of the department of modern languages at Simon Fraser University in British Columbia. This article was presented as a paper at the First International Congress of General Dialectology, Louvain–Brussells, August 23, 1960.

[1] *dreich* (wearisome).
[2] *quinie* (girl).
[3] *dreich, dreep* (drip), *dream, dreich, Breich* (place-name), *skreich* (scream).

By setting up the group (1) pin:fin (2) apple:addle, we obtain the following relations: (1) [p] which is distinct from [f]; (2) [p] which is distinct from [d]. But the grouping together of these various [p]'s is legitimate only when there is positive evidence of their constituting a positive entity.

The second point is therefore:

ii) The Principle of Complementary Distribution, by which various significantly alternating segments occurring at different points in the word-structure, thus northeast Scots **k/q** in **kni:, błaq**,[4] or in differing articulatory contexts, thus **lik, błaq**,[5] are identified as allophones of a phoneme. The result is a structural statement about the tongue, usually consisting of an inventory of phonemes plus specifications of their combinatory possibilities. This is usually set up in such a way that it applies to all the words in the language: it is a monosystemic type of description.

Now it is clear in the first place that sometimes the description of a language is quite well executed by using only the procedure I have classified under i): that is, to segment the word in the usual manner, and then to list all the altern-ances that may occur in a given segmental position, without changing the environment otherwise. This is exemplified for instance in J. C. Catford, *Vowel Systems of Scots Dialects* (*Transactions of the Philological Society*, 1957), in which it is shown that, by simply considering vocalic alternances in the restricted environment "stressed vowel plus-*t*", meaningful and valuable data can be obtained, in the form of a clear map showing a graduated complexity of vowel systems across the area. It might be objected that in this way we are getting an incomplete picture. On the other hand, certain pseudo-problems are prevented from arising. For example, in the Central Lowlands dialects of Scots a phoneme inventory would include two diphthong phonemes *əi* and *ae*, on the grounds of significant alternance in e.g. **pəi/pae**.[6] But this is the *only* environment in which the two are in significant alternance, viz. before zero consonant. In other contexts they are in complementary distribution, viz. **ae** before voiced fricatives and **r, əi** in other cases. Examples are: **baer, raez; rəis, hwəit, gəid**.[7] If we confine discussion to this micro-system, the distribution of diphthongs of the low-to-front type, we can set up the two environments "before zero consonant" and "before other consonants" as two different structural classes, each with its own series of alternants. Thus the first class will have two terms, and the second class will have one term with allophonic variation. In this way the question of how many phonemes are represented by **əi** and **ae** in the vowel sys' 'm as a whole is not permitted to arise.

I now wish to go further, and suggest that principle (i), the segmentation procedure, is not sacrosanct either, but may and should be abandoned in many

---

[4] *knee, black.*
[5] *leek, black.*
[6] *pey* (pay), *pie.*
[7] *byre* (cow-house), *rise, rice, white, guide.*

cases. As Z. S. Harris rightly observes (*Methods in Structural Linguistics*, Chicago 1951, p. 25, para 3.1):

> Utterances are stretches of continuous events. If we trace them as physiological events, we find various parts of the body moving in some degree independently of each other and continuously. . . . If we trace utterances as acoustic events, we find continuous changes of sound-wave periodicities.

In Harris's view, with which I concur, segmentation is a structure imposed by us on the material, to make utterances amenable to comparison. It follows from this that, if in a given case segmentation is less useful than another mode of analysis, it should be discarded, possibly to be replaced by such a technique as that described by R. H. Robins in *Aspects of Prosodic Analysis* (*Proceedings of the University of Durham Philosophical Society*, Series 1, B, Arts, No. 1, 1957), as follows:

> A great part . . . of the phonic material is referable to prosodies, which are, by definition, of more than one segment in scope or domain or relevance.[8]

In the rest of this paper, the subject of discussion will be prosodic features I label *clear* and *dark*. These terms are of course generalized from the customary designations for different types of lateral consonant, and refer to the presence of palatal and velar (sometimes also pharyngal) narrowing. An opposition of clear and dark occurs with varying phonological functions in many dialects of Scots, and a number of contrasting cases will be examined, and some suggestions made for their analysis.

Firstly, a case in which the opposition appears simply as a feature of certain consonantal articulations. In the Central Lowlands, the lateral consonant is always very dark, and the alveolar trill (or fricative) is palatalised: thus **ɫeːv, teɫ, ɽok, wɔːr**.[9] If, in a general classification of the consonants à la Trubetzkoy, we wished to oppose these two as "the liquids", their characters as "the clear liquid" and "the dark liquid" would give one possible statement of the opposition. It is interesting that this is the contrary of the typical system in Northern Irish dialects of Scots, where *l* is always clear and *r* a dark retroflex; and that a similar polarization, though not so noticeable, often occurs in the central Scottish middle-class speaker of English, presumably as a hypercorrection, such that *l* is not very dark, and *r* is a dark retroflex.

Now a more complicated case from the same Central Lowland dialects. As we have said, *l* in all positions is dark; but the other alveolar consonants, when final in the word, have clear quality: thus **mɔn, fɔs**,[10] Clear quality is heard not only in the consonant, but often as a vocalic on-glide; and it is

---

[8] This technique, Prosodic Analysis, is of course that associated with the name of J. R. Firth. It has been developed by his colleagues and students, primarily in London and also latterly in Edinburgh, but appears as yet too little known outside its country of origin. A valuable basic bibliography is given in the above-mentioned article by Robins.

[9] *lave* (remainder), *tale, rock, war.*

[10] *maun* (must), *fause* (false).

interesting that, when final *t* is represented by a glottal stop, this has also the clear on-glide: thus **la^i?**[11] Here we have a prosodic feature characteristic of word final position, in the presence of certain consonantal units. It is true, of course, that phonologically it can be attributed without difficulty to the final segments of the words in which it occurs; and indeed the instances I have quoted so far scarcely seem to have undergone any distinctively non-phonemic treatment. However, they were quoted to illustrate the occurrence of clear/dark contrast in Scots, and to prepare the way for cases of much greater complexity.

At the Cabrach, southern Banffshire, the following system of mono-syllables with a mid-front vowel occurs:

i) In final position, and before *x*, there is only a rather close No. 3 (in Cardinal Vowel terms)—thus **de:, pex.**[12]

ii) Before e.g. *k* and *v*, there is an alternance of a close No. 3 as above, with a slightly closer vowel ending in a close-front glide—thus **ek/ne^{i}k, grɛ:v/ de^{i}v.**[13]

iii) Before e.g. *t* and *m*, there is an additional alternant in which the close No. 3 ends with a centring glide, and the final consonant has perceptible dark resonance—thus **bet/be^{i}t/bɛət, hɛm/he^{i}m/ɛəm.**[14]

This phonological system might be stated in various ways. For instance, it might be said to have three mid-front vowel phonemes (with varying distri-butions) followed by various allophones of *k*, *t* etc.; or one vowel phoneme, separated from the consonant by the *i* phoneme, the *ə* phoneme, or zero. In the present analysis, however, a non-segmental approach will be adopted, according to which the three possible types of word will be said to have a prosodic feature of final neutrality, clearness or darkness. The advantage of this appears if we turn to what on the face of it would appear to be a quite distinct feature of these northeastern and eastern dialects, their so-called *vowel* harmony. It is most easily observed in the final syllable of such words as *lady, lassie, lucky*: of very frequent occurrence in this area of Scotland, due to the great number of diminutive formations, such as *doggie, hoosie* (house), *craftie* (croft). Here are a set of examples from Perthshire, grouped so as to display the phonological principles involved (which are stated below):

> **pisi, husi.**   **ledi, rodi, dʌgi.**
> **lese, kete, łase, tate, bote, łʌke.**[15]

In a phonemic analysis, it would be observed that the *i* and *e* phonemes (which also occur in stressed syllables, as may be seen above) alternate in final position according to rather complicated rules: -*i* occurring after *i* and *u* (and diph-

---

[11] *lat* (let).

[12] *day, pech* (to pant).

[13] *ache, neck, grave, deave* (to deafen).

[14] *bet, beat, bait, hem, hame* (home), *aim*.

[15] *piecie* (diminutive of piece), *hoosie, lady, roadie* (d. road), *duggie* (d. dog), *lacy, Katie, lassie* (girl), *tattie* (potato), *boatie* (d. boat), *lucky*.

thongs), and after voiced plosives (also voiced fricatives), but -*e* elsewhere. Such phoneme substitution constitutes vowel harmony *stricto sensu*.[16]

Reverting now to the Northeastern dialects represented by the Banffshire examples, here the system of final vowel alternances is more complicated. A set of examples, corresponding more or less to those quoted for Perthshire, would group themselves as follows:

pisi, husi.   ledi, rodi, dʌgi.
lese, kete, glase.
besəe, betəe, lasəe, tatəe, botəe, lʌqəe.[17]

The major opposition is of -**i** to -**əe**, corresponding to the Perthshire opposition -**i**/-**e**; but certain words that one might expect to have -**əe** end in -**e** instead, forming phonological oppositions as shown with the -**əe** words.

Here, then, there is a threefold system. The last line in the table cannot easily be stated in terms of vowel phonemes, for we cannot identify a vowel phoneme *əe* of general validity for the sound system of the dialect (though of course there would be no difficulty with *i* and *e*). But in addition, in this dialect area there is commonly a variation in the place and mode of articulation of the consonant preceding the final vowel, corresponding to the nature of the latter. Firstly, the dark resonance implied by the transcription əe begins with the consonant: this is uvular rather than velar in the case of *k*, and has velar (and/or pharyngal) narrowing if *s*. Regarding the manner of articulation: in the northeastern dialects in general, voiceless consonants in this position tend to a lenis articulation; but in the third (-əe) category this tendency goes even further, so that *k* and *p* are realised as voiced frictionless continuants, and *t* as a flap. Thus *lucky* and *tattie* are most often pronounced lʌɰəe (I have even heard '*ain* here!) and tarəe. All this may be summarised by saying that the disyllables in -y may have one of three final prosodies, viz:

  i) Close-front final vowel, plosives relatively firm (though lenis);

  ii) Mid-front final vowel, plosives as i);

  iii) The consonant has dark resonance, and looser closure if a plosive; the following vowel glides from a central (or back) to a mid-front position.

It seems reasonable to equate these three categories with those observed in the monosyllable. i) resembles that with final close-front glide, and ii) that with centring glide; ii) would then be treated as corresponding to the mono-

---

[16] Similar articulatory variations occur also south of this area. Thus, in the neighbourhood of Edinburgh the final vowel of *needy* is noticeably somewhat closer and fronter than that of *buddie* (body); the same dialect shows similar variation in a weak form, e.g. in ʌ pis ë kek and ʌ kʌp ä mʌł k (a piece of cake, a cup of milk). These phenomena, being described in the traditional manner as allophonic, would accordingly be held *not* to constitute vowel harmony. But their similarity to the vowel alternances north of the Tay is obvious, and this goes to justify any method of analysis by which they may all, if desired, be treated as a whole.

[17] Words not previously noted are *glassy* (adj.), *Bessie, Betty*.

syllable with zero glide. A formular representation of these phonological features could be made in some such way as the following:

bet	$(bet)^o$	lacy	$(lesi)^o$
beat	$(bet)^j$	hoosie	$(husu)^j$
bait	$(bet)^ə$	Bessie	$(besi)^ə$

We may also note the possibility of a still more analytical formulation, suggested by the alternance voiced/voiceless, correlated to prosodies **j/ø, ə** in disyllables. It might be appropriate to formulate thus:

lady $(ledi)^j$
Katie $(kedi)^o$
Betty $(bedi)^ə$

(This would of course exclude words with stem-vowel *i* or *u*, in which presence or absence of voice is an independent variable, as in **husi, buzi.**[18])

Nearly fifty miles from the Cabrach, at Gourdon on the south Kincardine-shire coast, a phonological system is found differing in various points from the former one, but equally complex and describable in similar terms. Some points to be noted are:

i) Both dialects have (*-et*) and (*-em*) with prosodies **j/ø/ə**; but whereas the Cabrach has **j/ø** in the case of (*-ek*) and (*-ev*), Gourdon has only (*-ek*)*ᵒ* and (*-ev*)*ᵉ*. Thus at Gourdon *ache, neck* are **ek, nek**; *grave, deave* are **greəv, deəv**.

(ii) Both dialects have all three prosodies in disyllables with final -y, but there are differences of distribution: thus Gourdon has **lede, rode** in place of **ledi, rodi**—ø-prosody occurs after a half-close stem-vowel irrespective of the intervening consonant.

Northeast of the line joining the Cabrach to Gourdon lies a well defined dialect area, centring on Buchan (northwestern Aberdeenshire). Within this area, the incidence of final prosodies of clearness, neutrality and darkness varies greatly, both in system and in detail within a given system. The simplest system appears to have only ø-prosody in monosyllables, so that *beat, bait, bet* are identical (unless, as is often noted, words of the *beat* type have **i** as in standard English); it has been noted, e.g. at Peterhead on the Buchan coast, near Turriff in northern Aberdeenshire, and on Donside in the south. Other informants have a contrast ø/ə in monosyllables, but there is enormous variation, the pattern of which is hard to discern, in the incidence of this, not only between places but between individuals. Thus, of two fishermen at a village near Peterhead, one had only **bet** for *bait, bet*; his neighbour sometimes did the same, but could also distinguish them as **beət, bet** respectively. A speaker may distinguish *sail, sell*—thus **seəł, sɛł**—but have **nɛł** for both *nail* and *Nell*. In the y-disyllables, the simplest system is a contrast of two prosodies, one of which is j, whereas the other may be ə (as at Peterhead) or φ (as in and near Aberdeen, and as in the Perthshire case quoted above). Here again there are

[18] *boozy.*

great local and individual variations. At the Cabrach, as mentioned above, *Bessie* and *Katie* are **besəe, kete;** at Rhynie, a few miles to the east, they both have -**əe** (but note -**e** in other words, e.g. in *lacy*); and at New Byth in the north they are **bese, ketəe.**

Variations of this kind are traditionally the typical subject matter of dialectology; but this portion of the northeastern sound system seems well beyond the usual limits of variation. I get the impression that there have been, upon an older sound system corresponding to that of the Cabrach (and therefore not very different from that of Gourdon), two trends at work: on the one hand, a native development, tending to simplify the system by eliminating the threefold prosodic contrast; on the other, a movement to conformity with standard English. In the resultant very fluid situation, I hope a prosodic approach as outlined above will give us insights into our material that would not be obtainable otherwise.

In conclusion, I acknowledge with pleasure my debt to Miss M. Green, of Moray House College of Education, Edinburgh. She was the first to use the *Linguistic Survey of Scotland* phonological questionnaire in the north-east, and it was she who originally drew my attention to the details of consonant articulation before the -y suffix, and to the existence of the alternant -**əe** (neither is apparently noted in Dieth's *Buchan Dialect*, till then our only source of detailed information). Basing this paper on my own field observations, I have also drawn freely on the great amount of data gathered by her. I have also derived great benefit from discussion with my colleague Mr. J. Y. Mather, whose research has been chiefly on areas (Shetland, Orkney, Caithness, Ulster), where a prosodic type of analysis seems equally promising.

Part Two

SOCIAL DIALECTS

Social Dialects

In the initial planning for what then was expected to become the Linguistic Atlas of the United States and Canada a recognition of greater social mobility in America than in Europe led to a break with the older practice of confining dialect investigation to the rural and relatively uneducated portion of the population. Professor Kurath decided to cover instead the entire range. Consequently, three categories of informants were established, Type I corresponding to the segment interviewed in the European atlases, Type II composed of middle-aged high school graduates, and Type III, less frequently represented, composed of younger college graduates presumably using the regional standard speech. All American fieldwork has used these same categories since then.

Raven I. McDavid, Jr., a fieldworker for the South Atlantic Atlas, first expressed an awareness of the wide implications of this diversified corpus of dialect information for scholars in the social sciences. His article in this Part was perhaps the first straw in what is now a strongly blowing wind.

Nearly twenty years later Kurath also found significance in a whole range of social correlations. His article suggests that the richest future study will be that of the speech of Type II informants.

But recent dynamic social ferment has focused attention rather upon the speech of relatively uneducated people of all ages in both urban and rural environments, principally the latter. One large group of such persons is composed of those whose first language is not English and whose English is marked by characteristics that tend to stigmatize the users when it is heard outside the group. Janet Sawyer pinpoints such a situation in her San Antonio study; that situation, however, has analogues in other communities and other sections of the United States.

The major group comprises native speakers of English whose dialects are noticeably different from any of the varieties of Standard English. Some of

these non-standard speakers whose educational needs are now receiving attention live in the rural areas of Appalachia; some live in rural areas of the deep
South; but the most conspicuous ones are those who live in urban centers where
the lack of control over Standard English is one of many factors leading to social
and economic disadvantage.

The linguistic methodology for studying these non-standard varieties in
relation to the environment was suggested by the procedures of the dialect
atlases but has undergone considerable modification, largely through the influence of William Labov, formerly of Columbia University. After a study of
linguistic and social correlations on Martha's Vineyard in which he used both
linguistic and sociological techniques, Labov perfected his synthesis of the two
in the research in New York City that led to his significant doctoral dissertation
in 1964, *The Social Stratification of English in New York City.* It was published
by the Center for Applied Linguistics in 1966.

Labov's approach has been deeply influential in subsequent investigation
both in New York under his direction and in other cities under the direction of
others. A Chicago study has been undertaken by Alva Davis of the Illinois
Institute of Technology; a Detroit study has just been completed by a team
working under Roger Shuy of Michigan State University; and a major investigation in Washington, D.C., begun by William A. Stewart of the Center for Applied
Linguistics, is now continuing under the leadership of Shuy, who has left
Michigan State to become head of the Center's sociolinguistic program.

Although the article by McDavid does not itself draw upon findings of
Labov, it opens the door to a comprehensive view of some of the language
problems raised by comparing features of Standard English with those of certain
non-standard dialects. In the next two articles Lee Pederson, at one time a
fieldworker for the Chicago survey, draws upon some of the data collected
therein. A meaningful byproduct of the study of the speech of diverse social
and ethnic groups, Pederson found, is information about the various lexical
designations and appellatives used by members and non-members to refer to a
specific group. The attitudes thus revealed are related to attitudes toward the
speech of the group. His first article thus partly introduces his second, which
concerns selected systematic linguistic features in the speech of a large Chicago
ethnic population.

As a warning to new workers in social dialect analysis, Mrs. Beryl Bailey
next writes that it is not enough to consider specific items in Negro speech.
Instead the investigator must search the regular correlations of these items in
order to arrive at the underlying system. She finds that at least some of the
systematic variations are attributable to a creole substratum.

Marvin D. Loflin's article reports an application of transformational
analysis in an attempt to make clearer the basic pattern or deep structure of a
central feature, the verb phrase. His study would suggest that the differences
between this speech and Standard English are actually in the deep structure;
they are not superficial matters to be dealt with on an item by item approach.

After pointing to some relevant and little-understood background in Negro speech history Stewart, in the second of his two companion articles, shifts the focus to a utilitarian objective that has stimulated and guided the current flurry of concern with this dialect. In discussing the pedagogical implications of the linguistic and social correlations he finds support for Mrs. Bailey's belief in the existence of a determining creole substratum that originated in an earlier widely used pidgin.

Labov's article then provides a careful analysis of the sociological complex, with its cross-currents of encouraging and inhibiting factors, that is involved in the efforts of schools to provide speakers of non-standard English with some control of Standard English.

A quite different area of social dialectology is represented by the closing article. Social dialects include not only the dialects of various social classes but also the special argots and cants of certain subcultures existing within and yet outside our society. These subcultures, some on the fringe of the law and some outside the law, are better known to Professor Maurer than to any other language scholar in the country. Three decades of close and privileged research have made him the unequaled authority in the language of the underworld. His article offers not only a concise overview of this little-studied language field but also an authoritative treatment of the speech of one of these subcultures, that of narcotic addicts. Lack of space prevents reprinting all of the accompanying glossary, but enough is used so as to exemplify the metaphors and semantic shifts that seem to be characteristic of subculture speech.

30

Dialect Geography and Social Science Problems

RAVEN I. McDAVID, Jr.

ALTHOUGH LINGUISTICS is one of the most rapidly developing of the social sciences, its position among them is not generally recognized, either by the layman, by the other social scientists, or even by some of the linguists themselves. The concealment of this relationship is due to several circumstances, not the least of which is the traditional modesty of science, which too often contents itself with recording and measuring, and leaves to others the derivation of broad conclusions from its findings.

But perhaps the most important block in the way of fully understanding the proper position of linguistics is that the teaching of language in our compartmentalized university curricula is almost exclusively done by departments of literature—English, Romance, Germanic, Slavic, and the like. English grammar is taught as a tool to enable the student to write acceptable literary essays; French or German or Russian grammar, as a tool to prepare the student for reading *Les Misérables* or *Faust* or *Anna Karenina*. These ends are not unworthy in themselves, but the emphasis upon them in our academic system prevents students from realizing that the command of a language is necessary not only for facile reading and fluent conversation but for the understanding of the culture in which the language is spoken. And the historical connection and superficial resemblances between the Indo-European languages most commonly taught in our universities often leads students to lose sight of basic differences in the grammatical systems of these languages—to say nothing of the existence in other societies of varying types of grammatical structure, as well as the types which we are accustomed to associate with the languages of Western Europe.

The great advances in the techniques of linguistics as a science have come since it became recognized as a social science by the anthropologists of the Boas–Sapir school. When the study of American Indian languages and cultures was systematically undertaken, it was soon discovered that just as the patterns of Indian culture could not be scientifically appraised by assuming the categories of Western European civilization as the norm from which everything else was a

Reprinted by permission of the University of North Carolina Press from *Social Forces* 25.168–72 (1946). The author is Professor of English at the University of Chicago.

deviant type, so the sound-types and grammatical categories of American Indian languages could not be appraised by assuming as universally normal the patterns of pronunciation and grammar found in Indo–European languages. From this realization came the beginnings of modern linguistics as a descriptive science, with the grammar of each language worked out according to the observations of trained fieldworkers without distortion by the patterns of the fieldworker's native language.[1] Along with this advance in linguistic techniques came the realization by cultural anthropologists that language is the medium through which the cultural relationships of a people are expressed, and that without the knowledge of linguistic principles by which an understanding of the native language may be attained, the anthropologist can attain only the most superficial description of a culture.

The way in which cultural patterns and attitudes are reflected in the language of the culture has been pointed out by many linguists—perhaps most brilliantly in the articles on Hopi by the late Benjamin L. Whorf.[2] It has been experienced by the linguists who prepared the textbooks on Far Eastern languages for the War Department and by the students who learned those languages. But it can also be found in the English language as spoken in various parts of the United States. Leaving out the obvious fact that the wide range of economic and military and political contacts between speakers of English and the speakers of other languages has resulted in the borrowing by English of a wide variety of foreign words for new things encountered in foreign cultures, the importance of language as a mirror of culture can be demonstrated by dialect differences in American English, as observed in fieldwork for the *Linguistic Atlas of the United States*.[3]

As in any discussion in the social sciences, it is necessary to dispose of a few myths—to show what simply is not so before we discuss what is so. It is definitely untrue that climate itself has any influence on pronunciation,

[1] Descriptive linguistics, of course, is far older. The Sanskrit grammarians, especially Panini (*circa* 600 BC), consistently approached language problems on the basis of what the language actually said. But their work was not known in Western Europe and had no influence upon the development of linguistic thinking until the nineteenth century. Even today the language-thinking of most teachers is in the normative tradition, deriving from the unrealistic metaphysics of the Greek grammarians and followed with more or less ludicrous results by Roman, medieval, Renaissance, and modern arbiters of usage. Their attitude reaches its ultimate absurdity in the publication of lists of "words everybody mispronounces" and "grammatical mistakes everybody makes."

[2] For example, "Languages and Logic," *The Technology Review*, 43, No. 6 (April 1941), pp. 2–6; "The Relation of Habitual Thought and Behaviour to Language," *Language, Culture, and Personality* (Sapir Memorial Volume, Menasha, Wisconsin, 1941), pp. 75–93.

[3] Fieldwork in the South Atlantic States was made possible for the writer, first, by a fellowship from the Julius Rosenwald Fund in 1941, and later by an honorary fellowship from Duke University and a grant by the American Council of Learned Societies. Observations on the distribution of linguistic forms in New England are based on the records of the *Linguistic Atlas of New England*, in the Middle West on the preliminary survey of the Great Lakes and Ohio Valley regions conducted by Professor Marckwardt of Michigan, otherwise on the writer's own experiences in the field.

(Southerners do not speak slowly because the climate makes them lazy. Mid-westerners do not talk through their noses because they have long damp winters and lots of cloudy weather. New Englanders do not talk rapidly because the climate is bracing.) As a matter of fact, many Southerners—especially the Gullah Negroes—talk very rapidly (as do the Burmans and Bengali, in an even hotter climate), and many New Englanders drawl. Pronunciation and rapidity of speech in a given dialect area have nothing to do with the climate but are a reflection of other forces, such as the kind of speech used by those who settled in the area and the subsequent contacts of the inhabitants with speakers of other dialects.

In any dialect area of the United States the fieldworker will observe the growing tendency toward uniformity and standardization arising from increasing ease of transportation and communication, radio and talking movies, and the extension of public-school education. Under the impact of these influences the old folk-words tend to disappear and are replaced by the commercial words for the same things. *Porch* replaces *piazza*, *veranda*, or *gallery*; *window-shades* (originally a commercial term in the Philadelphia area) has displaced *curtains* and *blinds* as a designation for the shades on rollers, and *dope* as a folk-term for Coca-Cola (the common folk-term in South Carolina and Tennessee as late as fifteen years ago) has given way to the commercially sponsored *Coke*.

With the spread of public education has come a certain linguistic snobbery and a tendency to assert spelling-pronunciations as the norm. That is, many common pronunciations, historically sound and normal in the pattern of a local dialect, are looked down upon because they are associated with illiteracy and the inability to spell, and new spelling-pronunciations are fostered as "correct" by teachers ignorant of the nature and development of the language but convinced (because they possess the skill) that the relatively recent and infrequent skill of writing is the norm to which the far older universal skill of speaking must be made to conform. Thus along the Atlantic seaboard the younger generation is taught it must sound the /h/ in *wheelbarrow* and *whetstone*;[4] the riming of *hearth* and *earth*, of *soot* and *cut*, of *creek* and *sick*, of *ewe* and *dough*, of *bleat* and *gate*, of *roil* and *tile* is discountenanced; and *sumach* is not allowed to begin with the sound everybody uses at the beginning of *sugar*. The snob-appeal of not using the same pronunciation as the uneducated or rustic people of one's own community reaches the limits of absurdity in the insistence of some teachers on the pronunciation of *either* and *neither* with the diphthong of *die*, or the attempt to force the "broad *a*" in words of the *ask*, *chance* type on students in areas where those words normally have the vowel of *hat* or a diphthong based upon it.[5] Fortunately these attempts generally have little influence, and the normal pronunciation-pattern of the community reasserts itself. Sometimes, also, a

[4] Where the fashion is to ape British Received Standard Pronunciation, teachers do try to force their students to drop the /h/ in *wheelbarrow* and the like. The snob-appeal is of course the same.

[5] See G. L. Trager, "One Phonemic Entity Becomes Two: the Case of 'Short A'," *American Speech*, 15 (1940), pp. 255-58.

speaker masters a few shibboleths but reverts to type when off guard, as the man in the subway whom Professor Sturtevant heard say ". . . and she didn't drop *eyether* one of them, *eether*," or the Negro informant in Charleston, South Carolina, who told me about his "ahnt," but in the next sentence spoke of "Aunt Susie," using the vowel of *hat*.

The tendency to abandon local folk-pronunciations and substitute pseudo-elegant or spelling-pronunciations is most characteristic of the newly risen middle class, who are anxious to differentiate themselves from the illiterate and less fortunate in their community. The uneducated person knows only the folk-usage; the person sure of his social position in the community feels under no necessity to change the pronunciation normal to him and his family. Thus in Charleston, upper-class speakers, even of the generation now in college, still use the palatal consonants in *car* and *garden* (conventionally transcribed *kyar* and *gyarden*), still say *whetstone* and *wheelbarrow* without an /h/, and many upper-class speakers unblushingly rime *earth* and *hearth* or pronounce *palm*, *calm*, and *tomato* with the vowel of *hat*.

From the extent of local dialect areas one can form an accurate picture of the extent of early settlements. Even if we did not know that Up-Country and Low-Country in South Carolina were settled by people from different parts of the British Isles, we might suspect it from the way they talk. The characteristic Charleston diphthongs in *date* and *boat* are found along the Carolina coast from Savannah to Georgetown, and reach inland to Sumter and Aiken and the neighborhood of Columbia—where the slow movement in from the coast ran up against the inundation of the Piedmont by the Scotch–Irish moving down from Pennsylvania. The term *bloody-noun* for a big bullfrog is another feature of coastal dialects, as is the term *mosquito-hawk* for *dragon-fly*, where the Up-Countryman normally says *snake-doctor*. In the Providence area in New England, and in a small area in Western Massachussetts settled from Providence, *eaceworm* is the local term for the *earthworm*. In Rhode Island one also hears the term *horning* for a burlesque serenade of newly married couples—a term that has been carried by settlers from Rhode Island to the Berkshires and Southwestern Vermont, and thence to Western New York. In the Middle West the settlers from the South carried with them the /z/ sound in *greasy*, and *corn-shuck* and *singletree*, where the settlers from the North brought *corn-husk* and *whiffletree*. The area settled predominantly from the South follows an irregular line a little south of parallel 40 in Ohio and Illinois, a little north of it in Indiana. Likewise local dialects preserve evidence of non-English-speaking settlers though the languages those settlers spoke may have disappeared. *Stoop* is a Dutch word for *porch* that has been taken into the English of the Hudson Valley and carried wherever settlers from that area have gone. In the South, *pindar* and *goober* for *peanut*, and *cooter* for *terrapin* (or sometimes for *turtle*), have spread far beyond the communities to which they were originally brought by West African Negroes. *Smearcase*, a Pennsylvania German word for *curd* or *cottage cheese*, has been found as far South as Greenville, South Carolina; in the English of the Middle

Atlantic Seaboard will probably remain the pronunciation of *Long Island* as *long-guyland* long after the descendants of immigrants to that area have forgotten their ancestors came from Southeastern Europe.

Similarly, trade and communication are reflected in the perpetuation of some words and pronunciations. In the Boston wholesale trading area, *tonic* is the common name for what is elsewhere known as *pop, soda pop, soft drinks,* or *cold drinks.* Around New Haven *callathump,* originally a slang term at Yale, is the designation of a burlesque serenade. The substitution of an *ee* glide for -*r* in such words as *bird, work,* and the like—a type of pronunciation commonly associated with Brooklyn and New Orleans—is also an old upper-class pro-nunciation in Manhattan and in the cotton-planting area of the deep South. It is found in the plantation area from north of Charleston to South Georgia, along the Gulf Coast to the mouth of the Mississippi, and up the Mississippi and its tributaries along the fertile bottom-lands as far inland as Decatur, Alabama. Thus the fact that the Tennessee River Valley in North Alabama is, like the Black Belt from Montgomery southward, historically an area of cotton culture, is reflected in the persistence of plantation-type speech in both sections, with the up-country type in between, in the hill-country around Birmingham.

Similarly, the isolation of a community is demonstrable by speech-forms quite different from those of neighboring communities. In Eastern New England -*r* is generally not pronounced in such words as *hard* and *car,* except in Marble-head, Cape Ann, and Martha's Vineyard—all relatively isolated communities. On Block Island, at the eastern end of Long Island Sound, *tippety-bounce* survives as the local name for *see-saw,* but nowhere else in New England. Among the mountain people of the Carolinas one still hears *fought* riming with *out,* or *search* riming with *starch.*

Although, as we have seen, climate has no effect on pronunciation, yet climate, topography, flora, and fauna are all reflected in the vocabulary of a community. In a flat country there will be none of the specific names for types of mountains—such as *pinnacle, bald, dome, knob*—that one finds in the Smokies. The Up-Countryman who has never seen a *salt marsh* would hardly be expected to have a name for it, nor would a Low-Countryman normally know the term *gully-washer* for a very heavy rain. In the Deep South one should not expect to find everyday words for kinds of snow, for kinds of sleds, or for coasting. The native of the Delta would not build *stone walls* around his cow-lot, nor would he have any need of a *stone-boat* to carry rocks out of his fields. The Charles-tonian knows almost nothing of the *sugar-maple,* the northern Vermonter at least as little about the *sycamore.* To the inlander who has never seen a *sea-turtle,* *turtle* and *terrapin* are likely to be synonymous.

The interrelationships between urban and rural life are also seen in the vocabulary. Where the city dweller has no contact with the farm, he will not know many of the more obvious parts of the vocabulary of farm life. And, conscious of a social difference which he interprets as his own superiority, he is likely to have in his vocabulary terms of contempt for the farmer more biting than those where there is free exchange of rural and urban population. The city dweller everywhere is unlikely to know the taboos of farm life—that the *bull*, *ram*, *stud*, and *boar* are rarely called by those names among farmers and almost never when women are present. And if he speaks of castrating animals, the urbanite will usually say *castrate* (or possibly *geld*), never *cut*, *change*, or *alter*. Many city dwellers have even said they thought a *boar* was an entirely different animal from a *hog*. And only a person who had had some experience with animals would certainly know what a *shote* is, or would refrain from using *pig* and *hog* synonymously.

The traditional economy of a region is brought out in little suggestions in the vocabulary. The farmers of South Carolina consistently have polite terms for the *bull*, the *stud*, and the *boar*—but a *ram* is never called anything else. The explanation is simple: sheep-raising was never an important occupation on the Carolina farm. In some parts of the South *potatoes* still means *sweet potatoes* (as in the favorite rural dish of *possum and potatoes*), the others being designated always as *Irish potatoes* or *white potatoes*; elsewhere in the South *potatoes* out of context is ambiguous and has to be qualified; in the North, *potatoes* normally means *Irish potatoes*. Where corn meal is the basic flour, there will be many kinds of *corn bread* in the diet. The farmer who stacks his hay in the field and leaves his cattle out of doors during the winter will hardly know of a *hay-mow* or a *cow-barn*. A society with a rural orientation might divide the day into *morning* and *evening*, with the dividing-point a one o'clock or two o'clock *dinner* followed by a rest in the heat of the day. This orientation may be carried over into the daily routine of the upper classes in a conservative place like Charleston, where a relative abundance of cheap servants perpetuates the custom of a heavy midday *dinner* and a relatively light *supper* after which the servants (or the mistress if the servants customarily go home when they have finished cleaning up after *dinner* and preparing the food for *supper*) find it a simpler chore to clean up. In the relatively servantless big city, the white-collar worker will eat a midday *lunch* somewhere near his office and wash the dishes after *dinner* when he gets home; the steelworker may carry his *dinner pail* with him, and eat *supper* at home. In rural South Carolina a *lunch* is something one eats between regular meals.

One's language also reflects the change in the size and organization of the family. The rural farmhouse—to say nothing of the larger city house—customarily had both a *parlor* and a *living-room*. The *parlor* was shut tight except for important events—weddings, funerals, the minister's calls, and the Sunday-dinner visits of grandparents, aunts, and uncles. Now there is less awe of grandpa and grandma and the minister; so they are invited to sit down with the family in the *living-room* and talk informally; and with smaller families, smaller homes, and higher rents, it would be foolish to set aside one room for infrequent "state" entertainments.

Nor does the everyday vocabulary fail to reveal the political, social, and religious structure of the community. The New England farmer hardly knows the term *county seat*; the *county* hardly enters into his political thinking, for all the important business of local government is handled by the *township* or *town*, in its annual *town meeting*. In the South and West, however, the township is little more than a surveyor's unit, and all the important records are kept by the *county* at the *county seat* or *courthouse*—in the South a carry-over from the days when voting was limited to the large property owners, when a plantation covered as much area as a New England *town*, and the plantation owners would get together in a committee meeting at some central point, the *county seat*, and choose the county officials. That the county system and county consciousness prevails even in parts of the South where plantations and slavery never flourished means only that the prevailing patterns of local government were fixed by those persons who dominated the early settlements.

The less democratic social organization of the South is also revealed in the local fondness for military titles, earned or honorary, and in such caste-conscious terms as *poor white trash*, used by both Negroes and whites. Where emphasis is less on family background and more on individual merits, as traditionally in rural New England, a person may be spoken of with contempt—but rarely as a member of a contemptible class. Nor, where rich and poor attend churches of the same denomination, should one expect to find terms like *jackleg preacher*, *yard-ax*, or *table-tapper*, which in the South are often applied to the untrained ministers who work at other occupations and devote their spare time to congregations of the less formally organized denominations to which most of the poorer and uneducated whites and Negroes belong. Similarly, a person who doesn't know the term *Mass* has probably had few contacts with Roman Catholics. And among the less sophisticated, the custom of *taking-on* at funerals, of making a great outward show of grief as a form of respect for the deceased, is more likely to be known and approved than among the uneducated.

And of course one's language reveals the prejudices in one's background. In rural New England *the Civil War* is generally known as *the Rebellion*, except by those cynics who still refer to it as *Abe Lincoln's War* or *The Nigger War*. In the South the usual folk-name among the older generation is *the Confederate War*. *The War between the States* and *the War for Southern Independence*, both of which have been sponsored by the Daughters of the Confederacy and sectionally-minded schoolteachers, have not caught on very much; in fact, the younger generation normally speaks unblushingly of *the Civil War*. Naturally, where there is frequent contact and at least potential economic competition, there will be more nick-names, derogatory and otherwise, for religious, racial, or immigrant minorities than where such contacts are few. The Southerner would normally have more such nicknames for the Negro, the New Yorker for the Italian or Jew. A curious reflection of such prejudices is the fact that around Beaufort, South Carolina (and to a lesser extent elsewhere in the South), *school-ma'am*, for *school-teacher*, is a term of contempt, or at least of mild opprobrium. In the folk-speech, especially in the phrase *Yankee school-ma'am*, it is commonly restricted to those teachers from the North who came down after the Civil War to educate the Negroes, and who still staff the Mather vocational school for Negro girls of Beaufort County.

Finally, there is fad-language. The fad may be associated with a particular occupation, or it may be concerned only with the pronunciation of a single word. Of the first type are the elegant terms that have grown up with the attempts of the undertaking business to acquire social respectability—the substitution of *casket* for *coffin, box,* or *pinto,* and of *cemetery, memorial park,* or *burial estate* for *graveyard* or *burying-ground*; of the latter the fluctuating pronunciations of *iodine, quinine,* and *mayonnaise* for each of which I have heard at least two different pronunciations from the same person at intervals of a few years. There is the notion that something is fashionable and one must keep up with fashion, not merely avoid the stigma of the rustic pronunciations already referred to.

These are only a few samples from the experience of one linguist in the field. For the social scientist interested in understanding social behavior, differences in local dialects have further significance. It is not improbable that the iteration of terms does much to fix the attitude of speakers toward social issues and social problems of which those terms are a manifestation. And certainly a social scientist must be careful in the terminology he uses in discussion with speakers of a dialect area different from his own. A classic example is the unfavorable Southern reception of Henry Wallace's "century of the common man," for to the average Southerner *common* is a term of contempt. The more one investigates American dialects, the more impressive is the evidence that linguistic phenomena are an essential part of the data that must be considered in the analysis of problems involving the social sciences.

31

Interrelation between Regional and Social Dialects

HANS KURATH

FOR NEARLY A CENTURY students of the spoken language have focused their attention on regional and local differences in *folk speech*, gathering information by systematic sampling of one kind or another and publishing their findings on maps, item by item. Relying upon these source materials, individual heteroglosses have been established, and dialect boundaries based upon bundles of such dividing lines, whether close-knit or spaced, have been drawn to exhibit the internal dialect structure of more or less extensive areas.

As a third step, attempts have been made to correlate the boundaries occurring in folk speech with settlement boundaries (migrations), with old and new political boundaries, with stable or shifting economic boundaries, with diocesan boundaries, with confessional barriers that discourage or prevent intermarriage, with physical features of the landscape that channel or hinder trade, and with the rise and fall of dominant cultural centers; in short, with a great variety of factors that are apt to hinder or favor communication.

Many inferences drawn from such correlations are well established; others are probable or at least suggestive. No one can fail to recognize the important new insights that have been achieved in this field of research with regard to the complicated nature of linguistic change in its relation to the various aspects of the life of a community or nation. And yet, considerable refinement in tracing the processes of diffusion and recession in linguistic usage are within our reach.

Two lines of research, already under way, will make for progress in dialectology—the study of living speech. One is the application of the concepts of structural linguistics to the raw data. The other is the systematic recording and treatment of the speech of at least two social levels in addition to that of the *folk* (the peasant or rustic, and the underprivileged city dweller): that of the *cultural elite* and the *middle class*. I shall address myself chiefly to the potential contribu-

Reprinted by permission of the publisher and the author from *Proceedings of the Ninth International Congress of Linguists.* 's-Gravenhage: Mouton, 1964. Pp. 135–143. The author, Emeritus Professor of English at the University of Michigan, was editor of the *Linguistic Atlas of New England* and director of the Atlantic coast surveys.

tion of the investigation of cultivated and middle-class speech to our understanding of linguistic change by diffusion.

Until recently the dialectologist has had at his disposal only a more or less
adequate record of regional folk usage, which enabled him to trace in realistic
fashion the influence of one folk dialect upon another folk dialect through direct
contact between the speakers. When confronted with features of vocabulary,
grammar, or phonology that did not seem to fit into either of the two adjoining
folk dialects, he resorted to "supra-regional" influence or adoption from the
national standard, i.e. to direct or indirect borrowing from a privileged class
dialect of another speech area. He arrived at this decision by a process of elimination. For lack of an adequate record of upper-class speech current within the
area of his immediate concern, or of adjoining or remote areas, he usually could
not go beyond a bald assertion. He could not trace the route or routes of such
infiltrations in precise terms.

A realistic account of this process is possible only when a record of middle-
class and upper-class usage within the area is available. To supply this information for the various European countries in which folk usage has been systematically recorded is surely one of the major tasks confronting the dialectologist.
This need was clearly foreseen forty years ago by Henry C. Wyld, when he
said in his *History of Modern Colloquial English*, p. 186: "It is remarkable that
while the English of illiterate elderly peasants has often been examined, with
the view of recording for posterity the rugged accents of the agricultural community . . . it has not been thought worth while to preserve the passing fashions
of speech of the courtly and polite of a former day."

Regional usage of the ever-growing middle group of speakers should in my
opinion be the dialectologist's primary object of future research. Without reliable,
detailed knowledge of usage on this social level, the influence of cultivated speech
upon folk speech, and vice versa, cannot be traced in realistic fashion, since the
social extremes do not influence each other directly. It is the middle group that
mediates between them.

In the United States a modest beginning has been made in this direction.
In the linguistic survey of the Eastern States, the usage of the social extremes—
the folk and the cultured—as well as that of the middle group was systematically
investigated. Of the 1500 informants, about 700 represent the folk, 650 the
middle class, and 150 the cultural elite. The inclusion of speakers from three
social levels, I may say, was dictated by the democratic organization of American
society, which knows no clearcut social classes. It is characterized by a continuous
gradation from level to level (except, perhaps, in some of the old cities on the
Atlantic seaboard) and by social mobility of the individual.

Drawing upon the data recorded for the Atlas of the Eastern United States,
I should like to illustrate, in a small way, the processes of expansion and recession
of several types of linguistic features from place to place and from class to class
in areas where both the area and the social dissemination of the variants is
known.

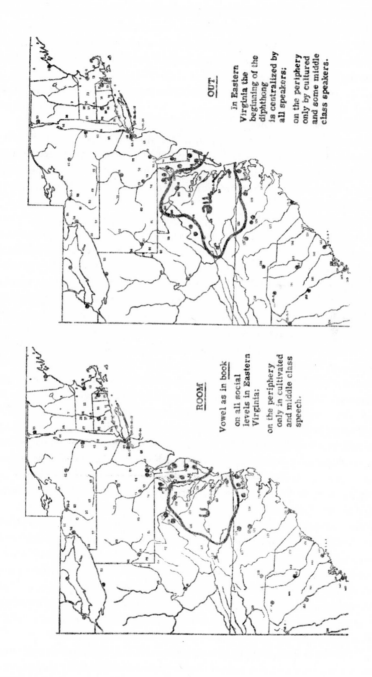

OUT

In Eastern Virginia the beginning of the diphthong is centralized by all speakers;

on the periphery only by cultured and some middle class speakers.

ROOM

Vowel as in book

on all social levels in Eastern Virginia;

on the periphery only in cultivated and middle class speech.

367

My sketch maps are somewhat simplified but adhere to well documented facts. I have chosen for my illustrations two markedly expansive focal areas, Virginia and Eastern New England. Six examples will show the density of documentation in the Atlantic States and the location of the focal areas dealt with in my examples.[1]

1   In Eastern Virginia and an adjoining part of Maryland, *room*, *broom* have the vowel of *pull* on all social levels. In adjoining areas the vowel of *pool* prevails in these words, but along the periphery of the Virginia area the vowel of *pull* has been adopted by some cultured and middle-class speakers. Since all speakers in the Atlantic States have the vowel contrast illustrated in *pull* vs. *pool*, the adoption of the Virginia pronunciation of *room*, *broom* on the periphery does not introduce a new phoneme; it merely changes the distribution (incidence) of shared phonemes.

2   Eastern Virginia has marked allophones of the diphthongal vowel in *house*, *out* on the one hand and in *down*, *cow* on the other. Before voiceless consonants, the diphthong starts approximately in the position for the vowel in *hut* and glides up swiftly; in all other positions it begins rather like the vowel in *hat* and glides up slowly. This feature is shared by all social groups within this area. On the periphery only some cultured speakers in Maryland and North Carolina exhibit these positional allophones, which they have clearly adopted from the Virginia speech area. To say *house* and *out* in the Virginian way carries social prestige. This innovation does not involve a phonemic change; it merely introduces an allophonic variation.

3   In a large area of the Upper South—Eastern Virginia and adjoining parts of Maryland and north-central North Carolina—historical post-vocalic /r/, as in *hear*, *care*, *car*, *door*, *forty*, is no longer pronounced as such on any social level. Along the periphery of this area, the /r/ generally survives in the speech of the folk and the middle class; but cultured speakers fairly regularly "drop" the /r/ in imitation of the prestige dialect of Eastern Virginia. The same process can be observed in the lower Hudson valley, which is dominated by "*r*-less" Metropolitan New York, and on the periphery of the "*r*-less" South Carolina–Georgia area.

Since the /r/ is thus replaced by an unsyllabic /ə/ in *hear*, *care*, *door*, and the sequence /ar/ in *hard*, *card* by a vowel differing from that in *hod*, *cod*, the adoption of these prestige features involves the addition of two new phonemes to the peripheral dialects. It is significant, however, that some of the innovators do not imitate the distinctive quality of the vowel in *hard*, *card*, but substitute for it a prolonged variant of the vowel they have in *hod*, *cod*. Such approximations or "compromises" are well enough known, when a feature of another dialect is adopted.

4   We know from earlier observations that the replacement of one phoneme by another occurs step by step, and that the process may extend over generations of speakers before the replacement is completed. This complicated process is

[1] The small numbers on the maps show the location of cultured speakers.

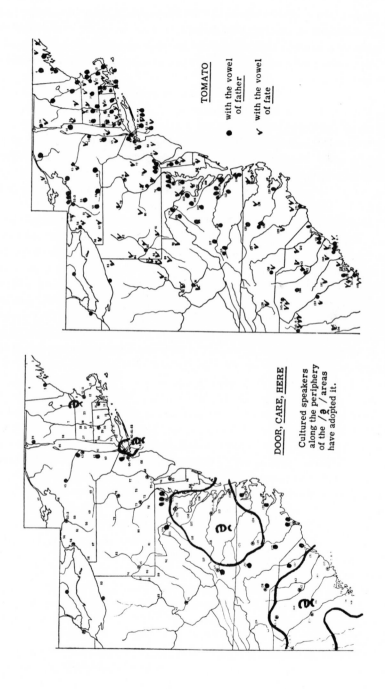

TOMATO

• with the vowel
  of father

v with the vowel
  of fate

DOOR, CARE, HERE

Cultured speakers
along the periphery
of the / ə / areas
have adopted it.

in need of thorough investigation. For best results, both the social and the regional dialects of an area must be sampled systematically and a rather large selection of pertinent items must be included in the survey, so that the changes can be traced from section to section, from social class to social class, and from word to word.

Walter S. Avis has investigated from this point of view the recession of the checked vowel /θ/ in such words as *whole, road*, which is in contrast with the free /o/ of *hole, rode*, etc., in the New England states. Having at his disposal a record of the incidence of /θ/ and /o/ in 24 words in the speech of 420 informants living in about 200 communities—150 belonging to the folk level, 220 to the middle group, and 50 to the cultured class—he can trace the replacement of checked /θ/ by free /o/ from area to area, from class to class, and from word to word.

Avis finds (a) that the recession of /θ/ proceeds in a northeasterly direction, i.e. from the industrial and urbanized southern section to the rural north; (b) that in communities where usage is divided, the younger and/or better educated speakers have adopted the free /o/; and (c) that the rate of replacement varies from word to word: that, for instance, the free /o/ has been adopted in *home, stone, road, smoke* by many speakers who retain the checked /θ/ in *toadstool, stone wall, back road, smokestack*, words that are in daily use on the farm but not in school. Curiously enough, some speakers hang on to the checked /θ/ in *the whole thing* and *wholly* long after they have discarded it in other words. Such "strays" are well known to the dialectologist, both as relics and as spurious innovations. See *Language*, 37 (1961), 544–58.

5   *Tomato* pronounced with the vowel of *father* is rather common in the cultivated speech of various sections of the Atlantic States, notably in New England (22/42), New York State (15/24), and Virginia (14/15). In New England and in Virginia north of the James River this pronunciation occurs also to some extent among the middle class, rarely elsewhere. About half of the cultured speakers interviewed rimed *tomato* with *potato*, as do the vast majority of the middle group. This dissemination of variant pronunciations is rather unique in America, indicating as it does a sharp class cleavage. It is apparently a recent fashionable acquisition of urbanites, perhaps in imitation of British English.

6   The past tense form *et* (riming with *let*) of the verb *eat* is current to some extent in most sections of the Atlantic States, notably in New England and New York State, along Chesapeake Bay, and in South Carolina. In New England, *et* is now quite rare in cultivated speech and is clearly yielding ground to *ate* (riming with *late*) also among the middle class, except in Maine, parts of New Hampshire, and the islands off Cape Cod. In 55 out of 66 communities where both forms were current in 1930, the younger and better-educated speaker used *ate*, the folk speaker *et*; and in about half of the 200 communities investigated only *ate*, with the vowel of *late*, was recorded. Here again we can observe the gradual dissemination of a linguistic feature from the top downward and from the urbanized southern section of New England in the direction of the

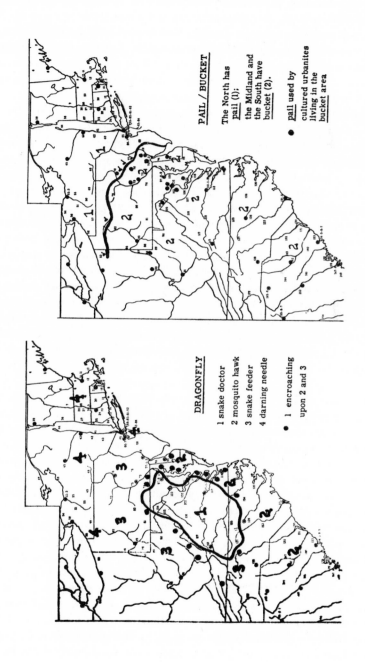

PAIL / BUCKET

The North has
pail (1);
the Midland and
the South have
bucket (2).

● pail used by
cultured urbanites
living in the
bucket area

DRAGONFLY

1 snake doctor
2 mosquito hawk
3 snake feeder
4 darning needle

● 1 encroaching
upon 2 and 3

371

rural northeast. It is of interest to observe that in England the trend has been in favor of *et.*

7   From Pennsylvania southward, three words for the dragon fly are widely current: *mosquito hawk* along the Atlantic coast, *snake doctor* in the piedmont of Virginia, and *snake feeder* in the Appalachians. From the Virginia piedmont and adjoining parts of Maryland and North Carolina, *snake doctor* is spreading. As usual, it is mostly the better educated speakers that have adopted the prestige word *snake doctor* (in 17 out of 20 communities with divided usage).

8   Two terms are current for a metal container used on the farm for drinking water or milk: *bucket* in the greater part of Pennsylvania and southward, *pail* in all of the North. The boundary line between them is rather sharply defined. However, there is evidence from social dissemination that in Pennsylvania *bucket* is spreading northward in middle-class speech. On the other hand, Northern *pail* has been adopted by cultured urbanities—and only by members of this group—not only in Philadelphia, but also in the cities along the Potomac and the Ohio River. Whereas the northward expansion of *bucket* is in all probability due to oral communication, the southward dissemination of *pail* in cultivated speech must clearly be attributed to the printed page or to schooling.

These examples illustrate the spreading of various features that do not affect the structure of the receiving dialect, as of checked /ʊ/ in *room*, the positional allophones of /au/ in *house, out,* the past tense *ate,* and the words *snake doctor* and *pail.* They also exemplify the spreading of features that involve a change in the phonemic system, as the introduction of unsyllabic /ə/ in *hear, care, four* and of free /ɑ/ in *car, garden,* and the loss of checked /θ/ in *road, whole.*

The data adduced show that this spreading takes place on social levels, cultured speakers being the first to adopt features of a neighboring prestige dialect. The middle class probably adopts these innovations from the cultured in their own communities, though direct contact with the middle group or the cultured in the adjoining area may also play a part. In the end such changes may find their way into the speech of the folk. It is readily granted that the latter events are in need of much fuller documentation than has been presented here.

Though structural innovations, such as the addition of phonemes to the native system, can be imported from a prestige dialect or from a foreign language, they are relatively rare. English is a striking example of this fact. Despite the wholesale adoption of words from French and Latin from the thirteenth century onward, Modern English has only two phonemes that are not native to it: the diphthong /oi/ of *joint, boil,* etc. (almost entirely replaced by the /ai/ of *pint, bile* in early Modern English, but then restored), and the medial consonant /ž/ of *measure, vision* (derived from the foreign sequence /zj/ < zi). The French rounded front vowels were doubtless used by bilingual speakers during the Middle Ages, but they were ultimately replaced by similar native sounds, as in *due* and *beef.*

The investigation of the adaptation of folk dialects to a national standard will shed light upon this important problem. I should like to present two cases to illustrate the behavior of dialects in this situation.

In his detailed study of the speechways of a mining community in Northern England (Byer's Green in Durham), Harold Orton found a rather marked influence of the Received Standard upon the local dialect, which differs sharply from the Received Standard in its system of vowels. Thus the native sequence /ia/ of *bake, gate* is sometimes replaced by /ē/; the /ia/ of *bone, home* by /ō/; the /au̯/ of *folk, soldier* by /ō/; the /i̯ɜ/ of *moon, book* and the /u/ of *hound, sound* by /öu̯/. All of these substitutions are prompted by the Received Standard of England, but none of them are accurate imitations of the phonemes occuring in Received Standard *bake, bone, moon, hound*. And, above all, none of these replacements introduce a new phoneme. Native /ē/ occurs in such words as *day, wait* (Middle English *ai*), native /ō/ in *coat, rose*, and native /öu̯/ is normal in *down, doubt* and in *blue, new*. Hence the integrity of the native system of vowels is fully preserved. There is no addition to the system, nor any loss. Only the number of instances of /ē, ō, öu̯/ is increased at the expense of /ia, au̯, i̯ɜ, u/.

In conclusion I shall present a German example. A South Bavarian folk dialect (Carinthian) adopts many words from Standard German and from the colloquial speech of a neighboring city (Villach); but, to my knowledge, not a single foreign phoneme has been adopted. There is no trace of the Standard German phoneme /z/ of *sagen, lesen*, or of the /p/ of *packen* (both *packen* and *backen* begin with the weak voiceless stop /b/). The rounded front vowels /ǖ, ü, ȫ, ö/ and the diphthong /oi/ of Standard German *Mühle, Sünde, König, Köpfe, neu* are not adopted, the native /ī, i, ē, e, ai/ being retained in such words. The native "centering" diphthongs /ia̯, ɛa̯, ɔa̯, ua̯/ of *lieb, schön, rot, gut* /lia̯b, šɛa̯n, rɔa̯t, gua̯t/, unless retained, are replaced by /ī, ē, ō, ū/, which occur as native phonemes in such words as *wissen, besser, hoffen, Butter* /wīsn, bēsr, hōfn, būtr/.

One would like to know whether other regional folk dialects behave in the same way, rejecting foreign phonemes and making adjustments within the native systems of sounds, when the speakers make concessions to a socially "superior" dialect. The dissemination of features from a privileged dialect has, of course, been documented again and again; but the crucial question of whether the receiving dialect stays within its own system of sounds and forms, when it accepts elements from another dialect, or whether it alters its systems, has hardly been asked.

DISCUSSION (by Barbara Strang)

Professor Kurath's paper records what is in effect the adding of a dimension to dialect studies. He speaks of making a "a modest beginning" in the analysis of the social dimension by distinguishing the folk from the middle class and the cultural elite, and in introducing the paper he specified this dimension as one to be measured in terms of quantity of education. What is surprising to a speaker of British English is that any single parameter, perhaps especially that one, yields useful results. There are four essentials for a situation of social dialect influence such as concerns him. There must be a prestige dialect, a mediating dialect, a non-prestige dialect, and also an awareness by the speakers of the socially inferior dialect that their usage does lack prestige. Such a situation is familiar in British English, but it is very complex in structure, for there are many different prestige groups with distinct linguistic characteristics. Perhaps to some extent those with a high quantity of education form an elite; but what is much more important is education at one place rather than another—one kind of school or one particular school, a particular university or service training establishment. Outside these considerations, there are many aristocracies, of birth, of wealth, of youth, etc. each of which, in its typical forms of English, may provide a goal for imitation by those aware of lack of privilege. And this less privileged group too is far from homogeneous, not only in its actual usage, but in its choice of a prestige-group whose English shall be a target-language. So we find that the influence of social upon regional dialects cannot be assessed in terms of a single dimension, but in terms of a complicated network of interactions between an indefinite range of prestige groups and an indefinite range of linguistic self-improvers.

32

Social Aspects of Bilingualism in San Antonio, Texas

JANET B. SAWYER

A RECENT DIALECT SURVEY of English in San Antonio Texas,[1] a community where over 40 percent of the people are Spanish-speaking immigrants from Mexico, yielded two important types of data: first, interviews with native speakers of English provided knowledge of the pronunciation features and vocabulary of a relatively unstudied part of Texas;[2] second, a study of the English spoken in the same community by Spanish-speaking informants revealed at least two degrees of second-language skill and unexpected evidence of the social stresses felt by speakers from a low-status culture who found no advantage in being identified as members of the Spanish-speaking minority.

The study of the pronunciation and vocabulary of the English-speaking informants, whom we will call *Anglos* in this report, following the custom of the community, was helpful in establishing the predominant influences upon the regional dialect. The informants were selected from various age, education, and culture groups within the Anglo community, and the tabulated records[3] gave the following pronunciation features as characteristic of San Antonio:

1. "Vocalized /r/": *here* [hɪə].
2. Diphthongal /æy/: *pass* [pæys].

Reprinted, by permission of the author and the University of Alabama Press, from *Publication of the American Dialect Society* No. 41 (1964), pp. 7–15. Professor Sawyer is a member of the English department of California State College at Long Beach.

[1] Janet B. Sawyer, "A Dialect Study of San Antonio, Texas, a Bilingual Community" (University of Texas diss., 1957).

[2] See E. Bagby Atwood, *The Regional Vocabulary of Texas* (Austin: University of Texas Press, 1962) for a more recent analysis of the larger dialect area.

[3] The items used for this study are those included in the worksheets made by Hans Kurath in 1939 (see note 4 below), as revised by E. Bagby Atwood for the Southwest regional study. The worksheets were supplemented by taped readings of Dagwood comic strips and other selections which provided additional information about pronunciation features in various styles of speech. For example, although in citation forms [aɪ] (in *five*) was often heard in the speech of certain Anglo speakers, in the reading of the comic strip, monothongal [aˑ] was more frequent for these same speakers.

3. Monophthongal "long i": *five* [faˑv].
4. Diphthongal /ɔw/: *fought* /fɔwt/.
5. /ɪ/ in certain unstressed syllables: *Dallas, wanted.*
6. /iw/ or /yuw/ after /t/, /d/, /n/: *tune, due.*

A comparison of these features with the known features of the dialect areas studied in the East[4] proved that such features are typical of the Southern dialect area, a somewhat surprising fact since a study of the immigration to San Antonio during the critical years between 1865 and 1880[5] states that 47 percent of the Anglo immigrants were from the Midland and South Midland speech areas, and only 44 percent were from the Gulf states. The prestige of the Southern settlers must have been high, judging from the persistence of the Southern speech characteristics. Of the six features listed above, only (1) is receding sharply in the speech of the youngest Anglo informants; (4) may be receding slightly.

In matters of lexicon, the survey disclosed that San Antonio English is not so strikingly Southern, partially because many of the words known to be characteristic of the South, such as *light-wood, chittling,* and *co-wench,* are obsolescent in this urban community. Words which spread from the South into the South Midland area appear with the greatest frequency in San Antonio. Terms such as *pully bone* and *clabber* are known to all the Anglo informants. Thus, in the Anglo community of San Antonio, we find a frequency of 53 percent for words common to the South and South Midland.

The English vocabulary of San Antonio has its distinctive regional flavor because of a continual contact with the Spanish culture and language during the early settlement years. We found numerous Spanish words pertaining particularly to Southwestern ranching and cattle raising: *burro, lariat, hackamore, tank, norther, acequia, arroyo, chaps, corral,* and *mesa* are in very common usage; however, others such as *nopal, guajilla, tuna, piñata, yobero* and *potro* were known only by the older members of the Anglo community, since the items they name are characteristic terms in a receding rural way of life.

The comparison of the English of seven Spanish-speaking informants, who will be referred to as *Latin* informants since the name *Latin-Americans* is the term preferred by this group, with the English of the seven Anglo informants made it possible to distinguish varying degrees of second-language skill. We were able to classify three informants as basically *unilingual* Spanish speakers, since they spoke Spanish exclusively at home and whenever possible away from

[4] Hans Kurath, M. L. Hanley, B. Bloch, G. S. Lowman, Jr., and M. L. Hansen, *Linguistic Atlas of New England* (3 vols. in 6 parts. Providence: Brown University, 1939–43); Hans Kurath, *A Word Geography of the Eastern United States* (Ann Arbor: University of Michigan Press, 1949); and E. Bagby Atwood, "Outline of the Principle Speech Areas of the Eastern United States" (mimeographed pamphlet, Austin, 1950).

A book which gives detailed information on the Linguistic Atlas materials was not available at the time that this dialect study of San Antonio, Texas, was made: Hans Kurath and Raven I. McDavid, Jr., *The Pronunciation of English in the Atlantic States* (Ann Arbor: University of Michigan Press, 1961).

[5] Homer Lee Kerr, "Migration Into Texas 1865–1880" (University of Texas diss., 1953).

home. (All of them were native second-generation residents of San Antonio with grade school educations.) Their English was characterized by constant interference from the phonological structure of Spanish, numerous errors in basic grammatical contrasts, and a limited, inaccurate use of English vocabulary. These informants were L2, a female midwife, 53 years old; L3, a male gardener, 46 years old; and L5, a female actress, 41 years old.

The remaining four Latin informants were classified as *bilinguals*, because their English was extremely competent. Very few errors occurred in their speech in either phonology or grammar, and they were able to respond to eight or more hours of interviewing in fluent English. These informants were L1, a retired female seamstress, 74 years old; L4, a female saleslady and housewife, 45 years old; L6, a male university graduate, 32 years old; and L7, a male university student, 21 years old.

In classifying these four informants as bilinguals, we do not mean that they had completely mastered English. Anyone speaking to either of the two women informants would immediately recognize the fact that English was not their native language. But they were competent within a limited vocabulary, and they had no difficulty making their ideas clear in English. Neither had had more than an elementary school education, but their jobs, which brought them into contact with English speakers, made it possible and even necessary for them to speak English well. The two male informants were much superior to them in the range and relative perfection of their English; L6, at least, was near the dividing line between bilingual Spanish and bilingual English, since he felt some embarrassment when speaking Spanish to anyone outside of San Antonio. Of course, neither L6 nor any of the other bilinguals felt completely at ease in English either.

The unilinguals experienced greater embarrassment and frustration when speaking English. However, L5, the unilingual actress, criticized the Spanish spoken in San Antonio, calling it "Tex.-Mex." Having been well-educated in cultured Spanish, thanks to the training of her Cuban husband and years in the Spanish theater, she disapproved of the way the Spanish speakers of the area interspersed English words among the Spanish words when speaking Spanish.

In order to ascertain the actual features of this Tex.-Mex., we also recorded the Spanish of the Latin informants and compared these records with those of Spanish students studying at the University of Texas from various parts of Mexico and the rest of the Spanish-speaking world. And no matter how diverse Tex.-Mex. may be in its vocabulary, the records proved that it is almost identical in its phonology to Mexican Spanish, so this dialect of Spanish was used in the comparative study of the two languages.[6]

The phonology of standard Southern English as spoken by the Anglo informants of San Antonio was the dialect of English used in judging the skill

[6] Harold V. King, "Outline of Mexican Spanish Phonology," *Studies in Linguistics*, X (1952), 51–62.

of the Latin informants since it seems reasonable to assume that the model they were striving to attain in English was not Northern or New England speech, or even "General American," but simply that variety of American English found in the Anglo community into which they were striving to integrate. Therefore, in making the analysis of the bilinguals' achievement, we did not consider them to be skilled if they used [aʊ] in *cow*, even if these phones happened to be found in this word in many varieties of American English, since the Anglo informants of San Antonio used only [æʊ] or [aʊ] in such words.

The English phonology of the unilingual Latins and the bilingual Latins can be briefly summarized:

Several vowel contrasts caused particular difficulty for the unilinguals:
1. /i/ and /ɪ/. The unilinguals commonly substituted Spanish /i/ (which lacks the high off-glide of English /i/) for English /ɪ/ in such words as *pig*.
2. /u/ and /ʊ/. The unilinguals commonly substituted Spanish /u/ (which lacks the lip-rounding off-glide of English for English /ʊ/ in such words as *pull*).
3. /æ/. This phoneme does not occur in Spanish, and the unilinguals commonly substituted either the close [e] or the open [ɛ] allophone of the Spanish /e/ in such words as *man*.
4. /ə/ also does not occur in Spanish. The unilingual Spanish speakers substitute either the [a] of Spanish /a/ or the [ɔ] allophone of Spanish /o/ in such words as *one*.

The bilingual informants very seldom had difficulty with the simple vowel contrasts. The most difficult vowel qualities for them were the [æʊ] (in *cow*), the monophthongal [a·] (in *five*), and the fronted [ʉ] (in *school*). L6, the university graduate, was the only Latin informant who had mastered these regional features.

A variety of errors occurred in the attempt of the Latins to produce the English consonant system. Those of highest incidence in the records of the San Antonio unilingual informants were the following:

1. Fricative allophones of Spanish stops such as [ß] often occurred in place of the labiodental [v] of English, following the Spanish distributional pattern. There is no /v/ phoneme in Spanish.
2. Final voiced consonants are often devoiced following the Spanish pattern, which permits only a few consonants to be final of word and commonly devoices those that do occur. Example: [wepʻ] for *web*; [pikʻ] for *pig*.
3. The fricatives and affricates /š/, /č/, and /ǰ/ often replace each other in a form of free variation. *Sheep* [čiˑp], *chair* [šɛr], *jump* [čəmp], and *fudge* [fəš] are typical occurrences in unilingual Latin speech.

Such phenomena were typical of unilingual speech. But such interference by the Spanish consonant system was rare in bilingual English. Apparently, the bilinguals had mastered the essential contrasts between the voiced and voiceless consonants and had learned the new phonemes which occur only as allophones in Spanish. The most difficult pattern for the bilinguals to master seemed to be the contrast between /s/ and /z/, which are separate phonemes in English. In Spanish, however, the [z] is an allophone of /s/, occurring only when /s/ is followed by a voiced consonant in close transition. In the speech of L5, one of the unilinguals, an example of this Spanish distributional pattern occurred: In the phrase "twice better" *twice* was pronounced as [twɑɪz], but when *uwice* occurred before pause, it was pronounced as [twɑis]. Although the bilinguals never made a total transfer of the Spanish pattern, the most persistent feature of "accent" in their speech (as well as in the speech of the unilinguals) is the occurrence of the tense voiceless [s] or the only partially voiced [z̥] in final position where [z] should occur in English. The high frequency of /s/ in both languages as a plural suffix and as a verb inflexional suffix may be one of the causes of the persistence of the difficulty in mastering the phoneme /z/ in English. It is a feature of the speech of even L6, who has attained most of the features of Texas English.

An interesting and unexpected feature of the pronunciation of the San Antonian bilinguals can be directly linked to the social pressures of the bilingual community, rather than to the interference of Spanish language habits. It became obvious after even the most superficial study of the community that the Latin-American population, commonly called *Mexicans*, or more derogatory terms such as *Meskans*, *pilau*, *greasers*, or *wet backs*, were regarded as inferior. One of the Anglo informants of a prominent San Antonio family commented, "Many of my friends and relatives don't think Negroes and Mexicans are human beings—just animals. I didn't even know we had many Mexicans in San Antonio until I came back from college in Virginia." The Latin informants were well aware of the situation. The granddaughter of L1, herself a skilled bilingual, talked of her difficulty in getting a job upon her return from a good position in a psychiatrist's office in a western city. "Every ad for a good job here in San Antonio says 'Only *Anglos* need apply'!"

How this almost insurmountable pressure would affect the language achievement of the bilinguals was not immediately clear. It would seem logical that the ultimate degree of their effort would be the mastery of English as spoken in San Antonio. But the bilinguals interviewed for this survey (and others observed at various times before and after this survey) had gone even further. So determined were they to erase any influence of their low-prestige language upon their use of English that they treated Spanish words in two very special ways. First, Spanish words that they could not avoid in English received different pronunciations depending upon who was listening. Second, Spanish words that could be avoided were not used even though they were the typical regional terms in the English-speaking community.

Let us illustrate each of these facets of bilingual behavior in greater detail. Whenever a Spanish word could not be avoided in English, for example, when a bilingual speaker had to pronounce a Spanish personal name or a Spanish place name, he pronounced it in two different ways. If the listener was also a bilingual speaker, he gave the word a Spanish pronunciation. If the listener was a member of the English-speaking prestige group, the bilingual gave the word an Anglicized pronunciation. The bilingual informants even pronounced their own names in two different ways in English: *Lorenzo*: [lořɛnso] to other bilinguals; [lowrɛnzow] to Anglos. Other examples follow: (In each case, the Spanish pronunciation has been given first.) *Dolores*: [dolóřɛs] or (dǝlórɛs]; *San Antonio*: [Sanantónio] or [sænæntówniǝ]; *burro*: [búřo] or [bɔ́row]; *plaza* [plásɑ] or [plǽzǝ]; *corral* [kořál] or [kǝrǽl]. The bilinguals gave the same double treatment for other indispensable borrowings from Spanish. It must be emphasized that this is not the way a speaker of Spanish from any Latin-American country or from Spain would treat Spanish words when speaking English. It would be a matter of pride to pronounce them in the true Spanish way and even to correct English speakers who mispronounced them. This writer remembers the horror of a bilingual from one South American country when he heard a San Antonio bilingual mispronounce his own Spanish name. The South American took an instant dislike to the Texan solely on the basis of this strange linguistic behavior.

As we mentioned above, if a Spanish word could be avoided in English, the bilinguals would not use it at all. In this they were like the unilinguals, who never used Spanish words in English. This was in direct contrast to the freedom with which all the Latin informants used *English* words in *Spanish*, the main distinguishing feature of San Antonio Spanish, according to various informants. (Examples: "Dame mi *pokebuk*." [Give me my *pocket book*.], or "Es un *eswamp*." [It's a *swamp*.].) Some of the Spanish words rejected in English by all the Latin informants were used normally by the Anglo informants: *corral, lariat, cinch, remuda, pilon, frijoles, chaps, hackamore, quirt*. Other words, which may have been borrowed from Latin or French rather than from Spanish, were also rejected by some of the Latin informants, because they were so similar to Spanish words: *gallery, melon, rancid*.

This rejection of the typical regional vocabulary of the English-speaking community illustrates the cultural isolation of even the bilingual speakers. In fact, if a Northern term happened to be more common in print, the Latin informants were likely to use that instead of the term preferred by all age levels in the Anglo group. Words such as *light bread, clabber*, and *corn shuck* were unknown to the Latin informants. They used the terms *corn husk* and *wish bone* rather than *corn shuck* and *pully bone*. The phrase *setting hen* was not known by even the most skilled bilingual Latin, L6, because such items are commonly learned in the home, and in the homes of the Latins only Spanish words for such things were used. Other terms typical of the regional English culture such as *Christmas Gift* or *snap beans* were unknown to the Latins, who used instead the general greeting, *Merry Christmas* and the commercial term *string beans*.

In evaluating our findings, we must remember that the number of bilinguals interviewed for this survey is out of all proportion to their number in the

Spanish-speaking community, since it was our intent to study bilingualism. Actually only a small number of people attempt to break through their isolation into the larger, prestige culture. Generally, they are content to consider themselves part of the Mexican culture and to live out their lives in relative security. Those who are more ambitious are called *agringados*, from the term *gringo*, with no compliment intended. Even members of the younger generation in the public schools generally stick together and talk Spanish outside of class. This is a sort of voluntary segregation; yet they would be the first to protest any actual segregation for the purpose of teaching them English as it should be taught to speakers of a second language. As a result, they are taught English along with the native speakers who need to learn the special kind of English known as formal written style. Those students who wish to become competent bilinguals adopt the "book-words" and formal usage rules of this special style for ordinary English speech situations, and this precise, elegant style often sets off a bilingual from the English-speaking community quite as much as the "errors" of the unilinguals do.

The isolation of the Latin American results in a series of social isoglosses separating their speech from that of the Anglo community. Although these lines cannot be drawn on the map like the geographical isoglosses which separate one dialect from another, they are quite as real and as enduring. In the long run, the acquiring of the regional standard speech depends upon acculturation, which means the elimination of social barriers. Only when this is achieved (a necessity, from the point of view of democracy) can social isoglosses be eliminated.

33

Terms of Abuse for Some Chicago Social Groups

LEE A. PEDERSON

EXPRESSIONS OF DERISION and contempt for members of racial, religious, and nationality groups form a complicated part of any urban lexicon. Sharing certain of the emotional, physical, and social characteristics of slang and the nomenclature of sex, ethnic pejoratives have been unevenly researched in American dialect investigations.[1] Like slang, many of these words and phrases are short-lived verbal fads and esoteric nonce words;[2] like the veiled language of sex, these terms are not always easy to elicit in a casual interview, and the forms collected are equally difficult to evaluate in the light of those restraints placed on an individual by society and the superego.[3] Despite these forbidding problems,

Reprinted by permission of the University of Alabama Press from *Publication of the American Dialect Society* 42.26–48 (1964). The author is Associate Professor of English at Emory University.

[1] The range of this investigation by the Atlas Project can be seen in Raven I. McDavid, Jr., and Virginia McDavid, "A Compilation of the Work Sheets of the Linguistic Atlas of the United States and Canada and Associated Projects" (Ann Arbor, mimeographed, 1951), especially, pp. 69 and 89 of both the basic compilation and of the Appendix. Atlas surveys have included neutral and derogatory terms for Italian, Irishman, Jew, mulatto, Mexican, Tex-Mex, French Canadian, Acadian French, Creole, and Gullah, but only terms for the Negro and the rustic have been included in all regional surveys and the Short Work Sheets. Similarly, names for members of various religious denominations —Baptist, Methodist, Catholic, Episcopalian, and Presbyterian—were included in the worksheets of a few regional surveys.

The best overall discussions and bibliographies of ethnic pejoratives are in H. L. Mencken, *The American Language* (New York, 1936), under "Euphemisms," pp. 285–300; H. L. Mencken, *The American Language: Supplement One* (New York, 1945), under "Euphemisms," pp. 595–639; and H. L. Mencken, *The American Language: The Fourth Edition and Two Supplements, abridged, with annotations and new material, by Raven I. McDavid, Jr., with the assistance of David W. Maurer* (New York, 1963), under "Terms of Abuse," pp. 367–89.

[2] At this stage of the investigation it is impossible to distinguish between the durable coinage and the nonce word. *Shawnty Irishman*, for example, as a variant of *Shanty Irishman*, may well be a folk etymology because there are now more Seans than shanties on the Irish South Side of Chicago.

[3] Consider the emendations in such songs as "Missouri Waltz" (*little baby* for *pickaninny*) or "Rockaby Your Baby with a Dixie Melody" (*soft and low* for "*Old Black*

TABLE 33.1: INFORMANTS

No.	Age	Sex	T.[a]	Neighborhood[b]	Ethnic Group	Occupation
1.	71	M	4	Chicago *South* (A)	WASP[c]	Insurance Exec.
2.	71	M	4	Oak Park (A)	WASP	Fire Inspector
3.	70	F	1	Kenilworth (A)	WASP	Housewife
4.	56	F	7	Glenview (A)	WASP	Housewife
5.	45	M	1	Chicago *South* (A)	WASP	Teacher
6.	41	M	8	Chicago *West* (D)	WASP	Truck Driver
7.	17	F	5	Evergreen Park (C)	WASP	Student
8.	86	F	8	Chicago *North* (C)	German-P	Housewife
9.	68	M	7	Chicago *North* (C)	German-P	Secretary
10.	56	F	4	Park Ridge (A)	German-P	Housewife
11.	56	M	3	Chicago *Northwest* (C)	German-P	Police Lieutenant
12.	57	M	5	Park Ridge (A)	Norwegian-P	Insurance Exec.
13.	61	F	4	Fox River Grove (B)	Czech-P	Housewife
14.	55	M	6	Chicago *West* (D)	Czech-C	Cashier
15.	23	F	4	Chicago *Northwest* (C)	Polish-C	Nurse
16.	28	M	3	Maywood (C)	Sicilian-C	Elec. Engineer
17.	79	M	7	Chicago *South* (D)	Irish-C	Postal Clerk
18.	55	M	4	Chicago *West* (E)	Irish-C	Social Worker
19.	50	M	7	Chicago *Northwest* (C)	Irish-C	Fire Marshall
20.	47	F	4	Chicago *South* (D)	Irish-C	Telephone Operator
21.	46	F	5	Chicago *South* (C)	Irish-C	Housewife
22.	45	M	1	Evanston (B)	Polish-J	Teacher
23.	23	F	4	Chicago *Northwest* (C)	Russian-J	Student
24.	84	M	4	Chicago *South* (B)	German-J	Advertising Exec.
25.	60	F	7	Chicago *South* (C)	German-J	Housewife
26.	27	M	6	Chicago *West* (E)	Mex-PR-C	TV Repairman
27.	85	M	4	Chicago *South* (B1)	Negro	Undertaker
28.	67	F	5	Chicago *South* (C1)	Negro	Personnel Clerk
29.	52	F	5	Chicago *South* (A1)	Negro	Housewife
30.	34	M	2	Gary (C1)	Negro	Social Worker
31.	24	M	7	Chicago *South* (D1)	Negro	Truck Driver

[a] *Education Types* are determined by the following criteria: (1) indicates a superior level of education, specifically a college degree with formal or informal graduate-level studies or reading, and extensive social contacts; (2) indicates a high level of education, specifically a college degree with less post-graduate studies or reading and fewer social contacts than Type 1; (3) indicates a college degree, specifically exposure to four years of higher education; (4) indicates a superior high-school education, perhaps intellectually and culturally superior to Type 3, but heavily dependent upon written authoritarian sources for vocabulary development and "preferred pronunciations"; (5) indicates a good high-school education; (6) indicates a high-school education, specifically exposure to four years of secondary schooling; (7) indicates a superior elementary-school education, perhaps intellectually and culturally superior to Type 6, but characterized by uncultivated speech; (8) indicates a good elementary-school education. None of the Type 9 or 10 completed this part of the interview.

[b] Chicago suburbs and neighborhoods are classified here according to the following designations: (A) indicates an upper or upper middle-class Caucasian community; (B) indicates an upper middle or middle-class Caucasian community; (C) indicates a middle or lower middle-class Caucasian community; (D) indicates a lower middle- or upper-lower-class Caucasian community; (E) indicates a lower-class Caucasian community. Corresponding Negro communities are indicated A1, B1, C1, and D1.

[c] WASP is used to designate white Anglo-Saxon Protestants, i.e. second- or third-generation Chicagoans of Northern European ancestry.

there is a need for systematic study of these terms, but this research cannot be sensibly undertaken until inventorial reports outline the problems and suggest procedures for more refined investigation. With these objectives in mind, a place was made in the worksheets for a social dialect study of American English spoken in Metropolitan Chicago in order to survey the range of lexical variation and to test the effectiveness of inquiry into the mysteries of name-calling among the citizens of that city.[4]

The present report identifies those informants who participated in this section of the interview and indicates their responses under the broad headings of racial, religious, and nationality groups. Although the investigation was begun with hopes of collecting a large body of exotic data concerning the peoples of the world as they appear through the eyes of urban Midwesterners, the field of inquiry was soon narrowed to those groups which are socially meaningful to the natives of Chicago.[5] These include, under racial groups; Negro, Caucasian, and Oriental; under religious groups, Jew, Catholic, and Protestant; and, under nationality groups, Irish, German, Scandinavian, Polish, Czechoslovakian, Lithuanian, Italian, Mexican, and Puerto Rican.

Of the thirty-eight primary informants interviewed in the Chicago survey, thirty-two were questioned on their use and knowledge of derogatory terms for members of the aforementioned social groups.[6] The six informants not questioned were either anxious to be finished with the interview or aggressively suspicious of its intent. In those cases it seemed advisable to sacrifice the section and concentrate on the collection of the basic corpus. Only one of thirty-two insisted she never used any terms of abuse and refused to repeat those expressions she had heard.[7] The remaining thirty-one primary informants are listed in Table 33.1.

Joe"). In the latter case the modification is understandable because "Old Black Joe," "Old Zip Coon" (the noblest ancestor of "Turkey in the Straw," which has also been modified), "Shine" (which was revived by Frankie Laine in the late 1940s), and many of the pedestrian favorites of Stephen Foster and George Gershwin are no longer heard on American radio.

[4] "The Pronunciation of English in Metropolitan Chicago: Vowels and Consonants" (University of Chicago diss., 1964).

[5] Omitted from the following classifications because insufficient evidence was collected, the Greeks and Serbo-Croatians should certainly be included by later investigators in Chicago.

[6] To understand the relationship of the terms collected in this part of the interview to the active and passive vocabularies of the informants, one must keep in mind that the interviewer did not have time to probe into the full significance of each term with each informant. For example, although *Jap*, *Chinaman*, *Swede*, and *Pole* are surely part of every informant's passive vocabulary, these terms did not emerge in every interview situation. This is one of the problems that future researchers in name-calling will have to take into consideration. In our current project in Minneapolis, we are experimenting with a rejection code, i.e. an arrangement of variants which the informant is asked to label as "primary," "possible," or "impossible" in his own speech. A summary of the aims of this project is given in "American English of the Ojibwa in Minneapolis: A Social Dialect Survey" (Minneapolis, mimeographed, 1965). In spite of this recent work, the Chicago experience suggests that, as with the language of sex and obscenity, it is practically im-

Of the fifteen social groups discussed in this report, only the Negro attracted designations from all thirty-one respondents. As the primary target of prejudice in the city today, the Negro received forty-one different terms of abuse in 104 responses. Of these only *nigger* has general currency. This was elicited from thirty of thirty-one informants, and the single exception (#18) had *nigrah* /nígrə/, which is a neutral designation in many parts of the South.[8]

Four other pejoratives were collected from both Negroes and Caucasians, but the distribution of the terms differs significantly. Three of six instances of *coon.* are in the speech of Caucasians who work in, or live on the periphery of, the Negro community (#5, 11, and 26), and the remaining three occur in the speech of the three oldest Negro informants (#27, 28, and 29). Of the other three variants, *darky, jig,* and *blackboy,* none is found in the speech of more than one Negro.

The widest variety of abusive terms, of course, are found exclusively in Caucasian speech. Most of these call attention to the stereotype racial characteristics of the Negro, viz. skin color: *eightball, chocolate drop, black, black bastard, load of coal, shithead, ebony, African, Ethiopian, blacky, painted goof, Schwarze,* and *sunburned Irish*; hair consistency: *burrhead* and *kinkyhead.* All of these except *blacky*[9] occur only in the speech of older informants, as does *shine,* which occurs in the speech of four Chicagoans, all over age forty-five. Terms most popular among young Caucasians are *jigaboo, booboo, blacky,* and *jungle bunny*; both middle-aged informants giving *jungle bunny* (#5 and 18) work with adolescents. The young Mexican Puerto-Rican informant (#26) has *nugget* and *ebony.* Both instances of the German–Yiddish loan *Schwerze* /švartzə/ were given by Slavic Jews (#22 and 23), and one WASP, a second-generation German, offered *swartzy* /swartzi/. Two tentatively specialized terms

---

possible to determine whether the informant uses the words or not unless they occur in free conversation.

[7] This first-generation Norwegian–American was perhaps inhibited by her casual acquaintance with my parents. As with the investigation of taboo data, very close friends and relatives or total strangers are the easiest informants with which to work; whereas, casual associates, especially friends and students, are among the most difficult.

[8] Although each informant was asked to give both neutral and derogatory terms for a "person of the same race as Martin Luther King, Congressman Dawson, Jackie Robinson, or Joe Louis" (unfortunately the frames varied and no rigorous control is suggested here), twenty-five initial responses were *nigger.* These include four of five Negro informants, which suggests, perhaps, that many responses had been conditioned by other parts of the interview, e.g. the taboo section. Among most uncultivated Caucasian speakers interviewed, however, *Negro* is unnatural in free conversation. *Colored people, colored folks, colored man,* and *the colored* were much more comfortably articulated than was *Negro.* Among these informants, *nigger* was said with no more intended vehemence or self-consciousness than was *Swede, Czech,* or *Pole.* Cultivated speakers, however, demonstrated the same nervousness with the word as they did with much of the taboo terminology of sex, i.e. whispers, altered breathing, and overly long pauses before articulation. Three cultivated Negroes, however, spoke of behavior characteristic of "low down" Negroes, viz. "someone acting like a nigger."

[9] According to a report of the Watts riots of 1965, "Get Whitey" was the battle cry of the Los Angeles Negroes.

TABLE 33.2: TERMS FOR RACIAL GROUPS

	Negro	Caucasian	Oriental
1.	nigger, darky, swartzy, African	—	—
2.	jig, black, nigger	—	yellow belly, squint-eyes
3.	nigger, colored folks, chocolate drop	—	—
4.	nigger, booboo	white trash	Jap
5.	nigger, coon, jungle bunny, black	white trash	Chink, Jap, slant-eyes, gook
6.	nigger, blacks, darky, colored man, black bastard, colored bastard	—	Chink
7.	nigger, jig, blacky, jigaboo, jungle bunny	—	li'l eyes
8.	nigger	—	—
9.	colored, nigger, half-breed	scum of the white race, Southerner, Southern hillbilly	Jap, Chinaman
10.	nigger, jigaboo	—	Chink
11.	nigger, coon, burrhead, shine, eightball, booboo	white trash, cracker, hillbilly, shit kicker	Jap, Chinaman, yellow belly
12.	nigger, black bastard	—	Chink
13.	nigger	—	Chinaman
14.	black bastard, colored bastard, dark cloud, painted goof, nigger	—	Chinaman
15.	nigger	—	Jap, Chink
16.	nigger, colored people	—	Chink
17.	nigger, shine, burrhead	—	yellow belly
18.	jungle bunny, jig, Ethiopian, darky, sunburned Irish, nigrah	ofay	Chink, slant-eyes, gook
19.	nigger, burrhead, shithead, load of coal	—	Chinaman, Jap, gink, gunk
20.	nigger, blackboy	—	—
21.	nigger, black, colored	—	Chink, Jap, yellowman
22.	nigger, shine, schvartza	—	Jap, Nip
23.	nigger, schvartza	—	Jap
24.	nigger, shine, kinkyhead	—	Chink, pigtail, Jap
25.	nigger	—	—
26.	nigger, blackboy, coon, nugget, ebony	gringo	Jap, Chink
27.	nigger, coon, jig	ofay	Chink
28.	nigger, coon	peckerwood, white trash, ofay, gray	—

Negro	Caucasian	Oriental
29. nigger, darky, coon, black fay, Uncle Tom	white trash, peckerwood, hillbilly, ofay	Chinaman
30. Negro, nigger, Ned, Cuff, blue, spade, spook	paleface, pink, gringo, ofay, fade, gray, Paddy, peckerwood, spick, redneck, hillbilly, cracker, ridgerunner, stump jumper, hunky	Chink
31. nigger, jazzbo, spook, blackboy	peckerwood, hunky, gray, ofay	Chink

were reported by a City of Chicago Fire Marshall (#19), who said that firemen frequently use *shithead* and *load of coal* to designate careless Negroes in slum areas. One Irishman (#18) gave *sunburned Irish* as a jocular expression, which reflects, perhaps, the deep contempt in which the Negro is held in those communities where he is a significant social force.[10]

Most of the terms collected exclusively from Negro informants are rare within the Caucasian social dialects of Chicago, e.g. *Cuff, Ned, blue, Uncle Tom*, and *black fay*.[11] *Spook, spade*, and *jazzbo* were also elicited only from Negroes in this survey, but these three, especially the first two, are common in the speech of Caucasian Chicagoans.

One of the most interesting sections of this catalogue of abusive terms is that which includes names for Caucasians. Seventeen Caucasian informants registered only silent surprise at the question or suspected that this line of inquiry was in some way aimed at the defamation of the "white race."[12] Apart from single instances of *white bastard* and *gringo*, all pejoratives for Caucasians were restricted to poor in-migrant Southerners, most of whom have their origins in Appalachia. These terms include *white trash, hillbilly, cracker, scum of the white race*, and the commonplace generic term for any rustic, *shit kicker*.

[10] See Table 33.4. Irish informant identifies a Puerto Rican as *nigger*, and Mexican-Puerto-Rican informant identifies an Irishman as a "nigger turned inside out."

[11] *Black fay* is applied to the modern counterparts of Uncle Tom. *Fay* is commonly used by Negroes to designate Caucasians, and, although this may well be—probably was, originally—a shortened form of *ofay*, the word might be better spelled *fey*, i.e. a fairy, pansy, fruit, homo, or queer, because all of these terms are widely used by Chicagoans of both races to identify a homosexual.

In *AL*, Mencken offers the following etymological note: "The word *ofay*, which may have come from the French *au fait* (signifying mastery), is in general use in the Negro press of the United States to designate a white person. It is possible that it originated in New Orleans. Its popularity, I suspect, is at least partly due to its brevity, which makes a good headline word" (p. 215). Later he notes, "Mr. William V. Glenn, of Harrisburg, Pa., suggests that it may be a pig-Latin form of *foe*, but that . . . seems unlikely" (*SI*, p. 637). Of Mencken's two explanations, McDavid favors the latter in *AL* (1963), p. 388. All five informants in Chicago assumed it to be pig Latin.

[12] After collecting a long list of pejoratives for Negro, I would ask, "And what derogatory or abusive or nasty terms would you give to members of your race?" A typical response was a suspicious glare and "What would *you* call them?"

Perhaps the most significant of all, however, was the response of one first-generation German American (#9), *Southerner*! The single instance of *ofay* was given in desperation by a middle-aged social worker (#18), who, after admitting he had heard no such terms used by Caucasians, recalled that "Negroes sometimes call whites *ofays*."[13]

Among the five Negro informants, only *ofay* was offered by each of them, and all insisted it was a mild term, probably, because of its currency in the bourgeois Negro press and radio. The youngest Negro (#31) said of *ofay*, "That's not derogatory; it just means *white*. The best of writers use that. It's the same as you using *Negro*." The most characteristic feature of Negro terms for Caucasian is the tendency to expand particularized designations for Caucasians to include all members of the race, e.g. terms for poor Southerners: *peckerwood, white trash, hillbilly, ridgerunner, stump-jumper, cracker*, and *redneck*, and terms for nationality groups: *hunky*,[14] *Paddy*, and *spick. Gringo* is apparently a loan from the Spanish speakers who share many parts of the ghetto with the Negroes, and *paleface* was probably borrowed from old western movies.[15] The remaining four terms, *pink, the Man, Miss Ann*, and *gray*, seem to be original.[16]

The only other racial group to attract pejoratives in the Chicago survey was the Oriental, and those terms were the least imaginative. Most of these are commonplace nicknames for Japanese, *Jap* and *Nip*, or Chinese, *Chink* and *Chinaman*, with a single occurrence of the relic *pigtail*. A few terms reflect stereotype racial characteristics, i.e. *yellow belly, yellowman, slant eyes, squint eyes*, and *li'l eyes*, but these occur much less frequently than do the nicknames and are more evenly distributed among all social classes, age groups, and education types. Although *gook* was reported by two middle-aged males (#5 and 18), it shows no sign of really taking hold in the urban lexicon. Informant #5 pronounces it /gǝk/, #18 /guk/, and #19 gave two apparently related forms

[13] See note 11.

[14] This is a further extension of the observation of Mencken, "*Hunk* and *hunkie* (or *hunky* or *hunkey*) are properly applicable to Hungarians only, but they have been extended to include all Europeans coming from the region east of the German lands and west of Russia, save only the Greeks. Berrey and Van den Bark report extensions, in the United States, signifying a country bumpkin, a numskull, a common laborer and a foreign-born miner of any nationality" (*AL* (1963), p. 371). In a description of Lonigan's activities in Chicago during 1924, James T. Farrell wrote, "The street car was crowded with home-going workers, a swaying mob of begrimed Hunkies, foreigners, who jabbered in broken English and their own tongues, and smelled of garlic" (*The Young Manhood of Studs Lonigan*, first published in 1934, in *Studs Lonigan: A Trilogy* (New York, 1938), p. 161).

[15] In *SI* Mencken reports, "The Negroes use various other sportive terms for whites, e.g. *pale-face, chalk*, and *milk*" (p. 637). McDavid adds *gray* to this list in *AL* (1963), p. 388.

[16] *Pink* is a fairly common nickname for light-skinned Negroes, e.g. the great Negro street musician Pink Anderson, who is paired with the Rev. Gary Davis on the Riverside album *American Street Songs* (RLP 12-611). *The Man* and *Miss Ann* refer more specifically to the boss and the fair, young white lady of the plantation, both of which, according to my informant (#30), are applied with respect for *the Man* and acknowledgment of beauty in *Miss Ann*. Both, of course, are used ironically, and both have been omitted from the table because they are not intended to designate all Caucasians. For *the Man*, see McDavid and Maurer, *AL* (1963), pp. 323 and 722.

/gəŋk/ and /gɪŋk/ both of which seem to be combinations of *gook* and *Chink*.[17]

Of the three religious groups listed in Table 3,[18] Jews are given a considerable number of pejoratives; Catholics, far fewer; and Protestants, practically none at all. Although sixty-nine responses were given for *Jew*, as compared with eighteen for *Catholic* and twelve for *Protestant*, only the *Jew* and *Catholic* received the same designations from more than a single informant; whereas, no designation for the *Protestant* has more than a single occurrence.

Fourteen of the twenty-six terms used abusively for *Jew* are simply variations on *Jew*, *Hebrew*, *Yiddish*, and *Israel*, viz. *Jew*, *Jewboy*, *Jew-bastard*, *dirty Jew*, *son-of-a-bitching Jew*, *fucking Jew*, *Hebrew*, *Hebe*, *yiddish*, *yiddisher*, *yid*, *yit*, *son of Israel*, and *Israeli*. Most of the remaining terms are drawn from the Hebrew and Yiddish lexicon of the Jewish sub-culture. All of these loans, however, have been structurally or semantically modified by outsiders, e.g. the nominal construction of a young Negro informant, *koshiator* /košietər/, which might be related to *kosher* and *negotiator* (cf. *shyster* and *Shylock*), but which more probably reflects an ignorance of the commonplace adjective, as is the case with the Irish informant who offered *kodger* /kojər/. Another Irish informant gave *schlemihl* as a generic term for Jew. This tendency might strengthen the argument that *sheeny* is from *schön* or *scheina—scheina*, *jaudea lischkol*[19] and explain the origin of *shonicker* as well.[20] Although *mocky*, as Mencken suggests, "may have some sort of relation to the word *mock*,"[21] it seems equally possible that it is derived from *macher*, a boaster (according to Mencken)[22] or a fixer (according to McDavid).[23] The most popular of these

---

[17] The pronunciation /guk/ seems literary, cp. *cook*, *book*, *look*, and the Iowa quarterback *Gary Snook*. In Korea (1950–51), /guk/ was usual, /gʊk/ was rare, and /gək/ was never used within earshot of me. *Slope* and *slope-head* were the most popular terms applied to all "indigenous personnel."

[18] From an anthropological standpoint, identification of these groups in terms of religion is perhaps silly. Current religious practices by the members of any of these groups have little, if anything, to do with contemporary prejudices.

[19] Mencken, *SI*, p. 613.

[20] Farrell uses this in *Young Lonigan* (1934), "Well, if you ask me, Barney is a combination of eight ball, mick, and shonicker" (p. 154). Again, "Two hooknoses, about Studs' size, did come along. Andy and Johnny O'Brien, the youngest in the gang, stopped the shonickers" (p. 173). *Hooknose* and *hooknosed* were not found in this survey, both of which seem to have lost currency in the city. In another Chicago novel, Theodore Dreiser's *Sister Carrie* (New York, 1932), first published in 1900, Drouet calls Burnstein, "a regular hook-nosed sheeny" (p. 148). Thus folk etymology derives *shonicker* from Yiddish *schnozzle*, viz. a large nose. My colleague Avrom Fleishman suggests a derivation from Hanukkah /xánškə/ with the palatalization in American English of the unfamiliar velar fricative (/x/ > /š/) and with either a derivational (agentive) suffix /ər/ or simply excrescent /r/.

[21] Informant #18 told me the term *mocky* "went back to the mock Christ," referring, I believe, to Antichrist, rather than to the cultural heritage of Jesus. It is not likely that Mencken had a Biblical allusion in mind, and, if he did, it would be difficult to identify. Of the fifty instances of *mock*, *mocking*, etc. in the King James Version, twenty-nine are from the Old Testament and those in the New Testament are by no means restricted to Jews, e.g. Matthew 20:17 "[The chief priests will] deliver him to the Gentiles to be mocked and scourged and crucified. . . ."

[22] Mencken *SI*, p. 434.   [23] McDavid *AL* (1963), p. 261.

TABLE 33.3: TERMS FOR RELIGIOUS GROUPS

	Jew	Catholic	Protestant
1.	kike, Hebrew	Roman, papist	—
2.	kike, Hebrew, sheeny	—	hard-shelled Baptist
3.	yiddisher, Shylock	—	—
4.	kike	—	—
5.	kike, sheeny, yid	—	Bible-Belter
6.	Jew-bastard, fucking-Jew, son-of-a-bitching-Jew	bead-puller, statue-lover, statue-wor-shipper	—
7.	kike	—	—
8.	dirty sheeny	—	—
9.	Hebrew, Hebe, kike, sheeny	—	—
10.	yit, sheeny, Hebe, kike	Turk, cross-back	revivalist
11.	sheeny, kike, mocky	cross-back, Roman	lefthander
12.	kike, Hebe, Christ-killer	bead-puller, Turk, cross-back	—
13.	yiddish	—	—
14.	kike, sheeny, dirty Jew, mocky	bastard Catholic, lousy Catholic, dirty Catholic	bastard Protestant, lousy Protestant, dirty Protestant
15.	Hebe	—	—
16.	Jew, kike	—	—
17.	sheeny, kike	one of the Pope's boys	anti-Catholic
18.	kike, yid, Hebe, mocky	papist, guppy-gobbler	bigoted Protestant
19.	kike, sheeny	—	Bible-back
20.	kike, schlemihl	—	crackpot
21.	kike, kodger	papist	—
22.	sheeny, yid, Christ-killer, Jewboy	—	—
23.	kike	—	—
24.	sheeny, shonicker, Christ-killer, Jew-bastard, cut-cock	—	—
25.	dirty Jew	—	—
26.	kike	—	—
27.	—	—	holy-roller
28.	kike, shyster, Hebe, son of Israel	—	—
29.	kike	—	—
30.	—	—	—
31.	Israele, koshiator	—	—

pejoratives is *kike*, which McDavid observes "is most commonly derived from the *-ki, -ky* ending of the surnames of many Slavic Jews, who first came to the United States in large numbers toward the end of the Nineteenth Century."[24] The remaining terms are relics from the recent past, viz. *cut-cock*, which had significance before the AMA recognized the hygienic value of circumcision, and *Christ-killer*, which had significance before the Ecumenical Congress

[24] *Ibid.*, p. 378.

decided to vindicate the Jews after almost two thousand years of folk and formal imputations.

Although *kike* was given twenty-seven times, only Irish Catholics (#17, 18, 19, 20, and 21) were in full agreement. Five of seven WASP's and three of four German Protestants also had that form. *Kike* was elicited from only one of four Jewish informants (#23), the youngest of that social group. Among Catholic and Protestant informants under age 30, two (#7 and 26) gave only *kike*, another (#16) gave *Jew* and *kike*, and the two without *kike* have broadly different backgrounds from the others: #15 is a Polish Catholic nurse with an excellent high-school education, and #31 is a Negro truck driver with an excellent elementary-school education.

Other terms with more than a single occurrence are *sheeny*, *Hebrew*, *Hebe*, and *yid*. Of these, *sheeny* is the most common. Given by all four German Protestants, this form is represented in the speech of all significant groups except the Negro, who has no instances of the term. *Hebrew* and *Hebe* were found among all social groups except the Jews themselves, but the Caucasian and Negro informants who use these terms have rather close similarities in both neighborhood and education. Six of seven live in neighborhoods ranked A to C, i.e. upper to upper middle class, and all of these have their origins in lower middle- or lower-class communities (#1, 2, 9, 12, 15, 18, and 27). Although none has completed more than secondary education, five are ranked Education Type 4. Among better-educated informants, *yid*, *yit*, *yiddisher*, and *yiddish* have wider currency. All four instances of *yid* and *yit* are from informants aged 45–56 (#5, 10, 18, and 22) of Education Types 1 and 4. Similarly, the single instances of *yiddisher* and *yiddish* are from #3 and #14, slightly older than the members of the aforementioned group, but of Education Types 1 and 4, respectively.[25]

The Catholic is identified by multiple responses of *papist*, *cross-back*, *Turk*, and *Roman*, and by single responses of *statue-lover*, *statue-worshipper*, *bastard Catholic*, *lousy Catholic*, *dirty Catholic*, *one of the Pope's boys*, and *guppy-gobbler*. All three instances of *cross-back* were elicited from Protestant informants (#10, 11, and 12), all of whom are closely similar in age, education, and ancestry.[26] Further, all grew up on the North Side of Chicago and remember the expression from childhood.[27] Two of three instances of *papist* are in the speech of middle-aged Irish Catholics (#18 and 21); whereas, *Roman* is found only among Protestants (#1 and 11), as are *bead-puller* and the single occurrences of *statue-lover* and *statue-worshipper*. Although *Turk* has been identified with the argot

[25] All instances of *yid*, *yit*, *yiddish*, and *yiddisher* were used without much malice and, usually, quite playfully. *Hebrew* and *Hebe*, conversely, were articulated with the kinds of paralinguistic and kinesic exaggeration one might expect in a Southern rustic's imitation of "network" pronunciation of *Negro*, i.e. /nígrô/ for the more comfortable /nígrə/.

[26] Informants #10 and 12 are husband and wife. Informants #10 and 11 attended the same high school but never met.

[27] Although the *OED* has one citation for *cross-back* (1611), it seems inadequate to bring it through three centuries with an expanded meaning from *crusader* to *Catholic*.

of the Roman Catholic clergy,[28] it was used in this survey only by #11 and 12, the two most improbable candidates for the Knights of Columbus in the full roster of informants. The remaining five entries—*lousy Catholic, bastard Catholic, dirty Catholic, one of the Pope's boys*, and *guppy-gobbler*—were offered by Catholics. The first three were recollected by a Czech (#14) with reference to interdenominational name-calling, rather than for hypocrites of the faith. The final two were given playfully by Irishmen (#17 and 18).[29]

As with terms for the Caucasian majority, this predominantly Protestant group of informants was hard put to recall many abusive terms for non-Catholic Christians. Of the twelve terms collected here, seven were provided by Catholics, but most of these referred either to the more energetic Protestant sects—*holy roller, Bible-belter* (i.e. an ingrown resident of the Bible Belt), *revivalist, hardshelled Baptist*, and *crackpot* (specifically, a Fundamentalist)—or to characteristics which are frequently applied to members of any imaginable social group, viz. *lousy Protestant, bastard Protestant*, and *dirty Protestant*. More specific epithets include *bigoted Protestant* (#18), *Bible-back* (#19), and *anti-Catholic* (#17), all of which were given by Irish Catholics. The only generic term received from a Protestant (#11) is *lefthander*, which is, perhaps, the best in the collection.[30]

The nine nationality groups included in Table 33.4 have preserved their traditional ghettos—most of which are near the core of the city;[31] in addition to these concentrations, second- and third-generation descendants of immigrants have developed middle-class communities to the south, north, and west—within and beyond the city limits.[32] This establishment of new territory is reflected in the complexity of the terms for nationality groups in Chicago. Besides maintaining abusive names for their old neighbors, these people have now coined in-group designations to distinguish among members of the same heritage.

[28] It may be no coincidence that Negro informants had no pejoratives for members of that church which had pioneered in race relations in Chicago long before it became fashionable.

[29] "Turk is used among Roman Catholic priests in the United States to designate a colleague of Irish birth: it is assumed that every such immigrant has a special talent for ecclesiastical politics, and hence gets on in the church" (Mencken *SI*, p. 603).

[30] After giving considerable attention to both Jews and Catholics, Informant #6 shrugged off the request for parallel terms for Protestants with, "Oh, they're all right."

[31] Scandinavians, Germans, and Czechs have been dislodged from the center of the city as the Negro ghetto extends its boundaries. The Polish community, described in some of the best works of Nelson Algren, are similarly threatened by Negroes, as well as Mexicans, Puerto Ricans, and Appalachian poor whites. Only the Irish of St. Gabriel's Parish, directly east of the Stock Yards, have managed to alter the course of "Dawson's Glacier," as Joseph C. Diggles calls it. The Lithuanians in nearby St. George parish now share territory with Mexicans and Puerto Ricans.

[32] In addition to the Irish, Polish, Lithuanian, and German Jewish neighborhoods on the South Side and the German, Scandinavian, Polish, Italian, and German–Slavic Jewish neighborhoods on the North Side, many of the communities of the inner suburban ring preserve distinct ethnic characteristics, e.g. Melrose Park (Italian), Cicero (Bohemian), and Skokie (German–Slavic Jewish).

This tendency to mark social levels within a nationality group with nick-names is best seen here among the Irish. The most commonplace of these is the distinction between *shanty-* and *lace-curtain Irish*,[33] i.e. those who remain in the lower-class communities near the center of the city (or, irrespective of residency, preserve the social traits of the shanty Irish) and those who move into lower middle-class communities and work hard to approximate the ideals of vulgar respectability. Three of five Irish informants (#17, 20, and 21) made this distinction, as did one well-educated WASP (#5), who regarded both as literary, and one truck-driving WASP (#6), who agreed with the three South-Side Irish. *Shanty Irish* occurred six more times in the speech of members of widely different social groups (#2, 8, 16, 19, 24, and 28), but there were no additional instances of *lace-curtain Irish*. The variant pronunciation /šɔnti iriš/ by one young WASP (#7) is mentioned earlier in note 2.

In addition to the old recessive forms *terrier* and *greenhorn*, Irish informants use *turkey* and *saltwater turkey* to designate a recent immigrant and *narrowback* for a second-generation Irishman who has neither the need, the desire, nor the physical equipment to do the work his father had to do.[34]

Among non-Irish informants, the more commonplace terms prevail, which include shortened forms of given names *Mick* and *Paddy* and reference to the stereotype, viz. *tough Irish, dirty Irish*,[35] and *chaw-mouth*, the latter of which refers to the Irishman's talkativeness and parallels the more common *flannel-mouth*.[36] *Drunken Irish*, which is perhaps the most widely known of all these, was offered by only one informant (#20), who is Irish herself.

The most popular terms for Germans have been carried over from World War I, viz. *hun, heinie, kraut, krauthead, Dutchman*, and *Dutch bastard*. Other expressions, *Prussian, Nazi*, and *Iroquois of Europe*, are more specific epithets for the German and his military aggressiveness.

---

[33] Mencken mentions only *shanty Irish*, and this is with reference to the title of Jim Tully's book (*AL*, p. 151). Both terms appear in *The Young Manhood of Studs Lonigan*, "Here's Shanty Irish Lonigan" (p. 295); "The Irish made a shanty Irishman out of Christ" (p. 334). Earlier, at Lucy Scanlan's house, Studs observes, "They were all trying to put on the dog, show that they were lace-curtain Irish, and lived in steam-heat" (p. 284).

[34] Although Irish informants interpret the designation as a reference to the linguistic peculiarities of recent emigrants from the Old Sod, e.g. "they sound like turkeys," more than half a century ago W. A. McLaughlin suggested, "May not *Turk*, Irish, be simply the Gaelic word *torc* in disguise? The pejorative *pig* has been long in many tongues the supreme but inadequate expression of absolute disgust, anger and disdain, and *torc* signifies, among other things, boar, pig" ("Some Current Substitutes for Irish," *Dialect Notes* IV, No. 2 (1914), 146–148, in Mencken, *SI*, p. 603). In *Young Lonigan*, Studs adds to McArdle's summary of Barney's genealogy, "And the Irish part is pig-Irish" (p. 154). In *The Young Manhood of Studs Lonigan*, Barney Keefe thus salutes Studs, "Lonigan, you pig-in-the-parlor mick!" (p. 148).

[35] E.g. the old parody of "The Wearin' of the Green": "The dirty, dirty Irishmen, they never wash their clothes 'cause there ain't no Chinese laundry where the River Shannon flows."

[36] Mencken *SI*, p. 602. Also, *The Young Manhood of Studs Lonigan*, "Keefe, you drunken flannel-mouth" (p. 148); "He's another one of these flannel-mouth Irish who thinks he's society stuff" (p. 291).

TABLE 33.4: TERMS FOR NATIONALITY GROUPS

	Irish	German	Scandinavian	Polish	Czechoslovak	Lithuanian	Italian	Mexican	Puerto Rican
1.	—	—	—	polack	—	—	wop	greaser	—
2.	tough Irish, shanty Irish	—	dumb Swede	—	—	—	wop, dago	—	—
3.	—	krauthead	Swede	—	—	—	—	—	—
4.	dirty Irish, mick	heinie, hun	Swede	bohunk	bohunk	—	—	—	—
5.	mick, shanty Irish, lace-curtain Irish	—	—	—	—	—	wop, dago	—	—
6.	shanty Irish, lace-curtain Irish	—	herring-choker	polack	—	—	dago, wop, hoodlum, gangster	spick, greaser, wetback, halfbreed, wetback, spick, greaseball	spick, greaser, wetback, halfbreed, wetback, spick, greaseball
7.	shawnty Irish-man	—	—	polack	—	—	wino	—	—
8.	shanty Irish, mick	Dutchman, hun	—	polack	czezski, butchski	—	—	—	—
9.	—	—	—	—	—	—	—	—	—
10.	—	kraut, hun	herring-choker	polack	bohunk	lugen	dago, wop	wetback	wetback
11.	saltwater, turkey, mick, chaw-mouth	heinie, kraut, hun, Dutchman	scoop	polack, yak, dyno, Stashu	bohunk, mushroom-picker	lugen	dago, wop, ginny	—	spick
12.	mick	Dutchman, heinie, krauthead	Swede, dumbsocks, Norski	polack	bohunk	—	dago, wop	spick	spick

	Irish	German	Scandinavian	Polish	Bohemian/Czech	Lithuanian	Italian		
13.	—	krauthead	—	polack	bohunk, bohak	—	ginny, dago	—	—
14.	Paddy	—	—	polack, dyno	lousy Czech	lugen	dago	—	—
15.	—	kraut	—	polack	—	—	wop	spick	spick
16.	shanty Irish	—	—	polack	bohunk	—	ginny, wop	wetback	spick
17.	turkey, terrier, lace-curtain Irish, shanty Irish, green-horn, narrow-back	heinie, krauthead	Scandie	Pole	bohak	lugen, Lit	dago	greaseball	—
18.	—	kraut, hun, Iroquois of Europe	Scandie, Swenska, herring destroyer	polack	bohunk	lugen	gin, greaseball, Siciliano, wop, dago	spick	spick
19.	shanty Irish, saltwater turkey, narrowback	hun, heinie, Dutchman, Prussian	—	—	—	—	dago, wop, walliyo, Siciliano, pizon	spick	spick, nigger
20.	shanty Irish, lace-curtain Irish, mick, drunken Irish, turkey	hun, Dutchman	Swede	polack	bohunk	lugen	dago, ginny	spick	spick
21.	mick, narrow-back, shanty Irish, lace-curtain Irish	kraut, bull-headed Dutchman, stubborn German	Swede	polack	bohunk	lugen	dago	spick	spick
22.	—	kraut, heinie, hun	—	Pole, polack	bohunk	—	dago		—

	Irish	German	Scandinavian	Polish	Czechoslovak	Lithuanian	Italian	Mexican	Puerto Rican
23.	—	kraut	—	polack	—	—	wop dago, spaghetti-eater	spick greaser	spick greaser
24.	Irish bastard, shanty Irish	krauthead, Dutch bastard	Scandi-huvian	polack, psecrev	—	—		—	—
25.	—	—	—	—	—	—	—	—	—
26.	shamrock, nigger turned inside out	—	—	poski	Czech, bohak	bohawk	wop, spaghetti-bender, Sicilian	—	speck P.R.
27.	mickey	Dutch	—	—	—	—	dago	—	—
28.	shanty Irish	heinie, Nazi, krauthead	—	polack	bohunk	lugen	wop	wetback	—
29.	—	Dutchman	—	—	—	—	—	—	—
30.	—	—	—	—	—	—	wop, ginny, dago	mick	—
31.	mick	kraut	—	polack	—	—	dago	wetback, spick	wetback, spick

Five of sixteen responses for Scandinavian were *Swede*. *Dumb Swede* and *dumb-socks*[37] were also applied to all Scandinavians, as were *scoop*, *Scandihuvian*, and *Scandie*. *Herring-choker*, *herring destroyer*, and *Norski* were restricted to Norwegians, and the anglicized *Swenska* (from *Svenska*), for Swedes.[38]

Unlike those inexpressive terms for Germanic nationality groups, more fully developed sets of pejoratives were gathered for Poles and Czechs, who are more recent arrivals and more distantly removed from the WASP subculture than are either the Germans or Scandinavians. Of all the abusives collected in this survey, the nineteen instances of *polack* were exceeded only by *nigger*.[39] Apart from *Pole* and a single occurrence of *bohunk*, the remaining terms are from the language of the Polish immigrants themselves. These are *dyno* and *yak*, both of which designate a recent immigrant, *psecrew* /pš-kə̀rɔ́v/ "dog-blood," *Poski* (from *Polski*), and *Stashu* "Stanley."[40] Of these, only *dyno* was elicited more than once (#11 and 15), both informants having extensive business and social contacts within the Polish subculture.

Terms for Czechoslovakian[41] include ten responses of *bohunk*, four of *bohak* /bóhák/, and single instances of *czezski*, *butchski*, *mushroom-picker*, *Czech*, and *lousy Czech*. *Bohunk* was elicited most frequently from members of those groups who are in close geographical proximity with the Bohemian communities, i.e. the Irish (#16, 18, and 21), Poles and Czechs themselves (#13 and 22), and those who work within the Bohemian subculture (#11 and 28). *Bohak* was given three times, twice by informants over age sixty (#13 and 17) and once by a young Mexican–Puerto-Rican (#26), the latter instance of which parallels the preservation of relic pronunciations among the lower social classes. Both of the very old forms *czezski* (or *chesky*) and *butchsky*[42] were offered by an

---

[37] In *Young Lonigan* the term *dumbsocks* is applied to Andy LeGere, a boy of French ancestry, p. 178.

[38] It must be remembered that the interviewer was a North Germanic type; better results might have been realized here by another fieldworker.

[39] Although neither this nor any of the other terms can be assigned properly as explicit references to the Polish–American stereotype, *polack* is used frequently to designate people and characteristics of the central European peasantry, e.g. "He talks like a polack" means he makes such phonemic substitutions as alveolar (or dental) stops for tip-dental fricatives, or "He dresses like a polack" means he does not dress tastefully. This is extended to descriptive modifiers, e.g. *polacky* furniture. These same characteristics are also attributed to Bohemians by the folk anthropologists.

[40] Polish exchange student, Mrs. Dorota Czarkowska-Starzecka, suggests that *dyno* /daínò/ is from the Polish form *daj-no* "give" (imperative, second person singular) and *yak* /yak/ from *jak sie masz* "how are you." Nelson Algren has an instance of the former in the speech of Frankie Majcinek (i.e. Dealer or Frankie Machine): "He's been shakin' down the greenhorns in here fourteen years. Someday he'll shake down the wrong dino" (*The Man with the Golden Arm* (New York, 1949), p. 20). Mencken has *dino* for Italian in *SI*, p. 606, but this, I believe, is a shortened form of Constantine and is pronounced dínò/, as it commonly is among Greek–Americans as a given name.

[41] No distinction was made by the interviewer or the informants to distinguish Bohemians (western Czechs) from other emigrants from that region. Indeed the term *Bohemian* was avoided by the interviewer to avoid confusing a nationality group with the forerunners of the Beatniks.

[42] These are explained by Mencken in *SI*, p. 602.

old German who remembered using those terms in her youth on the West Side of Chicago, where many poor European nationality groups begrudgingly shared territory. Although *mushroom-picker* was given only once, Czech informant #14 told of the recreational activities of first-generation Bohemians who combined picnicking with mushroom-gathering.[43]

One of the best indications of the linguistic-cultural relationships in these terms is seen in the pejoratives for the Lithuanian. All ten instances of *lugen* /lúgǝn/, *Lit*, and *bohawk* /bóhǝk/ are in the speech of Chicagoans with social or business contacts in the Lithuanian communities of the South Side.[44] *Lugen* is by far the most common, but this term is recorded by neither Mencken, Mathews, nor McDavid because its usage is quite specialized, even in Chicago.[45] Eight of the nine informants with names for Lithuanians, however, had *lugen*, with one Irishman offering *Lit* as an alternate, and the young Mexican–Puerto-Rican had only *bohawk*.

Thirty-eight of fifty pejorative responses for Italian are included in three forms, *dago* /dégò/, *wop* /wap/, and *ginny* /gíni/. Apart from *Siciliano* /šišǐlyánò/, which was given only twice, all other terms were unique within the survey; the latter include *gin* /gɪn/, *greaseball*, *wallio* /wálǐyò/, *pizon* /paízán/, *spaghetti-eater*, *spaghetti-bender*, *Sicilian*, *hoodlum*, *gangster*, and *wino* /wáɪnò/. Two of these are loans from Italian, *wallio* and *pizon*.[46] Three others refer to the Italian stereotype, *hoodlum*, *gangster*, and *Sicilian*, as do *spaghetti-eater* and *spaghetti-bender*. All of these are probably fairly widespread; *wino*, however, is used in a special sense here. It is a commonplace term in Chicago speech for a Madison Street or Clark Street drunken derelict (or an alcoholic, irrespective of social class), but I have never before heard it used to signify one who likes wine, i.e. likes wine even when stronger potables are available. This might suggest the young WASP (#7) either mixed her vague notion of the stereotype Italian with a word she had heard but does not use or that this is indeed a fresh usage. In Chicago *greaseball* is more commonly applied to Mexicans, Puerto Ricans, and, somewhat

---

[43] The ability of the Czech to laugh at himself is seen in the in-group designation "Bohemian matched luggage," i.e. two Sears–Roebuck shopping bags.

[44] The etymology of *lugen* could not be explained by any of the informants who used it or by any of the Lithuanians or Balto–Slavicists I have since consulted.

[45] All Chicago WASP informants were asked about the term *lugen*, but it is virtually unknown in their well-insulated subculture.

[46] My colleague Lawrence C. Mantini tells me that *wallio* is from the Tuscan dialect /wályò/. This is from *guaglione*, which means "boy" and has come to mean "someone clever or cunning." On the streets of Chicago, however, it is a mildly abusive term for Italian: ". . . we kep' right on goin' that way till we was doin' guys we never seen before even, Wallios 'n Greeks 'n a Flip from Clark Street. . . ." (Nelson Algren, "A Bottle of Milk for Mother," *Short Story Masterpieces*, eds. Robert Penn Warren and Albert Erskine (New York, 1954), p. 38, first published in *Neon Wilderness* (New York, 1941).

Paisan-o is "peasant, countryman, fellow countryman" in Italian. This is quite understandably extended to mean "friend" within the urban ghetto; thus, Nick and Grant address each other as *pizon* in Willard Mottley's Chicago novel *Knock on Any Door* (New York, 1947). The term connotes something closer to *dago* in the language of the street.

less frequently, to Greeks,[47] than it is to Italians. All of these terms are, however, without index value because they seem rather evenly distributed among all age, education, neighborhood, and ethnic groups.

Mexicans are called *spick* (nine times), *wetback* (four times), *greaser* (three times), *greaseball* (twice), and *halfbreed* (once). All of these designations are applied to Puerto Ricans as well. The only term which might distinguish a Mexican from a Puerto Rican is *mick*, used by a young Gary Negro (#30) who had no terms of abuse for the Irish. Terms used exclusively for Puerto Rican include *speck* and *P.R.* One informant (#11) gave *nigger* as an alternate designation for Puerto Rican.[48]

In four of six instances, *wetback* was applied to both Mexicans and Puerto Ricans; the two exceptions were offered by #16 and 28, both of whom restricted the term to Mexicans. Ten informants gave *spick* for both Mexicans and Puerto Ricans; two others (#11 and 16) used it to designate Puerto Ricans only, and #11 had no term at all for Mexicans.

In the collection of these terms, several important problems emerged, and all of these must be met if investigators intend to provide information that is sociologically useful and statistically meaningful in reflecting cultural and linguistic change. These problems concern the sample, the field instrument, and the interview. Ideally, these could be solved with a random sample, a powerful instrument, and a complete record of the segmental, paralinguistic, kinesic, and haptic systems,[49] none of which is within the grasp of the linguist today. An operational program, however, is within reach, and this should be planned with careful attention to the lessons learned over the past ninety years of European and American dialect investigation.

Systematic samples can be constructed within clearly defined social organizations, e.g. Negroes on the rosters of the Urban League and local county welfare departments will differ greatly in class, education, and regional dialect, as will Caucasians, however more subtly (from the WASP point-of-view), in various kinds of public and private schools or on the membership lists of country clubs. Religious and nationality groups are easily studied within parishes, presbyteries, and congregations. A multi-level investigation might include three generations, and such a sample could begin with a roster from either a kindergarten or a home for the aged. If the investigator limits himself to a specific problem and

[47] Greeks are called *grikola*, perhaps from schoolboy Latin *agricola*, and *asshole bandit*, probably with reference to the folklore of Hellenic culture.

[48] Informant #26, a Mexican–Puerto-Rican, spoke of himself as "probably a Negro," when asked to identify his race. Having none of the physical features usually associated with the American Negro, he seemed to have been conditioned by the kind of name-calling described above.

[49] Haptics is that sub-system of nonlanguage communication which conveys meaning through physical contact. William M. Austin observes, "In one sense all nonlanguage communications (kinesics, haptics, as well as 'vocalization') are paralinguistic but this term [i.e. paralinguistic] is now almost exclusively applied to significant, non-linguistic noises made in the vocal tract" ("Some Social Aspects of Paralanguage," *The Canadian Journal of Linguistics*, XI, No. 1 (Fall 1965), 31).

does not try to gather too many kinds of data, he might easily interview several hundred informants.

The development of a basic field instrument will always require extensive preliminary investigation and numerous adjustments afterwards.[50] The questionnaire might include the conventional LAUSC method, some carefully controlled frames,[51] several conversation situations in which the range of stylistic variation can be covered,[52] and the impressionistic reactions of the maligned themselves.[53] Most important of all, anthropological linguists in America must develop better techniques for eliciting free conversation.

Although the camera is not yet a practical field-recording instrument, its absence must be filled by the interviewer. Crucial information was lost in Chicago because the record does not include the complete kinesic (as well as paralinguistic) phenomena. Primary consideration in psycholinguistic fieldwork must be given to those elements of the message which the tape recorder cannot transcribe.[54]

[50] E.g. the work of Hans Kurath and his associates to construct the work sheets for the New England survey extended over four years, 1929–32 (Hans Kurath et al., Handbook of the Linguistic Geography of New England (Washington, D.C., 1939), pp. 148–49).

[51] E.g. those included in Frederic G. Cassidy and Audrey R. Duckert, A Method for Collecting Dialect, PADS, No. 20 (1953).

[52] See Martin Joos, The Five Clocks, supplement to IJAL, XXVIII, No. 2 (1962), and Raven I. McDavid, Jr.'s review of the monograph in College English, XXV, No. 3 (1963), 233–34. See also William Labov's "Stages in the Acquisition of Standard English" to appear in Social Dialects and Language Learning, edited by Roger W. Shuy for the NCTE, 1965. [See p. 473 in this book.]

[53] Labov, op. cit.

[54] As Labov and others have demonstrated, the fieldworker must settle for nothing less than the very best machine his project can afford.

34

Some Structural Differences in the Speech of Chicago Negroes

THIS IS A PROGRESS REPORT on a particular phase of the current investigation of speech habits among culturally deprived Chicagoans. In describing some structural differences in the speech of indigenous and in-migrant Negroes, this summary is a development of the preliminary research done in early 1963.[1] The current survey makes use of a more detailed questionnaire, takes into consideration a wider range of sociolinguistic factors, and includes a more extensive analysis than did the preliminary work of 1963. More important, this summary relies upon information collected for a recently completed survey, *The Pronunciation of English in Metropolitan Chicago: Vowels and Consonants* (1964), particularly with regard to the phonemic system. The most important sources for the current project are the standard works of American linguistic geographers, the extensive research of urban sociologists,[2] and the splendid efforts of Chicago social workers.[3] This report summarizes (1) the fieldwork done during the spring and summer of 1964, (2) a non-technical sociolinguistic classification of informants, and (3) the distribution of selected phonological, morphological, and lexical features.

Reprinted by permission from *Social Dialects and Language Learning* (Roger W. Shuy, ed.). Champaign, Ill.: National Council of Teachers of English, 1964. Pp. 28–51. For the author see the preceding article.

[1] Some of the goals and preliminary findings of the Chicago Cognitive Environment Study are summarized in "Nonstandard Negro Speech in Chicago," *Nonstandard Speech and the Teaching of English* (Washington, D.C.: Center for Applied Linguistics, 1964), pp. 16–23.

[2] E.g. Wirth's *The Ghetto*, Drake and Cayton's *Black Metropolis*, and Frazier's *Black Bourgeoisie*.

[3] This report is especially indebted to the help of Mrs. Gertrud Porteus, a leader of the Woodlawn Project at the Episcopal Christ Church, Mrs. Wilhelmina Blanks, a supervisor at the Cook County Department of Public Aid, Mrs. Olivia W. Filerman, former director of research for the Chicago Urban League, Father John Cermak, parish priest at Our Lady of Lourdes, and Mr. John Hobgood, New Residents Representative for the City of Chicago's Commission on Human Relations.

TABLE 34.1: TABLE OF INFORMANTS

20-Year Residents of Chicago: Group I

No.	S^1	A^2	N^3	E^4	Place of Birth	Mother's POB	Father's POB	Occupation	Y^5	Type[6]
1.	M	39	69	BS	Lawrenceville, Virginia	Virginia	Virginia	Social Worker	20	A17
2.	M	31	68	BS	Chicago, Illinois	Arkansas (rural)	Louisiana (rural)	Social Worker	31	B30
3.	M	57	40	JD	Humboldt, Tennessee	Tennessee	Tennessee	Lawyer	21	C32
4.	F	31	42	BA	Omaha, Nebraska	Alabama	Alabama	Restaurant Manager	28	C33
5.	F	67	68	13	Little Rock, Arkansas	Unknown	Unknown	Minister	35	C33
6.	M	57	38	12	Harrisburg, Illinois	Illinois (rural)	Illinois (rural)	Electrician	40	D39
7.	M	60	39	10	Chicago, Illinois	Louisiana	Tennessee	Clerk	60	D41
8.	F	30	30	10	Chicago, Illinois	Louisiana	Kentucky	Clerk	30	D44
9.	M	55	67	12	Sherman, Texas	Oklahoma	Texas	Cook	28	D44
10.	M	31	44	12	Chicago, Illinois	Mississippi	Mississippi	Janitor	22	D44
11.	F	46	69	10	Charleston, Tennessee	Tennessee	Tennessee	Housewife	25	E47
12.	F	42	42	9	Chicago, Illinois	Louisiana	Louisiana	Housewife	42	E47
13.	F	42	68	10	Chicago, Illinois	Jamaica	Jamaica	Housewife	37	E49
14.	M	67	42	8	Atlanta, Georgia	Georgia	Georgia	Porter	44	F53
15.	F	27	42	10	Mississippi	Mississippi	Mississippi	Housewife	21	F54
16.	F	46	67	8	Marvell, Arkansas	Unknown	Unknown	Housewife	20	F54
17.	F	50	67	7	Marvell, Arkansas	Unknown	Unknown	Housewife	24	F55
18.	M	56	54	4	Memphis, Tennessee	Tennessee	Tennessee	Laborer	20	F56
19.	M	40	...	6	Tuscaloosa, Alabama	Alabama	Alabama	Laborer	23	F60
20.	M	47	39	9	Baton Rouge, Louisiana	Louisiana	Louisiana	Watchman	25	G61

Recent Arrivals: Group II

No.	S[1]	A[2]	N[3]	E[4]	Place of Birth	Mother's POB	Father's POB	Occupation	Y[5]	Type[6]
1.	F	48	73	BA	Jacksonville, Florida	Florida	Florida	Housewife	12	A21
2.	F	43	49	BA	Los Angeles, California	Dallas, Texas	Pittsburgh, Pa.	Housewife	11	B25
3.	M	32	35	BS	West, Mississippi	Mississippi	Mississippi	Social Worker	2	C35
4.	M	45	42	11	Memphis, Tennessee	Mississippi	Mississippi	Janitor	17	E52
5.	F	42	29	12	Marigold, Mississippi	Mississippi	Mississippi	Clerk	1	F56
6.	F	35	...	9	Hattiesburg, Mississippi	Mississippi	Mississippi	Housewife	1	F57
7.	F	35	42	10	Montgomery, Alabama	Alabama	Alabama	Housewife	4	F58
8.	F	36	42	10	Lexington, Mississippi	Mississippi	Mississippi	Waitress	8	F59
9.	F	45	40	5	LaGrange, Georgia	Georgia	Georgia	Housewife	7	G65
10.	F	27	42	7	Macon, Mississippi	Mississippi	Mississippi	Housewife	7	G65

[1] Sex.
[2] Age.
[3] Neighborhood Community.
[4] Education.
[5] Years in Chicago.
[6] Sociolinguistic Type.

1. *The Fieldwork: Questionnaire, Interviews, and Fieldworkers.* The question-naire used in this survey was compiled by the project coordinators—Raven I. McDavid, Jr., Alva Lee Davis, and William M. Austin. McDavid and Davis are the adapters of the Atlas short worksheets for the North Central states; Mr. and Mrs. McDavid have made a compilation of all U.S. Atlas worksheets, and Austin has done pioneer work in the area of paraphonology.

Including numbers, days of the week, months of the year, verb forms, and regionally and socially significant lexical items, most of the entries in the question-naire are taken from the worksheets of the Linguistic Atlas of the United States and Canada. Most of these are household words which combine to establish a rather full phonological inventory. When combined with para- and supra-segmental phonology, the grammatical and lexical variants lead to the compli-cated problems of grammar, usage, style, and para-language.

The interviews were conducted in the homes of the informants in order to put them more nearly at their ease and to give the fieldworker a better oppor-tunity to evaluate their socio-economic status. All interviews were recorded on tape, and no full phonetic transcriptions were made in the homes. This un-fortunate dependence upon the machine precluded a rigorously accurate analysis of the phonology, e.g. labial fricatives were not always distinguishable from tip dentals.

Fourteen of the thirty Negro records were collected by John Willis, a graduate student in anthropology at the University of Chicago. Willis, a Negro, did a good job in gaining the confidence of the informants and in stimulating the free conversation which, perhaps, is the most valuable data collected. His lack of experience in the field led him to the occasional mistake of neglecting an item because it was difficult to elicit.

The remaining sixteen records were collected by this writer. These inter-views include a more nearly complete coverage of questionnaire items, but the free conversation in these records is usually distinctly inferior in richness of forms to those collected by Willis. Another questionable procedure in this writer's interviewing was the attempt to elicit responses in tightly controlled frames. For example, in trying to elicit the preterit of *swim*, instead of asking what a person did in the water yesterday, a typical frame was "Today he swims in the lake; yesterday he ————." The only lexical variant gathered with this sterile technique was *didn't*.

2. *The Informants: A Nontechnical Sociolinguistic Classification.* The original plan included the selection of twenty Negro informants, ten residents of the city for twenty or more years and ten recent arrivals. These informants were to represent the middle and lower socio-economic classes. When the fieldwork was completed, thirty informants had been interviewed, ten of whom were recent arrivals.

Table 34.1: Informants. The problem of classifying informants must be met in order to indicate sociological distribution. Unsatisfactory classification of informants is one of the serious defects of social dialectology in this decade. The precedent set in the New England Atlas—a distinction of three basic types with two subclasses (old-fashioned and modern)—was satisfactory in the regional surveys of the 30s and 40s, but the sociological implications of Mrs. Yakira Frank's analysis of Guy Lowman's field records in New York (1949) and David DeCamp's study of San Francisco speech (1955) suggest the need for further classification.

A readily available scale for this kind of investigation appears in W. Lloyd Warner's *Social Class in America*, and this was used to classify informants in *The Pronunciation of English in Metropolitan Chicago*. Warner's scale was used in that survey as a complement to a primary classification according to educational types. This was simply an analysis of the tripartite division of the New England Atlas into ten groups in order to distinguish the extent of academic inoculation, a problem growing up with mass college education since World War II.

These scales of ranking were unsatisfactory for social dialectology for obvious reasons: the New England Atlas did not undertake an analysis of social class and Warner did not include linguistic problems in his analysis. A non-technical scale is used here—non-technical because it has not yet been tested and the weights are arbitrary, but it can be called a scale because the informants are arranged according to the available personal data.

The seven categories include those factors available in the personal data sheets: (1) place of birth and years in Chicago, (2) education, (3) occupation, (4) parents' place of birth, (5) parents' education, (6) parents' occupation, (7) neighborhood and housing. For example, two of these categories are thus weighted:

1		2
1. Chicago born		1. Graduate of Integrated College
2. North-East-Western born	(20 yrs)	2. Student at Integrated College
3. North-East-Western born	(10 yrs)	3. Graduate of Segregated College
4. North-East-Western born	(less)	4. Student at Segregated College
5. Midland born	(20 yrs)	5. Graduate of Integrated HS
6. Midland born	(10 yrs)	6. Student at Integrated HS
7. Midland born	(less)	7. Graduate of Segregated HS
8. Southern born	(20 yrs)	8. Student at Segregated HS
9. Southern born	(10 yrs)	9. Elementary School Graduate
10. Southern born	(less)	10. Elementary School Student

Following this scale, Informant #I-1 has a total of 17 points; POB (5 of 10); Ed (3 of 10); O (1 of 10); PPOB (4 of 5); PEd (1 of 10); PO (1 of 10); H (1 of 10). Informant I-3, conversely, having attended the John Marshall Law School, has a better educational rank and as many years in Chicago, but, because his parents were not educated in integrated colleges and were not professionals and because he practices law, almost exclusively, within the Negro community, his total was 35.

The A to G classifications are established from these totals:

A   7 to 23   Highest sociolinguistic group
B   24 to 30   High sociolinguistic group
C   31 to 37   High-Mid sociolinguistic group
D   39 to 46   Mid sociolinguistic group
E   47 to 52   Low-Mid sociolinguistic group
F   53 to 60   Low sociolinguistic group
G   61 to 65   Lowest sociolinguistic group

This classification, then, provides a method for arranging the data in the present report and suggests the criteria to be included later in a statistically valid classification.

3. *Distribution.* The phonological and morphological features considered here include those which, in previous investigation in Chicago, showed a clear pattern of distribution on the basis of race, education, age, or socio-economic type and those which are regionally or socially distributed in the North, Midlands, and South. Neither syntactic structures nor suprasegmental phonemic patterns are included here because the most interesting evidence is in the free conversation, and those sections of the tape have not yet been thoroughly examined.

In Tables 34.2–10, the symbols *x* and *X* are used to indicate forms of the dominant Chicago dialect, i.e. of native Caucasians, ages thirty-five to fifty-five, of the middle socio-economic classes; the symbols *o*, *ϕ*, O are used to indicate forms which are not typical in the speech of that Caucasian group. Distribution based separately on age, region, or sex is not always given here because these factors too often overlap with criteria used to establish sociolinguistic types. For example, nine of ten recent arrivals are between ages twenty-seven and forty-five, six of these are of Mississippi ancestry, and eight of these ten are female.

Table 34.2: Tautosyllabic /r/ after Stressed Vowels. Three variants of the /ə/ + /r/ phonemes are distinguished here. These are (1) the constricted allophones [ɚ, ɝ], (2) the weakly constricted allophones [ə, ɜ], and (3) the unconstricted allophones [ɜ, ə]. A necessary distinction omitted from the table, and the preliminary analysis, is the loss of the nonsyllabic /ə/ after low-back vowels /ɔ, ɒ/ in *four* and *fourth*.

Table 34.2 shows a distinction between rounded and unrounded vowels because rounding versus unrounding seems to affect distribution. A much higher incidence of the unconstricted allophone occurs before rounded stressed vowels in the speech of members of all regional, social, and age groups. Among members of Group I, Types A–C, only two informants (I-3 and I-5) have a high incidence (i.e. more than half the occurrences) of the weak or unconstricted phone before unrounded vowels. Both informants are over age fifty-five and neither is closely associated with the Caucasian community. The single excep-

TABLE 34.2: TAUTOSYLLABIC /r/ AFTER STRESSED VOWELS

x is [ɚ, ɝ]
φ is [ə, ɜ]
o is [ə, ɜ]
– is *no response*

	Unrounded Vowels						Rounded Vowels					
A.	*beard* /i∼ɪ/						G.	*four* /o∼ɔ/				
B.	*careless* /ɛ∼æ/						H.	*fourth* /o∼ɔ/				
C.	*chair* /ɛ∼æ/						J.	*morning* (in *good morning*) /o∼ɔ/				
D.	*thirteen* /ə/						K.	*mourning* /o∼ɔ/				
E.	*furniture* /ə/						L.	*horse* /o∼ɔ/				
F.	*Birmingham* /ə/						M.	*hoarse* /o∼ɔ/				

No.	A.	B.	C.	D.	E.	F.	G.	H.	J.	K.	L.	M.
1.	x	x	x	x	x	x	x	o	x	φ	x	x
2.	x	x	φ	x	x	φ	o	o	φ	o	o	o
3.	φ	φ	o	φ	o	o	o	o	o	–	φ	o
4.	x	x	x	x	o	x	x	x	x	o	x	x
5.	o	o	φ	x	φ	–	φ	o	x	o	x	o
6.	x	x	x	x	x	x	x	x	o	o	x	x
7.	x	o	x	x	o	x	x	o	o	o	o	o
8.	x	x	x	x	o	φ	x	x	x	o	x	x
9.	x	φ	x	x	φ	x	x	o	x	x	x	o
10.	x	x	x	x	x	φ	o	o	o	o	o	o
11.	x	x	x	x	x	x	x	o	x	x	x	x
12.	x	φ	φ	–	φ	φ	φ	o	φ	o	o	o
13.	x	x	x	o	x	x	o	o	φ	x	o	x
14.	x	x	o	x	x	x	φ	φ	o	o	x	φ
15.	x	o	o	φ	o	φ	o	o	o	o	–	o
16.	o	x	x	φ	o	x	o	o	o	o	o	φ
17.	x	o	o	φ	o	x	o	o	o	o	o	o
18.	x	o	φ	φ	φ	φ	o	o	o	o	φ	o
19.	x	o	x	–	o	x	–	–	o	–	o	φ
20.	x	o	x	o	o	x	o	o	o	–	o	o
1.	φ	φ	x	–	x	x	o	o	o	x	o	o
2.	x	x	x	x	x	x	x	x	x	o	o	x
3.	φ	φ	x	φ	x	o	o	o	o	o	φ	o
4.	x	x	x	x	x	x	x	x	x	–	x	x
5.	x	o	x	φ	x	x	o	o	o	o	o	o
6.	φ	φ	o	x	φ	x	o	o	o	o	φ	φ
7.	φ	o	φ	x	φ	x	o	o	o	o	o	o
8.	o	o	o	o	φ	o	o	φ	o	o	o	x
9.	o	o	o	φ	o	o	o	φ	x	o	o	o
10.	o	–	o	o	–	φ	o	o	o	–	o	o

tion among Group II, Types A–C, is a young social worker who has been in Chicago only two years. All members of Type D have lived in Chicago twenty years or more and none of these has a high frequency of this recessive feature. Twelve of seventeen typed E–G, however, favor the recessive feature; these include seven of ten members of Group II. From Group I all three exceptions

TABLE 34.3: PHONES OF THE FIRST MEMBER OF /aɪ/ DIPHTHONG

x   is   [ɑ, ɑ., ɑ̃, ɑ̃.]
ϕ   is   [ɑ<, ɑ<., ɑ̃<, ɑ̃<., a>, a>., ã>, ã>.]
o   is   [a, a., aa, ã, ã.]
*   is   *an alternate phoneme*

A. *five*
B. *nine*
C. *twice*
D. *dining* (in *dining room*)
E. *China* (*dishes* or the *Peoples Republic*)
F. *spider* (in *spider web*)

G. *wife*
H. *right* (in *right ear*)
J. *tired*
K. *climbed*
L. *might*

No.	A.	B.	C.	D.	E.	F.	G.	H.	J.	K.	L.	
1.	x	x	x	x	ϕ	x	x	x	x	x	x	
2.	x	x	x	ϕ	ϕ	x	x	x	x	x	x	
3.	ϕ	ϕ	ϕ	x	ϕ	x	x	x	x	x	x	
4.	o	x	x	ϕ	ϕ	ϕ	ϕ	x	x	–	ϕ	
5.	ϕ	x	x	–	–	x	x	x	x	x	–	
6.	o	ϕ	ϕ	–	ϕ	ϕ	ϕ	ϕ	–	ϕ	ϕ	
7.	ϕ	x	x	–	x	ϕ	x	x	x	ϕ	x	
8.	x	x	x	x	ϕ	x	x	x	x	x	x	
9.	o	ϕ	o	ϕ	o	ϕ	x	ϕ	x	ϕ	x	
10.	o	ϕ	ϕ	ϕ	ϕ	ϕ	ϕ	*	ϕ	ϕ	x	* is /a/ in /rat/
11.	ϕ	ϕ	ϕ	ϕ	o	ϕ	ϕ	–	ϕ	ϕ	ϕ	
12.	o	o	ϕ	–	ϕ	ϕ	ϕ	ϕ	ϕ	ϕ	ϕ	
13.	x	x	x	x	x	ϕ	x	x	–	x	x	
14.	o	o	o	–	o	o	ϕ	ϕ	ϕ	*	ϕ	* is /ə/ in /kləm/
15.	ϕ	ϕ	–	x	x	x	x	x	x	*	–	* is /æ/ in /klæm/
16.	o	o	o	ϕ	o	ϕ	o	o	o	*	o	* is /æ/ in /klæm/
17.	o	ϕ	o	x	ϕ	o	o	o	o	*	o	* is /æ/ in /klæm/
18.	o	o	ϕ	ϕ	o	ϕ	ϕ	–	ϕ	o	ϕ	
19.	–	–	o	–	ϕ	ϕ	ϕ	ϕ	ϕ	ϕ	ϕ	
20.	ϕ	o	ϕ	–	o	ϕ	ϕ	ϕ	ϕ	–	ϕ	
1.	ϕ	x	ϕ	x	ϕ	x	–	x	x	x	x	
2.	ϕ	ϕ	x	ϕ	x	ϕ	ϕ	x	x	–	–	
3.	ϕ	ϕ	x	ϕ	o	ϕ	ϕ	x	x	x	x	
4.	ϕ	ϕ	ϕ	ϕ	x	ϕ	x	ϕ	x	x	x	
5.	o	ϕ	ϕ	ϕ	o	o	o	o	ϕ	o	–	
6.	ϕ	ϕ	ϕ	ϕ	ϕ	x	x	ϕ	ϕ	ϕ	ϕ	
7.	ϕ	ϕ	ϕ	–	o	ϕ	ϕ	ϕ	ϕ	x	ϕ	
8.	o	ϕ	ϕ	ϕ	ϕ	x	ϕ	ϕ	ϕ	o	ϕ	
9.	ϕ	ϕ	ϕ	x	x	x	ϕ	x	x	*	ϕ	* is /a/ in /klam/
10.	ϕ	ϕ	–	ϕ	ϕ	ϕ	ϕ	ϕ	x	ϕ	–	

are within six sociolinguistic points of Type D (I-11, I-13, I-14); from Group II, both exceptions are within nine points of Type D (II-4, II-5).

Before rounded vowels, the recessive feature has a high frequency occurrence in the speech of five members of Group I (I-2, I-3, I-5, I-7, and I-10). Eight of ten members of Group II favor the recessive feature. The exceptions again are the highly ranked II-2 and II-4.

TABLE 34.4: PHONES OF /ə/ INCLUDING ALTERNATE /ɛ/ AND SIMULTANEOUS /ər/

A. *shut* (in *shut the door*)
B. *brush* (noun)
C. *touch* (in *don't touch*)
D. *onions* (stressed vowel)
E. *husband* (stressed vowel)
F. *son*

G. *judge* (noun)
H. *pus*
J. *nothing* (response to *what's new?*)
K. *something* (response to *nothing*)
L. *hundred* (stressed vowel)
M. *once* (in *at once*)

No.	A.	B.	C.	D.	E.	F.	G.	H.	J.	K.	L.	M.
1.	Λ	Λ	Λ	Λ	Λ	Λ	ə>	Λ	Λ	Λ	Λ̃	Λ̃
2.	Λ<	Λ	–	Λ^γ	Λ^γ	Λ^γ	ə	γ	Λ	Λ	Λ	Λ
3.	Λ	ə<	Λ^I	Λ^γ	Λ^I	Λ^I	Λ^γ	Λ_<ᶜ	–	Λᶜ	Λ^I	Λ^I
4.	ə	ə	Λ	Λ	Λ^γ	Λ	Λ	Λ	Λ	Λ	Λ	Λ
5.	Λ	Λ^ə	Λ^γ	Λ	Λ^γ	Λ	Λ^γ	Λ^γ	Λ	Λ	ʁ	Λ
6.	ε>ə	ε<ᶜ	ə^ə	Λ^γ	–	Λ^ə	ε>ə	–	Λ<ᵊ	Λ<ᵊ	Λ<	Λ^ə
7.	ə	Λ	ə	Λ^I	Λ^I	Λ^I	Λ^I	Λ^I	ə	ə	Λ	Λ
8.	Λ	Λ	Λ	Λ	Λ̃	–	Λ	Λ	Λ	Λ	Λ	Λ̃
9.	Λᶜ	εᶜ	ə^ᶜ	Λ<ᶜ	Λ^γ	Λᶜ	ə	Λ^γ	Λᶜ	Λ^ə	Λᶜ	Λ̃^I
10.	Λ	ε>ə	Λ^ə	Λ^γ	Λ^ε	–	ε>	Λ>	Λ^ε	Λ^ε	Λ	Λ^ε
11.	–	ə̕>	Λ^ə	Λ̃^ə	Λ^ə	Λ^ə	Λ^γ	Λ^γ	–	Λ^ə	Λ̃	Λ^γ
12.	Λ.	ə	Λ<	Λ	Λ	Λ	Λ	Λ	Λ	Λ	Λ<	Λ
13.	Λ	Λ	Λ	Λ	ə^Λ_<	Λ	Λ	ə^Λ_<	Λ	Λ	Λ	Λ
14.	ə	Λ^γ	Λ	Λ^γ	Λ	Λ	ə<	ə	Λ	–	Λ	Λ^ə
15.	Λ	Λ<	–	Λ	Λ^γ	Λ	Λ^γ	Λ^γ	Λ^γ	Λ	Λ	–
16.	ε	ə̓	Λ^γ	Λ^γ	Λ^γ	Λ^γ	ə̕>	Λ^γ	Λ^γ	Λ	Λ̃	Λ̃
17.	ε	ε>	Λ^ə	Λ^γ	Λ^γ	Λ^γ	ə̕>	Λ^γ	Λ	Λ	Λ̃	Λ̃^>_V
18.	Λ^ə	ə̓	Λ^Λ	Λ^γ	Λ^γ	Λ^γ	–	Λ^ə	–	Λᶜ	Λ^γ	Λ^ə
19.	Λ^ε	ə<	Λ_<^Λ	Λ_<^Λ	Λ_<^Λ	Λ_<^Λ	ə<	Λ_<^Λ	–	–	–	–
20.	ε	ə	ə	Λ^γ	ə^I	Λ^γ	ə̕>	Λ	Λ	Λ	Λ	Λ^ə
1.	Λᶜ	Λᶜ	Λᶜ	Λ^γ	–	Λ^γ	Λ^I	Λ^γ	Λᶜ	Λᶜ	Λ	Λ^ə
2.	Λ^ə	ə>	Λ^ə	Λ^ə	Λ^ə	Λ^ə	ə>	Λ^γ	Λ^ə	Λ	Λ	Λ^Λə
3.	Λ	Λ	Λ	Λ^γ	Λ^γ	Λ	Λᶜ	Λ<	Λ	Λ	Λ	Λ>
4.	Λ^ə<	Λ<	ə^Λ	Λ_>^γ	ə	Λ^ə	Λ^γ	Λ^ə	–	Λ	Λ^ə	Λ^γ
5.	ə<	Λ	Λ	Λ̃^γ	Λ	Λᶜ	Λ^ə	Λ^γ	Λ	Λ	Λ	Λᶜ
6.	Λ	Λ^Λ	ə_>^Λ	ə_>^Λ	ə_>^Λ	ə_>^Λ	ə_>^Λ	ə_>^Λ	ə	ə	Λ^ə	Λᶜ
7.	Λ	ə̓ᶜ	Λ^γ	Λ	Λ^γ	ə	Λ^γ	Λ	Λᶜ	Λ	Λ	Λ̃
8.	Uᵥ^ə	Λ^ə	ə	Λ<	Λ^ə	ʁ^ə	Λ^U	Λ	Λ^ə	–	Λ^ə	Λ.^ə
9.	Λᶜ	ε	Λ_<^Λ	V^ᶜ	Λ^ə	Λ̃^ᶜ	ə	Λᶜ	Λᶜ	Λᶜ	Λ	Λᶜ
10.	ə̓ᶜ	ə̓ᶜ	Λ^I	Λ̃<	Λ	Λ<	Λ<·	–	Λ	Λ	Λə	–

[The Symbol ᶜ in this table represents a superior "barred i," Eds.]

Table 34.3: Initial Member of the /ai/ Diphthong. Seventeen allophones occur as initial members of the upgliding diphthong. These are distinguished by position (front to mid), by duration (unlengthened to extremely lengthened), and nasalization (strong nasalization versus weak or no nasalization). These allophones are classified in Table 34.3 only on the basis of position, i.e. the low-mid vowels typical of Chicago Caucasian speech, the fronted low-mid vowels or retracted low front vowels, and the low front vowels.

Both fronted variants, marked *o* and *ø* in the table, occur most frequently among lower ranked types (E–G). Of the twenty informants ranked E–G, only two have a preponderance of the low-mid vowel; both of these speakers, I-13 and I-15, received their full formal education in Chicago. Distribution by type is as follows:

Type			
A	17 of 21	4 of 21	0 of 21
B	13 of 20	7 of 20	0 of 20
C	23 of 40	15 of 40	2 of 40
D	21 of 51	25 of 51	5 of 51
E	14 of 41	24 of 41	3 of 41
F	11 of 97	52 of 97	34 of 97
G	6 of 28	20 of 28	2 of 28

Table 34.4: Phones of /ə/. The raw phonetic material is given in Table 34.4 because x's and o's would certainly obliterate the distinctiveness of these features. Several kinds of analysis are necessary: (1) monophthongs versus diphthongs, (2) fronted versus non-fronted elements irrespective of environments, (3) fronted-centralized versus backed irrespective of environment, and (4) fronted versus centralized versus backed irrespective of environment.

A preliminary analysis of these phones reveals one certain feature of distribution. The incidence of mid-central monophthongs in Caucasian speech in the city is clearly dominant. Among the Negroes interviewed in the summer of 1964, only four have no occurrences of the diphthongs. All four of these are of Group I (20-year residents of the city), and three of these are natives of the city.

An equally certain feature is the distinctiveness of the diphthong, especially with a fronted or retracted initial member. However insignificant from a phonemic standpoint, this is an unmistakably foreign sound to native Chicago Caucasians and is one of the features mentioned by informant I-1, who talked for some time about the Chicago Negro and his "Southern accent."

Table 34.5: Consonant Loss. Eighteen consonant phonemes are charted here. Each of these is lost in the speech of some informant, and none of these is usually lost in Caucasian speech except among very old or uneducated members of low socio-economic groups. These consonants were classified first as stops, fricatives, and sonorants, second as voiced or voiceless consonants, and third as phonemes occurring in syllable initial, medial, or final position. Two composite types of phonemes have social significance here. These are certain phonemes which include phonic members characterized as voicing and stoppage of the air stream and which occur in syllable initial position. The /d/ phoneme in *hundred*, the /b/ phoneme in *umbrella*, and the /d/ phoneme in *candles*, and the /d/ (alternating with /t/) phoneme of *vegetables*, all occurring in the second syllable are retained by all members of Group I, Types A–D, with two exceptions. Both of these informants, I-5 and I-6, are over age fifty-five and neither is a native of Chicago. Similar incidence is the loss of the syllable initial sonorants of /h/ in *forehead*

TABLE 34.5: CONSONANT LOSS

x is consonant retained
o is consonant lost
φ is alternate consonant (/t/ in *ninth* /naɪnt/)

A. /l/ in *help* /hɛlp/
B. /t d/ in *vegetables* /vɛjtəbəlz/
C. /h/ in *forehead* /forhɛd/
D. /d t/ in *hundred* /həndrɪd/
E. /d/ in *good* (*morning* /gʊd mɔrnɪŋ/
F. /b/ in *umbrella* /əmbrɛlə/
G. /b/ in *tube* /tub/
H. /t/ in *chest* /čɛst/
J. /t/ in *left-overs* /lɛft ovərz/

K. /θ/ in *fifth* /fɪfθ/
L. /θ/ in *ninth* /naɪnθ/
M. /t/ in *joints* /jɔɪnts/
N. /g/ in *bag* /bæg/
O. /j/ in *yeast* /jist/
P. /t/ in *yeast* /jist/
Q. /t/ in *caught* (*a*) *cold* /kɔt kold/
R. /d/ in *candles* /kændəlz/
S. /w/ in *Louisiana* /luwiziænə/

No.	A.	B.	C.	D.	E.	F.	G.	H.	J.	K.	L.	M.	N.	O.	P.	Q.	R.	S.
1.	x	x	x	x	x	x	x	x	x	x	x	x	x	x	x	x	x	x
2.	x	x	x	x	x	x	x	o	x	x	x	x	x	x	x	x	x	x
3.	–	x	x	x	x	x	x	x	o	o	x	x	o	x	o	o	x	o
4.	x	x	x	x	o	x	o	o	x	x	x	x	x	x	x	x	x	x
5.	–	o	x	x	x	x	x	o	–	o	o	x	x	o	x	–	o	o
6.	–	x	x	x	x	x	o	o	x	x	φ	o	o	o	x	–	x	o
7.	x	x	x	x	x	x	o	o	o	o	x	o	o	x	x	–	x	o
8.	x	x	–	x	x	x	x	x	x	x	x	x	x	o	x	–	x	o
9.	x	x	o	o	x	x	x	x	o	o	x	x	o	x	o	o	x	x
10.	–	x	x	x	x	x	x	o	o	o	x	x	o	x	o	o	x	x
11.	x	–	x	x	x	o	x	o	–	o	x	o	x	x	x	o	x	x
12.	x	x	x	x	o	o	x	x	x	o	o	x	o	o	x	x	o	o
13.	o	x	x	x	x	x	o	x	x	o	o	x	x	x	o	o	x	o
14.	–	x	x	x	o	x	o	x	–	x	x	o	x	o	x	–	o	o
15.	x	x	x	x	x	x	o	o	o	x	x	x	o	o	o	–	o	o
16.	o	x	x	o	x	o	x	o	x	o	x	–	x	o	o	o	x	o
17.	–	o	x	x	x	o	x	o	o	o	o	x	o	o	x	o	o	o
18.	–	o	o	o	x	x	x	x	o	o	x	x	o	x	x	o	o	o
19.	o	x	x	–	x	o	x	o	o	–	–	o	o	o	x	o	o	o
20.	o	o	o	o	x	o	x	o	o	o	φ	x	x	o	x	–	o	o
1.	x	x	o	x	x	x	o	o	o	o	–	x	–	x	x	–	x	o
2.	x	x	x	x	x	x	x	x	o	o	o	–	x	x	x	o	o	x
3.	x	x	x	x	x	x	–	x	–	x	x	–	o	x	x	o	o	–
4.	o	x	x	x	x	x	x	x	o	o	o	o	x	o	x	o	o	o
5.	o	o	x	x	x	x	x	o	o	o	x	o	x	o	x	o	o	o
6.	–	–	x	x	o	x	x	o	o	o	x	x	o	x	o	x	x	o
7.	–	x	x	x	x	x	x	o	x	o	x	x	x	x	x	x	o	o
8.	o	x	x	x	x	x	x	o	o	o	x	x	o	x	x	o	o	o
9.	o	o	x	x	x	x	o	x	o	o	o	x	x	o	o	o	–	o
10.	o	o	o	x	x	o	o	o	–	–	o	o	o	o	o	o	x	o

TABLE 34.6: INCIDENCE OF CONSONANT PHONEMES

A. *February*   x is /b/   o is /v/   * is consonant loss
B. *February*   x is /ru~rʊ/   o is /ju~jʊ/   * is consonant loss /ə/
C. *grease*   x is /s/   o is /z/
D. *greasy*   x is /s/   o is /z/
E. *this (year*   x is /ð/   o is /d/
F. *this (way*   x is /ð/   o is /d/
G. *wash) the (dishes*   x is /ð/   o is /d/   * is consonant loss
H. *with (milk*   x is /ð~θ/   o is /f/   φ is /d/
J. *without (milk*   x is /ð~θ/   o is /f/   φ is /d/
K. *mouth*   x is /θ/   o is /f/
L. *fourth*   x is /θ/   o is /f/
M. *rinses*   x is /s/   o is /š/
N. *chimney*   x is /n/   o is /l/
O. *Birmingham*   x is /m/   o is /n/   (/bermɪŋhæm/ vs. /bərnɪŋhæm/)

No.	A.	B.	C.	D.	E.	F.	G.	H.	J.	K.	L.	M.	N.	O.
1.	x	o	x	x	x	x	x	x	x	x	x	x	x	x
2.	x	x	x	x	x	o	x	x	x	x	x	o	x	x
3.	x	o	x	o	x	*	x	x	x	x	x	x	x	x
4.	x	o	o	x	x	o	x	x	x	x	x	x	o	x
5.	o	*	o	o	x	*	−	x	x	x	x	o	o	−
6.	x	x	x	x	x	*	−	x	x	x	o	o	o	x
7.	x	o	x	o	x	o	x	x	x	x	x	x	x	x
8.	x	*	o	o	x	o	o	x	φ	x	o	o	o	o
9.	x	o	x	x	x	−	x	x	x	x	x	x	x	x
10.	*	o	o	o	x	*	−	x	x	o	x	o	o	x
11.	x	*	o	o	x	−	x	x	x	x	x	o	o	x
12.	x	o	o	o	x	*	x	x	x	x	x	x	o	o
13.	x	x	x	x	x	*	o	x	x	x	x	o	o	x
14.	x	*	o	o	x	o	−	x	x	o	x	x	o	x
15.	x	*	x	−	x	−	−	−	−	x	x	x	x	x
16.	o	*	o	o	x	*	−	x	φ	o	x	o	o	x
17.	x	o	o	o	x	−	x	x	x	x	x	o	o	o
18.	o	o	x	o	x	−	x	x	x	x	x	o	o	x
19.	x	o	o	o	x	−	o	x	x	x	x	x	x	o
20.	o	*	x	o	x	o	x	o	o	x	o	x	o	o
1.	x	o	o	x	x	x	x	x	x	x	x	x	x	x
2.	x	*	o	x	x	−	x	x	x	x	x	x	o	x
3.	−	−	x	o	x	o	x	φ	x	x	x	−	o	x
4.	x	o	x	o	x	−	x	x	x	x	x	x	o	x
5.	x	o	o	o	x	x	x	x	x	x	x	x	x	x
6.	x	o	x	o	x	o	−	x	x	x	x	x	x	x
7.	o	*	o	o	x	−	x	x	x	x	x	x	o	x
8.	x	*	x	x	x	−	x	x	x	o	o	x	o	x
9.	x	*	x	o	x	x	x	o	o	−	o	o	o	o
10.	o	o	o	x	o	−	o	−	φ	x	o	o	x	o

TABLE 34.7: SYSTEMATIC ALTERNATION OF STRESSED VOWELS

A. *dairy*   x is /ɛ/   o is /æ/   φ is /ə/
B. *married*   x is /ɛ/   o is /æ/   φ is /ə/
C. *kerosene*   x is /ɛ/   o is /æ/   φ is /ə/
D. *parents*   x is /ɛ/   o is /æ/
E. *hoarse*   x is /ɔ/   o is /o/
F. *mourning*   x is /ɔ/   o is /o/
G. *tomorrow*   x is /a/   o is /ɔ/
H. *borrow*   x is /a/   o is /ɔ/
J. *palm*   x is /a/   o is /ɔ/   φ is /æ/
K. *wash* (noun)   x is /ɔ/   o is /a/
L. *wash* (verb)   x is /ɔ/   o is /a/
M. *water* (noun) x is /ɔ/   o is /a/
N. *faucet*   x is /ɔ/   o is /a/   φ is /aʊ/
O. *laundry*   x is /ɔ/   o is /a/   φ is /aʊ/
P. *haunted*   x is /ɔ/   o is /a/   φ is /aʊ/   O is /æ/

No.	A.	B.	C.	D.	E.	F.	G.	H.	J.	K.	L.	M.	N.	O.	P.
1.	x	o	x	o	o	o	o	o	x	x	x	x	x	x	x
2.	o	o	φ	o	o	x	o	x	x	x	x	x	o	x	o
3.	φ	o	–	o	o	–	o	o	x	x	x	x	x	o	φ
4.	x	o	x	o	o	o	x	x	x	x	x	o	x	x	x
5.	–	o	o	x	o	o	x	x	x	x	x	x	o	o	–
6.	x	o	x	o	x	o	x	x	x	x	x	x	o	x	o
7.	x	o	x	x	x	x	x	o	o	x	x	x	x	x	o
8.	x	o	x	o	x	o	x	x	x	x	o	x	o	o	o
9.	x	o	x	x	x	o	x	o	x	–	x	x	x	x	o
10.	x	o	–	x	o	x	x	x	x	o	o	–	φ	o	φ
11.	x	x	x	o	o	x	x	x	x	x	x	x	x	o	o
12.	x	–	o	o	x	o	x	x	x	o	x	x	x	o	o
13.	x	x	x	o	x	x	o	o	x	x	x	x	o	o	o
14.	x	φ	x	o	x	o	–	x	x	x	x	x	–	x	x
15.	o	o	–	x	o	o	x	x	x	x	x	x	o	o	–
16.	x	o	x	o	o	o	x	x	x	o	o	x	o	x	o
17.	o	–	–	o	o	o	x	x	φ	x	x	o	–	o	x
18.	x	–	x	o	o	o	o	o	x	x	x	x	o	o	o
19.	x	o	o	–	o	–	x	o	o	o	o	x	–	o	x
20.	–	o	–	o	o	–	x	o	x	o	o	x	φ	o	O

No.	A.	B.	C.	D.	E.	F.	G.	H.	J.	K.	L.	M.	N.	O.	P.
1.	x	o	x	x	x	o	x	x	x	x	x	x	x	o	o
2.	x	x	–	x	x	x	x	o	x	x	x	o	o	o	o
3.	o	o	x	o	o	o	x	o	x	x	o	x	o	φ	x
4.	φ	o	x	o	x	o	o	o	x	x	o	–	x	o	φ
5.	x	o	x	o	o	o	x	x	x	o	o	x	o	o	o
6.	x	–	o	o	o	o	x	o	x	o	o	–	o	o	x
7.	o	o	φ	o	o	o	x	x	x	x	o	o	o	o	x
8.	x	o	x	–	o	o	x	x	x	o	o	o	o	x	o
9.	φ	o	–	o	o	x	x	x	φ	o	o	x	o	o	O
10.	o	o	o	o	o	–	x	o	φ	o	x	x	o	o	–

TABLE 34.8: NON-SYSTEMATIC ALTERNATION OF VOWELS

A. *deaf*   x is /ε/   o is /i/   ø is both
B. *rather*   x is /æ/   o is /ə/   ø is /ε/
C. *aunt*   x is /æ/   o is /a/   ø is both
D. *shut*   x is /ə/   o is /ε/   ø is /ʊ/
E. *brush* (noun) x is /ə/   o is /ε/
F. *soot*   x is /ʊ/   o is /ə/
G. *roof*   x is /ʊ/   o is /u/
H. *window*   (2nd syllable)   x is /o/   o is /ə/
J. *widow*   (2nd syllable)   x is /o/   o is /ə/
K. *yellow*   (2nd syllable)   x is /o/   o is /ə/   ø is /u/
L. *tomorrow* (3rd syllable)   x is /o/   o is /ə/   ø is /u/
M. *tomato*   (3rd syllable)   x is /o/   o is /ə/   ø is /ɪ/
N. *Saturday* (2nd syllable)   x is /ə/   o is /ɪ/
O. *genuine* (3rd syllable)   x is /ɪ∼ə/   o is /aɪ/

	Stressed Vowels							*Weakly Stressed Vowels*						
No.	A.	B.	C.	D.	E.	F.	G.	H.	J.	K.	L.	M.	N.	O.
1.	x	ø	o	x	x	x	x	x	x	x	x	o	o	x
2.	x	x	o	x	x	x	x	x	x	x	x	x	x	o
3.	x	x	o	x	x	x	x	o	x	o	ø	x	o	x
4.	ø	x	o	x	x	x	x	x	x	x	x	x	x	o
5.	x	x	o	x	x	x	x	-	x	o	o	o	x	-
6.	x	x	o	o	o	x	x	x	x	o	x	o	x	o
7.	o	x	o	x	x	x	x	-	x	o	x	x	o	x
8.	x	ø	o	x	x	x	x	x	x	x	x	x	x	o
9.	x	-	o	x	o	x	x	x	o	-	o	x	o	o
10.	o	o	ø	o	o	o	x	o	-	o	o	o	x	x
11.	x	x	x	-	x	x	-	x	o	o	x	ø	o	o
12.	x	ø	o	x	x	o	x	x	x	o	x	o	x	o
13.	x	x	o	x	x	o	x	x	x	x	x	x	x	x
14.	x	ø	o	x	x	x	x	x	o	x	-	o	o	o
15.	x	-	o	x	x	o	x	x	x	o	x	o	o	-
16.	x	o	o	o	x	o	-	-	o	ø	o	o	o	x
17.	x	o	o	o	o	o	o	o	o	o	o	o	x	x
18.	o	o	x	x	x	o	o	o	x	o	o	o	x	o
19.	x	o	x	x	x	o	x	o	x	o	o	o	x	o
20.	o	o	o	o	x	o	o	o	x	o	x	o	o	x
1.	x	-	o	x	x	x	x	x	x	x	x	x	x	x
2.	x	x	o	x	x	o	x	x	x	x	x	x	x	x
3.	x	x	x	x	x	o	x	x	x	o	x	x	x	x
4.	ø	-	o	x	x	x	x	x	x	o	x	ø	x	o
5.	x	x	o	o	x	o	x	x	x	o	o	o	x	o
6.	x	o	x	x	x	x	o	x	o	o	o	o	o	x
7.	x	x	o	x	o	o	x	x	x	o	o	o	o	o
8.	x	x	o	ø	x	o	x	o	o	o	o	o	o	x
9.	ø	o	o	x	o	o	o	o	o	o	o	-	x	o
10.	o	-	x	o	o	o	o	o	o	o	o	o	o	-

TABLE 34.9: LEXICAL DIFFERENCES

A. x is *faucet* (at the sink)   o is *hydrant, pipe,* or *spigot*
B. x is *kerosene*   o is *coal oil* ϕ is both
C. x is *yolk* (of the egg)   o is *yellow* (of the egg)
D. x is *cobweb* (indoors)   o is *spiderweb* (indoors)
E. x is *chest* (of a man)   o is *breast* (of a man)
F. x is *got sick, got ill,*   o is *took sick* or ϕ is *came ill*
     or *was sick*   *took ill*
G. x is *stamp* (on the floor)   o is *stomp*
H. x is *bulge*   o is *stand out, stick out,* or *buffle out*
J. x is *afraid*   o is *scared* ϕ is *afeared* or *ascared*
K. x is *aunt*   o is *aunty* ϕ is both

No.	A.	B.	C.	D.	E.	F.	G.	H.	J.	K.
1.	x	x	x	o	x	x	o	x	x	x
2.	x	x	x	x	x	x	o	x	x	x
3.	x	o	x	x	x	o	o	x	o	x
4.	x	x	x	x	x	x	o	x	o	x
5.	x	ϕ	o	o	o	–	x	x	x	x
6.	x	ϕ	x	x	x	ϕ	o	x	o	x
7.	x	x	o	x	x	–	o	x	o	ϕ
8.	o	x	o	x	x	o	o	x	o	x
9.	x	ϕ	–	x	x	o	o	x	o	x
10.	x	o	o	o	o	x	x	x	o	x
11.	x	ϕ	o	x	x	o	o	x	o	x
12.	x	x	x	x	x	x	o	x	x	ϕ
13.	x	ϕ	x	o	x	o	x	x	o	x
14.	o	x	o	o	o	–	o	x	o	x
15.	x	–	x	o	x	x	o	o	x	o
16.	x	x	x	x	x	x	o	x	o	x
17.	o	o	–	o	x	x	o	o	o	x
18.	x	ϕ	o	x	x	x	o	x	o	ϕ
19.	o	ϕ	o	o	o	o	o	o	o	x
20.	o	o	o	o	o	o	x	o	x	o
1.	x	x	x	x	x	x	x	x	o	ϕ
2.	x	o	x	x	x	o	o	x	o	x
3.	x	x	x	o	x	x	o	x	x	x
4.	x	ϕ	x	x	x	–	o	x	ϕ	x
5.	x	ϕ	x	x	x	o	o	x	x	x
6.	x	o	x	x	x	o	o	x	o	x
7.	x	ϕ	x	x	x	x	x	x	x	x
8.	x	ϕ	o	x	x	–	o	–	o	x
9.	x	o	x	o	o	–	o	o	o	x
10.	x	ϕ	o	o	o	x	o	o	o	o

TABLE 34.10: VERB FORMS

Past Tense
A. *drive*   x is *drove*   o is *drive*   φ is *driv*   O is *drived*
B. *sit*   x is *sat*   o is *sit*   φ is *set*
C. *swim*   x is *swam*   o is *swim*   φ is *swum*   O is *swimmed*
D. *begin* x is *began*   o is *begin*   φ is *begun*
E. *dive*   x is *dived*   X is *dove*   o is *dive*   O is *divd*
F. *kneel* x is *kneeled*   X is *knelt*   o is *kneel*
G. *climb* x is *climbed*   o is *climb*   φ is *clum*
H. *eat*   x is *ate*   o is *eat*

Past Participle
J. *drown* x is *drowned*   o is *drow*   O is *drownded*
K. *bite*   x is *bitten*   φ is *bit*
L. *eat*   x is *eaten*   o is *eat*   φ is *ate*   O is *et*
M. *write* x is *written*   φ is *wrote*   O is *wrotten*
N. *drink* x is *drunk*   X is *drank*   o is *drink*   φ is *drinken*   O is *drinkt*
O. *do*   x is *done*   φ is *did*

No.	A.	B.	C.	D.	E.	F.	G.	H.	J.	K.	L.	M.	N.	O.
1.	x	x	x	x	x	X	x	x	x	x	x	x	X	x
2.	x	x	x	x	x	X	x	x	x	φ	x	x	X	x
3.	–	x	–	–	o	–	–	x	O	φ	x	x	–	–
4.	φ	x	φ	φ	X	X	–	x	x	x	x	o	O	–
5.	x	φ	x	x	–	X	x	x	o	φ	φ	o	X	φ
6.	x	φ	x	–	x	x	x	–	x	φ	–	o	–	φ
7.	x	x	φ	x	X	x	o	–	O	x	–	φ	X	φ
8.	x	x	o	x	X	x	x	x	O	x	x	φ	x	x
9.	x	x	x	x	X	–	o	x	x	φ	x	x	–	–
10.	x	x	x	x	x	x	x	–	x	φ	–	φ	O	–
11.	x	–	x	o	X	x	–	x	o	x	x	φ	o	φ
12.	x	φ	φ	x	o	x	x	x	O	φ	x	φ	φ	x
13.	x	x	x	–	x	x	–	–	x	x	φ	x	o	–
14.	x	φ	o	x	X	X	φ	x	O	φ	φ	x	X	φ
15.	x	φ	o	φ	–	–	o	–	O	φ	φ	–	O	–
16.	x	φ	o	x	–	o	o	o	O	φ	O	φ	o	φ
17.	x	φ	o	–	o	X	–	–	O	φ	o	φ	O	φ
18.	x	φ	o	–	o	X	–	–	O	φ	x	x	φ	φ
19.	o	φ	o	x	x	x	o	–	O	–	–	φ	o	φ
20.	x	φ	o	o	o	x	–	x	O	φ	φ	φ	O	–
1.	–	φ	x	x	X	X	x	x	x	x	–	x	–	–
2.	–	–	x	x	x	x	–	x	x	x	–	x	–	–
3.	x	x	x	x	X	X	x	x	x	x	x	x	O	x
4.	x	o	O	x	x	X	x	x	x	x	φ	x	–	φ
5.	x	x	x	x	x	X	o	x	x	x	x	x	X	x
6.	x	–	x	–	O	o	x	x	–	φ	–	x	o	–
7.	x	φ	o	φ	X	–	x	x	O	x	x	x	o	x
8.	x	φ	o	x	x	x	x	x	o	x	–	–	o	φ
9.	o	o	O	–	o	x	o	x	O	φ	φ	O	–	–
10.	x	x	o	o	x	o	o	o	o	φ	o	φ	x	φ

and /j/ in *yeast*. Three members of Group I, Types A–D, lose these consonants, and, like I-5 and I-6, informant I-9 is also over age fifty-five and a non-native Chicagoan. Among other forms in this table, the incidence is as expected. Members of Groups I and II of lower sociolinguistic types have a higher frequency of consonant loss than do the higher ranked informants.

It should be noted in passing that item *S* in this table, the /w/ of *Louisiana*, is obviously a syllable loss, but since there is no chart to illustrate that phenomenon, the feature is included in this table. The incidence of the four syllable utterance is quite atypical of Chicago Caucasian speech.

Table 34.6: Incidence of Consonant Phonemes. Four groups of consonant phonemes are classified in this table, the occurrence of the voiced spirant in *grease* and *greasy*, the alternation of the dental stop with the dental fricative in *this year*, *this way*, and *wash the dishes*, the alternation of the labio-dental fricative with the interdental fricative in *with, without, mouth,* and *fourth,* and the incidence of relic and assimilated forms in *rinses, chimney,* and *Birmingham,* i.e. /rɪnčɪz/, /čɪmli/, and /bərnɪŋhæm/.

The first pair reveals the same peculiar distributional pattern found earlier, i.e. a higher incidence of /z/ among native Chicago Negroes than among any Midland or most Southern-born immigrants. Here, indeed, seems the first clear feature of the Upsouth Negro dialect. The distribution in the 1963 analysis showed:

Chicago born Negroes	24 /z/ and 3 /s/
Midland born Negroes	5 /z/ and 5 /s/
Southern born Negroes	20 /z/ and 10 /s/

The current investigation shows:

Chicago born Negroes having	7 /z/ and 5 /s/
Midland born Negroes having	10 /z/ and 8 /s/
Southern born Negroes having	14 /z/ and 11 /s/

The factor to be considered here is that all informants were to be over age thirty in the current survey. In the previous investigations, high school age native Negroes were interviewed, and this powerfully influential group showed seventeen instances of /z/ to seven for /s/.

The incidence of dental stops for interdental fricatives appears much less frequently in the table than either Mark Twain or the script writers of Amos and Andy would have us believe. On the other hand, it must be remembered that questionnaire responses are perhaps more careful than free conversation, where there seems to be a higher frequency in the tapes. Almost every informant typed E–G has at least one occurrence of dental stop for dental fricative.

The fourth group of forms, M, N, O, in the table, have their highest frequency among older informants of all types and, to a somewhat lesser extent, among lower sociolinguistic types. This combination of factors, older age and lower sociolinguistic type, accounts for the higher frequency of these recessive forms among members of Group I. Eleven members of that group have at least two of three instances, and nine of these are over age forty; seven of eleven, however, are Types E–G. Both informants under age forty are of Type D, the bottom of the non-low section, with forty-four points. Both members of Group II with two or more occurrences of these forms are Type G with the maximum total of sixty-five sociolinguistic points.

Table 34.7: Systematic Alternation of Stressed Vowels. The incidence of vowels charted in this table are of three types: (1) those alternating /ɛ~æ/ before heterosyllabic /r/, items A–D, (2) those alternating /ɔ~o/ before tautosyllabic /r/, items E–F, (3) those alternating /ɑ~ɔ/ through the development of Middle English vowels, items G–P.

All fifteen of these items have sociolinguistic importance in their distribution among Chicago Area Caucasians. If we compare the Caucasian distribution with the incidence of these vowels among representative types from both races, we see some interesting similarities and differences. Furthermore, we find evidence to support the contention that investigative technique must be flexible and suited to the situation.

For example, /æ/ in items A–D in Caucasian speech occurs most frequently in the speech of informants under twenty-one, especially those of the highest socio-economic class. It is found to a lesser extent among informants twenty-one to forty-five, especially those particularly sensitive to "preferred" forms, and among those over age fifty with bicultural or bilingual ties.

The phonemic distribution of /ɔ~o/ in items E–F is a recessive feature in Caucasian speech in northeastern Illinois with the highest incidence shared by well educated urban and suburban informants and old rural informants living in the out-counties.

The incidence of /ɔ/ instead of /ɑ/ in items G–H is most frequent among the lowest socio-economic types of all urban and suburban age groups and equally consistent among the rural residents irrespective of class.

The occurrence of /ɑ/ for the usual /ɔ/ in items J–P is a distinctive feature of the speech of low socially classed urban Caucasians.

Finally the diphthong /au/ was not recorded in items N, O, P in Caucasian speech.

Items A–F are most effectively analyzed on the basis of regional dialects. The recessive features in *dairy, married, kerosene, parents, hoarse,* and *mourning* are also found in local Caucasian speech but, as reported in *The Pronunciation of English in Metropolitan Chicago* (1964), the highest incidence of those recessive features was found among Negroes, irrespective of social class. These recessive features, marked *o* in Table 34.7, are to be regarded, tentatively, as vestiges of Midland and Southern dialects.

Items G–J, when restricted to a large number of Negro speakers, demonstrate a pattern of distribution which parallels the incidence among Chicago Caucasians: the more highly educated informants have the unrounded allophones of /a/ in *tomorrow, borrow,* and *palm.*

In items K–L the development of Middle English /wa/ shows its neatest pattern of distribution in the pronunciation of *wash* (the verb or the noun), where the unrounded vowel /a/ occurs only in the speech of the lowest ranked members of Group I (I-10, 16, 19, and 20). Among the recent arrivals (Group II), ten to twelve instances of /a/ in *wash* occur in the speech of informants ranked F–G. No informant ranked A or B in either group has a single instance of this recessive form.

The development of the Middle English diphthong /aʊ/ shows the following social distribution of recessive features in *faucet, laundry,* and *haunted*:

Group I Types A–D 16 of 29 instances of /a/ or /aʊ/ instead of /ɔ/
            Types E–G 19 of 26 instances of /a/ or /aʊ/ instead of /ɔ/
Group II Types A–D 7 of 9 instances of /a/ or /aʊ/ instead of /ɔ/
            Types E–G 17 of 21 instances of /a/ or /aʊ/ instead of /ɔ/

Among native Chicago Negroes (all Group I):

Types A–D under age 40 8 of 9 instances of /a/ or /aʊ/ instead of /ɔ/
            over age 40 1 of 3 instances of /a/ or /aʊ/ instead of /ɔ/
Types E–G under age 40 4 of 6 instances of /a/ or /aʊ/ instead of /ɔ/

These figures again emphasize the spread of Caucasian recessive features, especially among the younger Chicago-born Negroes.

It is probably coincidental, but perhaps culturally explainable that all six instances of the /aʊ/ diphthong in N, O, P occur in the speech of male informants (I-3, I-10, I-20 and II-3, II-4) because most of these relate to female duties (the *dishes* and the *washing*).

Table 34.8: Nonsystematic Alternation of Vowels. The vowels in this table are distinguished as stressed and weakly stressed because the distributions within each set are somewhat different.

Among the stressed vowels, the occurrence of /i/ in *deaf*, /dif/, agrees with the observation of Kurath and McDavid concerning this alternation in the Atlantic states: incidence of the recessive form is highest among the lower social classes but the feature is also found among natives of the deep South and South Midland area:

I-4, I-7, and I-10 have parents from those areas.
I-18 and I-20 are ranked F and K.
II-4, II-9, II-10 are all natives of the deep South.

In Caucasian Chicago speech this form occurs only among members of the lowest socio-economic groups.

The incidence of the /ʌ/ phoneme in *rather*, /rʌðər/, occurs in seven of eight instances among members typed F–G, five of whom are of Group I. The occurrence of the /ɛ/ phoneme in /rɛðer/ corresponds roughly with the Kurath–McDavid observation, viz. that it is restricted to the speech of the folk and middle groups.

The most clearly distinctive feature of Chicago Negro speech is the occurrence of /a/ for usual /æ/ in *aunt*. The /æ/ phoneme was heard only seven times in this context and never among members of Types A–B.

The remaining items, D–G, are pretty well restricted to Types D–G of both groups with the highest frequency among Types F–G.

Similar distribution is found among the recessive forms of the weakly stressed vowels in this Table. The notable exceptions occur under items K–O among members of Group I, Types A–D, who have a rather high frequency of recessive forms (19 of 49). Conversely among the first three members of Group II, there is but one of fifteen instances.

Table 34.9: Lexical Differences. The paucity of lexical material with sociologically distributed variation reflects the thus far inadequate analysis of the Chicago lexicon. This is not to suggest that important information is not to be found in Chicago word studies, but this brief review does suggest that a more productive set of items should be established before moving to the next phase of the investigation.

Two aspects of the lexicon that should certainly be explored are Southernisms versus urbanisms and the intricacies of ingroup Negro slang. An item not shown in the Table is *soul food* which signifies the rib-stick results of fine southern cooking. About one-fourth of the informants knew the word, and Informant I-1 recalls the expression from his boyhood in Virginia. The term surely deserves more investigation and it is obviously wrong to assume, as we otherwise might, that it was coined by the Management of the Archways Restaurant in Chicago's South Side.

The recessive items in Table 34.9 are predominantly relics of Southern speech. Items G and J, *stomp* and *scared* have the highest frequency of occurrence and these forms, along with *aunty*, are the only recessive items which are not clearly old-fashioned.

The overall pattern of distribution shows all informants under age 40 with more than a few recessive forms to be Types D–G (I-8, I-10, II-8, II-10). All others having a high recurrence of recessive features are older and of Types E–G (I-11, I-14, I-16, I-17, I-18, I-19, I-20, and II-9). Notice that seven of these eight are of Types F–G.

Table 34.10: Verb Forms. As has been pointed out many times, standard verb forms in America are more important social class indicators than standard pronunciation, whereas in England the opposite is true. The items in this table certainly corroborate this observation. In six forms, B, C, G, J, K, and O, there is not a single instance of the standard verb form among Group I members of Types F and G, i.e. thirty-six of thirty-six instances of non-standard forms. With the exception of items A and F, all other verb forms in this table show a preponderance of non-standard forms in the speech of these seven informants.

Among the new arrivals, the incidence of standard forms is much higher among Types F–G, i.e. informants II-5 through II-10, than among the lower types of Group I. This is probably explained by the fact that the median grade level for Types F–G of Group I is 7.4 and for Types F–G of Group II is 10.6.

35

Towards a New Perspective in Negro English Dialectology[1]

BERYL LOFTMAN BAILEY

IN HIS ABRIDGMENT OF *The American Language*, Raven I. McDavid, Jr., gives a partial reproduction of H. L. Mencken's treatment of the dialect of Southern Negroes, as follows:

Of all the ethnic dialects on exhibition in the United States the one that has got the most attention, both from the literati and from students of linguistics, is that of the Southern Negroes. Tremaine McDowell says that it made its first appearance in American fiction in Part I of Hugh Henry Brackenridge's satirical novel "Modern Chivalry: Containing the Adventures of Captain Farrago and Teague O'Regan, His Servant," published in 1792, but it had been attempted in plays so early as 1775 and there were traces of it in other writings even before. Then, as ever since, Negro speech has shown a simplified—or at least different—grammatical structure. The origins of that structure were described by Krapp as the development of a dialect comparable to Pidgin English or Beach-la-Mar; and this dialect survives more or less in the Gullah of the sea islands of Georgia and South Carolina. But its vestiges are also to be found in the speech of the most ignorant Negroes of the inland regions, which still shows grammatical peculiarities seldom encountered in white Southern speech, however lowly, *e.g.*, the confusion of persons, as in "I *is*," "*Do* she?" "*Does* you?" "*Am* you de man?" and "He *am*"; the frequent use of present forms in the past, as in "He *been die*" and "He *done show* me"; the tendency to omit all the forms of *to be*, as in "He *gone*" and "Where you *at*?"[2]

In this condensation, McDavid has highlighted what seems to me to be a

Reprinted by permission from *American Speech* 40.171–77 (1965). Mrs. Bailey is Associate Professor of English at Hunter College.

[1] This article is the revised version of a paper which was read on March 14, 1965, at the Tenth Annual National Conference on Linguistics sponsored by the Linguistic Circle of New York.

[2] H. L. Mencken, *The American Language*. Fourth Edition and Two Supplements, Abridged, by Raven I. McDavid, Jr., with the Assistance of David W. Maurer (New York, 1963), p. 475. Although a great deal has been excised, the language of what has been retained is almost identical with that in H. L. Mencken, *The American Language*, *Supplement II* (New York, 1962), pp. 263–64.

curious juxtaposition of a very enlightened statement with an equally unen-
lightened—as well as completely non-structural and linguistically naïve—one.

One would have supposed that, following Krapp's suggestion made as far
back as 1924, there would have been some effort to investigate the historical
backgrounds of that dialect, so that the assertion could by this time be validated
or nullified. This would have necessitated, among other things, a description of
the dialect in terms of itself and not in terms of some other supposed norm, no
matter how feasible such a norm seemed to be. But the American Negro "dialect"
has not until recently been granted the autonomy which structuralism so freely
accorded to exotic languages and dialects in other parts of the world. It has
remained the stigmatized and unwanted "poor brother" of Standard English,
and hence the retention in so eminent a piece of scholarship as *The American
Language* of such statements as "confusion of persons," "the frequent use of
present forms in the past," and "the tendency to omit all the forms of *to be*"—
statements which, as I shall show, are only partially correct and serve merely to
obfuscate the true state of affairs. Surely the structuralists must have known
that this dialect is used for communication by a large section of our population
and that communication would necessarily break down if these elements of
structure were indeed "confused." I therefore maintain that only blind ethno-
centrism has prevented them from looking further for the real facts underlying
the grammatical structure of this dialect.

Recent developments in the study of the creole languages[3] indicate that
these languages show such amazing similarities in their grammatical structures
that it is convenient to set up a distinct creole typology in linguistics. Thus,
there are English-, Portuguese-, Spanish-, and Dutch-, as well as French-based,
creoles. We are indebted to R. W. Thompson, then at the University of Hong
Kong, for the suggestion that the pidgins of the Old World and the creoles of
the New World appear to have developed from some universal trade language
of pidgin, most probably Portuguese in origin. Thompson cited the similarities
in the verb system of these groups in support of his thesis. More recently,
William Stewart has hypothesized that this Portuguese-based pidgin was
re-lexified to yield the English, Dutch, and French pidgins which are the pro-
genitors of the creoles. This idea of a re-lexification which left the original
syntax almost intact is a very attractive one and should be further investigated.

As I have already indicated, the second section of the passage cited above
runs counter to the tenets of structuralism. It is significant that every one of
the examples given refers to the verb, and it is certainly surprising that the
verb should be discussed not in terms of the system of which it is a part but in
terms of another system from which it is known to have deviated.

I would like to suggest that the Southern Negro "dialect" differs from other
Southern speech because its deep structure is different, having its origins as it
undoubtedly does in some proto-creole grammatical structure. Hence, regard-

---

[3] I use the word *creole* to embrace all the mixed languages brought into the New
World by West African slaves, whatever the European source language may have been.

less of the surface resemblances to other dialects of English—and this must be expected, since the lexicon is English and the speakers are necessarily bidialectal —we must look into the system itself for an explanation of seeming confusion of persons and tenses.

In order to arrive at a satisfactory description of Jamaican creole, the dialect of Jamaican Negroes, I was compelled to modify the orthodox procedures considerably and even, at times, to adopt some completely unorthodox ones. The first problem that I had to face was that of abstracting a hypothetical dialect which could reasonably be regarded as featuring the main elements of the deep structure. This may sound like hocus-pocus, but indeed a good deal of linguistics is. A hocus-pocus procedure which yields the linguistic facts is surely preferable to a scientifically rigorous one which completely murders those facts. In all dialectology we are faced with the realization that our populations indulge in considerable code-switching, and consequently it is very difficult to find informants who do not switch codes to suit the occasion.

The American Negro, like the Jamaican, operates in a linguistic continuum. In describing Jamaican creole, I had to make arbitrary decisions as to which sentences should be included and which discarded in abstracting the basilect.[4] I discovered that the basilect is regularly spoken only by pre-school children and elderly people and by illiterates in the back country. All others, especially those who have had limited schooling, practice considerable code-switching, and any attempt to describe the entire continuum with its intermingling of co-structures would be doomed to failure. Fortunately, I was able to rely on my own *Sprachgefühl* as a native speaker of the language, and the general acceptance of my findings by other Jamaicans has more than vindicated my procedures.

Since I am not a native speaker of any Southern Negro dialect and since my investigations are still in the initial stage, I have, for the purposes of this article, looked into one such hypothetical language: that used by the narrator, Duke, in *The Cool World*.[5] The rationale here is that an author regularly packs his dialogue with those features which he knows to be most distinctive in the dialect which his characters speak. I am fully aware of the fact that this is not generally accepted as good linguistic procedure, but it seemed to me that this analysis could give some indication of the direction in which we have to move. Since, however, I have approached the Cool World language (CW) from my background in English (E) and Jamaican creole (JC), I suspect that I may be overlooking some crucial facts which only a native speaker can elucidate.

An analysis of Duke's speech reveals an absence of copulas. In Table 35.1, I list examples of that absence; the appropriate page numbers in *The Cool World* are enclosed by parentheses.

---

[4] William Stewart has proposed that we employ the word *basilect* to refer to the form most remote from English and the word *acrolect* to refer to the accepted form which most closely approximates English.

[5] Warren Miller, *The Cool World* (Boston, 1959).

TABLE 35.1: ABSENCE OF COPULA

BEFORE ADJECTIVES

1. I sure they aroun. (26)
2. "I glad he gone." Little Man say. (31)
3. Lu Ann fast asleep in the big bed. Lu Ann naked. (36)
4. You afraid of jail bait Big Man? (37)
5. For a while any way it clear. (90)
6. I keep trying to move away a little but the train too crowded. (106)

BEFORE NOMINALS

7. She a big woman not skinny like my mother. (11)
8. He one of us all right. (11)
9. Here come Duke Custis. He a cold killer. (12)
10. An she look at us one by one like it a line up. (31)
11. I mean you know I feel sorry because they people an they dont have a chance. (52)
12. Chester my best friend we friends since we was little kids. (61)

BEFORE ADVERBS AND PREPOSITIONAL PHRASES

13. I in a big hurry. (7)
14. But now I here at this place an they askin me questions. (10)
15. "I with you Duke Man," He say. (36)
16. When you out of something you always wish you was with it. (119)
17. Did you find out anything while you over in they territory? (122)
18. It a place where you can go when you in trouble. (129)

AFTER THE FILLER SUBJECTS "THERE" AND "IT"

19. It black dark and I cant hear only they breathin and the shuffelen of shoes. (27)
20. "It the truth." She say. "It the truth . . . ." (29)
21. "It true you bin a little un lucky." Fella say. (50)
22. Mostly they nothing but people on the street. (67)
23. They some women open up a business right in they house. (68)
24. They a lot of people on this street have Stomach Trouble. (68)

In the figure below, I provide a simple comparison of the phrase structure rules of nonverbal predications in English, Jamaican Creole, and Cool World. By *non-verbal predications* I mean those predications which do not make use of a verb, the term *verb* being limited here to that class of words which is so designated in Robert Livingston Allen's sector analysis of English. In that system words like *be, have, can,* and so on, fall into a special category whose primary function is to give time orientation to the predication. Consequently, I shall not here regard the auxiliary *be* as a verb. The statement of the English situation is, of course, extremely simplified; only the gross features are accounted for.

Phrase Structure Rules for Non-verbal Predications

$$E \qquad\qquad JC \qquad\qquad CW$$

$$P \rightarrow be + \left\{ \begin{array}{l} \text{Adj} \\ \text{Nom} \\ \text{Loc} \end{array} \right\} \qquad P \rightarrow \left\{ \begin{array}{l} \emptyset + \text{Adj} \\ a + \text{Nom} \\ (de) + \text{Loc} \end{array} \right\} \qquad P \rightarrow \emptyset + \left\{ \begin{array}{l} \text{Adj} \\ \text{Nom} \\ \text{Loc} \end{array} \right\}$$

The rules summarized in this figure may be stated as follows: English requires some form of *be* in all non-verbal predications; in *The Cool World*, predicates are used without any copula; and Jamaican Creole has a more complicated system, with zero before adjectives, an obligatory *a* before nominals, and a *de* which is often deleted before locatives.

While I claim a deep structural relationship between *JC* and *CW*, there has not been an identical development of the systems, and it is important that such identity not be assumed. Thus, if we take the second half of Sentence 9 in Table 35.1, "He a cold killer," we find that, with the exception of *he*—which in *JC* is some form of *him*—the sentences are identical. This is, however, only superficially so. In the *CW* version, there are just two units: the nominals *he* and *a cold killer*. In the *JC* version, there are three units: the nominals *he* and *cold killer* and the copula *a* which may not be omitted. Hence, if the Jamaican really wanted to stress the indefinite article, he would have to use *wan* and say, "Him a wan kuol kila."

The analysis further reveals that the system seems to have an unmarked form of the verb, which—like most unmarked forms—is non-committal as to time orientation, but that there are certain marked forms which are past and future respectively. It appears that *was* is reserved for events which are completely in the past, while *been* extends from the past up to, and even including, the present moment. *Be* is a simple future, with *gonna* the intentional future. Examples are supplied in Table 35.2.

TABLE 35.2: THE TENSE MARKERS "BEEN" ("WAS") AND "BE" ("GONNA")

1. . . . you just end up scared like you was walkin down a empty street at night. (10)
2. He knew we was smoken. (16)
3. . . . you was the sweetest baby so good. (23)
4. I going to see him soon Rod. I been busy with some other little things. (35)
5. They was two women workin at a table with a glass top. (46)
6. I been a salesman 20 years off an on. (50)
7. He been inside too much. (51)
8. You bin smokin with out me? (55)
9. They was just some guys with a racket. (67)
10. "You be back." Priest say lookin at me. "I know you be back Man." (9)
11. Be good to me and I be good for you. (26)
12. "I be here with em befor you are awake." I say. (39)
13. "I be all right." I tell her. (40)
14. I sure you gonna contribit some of you earned money to your mother. (46)
15. Things gonna be a lot different aroun here now Duke in command. (79)
16. Some time I jus gonna take off for that place like a big bird. (81)
17. "They be goin to the moon soon." He say. (88)
18. Thats whut I been thinking Priest. That I leave you say 5 then I be back next week some time with the 10. (96)
19. I see you been thru some trouble lately Boy. (90)
20. "We be waiting for you." Little Flower say. (142)

TABLE 35.3: THE NEGATION MARKERS "DON'T" AND "AIN'T"

1. That piece aint been worth no fifteen dollas since you was a little boy Priest. (8)
2. I aint paying that kind of bread for no iron like that. (8)
3. He aint comin back. (13)
4. He aint gonna get no money out of it. (34)
5. "I aint afraid of nothin." I tell her. (37)
6. "They aint never anything been right since." (40)
7. Aint nothing decent in our lives. (41)
8. He skinny still but he aint hungry lookin like he uset. (136)
9. Dont get the idee that I aint satisfied with my luck. (136)
10. But this aint the last chance Man. (146)
11. They dont come back aint no point coming back. (146)
12. I dont want to walk up the stairs to my place. (149)
13. I in it an I aint gonna chicken out but I dont have the heart for it no more. (149)
14. I been thinking about that. An they aint no plan. (151)
15. I dont know why he done it. (154)
16. I dont know how long I been sleeping there. (157)
17. I two people an this one aint me. (158)
18. I dont care if they aint room for him. (159)

The analysis also reveals that the American Negro system has a curious deployment of the negative markers *don't* and *ain't*, as shown by the examples in Table 35.3. *Ain't* is used consistently in nonverbal predications and before the tense markers; it also seems to be the form preferred before the progressive *-in* form of the verb. Whether this exhausts its limitations, and whether *don't* is used in all other cases, remains to be investigated.

Lastly, the analysis reveals that, in the American Negro system, the form *they* serves for the possessive pronoun *their*, as indicated by the examples in Table 35.4. The explanation could be a morphological one, since the pronoun *you* does not change its shape in the possessive (see Sentence 8 in Table 35.4); hence, we could reasonably conclude that *they* does not change. On the other hand, *CW* has such forms as *his, her, Lu Ann's,* and so on, which are clearly possessive. Then again, the locative *there* and the expletive *there* are also homophonous with the possessive *their*. Does this mean that the explanation is a phonological one? Or is the explanation both morphological and phonological? It is obviously impossible to decide on the basis of the corpus in *The Cool World*. The best we can do is to make an arbitrary decision, but clearly admitting that it is arbitrary and could easily have gone the other way.

One of the first things to be done is to train some of the native speakers of our Southern Negro dialects and to rely on their intuitions to throw light on those issues which are bound to remain unsolved, even after we have revised our approach along the lines suggested in this article. As I stated above, this has been an excursion into a literary text. But here, at least, I have been able to show that subsystems can be abstracted—subsystems which are so ordered as to make it possible to ignore certain categories which are basic in English.

TABLE 35.4: TREATMENT OF THE POSSESSIVE "THEIR"

1. Everybody look down at they feet. (14)
2. They must have over a 100 books in they apartment. (16)
3. . . . they come at me with they blades. (27)
4. They jus aint no place in a gang for girls. (35)[6]
5. In the day time those places full of kids and they mothers. (62)
6. People standen there with they mouths open watchin. (70)
7. . . . they gotta make they move right then and there . . . . (77)
8. An all the apartments have they own toilet so you dont have to go out in the hall an wait you turn. (95)
9. You find you self some pencil and paper an make a list. (101)[7]
10. I decide it then and they at the table by my self. (112)[8]
11. They aint drinkin it but only breathin it. Hold it up to they nose an taken deep breaths. (151)

[6] This sentence is included for comparison only.
[7] See n. 6.
[8] See n. 6.

36

On the Structure of the Verb in a Dialect of American Negro English

MARVIN D. LOFLIN

ANYONE WHO ATTEMPTS TO DESCRIBE the structure of the verb of non-standard Negro English (NNE)[1] must account for several facts; to begin with, there is no perfective form, *have + En*, comparable to the one posited for Standard English (SE). In particular, there are no surface realizations in simple sentences, ordinary yes/no questions, nor in tag questions. Thus, we find the following grammatical and ungrammatical sentences:

(a) (i) you done ate.
  (ii) *you've already eaten.[2]
  (iii) *you've already ate.
  (iv) ain't you eat yet?
  (v) you eat yet?
  (vi) didn't you eat yet?
  (vii) *haven't you eaten yet?
  (viii) you ate didn't you?
  (ix) *you've eaten haven't you?
  (x) he ate didn't he?
  (xi) he ain't eat did he?

Reprinted by permission of the author and of Mouton & Co., The Hague, publisher of *Linguistics*, a journal in which this article is to appear. Research for this study was supported by a grant from the U.S. Office of Naval Research. The author is Research Associate in the Center for Research in Social Behavior, University of Missouri.

[1] Essentially, the grammar fragment presented here was constructed on the basis of data obtained over a period of approximately one year (1966–67) from one male informant. He was 14 years old and a native of Washington, D.C. Two types of data acquisition techniques were employed: structured interview in an office and loosely directed conversations in a multiplicity of urban environments (parks, cafés, etc.). For additional insights and an extended reference sample, all the members of five families were interviewed in taped sessions and spontaneous conversations between children of various ages were taped. Transcriptions of tapes from these two additional sources were checked against the data from the primary informant.

[2] Sentences preceded with an asterisk (*) are ungrammatical in NNE.

(xii) *he's eaten hasn't he?

(xiii) he been eatin ain't he?

(xiv) *he's been eatin ain't he?

There is also an absence of nominalizations involving *have + En*. For example, sentences with subjects such as **his having bought the bicycle* ... do not occur. Hence, not only is *have + En* absent from simple sentences, negatives, and questions, but it is also absent from nominalizations.

We now present a well known analysis of SE auxiliary structure[3] in order to demonstrate how the structures encountered in NNE must necessarily be accounted for by a descriptive hypothesis different from that generally accepted for SE.

GRAMMAR I: Standard English

Aux $\longrightarrow$ Aux$_1$ (Aux$_2$)

Aux$_1$ $\longrightarrow$ (M) Tense

Aux$_2$ $\longrightarrow$ (Perf) (Imperf)

Perf $\longrightarrow$ have + En

Imperf $\longrightarrow$ be + Ing

Tense $\longrightarrow$ $\left\{ \begin{array}{c} \text{Pres} \\ \text{Past} \end{array} \right\}$

These rules generate at least the ... structures [in Diagram 1, pages 430–431].

At the very least, our observation will require that we exclude from our grammar *Perf* and its associated structure *have + En*. We effect further simplification by omitting *Aux$_2$* thereby obtaining Grammar II:

GRAMMAR II

Aux $\longrightarrow$ Aux$_1$ (Imperf)

Aux$_1$ $\longrightarrow$ (M) Tense

Imperf $\longrightarrow$ be + Ing

Tense $\longrightarrow$ $\left\{ \begin{array}{c} \text{Pres} \\ \text{Past} \end{array} \right\}$

The omission of *Perf* from the category sub-component of the base is, in effect, a claim that the deep structures of NNE and SE are different. Subsequently, we will discuss this problem and its implications in greater detail. However, for the time being, we wish merely to call attention to the fact that deep structure difference exists, and note that we make the claim because we find no evidence of the presence of *Perf* in several different structures where we might expect it.

The revision proposed in Grammar II accounts for the non-occurrence of *have + En* in our data but it presents new problems. In particular, how do we account for the *En* of *been* in (a) (xiii)? Low-level rules in a grammar of SE

[3] Charles J. Fillmore, "The Position of Embedding Transformations in a grammar," *POLA* 3r: 23 (1963). We have substituted the label *Imperf* for *Prog*.

Phrase Markers (PM)

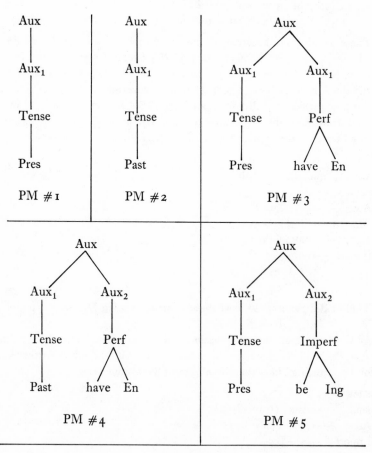

[Diagram 1.]

operate on the output of the auxiliary rules to transpose *En* to the right side of
the formative *be*. Obviously, we cannot exclude *have + En* from the grammar
of NNE and still obtain *be + En* in the way accepted for SE. For the time being,
let us postpone our discussion of the source of *been* in NNE and move on to
consider another form which occurs in NNE but not in SE.

An additional fact that must be accounted for in describing NNE is the
contrast between *be* and *is*. *be* is in a set with *Pres* (Present) and *Past* and is not
neutralized with the present form *is* (or any of its morphophonemic realizations
in agreement).

For example, we find

(b)   (i) I don't be mad except sometimes I be.
          (ii) *I don't be mad except sometimes I was.

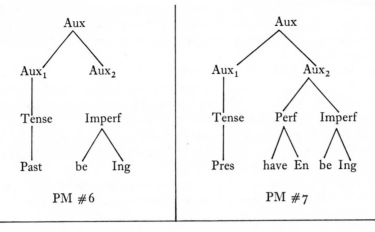

PM #6   PM #7

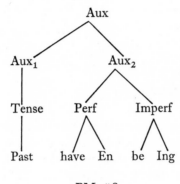

PM #8

[Diagram 1.]

(iii) *I don't be mad except sometimes I been.
(iv) *I don't be mad except sometimes I am.

If *be* and *am* were equivalent, we would expect (b) (iv) to be an acceptable paraphrase of (b) (i). These forms have different meanings and different distributions.

In SE we find

(c)   (i) I'm dancing right now.
         (ii) I'm dancing everytime you come in.

And note that the tenses of (c) (i) and (c) (ii) are the same; whereas in NNE we note

(d)   (i) *I be dancing right now.
         (ii) I (m) dancing right now.
         (iii) I be dancing everytime you come in.

Thus, in SE the *right now* and *everytime you come in* time adverbs are both compatible with *I'm* but in NNE these two time adverbs select different tense markers. Indeed, an attempt to substitute one for the other produces ungrammatical sentences.

We are now confronted with the task of revising Grammar II to reflect the results of our analysis of *be*. In the case of *have + En* our revision involved a simplification of the grammar in that Grammar II contains fewer grammatical categories and relations than does Grammar I. Our third descriptive hypothesis must be more complex than Grammar II in that it will have at least one more grammatical category; in addition, it will generate a set of phrase-markers different from either Grammar I or II.

We propose to treat *be* as the realization of a tense just as *is* and *was* are considered realizations of tenses. Such a treatment gives the following:

GRAMMAR III

$$\text{Aux} \longrightarrow \text{Aux}_1 \ (\text{Imperf})$$
$$\text{Aux}_1 \longrightarrow (\text{M}) \ \text{Tense}$$
$$\text{Imperf} \longrightarrow \text{Be} + \text{Ing}$$
$$\text{Tense} \longrightarrow \left\{ \begin{array}{l} \text{Pres} \\ \text{Past} \\ \text{A-Temporal}^4 \end{array} \right\}$$

[See Diagram 2.]

It is becoming more and more obvious that the set of rules postulated in Grammar I does not adequately account for the data confronting us in NNE. Consequently, at this stage, rather than continue to work from Grammar III we propose to abandon the descriptive apparatus of SE and put forward our hypothesis for the auxiliary structure of NNE.

We postulate the following:

GRAMMAR IV

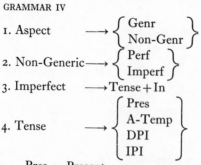

1. Aspect $\longrightarrow \left\{ \begin{array}{l} \text{Genr} \\ \text{Non-Genr} \end{array} \right\}$

2. Non-Generic $\longrightarrow \left\{ \begin{array}{l} \text{Perf} \\ \text{Imperf} \end{array} \right\}$

3. Imperfect $\longrightarrow \text{Tense} + \text{In}$

4. Tense $\longrightarrow \left\{ \begin{array}{l} \text{Pres} \\ \text{A-Temp} \\ \text{DPI} \\ \text{IPI} \end{array} \right\}$

Pres = Present
A-Temp = A-Temporal
DPI = Definite-Past-Imperfect
IPI = Indefinite-Past-Imperfect

[4] Cf. Marvin D. Loflin, "A Note on the Deep Structure of Nonstandard English in Washington, D.C." *Glossa* 1: 26–32 (1967), for a slightly different treatment of *be*.

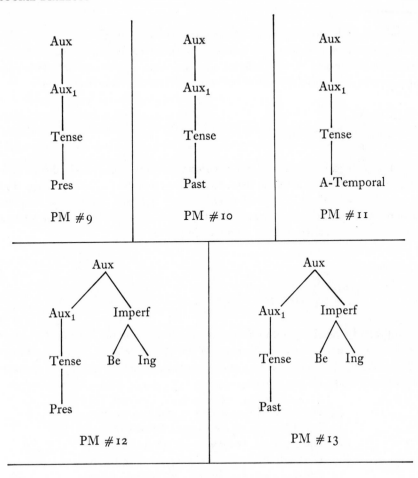

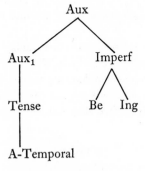

PM #14

[Diagram 2.]

These rules will generate the . . . P-markers [in Diagram 3].

Rule #1 of Grammar IV rewrites *Aspect* as consisting of two mutually exclusive categories: *Genr* (Generic) and *Non-Genr* (Non-Generic). This rule presupposes a base component which will generate the following string:

Noun Modifiers
$$X - Det + N + S - Y$$

The category—*Non-Genr*—is necessary for the rule which deletes the noun phrase of the constituent sentence in noun modified structures when *WH* is not selected. Thus, *The dude is offin me up got into trouble* is a complex sentence satisfying the structural description: $X - Det + N + S - Y$. If we assume that our base will also generate the following string:

Relativization
$$X - N \ (WH) \begin{Bmatrix} Def \\ Indef \end{Bmatrix} Y$$

it will then be possible to optionally select *WH* and obtain either *WH the dude* or *the dude* in the embedded sentence. When *WH* is selected in the generation of an embedded sentence such as our example there are no restrictions on verb inflections. Thus, we may obtain:

(e)   (i) The dude *who is offin me up* got into trouble.
         (ii) The dude *who off me up* got into trouble.
        (iii) The dude *who be offin me up* got into trouble.
        (iv) The dude *who was offin me up* got into trouble.
         (v) The dude *who been offin me up* got into trouble.
        (vi) The dude *who offed me up* got into trouble.

However, when *WH* is not selected two constraints operate: (1) the subject of the embedded sentence must be deleted and the verb must be inflected with either *ed* or *ing* (where *ed* is associated with passive). Consequently, we find

(f)   (i) The dude, offin me up, got into trouble.
         (ii) The dude, pushed from the chair, got into trouble.

but not

       (iii) *The dude, off me up, got into trouble.
       (iv) *the dude, push from the chair, got into trouble.

In addition to the Nom-deletion rule, a Nom-Modifier Shift rule is needed to place only *ed* and *In* affixed verbs before modified nouns. Such a rule will account for

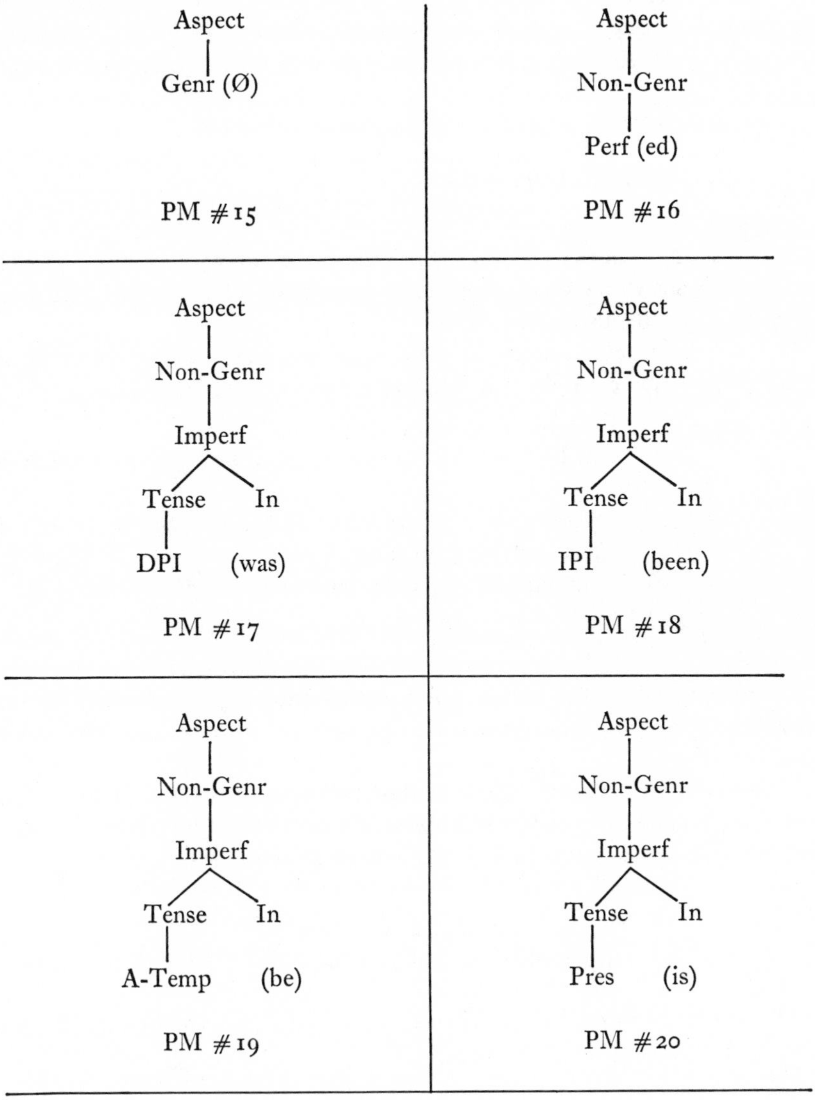

```
        Aspect                              Aspect
          |                                   |
       Genr (Ø)                           Non-Genr
                                              |
                                          Perf (ed)


        PM #15                              PM #16
```

```
        Aspect                              Aspect
          |                                   |
       Non-Genr                           Non-Genr
          |                                   |
        Imperf                             Imperf
         /  \                               /  \
      Tense  In                          Tense  In
        |                                   |
       DPI   (was)                         IPI   (been)

        PM #17                              PM #18
```

```
        Aspect                              Aspect
          |                                   |
       Non-Genr                           Non-Genr
          |                                   |
        Imperf                             Imperf
         /  \                               /  \
      Tense  In                          Tense  In
        |                                   |
     A-Temp  (be)                         Pres   (is)

        PM #19                              PM #20
```

[Diagram 3.]

(g)   (i) The drowning man . . .
          (ii) The drinking man . . .
         (iii) The murdered man . . .

but not

          (iv) *The drown man . . .
           (v) *The drink man . . .
          (vi) *The murder man . . .

The symbol *Genr* is utilized in all the rules wherein an infinitival is needed. An example of such a rule is the one Lees[5] refers to as Factive Nominal—Question-Word—Infinitival. It would have the following domain and change:

Factive Nominal—Question-Word Clause—Infinitival
$X - V + WH + PRO$ (Prev) Aspect $- Y \Rightarrow$
$X - V + WH + PRO$ (Prev) (to) Genr $- Y$

It is assumed in this rule that other rules have already operated to give the appropriate structural domain. A fuller description of infinitivals will reveal more precisely the distribution of *to*.

There are many sentences in NNE where this particle does not occur, although translation equivalents in SE would require it. For example,

(h)   (i) Man, I know what you go do—you probably go be sleeping all day.
           (ii) An so Blackie want de lady sing for him and de other man want de lady sing for him.
           (iii) An my muvah, see, she want take de car go to Safeway wit.
           (iv) I tol Michael come help me.

The optionality of *to* in this rule is intended to suggest the possibility that *to* may be obligatory in some embeddings, optional in others and obligatorily absent in others.

Genr also occurs with verbals marked [+Verb] in simple, complex, compound and compound-complex sentences. It is realized as zero (O) and accounts for such verb structures as those in the following sentences:

(j)   (i) We always eat dinner over there.
           (ii) They caught the old man cause he go round telling these stories all the time.
           (iii) *They caught the old man cause he went round tell these stories all the time.

It is interesting that the principal informant rejected (j) (iii). I noted to him that the action happened in the past and repeated the sentence to him. Thereupon, he looked surprised and said, "Yeah, but it happen all the time." This anecdote serves to illustrate a problem in NNE: Zero (O) may be the surface realization for either *Genr* or *Perf (ed)*. If we subcategorize verbs in SE by their morphophonemic realizations we obtain the following:

---

[5] R. B. Lees, *The Grammar of English Nominalizations*. The Hague: Mouton and Company, 1966, p. 62.

STANDARD ENGLISH:

Verb Class	Realization of Ed
A	t
B	d
C	ɨd
D	Stem Change (SC)
E	O

A = jump	B = rob	C = start	D = take	E = put
stop	cram	crate	shake	hit
walk	call	. . .	go	. . .
. . .	. . .		steal	
			strive	
			. . .	

Using the same criterion for grouping of NNE verbs we find:

NON-STANDARD NEGRO ENGLISH:

Verb Class	Realization of ED
F	t
G	t or O
H	d[6]
I	d or O
J	ɨd
K	ɨd or O
L	SC
M	SC or O
N	O

F = NONE	G = creep	H = sew	I = stay	J = NONE
	push	swear*	rob*	
	pass	strive*		
	jump*			
	walk*			
	stop*			

K = start*	L = ring	M = come	N = cut
lead	sink	say	hit
set	sting	send	but*
shut	steal*	go*	call*

*Also in the SE lists.

[6] Repetitions of words ending in *ED*, represented here by "d", vary from [t] to [d]. This potential voicing occurs only with classes H, I, J, and K.

First, we note the two sets of lists are not identical. Next, we note that there are no verbs which are only [t] or only [ɨd]. There are some, however, which are only *Stem Changing* (SC) and only [d].

The remainder are only O, or [t] or O, [d] or O, [ɨd] or O, or SC or O. When *ed* is realized as [t], [d], [ɨd], or *SC* there is no special problem. When it is realized as O there is. That problem is the determination of what grammatical category any given realization of O represents.[7] We obtain our answer by going elsewhere in the grammar. In negative and interrogative structures *ed* and *Genr* have different realizations. That is, they are only neutralized in surface structures which are not negative and not interrogative. Thus:

The negative of *ed* is *ain't* + V.
or *didn't* + V.
The negative of *Genr* is *don't* + V.
The tag question form of *ed* is . . . ain't he.
⠀⠀⠀⠀⠀⠀⠀⠀⠀⠀⠀⠀⠀⠀⠀⠀⠀. . . didn't he.
⠀⠀⠀⠀⠀⠀⠀⠀⠀⠀⠀⠀⠀⠀⠀⠀⠀. . . did he.
and the tag question form of *Genr* is . . . don't he.
⠀⠀⠀⠀⠀⠀⠀⠀⠀⠀⠀⠀⠀⠀⠀⠀⠀⠀⠀. . . do he.

Negative and interrogative forms such as these justify postulating deep structure entities (*Perf* and *Genr*) which may be neutralized, hence ambiguous, in surface structure realizations in NNE.

In this analysis I have opted in the direction of a grammatical solution because, on the one hand, a grammatical category (*Genr*) is already needed to account for the set of zero marked verbs which are negativized and inter-rogativized different from the *ed* marked verbs and, on the other hand, no consistent pattern of phonological or morphological conditioning has yet been determined.

In rule #2 we are given two aspects, *Imperf* and *Perf*, which we identify as Imperfective and Perfective. The perfective suffix *ed* occurs only with verbals marked [+Verb]; that is, we find no verbals marked [+Adj] terminating in a sound segment(s) which the native speaker associates with the perfective aspect.

Perfective negatives and perfective interrogatives are different from the corresponding generic and imperfective forms. Thus, we find

⠀⠀⠀(k)⠀⠀⠀(i) he ate yesterday. (Perf)
⠀⠀⠀⠀⠀⠀⠀⠀⠀(ii) he ain't eat yesterday. (Perf)
⠀⠀⠀⠀⠀⠀⠀⠀⠀(iii) *he don't eat yesterday.

---

[7] It also presents a serious practical problem. A teacher friend reports that in her predominantly Negro class of seventh graders in Alexandria, Virginia, the NNE speakers show a peculiar lack of competence in *ed* usage, sprinkling *ed* throughout their composi-tions, often placing it in environments where the so-called present tense of SE would be required.

    (iv) *he wasn't eat yesterday.
    (v) *he ain't been eat yesterday.
    (vi) *he don't be eat yesterday.
  (vii) he ate yesterday didn't he. (Perf)
 (viii) did he eat yesterday. (Perf)
   (ix) *he ate yesterday don't he.
    (x) *he ate yesterday don't he be.
   (xi) *he ate yesterday wasn't he.
  (xii) *he ate yesterday ain't he been.
 (xiii) *be he ate yesterday.
 (xiv) *was he eat yesterday.
  (xv) *is he eat yesterday.
 (xvi) *been he eat yesterday.

There occurs with the Imperfective (*Imperf*) a class of tense markers, one of which is the present tense (*Pres*). In the speech of young children (6–12 years) and the casual speech of the principal informant, *Pres* is realized as O; in older informants and in the careful speech of the informant there is agreement between the subject and the category, *Pres*. Thus, in careful speech we obtain *I'm eatin* (first person) and *he's eatin* (third person) but in casual speech we obtain *I eatin* and *he eatin*. When the present imperfect is unmarked it functions like the remaining tense markers; they all have only one form no matter what the person or the number; thus, we find:

(l)
$$
\left\{ \begin{array}{l} \text{I} \\ \text{you} \\ \text{he, she} \\ \text{we} \\ \text{they} \end{array} \right\}
\left\{ \begin{array}{l} \text{O (Present)} \\ \text{be (A-Temporal)} \\ \text{was (Definite Past)} \\ \text{been (Indefinite Past)} \end{array} \right\} \text{V} + \text{In}
$$

The case for the a-temporality (non-presentness) of *be*, which was introduced in the discussion of Grammar III above, hinges on examples of the following kind:

(m)   (i) They be here tomorrow.
         (ii) They be here all the time.
        (iii) They be dancing with each other.
            [The context was past; the informant said he went to a party where he sat out the dances in a corner; I asked him what the other people did there. Whereupon he gave me (m) (iii).]

It is possible to account for the ambiguity of *They be here* by stating that *be* in (m) (i) is a morphophonemically reduced form of *They will be here* (to-

morrow) and *be* in (m) (ii) is either a substitution for *is* or the realization of a completely different grammatical category. We have already concluded that *be* is not identical with *is*. However, I know of no way to account for the potential pastness, futurity and continuativeness of (m) (iii) except by positing an *A-Temporal* tense category as I have done here.

A *Tense* node (Rule #3) is required in the grammar to account for the deletion of *is*, *was*, *been* and *be* in the output of the Nom-Deletion and Nom-Modifier-Shift rules. It will be remembered that *is*, *was*, *been*, and *be* are not deleted at the same time *Nom* is deleted in the Nom-deletion rule; consequently, these four formatives are retained in the pre- and post-nominal modifiers formed by the Nom-Deletion and Nom-Modifier-Shift rules.

If we assume, as we have in our discussion of rules, that sentences are embedded by a recursive rule provided in the base we are, in effect, making the generalization that any and all sentences may be embedded. By virtue of a rule in the base which generates the *WH* formative we make it possible for Noun modification embeddings to be either relativized with the formatives *who*, *which*, etc., or without them. The first constraint we place on Noun modification embeddings is that there must be identity between the noun of the embedded sentence and the modified noun of the matrix sentence.

In the event *WH* is not selected, the constraint is that *Nom* of the constituent sentence is deleted when it is the subject or object of verbs inflected with *Non-Genr* categories and when the identity relations mentioned above hold. At this stage, all the post-nominal modifier sentences may be transposed and made pre-nominal modifiers. The verb affixes associated with the matrix sentence place constraints on the tenses of the embedded sentence. Rules to account for these constraints are introduced at this juncture. Following these rules would be those which delete *Tense* from the embedded modifier.

Early in the analysis sentences such as

> (n)   (i) The chicken béen ate something.
>   (ii) I béen washed the dishes.

—where the symbol (′) indicates emphatic stress—constituted a special problem. In particular, it had to be determined whether or not there were sentences in which *been* occurred with $V + ed$ without emphatic stress. If there were such sentences they would represent counter examples to the grammar presented here since, according to our formulation *been* co-occurs only with $V + in$.

Checking turned up

> (o)   (i) The chicken béen ate (something).
>   (ii) *The chicken been ate (something).
>   (iii) The chicken been ate by someone.
>   (iv) The dishes been washed by someone.
>   (v) I béen washed the dishes.

(vi) *I been washed the dishes.

(vii) The dishes been washed by me.[8]

Thus we concluded that *been* without emphatic stress does not occur with $V+ed$ (non-passive). We account for sentences such as (o) (i) and (o) (v) by postulating a formative E of emphatic stress which could be given in the rule rewriting VP and which could be converted in a later morphophonemic rule into appropriate realizations. E.g. $E+V+ed \Rightarrow b\acute{e}en+V+ed$.

In this article, an attempt has been made to construct a set of rules to explain the auxiliary structure of the verb in Non-standard Negro English. We began with the set of rules put forward to explain the auxiliary structure of SE and demonstrated how that set of rules did not adequately account for sentences in NNE. We then advanced our own formulation and discussed selected aspects of it.

In order to test the hypothesis that any two language varieties have the same deep structure it is obvious that we must construct grammars of the two language varieties which are the objects of the test. In the process of constructing grammars about which there is a question of deep structure identity, we must justify each relational entity in the categorial sub-component of each grammar. In other words, we must move away from the non-empirical approach wherein there is an *a priori* assumption of deep structure identity between two language varieties.[9] Behind such an *a priori* assumption is the notion that differences between dialects (styles? language varieties of the same language?) can be accounted for by low-level rules.[10] And conversely, any difference between any two language varieties that must be accounted for by high-level rules (supposedly, rules making up the categorial sub-component) must disqualify that pair of language varieties from being dialects of the same language. Restated, the assumption seems to be the following:

> Two or more language varieties V_1, V_2, V_3 ... V_n are *dialects* of the set L_1 if and only if the categorial sub-components of the bases of the grammars postulated for V_1, V_2, V_3 ... V_n are identical. Identity of categorial sub-components is necessary to define the membership of language varieties

[8] We tested for emphatic stress with passive sentences such as (o) (iii), (iv) and (vii) but failed to discover any with which the informant felt at ease. But, the informant avoided passive sentences in general. Hence, this gap may be accidental rather than grammatical.

[9] Essentially, Edward S. Klima makes this assumption in his insightful paper, "Relatedness between Grammatical Systems," *Language* 40:1–20 (1964), where he states, "Within different styles of one and the same language, however, comparison of syntactically differing systems is simplified by overall identity of grammatical elements; the words and their combination in constructions are essentially the same." (p. 2). He then proceeds to discuss rules to account for pronoun usage in four language styles.

Apparently, Peter S. Rosenbaum also makes this assumption in a short article entitled "Prerequisities for Linguistic Studies on the Effects of Dialect Differences on Learning to Read," *Project Literacy Reports*, No. 2 (Report of the Second Research Planning Conference held under the auspices of Project Literacy in Chicago, Illinois, August 6–8, 1964) Ithaca, New York: Cornell University, 1964, pp. 26–30.

V_1, V_2, V_3 ... V_n in the set L_1. Language varieties which have identical categorial sub-components also, of necessity, have identical deep structures.

Unfortunately, so far as I know, no one who works with this hypothesis has constructed a grammar for a non-standard variety of English. We must have grammars before we can claim anything about the nature of the differences between grammars. Research to date suggests that some differences between NNE and SE cannot be accounted for by low-level rules.

In the process of grammar construction we must justify each relational entity in the base of each grammar. If we do not undertake to justify each relational entity we may be misled by surface similarities. For example, in the discussion of *have+En* we found that *have+En* does not occur in negatives, questions, and nominalizations. It is likely that, if a speaker of NNE uses an occasional *have* form in a sentence it does not necessarily signify competence in the use of *have+En*. This would be especially true in the case of the principal informant. If the principal informant used a *have+En* form it would suggest learning in the directon of SE.

We also noted how surface differences might lead to unfounded hypotheses of deep structure differences. For example in a sentence such as *I béen washed the dishes* (non-passive), *been* was found to occur with $V+ed$. In spite of this, $béen+V+ed$ (where V = transitive verb and ($'$) = emphatic stress) can be shown to be the result of a simple morphophonemic adjustment involving emphatic stress.

Underlying the foregoing discussion is the assumption that every grammar may have a component that relates it (1) to, at least some or all other language varieties which have identical categorial sub-components and (2) very likely, to language varieties which, to varying degrees, differ in categorial sub-components.

Let us label this component the Language Variety Relationship (LVR) component. The LVR must have two sub-components—The Same Deep Structure (SDS) LVR and the Different Deep Structure (DDS) LVR. The two sub-components have fundamentally different roles.

SDS-LVR rules will truly be low level in the sense that they deal with no meaningful differences. That is, they relate varieties which have identical categorial sub-components and possibly different lexical, transformational, and phonological components. And DDS-LVR will account for differences between grammars with different deep structures. Precisely what a theory will be like

---

[10] This notion seems related to two facts of current work in transformation-generative grammar: (1) most of the discussion related to accounting for differences by low-level rules is concerned with phonology where the theoretical constructs do not have meaning in the sense intended in the discussion on the relevance of the semantic component in linguistic descriptions in J. Katz and P. Postal, *An Integrated Theory of Linguistic Description* (Cambridge: MIT, 1964); and, (2) there is a fundamental assumption that the output of the base must contain all the formatives upon which the semantic component is to operate, i.e. the transformational component does not insert meaningful formatives. Non-meaningful variation is accounted for by transformational rules. Rules that deal with non-meaningful variation are low-level rules.

which accounts for deep structure variation of this kind is not immediately obvious. What does a rule which rewrites *Aspect* as *Aux* mean? Or what does it mean to rewrite *Past* as *Perfective*? Ultimately we must answer questions of this sort if we are to account for deep structure differences between language varieties.

Some grammarians seem intent upon constructing a super grammar from which all dialects or languages might be derived.[11] This goal raises issues such as what would be the relationship between a native speaker and the super grammar when supposedly the super grammar would represent a competence the native speaker does not have. For example, let us suppose that the category *Perf* is in the *Aux* of English as per usual descriptions:

$$Aux \longrightarrow Aux_1 \ (Aux_2)$$
$$Aux_1 \longrightarrow (M) \ Tense$$
$$Aux_2 \longrightarrow (Perf) \ (Imperf)$$
$$Perf \longrightarrow have + En$$
$$Imperf \longrightarrow be + Ing$$
$$Tense \longrightarrow \left\{ \begin{array}{c} Pres \\ Past \end{array} \right\}$$

Acting on the assumption that SE is the super grammar from which NNE is to be derived, we would begin with this grammar claiming, I suppose, that NNE really has the structure represented by these rules; i.e. the real competence of native speakers of NNE is SE—it is merely that we cannot justify this hypothesis by recourse to data, native speakers, or motivations of a grammar-internal nature.

The super grammar approach entails problems, not the least of which is the predisposition on the part of its adherents to assume sameness and difference where they might not exist. A reasonable short range goal might be a component in each grammar such as suggested here to account for the differences between it and other grammars.

To summarize, we may state that identifiable relational entities in the *Aux* structure of NNE enter into different sets of relationships from identifiable relational entities in the *Aux* structure of SE. Specifically, there is an absence of *have+En* structures; there is no agreement between subjects and verbal forms other than *be*; *ed* and unmarked verbs traditionally identified with SE present tense may be neutralized; and *be* functions as a tense. These facts about NNE raise problems about the ways we might account for differences between SE and NNE and about accounting for differences between language varieties in general.

---

[11] This is a different problem from that associated with the quest for, and justification of, formal and substantive universals. See Noam Chomsky, *Aspects of the Theory of Syntax* (Cambridge, Mass.: MIT Press, 1965) pp. 27–30.

37

Sociolinguistic Factors in the History of American Negro Dialects

WILLIAM A. STEWART

WITHIN THE LAST FEW YEARS, the increased national commitment to bettering the lot of socially and economically underprivileged groups of Americans—the so-called "disadvantaged"—has caused educators to consider ways in which the schools may involve themselves in this task. Of the many possibilities, certainly one of the most obvious is to deal with the chronic language problems associated with many of the disadvantaged. Yet, although there is a general awareness that certain of the disadvantaged do have language problems, there is at the same time a lack of agreement as to what these problems entail, and therefore what to do about them. Some investigators (often educational psychologists) have maintained that the disadvantaged characteristically do not use verbal communication to the extent that members of the middle class do, and are thus impoverished in "communicative skills". To alleviate this situation, they have recommended programs aimed at encouraging the use of verbal communication of a variety of kinds by disadvantaged pupils. A few investigators have theorized that members of disadvantaged groups may even engage less in abstract thinking than do middle-class persons. For this there have been suggested programs designed to teach more perception and conceptualization on the part of the disadvantaged pupils.

On the other hand, linguists have tended to emphasize one other type of language problem which some disadvantaged groups often have, and for which evidence is quite accessible—being encountered every day in the nation's classrooms. This is the purely structural conflict between on the one hand the patterns of a non-standard dialect which an individual may have learned at home or in peer-group interaction, and on the other hand the equivalent patterns of Standard English—the language of modern technology and of the middle class. This is one kind of problem which many of the nation's schools ought to be

Reprinted by permission from *The Florida FL Reporter* 5, No. 2 (Spring, 1967), pp. 1–7. The author, former consultant with the Center for Applied Linguistics, is currently co-director of the Educational Study Center, Washington, D. C.

ready and willing to cope with. One indication of the readiness of the schools is the fact that traditional English teachers are rapidly abandoning the older "sloppy speech" and "lazy tongue" views of non-standard speech in favor of a realization that it usually represents the speaker's use of some language system which, though it may differ from Standard English in form and sometimes even in function, is nevertheless logical, coherent, and (in its own way) grammatical. Another indication of the readiness of schools to cope with the problem of dialect differences is the growth of a cadre of specialists in the teaching of English to speakers of other languages. With them, there has come into being a set of new techniques for teaching English to persons coming from a different language background.

Just as they are ready, America's schools certainly ought to be willing to deal with dialect-based problems, since there are a number of ways in which, by themselves, they can render a non-standard speaker dysfunctional in exchanges with Standard English-speaking members of the middle class. One way is for minor pronunciation differences between a non-standard and standard English—each one perhaps trivial by itself—to pile up in an utterance to such an extent that the non-standard version becomes unintelligible to a middle-class listener, even though in grammar and vocabulary it may be quite similar to its standard equivalent. Thus, a non-standard version of "I don't know where they live" might, in one dialect, become cryptic to the standard-speaking listener, merely because of its being pronounced something like *Ah 'own know wey 'ey lib.* Or, a Standard English speaker may misunderstand a non-standard utterance, even though he thinks he has deciphered it correctly, because it contains non-standard grammatical constructions which are unknown to him. For example, a middle-class listener may take a non-standard sentence *Dey ain't like dat* to mean "they aren't like that", when it really means "They didn't like that". The Standard-English speaker is simply unaware that *ain't* is this particular dialect's way of negating verbs in the past tense, as he is unaware that the usual equivalent in the same dialect of "They aren't like that" would be either *Dey not like dat* or *Dey don't be like dat* (the two variants indicating a difference in meaning which is not easily expressed in Standard English). Of course, similar breakdowns in intelligibility may also occur in the other direction, when the non-standard speaker tries to understand Standard English. Finally, even when he does succeed in making himself understood by his middle-class listeners, the non-standard speaker may still fall victim to the difference in social prestige between his dialect and Standard English. In other words, although middle-class persons may understand what he is saying, they may still consider him uncouth for saying it the way he does.

Professionally able though the schools may now be to embark on programs which would deal effectively with this kind of problem, the likelihood of their actually doing so in the near future is certainly not increased by the unwillingness of many educators and even some applied linguists to approach the problem in any but the most general terms. For, unfortunately, the technical know-how necessary to teach Standard English to speakers of non-standard dialects is simply not embodied in an awareness of the problem at the level of "Some children should probably be taught Standard English as a second dialect"—no matter how true such statements may be. The necessary know-how will begin to be adequate when and only when applied linguists can give, and educators will take seriously, details of the type "The verb system of such-and-such a non-standard dialect operates in such-and-such a way, and the verb system of Standard English operates in such-and-such a way, so that structural interference is most likely to occur at points *a*, *b*, and *c*. Therefore, the following lessons and drills in the Standard English verb system is what children who speak this non-standard dialect will need."[1]

One reason why there is little remedial English now being taught based upon a systematic comparison of the differences between non-standard dialects and Standard English is that information about one of the pedagogically most important features of non-standard dialects—their grammatical systems—is still largely lacking. This lack is due in great part to the fact that American dialect studies have traditionally emphasized differences in pronunciation and vocabulary, at the expense of information on systematic grammatical differences.

Now that linguists have begun to fill this information gap, however, they are finding their observations on language variation among the disadvantaged received with uneasiness and even hostility by many teachers, administrators, and community leaders. The reason for this is undoubtedly that the accurate description of dialect variation in American communities—particularly in urban centers—is turning out to show a disturbing correlation between language behavior on the one hand and socio-economic and ethnic stratification on the other.[2] The correlation is particularly controversial insofar as it involves the speech of large numbers of American Negroes, since at the present time Negro leadership (and this includes most Negro educators) is probably more achievement-oriented than any other. Because of this orientation, Negro elites tend not to welcome any evidence of uniform or stable behavioral differences between members of their own group (even lower-class ones) and those of the white-dominated middle class. Yet the fact is that Negroes account for most of the most pedagogically problematic non-standard dialect speakers in the larger cities, and also include within their group speakers of the most radically non-

[1] See William A. Stewart, editor, *Non-Standard Speech and the Teaching of English* (Washington, D.C., Center for Applied Linguistics, 1964).

[2] The American Dream notwithstanding, it is well known to social scientists that American society is stratified into a number of social classes and ethnic groups, and that each of these exhibits a "characteristic" configuration of customs, attitudes, roles, lifeways and, as it turns out, speech patterns. The literature on social and ethnic stratification is extensive, but good introductions are Egon Ernest Bergel, *Social Stratification* (New York, McGraw–Hill Book Co., 1962), and Tamotsu Shibutani and Kian M. Kwan, *Ethnic Stratification* (New York, The MacMillan Co., 1965). For an exhaustively documented study of the correlation between language variation and social class, ethnicity, and age in an American metropolis, see William Labov, *The Social Stratification of English in New York City*, (Washington, D.C., The Center for Applied Linguistics, 1966).

standard dialects of natively spoken English in the entire country.[3] Further-more, because *de facto* segregation in housing has caused non-standard-dialect-speaking Negroes to predominate in many schools and because these Negroes appear in many cases to have different kinds of problems with Standard English than non-standard-dialect-speaking whites have (even in the same area), the sweeping, for political purposes, of Negro dialect descriptions under the white-oriented geographic dialect rug would probably be more detrimental to dis-advantaged Negro children than it would be advantageous to Negro elites.[4]

On the other hand, linguists should realize that the fears and anxieties of Negro leaders about public discussion of ethnically correlated behavioral differences may have some foundation. It is possible, for example, that quite objective and innocently made statements about dialect differences between whites and Negroes might be interpreted by white racists as evidence of Negro cultural backwardness or mental inferiority, or even seized upon by black racists as evidence of some sort of mythical Negro "soul". Linguists should not censor their data, but they should make sure that their statements about Negro-white differences are not divorced from an awareness of the historical, social, and linguistic reasons why such differences may have come into existence and been maintained. Perhaps it would serve that end to point out here some of the sociolinguistic factors involved in the evolution of American Negro dialects, factors which explain why certain kinds of American Negro dialects are both different from the non-standard dialects of American whites, and more radically deviant from Standard English.

Although the linguistic history of the Negro in the United States can be reconstructed from the numerous literary attestations of the English of New World Negroes over the last two and a half centuries, and by comparing these with the English of Negroes in the United States, the Caribbean, and West Africa today, this has never been done for the English teaching profession. In presenting a historical sketch of this type, I realize that both the facts presented and my interpretations of them may embarrass or even infuriate those who would like to whitewash American Negro dialects by claiming that they do not exist—that (in spite of all sorts of observable evidence to the contrary) they are nothing but Southern white dialects, derived directly from Great Britain. I will simply make no apologies to those who regard human behavior as legitimate only if observed in the white man, since I feel that this constitutes a negation of the cultural and ethnic plurality which is one of America's greatest heritages.

---

[3] These two facts may not be entirely unrelated. For a graphic indication of the relatively more non-standard grammatical norms of Negro children over white children in a single city, see Figure 18 (page 53) in Walter Loban, *Problems in Oral English: Kindergarten Through Grade Nine* (Champaign, Ill. National Council of Teachers of English, 1966).

[4] For a discussion of Negro dialect in one urban community, see William A. Stewart, "Urban Negro Speech: Sociolinguistic Factors Affecting English Teaching" in Roger W. Shuy, editor, *Social Dialects and Language Learning* (Champaign, Ill. National Council of Teachers of English, 1965). The non-standard dialect patterns cited earlier in the present article are also Negro dialect.

On the other hand, I do regret that such a historical survey, although linguistically interesting, may at times conjure up out of the past memories of the Negro-as-slave to haunt the aspirations of the Negro-as-equal.

Of those Africans who fell victim to the Atlantic slave trade and were brought to the New World, many found it necessary to learn some kind of English. With very few exceptions, the form of English which they acquired was a pidginized one, and this kind of English became so well established as the principal medium of communication between Negro slaves in the British colonies that it was passed on as a creole language to succeeding generations of the New World Negroes, for whom it was their native tongue.[5] Some idea of what New World Negro English may have been like in its early stages can be obtained from a well known example of the speech of a fourteen-year-old Negro lad given by Daniel DeFoe in *The Family Instructor* (London, 1715). It is significant that the Negro, Toby, speaks a pidginized kind of English to his boy master, even though he states that he was born in the New World.

A sample of his speech is:[6]

Toby. Me be born at Barbadoes.
Boy. Who lives there, Toby?
Toby. There lives white mans, white womans, negree mans, negree womans, just so as live here.
Boy. What and not know God?

[5] In referring to types of languages, linguists use the terms *pidgin* and *creole* in a technical sense which has none of the derogatory or racial connotations of popular uses of these terms. When a linguist says that a variety of language is pidginized, he merely means that it has a markedly simplified grammatical structure compared with the "normal" (i.e. unpidginized) source-language. This simplification may be one way in which speakers of different languages can make a new language easier to learn and use—particularly if they have neither the opportunity nor the motivation to learn to speak it the way its primary users do. In addition, some of the unique characteristics of a pidgin language may be due, not to simplification, but to influences on it from the native languages of its users. What is important to realize, however, is that pidginized languages do have grammatical structure and regularity, even though their specific patterns may be different from those of the related unpidginized source-language of higher prestige. Thus, the fact that the sentence *Dem no get-am* in present-day West African Pidgin English is obviously different from its Standard English equivalent "They don't have it" does not necessarily indicate that the Pidgin English speaker "talks without grammar". In producing such a sentence, he is unconsciously obeying the grammatical rules of West African Pidgin English, and these determine that *Dem no get-am* is the "right" construction, as opposed to such ungrammatical or "wrong" combinations as *No dem get-am, No get dem-am, Get-am dem no,* etc. If a pidgin finally becomes the native language of a speech community (and thereby becomes by definition a creole language), it may expand in grammatical complexity to the level of "normal" or unpidginized languages. Of course, the resulting creole language may still exhibit structural differences from the original source-language, because the creole has gone through a pidginized stage. For more details, see Robert A. Hall, Jr., *Pidgin and Creole Languages*, (Ithaca, N.Y., Cornell U. Press, 1966).

[6] The same citation is given in a fuller form, along with a number of other attestations of early New World Negro speech, in George Philip Krapp, *The English Language in America* (New York, The Century Co., 1925), Vol. 1, pp. 255–65. Other attestations are cited in Tremaine McDowell, "Notes on Negro Dialect in the American Novel to 1821" *American Speech* V (1930), pp. 291–96.

> *Toby.* Yes, the white mans say God prayers,—no much know God.
> *Boy.* And what do the black mans do?
> *Toby.* They much work, much work,—no say God prayers, not at all.
> *Boy.* What work do they do, Toby?
> *Toby.* Makee the sugar, makee the ginger,—much great work, weary work,
> all day, all night.

Even though the boy master's English is slightly non-standard (e.g. *black mans*), it is still quite different from the speech of the Negro.

An idea of how widespread a pidginized form of English had become among the Negro population of the New World by the end of the seventeenth century can be gathered from the fact that it had even become the language of the coastal plantations in the Dutch colony of Surinam (i.e. Dutch Guiana), in South America. In an early description of that colony, the chapter on the Negro ends with a sample conversation in the local Negro English dialect. The dialogue includes such sentences as *Me bella well* "I am very well", *You wantee siddown pinkininne?* "Do you want to sit down for a bit?", and *You wantee go walka longa me?* "Do you want to take a walk with me?"[7] In these sentences, the use of the enclitic vowel in *wantee* recalls the same in DeFoe's example *makee*. Also, the speaker, like Toby, uses *me* as a subject pronoun. In the first Surinam sentence, we see an early example of a construction without any equivalent of the Standard English verb "to be". Toby also would probably have said *Me weary*, since the *be* in his first sentence was in all likelihood a past-tense marker (as it is in present-day West African pidgin English)—the sentence therefore meaning "I was born in Barbadoes". In the last Surinam sentence, a reflex of English *along* is used with the meaning of Standard English "with". It may or may not be accidental that in the Gullah dialect, spoken by the Negroes along the South Carolina coastal plain, the same phonemenon occurs, e.g. *Enty you wantuh walk long me?* "Do you want to take a walk with me?" Some Gullah speakers even still use *me* as a subject pronoun, e.g. *Me kyaan bruk-um* "I can't break it", and enclitic final vowels seem to have survived in such Gullah forms as *yerry*, *yeddy* "to hear".

Early examples of Negro dialect as spoken in the American colonies show it to be strikingly similar to that given by DeFoe for the West Indies and by Herlein for Surinam. In John Leacock's play, *The Fall of British Tyranny* (Philadelphia, 1776), part of the conversation between a certain "Kidnapper" and Cudjo, one of a group of Virginia Negroes, goes as follows[8]

[7] J. D. Herlein, *Beschryvinge van de volksplantinge Zuriname* (Leeuwarden, 1718), pp. 121–23. Herlein gives the Negro English dialogues in Dutch orthography. I have retranscribed these sentences in the kind of spelling which his English contemporaries would have used in order to show better the relationship between the Surinam dialect and the other examples. In the Dutch spelling, these sentences appear as *My belle wel, Jou wantje sie don pinkinine?*, and *Jo wantje gaeu wakke lange mie?*

[8] This citation also occurs in Krapp, and with others in Richard Walser, "Negro Dialect in Eighteenth-Century American Drama" *American Speech* XXX (1955), pp. 269–76.

Kidnapper. . . . . what part did you come from?

Cudjo.   Disse brack man, disse one, disse one, disse one, come from
                   Hamton, disse one, disse one, come from Nawfok, me come from
                   Nawfok too.

Kidnapper. Very well, what was your master's name?

Cudjo.   Me massa name Cunney Tomsee.

Kidnapper. Colonel Thompson—eigh?

Cudjo.   Eas, massa, Cunney Tomsee.

Kidnapper. Well then I'll make you a major—and what's your name?

Cudjo.   Me massa cawra me Cudjo.

Again, the enclitic vowels (e.g. *disse*) and the subject pronoun *me* are prominent features of the Negro dialect. In the sentence *Me Massa name Cunney
Tomsee* "My master's name is Colonel Thompson", both the verb "to be"
and the Standard English possessive suffix -*s* are absent. Incidentally, Cudjo's
construction is strikingly similar to sentences like *My sister name Mary* which
are used by many American Negroes today.

One possible explanation why this kind of pidginized English was so
widespread in the New World, with widely separated varieties resembling each
other in so many ways, is that it did not originate in the New World as isolated
and accidentally similar instances of random pidginization, but rather originated
as a *lingua franca* in the trade centers and slave factories on the West African
coast.[9] It is likely that at least some Africans already knew this pidgin English
when they came to the New World, and that the common colonial policy of
mixing slaves of various tribal origins forced its rapid adoption as a plantation
lingua franca.

In the course of the eighteenth century, some significant changes took
place in the New World Negro population, and these had their effect on language
behavior. For one thing, the number of Negroes born in the New World came
to exceed the number of those brought over from Africa. In the process, pidgin
English became the creole mother-tongue of the new generations, and in some
areas it has remained so to the present day.[10]

In the British colonies, the creole English of the uneducated Negroes and
the English dialects of both the educated and uneducated white were close
enough to each other (at least in vocabulary) to allow the speakers of each to
communicate, although they were still different enough so that the whites
could consider creole English to be "broken" or "corrupt" English and evidence,
so many thought, of the mental limitations of the Negro. But in Surinam, where
the European settlers spoke Dutch, creole English was regarded more objectively.
In fact, no less than two language courses specifically designed to teach creole

---

[9] See, for example, Basil Davidson, *Black Mother; The Years of the African Slave
Trade* (Boston, Little, Brown and Co., 1961), particularly p. 218.

[10] In the West Indies, creole English is usually called *patois*, while in Surinam it is
called *Taki-Taki*. In the United States, the only fairly "pure" creole English left today
is Gullah, spoken along the coast of South Carolina.

English to Dutch immigrants were published before the close of the eighteenth century.[11]

Another change which took place in the New World Negro population primarily during the course of the eighteenth century was the social cleavage of the New World-born generations into underprivileged field hands (a continuation of the older, almost universal lot of the Negro slave) and privileged domestic servant. The difference in privilege usually meant, not freedom instead of bondage, but rather freedom from degrading kinds of labor, access to the "big house" with its comforts and "civilization", and proximity to the prestigious "quality" whites, with the opportunity to imitate their behavior (including their speech) and to wear their clothes. In some cases, privilege included the chance to get an education and, in a very few, access to wealth and freedom. In both the British colonies and the United States, Negroes belonging to the privileged group were soon able to acquire a more standard variety of English than the creole of the field hands, and those who managed to get a decent education became speakers of fully standard and often elegant English. This seems to have become the usual situation by the early 1800s, and remained so through the Civil War. In Caroline Gilman's *Recollections of a Southern Matron* (New York, 1838), the difference between field-hand creole (in this case, Gullah) and domestic servant dialect is evident in a comparison of the gardener's "He tief one sheep—he run away las week, cause de overseer gwine for flog him" with Dina's "'Scuse me, missis, I is gitting hard o' hearing, and yes is more politer dan no" (page 254). A more striking contrast between the speech of educated and uneducated Negroes occurs in a novel written in the 1850s by an American Negro who had traveled extensively through the slave states. In Chapter XVII, part of the exchange between Henry, an educated Negro traveler, and an old "aunty" goes as follows:[12]

"Who was that old man who ran behind your master's horse?"

"Dat Nathan, my husban'."

"Do they treat him well, aunty?"

"No, chile, wus an' any dog, da beat 'im foh little an nothin'."

"Is uncle Nathan religious?"

"Yes, chile, ole man an' I's been sahvin' God dis many day, fo yeh baun! Wen any on 'em in de house git sick, den da sen foh "uncle Nathan" come pray foh dem; "uncle Nathan" mighty good den!"

After the Civil War, with the abolition of slavery, the breakdown of the plantation system, and the steady increase in education for poor as well as affluent Negroes, the older field-hand creole English began to lose many of its

[11] These were Pieter van Dijk, *Nieuwe en nooit bevoorens geziende onderwijzinge in het Bastert Engels, of Neeger Engels* (Amsterdam, undated, but probably 1780), and G. C. Weygandt, *Gemeenzame leerwijze om het Basterd of Neger-Engelsch op een gemakkelijke wijze te leeren verstaan en spreeken* (Paramaribo, 1798).

[12] Martin R. Delany, *Blake; or the Huts of America*, published serially in *The Anglo-African Magazine* (1859). The quotation is from Vol. 1, No. 6, (June 1859), p. 163.

creole characteristics, and take on more and more of the features of the local white dialects and of the written language. Yet, this process has not been just one way. For if it is true that the speech of American Negroes has been strongly influenced by the speech of whites with whom they came into contact, it is probably also true that the speech of many whites has been influenced in some ways by the speech of Negroes.[13]

Over the last two centuries, the proportion of American Negroes who speak a perfectly standard variety of English has risen from a small group of privileged house slaves and free Negroes to persons numbering in the hundreds of thousands, and perhaps even millions. Yet there is still a sizeable number of American Negroes—undoubtedly larger than the number of standard-speaking Negroes—whose speech may be radically non-standard. The non-standard features in the speech of such persons may be due in part to the influence of the non-standard dialects of whites with whom they or their ancestors have come in contact, but they also may be due to the survival of creolisms from the older Negro field-hand speech of the plantations. To insure their social mobility in modern American society, these non-standard speakers must undoubtedly be given a command of Standard English; that point was made in the early part of this paper. In studying non-standard Negro dialects and teaching Standard English in terms of them, however, both the applied linguist and the language teacher must come to appreciate the fact that even if certain non-standard Negro dialect patterns do not resemble the dialect usage of American whites, or even those of the speakers of remote British dialects, they may nevertheless be as old as African and European settlement in the New World, and therefore quite widespread and well established. On various occasions, I have pointed out that many speakers of non-standard American Negro dialects make a grammatical and semantic distinction by means of *be*, illustrated by such constructions as *he busy* "He is busy (momentarily)" or *he workin'* "he is working (right now)" as opposed to *he be busy* "he is (habitually) busy" or *he be workin'* "he is working (steadily)", which the grammar of Standard English is unable to make.[14] Even this distinction goes back well over a century. One observer in the 1830s noted a request by a slave for a permanent supply of soap as "(If) Missis only give we, we be so so clean forever", while *be* is absent in a subsequent report of someone's temporary illness with "She jist sick for a little while".[15]

Once educators who are concerned with the language problems of the disadvantaged come to realize that non-standard Negro dialects represent a historical tradition of this type, it is to be hoped that they will become less embarrassed by evidence that these dialects are very much alike throughout the country while different in many ways from the non-standard dialects of whites,

[13] See Raven I. McDavid, Jr., and Virginia Glenn McDavid, "The Relationship of the Speech of American Negroes to the Speech of Whites" *American Speech* XXVI (1951), pp. 3–17.

[14] See, for example, *The Florida FL Reporter*, Vol. 4, No. 2 (Winter 1965–66), p. 25.

[15] Frances Anne Kemble, *Journal of a Residence on a Georgian Plantation in 1838–39* (New York, 1862). The first quotation is from page 52, and the second is from page 118.

less frustrated by failure to turn non-standard Negro dialect speakers into Standard English speakers overnight, less impatient with the stubborn survival of Negro dialect features in the speech of even educated persons, and less zealous in proclaiming what is "right" and what is "wrong". If this happens, then applied linguists and educators will be able to communicate with each other, and both will be able to communicate with the non-standard-speaking Negro child. The problem will then be well on its way toward a solution.

38

Continuity and Change in American Negro Dialects

WILLIAM A. STEWART

IN A PREVIOUS ARTICLE on the history of American Negro dialects[1] I cited examples of the kind of literary and comparative evidence which exists for determining earlier stages of these dialects, and which practically forces the conclusion that the linguistic assimilation of the Afro-American population to the speech patterns of English-speaking American whites was neither as rapid nor as complete as some scholars have supposed.[2] Of the Negro slaves who constituted the field labor force on North American plantations up to the mid-nineteenth century, even many who were born in the New World spoke a variety of English which was in fact a true creole language—differing markedly in grammatical structure from those English dialects which were brought directly from Great Britain, as well as from New World modifications of these

Reprinted by permission from *The Florida FL Reporter* 6, No. 1 (Spring, 1968, pp. 3-4, 14-16, 18). For the author see the preceding article.

[1] William A. Stewart, "Sociolinguistic Factors in the History of American Negro Dialects" *The Florida FL Reporter*, Vol. 5, No. 2 (Spring, 1967). [See p. 444 in this book.]

[2] E.g. "The Negroes born in this country invariably used, according to these records, good English." Allen Walker Read, "The Speech of Negroes in Colonial America" *The Journal of Negro History*, Vol. 24, No. 3, (the quote is from page 258). The records which Read refers to are for the most part runaway slave advertisements published before the American Revolution. Of course, the evidence which they supply on slave speech is indirect (i.e. they give impressions of the particular slave's competence in English, but no examples of that English), since the information was merely intended to help identify the runaway. If these indirect records say what Read interprets them as saying, then they are certainly at variance with what direct evidence (quotations in slave dialect) is available from the same period. Furthermore, the far larger number of attestations of slave speech during the nineteenth century which show widespread use of non-standard dialect, together with a similar situation observable today, would mean that American Negro speech generally became less standard after that first generation of American-born slaves. Needless to say, such a process would be difficult to explain either structurally or historically. The trouble with Read's conclusion seems to be that, in interpreting such advertisements, he did not consider the possibility that in the parlance of slave owners a term like "good English" might have meant something very different when applied to Negroes than it would have if applied to whites. Indications that this was probably the case seem to exist in the advertisements quoted on pp. 252-53.

in the mouths of descendants of the original white colonists.[3] And, although this creole English subsequently underwent modification in the direction of the more prestigious British-derived dialects, the merging process was neither instantaneous nor uniform. Indeed, the non-standard speech of present-day American Negroes still seems to exhibit structural traces of a creole predecessor, and this is probably a reason why it is in some ways more deviant from Standard English than is the non-standard speech of even the most uneducated American whites.

For the teacher, this means that such "Negro" patterns as the "zero copula",[4] the "zero possessive"[5], or "undifferentiated pronouns"[6] should not be ascribed to greater carelessness, laziness, or stupidity on the part of Negroes, but rather should be treated as what they really are—language patterns which have been in existence for generations and which their present users have acquired, from parent and peer, through a perfectly normal kind of language-learning process.[7]

Since the main purpose of the earlier article was to document the use of creole English by native-born American Negroes during the colonial and ante-bellum periods, almost nothing was said about the course of Negro dialects since Emancipation. But, as anyone can see who compares written samples of

---

[3] The Gullah (or Geechee) dialect, spoken by many Negroes along the South Atlantic coast, appears to be a fairly direct descendant of the older kind of plantation creole.

[4] The term "zero copula" refers to the absence of an explicit predicating verb in certain dialect constructions, where Standard English has such a verb (usually in the present tense). Compare non-standard Negro dialect *He old, Dey runnin'*, and *She a teacher* with Standard English "He is old", "They are running" and "She is a teacher".

[5] The term "zero possessive" refers to the absence of an explicit suffix in noun–noun constructions, where Standard English has such a suffix. Compare non-standard Negro dialect *My fahver frien'* with standard English "My father's friend."

[6] The term "undifferentiated pronoun" refers to the use of the same pronoun form for both subject and object, and sometimes for possession as well. The pronominal form used may be derived from either the Standard English object form, or the subject form. Compare such non-standard forms as *Him know we, Him know us*, (beside *He know us*) with the Standard English "He knows us" to which they are equivalent. Or compare *He fahver* (beside *His fahver*) and *We house* (beside *Our house*) with Standard English "His father" and "Our house".

[7] If the term "Negro dialect" is understood to refer to non-standard varieties of American English whose more unique (i.e. non-white and non-British) structural features are simply due to the historical influence of an earlier plantation creole, then it should be clear that such a term does not imply any direct genetic determination of speech patterns, in spite of its ethnic reference. The "Negro" in "Negro dialect" is merely a recognition of the fact that the creole predecessor for such structural features was itself the result of African migration to and acculturation in Anglo-Saxon America, and that those present-day dialects which show the greatest influence from such a creole are precisely those which are used by the descendants of the Negro field hands who originally spoke it. In addition, the speech of American Negroes is often characterized by special kinds of syllable and breath dynamics, as well as unique uses of pitch, stress and volume. But even these language habits are always socially learned and transmitted ones, although it is difficult to tell whether they represent survivals of African speech habits, creole speech habits, or are more recent innovations. That they are not the product of any special Negro vocal physiology should be obvious from the fact that some whites can mimic such features quite well, while there are some Negroes in whose speech the same features are not normally present.

Negro dialect from around the Civil War with Negro dialect today, there have been changes. And, equally interesting, one can also see that there are still many similarities between the two. An overview of the interacting processes of continuity and change in American Negro dialects as they relate to one important aspect of language variation—grammatical structure—will help educators to put the classroom language problems of today's disadvantaged Negro children into a clearer perspective.

One of the more important changes which have occurred in American Negro dialects during the past century has been the almost complete decreolization of both their functional and lexical vocabulary. Although this process actually began long before the Civil War (particularly in areas with a low proportion of Negroes to whites), the breakdown of the plantation system apparently accelerated it considerably, even in the coastal areas of South Carolina and Georgia. In the process, overt creolisms which were so common in early attestations of slave speech, such as *been* for marking past action (with no basic distinction between preterite and perfect), undifferentiated pronouns for subject and object (e.g. *me, him,* and *dem* also as subject pronouns and *we* also as an object pronoun), a single subject pronoun form (usually *him* or *he*) for masculine, feminine and neuter in the third person singular, *-um* (or *-am*) as a general third person (all genders and numbers) object suffix, *no* as a verbal negator, and *for* as an infinitive marker became quite rare in even the more non-standard speech of Negroes born after Emancipation.[8]

However, the speed and thoroughness with which the plantation fieldhand dialects were thus made more "proper" varied both according to the region and according to the social characteristics of the speakers themselves. Because people

[8] Judging from the literary treatment of Negro dialect, these features were characteristic of the non-standard speech of even New England Negroes up to the close of the eighteenth century. Within the first decades of the nineteenth century, however, the northern limit of their common occurrence in adult speech appears to have receded to the Delaware region, and to somewhere in the Carolinas by the middle of the same century. Of course, most of these creolisms still occur in Gullah—at least sporadically. And it is likely that the *for to* infinitives of some Deep South Negro dialects are the result of incomplete de-creolization (the adding of non-creole *to*, without giving up the creole *for*), rather than the borrowing of a white non-standard dialect pattern, as some might suppose. In the first place, such white dialects (Appalachia, Georgia, etc.) usually have a contrast between *to* and *for to*, e.g. *I come to see it* (i.e. "It dawned on me") vs. *I come for to see it* ("I came in order to see it"), while many Negro dialects in which *for* occurs do not make such a distinction. In the second place, there is piecemeal evidence of the addition of *to* after *for* along the South Atlantic coast, where the change has been relatively recent. For example, in *Drums and Shadows: Survival Studies Among the Georgia Coastal Negroes* (Athens, Ga. 1940, p. 144) a team of the Georgia Writers' Project interviewed an old lady (then approximately one hundred years old) who, speaking of an African-born slave whom she knew in her youth, recalled "I membuh he say 'Lemme cook sumpm fuh nyam.' He mean sumpm fuh to eat". Notice also the de-creolization of the Gullah and Caribbean Creole English verb *nyam* "to eat". In some areas, the changeover was not so complete, cf. a literary reflection of a Gullah Negroe's alternation between the same two verbs in Ambrose E. Gonzales, *The Captain: Stories of the Black Border* (Columbia, S. C.: The State Co., 1924, p. 149), "You hab mout' fuh nyam da' haa'd hoecake you juntlemun gi' you fuh eat".

learn most of their language forms from others, the change took place more rapidly and completely in areas where speakers (white or Negro) of more-or-less standard varieties of English were present in numbers than it did in areas with a high concentration of field laborers. On the other hand, because children generally are more affected by the language usage of other children than by that of grownups, and because lower-class child peer groups tend to remain rather isolated from the stylistic innovations of adult discourse, the change took place more slowly and less thoroughly in the speech of young children than it did in that of adolescents and adults.

The result of this uneven "correction" of the older plantation dialects was that, while they seemed to have died out by the end of the nineteenth century (particularly outside the South Atlantic coastal area and the Mississippi Basin), juvenile versions of them actually continued to survive in many Negro speech communities as "baby talk" or "small-boy talk".[9] That is, the older non-standard (and sometimes even creole-like) dialect features remained in use principally by younger children in Negro speech-communities—being learned from other young children, to be given up later in life when "smallboy talk" was no longer appropriate to a more mature status.[10] And even though the adult dialects which these child dialects were ontogenetically given up for were also structurally

[9] The impression that the rustic and creole features of the older plantation dialects died out entirely during this period is easy to get, considering that the speech of children hardly appears at all in the records of folklorists or dialectologists, or even in the fictional use of dialect, since the main concern of the social scientist and the novelist alike has been the adult. Evidence that the older dialects have in fact survived in the speech of children is only now coming to light through recent studies of present-day Negro speech communities. See William A. Stewart "Urban Negro Speech: Sociolinguistic Factors Affecting English Teaching" in Roger W. Shuy, editor, *Social Dialects and Language Learning* (Champaign, Ill: National Council of Teachers of English, 1965), particularly pp. 16–18, and J. L. Dillard, "Negro Children's Dialect in the Inner City" *The Florida FL Reporter*, Vol. 5, No. 3 (Fall, 1967). It would seem that the preservation of a more conservative dialect by young children in communities where the older language forms are being encroached upon by imported ones is not limited to Negro communities. During a recent sociolinguistic survey of the Appalachian region, I found full-fledged mountain dialect still being used by pre-school-age white children in communities where it had been abandoned by all but the oldest adults.

[10] Like Dillard, I feel that this constitutes the most plausible explanation of the sporadic but not infrequent occurrence in the speech of lower-class Negro children of such "mistakes" as *been* as a general past-time marker (e.g. *He been hit me*), pronominal forms which are undifferentiated for case or gender (e.g. *Me gonna try* and *He out playin'*—the latter said in reference to a girl), etc., since these same features were quite normal in older forms of Negro dialect (and still are in Gullah) and since there is, after all, an uninterrupted chain of language transmission from those earlier speakers to Negro children of the present day. Because some of the features are similar (at least superficially) to ones which are characteristic at certain stages of language development in virtually all English-speaking children, most specialists have attributed the Negro child patterns to developmental causes. However, since the Negro patterns are sometimes used by children who are well beyond the developmental stage (which normally ends at age 3.6 or 4 for whites), this would imply that Negroes develop linguistically more slowly than do whites. And, since there are even Negro octogenarians who use these forms, one would be forced to the absurd conclusion that some Negroes must not have completed the developmental process at all.

non-standard and identifiably Negro in most cases, they were still more standard—enough, at least, so that conspicuous retentions of child-dialect forms in
the speech of an adult could sometimes result in the accusation that he or she
was "talking like a child" or simply "talking bad".[11]

Interestingly enough, the use of an older, more conservative form of Negro
dialect as child speech was not always limited to Negroes. In the Old South,
many upper-class whites went through a similar linguistic metamorphosis from
the non-standard dialect of their Negro playmates to the relatively Standard
English of their adult station in life. As John Bennett described the situation for
the Charlestonian aristocracy of his day:

It is true that, up to the age of four, approximately, the children of the best
families, even in town, are apt to speak an almost unmodified *Gullah*, caught from
brown playmates and country bred nurses; but at that age the refinement of
cultivation begins, and "the flowers o' the forest are a' weed awa!"[12]

It was undoubtedly in this manner that such white Southern writers as
Joel C. Harris and Ambrose E. Gonzales first acquired their knowledge of the
Negro dialects which they immortalized in print.[13]

[11] In Washington, D.C., I know of an adolescent Negro who for some reason had
retained many child-dialect features in his speech. His peers characterized his speech by
saying that "He talk just like a small boy". And in her *Folk-Lore of the Sea Islands,
South Carolina* (Cambridge, Mass.: American Folklore Society, 1923), Elsie Clews
Parson gives a Negro folk-tale (No. 148, The Girl Who Learned to Talk Proper) in which
the speech of a young lady who was said to "talk very bad" is marked by the use of creole
pronominal forms (e.g. "Me ain' col', suh!"). It is interesting that the conclusion of this
tale also shows popular recognition of the effect of out-migration on speech habits, since
the same girl did finally "learn to talk proper" when an outsider married her and "kyarried
her to his country".

[12] John Bennett, "Gullah: A Negro Patois" *The South Atlantic Quarterly*, Vol. 7
(Oct. 1908) and Vol. 8 (Jan. 1909), quote from Vol. 7, p. 339. This same process had
evidently been going on for at least a century and a half before Bennett's time. It was noted
during the first half of the eighteenth century by G. L. Campbell, a British traveler to the
American colonies. "One Thing they are very faulty in, with regard to their Children,"
he wrote of the white planters in the July 1746 number of *The London Magazine*, "which
is, that when young, they suffer them too much to prowl amongst the young Negroes,
which insensibly causes them to imbibe their Manners and broken Speech." Quoted in
Allen Walker Read, "British Recognition of American Speech in the Eighteenth Century"
Dialect Notes, Vol. 6, Part 6 (July 1933), p. 329. Since even the most aristocratic British
children undoubtedly picked up non-standard English or Scottish dialects from children
of the servant class, it must have been the "broken" (i.e. creolized) character of colonial
Negro speech which Campbell found so disagreeable in the North American situation.

[13] Elsewhere ("Urban Negro Speech . . .," *loc. cit.*, p. 13, fn. 7), I have taken Ambrose
E. Gonzales to task for his racistic explanation of some of the structural characteristics
of the Gullah dialect. At the same time, one can see how he would come to such a point
of view, since he was obviously unaware of pidginization as a linguistic phenomenon,
and therefore unable to account scientifically for its operation in the speech of the Gullah
Negroes. In addition, a genetic explanation of language differences fitted quite comfortably
into the rhetoric of the caste-cloven society of which Gonzales was so much a product.
This theoretical weakness notwithstanding, Gonzales' literary rendition of Gullah was
superb. Considering the accuracy of his dialect phonology and syntax, and the ease with
which he handled subtle dialect differences and even individual switching behavior, he
can certainly qualify as America's greatest dialect writer. For a similar opinion of Gonzales,

Today, genteel Southern whites no longer learn non-standard Negro dialects as children, since the social conditions which once prompted them to do so have now become part of history. In their pre-school childhood, however, many Negroes still learn and use such dialects, and although they may modify these in later life, few ever attain anything like the elegant Standard English which was the familial and social heritage of the older white aristocrats. Yet, when they enter the Standard English milieu of the school, Negro children from this kind of language background are expected to compete linguistically with children (usually white) who have known and used Standard English all their lives. Of course, a few of these Negro children do succeed, not because of good teaching, but because of their own exceptional abilities. But a far greater proportion of these children—the average ones, as well as the few who are truly below average —fail conspicuously. And, because there is obviously some sort of ethnic correlation between pupil success and failure in newly integrated school situations, the embarrassed educational establishment and the frustrated public enter into a crisis relationship. Some whites charge (privately, at least) that the schools are being given the impossible task of teaching unteachable Negroes. And some Negroes charge (not so privately) that white educators are involved in a conspiracy to deliberately keep Negro children from learning. Parents protest blindly, and school administrators run helter-skelter, holding councils of despair with colleagues who understand the problem no better.

A basic reason why so many Negro children fail in school is not that they are unteachable, but that they are not being taught efficiently or fairly. And this fact may have little or nothing to do with a white conspiracy against integrated schools. Rather, it may be the result of a far less deliberate yet equally devastating insensitivity of the educational process to the social and cultural characteristics of the school population. This is probably nowhere more striking than in the area of language since, as speakers largely of non-standard dialects which are among the most deviant from Standard English now being used in America, many Negro children are burdened at every turn with achievement barriers in the form of extra (and uncompensated for) language learning requirements. For example, all children are expected to learn how to read in school. But, for many Negro pupils, the problem is made more difficult by the fact that they are unfamiliar, not only with the sound-spelling-meaning correspondences of many of the words, but even with the grammatical patterns which these words make up in their reading lessons. Consequently, the reading achievement of these children becomes dependent upon their own success in deciphering Standard English sentence structure. And the same type of problem is reflected in other subject areas in the schools. The irony, here, is that the traditional educational system is itself creating much of the pedagogical disadvantagement of its linguistically different pupils by requiring them to accomplish, on their own, as

see Ann Sullivan Haskell *The Representation of Gullah-influenced Dialect in Twentieth Century South Carolina Prose: 1922–30* (University of Pennsylvania Ph.D. Dissertation, 1964), pp. 238–41.

much again as middle-class pupils from a Standard English background are expected to accomplish with expert help.

In many ways, the plight of the Negro child who enters school speaking a non-standard dialect is similar to that of a foreign-language-speaking child entering an American school. And, while it can be argued that no Negro dialect is as different from Standard English as is, say, Spanish, this does not necessarily mean that the linguistically different Negro's task is that much easier. For, while the boundaries between a full-fledged foreign language and English are usually clear cut (the Spanish-speaking child, for example, will usually know at any given point whether Spanish or English is being used, and so will the teacher), the many similarities between any Negro dialect and Standard English makes it difficult to tell exactly where one leaves off and the other begins.[14] Thus, even the linguistic similarities between a non-standard dialect and Standard English can be pedagogically and psychologically disadvantageous, since they can camouflage functional differences between the two linguistic systems. Furthermore, while a wealth of linguistic knowledge and pedagogical know-how is currently brought to bear on the language problems of the child who speaks a foreign language such as Spanish, no similar competences have yet been developed to help the child who speaks a non-standard dialect, although his needs are just as great—and his numbers greater. Considering his educational prospects as they stand at present, the linguistically different Negro child might well say "I look down de road an' de road so lonesome".

Although English teachers, speech therapists, and other language-oriented educators are now dedicating themselves more than ever to the task of helping disadvantaged children—and especially disadvantaged Negro children—acquire proficiency in Standard English, very few of these dedicated professionals have demonstrated any real understanding of the language characteristics of the communities from which these children come. For their part, teachers of English to Spanish-speaking Mexican, Puerto Rican or Cuban children know that an understanding of the structure of Spanish will give insights into the problem which such children have with English, and these teachers would be shocked by any suggestion that a comparative approach to the language of the school and the language of the child is unnecessary. In contrast, teachers of English to disadvantaged Negro children have generally remained aloof from the serious study of non-standard Negro dialect.

This lack of interest on the part of many English teachers in the non-standard language of Negro children is in large part the product of a normative view of language which has long been the mainstay of traditional teacher training.

[14] Because the structural relationships which hold between the two "dialects" in such a case are in part like those between completely foreign languages and in part like those between two style levels of a single language, I have coined the term "quasi-foreign language situation" to describe it. See my "Foreign Language Teaching Methods in Quasi-Foreign Language Situations" in William A. Stewart, editor, *Non-Standard Speech and the Teaching of English* (Washington, D.C.: Center for Applied Linguistics, 1964).

Either overtly or by implication, the teacher-to-be is taught that the kind of usage which is indicated in grammar books, dictionaries and style manuals, (and which is presumably followed by educated speakers and writers) represents a maximum of structural neatness, communicative efficiency, esthetic taste and logical clarity. Once this normative view has been inculcated in the prospective teacher (and it must be admitted that popular beliefs about "correct" and "incorrect" language practically guarantee this) then the teacher will quite naturally regard departures from the norms of Standard English as departures from structure, clarity, taste, and even logic itself.[15]

Of course, there have always been exceptional teachers who have seen that chronic deviations from Standard English usage on the part of their pupils may indicate simply their normal use of some other variety of English, with its own structure and logic. William Francis Allen was an early example of a teacher who not only discovered this, but came to realize that even apparent "ignorance" in coping with logical or experiential problems could sometimes be traced to mere difficulty with the language in which the problems were posed. He recorded the following incident, which occurred while he was teaching Gullah Negro children on Port Royal Island, South Carolina, during the Civil War.

I asked a group of boys one day the color of the sky. Nobody could tell me. Presently the father of one of them came by, and I told him their ignorance, repeating my question with the same result as before. He grinned: "Tom, how sky stan'?" "Blue," promptly shouted Tom.[16]

But in attempting to teach Standard English to children who speak a non-standard dialect, even those teachers who understand that there is a language conflict involved, and who would accordingly like to borrow techniques from foreign-language teaching methodology, are likely to find their efforts hampered by too limited a knowledge of the structural characteristics of whatever non-standard dialect the children speak. For, in all too many cases, the best pedagogical grasp of the structural features of a particular non-standard dialect will consist of little more than a list of certain "folk" pronunciations and an awareness of the use of such grammatical shibboleths as *ain't* and the double negative. Unfortunately, this kind of superficial knowledge of the structural details of the speech of disadvantaged children will not only prevent the teacher or therapist from understanding the reasons for many of these children's "mistakes" in Standard English, but it is also likely to lead to an inadvertent

[15] Linguistic and cultural relativists will be pleased to learn that the dialect tables have been turned on the normativists at least once. In his essay, John Bennett (*op. cit.*, Vol. 7, p. 340) reports that Gullah-speaking Negroes passed judgment on visiting Yankees with "Dey use dem mout' so funny!"

[16] William Francis Allen, Charles Pickard Ware, and Lucy McKim Garrison, *Slave Songs of the United States* (New York: 1867), p. xxvii. What the father of the boy knew was that, in Gullah, observable characteristics are usually indicated by means of the verb *stan'* (or *'tan'*) which can be translated roughly as "look," "seem" or "appear".

lumping together of children who speak different dialects (and therefore who have different kinds of problems with Standard English) under a generalized remedial English approach which would not take these differences into account. In the likely event that both Negroes and whites make up the disadvantaged student population of a school system, this egalitarian approach to their language problems may prove almost irresistible in the face of a particularly unsophisticated kind of social liberalism, currently in vogue among educators, which regards it as a manifestation of racism to entertain even the most well qualified hypothesis that differences in ethnicity (such as being "white" or "Negro" in America) might possibly correlate with differences in behavior (in language usage, for example). In fact, so strong is the hold upon today's educators of this sociologically simplistic philosophy, with its "all children are the same" credo, that many educators and teachers even find uncomfortable the anthropologist's contention that correlations between ethnicity and behavior are not only possible but probable, when one considers that ethnicity is more of a social phenomenon than a physiological one, and that so much of human behavior is socially conditioned rather than genetically determined. And instead of seeing the chronic failure of disadvantaged Negroes in integrated school situations as a strong indication that this "sameness" credo is inadequate and counter-productive in terms of the real goals of education, many educators let such unpleasant realities force them into clinging all the more blindly and tenaciously to their simplistic views of the matter.

But the failure to perceive structural differences between the non-standard dialects of American Negroes and those of American whites has not been unique to English teachers and speech therapists. Some prominent dialectologists also have claimed that Negro dialects represent, at the most, a minor statistical skewing of white dialect features.[17] And still others have passed over the subject altogether.[18]

[17] As one dialect geographer expressed his view of the matter, "the range of variants is the same in Negro and in white speech, though the statistical distribution of variants has been skewed by the American caste system". Raven I. McDavid, Jr., "American Social Dialects" *College English*, Vol. 26, No. 4 (January, 1965), p. 258, fn. 7. In an even more recent article, McDavid rejects the idea of a pidgin or creole background for American Negro dialects, saying "To a naive social scientist, what is generally known about the operations of the domestic slave trade should be sufficient to refute such an argument". Raven I. McDavid, Jr., "Needed Research in Southern Dialects" in Edgar T. Thompson, editor, *Perspectives on the South: Agenda for Research* (Durham, N.C.: Duke University Press, 1967), p. 122. In view of the numerous attestations of the actual use of pidgin and creole forms of English by American Negro slaves in the contemporary literature (see my "Sociolinguistic Factors in the History of American Negro Dialects" *loc. cit.*, for a few references), it is difficult to imagine any historical basis for McDavid's statements. Since he must have seen at least the reprintings of some of these in scholarly books and articles, it can only be that he has not considered the linguistic implications of their rather non-European grammatical structure. Furthermore, if there is anything in what is known about the slave trade, slave life, or plantation social stratification in America which would call into question these early attestations of pidgin and creole English, it is strange that it has never been articulated in such standard works on American Negro slavery as Philip Alexander Bruce, *Economic History of Virginia in the Seventeenth Century* (New York: The MacMillan Co., 1895); Ulrich B. Phillips, *American Negro Slavery*

One further reason why both language teachers and dialectologists have failed to appreciate the extent to which non-standard Negro dialects may differ from non-standard white dialects (even in the Deep South) may simply be that such differences now remain mostly in syntax (i.e. grammatical patterns and categories) rather than in vocabulary or lexicophonology (i.e. word forms), and are thus not normally uncovered by the word-comparison techniques which dialectologists and non-linguists rely on so heavily. Yet, a comparison of the grammatical details of white and Negro non-standard dialects suggests a very different kind of historical relationship than is evident from a comparison of words alone. This can be illustrated by the comparison of a Standard English (STE) conjunctive sentence like "We were eating—and drinking, too" together with its equivalents in representative varieties of Southern white non-standard basilect (WNS), Negro non-standard basilect (NNS), and Gullah Basilect (GUL):[19]

STE: We were eating—and drinking, too.
WNS: We was eatin'—an' drinkin', too.
NNS: We was eatin'—an' we drinkin', too.
GUL: We bin duh nyam—en' we duh drink, too.

If one compares only the forms of the equivalent words in these sentences, NNS (Negro non-standard) appears to be virtually identical to WNS (white non-standard), with both of them about equally different from STE (Standard English).[20] Judged by the same criteria, GUL (Gullah) appears to be radically different from all the others, including NNS.

(New York: D. Appleton and Co., 1918) and his *Life and Labor in the Old South* (Boston: Little, Brown and Co., 1929); Marcus William Jernegan, *Laboring and Dependent Classes in Colonial America: 1607–1783* (University of Chicago Press, 1931); Frederick Bancroft, *Slave-Trading in the Old South* (Baltimore: J. H. Furst Co., 1931): Kenneth M. Stampp, *The Peculiar Institution: Slavery in the Ante-Bellum South* (New York: Alfred A. Knopf, Inc., 1956); Herbert S. Klein, *Slavery in the Americas: A Comparative Study of Virginia and Cuba* (University of Chicago Press, 1967).

[18] None of the four recent publications on American dialects which have been written for the use of English teachers contain any substantive reference to Negro dialect—not even a simple statement of the historical and definitional issues involved in the concept. This omission is probably due to the tacit acceptance on the part of the various authors of the theory that most Negro speech is identical to Southern varieties of white speech, and therefore that the description of the latter in their manuals takes care of Negro speech as well. These four publications are: Jean Malmstrom and Annabel Ashley, *Dialects— USA* (Champaign, Ill.: National Council of Teachers of English, 1963); Jean Malmstrom, *Language in Society* (New York: The Hayden Book Co., 1965); Carroll E. Reed, *Dialects of American English* (Cleveland: World Publishing Co., 1967); Roger W. Shuy, *Discovering American Dialects* (Champaign Ill.: National Council of Teachers of English, 1967).

[19] The term *basilect* refers to that variety of a particular dialect which is structurally the most deviant from standard English. See William A. Stewart, "Urban Negro Speech: Sociolinguistic Factors Affecting English Teaching" *loc. cit.*, particularly pp. 15–17.

[20] The literary dialect spellings which I have used in these examples may well make the individual words in WNS and NNS seem more alike than they actually are when pronounced. But, for the sake of argument, I would just as soon allow for the possibility that some words might have identical phonological forms in the different dialects.

Because of such word-form similarities and differences, many dialectologists have concluded that, while Gullah itself may be a creolized form of
English (rather than a direct descendant of any British dialect or dialects),
there is no evidence that other kinds of American Negro speech are related to
it in any direct way.[21] For, according to the same kind of word-form comparisons, these represent little more than the use by Negroes of dialect patterns
which are also used by (and presumably borrowed from) whites in the Deep
South.

However, a comparison of the sentence structure of these dialects shows a
somewhat different kind of relationship. In the foregoing equivalent sentences,
this is evident in the treatment of the subject pronoun and the tense-marking
auxiliary (or copula). For, although STE, WNS, NNS, and GUL can all repeat
the subject pronoun and auxiliary in a conjunctive clause (e.g. STE "We were
eating—and we were drinking, too"), this is not generally done in any of them.
Instead, one or both will usually be omitted (provided, of course, that the
subject and temporal referents remain the same). But in terms of what they
omit, these dialects split along lines which are different from those indicated by
word-form similarities and differences. Both STE and WNS normally omit
both the subject pronoun and the auxiliary in a conjunctive clause, although the
tense-marking auxiliary must be present if the subject is not omitted. But
NNS, like GUL, often repeats the subject pronoun in a conjunctive clause
while omitting the auxiliary—even when this indicates past tense.[22]

An example of the same phenomenon in American Negro speech at the
beginning of the nineteenth century is to be found in A. B. Lindsley's play
Love and Friendship (New York: 1807). A Negro says: "I tink dey bin like sich
a man de boss, for dey like for be tumel 'bout." Side by side with *dey bin like*
in the first clause is *dey like* in the second one, even though the context makes it
reasonably clear that both mean "they liked".[23]

If, in such features as the omission of a redundant auxiliary (while retaining

---

[21] This concession as to the creole nature of Gullah was largely forced upon an
intensely Anglo-centric American dialect-studies tradition by Lorenzo Dow Turner's
Africanisms in the Gullah Dialect (University of Chicago Press, 1949) which, though it
concentrated more on African survivals than on creole influences and dealt more with
naming practices than with linguistic structure, did at least make the point rather strongly
that Gullah is a creolized form of English.

[22] Those who have had enough contact with Negro non-standard dialects to know
that constructions like *We tryin'* usually indicate the present tense (i.e. STE "We are
trying") might assume that the superficially similar construction *we drinkin'* in the NNS
sentence *We was eatin'—an' we drinkin', too* also indicates the present tense—the whole
thereby meaning "We were eating—and we are drinking, too" with an erroneous lack
of tense agreement between the two clauses. Although it is true that *we drinkin'* does
mean "we are drinking" in most circumstances (cf. NNS *We drinkin' right now*), in the
sentence cited the phrase really represents *we was drinkin'* with the past tense marker *was*
omitted. By the same token, GUL *we duh drink*, can mean "we are drinking" as well,
but represents *we bin duh drink*, with the past tense marker *bin* omitted, in the sentence
cited.

[23] Quoted in George Philip Krapp, *The English Language in America* (New York:
The Century Co., 1925), Vol. 1, pp. 258–59.

the redundant subject pronoun), Gullah and other non-standard Negro dialects part company with Standard English and non-standard white dialects (of both America and Great Britain), they do have counterparts in a number of pidgin and creole forms of English which, though used far from the shores of the United States and in widely separated places, are all the legacy of the African slave trade. To illustrate how much these forms of English resemble Gullah and other non-standard Negro dialects with respect to auxiliary omission, the same equivalent sentences are given in Jamaican Creole (JMC), Sranan (SRA), the creole English of Surinam in South America, and West African Pidgin English (WAP):[24]

JMC: We ben a nyam—an' we a drink, too.
SRA: We ben de nyang—en' we de dringie, too.
WAP: We bin de eat—an' we de dring, too.

In addition to the grammatical correspondences, the word-form similarities of these languages with Gullah will be apparent.[25]

These correspondences are much too neat to be dismissed as mere accident. Rather, they seem to indicate that at least some of the particular syntactic features of American Negro dialects are neither skewings nor extensions of white dialect patterns, but are in fact structural vestiges of an earlier plantation creole, and ultimately of the original slave-trade pidgin English which gave rise to it.

This kind of evidence—existing in abundance for those who will admit it —calls for a complete reassessment of the relationships between British dialects,

---

[24] For comparative purposes, I have written these languages in a spelling which is as close to that of Standard English as the literary dialect spellings used in the preceding set of equivalent sentences. Scientific (phonemic) orthographies have been devised for these languages, however, and in them the same sentences would appear as: JMC *We ben a nyam—an we a dringk, tu;* SRA *we ben njan—en we de dringi, toe;* WAP *Wi bin de it—an we de dring, tu.* See Frederic G. Cassidy, *Jamaica Talk* (London: Macmillan Co., Ltd., 1961); Beryl L. Bailey, *Jamaican Creole Syntax* (Cambridge University Press, 1966); A. Donicie, *De Creolentaal van Suriname* (Paramaribo: Radhakishun and Co., 1959); Gouvernement van Suriname, Bureau Volkslectuur, *Woordenlijst van het Sranan-Tongo* (Paramaribo: N. V. Varekamp & Co., 1961); Gilbert D. Schneider, *West African Pidgin English* (Ph.D. Thesis, Hartford Seminary Foundation, 1966); David Dwyer, *An Introduction to West African Pidgin English* (African Studies Center, Michigan State University, 1967).

[25] The past tense markers in this series are *ben* (JMC, SRA) and *bin* (WAP), the latter having a common variant—*be.* The preverbal *a* in JMC is a modern reduction of an older *da,* obviously related historically to GUL *duh,* as well as to SRA and WAP *de.* In fact, the preverbal *a-* in some Southern Negro dialects (e.g. *he a-workin'*) may well derive from just such a source, rather than from the verbal prefix *a-* of many white dialects. This seems likely in view of the fact that, in those white dialects in which such a prefix is used functionally, there is usually a contrast between its presence and its absence (e.g. *he's workin'* "he is working within view" vs. *he's a-workin'* "he is off working somewhere"), while Negro dialects with preverbal *a-* use it like Gullah uses preverbal *duh*—for the simple durative. Finally, Gullah actually has *a* (or *uh*) as a variant of *duh,* especially after *bin.*

white American dialects, Negro American dialects (including Gullah), and the pidgin and creole English of Africa and the Caribbean. In particular, a new and more careful look at the question of American Negro dialects needs to be taken by those working within orthodox American dialectology—most of all by those who have made an almost exclusive use of American Dialect Atlas materials and techniques. High on the list of priorities for determining Negro and white dialect relationships should be: (1) the relationship between Gullah and other Negro dialects, and (2) the relationship between Negro dialects (other than Gullah) and white dialects. In such a reassessment, many new insights into the history of these relationships will be gained from studies of the syntax, not only of present-day dialects, but also of literary attestations of early Negro and white non-standard dialect, and by comparative studies of European, pidgin, and creole dialects of English.

All-in-all, it looks very much like the word-form similarities between non-standard Negro dialects and non-standard white dialects are the result of a relatively superficial merging process, in which creole-speaking Negroes tried to make their "broken" (i.e. creole) English become more like that of the whites by means of minor pronunciation changes and vocabulary substitutions. But the creole grammatical patterns of these Negroes' speech, being less amenable to conscious manipulation, remained more resistant to this substitution process.[26] In an earlier article on urban Negro dialect in Washington, D.C., I pointed out how Negro children who reach school age speaking a radically non-standard dialect often modify it in the direction of standard English in a similarly superficial fashion as they grow older.[27] It is interesting to consider that, in the language-socialization process of their individual lifetimes, many American Negroes may actually repeat something of the larger process of Negro dialect history.

Now, the pedagogical implications of a historical relationship of this kind between Negro and white non-standard dialects and, more particularly, between non-standard Negro dialects and Standard English ought to be clear. For, if American Negro dialects have evolved in such a way that structural similarities with other dialects of American English (including Standard English) are

---

[26] Even persons who are quite familiar with American Negro dialects may be led, by dissimilarities in word-forms, to overestimate the difference between them. For example, as keen an observer of dialect as E. C. L. Adams stated in *Nigger to Nigger* (New York: Charles Scribner's Sons, 1928), p. viii, that the speech of the Congaree Negroes of inland South Carolina was "absolutely distinct" from the coastal Gullah. Actually, the many striking syntactic similarities between the two dialects would suggest that the former is only a slightly de-creolized form of the latter. Observers of Gullah, from John Bennett on, have all remarked on how the older "pure" form of the language has been undergoing modification (i.e. de-creolization), particularly in the cities and towns. Seeing this "modified Gullah" always as a new phenomenon, they never expressed any awareness of the possibility that they might have been watching a continuation of the same process which earlier gave rise to the contemporary forms of other American Negro dialects.

[27] William A. Stewart, "Urban Negro Speech: Sociolinguistic Factors Affecting English Teaching" *loc. cit.*, p. 17.

greatest at the superficial word-form level, then it is possible for these similarities to mask any number of grammatical differences between them. And the teacher, concentrating on the more obvious word-form differences, is quite likely to miss the grammatical differences in the process—thereby leaving them to persist as apparent malapropisms, awkward turns of phrase, and random "mistakes" in speech and composition through grade school, high school, and frequently even through higher education.

As the grammatical study of non-standard Negro dialect progresses, it is quite probable that many more differences will be found between Negro and white speech patterns, and it may well turn out that at least some of these will also be traceable to a creole English, pidgin English, or even African language source. Of course, such discoveries are bound to cause embarrassment to those superficially liberal whites who will accept the Negro for what he is only if his behavioral patterns prove to be as European as their own, and they will be disquieting to those racial image-conscious Negroes who are so often pre-occupied with the question "What will the white folks think?" But quite apart from whether he thinks they are a help or a hindrance in integration, good or bad for the Negro's racial image, the dedicated educator should welcome the discovery and formulation of such ethnically correlated dialect differences as do exist. For, only when they are taken into account in the teaching process will the linguistic cards cease to be stacked against the disadvantaged Negro pupil in the nation's classrooms.

39

A Checklist of Significant Features for Discriminating Social Dialects[1]

RAVEN I. McDAVID, Jr.

AS AN AID TO THE TEACHER who is interested in a more efficient approach to the problem of teaching a standard variety of English—for public roles—to those who use non-standard varieties at home, the following list of features, all of which are both systematic and significant, has been drawn up, partly from the collections of the regional linguistic atlases, partly from more intensive local studies.

The emphasis is on those features of the language that recur frequently and are therefore most amenable to pattern drills. It must not be inferred that other, less well-patterned features of English are unimportant as social markers, but only that they do not lend themselves to productive drill. Discriminating the principal parts of irregular verbs, as past tense *saw* and past participle *seen*, is a part of the linguistic behavior that constitutes Standard English, but the pattern *see-saw-seen* is duplicated only by such compounds of *see* as *foresee*. On the other hand, the discrimination between *I see* and *he sees* is a part of a pattern of subject-verb concord that is faced every time a subject is used with a present tense verb.

The list is concerned with social dialects of English and does not include all the problems faced by the native speaker of some other language. For each such situation one needs special contrastive studies like those currently being published by the University of Chicago Press. Native speakers of Spanish, for instance, have special difficulties with the English consonant clusters /sp-, st-, sk-/ at the beginnings of words; native speakers of Czech or Finnish need to learn the accentual patterns of English; native speakers of continental European languages need to master the perfect phrase in such expressions of time as *I*

Reprinted by permission from *Dimensions of Dialect* (Eldonna Evertts, ed.). Champaign, Ill.: National Council of Teachers of English, 1967. Pp. 7–10. The author, previously identified in this book, is Professor of English at the University of Chicago.

[1] This list will be incorporated in a manual of social dialects being prepared by Alva L. Davis of the Illinois Institute of Technology under a grant from the U.S. Office of Education.

have been in Chicago for five years; native speakers of almost every other language need to learn a finer meshed set of vowel distinctions, as between *peach* and *pitch*, *bait* and *bet* and *but*, *pool* and *pull*, *boat* and *bought*, *hot* and *hut*.

The origins of these features are of indirect concern here; that they are of social significance is what concerns us. In general, however, it is clear that most of them may be traced back to the folk speech of England, and that in the United States none of them is exclusively identified with any racial group, though in any given community some of them may be relatively more frequent among whites or among Negroes.

This list is restricted to features that occur in speech as well as in writing. It is recognized that regional varieties of English differ in the distance between standard informal speech and standard formal writing. They vary considerably in the kinds of reductions of final consonant clusters, either absolutely or when followed by a word beginning with a consonant. The plural of sixth may be /sɪks/, homonymous with the cardinal numeral; *burned a hole* may be pronounced /bɔ́rnd ə hól/ but *burned my pants* /bɔrn mài pǽnts/. Similarly, the copula may not appear in questions as *They ready? That your boy? We going now? She been drinking?* The auxiliary *have* may not appear even as a reflex of /v/ in such statements as *I been thinking about it* or *we been telling you this*. In families where the conventions of written and printed English are learned early as a separate subsystem, differences of this kind cause little trouble but for speakers of non-standard dialects who have little home exposure to books, these features may provide additional problems in learning to write. It is often difficult for the teacher to overcome these problems in the students' writing without fostering an unnatural pronunciation.

It should be recognized, of course, that cultural situations may change in any community. To take the southern dialectal situation, with which I am most familiar. Forty years ago there was a widespread social distinction in the allophones of /ai/. The monophthongal [a·] was used by all classes finally, as in *rye*, or before voiced consonants as in *ride*; before voiceless consonants, however, educated speakers had a diphthong and any uneducated speakers used the monophthong, so that *nice white rice* became a well known social shibboleth.[2] In recent years, however, the shibboleth has ceased to operate, and many educated Southerners now have the monophthong in all positions, and their numbers are increasing. This observation was also made last spring by James B. McMillan, of the University of Alabama, who added that in his experience the falling together of /ai/ and /a/ before /-r/, so that *fire* and *far*, *hired* and *hard*, become homonymous, was still restricted to non-standard speech. Yet last August I noticed that this homonymy was common on the Dallas radio, in the formal speech of the editor of the women's hour.

It should not be assumed, furthermore, that one will not find other systematic

---

[2] This observation was made, *inter alia*, in my analyses of the pronunciation of English in the Greenville, S.C., metropolitan area, at meetings of the Linguistic Society in New York City (December 1938) and Chapel Hill, N.C. (July 1941).

features discriminating local dialects. Nor should we be so naive as to expect the speakers of any community to cease regarding the speech of outsiders as *ipso facto* inferior because it is different—even though these outsiders may be superior in education and social standing.

We are all ethnocentric after our own fashion; in our localities, we may consider some differences important whether they are or not—and if enough people worry about them some of these may become important. This is the traditional origin of neuroses. Meanwhile, it is probably good sense as well as good humor to recognize that though the white middle-class Chicagoan often considers the loss of /r/ in *barn* and the like a lower-class feature, the cultivated Southerner associates the middle western /r/ in such words with the speech of poor whites—and that the distinction between *wails* and *whales* is socially diagnostic nowhere in the English speaking world. The features here are diagnostic everywhere, though not all of them occur in every situation where differences in social dialects are important.

39.1   Pronunciation

1   The distinction between /θ/ as in *thin* and /t/ in *tin*, /f/ in *fin*, /s/ in *sin*.

2   Failure to make the similar distinction between /ð/ in *then* and /d/, /v/, /z/.

3   Failure to make the distinction between the vowels of *bird* and *Boyd*, *curl* and *coil*.

A generation ago this contrast was most significant among older speakers of the New York metropolitan area. It has become less important, since few younger speakers confuse these pairs. But it still should be noted, not only for New York City but for New Orleans as well.[3]

At one time a monophthongal /ai/ in the South was standard in final position and before voiced consonants, as in *rye* and *ride*, but substandard before voiceless consonants as in *right*. This is no longer true; many educated Southerners have monophthongal /ai/ in all positions and the number is increasing.

4   The omission of a weak stressed syllable preceding the primary stress, so that in substandard speech *professor* may become *fessor*, *reporter* become *porter*, and *insurance* become *shoo-ance or sho-unce*.

5   A statistically disproportionate front-shifting of the primary stress giving such forms as *po*-lice, *in*-surance, *ee*-ficiency and *gui*-tar, etc.

Front-shifting is characteristic of English borrowings from other languages; in *bal*cony it is completely acceptable, in *ho*tel and *Ju*ly, acceptability is conditioned by position in the sentence.

---

[3] The monophthongal southern /ai/ disturbs many easterners and middlewesterners. Some Philadelphians, for instance, allege that southerners confuse *ride* and *rod*; some Detroiters, that they confuse *right* and *rat*. They do not; the confusion exists in the mind of the eastern and middlewestern observer.

6 Heavy stress on what is a weak stressed final syllable in standard English, giving acci*dent*, ele*ment*, presi*dent*, evi*dence*, etc.

39.2 Inflection

Noun

7 Lack of the noun plural: Two *boy* came to see me.
8 Lack of the noun genitive: This is *Mr. Brown* hat.

Pronoun

9 Analogizing of the /-n/ of *mine* to other absolute genitives, yielding *ourn, yourn, hisn, hern, theirn*.
10 Analogizing of the compound reflexives, yielding *hisself, theirselves*.

Demonstratives

11 Substitution of *them* for *those*, as *them* books.
12 Compound demonstratives: *these-here* dogs, *them-(th)ere* cats.

Adjectives

13 Analogizing of inflected comparisons: the *wonderfullest* time, a *lovinger* child.
14 Double comparisons: a *more prettier* dress, the *most ugliest* man.

Verb

15 Unorthodox person-number concord of the present of *to be*. This may be manifest in generalizing of *am* or *is* or *are*, or in the use of *be* with all persons.
16 Unorthodox person-number concord of the past of *be*: I *were* or we *was*.
17 Failure to maintain person-number concord of the present indicative of other verbs: *I does, he do*. (This is perhaps the most clearly diagnostic feature.)

Note that three third person singular forms of common verbs are irregular: *has, does* /dʌz/, *says* /sɛz/; in the last two the spelling conceals the irregularity, but many speakers who are learning this inflection will say /duz/ and /sez/.

18 Omission of /-ɪŋ/ of the present participle: He was *open* a can of beer.

Note that both /ɪŋ/ and /ɪn/ may be heard in standard speech, depending on region and styles.

19 Omission of /-t, -d, -əd/ of the past tense: *I burn a hole* in my pants yesterday.

Note that before a word beginning with a consonant the /-d/ may be omitted in speech in *I burned my* pants. Those who have this contextual loss of the sound need to learn the special conventions of writing.

20 Omission of /-t, -d, -əd/ of the past participle.

21   Omission of the verb *to be* in statements before a predicate nominative. *He a good boy.*

Note that in questions this omission may occur in standard oral English, though it would never be written in standard expository prose.

22   Omission of *to be* in statements before adjectives: *They ready.*

23   Omission of *to be* in statements before present participles: *I going* with you.

24   Omission of *to be* in statements before past participle: *The window broken.*

25   Omission of the /-s, -z,-əz/ reflex of *has* before *been* in statements: *He been drinking.*

Note that this omission may occur in questions in standard oral English, and also that in standard oral English many educated speakers may omit the /-v/ reflex of *have*: *I been thinking about it*; *we been telling you this*, though it would not be omitted in standard expository prose.

26   Substitution of *been, done,* or *done been* for *have*, especially with a third person singular subject: *He done been finished.* In other situations the /-v/ may be lost, as in #25 (the preceding situation).

40

Stages in the Acquisition of Standard English

WILLIAM LABOV

40.1   Introduction: The Significance of Urban Language Problems for Linguists

IT IS FREQUENTLY SAID that children learn to speak the English language long before they learn to read and write it, and in its most obvious sense this statement can hardly be disputed. It is evident that the six-year-old child has mastered the greatest part of the machinery of spoken English. Yet there are many stages in the learning of spoken English which cannot be reached until much later in life, and there are skills in the speaking of English which the grade school child knows nothing about. In the following discussion, I would like to present evidence for the existence of such stages in the acquisition of Standard English, and show how this is related to the educational process in the schoolroom. Most of the data will be drawn from a study of the New York City speech community, and primarily from a survey of the Lower East Side of New York completed this year.[1]

This work is part of a continuing interest on my own part, as a linguist, in the study of speech in its community context. One of the major questions that remain unsolved for linguists is the mechanism by which languages evolve and change, and the process that has led to the great diversity of languages in the world today. Part of the answer can be found by a close examination of contem-

Reprinted by permission from *Social Dialects and Language Learning* (Roger W. Shuy, ed.). Campaign, Ill.: National Council of Teachers of English, 1964. Professor Labov, formerly a member of the department of Linguistics at Columbia University, became professor of Linguistics at the University of Pennsylvania in 1970.

[1] The most complete report of this work is given in "The Social Stratification of English in New York City," Columbia University dissertation, 1964. The use of quantitative indexes is discussed in some detail in "Phonological Correlates of Social Stratification," in Gumperz and Hymes (eds.), *The Ethnography of Communication*, appearing as the December 1964 issue of the *American Anthropologist*. One aspect of linguistic change of special interest for the problem of school dialects is presented in "Hypercorrection by the Lower Middle Class as a Factor in Linguistic Change," in the proceedings of the UCLA Conference on Sociolinguistics, Los Angeles, 1964.

porary changes that are taking place in the speech community. The case of New York City has a special interest, because of the usually high degree of fluctuation in speech forms that has been reported. Previous investigators had written of extensive variation that was "thoroughly haphazard," and "the product of pure chance."[2] Our studies of the variable elements in New York City speech have shown that this is far from the case: that the use of these language variants is determined by a pattern of social and stylistic norms. We find that there is a continuous and measurable influence of social factors upon language change. We also find, in the course of this work, a series of challenging questions which have immediate application to the problems of education: Why is it that young people, who are exposed to the Standard English of their teachers for ten or twelve years, still cannot use this form of speech no matter how badly they need it? Why is it, Negro parents ask me, that young Negro people who are raised in the North, of northern parents, speak like southerners?

The answers to these questions do not lie in the study of conscious choice. Most of the factors that influence speech performance lie well below the level of conscious awareness. It is therefore possible for us to use the evidence of speech variation in overt behavior to infer the deeper, underlying processes which must be understood if we are to solve the urgent problems of the urban schools. To present the evidence clearly, it will first be necessary to discuss the methods used to study the sociolinguistic structure of the New York City speech community.

40.2   Methods for the Study of Urban Dialects

a. *Sampling the Population.* In studying the urban dialects of the eastern United States, we are quite fortunate in being able to build upon the results of the Linguistic Atlas, which employed the highly systematic methods of dialect geography to study regional variation in the speech patterns of the most stable sections of the population. Kurath further refined and sharpened the methodology of European dialect geographers, and the American Atlas provides a reliable base for our present investigations of urban speech communities. It shows us the traditional regional pattern and allows us to recognize the intrusion of other regional features into the community.[3]

A simple approach to the study of urban speech communities would be to apply the methods of dialectology to social strata and attempt to isolate the characteristic speech forms of class groups, ethnic groups, and racial groups.

[2] Cf. A. F. Hubbell, *The Pronunciation of English in New York City* (New York: King's Crown Press, 1950), p. 48.

[3] H. Kurath, *Handbook of the Linguistic Geography of New England* (Providence: American Council of Learned Societies, 1939). In the study of New York City, various publications based on the Atlas materials were valuable sources of background data, particularly Y. Frank, "The Speech of New York City" (University of Michigan dissertation, 1948), and H. Kurath, *A Word Geography of the Eastern United States* (Ann Arbor: University of Michigan Press, 1949).

Such an approach would not be adequate, for a number of reasons. Dialectology begins with the laying out of a geometric grid that divides the area to be investigated into sectors; the fieldworker finds one or more informants within each sector of the grid. An informant must have certain specific characteristics—his age, his education, and his history of residence are important—but within a particular subgroup he is only one of many. It is assumed, for example, that the subgroup of old, uneducated, local residents is reasonably homogeneous. The choice of this typical informant must be dictated partly by convenience, partly by the informant's working habits and his willingness to talk for several days.

The method works well, for several reasons: (1) the important variable is specified in advance as geographic location, and there is no doubt about that; (2) if any characteristics of the informant make him atypical, his eccentricity will show up clearly on the finished maps, for dialect maps are self-confirming; the important regional markers appear as areas of solid agreement, and atypical cases stand out as isolated dots in a large area of uniformity; (3) in dialect geography, we are usually investigating separate speech communities which have little contact with each other, and contamination by direct contact is low.

In studying a complex urban area, these favorable factors are not present. We do not know the significant variables in advance, and there is far more contact within the different segments of the population. We cannot pick out a typical informant by chance or convenience and *then* describe his social characteristics. Instead, we must plan in advance to describe a specific population and then select a representative group from that population. One of the basic approaches to this problem is that of survey methodology. A set of informants is randomly drawn from an exhaustively enumerated portion of the community, and then considerable effort is made to interview every one of these informants. The more inconvenient it is to speak to an informant, the more effort is made to contact him. At the end, there always remains a small group that has refused the interview or eluded the fieldworkers. This group must be sampled in turn by a more intensive approach, to determine whether or not it differs in any important aspect of speech behavior from the main body of informants.[4]

In New York City, this method was carried out for the 100,000 residents of the Lower East Side by utilizing a sample already constructed for a sociological survey.[5] We thus gained all of the rigor of the survey approach, with the

[4] Methods for sampling refusals are discussed in "The Social Stratification of English in New York City," cited above, Appendix D. There are many ways of surveying a population, and the most accurate means are undoubtedly those based upon the procedures of survey methodology. Supplementary surveys of special cross sections, however, can be carried out much more quickly and can provide a great deal of useful information. A rapid survey of one characteristic of department store employees is discussed in Chapter III of the reference cited above, which tested the general hypothesis that any groups of New Yorkers who show socioeconomic stratification will also be stratified by their use of (r).

[5] This sample was constructed by Mobilization for Youth's research staff after an exhaustive enumeration of all of the residents of the area. They selected 1250 informants

data on the social characteristics of the informants, so that we could concentrate entirely upon their linguistic behavior.

b. *The Isolation of Contextual Styles.* The dialect geographer attempts to isolate the regionally significant variables in the speech of his informants, and these are usually consistent for any one informant. The method of dialectology is therefore not overly concerned with the problem of style: the interviewer is usually quite skilled in putting the subject at ease, and he uses his own judgment in discarding replies that seem to be overly careful. But in urban studies, many of the significant variables are not constant in the speech of the informants; they vary continuously over the full range of possibilities. Furthermore, the informant is not necessarily an eager and congenial respondent: he may be pressed for time, suspicious, or only half willing in his response, and the fieldworker cannot expect complete success in creating the same informal atmosphere for each interview. Different class groups have different conceptions of the appropriate style of speech for an interview. In our interviews, we assumed that informants would normally use a style of speech that they, consciously or unconsciously, considered appropriate for the interview situation. We defined this style as careful speech. We made no attempt to judge from our own immediate impressions whether this was careful or casual: we assumed that the speaker had another style, a *more* casual style, that he used with his family or friends when the interviewer was not present.

The problems produced by wide changing variability and by the appropriateness of careful speech in an interview were the problems that previous studies of New York City could not solve. We set about finding ways to isolate, elicit, and define the most casual style of the speaker, within the framework of the interview. The interview itself was constructed about several topics which were designed to elicit casual or spontaneous speech. One of these was a discussion of childhood rhymes and folklore. We found, for example, that careful speech could not be used by the informant when he repeated such rhymes as:

> Glory, glory, hallelujah
> The teacher hit me with a ruler,
> The ruler turned red

---

and completed interviews with 988. The linguistic survey, conducted two years later, was concerned with the 450 adult native speakers of English in the MFY sample. Thirty percent of these had moved from the area; of the remainder, 195 were randomly selected as the target sample for the linguistic survey. A total of 81 percent, or 157 informants were interviewed by the methods described. The data given here are based on 81 informants interviewed at length who were born and raised in New York City. [The comparable analysis for those who were raised outside of New York City allows us to distinguish those patterns which are peculiar to the city itself.] It should be noted that the pattern of social and stylistic stratification given here is so regular that it appears in subsections of the sample as small as 25 informants. Linguistic behavior, as measured here, is far more regular than most other forms of social behavior. It can be stated with considerable certainty that such relatively small samples are adequate for many forms of linguistic research if the informants are selected in a systematic manner and the biases of selection are minimized.

And the teacher fell dead
And that was the end of her.[6]

Another topic which was effective in overcoming the constraints of careful speech was the "danger of death." The informant was asked, at a particular point in the interview sequence, if he had ever been in a situation where he was in serious danger of being killed. If the informant had such an experience to retell, he usually became involved in the emotional tension of the situation as he recalled it, and he no longer concentrated on the task of maintaining careful speech patterns.

In these two situations and three others, we found that casual or spontaneous speech was likely to occur. The actual occurrence of this style was defined by the presence of at least one of five "channel cues": changes in tempo, volume, pitch, breathing, or laughter. If any one of these cues was present in one of the five situations designated, we measured the linguistic variables of that utterance under the heading of "casual speech." Then, in the more formal direction, we added a series of contexts in which more and more attention was paid to speech: the reading of a text, the pronunciation of isolated words, and the comparison of minimal pairs of words that differed only by the variable in question.

c. *The Phonological Variables*. Five chief phonological variables were measured throughout the various styles and various social groups in the New York City population. One of these was the form of the first consonant of *thing*, *three*, *thought*, etc. Sometimes New Yorkers say [θɪŋ], with a fricative consonant; sometimes they use a stop consonant [tɪŋ] and sometimes a combination of the two, an affricate as in [tθɪŋ]. The prestige form, as elsewhere in the United States, is the fricative form, [θɪŋ]. In our analysis of the tape recorded interviews, every single occurrence of this variable was counted—not only those in stressed, short replies—and from this count a quantitative index was constructed. If a person always said [θɪŋ], his index score would be (th)-oo. If he always used stops, as in [tɪŋ], his score would be (th)-200. In practice, no native speaker uses only stops: scores varied from oo to a high of 150. A typical performance for one informant, a white collar worker, would be:

	Casual speech	Careful speech	Reading style	Word lists
(th)-	35	20	05	00

A working man, of Italian background, would typically show the same pattern of declining index scores with increasing formality, but at a higher level:

105	75	35	25

[6] Note that *hallelujah* and *ruler* rhyme; this is perfectly regular in the [r]-less pattern of casual speech, but in the careful speech of many New Yorkers, *ruler* will be pronounced [rulɚ] and the two words will not rhyme at all. In casual speech, we also find that the final word *her* may be pronounced as [hʌ], with considerably greater effect than the careful style, [hɚ].

A college-educated professional might show only a trace of the non-standard form and follow the same pattern at a lower level:

19   15   00   00

When the values for all of the informants in the survey are calculated and averaged, the regular pattern in Figure 40.1 is obtained. Here the horizontal axis represents the range of contextual styles, and the vertical axis the range of (th) index scores. The immediate interest here is in the relation between socio-economic stratification and the use of (th), so the average index scores for a number of socio-economic subdivisions of the population are plotted and connected along straight lines. The socio-economic ratings are based upon an objective index which is the combination of three indicators: the occupation of the informant, his education, and the income of his family in relation to its size.[7] The ten-point scale for this index is broken up into subgroups which are

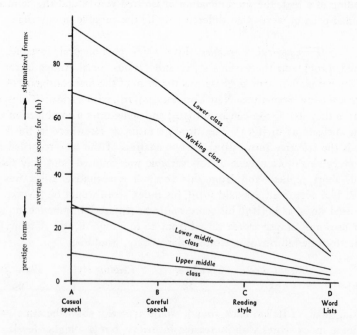

Figure 40.1: Class stratification of (th): the initial consonant of *thing, through, three,* etc.

[7] For details on this index, see "The Social Stratification of English in New York City," Ch. VII.

named informally in Figure 40.1. The result is a regular pattern of stylistic and social stratification, in which the two lower groups, "working-class" and "lower-class" informants, show a much higher degree of non-standard forms than the "middle-class" groups.

There are two aspects to this regular pattern. On the one hand, we see regular social stratification at every level of stylistic performance. From the middle-class standpoint, the stigmatized form [tɪŋ] is a marker of lower-class and working-class speech. Although the middle-class speaker uses a small percentage of stigmatized forms himself, he is not aware of this fact. From his point of view, socio-economic differentiation is the most obvious kind of regularity. Yet the opposing aspect is equally striking in an examination of Figure 40.1. Almost all New Yorkers behave in the same way in their regular transition from a greater to a lesser use of stigmatized forms with increasing formality of context. The other variables studied reveal this same duality of stratification in the speech community.

d. *The Subjective Evaluation of Linguistic Variables.* The preceding discussion has shown that New Yorkers generally agree in their social evaluation of (th), if we are to judge by their regular shift of style towards the standard fricative form. A few individuals, mostly from the lower class, do not show this shift: they are "outside" the pattern, and they will be a group of particular interest to us in studying the problems of teaching Standard English. But first we would like to penetrate more deeply into the question of subjective evaluation. Is there any connection between the pattern of performance and the attitudes and value judgments of the speakers? The problem is complicated because people react to speech as a whole, and they seldom are aware of what they like or dislike in the speech pattern of others. There is no socially regulated vocabulary that can be used to communicate this information.

In the study of New York City, a test was developed which successfully isolated and measured the unconscious subjective reactions of the informant to individual variables in the speech of others.[8] The uniform nature of these reactions was surprising. Although New Yorkers vary widely in their use of (th), most of them can detect low-prestige variants of this feature in the speech of others and downgrade the speaker who uses the non-standard forms. For example, the proportion of informants who showed the ability to detect and stigmatize non-standard (th) forms in the subjective response test was 82 percent. The greatest concentration of those who were insensitive to (th) was among lower-class speakers.

	% of (th)-insensitive subjects
Lower class	42
Working class	24

[8] The details of this test are given in the reference cited above, Ch. XI, and in "Subjective Dimensions of a Linguistic Change in Progress," a paper given before the Linguistic Society of America, Chicago, December 1963. Further discussion of subjective reactions is given below.

Lower middle class	19
Upper middle class	8

Furthermore, it was surprising to learn that those who showed the highest use of the non-standard forms in their own speech were often among the most sensitive in detecting and stigmatizing these forms in the speech of others.[9] Although the informants of Italian background showed many more [t] and [tθ] forms in speech than those of Jewish background, they showed only half as many who were insensitive to (th): 14 percent for the Italians as against 27 percent for the Jewish group. An even more striking comparison can be made between men and women. Men showed much higher index scores for (th) than women: in fact, they used on the average more than twice as many non-standard forms. But only 9 percent of the male informants were insensitive to (th) in the

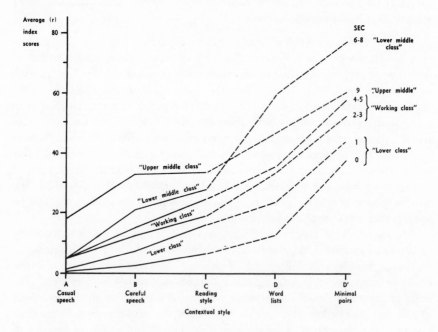

Figure 40.2: Class stratification of (r) in *guard, car, beer, beard*, etc.

[9] It should be noted that this test does not attempt to measure the entire range of subjective evaluations possible, but only those which reflect the suitability of a speech form for various levels in the occupational hierarchy. The subject marked each of the samples of speech that he heard according to the highest of seven job classifications which the speaker could hold, "speaking as she does." These ratings show the subject's recognition of the value system overtly endorsed by the schools and other social institutions: it is essentially a middle-class value system. Other value systems exist, and their analysis is important for an understanding of the speech community.

subjective reaction test, and 30 percent of the women were insensitive to this variable.

On the whole, it appears that the subjective responses of speakers are more uniform than performance. When a new prestige pattern enters the language, it is accepted on the level of unconscious subjective response before it achieves uniformity in actual usage. The case of final and pre-consonantal (r) in New York City illustrates the dramatic character of such a shift in response. Figure 40.2 shows the pattern of social and stylistic variation in the use of (r); again, the horizontal axis shows the range of stylistic contexts, and the vertical axis shows the average index scores for the new prestige feature (r).[10] It is evident that all classes agree, from their pattern of shifting, that the pronunciation of a constricted [r] in words like *guard, car, board*, etc., is appropriate for more formal contexts. On the other hand, only upper middle-class speakers show any degree of [r]-pronunciation in casual speech; in everyday life, the great majority of New Yorkers are [r]-less. In Figure 40.3, we can study the development of

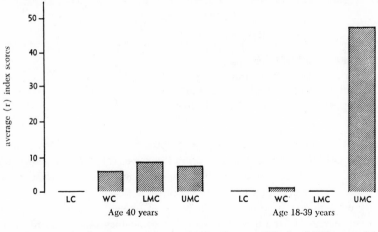

LC: "Lower class," SEC groups 0-1   LMC: "Lower middle class," SEC groups 6-8
WC: "Working class," SEC groups 2-5   UMC: "Upper middle class," SEC group 9

Figure 40.3: Class stratification of (r) by age in casual speech.
average (r) index scores

[10] In the notation used here, parentheses enclose a *linguistic variable*, while brackets indicate, as usual, a phonetic transcription. The variable (r) is the percentage of plainly constricted phones in all of the words where historical [and orthographic] *r* appears in final and preconsonantal position. The word classes in which *r* follows a mid-central vowel—*her, were, bird, work*, etc.—are not included, as these form separate indexes. Where the following word begins with a vowel, as in *four o'clock*, the occurrence of *r* is noted as an example of intervocalic, not final position.

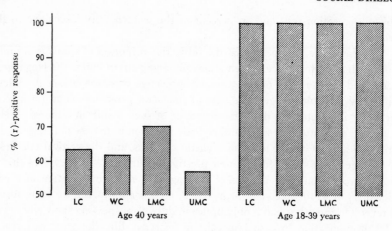

Figure 40.4: Subjective evaluation of (r) by class and age groups.
% (r)-positive response

LC: "Lower class," SEC groups 0–1
WC: "Working class," SEC groups 2–5
LMC: "Lower middle class," SEC groups 6–8
UMC: "Upper middle class," SEC group 9

[r]-pronunciation in casual speech by age groups. For those over forty years old, there is no significant social stratification in the use of (r). All class groups show a low level. But for those under forty, we see that upper middle-class speakers use a quite high degree of constricted (r) in their casual speech, and all other classes are absolutely [r]-less. Thus in terms of objective performance, we do not see an increase in the use of [r] so much as an increase in stratification of this variable.[11]

Figure 40.4 shows the percentages of those whose subjective response is consistent with the recognition of [r] as a prestige form. The older groups, those over forty years old, show a level of (r)-sensitivity which is close to chance expectation. But the younger group, those under forty, are absolutely uniform in their response: 100 percent agree in recognizing the prestige status of [r].

Thus we see that subjective response outruns performance in the process of linguistic change. Variations in the structure of the speech community are to be

[11] The evidence of the department store survey, noted above, confirmed the findings of the survey of the Lower East Side in this respect. The distribution of (r) among department store employees by age levels showed no overall increase if the three stores were taken together; we did find an increase in stratification, for the differences between the stores were by far the greatest for the youngest employees.

seen most clearly as variations in subjective evaluation, rather than fluctuations in performance.

In addition to the subjective response test, a *self-evaluation test* was used in which the informant was asked to choose one of several pronunciations as the form that he actually employed most often. The answers to these questions had no relation to performance, but they did reflect the pattern of evaluative norms that the informants had already given us in their shifts of style and in their subjective response tests. At least as far as sound patterns are concerned, the speaker hears himself as speaking the norm that he considers correct.

We were interested in exploring further the speakers' feelings of security or insecurity about their own speech: that is their anxiety or motivation for improving their speech in terms of middle-class values. For this purpose, we turned to words which had socially significant variants and which had received a great deal of public attention. Alternate pronunciations were given for eighteen such words, such as [ant, ænt], [lɛnθ, lɛŋθ], [ɛskəletɚ, ɛskjʊletɚ]. The informant was asked to circle the number of the variant that he considered correct. He was then asked to check the form that he usually used. The number of items in which the choices were different formed the "index of linguistic insecurity." This index represented the willingness of the speaker to recognize an exterior standard of correctness. For upper-middle class speakers, the index was low: one or two out of a possible eighteen. For lower-class speakers, it was often zero: as one person said, "How could I speak any other way than I do?" Working-class speakers showed higher indexes, but by far the greatest amount of such insecurity was shown by lower middle-class speakers: white-collar workers, substitute teachers, and the higher ranks of skilled workers. The term *insecurity* expresses only one aspect of the situation; one can look at the matter the other way around and say that this recognition of an external standard of correctness is an inevitable accompaniment of upward social aspirations and upward social mobility.

Through the various means described here, we succeeded in penetrating deeper into the structure of linguistic behavior than earlier studies of urban speech had done. We would now be inclined to define a speech community as a group of people who share a set of common norms in regard to language, rather than as a group of people who speak in the same way.

40.3   The Acquisition of Standard English by Children

a. *The Gradual Development of Adult Norms.* The first section of this paper was concerned with the various types of linguistic behavior shown by adults. We can now turn to the question of the acquisition of these norms and levels of behavior by children. The sample of informants under twenty years old was not as systematic as the sample of adults in the study of New York City; we depended primarily upon the children of our adult informants, and it was not possible to obtain a high percentage of the total sample population. Fifty-eight children of the New York City informants were interviewed, ranging from eight to nineteen years of age. The evidence brought forward in this section is consistent with that of the preceding, but the type of sampling used does not permit the same high level of confidence in the conclusions. We may consider the following outline of the acquisition of the levels of competence in Standard English as a series of tentative statements to be confirmed by further study in the New York City area.[12]

First of all, we may look at the overall performance of young people in all of the measures outlined above: their use of the linguistic variables in the various contextual styles, their subjective response tests, and their self-evaluation tests. The overall percentage of cases in which they follow the predominating pattern of the adult community climbs gradually as they approach adult status:

Age	% conformity with adult norms
8–11	52
12–13	50
14–15	57
16–17	62
18–19	64
(20–39	84)

We can view this process of acculturation most clearly if we examine families with more than one informant below the age of twenty. The table given above reflects a rather uneven distribution of informants in the various age groups; but if we take brothers and sisters within the same family, we can minimize fluctuations due to factors other than age. Figure 40.5 shows the percentage of agreement with adult norms shown by members of twenty-eight families. Here the horizontal axis represents the age of the informants, and the vertical axis the percentage of agreement. Points representing members of the same family are connected along straight lines.

Figure 40.5 shows graphically the process of acculturation which is often described in less specific terms. The linguistic indicators give us a precise measure of the extent to which the young person has grasped the norms of behavior which govern the adult community. It can be seen that some families begin this process relatively high in the continuum: middle-class families are to be found near the

---

[12] The data given in this paper as a whole apply primarily to New York City. There is reason to think that the behavior of the Lower East Side informants is characteristic of linguistic behavior within the city as a whole, and that regional differences within New York are minor. Several supplementary studies have given essentially the same results as the survey of the Lower East Side. On the other hand, it has been possible to show in great detail how New York City informants differ from those who were raised outside of the city. The two variables discussed here, (th) and (r), are the ones which are most general in their application, and which are essentially the same for the New York and non-New York informants. The principles of sociolinguistic organization illustrated here are therefore more general than the limitation to New York City would imply.

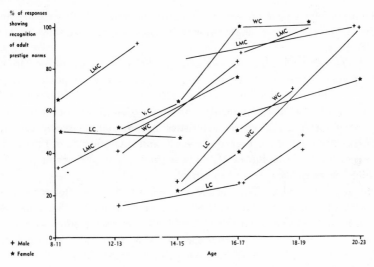

Figure 40.5: Acquisition of prestige norms in families with two or more children

top of the diagram, together with a few working-class families. Some working-class families, and all of the lower-class families, are to be seen operating at a much lower level of conformity to adult norms. Despite this great variation in relative position, we see that the slope of most of the lines is similar. Some working-class and most lower-class families are apparently too far removed from the middle-class norms to assimilate them efficiently, and we can see that those youngsters who are below 50 percent at eighteen or nineteen years old will probably not reach any significant degree of conformity while they still have the learning ability to match performance to evaluation. At the ages of thirty-five or forty, these individuals may be able to evaluate the social significance of their own and other speech forms, without being able to shift their own performance. At the same time, there is also a correlation between those families that expressed the most hostility to middle-class norms of social behavior, and those who appeared low on Figure 40.5. We can infer that there are other values operating to produce the differential of Figure 40.5, beyond mere differences in familiarity with middle-class patterns.

b. *Levels in the Acquisition of Spoken English.* From some of the evidence discussed above, and from other details obtained in the interviews with young people, we can construct a model of six stages of the acquisition of the full range of spoken English.

1 *The basic grammar.* The first level is the mastery of the main body of grammatical rules and the lexicon of spoken English, in such a form that the child can communicate his basic needs and experiences to his parents. This

stage is normally achieved under the linguistic influence of the parents—that is the case with all of our younger informants, who are at least third generation New Yorkers.

2   *The vernacular*. The second stage is the most important one from the point of view of the evolution of the language. In the pre-adolescent years, roughly ages five to twelve, the child learns the use of the local dialect in a form consistent with that of his immediate group of friends and associates. At this stage, neighborhood dialect characteristics become automatically established responses in the pattern of everyday speech, and the influence of the parents is submerged under the influence of the peer group. It is during this period that the child begins to learn to read in school.

3   *Social perception*. The third stage begins with early adolescence, as the child begins to come into wider contact with the adult world. The social significance of the dialect characteristics of his friends becomes gradually apparent to him as he becomes exposed to other speech forms, even while he himself is still confined to the single style of his own vernacular. At the age of fourteen or fifteen children begin to respond to the subjective reaction test with patterns that resemble the adult pattern.

4   *Stylistic variation*. In the next stage, the child begins to learn how to modify his speech in the direction of the prestige standard, in formal situations, or even to some extent in casual speech. The great turning point seems to be exposure to a group larger than the neighborhood group in the first year of high school. In our sample, for instance, we find that the number of stops and affricates used for (th) differs greatly between those speakers who have never been to high school and those who have had at least one year.

5   *The consistent standard*. It is not enough to be able to use standard speech forms sporadically. The ability to maintain standard styles of speech for any length of time is often not acquired at all. At best, some New Yorkers may be able to add a few corrected forms to their speech patterns. The ability to switch to a consistent style of speech and maintain that style with reasonable consistency is acquired primarily by the middle-class groups. In Figure 40.2, such consistency can be seen as a goal of the lower middle-class group. The lower middle-class line for (r) ranges from a very low position to the highest position, crossing over the upper middle-class line in the two most formal styles of speech. This mobility of the lower middle class is apparently an important factor in the evolution of new and consistent styles of speech.[13]

6   *The full range*. Some speakers attain complete consistency, or something close to it, in range of styles appropriate for a wide range of occasions. Comparatively few New Yorkers attain this level of skill in speaking, and those who do are mostly college-educated persons with special interest in speech. In the case of (th), quite a few of our subjects did use the fricative form all of the time. We also found that there were many subjects who did not depart at all from standard syntax and word morphology. This mastery of the prestige forms

[13] See "Hypercorrection by the Lower Middle Class . . ." cited above.

seemed to accompany a certain rigidity of linguistic style: few of these speakers seem to have retained the ability to switch "downwards" to their original vernacular. On the other hand, there was a continual shift in the percentage of (r) used, but not one of our informants who was raised in New York City had achieved complete consistency in the use of the prestige form.[14]

From this outline, it is plain that the relations between learning to speak and learning to read are not as simple as they have been sometimes said to be. The pattern of the vernacular is not fully formed when the child first learns to read, and there are many further steps in the mastery of spoken English which are still beyond his horizon. And success or failure in learning to read may have a strong effect upon the development of these other verbal skills.

By examining linguistic changes in progress, we have seen that the ability to perceive the social significance of dialect differences precedes the acquisition of consistent prestige styles in Standard English. For example, in the subjective evaluation of (r), we find that there is a sudden increase in the recognition of the prestige status of (r) for the group of sixteen–seventeen-year-olds. For eighteen–nineteen-year-olds, there is almost the same total agreement in the recognition of (r) as for the young adults, the twenty to thirty-nine-year-olds. At the same time, only the upper middle-class speakers show any ability to use (r) in their everyday speech. Since the great majority of the members of the adult community agree in the evaluation of speech forms, why then do most New Yorkers fail to acquire levels (5) and (6) in the series sketched above?

c. *Obstacles to the Acquisition of Standard English.* The regular patterns of social stratification in the use of linguistic variables reflect a balance of forces, rather than a simple, overall trend. On the one hand, the vernacular of the New York City speech community evolves in its own consistent pattern, following a mechanism that is not yet wholly understood. On the other hand, the New York City speech community has also maintained prestige patterns borrowed from other communities: from England, New England, or most recently, from (r)-pronouncing areas outside of the city. While almost everyone recognizes the middle-class values inherent in this borrowed prestige pattern, there is a wide range of differences in the actualization of this pattern. We can consider the following bases for such a range of performance.

1   *Isolation.* It is possible that working-class and lower-class speakers are simply not as familiar with the prestige norms as middle-class speakers—that they have less opportunity to hear the prestige dialect. At one time, this may have been an important factor, but it is clearly becoming less important with the

[14] Throughout this paper, I have used the conception of stylistic levels which is most commonly employed in the discussion of social variation. However, this approach in the New York City speech community leads to a multiplication of structural devices that seems increasingly unrealistic as we gather more data. It is possible to view the sociolinguistic structure as a single complex, within which continuous variation occurs along the social and stylistic dimension. Cf. "The Linguistic Variable as a Structural Unit," paper given before the Washington Linguistics Club, Washington, D.C., November 1964.

development of the mass media. The great majority of prestige figures on radio and television in the New York City area use the prestige dialect consistently. Furthermore, the conditions of daily life in a large city permit a considerable amount of interaction between speakers of various levels.

2 *Structural interference.* It is also possible that there are mechanical constraints upon the linguistic performance of some speakers, proceeding from differences in the structure of their vernacular and the structure of the prestige pattern.

We can see such interference in the case of a young New Yorker who enters the sixth grade speaking a vernacular in which *bad, bared,* and *beard* are completely homonymous, together with thousands of other words in these classes. If we add to this list the homonymy of *laud, lord,* and *lured; god* and *guard; dot* and *dart; pin* and *pen;* it is apparent that a great many new distinctions must be learned if the child is to master the Standard English spoken by the teacher.

In the case of the new population of in-migrants from the South who speak a non-standard dialect, or in the case of the Puerto Rican group, such interference may be important. It is not as likely to be a strong factor in the speech of the main body of New Yorkers, who began to acquire early in life the pattern of stylistic shifting which carries them from their basic vernacular to the prestige forms.

Nevertheless, an important step in the study of any such system of social stratification is to attempt an analysis of the vernacular of each social group showing the internal relations of the elements within each system. (See footnote 14.) This analysis will be essential for the understanding of linguistic change, and it will isolate the differences between systems which must be adjusted in the mastery of Standard English.

3 *Conflict of value systems.* It can easily be seen that any systematic differences between dialects of English in New York City are small in comparison with the similarities. One can hardly imagine a theory of mechanical constraints which could account for the dilemma proposed at the beginning of this paper: How is it that young people who are exposed to the Standard English of their teachers for twelve years cannot reproduce this style for twelve minutes in a job interview? The problem is parallel to the more serious question as to how a student can sit through eight to ten years of school without learning to read more than a few words. Those who feel that they can solve this problem by experimenting with the machinery of the learning process are measuring small causes against large effects. My own feeling is that the primary interference with the acquisition of Standard English stems from a conflict of value systems.

Language may be looked upon as a system for integrating values. Linguistics has made the most progress in analyzing the cognitive component; but many elements of language (certainly not all) are imbued with non-cognitive values as well, and the total information conveyed in these non-cognitive functions may outweigh the cognitive information. In our subjective reaction tests we have studied only those values which follow the middle-class patterns: the suitability of a speech form for various occupations. But there are other values, values which support the use of the vernacular style of the working class, and the social stratification of language seen in Figures 40.1–5. There are many New Yorkers, for example, who feel no desire to be identified with middle-class, white-collar workers. They deliberately turn aside from white-collar jobs in seeking lower-skilled, lower-paid manual work. Identification with the class of people that includes one's friends and family is a powerful factor in explaining linguistic behavior. Furthermore, I believe that we can establish that the working-class style of casual speech has values strongly associated with masculinity. In the work now being carried on in Harlem and other parts of New York City, we plan to explore these value systems.

There are also negative factors in the conflict of value systems. The adolescent peer group exerts strong pressure against any deviation in the direction of middle-class standards. This is a type of behavior that we would like to investigate in more detail; there is a great deal of anecdotal evidence of such pressure, but it consists mostly of recollections of striking incidents in the past. Evidence to the contrary—group approval of the verbal proficiency of a member—might not be so striking and therefore would not appear in anecdotal evidence. Therefore we need observations of group pressures upon language behavior as these pressures operate. If it is true adolescent groups do not permit free experimentation with middle-class language styles, and that they penalize members who try to put into practice the teaching of the schools,[15] then the practical problem of urban dialect engineering will have such group constraints as a major focus. It will be necessary to build into the community a tolerance for style shifting which is helpful in educational and occupational advancement.

Another negative factor undoubtedly exists in the conflict of values symbolized by the difference between the teachers' speech and the students. Although English teachers have been urged for many years to treat the non-standard vernaculars as simply "different" from Standard English, it is clear that the prevailing attitude is that the students' vernacular is "bad English," "incorrect," and "sloppy" speech. It would be surprising if this were not so. The survey of New York City shows that such opinions of the teacher reflect an almost universal sentiment of the speech community.[16] The conflict is a covert one: both teacher and student may be only partly aware of the value systems which bring them into unyielding opposition.

Most teachers in the New York City system probably follow the pattern of group 6–8 in Figure 40.2 for a great many features of speech. In casual speech,

[15] The current program for research in Harlem among teenage speakers is designed to obtain further evidence on this point. No one would deny that such tendencies exist; the question is, to what extent do they influence behavior? Only quantitative methods can answer such questions; after a certain point, anecdotal evidence only confuses the issue.

[16] Again, one should note that this agreement extends only to those attitudes which reflect the middle-class value system.

they unconsciously use forms which they themselves stigmatize in the speech of others. When they pronounce words in isolation, they use an even higher percentage of prestige forms than those who use these forms naturally in casual speech. Their performance is governed by certain norms, and these norms are the sounds or images that they hear themselves use. Thus the teacher will frequently condemn students in strong, moralistic terms for the use of speech forms that she frequently uses herself without being aware of them. There are undoubtedly many non-standard forms used by the students that the teacher does not use, but the essential fact is that the teacher has no more tolerance for style shift than the adolescent groups mentioned above. Neither teacher nor student is aware of the fact that they both follow the same pattern of style shifting in their language, though at different levels. The teacher struggles to impose a fixed standard, which she mistakenly believes she follows herself, upon youngsters who mistakenly believe that they also make no concession to the other side in daily life. In the data from the New York City survey, we see some evidence for the view that teachers may be transferring to the students their own inner conflicts; they recoil from a kind of behavior that is still very much a part of their own personalities. On the other hand, the student may rightfully feel that the teacher threatens him in trying to abolish completely the speech pattern that identifies him as a member of his own group: this is the group that he respects, that awards him prestige, that establishes his masculinity.

These comments suggest that the conflict of values should be investigated in the classroom itself. The foregoing remarks are merely extrapolations from observations made in a community study, and they are based on the least favorable case, in which a male student faces a female teacher. But the view given here becomes somewhat more plausible when we consider the even more serious problem produced by the new polarization within the New York speech community.

40.4   Opposing Value Systems Within The New York City Speech Community

The view of the speech community given so far is not complete. There are signs of a developing lower-class group which is breaking away from the pattern shown in Figures 40.1 through 40.5, a group which has adopted other reference points and other values, and is drifting in a different direction from the main group.

Evidence for such a trend can be seen in some of the details of the phonological system. Whereas the traditional New York City system is continuing to evolve towards higher and higher in-gliding vowels in word groups such as *bad*, *ask*, *dance*, *where*, etc., and *off*, *talk*, *law*, etc., there is an opposing trend towards lower in-gliding vowels in these groups. Similarly, we find that the traditional New York City system shows a systematic backing of the first element in the

diphthong of *my*, *side*, *why*, etc., while a separate trend exists towards the fronting of this element and the loss of the up-glide. These contrary directions are
all the more striking when they are seen against a view of the overall structure
of New York City speech.[17] The great majority of working-class and middle-
class speakers follow the first direction mentioned, which continues the evolution
which began in the nineteenth century. The second direction is characteristic of
a sizeable group of Negro speakers, Puerto Ricans, and lower-class white
speakers who live in close contact with these other groups.

The differences in speech performance are matched by a new polarization
of values developing in New York City. The old polarization of ethnic groups
showed a number of equally balanced interest groups: Italians, Jews, Negroes,
Irish, who determined the political character of the city as well as its informal
social structure.[18] The newer pattern shows that a growing minority of Negroes,
Puerto Ricans, and lower-class whites reject the value system implied by the
dominant speech pattern and adopt a new reference point in which southern
Negro speech is central.

This new development is best illustrated by considering the overt attitudes
expressed by New Yorkers about speech itself. Most white New Yorkers do not
like the sound of New York City speech. Almost all of our informants agree that
they would be complimented if they were told that they did *not* sound like New
Yorkers. As far back as we can go, the city's prestige patterns have always been
borrowed from other regions. On the other hand, many white New Yorkers like
the sound of white southern speech. The attitudes of most Negro informants
are quite the reverse. They like almost any type of northern speech, and dislike
Southern speech intensely. Southern speech is considered "rough," "uneducated," "bad" speech. One excerpt from an interview with an older Negro
informant in New York City will illustrate this value pattern vividly. Mr.
Joseph McSorley was born and raised in New York City sixty years ago. He
works as a guard at a YMCA building, and although he has had little formal
education, he is a well read, well spoken man. In answer to the question on the
danger of death, he told of an incident in which he was asked to investigate a
report that someone had a gun in his room and had threatened some other
tenant with it. In this narrative, Mr. McSorley used two very different voices:
his own quiet, pleasant, and cultivated northern manner, and a rough, rapid
style with many strongly southern characteristics and a tone of voice that was
rasping and whining. The first style is indicated in regular type below—the
second in capitals.

I go up whistlin', let him know I'm comin', shakin' my keys, you know.
'Hey, Bill! What are you doin'?"
"WHADA YOU WANT?"

[17] See "The Social Stratification of English in New York City," cited above, Ch. XII.
[18] The ethnic composition of New York City is described in N. Glazier and D.
Moynihan. *Beyond the Melting Pot: The Negroes, Puerto Ricans, Jews, Italians and Irish
of New York City* (Cambridge: M.I.T. and Harvard University Press, 1963).

I said, "What are you doin'?"

"I AIN'T DOIN' NUTTIN', JOE."

I said, "Well, they claim a little disturbance up here, somebody says you chased them with something. What did you chase them with?"

"OH JOE, I AIN'T GOIN' BOTHER 'EM. I WASN'T DOIN' NOTHIN'."

I said, "Open the door, Bill. Let me look." So he opened the door and I went in there. He did have a gun. So I said, "You better get rid of that because down at the desk, they're calling for the police department."

"I GOT A P'MIT FO' IT."

I said, "You better show it to the cops when they come."

"O.K. JOE, O.K."

The voice that Mr. McSorley usually used is not easily identified as that of a Negro by most listeners, but the second voice was plainly that of a southern Negro. At the end of the interview, I complimented Mr. McSorley on his ability to sound like two different people. He was quite mystified by my remark. He had no idea that he had used any voice other than his usual one; yet his niece, who had been listening, agreed that he had done so, and she told him that he had sounded "just like a southern Negro." Finally I asked Mr. McSorley what sort of a man Bill was—what was his background. "I don't know," said Mr. McSorley, "some kind of a Hungarian, I think."

In this incident we see a process of unconscious substitution taking place in accordance with the value system of the speaker. The man Mr. McSorley was imitating used a speech pattern that was evidently rough and uneducated, but unfamiliar in detail to him. In representing this style, he automatically and unconsciously substituted the only rough uneducated low-prestige dialect with which he was intimately familiar—that of non-standard southern Negro English.

Mr. McSorley is typical of the many Negro New Yorkers who are puzzled by the recent trend towards southern speech among the young people he knows. He finds it hard to understand why people would go out of their way to talk in a rough, uneducated way. In actual fact, this polarization of linguistic values about a new norm is a sign of a cultural split in New York City which goes beyond language. We find that even lower-class whites who live in apparent hostility with Negroes have unconsciously adopted the Negro delinquent youth as a reference group for their own behavior.[19] This trend is dramatically evident in a section of another interview from the Lower East Side survey. The subjects were six brothers, from thirteen to nineteen years old, from an Irish-Italian family that would be rated on most indicators near the lower end of the socio-economic scale. In their social attitudes and aspirations most of the Riley brothers show overt hostility to middle-class values. The most vocal is the second oldest,

---

[19] "Reference group" is used here in the technical sense introduced by Herbert Hyman in *The Psychology of Status*, 1942, and utilized by Robert Merton in *Social Theory and Social Structure* in 1949. When an individual or a group adopts the values of some other group outside of their own network of social contacts, that other group is said to serve as a reference group for them.

Jimmy Riley, the natural joker and storyteller of the group. At eighteen, he had resisted all of the schools' efforts to teach him white-collar skills, and more or less decided to become a longshoreman, like his father. In his account of a situation in which he was in danger of being killed, he told of being attacked by a group of Negroes. In the course of the narrative, he drifted into a style of speech which is remarkably like that of the Negro boys who are his immediate enemies:

I went ice skatin' in Jersey—Hoboken. Came back two o'clock in the mornin'. Whole bunch of guys went—I come back, everybody says, "I'm hongry, I'm hongry." I say, "I'll be right back."

I go next door for a pizza. I come out, and there's five big niggers standin' there. They say, "Gimme that!" I say, "Give you *wot*." Yerr whop! I went down. They kicked me, everything. Boom!

I got up, 'n' ran in the house, 'n' grabbed a steak knife and chased them. A guy jumped into his car and chased them. Spanish guy named Rickey, he took out a bread knife, ran down the subway, and scared an old lady silly. Thought he was gonna kill her.

Bright cop comes over—cullud ['kʌlʌd] cop. "Wha' happened?" I say, "Five of your bright people jumped me." He says, "What were dey?" I say, "Yeah, they were colored." He says, "Den they—they ain't my people." I said, "You cullud." He says, "They ain't my people." I say, "O.K., g'bye, f'get everyt'ing. Went t'the hospital."

Again, this stylistic behavior proved to be quite unconscious. When one of Jimmy Riley's own brothers told him that he sounded like a nigger himself when he was telling the story, he was quite surprised. Yet he had quoted himself saying "You cullud," a form of predication without the copula which is highly characteristic of Negro speech as opposed to other vernacular speech forms.

In the case of Jimmy Riley, we see a constellation of factors that seems to lead to low educational achievement, lack of occupational skills, and unemployment. His speech patterns are sensitive indicators of these trends. It is not likely that any change in the methods of teaching English will be powerful enough to cope with problems such as these. I think, however, that we must be aware of these problems, because they reflect social processes that will continue to operate to produce similar results in the future. No amount of research into the mechanism of language learning will remove these larger social forces from the scene. The polarization of linguistic behavior serves as an excellent indicator of the social processes that are occurring, but these indicators do not give us any immediate program for corrective action, or even for amelioration. The linguist is essentially an analyst, not an educator; it would seem that his goal in attacking the problems of the urban schools is to give the educators information with which they can build programs and check the results of their efforts.

40.5 Some Directions for Research on Urban Schools Problems

a. *Describing the Structure of Non-standard English*. The first task of the linguist in any community is a descriptive one. There is little to say about educational problems, or motivation, or interference, until one can give an account of the linguistic behavior of the native speakers of the particular speech community in question. From the evidence brought forward in the present conference, we know that there are striking similarities in the linguistic problems that have arisen in many different cities across the United States. Nevertheless, we can take nothing for granted in approaching the language of Detroit, or Wilmington, or Newark: the following suggestions will outline several lines of research which will give us the data we need on actual linguistic behavior.

1 *Isolating the chief variables.* It is necessary to have a clear idea of what features are constant in the speech of a given area and which tend to fluctuate. Wherever social forces interact with linguistic behavior, we find variation, and this variation is usually the focal point of social values. The traditional method has been to record the mistakes that children make in the classroom; certainly this is important, and it should be done. The teachers in any and all parts of the school system can help the linguist by giving him a quantitative tabulation of the grammatical and lexical errors that children make in their written and oral work. To interpret these errors, it is of course necessary to give an exact account of the form of Standard English from which they deviate and also to show which deviations are not considered errors but are tolerated as acceptable variation. For this latter task, the educator may need direct help from the linguist in the classroom, as he observes the type of Standard English used by the teacher and administrators of the school.

A more systematic approach to the isolation of the variables can be followed by the linguist in his exploratory interviews and observations in the community. From this work, he can begin to divide variables into two types: those which show *social variation,* but are essentially constant in the speech of any one person and those which also show *stylistic variation,* shifting in occurrence or frequency from one style or context to another.

2 *Structural descriptions.* The next step is undertaken by the linguist. He must attempt to organize the constant and variable factors in the speech of the community, or any subsection of the community, into a structural description. As we know, a complete structural description is hardly possible, since it has never been accomplished for any variety of English. The linguist therefore concentrates upon certain areas of language which he knows are most tightly organized, such as the phonological system, or the system of verbal auxiliaries, and pays particular attention to those areas that are marked by the greatest variation.

A structural description of this type serves three chief purposes: (a) It enables the linguist to locate other variables in the system which have not been noticed before. At alternate and opposite points in the structure, it is not uncommon to find parallel variation; furthermore, pressure from variation at one point frequently produces shifts or mergers with neighboring elements; (b) The structural analysis frequently explains one form of linguistic behavior as a structural consequence of other forms. Several isolated examples of differences between Standard and non-standard English may actually be instances of a single difference in the operation of a more general rule; (c) The structural description may show that forms which are superficially identical with Standard English (or with other forms within the same system) are actually different in syntactic or semantic value. In a highly organized system, the value of each term is based upon its relation with all other terms, so that a different organization or inventory of terms will affect the meaning of all the terms. We find such underlying differences frequently in pronoun systems, or in the tense and modal systems of the verb.

3 *Social and stylistic distribution.* The distribution of the variables throughout the speech community must be studied in order to assess the social significance of the different forms and systems that have been isolated. Some of the methods used and the purposes of such a description are outlined in this paper. It is not always necessary to construct a random sample of all of the individuals in the speech community. More rapid samples can be made by various methods, in the school system and through other institutions.[20] The greater the degree of social and stylistic variation, the more necessary to avoid the bias of *convenience* in selecting informants, and to avoid the bias produced by approaching informants through formal institutions such as the school. For this work, the linguist can draw upon other social scientists for assistance, and whenever possible, he should couple his study with other social surveys so as to devote the maximum energy to the study of language itself. One of the great advantages of a representative survey of linguistic behavior is that it allows us to study change. Through the distribution of linguistic forms through various age levels in the population, we can infer the existence of linguistic and social change; even more valuable information eventually can be derived by repeating the study at a later time. If, on the other hand, we remain content with an impressionistic account of a particular dialect derived from the study of a few "typical" informants, we will have no means of measuring these observations against any later research.

4 *The influence of other languages.* In many areas of the United States, we must consider the effect of languages other than English upon the linguistic behavior of particular ethnic groups and perhaps upon the entire population. For this purpose, it is necessary to provide formal descriptions of the particular dialect of the foreign language which is used, and of the English used by the second- and third-generation members of that ethnic group, and then to chart the possible relations between these.[21] While the main task of this description

[20] In a recent study in the Phoenix Union Central High School of Phoenix, Arizona, it was possible to obtain a great deal of information about the sociolinguistic structures of Phoenix in a few days, by interviewing classes of students as a whole. Of the many favorable circumstances, not least was the cooperative and helpful attitude of the school administration.

[21] The lines of research to be followed here have been laid out in some detail by Uriel Weinreich in *Languages in Contact* (New York: Linguistic Circle of New York, 1953).

falls upon the linguist, the teacher can help greatly by making separate reports of the errors made by students with the foreign language background in question and giving some estimate of the relative difficulty encountered in changing these patterns.

b. *The Social Significance of Non-standard English.* Information on the social distribution of speech forms tells us a great deal about social significance, but it is possible to make a more direct attack upon this question. In order to make intelligent decisions about which forms of language require correction or suppletion with alternate forms, we have to know which markers of linguistic behavior have serious effects upon the life chances of the individual. In different areas, we might find the same non-standard forms, but with radically different social significance. For example, one can hear stops and affricates used for /θ/ and /ð/ in the Southwest, but there this feature does not seem to have the same strong social impact as in Chicago or New York.

The methods required to measure subjective evaluation are complex, and they are not generally available to linguists or educators. The school system can, however, provide information on the ability of students to perceive the differences between standard and non-standard variants. The ability of the student to hear the difference between two forms consistently is closely correlated with their social significance.[22]

The information on subjective evaluation can be used to classify linguistic variables into three basic categories:

> *indicators,* which show social variation but usually not stylistic variation, and have little effect upon the listener's judgment of the social status of the speaker
>
> *markers,* which show both social and stylistic variation, and have consistent effects upon the conscious or unconscious judgment of the speaker's status by the listener
>
> *stereotypes,* which are the overt topics of social comment in the speech community, and may or may not correspond to actual linguistic behavior.

It is evident that most of the attention of the educators will be concentrated upon the markers and upon systems which contain a great many markers. Thus we may find that there are regular characteristics of Negro speakers which are indicators, but do not function as markers, and there would be little justification for including these elements as "errors," "mistakes," or deviations from Standard English.

[22] In a study of 53 delinquent youths at New York City's Youth House, carried out in the summer of 1964, we obtained information on the speaker's ability to perceive a series of phonological contrasts. The contention that native speakers can hear phonemic distinctions much better than nonphonemic distinctions was not borne out by the evidence. Instead, one might say that the ability to perceive distinctions is determined largely by the social significance of the distinction to the listener.

The study of subjective evaluation must be carried out in many different communities if we are to resolve questions raised concerning the cultivated regional varieties used in the South. If indeed there are many students who enter northern school systems using such varieties, it is important to discover how the northern speech community evaluates them. As far as the children's vernacular is concerned, we have every reason to think that pressure from their friends and associates will lead to the adoption of the local forms. Whether or not the school should take any position at all on the status of cultivated Southern speech probably depends more upon the frequency of such cases than any other factor.

c. *The Acquisition of Standard English*. This topic has been the principal concern of the present paper, and some of the tentative findings have been outlined on the basis of the New York City study. Future research programs would necessarily be concerned with testing preliminary notions on all of the aspects of language acquisition for many communities. One important focus of such research would be this question: given a regular pattern of social and stylistic stratification, how can one give lower-class children the same wide range of stylistic variation that is open to middle-class children? It would seem that there are two main types of solutions: early training which permits lower-class children to enter the acquisition route (Figure 40.5) at a higher point than they normally would, or special training which increases the normal rate of acquisition of Standard English.

d. *Resistance to the Acquisition of Standard English*. The three areas of research outlined above are only preliminary to the major question of analyzing the reasons why those who are exposed to Standard English, and who need the ability to use Standard English, do not learn this form of the language. We can point to four major aspects of this question, recapitulating in part the discussion of 2c above.

1   *Structural interference*. The results of research under section *a* above can be applied to the analysis of interference between the underlying vernacular and the standard language as it is taught in the schools. Teaching methods which focus upon the contrastive points of interference can then be formulated.

2   *Opposing motivations*. Although it has been shown that most New Yorkers endorse the value of Standard English, we have also seen that there must exist opposing motivations which must be made explicit in further research. Furthermore, it is necessary to find the particular variables upon which these opposing value systems are focused. All variables may not bear equal weight in this respect.

3   *Resistance in the peer group*. Small group studies are required to show in detail the means by which the adolescent and pre-adolescent group behavior interferes with the acquisition of second dialects.

4   *Teacher-student interaction*. Studies in the classroom are needed to

investigate the type of adjustment in language behavior which the teacher makes to the vernacular of the students and which the students make to the normal style of the teacher. It is possible that teachers who show a wider range of stylistic performance in their own speech have greater (or lesser) effectiveness in persuading students to accept a form of Standard English. Research of this type would require close cooperation between educators and linguists. While linguists may provide indexes for measuring linguistic interaction in the class-room, they have no means of measuring teacher effectiveness.

This brief outline is intended to summarize the main directions for research in urban dialects which would help to answer the questions raised in the conference as a whole. For many of the problems mentioned, the joint efforts of linguists, social scientists, and educators will be needed. Their approaches appear to be complementary rather than contradictory, and there is every reason to think that considerable progress can be made through such cooperation.

DISCUSSION

Roger W. Shuy, Michigan State University
William Stewart, Center for Applied Linguistics
Charles Ferguson, Center for Applied Linguistics
Ruth Golden, Detroit Public Schools
Thomas Creswell, Chicago Teachers College, South
Raven I. McDavid, Jr., University of Chicago
Muriel Crosby, Wilmington, Delaware, Public Schools

The applicability of Labov's work to other urban areas was discussed at length. It was generally agreed that one might expect quite different results if he were to apply Labov's technique to other areas but that Labov's great contribution is in presenting an empirical model that can be applied to a variety of situations and in pointing out variables that can lead to comparative studies which use virtually the same parameters.

A second topic of discussion centered on the pedagogical applications of this approach. Labov stated that a great deal more study will have to be made before language engineering for the lower classes can be successful. Since the homes of many lower-class and working people do not provide the pressures toward upward social mobility that middle-class homes provide, we must build into the group, starting from a level not much above the nursery school and going on through high school, a tolerance for practice in second role playing.

Since he mentioned only two of the five indices of Standard English in New York City, Labov was asked to enumerate all five. They are:

1. The use of *r* in post-vocalic and pre-consonantal position (*guard, horse,* but not including *work* and *shirt*—which are special cases).
2. The vowel in *bad, ask, dance, had, cash.*

3. The stressed vowel in *awful, coffee, office.*
4. The use of (θ) in *thing* and *thin.*
5. The use of (ð) in *then* and *the.*

Labov also mentioned that one of the most important social contrasts in American English is found in the /ɑ/ ~ /ɔ/ collapse. He estimated that people in about half the geographic area of the U.S. have no contrast between "hock" and "hawk" or between "cot" and "caught."

41

The Argot of Narcotic Addicts

DAVID W. MAURER

41.1   The Social Aspects of Argot Formation

IT IS BASIC TO HUMAN SOCIAL ORGANIZATION that whenever people are closely associated, they develop certain special aspects of language, often on several different levels. Most trades and occupations, for instance, carry with them a specialized vocabulary which not only is useful in the performance and perpetuation of the work pattern, but gives status to the worker. Thus printers, sailors, railroaders, physicians, etc., develop a sort of occupational language which is functional as well as social in its nature.

Sometimes these specialized linguistic phenomena are associated with religion or sacred ritual, and, among primitive peoples, we may find the language used by warriors on the warpath, or the language used by priests or medicine men, considered as sacred and often kept completely secret from the outgroup. The presence of these sacred languages among Stone Age people shows us that this tendency in language is very very old, and perhaps fundamental to human society.

When we go into the underworld we find that the forces which motivate the formation and use of secret or semi-secret languages are intensified. First, legitimate society is organized against the professional criminal, who may experience both social and economic ostracism during his entire lifetime. Professional criminals, on the other hand, have formed a counter-organization in order to protect themselves as best they can from the pressures of legitimate society expressed through the law.

Second, because the criminal organization is much tighter than the organization of the legitimate world, it is extremely powerful, and part of its power emanates from the close-knit structure made possible by the fact that all criminals share certain habits, certain stigmata and certain security problems in common. Within some occupational groups, this group-solidarity is greater than in others, but in all groups it is observable to some degree, and finds expression not only in mannerisms, beliefs and customs, but most characteristically in the use of language. Speech patterns reflect the behavior patterns of the group, as well as

Reprinted by permission from David W. Maurer and Victor H. Vogel, *Narcotics and Narcotic Addiction*, 3d ed., Springfield, Ill., Charles C. Thomas, 1967. Dr. Maurer, the principal author of this chapter (pp. 318–46) is Professor of English at the University of Louisville. The entire glossary is too long for inclusion here, but the first two letters of the alphabet are offered to provide examples.

the traditions and group subculture, insofar as this rudimentary culture dif-
ferentiates the criminal group from legitimate society on the one hand, and
from other criminal groups on the other. To a greater or lesser degree the
language of the group is semi-secret; it is, in effect, a union card, for it is difficult
for an outsider to know and use the argot like a professional. These argots are
keys to the behavior patterns as well as the techniques used by various specialized
criminal groups.

Third, the modern underworld is composed of four or five major social and
occupational divisions, within which there are literally hundreds of specific
criminal activities. A professional criminal is usually identified loosely with one
of the social divisions and speaks the idiom common to that division, in addition,
of course, to Standard English, on whatever level he would normally use it.
Furthermore, he knows and uses the specialized vocabulary of the specific
racket or rackets with which he makes his living. These aspects of language in
the underworld are called argots, and a confidence man, for instance, would
speak the general argot of the *grift*, with special reference to the *big-con* or the
short-con; he might further specialize his vocabulary according to the individual
con games which he consistently practices. Some widely experienced operators
will know and use several argots, and have a peripheral knowledge of several
more, but these individuals are increasingly rare.

We now know that each of the many subdivisions of professional criminals
constitutes what we might call a subculture or microsystem, which is a cultural
entity differing both in behavior pattern and language from the dominant culture.
Some of these subcultures are almost outside the dominant culture and have
little in common with it—as, for instance, the gypsies. Others, like the confidence
rackets, share many cultural indices with the dominant culture, and simulate
the behavior of successful business men so well that good big-con men are
usually accepted in very respectable financial circles; they have to be to operate.
While we do not know exactly how subcultures begin, we suspect that both
criminal and noncriminal subcultures are language-generated, and much of the
socio-linguistic evidence collected by Dr. Maurer during many years of sociolinguistic fieldwork among criminals tends to strengthen this suspicion.

When a professional criminal learns his occupation, as, for instance, thievery,
with specialization as a pickpocket, he starts with the very specialized techniques
of pocket-picking in terms of a specific language. More than that, he constantly
thinks of his occupation in terms of that language and discusses his work with
other pickpockets in terms of their common language. In other words, his
entire occupational frame of reference is both technical and linguistic, and the
language is fundamental not only to the perpetuation of the craft of thievery
but to its practice.

Last, a professional criminal usually takes great pride in his craft. He
identifies himself with it very closely and rationalizes its importance in the
underworld and his importance within the group in a way which is satisfying to
his own sense of self-importance. To each individual, a knowledge of the

language of his own craft, as well as perhaps that of several others, is a mark of status in the underworld. Also, it furnishes identification and provides him with recognition. Among people who live and work constantly under a legal, social and perhaps moral stigma, this element of recognition is very important.

Thus we see that the formation of specialized argots within the underworld is a natural phenomenon, and we know from having explored many of the highly specialized rackets, together with their appropriate argots, that a vast body of secret and semi-secret language is used by people in the underworld. As yet it is imperfectly explored, and its relationship to the legitimate language has not been fully charted. However, we have observed that professional criminals operating in a certain technical and social area developed a specialized argot, while non-professional or occasional criminals performing similar criminal acts as individuals do not know or develop a specialized language pattern. For instance, a professional killer or *torpedo* for a racket mob will know and use the argot of his profession fluently; a psychopathic murderer who might well have committed more murders in a lifetime than the professional killer will not develop any standardized language pattern in connection with murder. A bank teller might indeed embezzle more money over a period of years than a competent professional *heel-thief* would steal (and both would take it from behind the cashier's window), yet the embezzler would have no knowledge of the argot spoken by the thief, nor would be form an argot to be used in speaking or thinking about his own criminal activities. An individual forger will never develop an argot on his own, but professional passers of forged checks have a well defined argot, though they almost always work alone. While legitimate gamblers have some slang (largely borrowed from professionals), those who gamble professionally in the underworld have a large and highly developed argot.

We now know that the so-called "underworld" is nothing more than an aggregate of criminal subcultures, all parasitic on the dominant culture and each distinct from the others to a variable degree. Each of these subcultures has its own characteristic behavior pattern, including mores, technology, modes of defense against the dominant culture, attitudes toward professional bisexuality, etc. Language is one of the most significant of these subcultural indices.

Argots, then, are a reflection of social structure. They are learned and transmitted and used within organized grops in the practice of a criminal profession. They are indeed the earmark of the professional. They are used almost entirely within the in-group and are spoken almost exclusively in the presence of other members of that group. Contrary to popular belief, argots are seldom used to deceive victims, to mystify non-criminals or to fool the police. In fact, they are seldom used at all in the presence of outsiders.

Because argots reflect the way of life within the group, and the way of life within many professional criminal groups is insecure and sometimes dramatic, the language pattern of those groups is often vivid and salty. For thousands of years the argots of professional criminals in many languages have constituted a fresh source of vivid phraseology which is used to enrich the standard languages spoken and written by non-criminals. As far back as the *Satyricon* of Petronius, for instance, we find that much of the author's freshness stems from his lively use of the argots of the Roman underworld. In the Golden Age of Spanish literature, it was fashionable for writers, some of them great, to affect the usage of thieves, vagabonds, and swindlers; this custom was carried so far that today, much of the writing of an author like Francisco de Quevedo defies exact translation; in fact, during the seventeenth century, a whole literary genre, the picaresque novel, concerned itself with the adventures of thieves, written in what passed for a reasonable facsimile of their own language. This school of writing was popular not only in Spain, but all over Europe. Shakespeare borrowed freely from the underworld argots of his day, and other Elizabethans, like Thomas Dekker, acquired a very accurate first-hand knowledge of criminal argots. Such masters as Defoe, Fielding, Smollett, and Sterne flavored their literary vocabularies not only with older underworld terms, but with contemporary eighteenth-century argot phrases which were strong and colorful. Today, most popular slang is borrowed or discarded from the underworld, but the closed corporations of modern big-time crime make current argots less accessible to modern writers than were the argots of the Renaissance, when it was fashionable for gentlemen and writers to rub shoulders with rogues.

However, it is only within recent years that linguists have realized the importance and the extent of the contribution which criminal groups make to standard usage in all civilized languages. Naturally, when words and phrases from criminal groups become widely used by outsiders, those words are usually replaced by others known only within the profession, so that criminal argots are often less stable than standard language, with a high birth rate of words balanced by a high death rate within the ingroups, and a relatively low survival rate compared to standard language. These birth, death, and survival rates are also influenced by the fact that most criminal argots are not generally written, and almost never printed. Argots live principally in the minds and on the tongues of individual speakers, and the turnover in terminology is frequently very great, especially among those argots which, through contact with legitimate people, become known outside the ingroup. Some criminal argots, however, remain surprisingly stable, with a portion of the vocabulary becoming almost traditional. While in this study we are mainly concerned with words, or lexical elements, it should be noted that argots differ from the standard language in some aspects of structure, and especially in intonation, pitch, and juncture. These are now being investigated in the argots used by professionals.

The importance of a study of argots has been recognized only recently, with the realization among psychologists, anthropologists, and linguists that the language of any group is one of the most reliable keys to the culture pattern; and, since this culture pattern is not so obvious or so easily observed as the life pattern of the groups which do not operate outside the law, a knowledge of the argot is not only useful in penetrating the ingroups, but is essential to understanding the motives, the techniques, and the attitudes of the professional criminal.

A study of these linguistic phenomena implies a simultaneous anthropological study of the subcultures in the same depth with which some primitive cultures have been studied. At present, we can only make some generalizations about them with some degree of validity.

First, subcultures and specialized linguistic phenomena seem to arise spontaneously and simultaneously; language seems to lie at the heart of their cultural genesis. They develop against the background of a dominant culture already highly sophisticated in handling symbols, and this tends to shape the subcultures into entities of special symbolism, all of which tends to nurture a heightened sense of group identity.

Second, subcultures really begin to expand and intensify and differentiate when pressures from the dominant culture are generated. In fact, it appears that, without some of these pressures, subcultures become abortive or tend to atrophy. There must be a threat from the dominant culture—or from other subcultures—and this threat intensifies the internal pressures already at work. The language indigenous to the subculture tends to intensify the attitudes, values, and technology which characterize the group. The development of techniques, especially those which may be a threat to the dominant culture, may be disapproved or suppressed, which excites increased linguistic activity, usually accompanied by an intensification of internal cohesive forces and an increased emphasis on secrecy.

This special language or argot is a strong influence toward homogeneity; through it, group identity is further developed, and, as the subculture becomes stronger, it tends to pull away from the dominant culture, becoming more aware of itself as its communication system becomes more versatile. It comes to believe what it hears, and is more positive in what it says. The behavior pattern shapes itself ever closer to what the group says it is and what its acts prove it to be.

Third, when the dominant culture senses the presence of a criminal subculture, it tends to draw away, and this dichotomy increases the differentiation, which process is speeded up as social distance becomes more and more obvious.

It is not accidental that the dominant culture usually first becomes aware of an emerging criminal subculture through the leakage of terms and idioms from this group. At first these new expressions provoke humor, derision, and some curiosity in the dominant culture. As soon as it becomes apparent that they have linked with them a hostile and even sinister behavior pattern, the dominant culture manifests first fear, then hostility. The dominant culture may counterattack with suppressive measures—usually enacting a new law or the shoring up of an old one—for society has a firm belief that a new law, and preferably a very stiff one, will take care of everything. Increased pressure provokes stronger resistance, and there is now a minor power struggle in the making. By this time, the subculture has structured a set of laws of its own—often more severe and more rigorously enforced than those of the dominant culture—and has no intention of accepting the laws of the dominant culture. However, we of the dominant culture still cling to the myth that we can convert professional criminals into law-abiding citizens if we only apply enough law, enough psychiatry, or both.

Last, we might note that this hostility between the dominant culture and various criminal subcultures has characterized the growth of American civilization. Indeed, there have been times in our history—and this by no means excludes the present—when highly organized criminal subcultures have taken over entire communities and even large cities. When these subcultures maintain an exclusive membership, a tight code of enforcement and the utilization of pressures from the dominant culture to strengthen their own sub-system, they become formidable indeed. Such a group is the modern Mafia, which is well-nigh untouchable. Sometimes these subcultures have been battled, in the past often in bloody fashion, by vigilante-type splinter groups from the dominant culture, with very little real law involved in the struggle. Sometimes, also, the dominant culture has been dismayed when the very people who subdued the criminal subcultures (which are usually only driven out, not exterminated or effectively subdued) turned out to be mere exploiters of these groups for their own profit after the furor died down. This is the cycle of so-called "reform" governments on the local level in the United States.

41.2   Argots and the Narcotic Addict

Narcotic addicts fall into two main groups. First, there are those legitimate people who become addicted but who do not resort to organized crime to support their habits. They do not secure their drugs from underworld sources or habitually associate with underworld characters. These people have no knowledge of the argot of the underworld narcotic addict, and modify or utilize colloquial or medical terminology when they think of or discuss the use of drugs. A second larger group of addicts inhabits the underworld, lives by a criminal profession, secures its drugs from underworld dealers or peddlers and associates with other addicts. These addicts know and use the argot of the underworld addict. It is with this group that we are particularly concerned.

It is important to note that addiction is very common in some underworld professions and rare in others, that it is acceptable in some professions, even highly respectable ones (from the underworld point of view) and not acceptable in others. For example, among professional thieves the incidence of narcotic addiction is very high, and addiction is socially acceptable among most thieves, especially pickpockets and shoplifters. The authors estimate addiction among thieves at between 60 and 70 percent, depending upon the type of thievery. On the other hand, among stick-up mobs, bank robbers, payroll bandits, etc., the incidence of narcotic addiction is very low, and addiction is looked upon as a sign of weakness and unreliability.

We should also note that different groups of professional criminals have differing attitudes toward the use of various drugs. Old-time safecrackers, for example, accepted the smoking of opium as a gentleman's vice, and this toleration of the use of opium is still found in some of the higher brackets among the underworld, noticeably among big-time professional gamblers and big-time confidence men. These same groups, and especially the old-timers in these groups, tended to reject the use of the needle along with morphine, heroin, etc., although some of them accepted the needle as a substitute for the pipe only because the smoking of opium while traveling was too cumbersome and too dangerous. There is also a tendency at the present time for those criminal groups who accept the use of narcotics by needle to look down upon those who use narcotics by other methods, or those who use other types of drug. A mob of professional thieves who use morphine, for instance, would not accept a marihuana user on a level of equality; in fact, they would distrust him completely and would probably refuse to recognize marihuana as a drug of addition. Among modern heroin users, however, this pattern is changing, since so many of them started with marihuana and consequently carry over into heroin addiction their earlier argot usage connected with marihuana. In a sense, they have "corrupted" the argot of the users of hard drugs by needle in something of the same manner that needle addicts "corrupted" the argot of the old-time opium smoker.

Among underworld addicts, the use of various drugs, then, carries with it varying status in different groups, with opium smoking still remaining the almost inaccessible preference of the aristocrats of the underworld. Furthermore, among some underworld groups, the size of the habit is an important index to status, with those who support large habits feeling more important and receiving more recognition than those who have small habits, this recognition being more common among professionals in the lower brackets. This differentiation is in part influenced by economic considerations, since, with drugs at the present high prices, a professional who can support a large habit must *ipso facto* be sufficiently successful at his profession. However, among opium smokers, the support of a small regular habit is considered a gentleman's privilege, but at the same time, successful big-time criminals do not as a rule regard over-indulgence in opium as a mark of distinction; in fact, quite the reverse. The opium addict who can hold his habit down to a reasonable level is considered "smart." The same thing is true of alcohol, for it implies a high degree of self-control. *Big-con* men, for example, almost never drink while they are working.

Also in the underworld a distinction is made between the individual who supports a narcotic habit as a luxury which interferes to a small extent or not at all with the practice of his profession, and the one who works at a criminal profession for the sole purpose of supporting a habit. Usually, the latter type tends to degenerate in his profession, to lose status among his associates and to go downhill rapidly.

Professional criminals who use narcotics have a tendency to work together; thus, a non-addict may work temporarily with a mob whose members are addicted, but he will probably not enjoy this association, nor will a non-addict mob accept without reservations a member who is addicted, despite his skill or special abilities. Temporary or fill-in work would be an exception. This acceptance or rejection, while partly based on moral and social reasons, is primarily a result of the physical limitations which addiction places upon an individual. An addict must maintain regular contact with sources of supply; he must withdraw from his work at very regular time intervals in order to take drugs, which may appear to others to be an unsavory and time-consuming process; the transportation of drugs and equipment may be difficult among traveling mobs; and the possession of these articles constitutes a safety hazard for the rest of the mob, since drugs and equipment for using them might cause the arrest of a mob or involve the entire mob in difficulties not connected with the usual hazards of their work. Furthermore, among non-addict criminals, the taking of narcotics is often looked upon as distasteful, and non-addicted professionals have a tendency to distrust addicts; however, addicts work rather well together in mobs since their problems are the same, and since they have all accepted the phenomenon of addiction. Thus a pickpocket mob will stop work at certain intervals to take narcotics, one member of the mob may do the purchasing of narcotics for the entire mob, and needles and accessories sometimes are shared, though a certain class of addicts prefer not to share this equipment.

In addition to associations on the road or in the course of a criminal occupation, narcotic addicts have a tendency to gather in taverns, restaurants, saloons, and other places where it is convenient to meet. Sometimes these establishments supply drugs, or someone living near them can be contacted in order to secure drugs. Also, addicts sometimes congregate in the places where drugs are supplied to users. Some addicts cannot use the needle themselves or prefer not to, and require the services of an attendant to make the injection.

Where opium is smoked, a chef (either professional or amateur) is always available to cook the pills for the smokers. In these establishments (usually referred to in literature as "opium dens" but known to the addicts as *hop joints* or *lay down joints*), conversation is lively, and addicts enjoy associating with their friends. Among opium smokers, especially where the smoking is done in groups, conversation is a notable concomitant to smoking; the general sense of well-being and mental relaxation tends to stimulate conversation. This tendency to converse, often on a high intellectual level, has been noted by non-criminal opium smokers—such as the artists and writers of Paris and other bohemian centers—but seems to be notably absent among needle addicts, who like to "coast" and enjoy the drug subjectively.

At these meeting places, addicts confer and gossip freely, and here the argot is coined and transmitted. Since many of these addicts are in trouble with the law rather frequently, they carry the argot into the jails and eventually into the prisons.

In both these institutions, addicts have a tendency to congregate and to connive in order to secure drugs, a procedure which is not too difficult in most correctional institutions if the addict or his friends outside have any money. In prisons, the argot of the narcotic addict is recognized as different from the argot of the other professional groups, and the association of addicts in prisons tends to stimulate the production and use of argot.

Within the past few years, the close fraternity of addiction (which was previously tightly closed to outsiders) has been invaded by literally thousands of newcomers, many of them youngsters under twenty-one who, twenty years ago, could never have penetrated the underworld circles where they now circulate freely. While underworld opiate addicts formerly excluded the "weed-heads" or marihuana addicts from their company, the marihuana traffic has now become vast and immensely profitable; furthermore, marihuana paves the way for heroin, and youngsters now become opiate addicts almost overnight. Twenty years ago, most drug addicts were over thirty, and a juvenile addict had yet to be encountered. All this activity has not only introduced a vast new class of addicts, but has also disturbed the argot. Phraseology which, thirty years ago, was standard and well stabilized to opium smokers or needle addicts, is now used in all sorts of new and unorthodox ways by the younger generation of addicts; furthermore, the drastic changes in the bootleg market and in the drugs available, as well as in the rackets adopted by addicts to support their habits, have forced the incorporation of many new terms and the corruption of many older ones. The conservative, sometimes dignified and intelligent opium smoker has given way to an increasing number of cool needle-pushers and marihuana smokers who are not only playing havoc with the drugs of addiction, but with the argot as well. Consequently, one hears some surprising adaptations and applications of what was formerly a fairly stable argot.

Also, among addicts there is a very close relationship between argot usage and the psychic and physical effect of drugs. As addicts verbalize their reactions to drugs, they also reinforce the effect which these drugs have on them, and the association of certain terms with specific experiences tends to create an associative pattern which undoubtedly plays a part in the satisfaction which the addict gets from the use of the argot. Many terms in the argot describe vividly and graphically not only the effects which drugs or abstinence from drugs produce, but also, by use of metaphor and suggestion, relate the sensations derived from drugs to other physical and emotional sensations, notably those connected with sex.

Although many underworld people are strongly inclined to be gregarious, addicts are especially so; as soon as two or more gather, the conversation turns to drugs, which may be consumed simultaneously with the visiting and gossiping that goes on among the users.

This tendency to give drugs a prominent place in the conversation increases noticeably when addicts gather in places where drugs are not readily available, such as a prison, a narcotic hospital or jail, where the talk of narcotics is continuous and intense.

Historically, the argot of the narcotic addict is interesting for several reasons. First of all, it seems to spring from the language used by opium smokers; some old-time smokers have retained the basic argot, much of it Chinese or

Oriental in origin, which they learned thirty or forty years ago; however, as pipe smokers were forced by circumstances to take up the needle and substitute morphine or heroin for opium, a good deal of the pipe smokers' argot was adapted to the use of narcotics injected hypodermically. Now many younger addicts are quite unaware that much of their argot is derived from the opium traffic. Also, marihuana smoking on a large scale is relatively new in the United States; marihuana apparently entered through New Orleans about 1910. It became obvious as a problem about 1935, and its use has since expanded tremendously, so that there are now more marihuana smokers than all other types of narcotic addicts combined. For a time the users of opiate drugs refused to accept marihuana smokers into the fraternity, and the argot of marihuana smokers was looked upon with contempt by opiate addicts. Now, however, with many young marihuana smokers turning to heroin and with marihuana recognized as the link between the use of heroin or heroin and cocaine mixed, the argot of the marihuana smoker is no longer so distinct a phenomenon, and some of it is being accepted into the general argot of the narcotic addict.

It is probable that the smoking of marihuana has been carried on in the United States from Colonial days to the present, though on a very small scale and in isolated communities. The impetus which brought about the present popularity of marihuana in the last few years seems to have come from Mexico, Central America and Cuba. Because of the close association between swing music and the consumption of marihuana, the marihuana smoker has not only adopted much of the slang and argot characteristic of swing music, but has contributed heavily to it. Some of it also comes from the black-and-tan joints, the tea pads, and the brothels of such large metropolitan centers as Los Angeles, San Francisco, San Antonio, New Orleans, Memphis, Louisville, St. Louis, Chicago, Cleveland, Pittsburgh, and New York. The important centers in the evolution of the slang of swing music, however, have been New Orleans, Chicago, and New York. Furthermore, many youngsters are quite familiar with the language of swing, including some of the argot of the marihuana smoker, and use it freely even though they are not addicted.

The argot of the marihuana smoker, then, is somewhat different from the argot of opiate users in character, imagery, connotation, and in the life pattern reflected. Compared to the argot of opiate users it appears to the authors to be thin, obscure, and affected. It reflects the very different type of person who uses marihuana, the marihuana addict usually being young, naive, unseasoned, and parasitic, while the opiate addicts, especially the old-timers, are cynical, sharp-witted, mature, and rich in life experience. Especially among the ranks of the opium smokers there are some brilliant minds to whom the carefully turned phrase and the meaningful metaphor are very important.

To some extent, the argot of the addict is affected by the kind of drug he consumes and the method by which he takes it. For instance, addicts who sniff cocaine or heroin may have very little knowledge of the argot of the needle addict—until their increased tolerance forces them to substitute injection for sniffing; if they continue to take cocaine or heroin by inhalation indefinitely (a very unusual circumstance), they might never become aware of the argot of the needle addict; however, most needle addicts are familiar with the phraseology of those who sniff drugs, since large numbers of needle addicts were formerly inhalers. Users of drugs like Benzedrine and the barbiturates may never become familiar with the argot of the opiate addicts unless they are thrown with these addicts in intimate association. Even so, users of Benzedrine are looked upon by opiate addicts in much the same light as are marihuana smokers. Perhaps they are even less acceptable to the fraternity than users of marihuana. Also, it is noticeable that the users of barbiturates and Benzedrine have contributed very little to the argot of narcotic addiction. Neither have the addicts who take drugs by mouth been very active in developing the argot, with the possible exception of opium addicts, who eat opium or drink it in solution; these addicts usually know the argot of opiate addiction and use it, largely because sooner or later they go to the needle themselves.

The argot used by narcotic addicts, then, reflects rather vividly the way of life of the addict—the ecstasy of narcotics, the necessity for escape from the world of reality, the compensatory effect of drugs upon the inadequate personality, the constant preoccupation with the needle as a symbol, the eventual exclusion of all other motives for living, and the complete preoccupation with the necessity for securing drugs. There is also the ever-present evidence of the substitution of drugs for sexual activity. A study of this argot has already proved of value to psychoanalysts, psychiatrists and sociologists, since through the argot the addict unwittingly reveals a considerable portion of the unconscious which is preoccupied with addiction.

On the whole, relatively little of the argot of the underworld addict passes into general usage while it is currently popular in criminal circles, although, as time goes by, a rather large body of archaic or obsolescent argot finds its way into the language of the dominant culture. As new terms appear, the ones which they replace often are discarded, sometimes because they are already beginning to be used by "squares." A great number of terms, however, seem to remain in the argot for a long time and do not seep out into the dominant culture. Much of the argot which does get out develops meanings somewhat different from those used within the addict subculture. However, the argot used by underworld addicts is definitely expanding in size, and it is still obscure to the outsider. Therefore, a rather comprehensive glossary of words and phrases associated with addiction is appended.

Several points should be made regarding this material, which has been collected from practically all regions of the United States where addiction is at all common. It represents the usage of literally hundreds of addicts, although it is unlikely that any one addict would know all the terms included, since no single addict is familiar either with all geographical regions or all the social classes from which the usage has been collected. Certain subcultures are open to some addicts, closed to others; from these subcultures, only the terms used by these criminals *as addicts* have been included, since otherwise the whole of these specialized languages would have to be treated. However, with the proliferation of addicts into some subcultures from which they were largely excluded fifteen or twenty years ago, even in the marginal status which they now have, some of the words from these specialized subcultures are beginning to appear in the general usage of addicts. Also, only a small portion of the data collected on each word can be included here because of the need for condensation.

Readers with a linguistic background who use this material will note immediately that there is an apparent inconsistency in the forms used in each main entry. This is deliberate, since many terms have incomplete paradigms, with the form listed usually being the most common, or in some cases, the only form used. For example, some terms occur only in the plural, others only or mostly in a participial form. Verbs defined as infinitives usually have a complete, or hypothetically complete, set of paradigms. Many idioms have a variable usage, and only one or two illustrations are given from the many recorded.

Cross-referencing is somewhat irregular, since many items which are near-synonyms but have slight differences in meaning need to be linked together for the general reader. There has been a rather close cross-referencing of terms intimately connected with drugs and addiction, since that is the main concern of this book, while terms less closely associated with addiction are not cross-referenced or rather loosely treated in this respect. The spelling is somewhat arbitrary, since most of the words are taken from verbal usage and must be rendered in graphics according to the best judgment of the writers. There simply is no authority to consult in this connection, for the great bulk of this linguistic material was first put into print by Dr. Maurer, who always reserves the privilege of altering spelling in the light of new information, usually of an etymological nature. For example, one term for marihuana was first recorded as *greefo* or *griffo*, until its probable relationship to Mexican Spanish *potación de guaya* (drink of grief) was noted, after which the variant *griefo* was added. *Potación de guaya* (marihuana pods soaked in wine or brandy) is an old Mexican term, incidentally also probably the source of the very modern *pot* for marihuana to be smoked. Addicts are seldom if ever aware of these etymological connections.

It will be noted that the qualification *obsolescent* appears after a number of terms. This means only that a number of informants have expressed the idea that a given term is out of date, or not so much used as more popular ones, or the informant indicated that he knows the word but does not use it himself. However, the situation with regard to obsolescence varies dramatically from area to area, with a word which is already old-fashioned in one area being at the height of popularity in another. Sometimes these popular words are new contributions; more often they are simply older terms rediscovered and used in their original sense, or given new meanings. Often these words are modifications or corruptions of older terms which the current generation regard as new only because they have never heard the older form. And so, while obsolescence is a kind of cyclical phenomenon, it is rare that a word can be labeled truly obsolete, for about the time that label is applied, it is almost certain to pop up in another area or among a different class of addicts; it has merely been kept alive in some obscure circles which have not been currently studied. It is notable that, thirty or thirty-five years ago, younger addicts learned the argot from their elders and imitated it rather carefully; today, because of the preponderance of younger addicts, the older ones seem to go along with the language currently in use in order to maintain status and identity within the subculture. In general, a movement of terms from East to West has been observed, although there are many exceptions to this, and new words tend to generate and reach popularity in any center where a number of addicts congregate. However, it is a common experience to find that a new term on the East Coast is unknown on the West Coast, and by the time it reaches the West Coast—if it does—it may well be obsolescent in the East. At the same time, one can observe terms used on the West Coast, or from the Chicago or Detroit areas, which are unknown in the East, though eventually they may appear there.

Phonologically, there is little to say about the argot of addicts at the present time, largely because this phase is difficult to study, and because the evidence is far from complete. However, we might oversimplify a bit and say that the phonology of addicts tends to follow that of the geographical regional dialect as well as the social level to which they are indigenous. At the same time, there are some para-linguistic and kinesic factors which, though very subtle, seem to be almost universal among American underworld addicts, who readily recognize one another by these means, even though they may be hard put to it to explain exactly and specifically how they do this. A trained observer, however, can, after sufficient experience with addicts, readily isolate and identify some of these.

While this glossary is by no means complete, pains have been taken to see that it is representative. Consequently, there is a sprinkling of terms from the institutional argot of narcotics hospitals, jails, and prisons which, several years ago, would not have been characteristic. Also there are some terms for the "hustle" or small-time racket by which the addict supports his habit; often these are modifications, corruptions, or improper applications of terms already established in other rackets, for they have been hastily adapted by young addicts who have had no real experience in the rackets proper before drugs forced them into some form of criminal activity. There are also a number of terms which originated or were adapted by Negro addicts, reflecting not only the preponderance of addiction among Negroes, but the spreading psychology of the so-called white Negro as well.

REFERENCES

Note: There are no references to previously published material in [this chapter] because the authors felt that it was desirable to include a fresh study of the argot, based on fieldwork done during 1965–66. However, the following titles are relevant to any consideration of the argot, at least in an historical sense, because of the obscure nature of addicts' usage and in the light of the widespread changes which have taken place in that usage within the past decade.

1. BERREY, LESTER V., and VAN DEN BARK, MELVIN: *The American Thesaurus of Slang.* New York, Thomas Y. Crowell, 1942. (Contains some data on the argot of addicts, very loosely edited, based on the work of D. W. Maurer, with acknowledgments in the fifth and subsequent printings.)

2. COWDRY, E. V. JR., and GOTTSCHALK, L. A.: *The Language of the Narcotic Addict.* The United States Public Health Service Hospital, Fort Worth, Texas, 1948.

3. GOLDIN, HYMAN E., O'LEARY, FRANK, and LIPSIUS, MORRIS: *Dictionary of American Underworld Lingo.* New York, Twayne Publishers, 1950. (Contains some sound data on the usage of addicts, especially in prisons.)

4. MAURER, DAVID W.: Junker lingo: A by-product of underworld argot. *American Speech,* 8:2 (Apr.), 1933.

5. MAURER, DAVID W.: The argot of the underworld narcotic addict, Part I. *American Speech,* 11:2 (Apr.), 1936. Reprinted by the United States Public Health Service, 1936.

6. MAURER, DAVID W.: Addenda to addicts' argot. *American Speech,* 11:3 (Oct.), 1936.

7. MAURER, DAVID W.: The argot of the underworld narcotic addict, Part II. *American Speech,* 13:3 (Oct.), 1938. Reprinted by The United States Public Health Service, 1938.

8. MAURER, DAVID W.: *The Big Con: The Story of the Confidence Man and the Confidence Game.* New York, Bobbs-Merrill, 1940. (Contains notes on the use of narcotics among confidence men and consequent reflection in their argot.)

9. MAURER, DAVID W.: The argot of forgery. *American Speech,* 16:4 (Dec.), 1941. (Contains notes on addiction among forgers and passers of forged checks.)

10. MAURER, DAVID W.: Speech of the narcotic underworld. *The American Mercury,* 62:266 (Feb.), 1946.

11. MAURER, DAVID W.: Marijuana addicts and their lingo. *The American Mercury,* 63:275 (Nov.), 1946.

12. MAURER, DAVID W.: *The Technical Argot of the Pickpocket and Its Relation to the Culture-Pattern.* A paper presented before the Modern Language Association, Detroit, Michigan, December, 1947. (Contains notes on the use of drugs among thieves and pickpockets, with consequent reflection in the argot. Also, *Whiz Mob: A Correlation of the Technical Argot of Pickpockets With Their Behavior-Pattern.* Publication No. 24 (Book) of the American Dialect Society, 1955. Publication No. 31, 1959 contains a word-finder list for the above book. Trade edition, New Haven, College and University Press Services, Inc., 1964, 216 pp.

13. MAURER, DAVID W.: *The Argot of the Criminal Narcotic Addict.* A paper presented before the Foreign Language Conference, The University of Kentucky, April 25, 1952.

14. MAURER, DAVID W.: *Reflections of the Behavior-Pattern in the Argot of Under-*

world Narcotic Addicts. A paper presented before The American Dialect Society at the convention of The Modern Language Association, Boston, Boston, December 29, 1952.

15. PARTRIDGE, ERIC: *A Dictionary of the Underworld, British and American.* New York, Macmillan, 1950. (Contains data on the usage of addicts, rather loosely edited, based on the work of D. W. Maurer, with acknowledgments in the second American edition.)

16. PROVOST MARSHAL GENERAL'S SCHOOL: *Glossary of Colloquial Terms Used by Narcotic Addicts, and Commercial Preparations Containing Narcotic Drugs.* (Vol. II of *Narcotics and Other Drugs.*) Camp Gordon, Ga., 1952. (Argot materials contributed by D. W. Maurer.)

GLOSSARY

A.B. An adverse behavior report (Lexington). Elsewhere, often called a *gunsel*, a kind of obscure pun on adverse (perverse) behavior, since a *gunsel* is a kind of "pervert". See *shoot (him) down.*

ab or **abb.** An abscess which forms at the site of injection on needle addicts, largely as a result of impure drugs or unsterile needles. For details see text and photographs. Addicts are sometimes literally covered with draining sores. Barbiturates also produce abscesses. Also *Raspberry, cave.* See Fig. 4. "The worst abs I ever saw were caused by yen shee, cooked and shot in the line or in the skin." "Yen shee will not cause an ab if shot in a vein or deep in muscle. Worst abs are caused by Nembutal when the vein is missed."

Abe. A five dollar bill. Also *Lincoln, nickel, fin,* etc.

ace. 1. A one-year sentence. Also *bullet.* "He laid an ace on me for that score." 2. One of anything. 3. Or *ace note.* A one dollar bill. Also *Abe.*

acid. Lysergic acid diethylamide (LSD-25), a powerful psychomimetic drug, produced synthetically, which duplicates in a highly concentrated form the same hallucinogenic agent found in peyote, mescaline and psilocybin. It appears on the contraband market in the form of powder, liquid in ampules, and sugar lumps on which a drop of the concentrated drug has been deposited. Much used by amateur experimenters, but of little or no interest to opiate addicts. See text for a detailed discussion.

acid dropper. One who uses LSD. Also *acid head.*

acid head. A user of LSD. Also *acid dropper.*

acid test. The experience involved in taking LSD. A common phrase among users is, "Can you pass the acid test?" (meaning, Can you take the psychological consequences of using this drug? Have you been initiated to it?)

action. 1. The selling of narcotics. 2. Anything pertaining to criminal activities. "All the action is going on at Pete's pad" (meaning *planning*). See also *happenings, skams.*

all lit up or **lit up.** To be under the influence of narcotics; to be obviously experiencing the euphoria immediately following an intravenous injection. Usually restricted to needle addicts, especially *speed ball* shooters. Also *coasting, floating, hitting the gow, hitting the stuff, in high, on stuff, on the gow, picked up,* some with specialized meanings.

"He was racing his motor and all lit up too." "Their eyes shine and stay lit up. . . ." Commonly used by squares to refer to anybody under influence of anything. Not commonly used by West Coast addicts. See *geed up, ripped, smashed, wired up, charged, zonked, stoned, loaded, knocked out*.

amp. A 1 cc Methedrine ampule, legitimate.

around the turn. For an addict who is *kicking the habit* to have passed through the worst of the withdrawal syndrome, which reaches its maximum intensity in from thirty-six to seventy-two hours from the last regular injection. Also *over the hump, reach the pitch*. Present-day addicts without habits so severe as in former years often use it to refer to the last day of withdrawal. "Doc, give me a pick up and it'll put me around the turn."

artillery. The outfit used to inject drugs hypodermically, that is, usually, a medicine dropper fitted with a hollow needle. Specialized to needle addicts. Also *Bay State, emergency gun, gun, hype, joint, Luer, nail, needle, works*, some with specialized meaning. ". . . it (a needle) is referred to as a spike usually, and a dropper is a dripper. Put them together and you have artillery."

ask for the cotton. 1. To ask for another addict's filtering cotton in order to squeeze out the residue for a very small shot. An indication that the addict is broke and out of drugs. "He was around T.O. asking for the cotton a few weeks ago." 2. By extension, to dislike a person. "I wouldn't ask that bum for the cotton."

attitude, show an attitude, have an attitude, etc. Hostile or aloof and uncooperative. "I pegged him for a lame with an attitude. . . ."

away. Incarcerated.

away from the habit. To be *off drugs*. Also *to break the habit, to be off,*

to catch up, to fold up, on the up and up, washed up, cleaned up.

back up. 1. To allow the blood to come back into the glass (dropper or glass syringe) during a vein shot. See *register, jack off, booting*. "He always liked to back up a shot three or four times." 2. To refuse to make a connection because of suspicion that the addict (or the peddler) may be a stool pigeon. Also to *blow the meet*. 3. To fold up or back away from something.

bag. 1. A quantity of drugs packaged in small paper or cellophane parcels, *e.g.*, five dollar bags. Also *balloon*, though a *balloon* is usually a condom or small rubber balloon. See *bindle*. 2. To put in a classification as convict, thief, con man, etc.

balloon. A quantity of drugs packaged in small paper, cellophane or rubber parcels. See *bindle*.

bambalache. Marihuana (New York). See *muggles*.

bamboo. An opium pipe. Specialized to opium smokers. Obsolescent. Also *gong, gonger, dream stick, hop stick, joy stick, saxophone, stem, stick, yen cheung, crock, gongola, log*. "Seems like I can't get my habit off this morning. Let's have another crack at that bamboo. . . ."

bang. 1. An injection of narcotics, usually taken intravenously, but may refer also to subcutaneous injecttions. Restricted to needle addicts, and usually means morphine, heroin or cocaine, or a combination. Also *bang in the arm, fix up, geezer, jolt, pop, shot, bird's eye, skin shot, vein shot, speed ball, jab*, with specialized meanings. All these terms indicate a ration of drug prepared for injection, as contrasted to a *bindle, check, deck*, etc., which indicate units of drug as they are sold retail. "I'll loan you a bang till you score. . . ." 2. The thrill or drive experienced immediately after a vein shot; euphoria. Restricted to needle addicts. Also *bing, boot, drive, jab off, kick or kicks, belt, buzz, flash, charge.* "I took four shots of that flea powder and couldn't get no bang out of it." "Yeah, I noticed I didn't get the right bang out of that last shot myself." 3. The lift or exhilaration experienced from taking drugs in any manner. "Now I'm on horse, I can't get no bang out of muggles any more." 4. To inject narcotics, especially in the vein, but may refer to *skin shooting* also. Also to *shoot,* to *get with it.* See *bang in the arm.*

bang in the arm. Usually shortened to *bang.* An injection of narcotics. Obsolescent. See *bang* 1. "A bang in the arm and we'll be dead ready for that trip tonight."

Bay State. A standard medical hypodermic syringe, usually of glass with metal reenforcement, using a plunger and screw type needle. Derived from the trade name of the syringe. Seldom used by underworld addicts. Also *Luer* (for a standard syringe). "She wouldn't use anything but a Bay State to fix, but I liked a dripper. . . ."

bean. A Benzedrine tablet or capsule. See *benny.*

bean trip. Intoxication from ingesting Benzedrine; a *benny jag.*

bear down on (one). For a habit to come on, especially the early withdrawal symptoms. See *habit.*

beat. 1. To cheat. 2 Sick for lack of drugs. 3. Down and out. 4. To rob. See *knock off* 4.

beat a till. To steal from a cash register. See *till tapping.*

beat the gong. To smoke opium. See *hit the gong, kick the gong.*

beat the rap or **beat the beef.** To be acquitted of a charge.

bee that stings. A drug habit, especially one coming on; *a monkey on my back.* See *habit.*

bees and honey. Money. From "Australian" rhyming argot, in which the meaning rhymes with the second element in the phrase and is filled in by the one who hears it. *E.g.,* "twist and twirl" means "girl".

beetlebrow. An aggressive female homosexual.

behind stuff. Using heroin.

belly habit. A drug habit satisfied by taking drugs orally. See *mouthhabit.*

belt. 1. The euphoria following an injection of narcotics. See *bang* 2. 2. A shot, or a quantity of drugs to be injected. "Gimme a belt of stuff."

bending and bowing. To be under the influence of narcotics. Obsolescent, See *high, all lit up.*

benny. Benzedrine (amphetamine) in tablets, capsules or inhalers. Also *whites, crosses, beans, blancas* (Mexican), referring to capsules.

benny jag. Intoxication from ingesting Benzedrine. Also *wired on whites, bean trip, white scene.* See *benny.*

Bernice, Burnese, Bernies. Crystallized cocaine used either for inhaling or for mixing with morphine or heroin in the form of hypodermic injections. Sold in papers or capsules. Also, *C, Corine, Carrie, coke, Cecil, Cholly, happy dust, heaven dust, dust, snow, star dust,* and other similar terms beginning with *C.*

"... soon as I get Bernice we'll go for a ride."

big man. The brains behind a dope ring; the one who seldom takes the rap. Most traffic in narcotics is controlled by gangsters of a vicious type, often with sound political connections. The *big man* wholesales drugs to dealers and for peddlers, and may racketeer them for protection and the privilege of selling. *Big men* are usually not addicted.

bindle. A quantity of narcotics (usually restricted to morphine, heroin, and cocaine) prepared for sale, as contrasted to a *ration*, which is prepared for injection. Both *bindles* and *rations* vary widely in size and strength. Also *cap, card, check, cigarette paper, cube, deck, O., O.Z., piece, ballon, half load, load, bundle, bag,* with specialized meanings. ". . . and this connection had bindles for five dollars, ten dollars and twenty dollars, good H, too."

bing. An injection of drugs. Also *bingo, bird's eye, fix, gee, go, jab, pop, load, penitentiary shot, pick up, pin shot, geez* or *geezer, point shot, prod, prop,* with specialized meanings. See *bang.*

bird cage hype. A down and out underworld addict, probably so called because he often lives in a *bird cage joint* or flophouse where the cots are separated by chicken wire. There is also a saying that a down and out addict "has a bird cage on one foot and a boxing glove on the other." "He's just a bird cage hype stemming his score dough." Obsolescent. Current popular term, *gutter hype.*

bird's eye. 1. A half size or small ration of narcotics. "A bird's eye is generally what a junker takes in his first bang after being on vacation for a while. . . ." 2. A small pill of opium, especially opium prepared for smoking. This is the smallest size. The next in sequence are *buttons* and *high hats.* 3. A very small quantity of drugs. "When Whitey bought the cap I took just a tiny bit—a bird's eye—and gave the rest to him." 4. A small quantity of narcotic solution held in the *joint*

for another addict to take; equivalent to "butt's" on a cigarette. "Save me two or three points of that for a bird's eye." Also *taste, lightweight taste.*

bit. A prison sentence. Also *jolt, stuff.* "I started in San Quentin and finished my stuff in Chino."

bitch or **the bitch.** The death penalty or life imprisonment. Also used for a long sentence given to a habitual criminal. Clipped back from *habitch,* in turn clipped from habitual.

biz or **business.** 1. An outfit (*joint* and *spoon*) for taking drugs hypodermically. Also *factory, joint, layout, machinery, works,* etc. See artillery. "Have you got the business? I'm sick." 2. The hypodermic needle as separate from the syringe. Also *harpoon, point, tom cat,* with specialized meanings. "Let me use the business." 3. Narcotics in general. See junk. "What I want is the business." 4. The "third degree" administered by the police. "Everyone gets the business from those dicks in Cincy." 5. Death or a beating given a stool pigeon. "They finally gave that rat from Chi the business." 6. As *B.I.Z.* To emphasize the action, with each letter pronounced separately. "That dude is really taking care of the B.I.Z." (He is being successful in criminal activity.) 7. The end of anything. 8. Bad or fake dope. See *blank.*

black and white. A policeman.

black shit. Smoking opium. See *black stuff.*

black stuff. 1. Opium prepared for smoking, as contrasted to crude gum. Also *gee yen, hop, gum, mud, pen yen, san lo, tar, black shit, yen shee, ah pen yen, dai yen, fi doo nie, hok for, sook nie, li yuen, gee, gonger* 3, *lem kee,* with specialized meanings. 2. Laudanum is now being called *black stuff* by extension. 3. Concentrated paregoric cooked down for injection. 4. Dark brown heroin that comes from Mexico.

blackjack. Paregoric which has been cooked down to be injected in a concentrated form. See *P.G.*

blancas. Benzedrine tablets (Mexican).

blank. 1. A quantity of bad or fake dope. Also *turkey, sugar, flea powder, talcum powder, queer* 5, *business* 8. 2. An individual who is nothing, especially as far as the rackets are concerned.

block. 1. A *cube* of morphine as sold by the can (or ounce). "It comes 120 to 130 blocks to the ounce." 2. Crude bootleg morphine. 3. A kilo (2½ lb.) of bulk marihuana.

block buster. See *yen shee baby*.

bloomer girls or **bloomer broads.** Shoplifters who wear specially constructed underwear in which stolen articles are concealed. See *hustling drawers*.

blow. To inhale narcotics in powder form, usually heroin, though cocaine was formerly popular taken by sniffing it up the nose, usually from the back of the hand. Narcotics in tablet form are crushed between two coins before inhaling. ". . . when I could get a dozen heroin tablets for fifty cents, I'd blow one just before I went on (the stage) and one as soon as my act was over. . . ." "You know Slim. Well, he first started blowing C around a layout." Also *horn, snort*. 2. To smoke marihuana, as to *blow weed*.

blow a pill. To smoke opium.

blow a shot. To waste drugs by missing a vein, or because of a break or malfunction of the equipment. Restricted to needle addicts. ". . . never seen it fail. On short stuff I'll always blow a shot." Also *skin* or *skin the punk*. 2. To spill the solution.

blow the meet. To fail to keep an appointment, usually because of suspicion on the part of either addict or peddler. ". . . considered high treason for a peddler to blow a meet, he will lose his customers quick . . . it's bad for the addict, too." "It takes a pinch or its equal to make me blow a meet." Also *hang him up, blow the scene*.

blow the scene. 1. To fail to keep an appointment, especially for the sale or purchase of narcotics. Also *hang (someone) up, blow the meet*. 2. To flee; to leave precipitously.

blow weed. To smoke marihuana.

blue birds or **blues.** Sodium Amytal in capsules. Also *blue heaven, blues, jack up*.

blue grass. To obtain a commitment to the Lexington Hospital under certain conditions. If an addict breaks those conditions, he usually serves a year in jail. This term is now loosely applied to similar situations elsewhere, although the practice is not much used now in Kentucky. Used as adjective, noun or verb. "If you leave Lexington, the Kentucky authorities will place a charge against you for drug addiction unless you recommit yourself and stay until you're pronounced cured. This is called a blue grass commitment."

blue heaven. Sodium Amytal in capsules. Also *blue birds, blues, blue heaven, jack up*.

blue velvet. 1. Sodium Amytal. See *blue birds, blue heaven*. 2. Pyribenzamine.

boat sailed or **boat's in.** Said when narcotics are successfully smuggled into prison. See *drive* 4.

bo bo bush. Marihuana. See *muggles*.

bogart. To take more than one's share, usually by violence.

bogus beef. See *meat ball rap*.

bogus smack. See *blank*.

bogus trip. False information regarding drugs or peddlers.

bombita. An amphetamine capsule; from Mexican Spanish for "little bomb."

bonaroo. 1. Good narcotics, uncut or cut only a little; the best. 2. Wearing starched, pressed clothing in a prison or a narcotics hospital. "That dude was looking bonaroo when he flashed at the board (parole board)."

bonche. A group of marihuana smokers using the drug. Also *cofradia* (Cuba and New York City).

bonita. Mexican Spanish, slang term for milk sugar, which is used to adulterate heroin.

boo gee. The *gee rag* used to make a tight connection between syringe and needle. Probably a variant or corruption of the medical term *boogie*. Rare. Also *geep, boat, collar*. See *gee rag*. 2.

book. The maximum penalty, usually in the phrase, "He threw the book at me," "He gave me the book." Also *stuck it to me* (West Coast).

boomer. An addict who moves frequently. Borrowed from the lingo of the old-time railroaders, meaning a railroader who drifted from job to job, working a while at each, or riding freights when he had no work. *Cf.* German *bummeler, bummel-zug*, etc. Also *globe trotter, drifter, floater, boot and shoe*.

boost. To shoplift. Probably the most common way of supporting a habit, excepting prostitution. The noun form is often recorded in such idioms as *rooting on the boost, on the boost, working the boost*.

booster. A professional shoplifter, male or female.

booster stick. 1. A cigarette of treated marihuana, reputedly potent. Also *gold leaf special*. 2. An ordinary cigarette, the tip of which is dipped in a concentrated essence of marihuana preserved in alcohol. It is lit, blown out when it flames, and inhaled.

boosting drawers. See *hustling drawers*.

boot. 1. Euphoria following injection. See *bang, belt, flash, gassed, stoned*. 2. The *gee rag* used to make a tight connection between needle and dropper. 3. To back blood into the dropper, allow it to mix with the drug, then shoot it back. Also *verification shot*.

boot and shoe. 1. Down and out, as applied to an underworld addict. Probably derived from the bizarre garb worn by some addicts, especially those who make a living by begging or panhandling. "The boot and shoe junkies made that joint a hangout, so it was really hot." The plural is sometimes used with adverbial function. "All hypes eventually go boot and shoes." Also *bird cage hype, broker*.

booter. One who uses *boot shots*. See *boot* 3.

boots on. In on the know, informed. Recorded as *have (one's) boots on, keep (one's) boots on*, etc. "Tell Joe to put his boots on, to wise up."

boss. Wonderful or choice. Also *righteous, groovy, solid, out of sight, something else, too much, (the) end*.

boss habit. A very heavy habit.

bottoms. A male homosexual who is the passive receptor in pederasty. Also *sissy, stuff, sex punk, rap and bag it, queen pussy, boy girl*.

bow sow. Narcotics. West Coast, obsolescent.

box. 1. A record player. 2. The vagina. 3. A carton of cigarettes. 4. Radio.

5. Television. 6. A safe.

box of L. 100 ampules of Methedrine in a pharmacist's box.

boy. Heroin. See *Racehorse Charlie.*

boy girl. 1. See *bottoms.* 2. A person who adopts the mannerisms of the opposite sex.

brace and bits. The breasts. From "Australian" rhyming argot.

bread. Money.

break the habit or **break.** 1. To go *off drugs.* See *kick the habit.* "I have to break the habit for I have a State case coming up." 2. To suffer severe localized withdrawal distress. An opium smoker may say, "I always break the habit in my stomach."

brick gum or **brick.** 1. Crude opium after it is cooked into smoking opium or prepared opium. "Sometimes it comes in bricks weighing a pound, and sometimes in odd-shaped lumps." "Used to get brick gum for $40.00 to $60.00 a pound; now it's $300.00 to $450.00." 2. *Brick* (only). A kilo of marihuana (2½ lb.).

bring up. To distend the vein into which the *shot* will be injected by holding up the circulation with a cord or tourniquet, simultaneously massaging the skin over the vein toward the tourniquet. Also *tie off,* which is more popular on the West Coast.

britch. A pocket, especially a side pants pocket. Borrowed from pickpockets, who seldom use *britch* alone, but rather *right britch* or *left britch,* and then only for side pants pockets.

Brody. 1. A feigned "fit" or spasm staged by an addict to elicit sympathy and perhaps a ration of narcotics from a physician. Obsolescent. Also *cartwheel, circus, wingding, figure eight, twister, toss out, meter, Duffy, bitch,* as in *pitch a bitch.* "He threw a Brody for the

croaker and scored for some stuff." 2. A long chance, derived from the dive of Steve Brody from Brooklyn Bridge, ". . . an awful Brody he took, but he made a clean get."

broker. A down and out addict. See *boot and shoe.*

brown eye. Coitus *per anum.*

buffalo. A five-year sentence. Obsolescent. Also *nickel, fin.*

bug. 1. To inject an irritant such as kerosene or the creosote disinfectant often used in jails into the muscles or beneath the skin to produce a swelling or abscess; used to solicit narcotics from a doctor. "That time seven guys bugged themselves and got junk for a while, also a rest. . . ." 2. To annoy someone especially a guard in a prison or jail. "Steve had two speeds, slow and slower. He'd slip into slower to bug the hack." 3. To tap a telephone line. 4. An abscess or sore, self-inflicted and used to solicit narcotics from physicians. Probably derived from the *bugs* or sores cultivated by old-time beggars.

build up the habit or **a habit.** To increase one's tolerance to narcotics by gradually increasing the dosage, usually inevitable with opiates. "A guy can build up one hell of a habit using Dilaudid before he realizes it." Also *strung out, hooked, got a thing going.*

bull. 1. A policeman. Also the *man, the heat, screw, black and white, hudda* (Mexican). 2. An aggressive female homosexual, clipped from *bulldyker* sometimes rendered as *bulldagger, q.v.*

bull horrors. The delusions often experienced by cocaine addicts; part of the anxiety complex produced by the drug and sometimes reinforced by paranoid tendencies in the user. Policemen (*bulls*) and detectives often figure prominently in these delusions, hence the term, 'Monty had the bull horrors bad. . . ."

bulldagger. Variant of *bulldyker*. See *bull* 2. Also *butch*.

bullet. A currently popular expression for one year sentence, supplanting *ace* on the West Coast.

bum beef or **bum steer.** False complaint or information, which is usually given deliberately to the police.

bum kick. Boring, unpleasant.

bum rap. An arrest or conviction for a crime the man actually did not commit, as distinguished from denying it. See *rap* 2, *rap partner*, *rap sheet*,

bum steer. False or unreliable information about drugs or peddlers. "You gave me a bum steer, Jack, about that joint. . . ." Also *bogus trip, bum wire, jive*.

bum wire. False information regarding peddlers or drugs.

bummer. Anything boring or unpleasant.

bundle. 1. A quantity of narcotics for sale. Variant of *bindle*. 2. A sum of cash, especially a roll.

bunk habit. 1. The desire to hang about where opium is being smoked; actually, a mild opium habit can be contracted from continually breathing smoke-filled air. See *bunk yen, lamp habit* 3. "His girl don't smoke but she has a bunk habit." 2. An opium habit (smoking). 3. A tendency to sleep a great deal; used to refer to addicts of any kind by extension. "They ought to call her The Pajama Kid; she has an awful bunk habit."

bunk yen. 1. A small opium habit requiring only two or three pills to satisfy. Also *bunk habit* 2, *lamp habit* 3. ". . . well, he only had a bunk yen, but he would get so

sick. . . ." 2. The slight addiction acquired from breathing the smoke-filled air in a *lay down joint* or in a room where opium is regularly smoked. Also *bunk habit* 1. "I used to let the pup lay down with us, and he finally got a bunk yen. . . ." (Many West Coast prostitutes formerly had Pekingese or other lap dogs who were obviously addicted.) "Some Chinese broads did not smoke, but had a bunk yen just from cheffing. . . ."

burn. 1. To cheat. 2. To cheat or steal from someone. 3. To sell bad or fake drugs. "I burnt that poop butt. I sold him some Ajax." 4. The initial exhilaration following the injection of opiates. See *jaboff*.

burned out. A sclerotic condition of the veins resulting from abscesses and continued puncturing. Also *up and down the lines*. ". . . had to go to the skin, all his lines are burned out." See *soul searching, up and down the lines*.

Burnese. Variant of Bernice, *q.v.*

bush. Marihuana.

business. See *biz*.

bust. 1. To arrest or be arrested. See *put away, down, nailed, clouted, snatched, rousted, knocked off, knocked out*. 2. To catch someone redhanded. "I knew I'd bust Jimmy dipping if I left the smack on the table."

bust the main line. To inject narcotics intravenously. Also *to shoot, to take it in the vein, to take it main, hit the sewer, send it home, geeze* or *geez*.

From my dropper I'll shake the dust
From my spike I'll scrape the rust,
And my old main line I'll bust. . . .

busted on a buzzer. See *meat ball rap*.

butch. See *bull*. A *butch* is not necessarily a *bull*, however. She may simply be the active lesbian partner.

butch game. 1. An ultimatum to co-operate or suffer heavy penalty. Also *murder game*. 2. The technique used by a lesbian prostitute beating her trick for money without going through with the sexual act.

button. A pill of smoking opium, in size between a *bird's eye* and a *high hat*. See *bird's eye*. 2. A nodule of peyote, not addicting but used experimentally by some "far-out" beatniks.

buy. 1. A narcotic peddler. 2. A purchase of narcotics.

buy money. The money used to purchase drugs. See *connection dough*, *score dough*.

buzzer. 1. A homosexual. 2. A prison guard. 3. An enforcement officer's badge. "We got his leather that had his buzzer in it."

Bibliography

Articles marked with an asterisk are included in this volume.

AARONS, ALFRED C., BARBARA Y. GORDON, and WILLIAM A. STEWART
    1969   eds., *Linguistic-Cultural Differences and American Education.* Special Anthology issue, *Florida FL Reporter* 7, No. 1.

ABEL, JAMES W.
    1950   *A Study of the Speech of Six Freshmen from Southern University (Negro).* Ph.D. dissertation, Louisiana State University.

ABERCROMBIE, DAVID
    1954   "The recording of dialect material," *Orbis* 3.231–35.

AIKEN, JOHNNYE
    1938   *The Speech of Haynesville, Louisiana, at Three Age Levels.* Ph.D. dissertation, Louisiana State University.

ALATIS, JAMES E.
    1970   ed., *Linguistics and the Teaching of Standard English to Speakers of Other Languages or Dialects.* Report of the 20th annual round table meeting on linguistics and language studies. Washington: Georgetown University Press, monograph 22.

ALDERSON, WILLIAM L.
    1953   "Carnie talk from the West Coast," *American Speech* 28.112–19.

ALLEN, HAROLD B.
    1952   "The Linguistic Atlas of the Upper Midwest of the United States," *Orbis* 1.89–94.
    1956   "The linguistic atlases: our new resources," *English Journal* 45.188–94.
    1957   "On accepting participial *drank*," *College English* 18.263–65.
    1958a "Distribution patterns of place-name pronunciations," *Names* 6.74–79.
    1958b ed., "Linguistic geography," in *Readings in Applied English Linguistics.* 1st edition. New York: Appleton-Century-Crofts. Pp. 137–91.
 *1958c "Minor dialect areas of the Upper Midwest," *Publication of the American Dialect Society* 30.3–16.
    1958d "Pejorative terms for midwest farmers," *American Speech* 33.260–65.
    1959a "Canadian-American differences along the Middle Border," *Journal of the Canadian Linguistics Association* 5.17–25.
    1959b "*Haycock* and its synonyms," *American Speech* 34.144–45.

1959c "No epitaphs for *depot*," *American Speech* 34.233–34.
1960 "Semantic confusion: a report from the atlas files," *Publication of the American Dialect Society* 33.3–13.
1964a ed., "Linguistic geography," in *Readings in Applied English Linguistics*, 2nd edition. New York: Appleton-Century-Crofts. Pp. 201–69.
*1964b "The primary dialect areas of the Upper Midwest," in Allen (1964a). Pp. 231–41. Also in Marckwardt (1964) as "Aspects of the linguistic geography of the Upper Midwest," pp. 303–14.

ARNOLD, DAVID B.
1962 *Linguistic Variation in a New England Community*. Ph.D. dissertation, Harvard University.

ASHCOM, B. B.
1953 "Notes on the language of the Bedford, Pennsylvania, subarea," *American Speech* 28.241–55.

ATWOOD, E. BAGBY
*1950a "*Grease* and *greasy*: a study of geographical variation," *Studies in English* 29.249–60.
1950b "The pronunciation of *Mrs.*," *American Speech* 25.10–18.
1951 "Some Eastern Virginia pronunciation features," in *English Studies in Honor of James Southall Wilson*, Fredson Bowers, ed. *University of Virginia Studies*, Vol. 4. Charlottesville: University of Virginia Press. Pp. 111–24.
1953a "A preliminary report on Texas word geography," *Orbis* 2.61–66.
1953b *A Survey of Verb Forms in the Eastern United States*. Ann Arbor: University of Michigan Press. Reviewed by H. B. Allen, *American Anthropologist* 56.315 (1954); N. E. Eliason, *Modern Language Notes* 49.282 (1954); A. H. Marckwardt, *Language* 30.74–78 (1954); C. K. Thomas, *Quarterly Journal of Speech* 40.81–82 (1954); C. M. Wise, *Southern Speech Journal* 19.341–42 (1954); A. L. Davis, *American Speech* 30.121–23 (1955).
1958 "Linguistic geography in the United States," *Proceedings and Transactions. Fifth International Congress of Onomastic Sciences*. Salamanca. Pp. 3–12.
1961 "Words of the Southwest," *The Round Table of the South-Central College English Association* 2.1.
1962 *The Regional Vocabulary of Texas*. Austin: University of Texas Press. Reviewed by W. Labov, *Word* 19.266–72 (1963); D. M. McKeithan, *Southwestern Historical Quarterly* 67.158–63 (1963); G. R. Wood, *American Speech* 38.220 (1963); R. I. McDavid, Jr., *Journal of English and Germanic Philology* 63.841–46 (1964); C. E. Reed, *Language* 40.296–98 (1964); J. N. Tidwell, *Journal of American Folklore* 77.163–64 (1964).
*1963 "The methods of American dialectology," *Zeitschrift für Mundartforschung* 30:1.1–29

AUSTIN, WILLIAM M.
1965 "Some social aspects of paralanguage," *Canadian Journal of Linguistics* 9.31–39.

AVIS, WALTER S.

1953 "Past participle *drank*: Standard American English?" *American Speech* 28.106–11.

1954 "Speech differences along the Ontario–United States border. I. Vocabulary," *Journal of the Canadian Linguistics Association* 1.13–19.

*1955a "*Crocus bag*: a problem in areal linguistics," *American Speech* 30.5–16.

1955b "Speech differences along the Ontario–United States border. II. Grammar and syntax," *Journal of the Canadian Linguistics Association* 1.14–19 regular series.

1956a *The Mid-Back Vowels in the English of the Eastern United States*. Ph.D. dissertation, University of Michigan.

1956b "Speech differences along the Ontario–United States border. III. Pronunciation," *Journal of the Canadian Linguistics Association* 2.41–59.

*1961 "The 'New England short o': a recessive phoneme," *Language* 37.544–58.

1964 "Problems in the study of Canadian English," *Communications et Rapports du Premier Congrès International de Dialectologie Générale*. Louvain: Centre International de Dialectologie Générale. Pp. 183–91.

BABCOCK, C. MERTON

1949 "The social significance of the language of the American frontier," *American Speech* 24.256–63.

BABINGTON, MIMA, and E. BAGBY ATWOOD

1961 *Lexical Usage in Southern Louisiana. Publication of the American Dialect Society* 36.

BAILEY, BERYL LOFTMAN

*1965 "Toward a new perspective in Negro English dialectology," *American Speech* 40.171–77.

1966 *Jamaican Creole Syntax*. Cambridge, England: Cambridge University Press.

1968 "Some aspects of the impact of linguistics on language teaching in disadvantaged communities," *Elementary English* 45.570–78, 626.

BARRETT, MADIE WARD

1948 *A Phonology of Southeast Alabama*. Ph.D. dissertation, University of North Carolina.

BERNSTEIN, BASIL

1962 "Social class, linguistic codes, and grammatical elements," *Language and Speech* 5.221–40.

1964 "Elaborated and restricted codes," in Gumperz and Hymes (1964). Pp. 55–69.

BIGELOW, GORDON E.

1955 "More evidence of early loss of [r] in Eastern American speech," *American Speech* 30.154–56.

BLOCH, BERNARD

1935 *The Treatment of Middle English Final and Preconsonantal R in the Present-Day Speech of New England*. Ph.D. dissertation, Brown University.

*1939 "Postvocalic /r/ in New England speech," *Actes du quartième Congrès internationale de linguistes*. Copenhagen: Munksgaard. Pp. 195–99.

1941   "Phonemic overlapping," *American Speech*. 16.278–84.

BLOK, H. P.
1959   "Annotations to Mr. Turner's 'Africanisms in the Gullah dialect'," *Lingua* 8.306–21. [See Turner (1949)]

BLOOMFIELD, LEONARD
1933   *Language*. Holt, Rinehart and Winston. [Chapter 5 (Chicago pronunciation), pp. 91–92; Chapter 19, "Dialect geography," pp. 321–45.]

BOESEN, MARY L., B. V. M.
1968   *Contextual Incidence of Verb Forms in the Speech of Selected Sixth Grade Minneapolis-Born Children*. Ph.D. dissertation, University of Minnesota.

BOTTIGLIONI, GINO
*1954   "Linguistic geography: achievements, methods, and orientations," *Word* 10.375–87.

BRENGELMAN, FREDERICK H.
1957   *The Native American English Spoken in the Puget Sound Area*. Ph.D. dissertation, University of Washington.

BRIGHT, WILLIAM
1966   ed., *Sociolinguistics: Proceedings of the UCLA Socio-Linguistics Conference, 1964*. The Hague: Mouton.
1967   "Language, social stratification, and cognitive orientation," in Lieberson (1967). Pp. 185–90.

BRIGHT, WILLIAM, and A. K. RAMANUJAN
1964   "Sociolinguistic variation and language change," in Lunt (1964). Pp. 1107–13.

BROADDUS, JAMES
1957   *The Folk Vocabulary of Estill County, Kentucky*. M.A. thesis, University of Kentucky.

BRONSTEIN, ARTHUR J.
1949   *A Study of Predominant Dialect Variations of Standard Speech in the United States during the First Half of the Nineteenth Century*. Ph.D. dissertation, New York University.
1962   "Let's take another look at New York City speech," *American Speech* 37.13–26.

BROOKS, CLEANTH
1935   *The Relation of the Alabama-Georgia Dialect to the Provincial Dialects of Great Britain*. Baton Rouge: Louisiana State University Press. [See also Ives (1955a).]

BUCK, JOYCE F.
1968   "The effects of Negro and white dialectal variations upon attitudes of college students," *Speech Monographs* 35.181–86.

CAFFEE, NATHANIEL M.
1935   *A Phonological Study of the Speech of a Homogeneous Social Group in Charlottesville, Virginia*. Ph.D. dissertation, University of Virginia.
1940a   "Some notes on consonant pronunciation in the South," in Caffee and Kirby (1940). Pp. 125–32.

1940b "Southern 'l' plus a consonant," *American Speech* 15.259–61.

CAFFEE, NATHANIEL M., and THOMAS A. KIRBY
1940 eds., *Studies for William A. Read*. Baton Rouge: Louisiana State University Press.

CAPELL, ARTHUR
1966 *Studies in Sociolinguistics*. The Hague: Mouton. Reviewed by S. A. Tyler, *Language* 44.197–98 (1968).

CARMONY, MARVIN DALE
1965 *The Speech of Terre Haute: A Hoosier Dialect Study*. Ph.D. dissertation, Indiana University.

CARR, DONNA HUMPHREYS
1966 *Reflections of Atlantic Coast Lexical Variations in Three Mormon Communities*. M.A. thesis, University of Utah.

CARR, ELIZABETH B.
1960 "A recent chapter in the story of the English language in Hawaii," *Social Process in Hawaii* 24.54–62.

CARRANCO, LYNWOOD, and WILMA RAWLES SIMMONS
1964 "The Boonville Language of Northern California," *American Speech* 39.278–86.

CARROLL, WILLIAM S., and IRWIN FEIGENBAUM
1967 "Teaching a second dialect and some implications for TESOL," *TESOL Quarterly* 1:3.31–39.

CASSIDY, FREDERIC G.
1941 "Some New England words in Wisconsin," *Language* 17.324–39.
1953 *A Method for Collecting Dialect*. Publication of the American Dialect Society 20. Reviewed by A. R. Dunlap, *American Speech* 29.201–5 (1954); H. B. Allen, *Language* 32.549–53 (1956).

CATFORD, JOHN C.
1957 "The linguistic survey of Scotland," *Orbis* 6.105–21.

CHALK, SARAH SLAY
1958 *A Vocabulary Study of Dallas County, Texas*. M.A. thesis, University of Texas, Austin.

CLIFTON, ERNEST S.
1959 "Some /u/–/ju/ variations in Texas," *American Speech* 34.190–93.

CLOUGH, W. O.
1954 "Some Wyoming speech patterns," *American Speech* 29.28–35.

COHEN, MARCEL
1956 "Social and linguistic structure," *Diogenes* 13.38–47.

COHEN, PAUL S., WILLIAM LABOV, and CLARENCE ROBBINS
1966 "A preliminary study of the structure of English used by Negro and Puerto Rican speakers in New York City—an outline of research results," *Project Literacy Reports No. 7*. Ithaca: Cornell University. Pp. 13–17.

COLMAN, WILMA
1963 *Mountain Dialects in North Georgia*. M.A. thesis, University of Georgia.

COOPER, DEANNA, KARIN MATUSEK, and DIANNE WOOD
   1967 "Short 'o' vowels in Eastern Massachusetts speech," *Speech Monographs* 33.93–94.

CORBIN, RICHARD, and MURIEL CROSBY
   1965 eds., *Language Programs for the Disadvantaged; The Report of the NCTE Task Force on Teaching English to the Disadvantaged*. Champaign: National Council of Teachers of English.

CRAWFORD, BERNICE FLAKE
   1950 *Some Lexical Variants in Pioneer Ellis County*. M.A. thesis, North Texas State University.

CURRIE, EVA G.
   1950 "Linguistic and sociological considerations of some populations of Texas," *Southern Speech Journal* 15.286–96.

CURRIE, HAVER C.
   1952 "A projection of sociolinguistics: the relationship of speech to social status," *Southern Speech Journal* 17.28–37.

DAKIN, ROBERT F.
   1967 *The Dialect Vocabulary of the Ohio River Valley: A Survey of the Distribution of Selected Vocabulary Forms in an Area of Complex Settlement History*. Ph.D. dissertation, University of Michigan.

DAVIS, ALVA L.
   1949 *A Word Atlas of the Great Lakes Region*, Ph.D. dissertation, University of Michigan.
   1951 "Dialect distribution and settlement patterns in the Great Lakes region," *Ohio State Archeological and Historical Quarterly* 50.48–56.
   1966 "Social dialects and social change," *Instructor* 75:7.93, 100.

DAVIS, ALVA L., and RAVEN I. MCDAVID, JR.
   *1949 "*Shivaree*: an example of cultural diffusion," *American Speech* 24.249–55.
   1950 "Northwest Ohio: a transition area," *Language* 26.264–73.

DAVIS, LAWRENCE M.
   1967 "The stressed vowels of Yiddish-American English," *Publication of the American Dialect Society* 48.51–59.

DEARDEN, ELIZABETH JEANNETTE
   1941 *Dialect Areas of the South Atlantic States as Determined by Variations in Vocabulary*. Ph.D. dissertation, Brown University.

DE CAMP, DAVID
   1958 "The pronunciation of English in San Francisco," *Orbis* 7.372–91.
   1959 "The pronunciation of English in San Francisco," *Orbis* 8.54–77.

DEUTSCH, MARTIN
   1965 "The role of social class in language development and cognition," *American Journal of Orthopsychiatry* 35.78–88.

DICKINSON, DONALD
   1952 *Speech Characteristics of the Rio Grand Valley, New Mexico*. M.A. thesis, University of New Mexico.

DILLARD, J. L.
   1967a "The English teacher and the language of the newly integrated student,"
           The Record—Teachers College 69:2.115–20.
   1967b "Negro children's dialect in the inner city," *Florida FL Reporter* 5:3.
           7–8, 10.
   1968   "Non-standard Negro dialects—convergence or divergence?" *Florida FL
           Reporter* 6:2. 9–10, 12.

DOWNER, JAMES W.
   1958   *Features of New England Rustic Pronunciation in James Russell Lowell's
           Biglow Papers.* Ph.D. dissertation, University of Michigan.

DRAKE, JAMES A.
   1961   "The effect of urbanization upon regional vocabulary," *American Speech*
           36.17–33.

DUCKERT, AUDREY
   1956   "*Gutter:* its rise and fall," *Names* 4.146–54.
  *1963   "*The Linguistic Atlas of New England* revisited," *Publication of the
           American Dialect Society* 39.8–15.

ELDERS, ROY
   1949   *The Stressed Back Vowels in the Speech of Parker County.* M.A. thesis,
           North Texas State University.

ELIASON, NORMAN L.
   1956   *Tarheel Talk: An Historical Study of the English Language in North
           Carolina to 1860.* Chapel Hill: University of North Carolina Press. Re-
           viewed by D. E. Baughan, *American Speech* 32.283–86 (1957); T. Pyles,
           Language 33.256–61 (1957); R. H. Spire, *Journal of Southern History*
           32.375–76 (1957); H. Galinsky, *Anglia* 76.160–65 (1958); R. Walser, *North
           Carolina Historical Review* 34.64–67 (1958).

EMERSON, O. F.
   1891   "The Ithaca dialect," *Dialect Notes* 1.85–173.

EVERETT, RUSSELL I.
   1958   *The Speech of the Tri-Racial Group Composing the Community of Clinton,
           Louisiana.* Ph.D. dissertation, Louisiana State University.

FARRISON, WILLIAM E.
   1937   *The Phonology of the Illiterate Negro Dialect of Guilford County, North
           Carolina.* Ph.D. dissertation, Ohio State University.

FASOLD, RALPH W.
   1969   "Tense and the form *be* in Black English," *Language* 45.763–67.

FISCHER, JOHN L.
   1958   "Social influences on the choice of a linguistic variant," *Word* 14.47–56.

FISHER, HILDA B.
   1950   *A Study of the Speech of East Feliciana Parish, Louisiana.* Ph.D. disserta-
           tion, Louisiana State University.

FLUJE, DOROTHEA L.
  1938   *A Study of the Speech of Dutchtown, Louisiana, Using Three Age Levels.* M.A. thesis, Louisiana State University.

FOLK, MARY LUCILE PIERCE
  1961   *A Word Atlas of Northern Louisiana.* Ph.D. dissertation, Louisiana State University.

FORRESTER, CHRISTINE DUNCAN
  1952   *A Word Geography of Kentucky.* M.A. thesis, University of Kentucky.

FOSCUE, VIRGINIA O.
  1967   *Background and Preliminary Survey of the Linguistic Geography of Alabama.* Ph.D. dissertation, University of Wisconsin.

FOSTER, DAVID WILLIAM, and ROBERT J. HOFFMAN
  1966   "Some observations on the vowels of Pacific Northwest English (Seattle area)," *American Speech* 41.119–22.

FRANCIS, W. NELSON
 *1959   "Some dialect isoglosses in England," *American Speech* 34.243–57.
 *1961   "Some dialectal verb forms in England," *Orbis* 10.1–14.

FRANCIS, W. NELSON, JAN SVARTIK, and GERALD M. RUBIN
  1969   "Computer-produced representation of dialectal variation: initial fricatives in Southern British English," *Coling 1969* (International Conference on Computational Linguistics, 1969. Preprint No. 52). Stockholm: Research Group for Quantitative Linguistics.

FRANK, YAKIRA
  1948   *The Speech of New York City.* Ph.D. dissertation, University of Michigan.

FURFEY, PAUL H.
  1944   "The sociological implications of substandard English," *The American Catholic Sociological Review* 5.3–10.

GARBUTT, CAMERON W.
  1952   *A Study of the Dialectal Characteristics of the Older Generation Living in the Three Southernmost Counties of Illinois: Alexander, Pulaski, and Massac.* Ph.D. dissertation, Louisiana State University.

GEORGE, ALBERT D.
  1958   *Some Louisiana Isoglosses, Based on the Workbooks of the Louisiana Dialect Atlas.* Ph.D. dissertation, Louisiana State University.

GREEN, ELIZABETH
  1932   *A Dialect Survey of Mobile, Mobile County, Alabama.* M.A. thesis, Alabama Polytechnical Institute.

GREET, W. CABELL
  1933   "Delmarva speech," *American Speech* 8.56–65.
  1934   "Southern Speech," in *Culture in the South,* W. T. Couch, ed. Chapel Hill: University of North Carolina Press. Pp. 594–615.

GREET, W. CABELL, and WILLIAM BROWN MELONEY
  1930   "Two notes on Virginia speech," *American Speech* 5.94–96.

GROOTAERS, WILLEM A.
1959 "Origin and nature of the subjective boundaries of dialects," *Orbis* 8.355–84.

GUEST, CHARLES B.
1941 *A Survey of the Dialect of the Lee County, Alabama, Negro.* M.A. thesis, Alabama Polytechnical Institute.

GUMPERZ, JOHN J.
1966 "On the ethnology of linguistic change," in Bright (1966). Pp. 27–49.

GUMPERZ, JOHN J., and DELL HYMES
1964 eds., *The Ethnology of Communication. Amercian Anthropologist* 66, No. 6, Pt. 2. Special Publication.

HAIR, P. E. H.
1965 "Sierra Leone items in the Gullah dialect of American English," *Sierra Leone Language Review* 4.79–84.

HALE, LULU
1930 *A Study of English Pronunciation in Kentucky.* M.A. thesis, University of Kentucky.

HALL, JOE T.
1932 *A Dialect Study of Langdale, Chambers County, Alabama.* M.A. thesis, Alabama Polytechnical Institute.

HALL, JOSEPH S.
1942 *The Phonetics of Great Smoky Mountain Speech. Amercian Speech,* Reprints and Monographs No. 4. New York: Columbia University Press. Reviewed by A. H. Marckwardt, *Quarterly Journal of Speech* 28.487 (1942); R. I. McDavid, Jr., *Language* 29.184–95 (1943).

HANKEY, CLYDE T.
1960 *A Colorado Word Geography. Publication of the American Dialect Society* 34.
1961 "Semantic features and eastern relics in Colorado diaect," *American Speech* 36.266–70.
1965 "*Tiger, tagger* and [aɪ] in Western Pennsylvania," and "Diphthongal variants of [ɛ] and [æ] in Western Pennsylvania," *American Speech* 40.226–29.

HANLEY, MILES L.
1925 "Observations on the broad A," *Dialect Notes* 5.347–50.

HANLEY, THEODORE D.
1950 *An Analysis of Vocal Frequency and Duration Characteristics of Selected Samples of Speech from General American, Eastern American, and Southern American Dialect Regions.* Ph.D. dissertation, University of Iowa.

HARDY, ZELMA B.
1950 *A Vocabulary Study of Kerr County, Texas.* M.A. thesis, University of Texas, Austin.

HARRIS, RACHEL S.
1933 "New England words for the earthworm," *American Speech* 8:4.12–17.

1937 *The Speech of Rhode Island: The Stressed Vowels and Diphthongs.* Ph.D. dissertation, Brown University.

HARTMAN, JAMES W.
1967 *Pressure for Dialect Change in Hocking County, Ohio.* Ph.D. dissertation, University of Michigan.

HAUGEN, EINAR
1966 "Linguistics and language planning," in Bright (1966). Pp. 50–71.

HAWKINS, JANE DADDOW
1942 *The Speech of the Hudson Valley.* Ph.D. dissertation, Brown University.

HAYES, ROBERT W.
1958 *A Phonological Study of the English Speech of Selected Japanese Speakers in Hawaii.* M.A. thesis, University of Hawaii.

HAYNES, RANDOLPH A., JR.
1954 *A Vocabulary Study of Travis County, Texas.* M.A. thesis, University of Texas, Austin.

HEFLIN, WOODFORD A.
1942 *Characteristic Features of New Mexico English between 1805 and 1890.* Ph.D. dissertation, University of Chicago.

HEMPL, GEORGE
*1896 "*Grease* and *greasy*," *Dialect Notes* 1.438–44.

HEWITT, RYLAND H., JR.
1961 *The Pronunciation of English in the Province of Maine, 1636–1730.* Ph.D. dissertation, Cornell University.

HILL, TREVOR
*1963 "Phonemic and prosodic analysis in linguistic geography," *Orbis* 12.449–54.

HORMANN, BERNHARD L.
1960 "Hawaii's linguistic situation: a sociological interpretation in the new key," *Social Process in Hawaii* 24.6–31.

HOUSTON, SUSAN H.
1969 "A sociolinguistic consideration of the Black English of children in northern Florida," *Language* 45.599–607.

HOWREN, ROBERT RAY, JR.
1958 *The Speech of Louisville, Kentucky.* Ph.D. dissertation, Indiana University.
1962 "The speech of Okracoke, North Carolina," *American Speech* 37.163–75.

HUBBELL, ALLAN F.
1940 "*Curl* and *coil* in New York City," *American Speech* 15.372–76.
1950 *The Pronunciation of English in New York City: Consonants and Vowels.* New York: King's Crown Press, Reviewed by C. M. Wise, *Quarterly Journal of Speech* 37.227–30 (1951); C. K. Thomas, *American Speech* 26.122–23 (1951).

HUNT, ELISE
1938 *A Study of the Speech of a Haynesville, Louisiana, Family.* M.A. thesis, Louisiana State University.

HYMES, DELL
    1962   "The ethnography of speaking," in *Anthropology and Human Behavior*,
            T. Gladwin and W. Sturtevant, eds. Washington, D.C.: Anthropological
            Society of Washington, Pp. 15–53.
    1968   "Sociolinguistics," *Language Sciences* 1.23–26.

INGLEDUE, GRACE
    1938   *A Study of the Speech of Three Generations in One Family and in the Like
            Generations of Three Different Families in Monroe, Louisiana*. Ph.D. dis-
            sertation, Louisiana State University.

IVES, SUMNER A.
    1950a   *The Negro Dialect of the Uncle Remus Stories*. Ph.D. dissertation, Uni-
            versity of Texas, Austin.
    1950b   "A theory of literary dialect," *Tulane Studies in English* 2.137–82.
    1952   "American pronunciation in the *Linguistic Atlas*," *Tulane Studies in
            English* 3.179–93.
   *1953a   "Pronunciation of *can't* in the eastern states," *American Speech*
            28.149–57.
    1953b   "Vowel transcriptions in a Georgia field record," *Tulane Studies in
            English* 4.147–69.
    1954   *The Phonology of the Uncle Remus Stories. Publication of the American
            Dialect Society* 22.
    1955a   "Dialect differentiation in the stories of Joel Chandler Harris," *American
            Literature* 28.88–96. [See also Brooks (1935).]
    1955b   "Use of field materials in the determining of dialect groupings," *Quarterly
            Journal of Speech* 41.359–64.

IVIĆ, PAVLE
    1962   "On the structure of dialect differentiation," *Word* 18.33–53.
    1964   "Structure and typology of dialectal differentiation," in Lunt (1964).
            Pp. 115–19.

JACKSON, ELIZABETH HOPE
    1958   *An Analysis of Certain Colorado Atlas Field Records with Regard to
            Settlement History and Other Factors*. Ph.D. dissertation, University of
            Colorado.

JAFFE, HILDA
    1966   *The Speech of the Central Coast of North Carolina: The Carteret County
            Version of the Banks 'Brogue'*." Ph.D. dissertation, Michigan State Uni-
            versity.

KER, ANNA SUE CAROTHERS
    1956   *The Vocabulary of West Texas: A Preliminary Study*. M.A. thesis, Texas
            Technological College.

KEYSER, SAMUEL J.
    1962   *The Dialect of Samuel Worcester*. Ph.D. dissertation, Yale University.

KIMBALL, ARTHUR G.
    1963   "Sears-Roebuck and regional terms," *American Speech* 38.209–13.

KIMMERLE, MARJORIE M.
  1950 "The influence of locale and human activity on some words in Colorado,"
         American Speech 25.161–67.
  1952 *"Bum, poddy,* or *penco," Colorado Quarterly* 1.87–97.

KIMMERLE, MARJORIE M., RAVEN I. McDAVID, JR., and VIRGINIA G. McDAVID
  1951 "Problems of linguistic geography in the Rocky Mountain area," *Western
         Humanities Review* 5.249–64.

KINDIG, MAITA M.
  1960 *A Phonological Study of the English Speech of Selected Speakers of Puerto
         Rican Spanish in Honolulu.* M.A. thesis, University of Hawaii.

KLIMA, EDWARD S.
  1964 "Relatedness between grammatical systems," *Language* 40.1–20.

KRIGER, ALBERT
  1942 *A Study of the Speech of Clinton, Louisiana, at Three Age Levels.* M.A.
         thesis, Louisiana State University.

KURATH, HANS
  1928 "The origin of the dialectal differences in spoken American English,"
         Modern Philology 25.385–95.
  1929 "Bibliography on American pronunciation, 1888–1928," *Language*
         5.155–62.
  1933 "New England words for the seesaw," *American Speech* 8:2.14–18.
  1939a *Handbook of the Linguistic Geography of New England.* Providence:
         Brown University.
  1939b (director and editor), *et al. Linguistic Atlas of New England.* 3 vols. in 6.
         Providence: Brown University, 1939–43.
  1940a "Dialect areas, settlement areas, and cultural areas in the United States,"
         in *The Cultural Approach to History,* C. F. Ware, ed. New York:
         Columbia University Press. Pp. 331–51.
  1940b *"Mourning* and *morning,"* in Caffee and Kirby (1940). Pp. 166–73.
  1943 "Linguistic Atlas of New England," *American Philosophical Society
         Proceedings* 74.227–43.
  1949 *A Word Geography of the Eastern United States.* Ann Arbor: University
         of Michigan Press. Reviewed by E. B. Atwood, *Word* 6.194–97 (1950);
         R. J. Menner, *American Speech* 25.122–26 (1950); C. K. Thomas,
         Quarterly Journal of Speech 36.262–63 (1950); J. B. McMillan, *Language*
         27.423–29 (1951); H. L. Smith, Jr., *Studies in Linguistics* 9.7–12 (1951).
  1951 "Linguistic regionalism," in *Regionalism in America,* Merril Jensen, ed.
         Madison: University of Wisconsin Press. Pp. 297–310.
  1961 "Area linguistics and the teacher of English," *Language Learning* Special
         Issue 2.9–14.
  1962a "Areal linguistics in the U.S.A.," *Orbis* 11.57–60.
  1962b "Regional features in cultivated American pronunciation," *Michigan
         Quarterly Review* 1.234–48.
 *1964a "British sources of selected features of American pronunciation: problems
         and methods," in *In Honor of Daniel Jones,* Dennis B. Fry, *et al.,* eds.
         London: Longmans, Green. Pp. 146–55.

*1964b "Interrelation between regional and social dialects," in Lunt (1964). Pp. 135–43.

1964c *A Phonology and Prosody of Modern English.* Heidelberg: C. Winter; Ann Arbor: University of Michigan Press. Reviewed by J. H. Sledd, *American Speech* 40.201–5 (1965); C. L. Laird, *English Language Notes* 3.315 (1966); R. I. McDavid, Jr., *Modern Philology* 64.182 (1966); A. A. Hill, *Journal of English Linguistics* 1.74–75 (1967).

1965 "Some aspects of Atlantic Seaboard English considered in their connections with British English," *Communications et Rapports du Premier Congrès International de Dialectologie Générale.* Louvain: Centre International de Dialectologie Générale. Pp. 236–40.

1966 "Regionalism in American English," in *The English Language in the School Curriculum*, Robert F. Hogan, ed. Champaign: National Council of Teachers of English. Pp. 161–75.

1968 "The investigation of urban speech," *Publication of the American Dialect Society*, 49.1–7.

KURATH, HANS, and RAVEN I. MCDAVID, JR.

1961 *The Pronunciation of English in the Atlantic States.* Ann Arbor: University of Michigan Press. Reviewed by A. J. Bronstein, *Quarterly Journal of Speech* 48.440–41 (1962); N. E. Eliason, *South Atlantic Quarterly* 61.121–22 (1961); T. Hill, *Modern Language Review* 57.624–25 (1962); R. M. Dorson, *Ohio History* 72, 73–75 (1963); S. J. Keyser, *Language* 39.303–16 (1963); W. S. Avis, *Canadian Journal of Linguistics* 9.63–70 (1965); F. H. Beukema, *Orbis* 16.577–79 (1967).

LA BAN, FRANK KENNETH

1965 *The Phonological Study of the Speech of the Conchs, Early Inhabitants of the Florida Keys, at Three Age Levels.* Ph.D. dissertation, Louisiana State University.

LABOV, WILLIAM

1963 "The social motivation of a sound change," *Word* 19.273–309.

1964 "Phonological correlates of social stratification," in Gumperz and Hymes (1964). Pp. 164–76.

*1965 "Stages in the acquisition of Standard English," in Shuy (1965). Pp. 77–103.

1966a "Hypercorrection by the lower middle class as a factor in linguistic evaluation," in Bright (1966). Pp. 84–113.

1966b "Some sources in reading problems for Negro speakers of non-standard English," in *New Directions in Elementary English*, Alexander Frazier, ed. Champaign: National Council of Teachers of English. Pp. 140–67.

1966c *The Social Stratification of English in New York City.* Washington: Center for Applied Linguistics. Reviewed by Glen G. Gilbert, *Language* 45.469–76 (1969).

1966d "The linguistic variable as a structural unit," *Washington Linguistics Review* 3.4–22.

1967   "The effect of social mobility on linguistic behavior," in Lieberson (1967). Pp. 58–75.

1969   "Contraction, deletion, and inherent variability of the English copula," *Language* 45.715–62.

LABOV, WILLIAM, and PAUL COHEN

1967   "Systematic relations of Standard and non-Standard rules in the grammars of Negro speakers," *Project Literacy Reports No.* 8. Ithaca: Cornell University. Pp. 66–84.

LAWRENCE, VIVIAN S.

1960   *Dialect Mixture in Three New England Pronunciation Patterns: Vowels and Consonants.* Ph.D. dissertation, Columbia University.

LE COMPTE, NOLAN, P., JR.

1961   *A Word Atlas of Terrebonne Parish.* M.A. thesis, Louisiana State University.

1967   *A Word Atlas of La Fourche Parish and Grand Isle, Louisiana.* Ph.D. dissertation, Louisiana State University.

LE COMPTE, NOLAN P., JR.

1968   "Certain points of dialectal usage in South Louisiana," *Louisiana Studies* 7.149–58.

LEVINE, LEWIS, and HARRY J. CROCKETT, JR.

1967   "Speech variation in a Piedmont community: postvocalic *r*," in Lieberson (1967). Pp. 76–98.

LIEBERSON, STANLEY

1967   ed., *Explorations in Sociolinguistics. International Journal of American Linguistics* 33, No. 4, Pt. 2.

LOFLIN, MARVIN D.

1967   "A note on the deep structure of nonstandard English in Washington, D.C.," *Glossa* 1.26–32.

1969   "Negro Nonstandard and Standard English: same or different deep structure?" *Orbis* 18.74–91.

*1970   "On the structure of the verb in a dialect of American Negro English." [Also to appear in *Linguistics*.]

LOMAN, BENGT

1967   ed., *Conversations in a Negro American Dialect.* Transcribed by Bengt Loman. Washington: Center for Applied Linguistics.

LOWMAN, GUY S.

1936   "The treatment of /aʊ/ in Virginia," *Proceedings of the Second International Congress of Phonetic Scientists.* Cambridge, England: Cambridge University Press. Pp. 122–25.

LUCKE, JESSIE R.

1949   *A Study of the Virginia Dialect and Its Origin in England.* Ph.D. dissertation, University of Virginia.

LUNT, HORACE G.
   1964   ed., *Proceedings of the Ninth International Congress of Linguists, Cambridge, Massachusetts, August 27–31, 1962.* The Hague: Mouton.

MCBRIDE, JOHN S.
   1936   *Hill Speech in Southwestern Tennessee.* M.A. thesis, Columbia University.

MCDAVID, RAVEN I., JR.
   1940   "Low-back vowels in the South Carolina Piedmont," *American Speech* 15.144–48.
   1942   "Some principles for American dialect study," *Studies in Linguistics* 1:12.1–11.
   1943   "Provincial sayings and regional distributions," *American Speech* 18.66–68.
   1944   "The unstressed syllabic phonemes of a southern dialect: a problem in analysis," *Studies in Linguistics* 2.51–55.
  *1946   "Dialect geography and social science problems," *Social Forces* 25. 168–72.
   1948a "The influence of French on Southern American English: evidence of the Linguistic Atlas," *Studies in Linguistics* 6.39–43.
   1948b "Postvocalic /-r/ in South Carolina: a social analysis," *American Speech* 23.194–203.
   1948c "Application of the *Linguistic Atlas* method to dialect study in the South-Central area," *Southern Speech Journal* 15.1–6.
   1949a "Derivatives of Middle English [o:] in the South Atlantic area," *Quarterly Journal of Speech* 35.496–504.
   1949b "Grist from the atlas mill," *American Speech* 24.105–14.
   1949c "/r/ and /y/ in the South," *Studies in Linguistics* 7.18–20.
   1950   "Our initial consonant 'h'," *College English* 11.458–59.
   1951a "Dialect differences and inter-group tensions," *Studies in Linguistics* 9.27–33.
   1951b "The folk vocabulary of New York State," *New York Folklore Quarterly* 7.173–91.
   1951c "Midland and Canadian words in Upstate New York," *American Speech* 26.248–56.
   1952a "The Linguistic Atlas of New England," *Orbis* 1.95–103.
   1952b "Some social differences in pronunciation," *Language Learning* 40.12–16.
   1953a "Notes on the pronunciation of *catch*," *College English* 14.290–91.
   1953b "*Oughtn't* and *hadn't ought*," *College English* 14.472–73.
   1954   "Linguistic geography in Canada: an introduction," *Journal of the Canadian Linguistic Association* Introductory number, 3–8.
   1955   "The position of the Charleston dialect," *Publication of the American Dialect Society* 23.35–53.
   1956   "Social differences in pronunciation: a problem in methodology," *General Linguistics* 2.15–21.
   1958a "The dialects of American English," Chapter 9 in W. Nelson Francis, *The Structure of American English.* New York: Ronald Press. Pp. 480–543.
   1958b "Linguistic geography and the study of folklore," *New York Folklore Quarterly* 14.242–62.

1958c "Linguistic geography and toponymic research," *Names* 6.65–73.

1960a "The second round in the dialectology of North American English," *Journal of the Canadian Linguistic Association* 6.108–15.

1960b "A study in ethnolinguistics," *Southern Speech Journal* 25.247–54.

1961 "Structural linguistics and linguistic geography," *Orbis* 10.35–46.

1964a "The dialectology of an urban society," *Communications et Rapports du Premier Congrès International de Dialectologie Générale*. Louvain: Centre International de Dialectologie Générale. Pp. 68–80.

1964b "Needed research in American English," *Publication of the American Dialect Society* 41.22–41.

1965a "American social dialects," *College English* 26.254–59.

1965b "The cultural matrix of American English," *Elementary English* 42.13–22.

1965c "Dialectology and the integration of the schools," *Transactions of the Yorkshire Dialect Society* 11, lxv. 18–27.

1966a "Dialect differences and social differences in an urban society," in Bright (1966). Pp. 72–83.

*1966b "Sense and nonsense about American dialects," *Publications of the Modern Language Association* 81:2.7–17.

*1967a "A checklist of significant features for discriminating social dialects," in *Dimensions of Dialect*, Eldonna Evertts, ed. Champaign: National Council of Teachers of English. Pp. 7–10.

1967b "Historical, regional, and social variation," *Journal of English Linguistics* 1.24–40.

1967c "Needed research in southern dialects," in *Perspectives on the South: Agenda for Research*, Edgar T. Thompson, ed. Durham: Duke University Press. Pp. 113–24.

McDAVID, RAVEN I., JR., and WILLIAM M. AUSTIN

1966 *Communication Barriers to the Culturally Deprived*. USOE Cooperative Research Project 2107.

McDAVID, RAVEN I., JR., and VIRGINIA G. McDAVID

1951 "The relation of the speech of American Negroes to the speech of the whites," *American Speech* 26.3–17.

1952 "*h* before semivowels in the Eastern United States," *Language* 28.41–62.

1956 "Regional linguistic atlases in the United States," *Orbis* 5.349–86.

1960 "Grammatical differences in the North Central States," *American Speech* 35.5–19.

1964 "Plurals of nouns of measure in the United States," in Marckwardt (1964). Pp. 271–302.

McDAVID, VIRGINIA G.

1956 *Verb Forms of the North Central States and the Upper Midwest*. Ph.D. dissertation, University of Minnesota.

1963 "*To* as a preposition of location in linguistic atlas materials," *Publication of the American Dialect Society* 39.8–15.

McGUIRE, WILLIAM J., JR.

1939 *A Study of Florida Cracker Dialect Based Chiefly on the Prose of Marjorie Kinnan Rawlings*. Ph.D. dissertation, University of Florida.

McIntosh, Angus

1952   *An Introductory Survey of Scottish Dialects.* Edinburgh: Thomas Nelson.
        Reviewed by E. B. Atwood, *Journal of English and Germanic Philology*
        53.224–27 (1953); F. G. Cassidy, *American Speech* 29.122–25 (1954);
        R. I. McDavid, Jr., *Language* 30.414–23 (1954).
1961   "Patterns and ranges," *Language* 37.325–37.

McMillan, James B.

1939   "Vowel nasality as a sandhi-form of the morphemes *-nt* and *-ing* in
        Southern American," *American Speech* 14.120–23.
1946   *A Phonology of the Standard English of East Central Alabama.* Ph.D.
        dissertation, University of Chicago.

Malmstrom, Jean

1958   *A Study of the Validity of Textbook Statements about Certain Contro-
        versial Grammatical Items in the Light of Evidence from the Linguistic
        Atlases.* Ph.D. dissertation, University of Minnesota.
1959   "Linguistic Atlas findings versus textbook pronouncements on current
        English usage," *English Journal* 48.191–98.

Malmstrom, Jean, and Annabel Ashley

1963   *Dialects U.S.A.* Champaign: National Council of Teachers of English.

Marckwardt, Albert H.

1940   "Folk speech in Indiana and adjacent states," *Indiana History Bulletin*
        17.120–40.
1941   "Middle English ŏ in the American English of the Great Lakes area,"
        Papers of the Michigan Academy of Arts, Sciences, and Letters 26.56–71.
1942   "Middle-English *wa* in the speech of the Great Lakes region," *American
        Speech* 17.226–34.
1948   "*Want* with ellipsis of verbs of motion," *American Speech* 23.3–9.
1952   "Linguistic geography and freshman English," *CEA Critic* 14.1.
*1957   "Principal and subsidiary dialect areas in the North Central States,"
        Publication of the American Dialect Society 27.3–15.
1958   *American English.* New York: Oxford University Press.
1964   ed., *Studies in Language and Linguistics in Honor of Charles C. Fries.*
        Ann Arbor: English Language Institute, University of Michigan.

Martin, Rudolph, Jr.

1960   "Four undescribed verb forms in American Negro English," *American
        Speech* 35.238–39.

Mathews, Mitford M.

1948   *Some Sources of Southernisms.* University, Ala.: University of Alabama
        Press.

Maurer, David W.

1936   "The argot of the underworld narcotic addict: Part I." *American Speech*
        11.116–27, 222.
1938   "The argot of the underworld narcotic addict: Part II," *American
        Speech* 13.179–92.
1939   "Prostitutes and criminal argots," *American Journal of Sociology* 44.
        546–50.

1940 "The argot of the confidence men," *American Speech* 15.113–23.

1941 "The argot of forgery," *American Speech* 16.243–50.

1944 " 'Australian' rhyming argot in the American underworld," *American Speech* 19.183–95.

1946 "Marijuana addicts and their lingo," *American Mercury* 63.571–75.

1947 "The argot of the three-shell game," *American Speech* 23.161–70.

1949 "The argot of the moonshiner," *American Speech* 24.3–13.

1951 *The Argot of the Racetrack. Publication of the American Dialect Society* 16.

1955 *Whiz-Mob: A Correlation of the Argot of Pickpockets with Their Behavior Patterns. Publications of the American Dialect Society* 24.

1959 "A word-finder list for whiz-mob," *Publication of the American Dialect Society* 31.14–30.

1963 *The Big Con: The Story of the American Confidence Man and the Confidence Game.* Trade edition, revised and updated. New York: New American Library of World Literature.

1969 "The importance of social dialects," *Newsletter of the American Dialect Society* 1:2.1–8.

MAURER, DAVID W., and VICTOR H. VOGEL

*1967 "The argot of narcotics addicts," Chapter 10 in *Narcotics and Narcotic Addiction.* 3rd edition. Springfield, Ill.: Charles C. Thomas. Pp. 318–46.

MENCKEN, H. L.

1936 *The American Language.* 4th edition. New York: Alfred A. Knopf.

1946 *The American Language. Supplement I.* New York: Alfred A. Knopf.

1948 *The American Language. Supplement II.* New York: Alfred A. Knopf.

1963 *The American Language.* Abridged by Raven I. McDavid, Jr., with the assistance of David W. Maurer. New York: Alfred A. Knopf. Reviewed by W. Card, *College English* 25.230–31 (1963); H. R. Wilson, *Canadian Journal of Linguistics* 10.70–72 (1964); W. C. Greet, *American Speech* 40.58–61 (1965); L. A. Pederson, *Orbis* 14.63–74 (1965); H. B. Woolf, *English Studies* 47.102–18 (1966).

MERRITT, WANDA F.

1943 *A Study of the Speech of West Texas Students in Hardin-Simmons University.* M.A. thesis, Louisiana State University.

MILLER, VIRGINIA R.

1953 "Present-day use of the broad A in Eastern Massachusetts," *Speech Monographs* 20.235–46.

MONCUR, JOHN P.

1956 "A comparative analysis of [u ~ ʊ] variants in the San Francisco and Los Angeles areas," *Quarterly Journal of Speech* 42.31–34.

MOULTON, WILLIAM G.

1962 "Dialect geography and the concept of phonological space," *Word* 18.23–32.

1968 "Structural dialectology," *Language* 44.451–66.

NELSON, AGNES DENMAN

1958 *A Study of English Speech of Hungarians of Albany, Livingston Parish, Louisiana.* Ph.D. dissertation, Louisiana State University.

NEW YORK CITY BOARD OF EDUCATION
    1967   *Nonstandard Dialect.* Champaign: National Council of Teachers of
           English.

NEWTON, EUNICE S.
    1962   "The culturally disadvantaged child in our verbal schools," *Journal of
           Negro Education* 31.184–87.
    1964   "Planning for the language development of disadvantaged children and
           youth," *Journal of Negro Education* 33.264–74.

NORMAN, ARTHUR M. Z.
   *1956   "A southeast Texas dialect study," *Orbis* 5.61–79.

O'HARE, THOMAS J.
    1964   *The Linguistic Geography of Eastern Montana.* Ph.D. dissertation,
           University of Texas, Austin.

OLIVER, RAYMOND
    1966   "More carnie talk from the West Coast," *American Speech* 41.278–83.

O'NEIL, WAYNE A.
    1968   "Transformation dialectology: phonology and syntax," in Ludwig E.
           Schmitt, ed., *Verhandlungen des Zweiten Internationalen Dialektologen-
           kongresses, Marburg/Lahn, 5–10 September 1965.* Vol. 2. Wiesbaden:
           Steiner. Pp. 629–38. (*Zeitschrift für Mundartforschung,* Nr. 4.)

ORBECK, ANDERS
    1927   *Early New England Pronunciation as Reflected in Some Seventeenth-
           Century Town Records.* Ann Arbor: George Wahr.

ORTON, HAROLD
   *1960   "The English Dialect Survey: Linguistic Atlas of England," *Orbis*
           9.331–48.

ORTON, HAROLD, and EUGEN DIETH
    1962   *Survey of English Dialects: Introduction.* Leeds: E. J. Arnold (for the
           University of Leeds).

ORTON, HAROLD, and WILFRED J. HALLIDAY
    1962   eds., *Survey of English Dialects.* Vol. 1, *Basic Material: Six Northern
           Counties and Man.* Part 1. Leeds: E. J. Arnold (for the University of
           Leeds). Pts 2 and 3, 1963.

ORTON, HAROLD, and MARTYN F. WAKELIN
    1962   *Survey of English Dialects: Southern Counties* Part I, Leeds: E. J. Arnold.
           An Annotated Bibliography of Southern Speech. Atlanta: South-eastern
           Educational Laboratory.

PACE, GEORGE B.
   *1960   "Linguistic geography and names ending in *i,*" *American Speech* 35.
           175–87.
    1965   "On the Eastern affiliation of Missouri speech," *American Speech*
           40.46–52.

PARDOE, EARL
    1937   *A Historical and Phonetic Study of Negro Dialect.* Ph.D. dissertation,
           Louisiana State University.

PEARCE, T. M.
  1932 "The English language in the Southwest," *New Mexico Historical Review* 7.210–32.
  1958 "Three Rocky Mountain terms: *park, sugan,* and *plaza,*" *American Speech* 33.99–107.

PEDERSON, LEE A.
  1962 "An introductory field procedure in a current urban survey," *Orbis* 11.465–69.
  1964a "Nonstandard Negro speech in Chicago," in Stewart (1964). Pp. 16–23.
  *1964b "Terms of abuse for some Chicago social groups," *Publication of the American Dialect Society* 42.26–48.
  1965a *The Pronunciation of English in Metropolitan Chicago. Publication of the American Dialect Society* 44.
  1965b "Social dialects and the disadvantaged," in Corbin and Crosby (1965). Pp. 236–49.
  *1965c "Some structural differences in the speech of Chicago Negroes," in Shuy (1965). Pp. 28–51.
  1966 "Negro speech in *The Adventures of Huckleberry Finn,*" *Mark Twain Journal* 13.i, 1–4.
  1967 "Middle-class Negro speech in Minneapolis," *Orbis* 16.347–53.
  1968 "The speech of Marion County, Missouri; phonemics for Mark Twain's Missouri dialects," *American Speech* 42. 261–78.

PENZL, HERBERT
  1934a *The Development of Middle English a in New England.* Ph.D. dissertation, Vienna.
  1934b "New England terms for 'poached eggs'," *American Speech* 9.90–95.
  1938a "Relics with *broad a* in New England speech," *American Speech* 13.45–49.
  1938b "The vowel in *rather* in New England," *Publications of the Modern Language Association* 53.1186–92.
  1940 "The vowel-phonemes in *father, map, dance* in dictionaries and New England speech," *Journal of English and Germanic Philology* 39.13–32.

PERRY, LOUISE SUBLETTE
  1940 *A Study of the Pronoun hit in Grassy Branch, North Carolina.* M.A. thesis, Louisiana State University.

PICKFORD, GLENNA R.
  1956 "American linguistic geography: a sociological appraisal," *Word* 12. 211–33.

PORTER, RUTH SCHELL
  1965 *A Dialect Study in Dartmouth, Massachusetts. Publication of the American Dialect Society* 43.

POTTER, EDWARD E.
  1955 *The Dialect of Northwestern Ohio: A Study of a Transition Area.* Ph.D. dissertation, University of Michigan.

POUND, LOUISE
  1905 "Dialect speech in Nebraska," *Dialect Notes* 3.55–67.
  1927 "The dialect of Cooper's Leatherstocking," *American Speech* 2.479–88.

1945   "Folklore and dialect," *California Folklore Quarterly* 4.46–53.
1952   "The American Dialect Society: a historical sketch," *Publication of the American Dialect Society* 17.3–28.

PUTNAM, G. M., and EDNA M. O'HERN
1955   *The Status Significance of an Isolated Urban Dialect.* Language Dissertations No. 53. *Language* 31, No. 4, Part 2.

PYLES, THOMAS
1952   *Words and Ways of American English.* New York: Random House.

RANDOLPH, VANCE
1927a "The grammar of the Ozark dialect," *American Speech* 3.1–11.
1927b "The Ozark dialect in fiction," *American Speech* 2.283–89.

RANDOLPH, VANCE, and GEORGE P. WILSON
1953   *Down the Holler: A Gallery of Ozark Folk Speech.* Norman: University of Oklahoma Press. Reviewed by E. H. Criswell, *American Speech* 28.285–88 (1953); C. W. Garbutt, *Quarterly Journal of Speech* 39.374–75 (1953); R. I. McDavid, Jr., *Journal of American Folklore* 67.327–30 (1954).

RASH, CORALEE
1941   *A Dialect Study of Kinston, Chambers County, Alabama.* M.A. thesis, Alabama Polytechnical Institute.

RAWLES, MYRTLE READ
1966   " 'Boontling'—esoteric speech of Boonville, California," *Western Folklore* 25.93–103.

REED, CARROLL E.
1952   "The pronunciation of English in the state of Washington," *American Speech* 27.186–89.
1956   "Washington words," *Publication of the American Dialect Society* 25.3–11.
1958a "Frontiers of English in the Pacific Northwest," *Proceedings of the Ninth Pacific Northwest Conference of Foreign Language Teachers.* Seattle: University of Washington. Pp. 33–35.
1958b "Word geography of the Pacific Northwest," *Orbis* 7.372–91.
*1961a "Double dialect geography," *Orbis* 10.308–19.
*1961b "The pronunciation of English in the Pacific Northwest," *Language* 37.559–64.
1967   *Dialects of American English.* Cleveland: World. Reviewed by H. B. Allen, *Journal of English Linguistics* 2.130–34 (1968).

REED, DAVID W.
1949   "A statistical approach to quantitative linguistic analysis," *Word* 5.235–47.
*1954 "Eastern dialect words in California," *Publication of the American Dialect Society* 21.3–15.
1964   "Establishing and evaluating social boundaries in English," in Marckwardt (1964). Pp. 241–48.

REED, DAVID W., and JOHN L. SPICER
1952   "Correlation methods of comparing idiolects in a transition area," *Language* 28.348–59.

REESE, GEORGE H.
  1941 "The pronunciation of *shrimp*, *shrub*, and similar words," *American Speech* 16.251–55.

REINECKE, JOHN E.
  1938 "Pidgin English in Hawaii: a local study in the sociology of language," *American Journal of Sociology* 43.778–89.

REINECKE, JOHN E., and AIKO TOKIMASA
  1934 "The English dialect of Hawaii," *American Speech* 9.48–58, 122–31.

REYNOLDS, JACK A.
  1934 *The Pronunciation of English in Southern Louisiana*. M.A. thesis, Louisiana State University.

ROBERTS, MARGARET M.
  1967 *The Pronunciation of Vowels in Negro Speech*. Ph.D. dissertation, Ohio State University.

ROGERS, CATHERINE
  1940 *A Dialect Study of Camp Hill, Talapoosa County, Alabama*. M.A. thesis, Alabama Polytechnical Institute.

ROWE, H. D.
  1957 "New England terms for *bull*," *American Speech* 32.110–16.

RUSH, LAURA BELLE
  1951 *A Lexical Survey of Twelve Selected Terms in Iowa*. M.A. thesis, University of Iowa.

SAPON, STANLEY
  1953 "A methodology for the study of socio-economic differentials in linguistic phenomena," *Studies in Linguistics* 11.57–68.

SAPORTA, SOL
  1965 "Ordered rules, dialect differences, and historical processes," *Language* 41.218–24.

SATTERFIELD, CECILE
  1939 *Dialect Studies of Marburg School District, Autauga County, Alabama*. M.A. thesis, Alabama Polytechnical Institute.

SAWYER, JANET B.
  1957 *A Dialect Study of San Antonio, Texas: A Bilingual Community*. Ph.D. dissertation, University of Texas, Austin.
  1959 "Aloofness from Spanish influence in Texas English," *Word* 15.270–81.
 *1964 "Social aspects of bilingualism in San Antonio, Texas," *Publication of the American Dialect Society* 41.7–15.
  1965 "Dialects, education, and the contributions of linguists," in Corbin and Crosby (1965). Pp. 216–20.

SHEWMAKE, EDWIN F.
  1925 "Laws of pronunciation in Eastern Virginia," *Modern Language Notes* 40.489–92.
  1927 *English Pronunciation in Virginia*. Davidson, N. C.: the author. Reviewed by H. Kurath, *American Speech* 3.478–79 (1928).
  1943 "Distinctive Virginia pronunciation," *American Speech* 18.33–38.

SHUY, ROGER W.

1962 The Northern-Midland Dialect Boundary in Illinois. Publication of the
      American Dialect Society 38.

1965 ed., Social Dialects and Language Learning. Champaign: National Council
      of Teachers of English.

1966 "An automatic retrieval program for the Linguistic Atlas of the United
      States and Canada," in Computation in Linguistics: A Case Book, Paul
      Garvin and Bernard Spolsky, eds. Bloomington: Indiana Press. Pp.
      60–75.

1966–67 "Dialectology and usage," Baltimore Bulletin of Education 43:2–4.
      40–51.

1967 Discovering American Dialects. Champaign: National Council of Teachers
      of English.

1968 "Detroit speech: careless, awkward, and inconsistent, or systematic,
      graceful, and regular?" Elementary English 45.565–69.

SHUY, ROGER W., WALTER A. WOLFRAM, and WILLIAM K. RILEY

1967 Linguistic Correlates of Social Stratification in Detroit Speech. USOE
      Cooperative Research Project 6–1347.

1968 Field Techniques in an Urban Language Study. Washington: Center for
      Applied Linguistics.

SIMPSON, CLAUDE M., JR.

1936 The English Speech of Early Rhode Island, 1636–1700. Ph.D. dissertation,
      Harvard University.

SKILLMAN, BILLY G.

1953 Phonological and Lexical Features of the Speech of the First Generation
      Native-Born Inhabitants of Cleburne County, Arkansas. Ph.D. dissertation,
      University of Denver.

SLEATOR, MARY DOROTHEA

1957 Phonology and Morphology of an American English Dialect. Ph.D. dis-
      sertation, Indiana University.

SLEDD, JAMES H.

1966 "Breaking, umlaut, and the southern drawl," Language 42.18–41.

SLOBIN, DAN

1967 ed., A Field Manual for Cross-cultural Study of the Acquisition of Commu-
      nicative Competence. Berkeley: University of California.

SMITH, HARLEY A.

1936 A Recording of English Speech Sounds at Three Age Levels in Ville Platte,
      Louisiana. Ph.D. dissertation, Louisiana State University.

SMITH, RILEY B.

1969 "Interrelatedness of certain deviant grammatical structures in Negro
      nonstandard dialects," Journal of English Linguistics 3.82–88.

SO RELLE, ZELL RODGERS

1966 Segmental Phonology of Texas Panhandle Speech. Ph.D. dissertation,
      University of Denver.

STANKIEWICZ, EDWARD

1957 "On discreteness and continuity in structural dialectology," *Word* 13.44–59.

STANLEY, OMA

1937 *The Speech of East Texas. American Speech*, Monograph No. 2. New York: Columbia University Press. Reviewed by C. K. Thomas, *Quarterly Journal of Speech* 24.693 (1938).

1941 "Negro speech of East Texas," *American Speech* 16.3–16.

STEELE, RALPH

1938 *A Study of the Speech of Lake Charles, Louisiana, at Three Age Levels.* M.A. thesis, Louisiana State University.

STEPHENSON, EDWARD A.

1956 "Linguistic resources of the Southern Historical Collection," *American Speech* 31.271–77.

1958 *Early North Carolina Pronunciation.* Ph.D. dissertation, University of North Carolina.

1968 "The beginnings of the loss of postvocalic /r/ in North Carolina," *Journal of English Linguistics* 2.57–77.

STEWART, WILLIAM A.

1964 ed., *Non-Standard Speech and the Teaching of English.* Washington: Center for Applied Linguistics.

1965 "Urban Negro speech: sociolinguistic factors affecting English teaching," in Shuy (1965). Pp. 10–19.

1966–67 "Nonstandard speech patterns," *Baltimore Bulletin of Education* 43:2–4.52–65.

*1967 "Sociolinguistic factors in the history of American Negro dialects," *Florida FL Reporter* 5:2.1–4.

*1968 "Continuity and change in American Negro dialects," *Florida FL Reporter* 6:1.3–4, 14–16, 18.

STOCKWELL, ROBERT P.

*1959 "Structural dialectology: a proposal," *American Speech* 34.258–68.

SWADESH, MORRIS

1935 "The vowels of Chicago English," *Language* 11.148–51.

TARPLEY, FRED A.

1960 *A Word Atlas of Northeast Texas.* Ph.D. dissertation, Louisiana State University.

THOMAS, ALAN R.

1967 "Generative phonology in dialectology," *Transactions of the Philological Society* 179–203.

THOMAS, C. K.

1932 "Jewish dialect and New York dialect," *American Speech* 7.321–26.

1935 "Pronunciation in Upstate New York (I)," *American Speech* 10.107–12; (II), 10.208–21; (III), 10.292–97.

1936 "Pronunciation in Upstate New York (IV)," *American Speech* 11.68–77; (V), 11.307–13.

1937   "Pronunciation in Upstate New York (VI)," *American Speech* 12.122–27.
1942   "Pronunciation in Downstate New York (I)," *American Speech* 17.30–41; (II), 17.149–57.
1944   "The dialectal significance of the non-phonemic low-back vowel variants before r," in *Studies in Speech and Drama in Honor of Alexander M. Drummond*. Ithaca: Cornell University Press. Pp. 244–54.
1947   "The place of New York City in American linguistic geography," *Quarterly Journal of Speech* 33.314–20.
1951   "New York City pronunciation," *American Speech* 26.122–23.
1958   "The linguistic Mason and Dixon line," in *The Rhetorical Idiom*, Donald C. Bryant, ed. Ithaca: Cornell University Press. Pp. 251–55.
*1961 "The phonology of New England English," *Speech Monographs* 28. 223–32.

TIDWELL, JAMES N.
1948   *The Literacy Representation of the Phonology of the Southern Dialect.* Ph.D. dissertation, Ohio State University.

TJOSSEM, HERBERT K.
1956   *New England Pronunciation before 1700.* Ph.D. dissertation, Yale University.

TODD, JULIA M.
1965   *A Phonological Analysis of the Speech of Aged Citizens of Claiborne County, Mississippi.* Ph.D. dissertation, Louisiana State University.

TRAGER, GEORGE L.
1955   "The language of America," *American Anthropologist* 57.1182–93.

TRESIDDER, ARGUS
1941   "Notes on Virginia speech: the diphthong [au]," *American Speech* 6.112–20.
1943   "Sounds of Virginia speech," *American Speech* 18.261–72.

TROIKE, RUDOLPH C.
*1969 "Overall pattern and generative phonology."

TSUZAKI, STANLEY M.
1966   "Hawaiian-English: pidgin, creole, or dialect?" *Pacific Speech* 1:2.25–28.

TUCKER, WHITNEY R.
1944   "Notes on the Philadelphia dialect," *American Speech* 19.37–42.
1964   "More on the Philadelphia dialect," *American Speech* 39.157–58; discussion 40.226–29 (1965).

TURNER, LORENZO
1945   "Notes on the sounds and vocabulary of Gullah," *Publication of the American Dialect Society* 3.13–28.
1949   *Africanisms in the Gullah Dialect.* Chicago: University of Chicago Press. Reviewed by R. I. McDavid, Jr., *Language* 26.323–33 (1950); J. B. McMillan, *Alabama Review* 3.148–50 (1950); G. P. Wilson, *Quarterly Journal of Speech* 36.261–62 (1950); M. Swadesh, *Word* 7.82–84 (1951).

UDELL, GERALD
1966   *The Speech of Akron, Ohio.* Ph.D. dissertation, University of Chicago.

ULSTER FOLK MUSEUM

1964 *Ulster Dialects. An Introductory Symposium.* Holywood, Co. Down, Northern Ireland: Ulster Folk Museum.

UNDERWOOD, GARY N.

1968a "Semantic confusion: evidence from the Linguistic Atlas of the Upper Midwest," *Journal of English Linguistics* 2.86–95.

1968b "Vocabulary change in the Upper Midwest," *Publication of the American Dialect Society* 49.8–28.

1970 *The Dialect of the Mesabi Iron Range in its Historical and Social Context.* Ph. D. dissertation, University of Minnesota.

VACHEK, JOSEPH

1960 "On social differentiation of English speech habits," *Philogogica Pragensiy* Roč 3, Cislo 4: 222–27.

VAN RIPER, WILLIAM R.

1958 *The Loss of Post-Vocalic /r/ in the Eastern States.* Ph.D. dissertation, University of Michigan.

1961 "Oklahoma words," *The Round Table of the South-Central College English Association* 2.3.

VANDERSLICE, RALPH, and LAURA S. PIERSON

1967 "Prosodic features of Hawaiian English," *Quarterly Journal of Speech* 43.156–66.

VOEGELIN, CHARLES F., and FLORENCE M. VOEGELIN

1964 "Hawaiian pidgin and mother tongue," *Anthropological Linguistics* 6:7.20–56.

WAGNER, H.

1959 *Linguistic Atlas and Survey of Irish Dialects,* Vol. 1. Dublin: Institute for Advanced Studies.

WALKER, SAUNDERS

1956 *A Dictionary of the Folk Speech of the East Alabama Negro.* Ph.D. dissertation, Western Reserve University.

WALKER, URSULA GENUNG

1968 *Structural Features of Negro English in Natchitoches Parish.* M.A. thesis, Northwestern State College of Louisiana.

WALSER, RICHARD

1955 "Negro dialect in eighteenth-century American drama," *American Speech* 30.269–76.

WEBER, ROBERT H.

1964 *A Comparative Study of Regional Terms Common to the Twin Cities and the Eastern United States.* Ph.D. dissertation, University of Minnesota.

WEINREICH, URIEL

*1954 "Is a structural dialectology possible?" *Word* 10.388–400.

WETMORE, THOMAS H.

1959 *The Low-Central and Low-Back Vowels in the English of Eastern United States. Publication of the American Dialect Society* 32. Reviewed by C. K.

Thomas, *American Speech* 36.201–3 (1961); M. L. Gateau, *Word* 18.362 (1963).

WHEATLEY, KATHERINE, and OMA STANLEY
1959   "Three generations of East Texas speech," *American Speech* 34.83–94.

WHITEHALL, HAROLD
1947   "The orthography of John Bate of Sharon, Connecticut (1700–1784)," *American Speech* 22:1, Part 2, 3–56.

WHORF, BENJAMIN LEE
1943   "Phonemic analysis of the English of Eastern Massachusetts," *Studies in Linguistics* 2.1–40. [Comments by G. L. Trager, 41–44.]

WILLIAMSON, JUANITA V.
1961   *A Phonological and Morphological Study of the Speech of the Negro of Memphis, Tennessee.* Ph.D. dissertation, University of Michigan.

WILSON, GORDON
1963   "Studying folklore in a small region—IV: regional words," *Tennessee Folklore Society Bulletin* 29.79–87.
1964a   "Studying folklore in a small region—V: pronunciation," *Tennessee Folklore Society Bulletin* 30.119–26.
1964b   "Words relating to plants and animals in the Mammoth Cave region," *Publication of the American Dialect Society* 42.11–25.
1965a   "Mammoth Cave words—I. around the house," *Kentucky Folklore Record* 11.5–8.
1965b   "Mammoth Cave words—II. around the house some more," *Kentucky Folklore Record* 11.28–31.
1965c   "Mammoth Cave words—III. neighborhood doings," *Kentucky Folklore Record* 11.52–55.
1965d   "Mammoth Cave words—IV. more neighborhood doings," *Kentucky Folklore Record* 11.78–81.
1966a   "Mammoth Cave words—V. some good regional verbs," *Kentucky Folklore Record* 12.15–20.
1966b   "Mammoth Cave words—VI. some folk nouns," *Kentucky Folklore Record* 12.67–71.
1966c   "Mammoth Cave words—VII. some more folk nouns," *Kentucky Folklore Record* 12.93–98.
1966d   "Mammoth Cave words—VIII. some useful adjectives," *Kentucky Folklore Record* 12.119–22.

WISE, C. M.
1933   "Southern American dialect," *American Speech* 8.37–43.
1945   "The Dialect Atlas of Louisiana—a report of progress," *Studies in Linguistics* 3.27–42.

WISE, HARRY S.
1937   *A Phonetic Study of the Southern American* [aɪ]. M.A. thesis, Louisiana State University.

WOOD, GORDON R.
1960   "An atlas survey of the interior South," *Orbis* 9.7–12.

1961   "Word distribution in the interior South," *Publication of the American Dialect Society* 35.1–16.

*1963   "Dialect contours in the southern states," *American Speech* 38.243–56.

1967   *Sub-Regional Speech Variations in Vocabulary, Grammar and Pronunciation.* USOE Cooperative Research Project 3146.

1969   "Dialectology by computer," *Coling 1969* (International Conference on Computational Linguistics, Preprint No. 19). Stockholm: Research Group for Quantitative Linguistics.

1970   *Word Dissemination: A Study of Regional Words in Eight of the Southern States.* Carbondale: Southern Illinois University Press.

Author and Subject Index

Boldface numerals indicate the page limits of an article by the writer whose name occurs as the entry.

absence of copula. *See* zero copula
Acadian French, 145
acoustic phonetics, 319 n
acquisition of Standard English:
  by children, 483 ff
  obstacles to the, 487
Adams, E. C. L., 466 n
Aebischer, Paul, 293 n
age differential, 197–198
Alexander, Henry M., 181 n
Algren, Nelson, 397 n, 398 n
Allen, Harold B., 25 n, 27–28, 52, 54, **83–93**, **94–104**, 94 n, 122 n, 166 n, 181 n, 217 n, 299
Allen, William Francis, 461
allophone, 23
allophones, in southeast Texas, 428 ff
allophonic variation, 368, 372
ambiguity, 96
American Council of Learned Societies, 11, 315 n
American Dialect Dictionary, 8
American Dialect Society, 6–8
American Glossary, 6
Americanism, 5
The American Language, 8
anglicization, resistance to, 279
Appalachian dialect, 456 n
archiphoneme, 325, 327
argot:
  definition of, 42

of the marijuana smoker, 509
and the narcotic addict, 505 ff
of narcotic addicts, bibliography of, 513 ff
in relation to group culture, 502–503
Ascoli, G., 286
Ashley, Annabel, 463 n
a-temporal *be*, 439–440
Atlantic states, atlases of, 10 ff
atlas, publication cost of, 18
Atlas linguistique de la France, 43, 288, 294, 298
Atlas of the Iberian Peninsula, 295
attitude toward language forms, 159
Atwood, E. Bagby, 3, **5–35**, 20 n, 44, 52–53, 79, 79 n, 83, 132 n, 135 n, 137, 145 n, 150 n, 152, **160–168**, 169 n, 173 n, 181 n, 210 n, 255 n, 255 ff, 257, 263 n, 375 n, 376 n
Atwood, Mary (Mrs. E. Bagby), 5 n
Austin, William M., 322, 399 n, 404
auxiliary, 429
Avis, Walter S., 68, 153, **185–195**, 185 n, **200–215**, 200 n, 201 n, 202 n, 213 n, 214 n, 215 n, 370
Ayres, Harry M., 10 n

Babington, E. Mima, 33
Bach, Adolf, 310 n
Bach, Emmon, 324 n, 326 n

553

The following list generally includes diaphonemes and phonemes, but not allophones.

Word and Phrase Index

Boldface numerals indicate reference is to a figure.

flapjack, 109, 114

flat, 95

flitters, **243**

floor, 62, 64

Florida, 59–60, 149

flowers, 63, 116

flying jenny, 132–133

fog, 61, 88, 117–118, 120, 149, **253**, 253, **276**, 277

foggy, 59, 61, 88, 149, **276**, 277

follow, 62

folk, 373

folks, 201, 203, 208, 211, 214

food, 269, 337–338

foot, 147

forehead, 411

foreign, 60

forenoon drinking, **239**

forenoons, **239**

forest, 60

fork, 64

form, 320

forty, 22, 64, 116–118, 120, 368

fought, 148, 361

found, 63

fount, 341

four, 22, 62, 64, 117–118, 120, 372, 407

four-legged emmet, **241**

fourth, 407, 412, 417

freestone, 141, 202, 208

French harp, 86, 124

fried cake(s), 87–88, **276**, 277

frijoles, 380

fritter(s), 113, 125

frog, 61, 72, 149

frost, 117–118, 269

froze, 203

frying pan, 111

fucking Jew, 398–399

fudge, 378

full, 269

fund, 341

funnel, **241**, 242

fur, 266–267

furniture, 407

furrow, 147

furry, 320

gallery, **130**, 141, 359, 380

gan, **256**

gangster, 394, 398

garage, 60, 64

garbage, 147

garden, 116, 118, 147, 267, 360, 372

gate, 138, 359, 373

geld, 362

genuine, 90, 414

gesture, 52

get, 59

ghosts, 203

ghyll, **249**

giant, 332

gibby lamb, **252**

gin, **256**, 395, 398

gink, 386

ginny, 394–395, 398

girl, 63, 147, 196

gladioli, 223 n, 225

glass, 60, 116, 118–119, 147

glow-worm, 72, 109, 114, 203

go, 62, 203

goal, 88, 203

goat, 203

go-devil, **103**

goit, **249**

gong, 61

gonna, 425

goober, 360

good, 202, 269, 411

gook, 396, 398

goose, 337

got ill, 415

got sick, 415

granny, 112

granny woman, 113

grass, 160 n

grate, 111

grave, 358

graveyard, 364

gray, 396–397

graze, 160 n

grease, v., 7, 116, 146, 154 ff, **160**, **164**, 412, 417

greaseball, 394–395, 398–399

greased, 64

greaser, 379, 394, 396, 399

greasy, 7, 14, 59, 64, **76**, 119, 152, 154 ff, 160 ff, **274**, 277, 360, 412, 417

great beams, 113

greaves, **242**

green beans, 113

greenhorn, 393, 395

grew, **261**, 262

Date Due

DE 1 '72			
DE 15'72			